AF600589

HOMER AND THE QUESTION OF STRIFE FROM ERASMUS TO HOBBES

JESSICA WOLFE

Homer and the Question of Strife from Erasmus to Hobbes

UNIVERSITY OF TORONTO PRESS
Toronto Buffalo London

Toronto Buffalo London
www.utppublishing.com

ISBN 978-1-4426-5026-8

Library and Archives Canada Cataloguing in Publication

Wolfe, Jessica, author
Homer and the question of strife from Erasmus to Hobbes / Jessica Wolfe.

Includes bibliographical references and index.
ISBN 978-1-4426-5026-8 (bound)

1. Homer—Appreciation. 2. Homer—Influence. 3. Homer— Translations. 4. Homer—Criticism and interpretation. 5. Epic poetry, Greek—History and criticism. 6. Social conflict in literature. 7. European literature—Renaissance, 1450–1600—History and criticism. I. Title.

PA4037.A2W64 2015 883'.01 C2015-903435-3

University of Toronto Press acknowledges the financial assistance to its publishing program of the Canada Council for the Arts and the Ontario Arts Council, an agency of the Government of Ontario.

Canada Council for the Arts Conseil des Arts du Canada

Funded by the Government of Canada Financé par le gouvernement du Canada

To Reid Barbour

"For nothing is greater or better than this ... to keep house together, sharing one heart and mind."

Homer, *Odyssey* 6.182–4

Contents

Illustrations

Acknowledgments

This book took longer to complete than Odysseus spent travelling homeward to Ithaca, and I met with almost as many obstacles along the way. Thankfully, I was assisted by a generous and brilliant pantheon of friends and colleagues who filled my sails with Aeolian winds, gave me prudent Hermetic guidance, and administered Nepenthe and Moly when needed.

At the very beginning of this project, six weeks at the Vatican Library, made possible by the hospitality of the American Academy in Rome, followed by a short-term fellowship at the Henry E. Huntington Library, helped to enrich the book as well as the pleasure of researching it. A year-long colloquium at the Folger Shakespeare Library, led by Leonard Barkan and Nigel Smith, offered a congenial and rigorous audience for an early chapter. I am grateful to the readers and editors at *Renaissance Quarterly*, *College Literature*, and *Renaissance Papers* for their help and encouragement in publishing instalments of the project.

At eight consecutive Renaissance Society of America conferences, enthusiastic and learned audiences helped to shape different portions of this work; among them, Achsah Guibbory, Claire Preston, Debora Shuger, and Will West have helped to turn this event into an annual *nostos*. I was fortunate to have the opportunity to present my research at a number of smaller conferences and invited lectures, and I am grateful to the intellectual and financial generosity of hosts, fellow participants, and audiences at East Carolina University (David Wilson-Okamura and Charles Fantazzi), Brown University (Coppélia Kahn), U. Tennessee Knoxville (Rob Stillman and Anthony Welch), U. Wisconsin Madison (David Loewenstein and Henry Turner), SUNY Buffalo (Andy Stott), Kings College London (David Ricks and Michael Silk), U. Indiana Bloomington (Sarah Van der

Laan, Eric MacPhail, and Massimo Scalabrini), U. Maryland College Park (Jerry Passannante and Kent Cartwright), and UC Berkeley (Victoria Kahn and Joanna Picciotto). The scholars I met at these and other events helped make this a better and a more exciting book, but none more than Kathy Eden, Carol Kaske, and David Quint. I am deeply grateful to Ann-Louise Aguiar and staff of the *Corinthian II* for giving me the opportunity to lecture my way through the Aegean on a boat that traced its Odyssean way from Troy, to Nestor's bathtub, and finally to Ithaca.

At the University of North Carolina, I was fortunate to receive support from the Institute of the Arts and Humanities, the Spray-Randleigh Foundation, the program in Medieval and Early Modern Studies, and the University Research Council's Small Grant program. But the true wealth of UNC's contribution to this book comes in the form of its undergraduate and graduate students, who have studied Homer and the epic tradition with me (and I with them) for the past decade. In particular, the program in Comparative Literature offers a seemingly endless supply of students whose commitment to the classics and their enduring relevance makes teaching an utter pleasure. An abundance of gifted doctoral students at UNC has enriched my own research as well as the joy of belonging to an intellectual community that prizes cooperation and humility as much as excellence.

Several of my UNC colleagues deserve special mention for their loyal friendship and their exemplary dedication to teaching and scholarship: Gregg Flaxman, Mary Floyd-Wilson, Shayne Legassie, and above all Darryl Gless, who died just weeks before this book went to press: an exemplary colleague, devoted friend, and merry travel companion, Darryl's kindness and good humour will be sorely missed. One dear friend, Jerry Passannante, has been a steadfast intellectual ally, a confidant, and a "second self" since we first met in 2003. One even dearer friend, my husband Reid, has been both steersman and anchor on this long voyage, playing the role of Penelope to perfection as he waited patiently for this book to find its long way home. Our life together has confirmed the wisdom of Diomedes: when two go together, they make each other wiser, wittier, and more successful.

June 2014, Durham, NC

Abbreviations

ACMRS	Arizona Center for Medieval and Renaissance Studies
Aen.	Virgil, *Aeneid*. In *Eclogues. Georgics. Aeneid.* 2 vols. Translated by H. Rushton Fairclough. Cambridge, MA: Harvard University Press, 1934–5
AJP	*American Journal of Philology*
ASD	Desiderius Erasmus. *Opera Omnia Desiderii Erasmi Roterodami.* Amsterdam, 1969–
CA	*Classical Antiquity*
CJ	*Classical Journal*
CL	Rabelais, François, *Cinquième Livre*. In *Gargantua and Pantagruel*. Translated by J.M. Cohen. London: Penguin, 1955
CLS	*Comparative Literary Studies*
CP	*Classical Philology*
CQ	*Classical Quarterly*
CW	John Milton, *The Works*. 21 vols. Edited by Frank Allen Patterson. New York: Columbia University Press, 1931–8
CWE	Desiderius Erasmus, *Collected Works*. Toronto, 1994–
DK	Diels, Hermann, and Walther Kranz, *Die Fragmente der Vorsokratiker.* Zurich, 1985
DRN	Lucretius, *De Rerum Natura*. Translated by W.H.D. Rouse. 2nd ed. Cambridge, MA: Harvard University Press, 1982
ELH	*English Literary History*
ELR	*English Literary Renaissance*
ERSY	*Erasmus of Rotterdam Society Yearbook*
EW	Thomas Hobbes, *The English Works of Thomas Hobbes of Malmesbury*. 11 vols. Edited by Sir William Molesworth. London: Bohn, 1839–45

FQ	Edmund Spenser, *The Faerie Queene*. Edited by Thomas P. Roche, Jr. New York: Penguin, 1978
G	Rabelais, François, *Gargantua*. In *Gargantua and Pantagruel*. Translated by J.M. Cohen. London: Penguin, 1955
Georg.	Virgil, *Georgics*. In *Eclogues. Georgics. Aeneid.* 2 vols. Translated by H. Rushton Fairclough. Cambridge, MA: Harvard University Press, 1934–5
HH	Thomas Hobbes, *Translations of Homer*. 2 vols. Edited by Eric Nelson. Oxford: Clarendon Press, 2008
HLQ	*Huntington Library Quarterly*
IJCT	*International Journal of the Classical Tradition*
Il.	Homer, *Iliad*. 2 vols. Translated by A.T. Murray. Cambridge, MA: Harvard University Press, 1999
Inst. Orat.	Quintilian, *Institutio Oratoria*. 4 vols. Translated by H.E. Butler. Cambridge, MA: Harvard University Press, 1993
JHI	*Journal of the History of Ideas*
JHS	*Journal of Hellenic Studies*
LB	Erasmus, *Opera Omnia*. 10 vols. Edited by J. Leclerc. Leiden, 1703–6
Metam.	Ovid, *Metamorphoses*. 2 vols. 3rd ed. Translated by Frank Justus Miller. Cambridge, MA: Harvard University Press, 1977–84
MLN	*Modern Language Notes*
MP	*Modern Philology*
MQ	*Milton Quarterly*
MRTS	*Medieval and Renaissance Texts and Studies*
MS	*Milton Studies*
Od.	Homer, *Odyssey*. 2 vols. 2nd ed. Translated by A.T. Murray. Cambridge, MA: Harvard University Press, 1995
P	Rabelais, François, *Pantagruel*. In *Gargantua and Pantagruel*. Translated by J.M. Cohen. London: Penguin, 1955
PL	John Milton, *Paradise Lost*. Edited by Alistair Fowler. Harlow: Longman, 1971
PMLA	*Publications of the Modern Language Assocation*
QL	Rabelais, François, *Quart Livre*. In *Gargantua and Pantagruel*. Translated by J.M. Cohen. London: Penguin, 1955

Rep.	Plato, *Republic*. 2 vols. Translated by Paul Shorey. Cambridge, MA: Harvard University Press, 1937
RQ	*Renaissance Quarterly*
SCJ	*Sixteenth-Century Journal*
SEL	*Studies in English Literature 1500–1900*
ShS	*Shakespeare Studies*
SP	*Studies in Philology*
TAPA	*Transactions of the American Philological Association*
TL	Rabelais, François, *Tiers Livre*. In *Gargantua and Pantagruel*. Translated by J.M. Cohen. London: Penguin, 1955
TSLL	*Texas Studies in Language and Literature*
WD	Hesiod, *Works and Days*. In *Hesiod, the Homeric Hymns, and Homerica*. Translated by H.G. Evelyn-White. Cambridge, MA: Harvard University Press, 1936
YP	Milton, John, *Complete Prose Works*. 8 vols. Edited by Don M. Wolfe. New Haven, CT: Yale University Press, 1953–82

HOMER AND THE QUESTION OF STRIFE FROM ERASMUS TO HOBBES

Introduction: Homer and the Question of Strife

"Shall we, like Homer, invoke the Muses to tell us how discord first arose?"
– Plato, *Republic*[1]

The *Iliad* of Our Age

In an eccentric 1655 work called the *Vera Historia Romana*, the French Jesuit Jacobus Hugo proposes to interpret the *Iliad* and *Odyssey* as allegories of the Roman Catholic Church. Homer's Achaean troops play Evangelists to Achilles's Christ, while the *Odyssey* narrates the "sea journey of Peter (the Church)" [*cursum navis Petri (Ecclesiae)*], a voyage prolonged by hair-raising encounters with various heretical sects including the Syrians and Gentiles (played by Scylla and Charybdis) and the Lutherans (the Lotophagi).[2] Thanks to Hugo's creative anagrammatizing of the reformer's first name, Martin Luther is cast as the arrogant suitor Antinous, whose grasping sidekicks represent Beza, Melanchthon, and other schismatics. Some of Hugo's allegories are admittedly hackneyed – it is hardly surprising to discover that Aeolus symbolises the divine breath of the Holy Spirit – but others reflect his creative flair.[3] Hugo interprets the unravelling and reweaving of Penelope's shroud as a symbol of the destruction and rebuilding of the Temple of Jerusalem, while Patroclus, thanks to a bilingual rebus (*Petros* + *clavis*), represents Peter and his keys, symbol of the authority of the Roman Catholic Church.[4]

Most Renaissance readers of Homer do not resort to the allegorical flights of fancy typical of the *Vera Historia Romana*. Many openly disdain such hermeneutic methods. But even those readers disinclined to regard Homer's poems as typological precursors of Christian history or doctrine nonetheless regard the events narrated by Homer's poems as vividly refracted in contemporary events. In his *Politica*, written during the Dutch Wars of Independence, the Flemish scholar Justus Lipsius explains the "cause of the present troubles" [*Caussa…turbarum hodie*] in Homeric terms. He laments the "flames of sedition" [*seditionum flamma*] burning in Europe by citing *Il.* 16.387, "they damage the rights of the people, / evade justice, and feel no fear for the words of the gods," and *Il.* 1.196, "God sends punishment for these facts, and will send more."[5] Other Renaissance writers likewise assess contemporary conflicts according to a Homeric measure. In his *Rerum Senilium Libri*, Francesco Petrarch argues that the Trojan horse represents "the onset of civil discord," since once opened, it unleashes various evils including "hostile cunning" (represented by Odysseus), "arrogance and the urge for revenge" (Neoptolemus), and "jealousy and rancor" (Menelaus).[6] Almost two centuries later, in his 1535 *De Transitu Hellenismi ad Christianismum*, the French humanist Guillaume Budé compares certain of Luther's followers to "Epeus, the artificer of the fatal horse of Homer's noble poem," arguing that the Reformers have started a conflagration that has "caused the Church more atrocious violence [*contentionis*] and destruction of religion than was aroused between Troy and Greece by the infamous apple of discord."[7]

Such allusions to the fall of Troy or to the apple of discord are favoured by sixteenth-century writers eager to condemn – or simply to find a precedent for – the violence and religious strife sweeping across Europe. An anthology of political observations entitled *The Treasurie of Auncient and Moderne Times* appears to be contemplating current events rather than ancient history when it interprets the fall of Troy as the consequence of factionalism among men who became "al dissonant in their opinions, and f[a]ll into many Sects, and diverse labyrinths of excogitated fallacies."[8] While some writers of the period diagnose the fall of Troy in remarkably contemporary terms, others invoke instances of conflict or disunity in Homeric epic as a means of cautioning against contemporary sectarian controversies. In *Behemoth*, Thomas Hobbes blames the English Civil War on the contentiousness and sophistry of school divines by asserting that the "universities have been to this nation, as the wooden horse was to the Trojans."[9]

The practise of reading classical poets in light of present occasions is by no means limited to Homeric epic during the Renaissance. Lucan's *Pharsalia* and Virgil's *Georgics* help Renaissance readers articulate the horrors of civil war; the Greek tragedians help them critique tyranny; Latin satirists such as Martial and Persius help them excoriate moral and political corruption in city and court. But Homer's *Iliad* and *Odyssey* are interpreted in terms of their contemporary relevance more persistently – and more variously – than these other works, so much so that certain episodes and characters from both poems provide an idiom – a mythographic shorthand, as it were – to describe and analyse conflict. At times, this idiom is so conventional that it may appear inconsequential for the history of Homer's reception. Yet when Paolo Sarpi, musing on the threat of fractured unity at the Council of Trent, calls the protracted set of negotiations over the future of the Catholic Church "the Iliade of our age," the statement is not just a rhetorical ornament but rather symptomatic of a more widepsread tendency to interpret Homer's two poems as fables of discord that possess potent contemporary applications.[10] Like the *Iliad*, after all, the Counter-Reformation began with a council, one that aggravated conflict rather than remedying it. Other Renaissance writers also interpret Homeric council scenes according to a contemporary political measure, and such interpretations reflect the political convictions of their bearers. Whereas Hobbes discerns in Homeric council scenes a series of cautionary tales about the perils of parliamentary rule and the accompanying threat of rhetorical display as a tool of governance, defenders of republicanism from Etienne de la Boëtie to John Milton locate very different political and theological lessons in the council scenes of the *Iliad* and *Odyssey*. For similar reasons, we find the council of the Homeric gods a frequent subject in the visual arts of the late sixteenth and early seventeenth centuries. Artists including Carlo Cesio, Cornelis Cort, Peter Paul Rubens, and Joachim Wtewael represent the Homeric gods in dynamic and even chaotic groupings in the Olympian council, compositions that refract contemporary anxieties about the effectiveness of consiliar government.

The strategy of reading contemporary conflicts such as the Reformation or the English Civil War through the lens of Homeric epic informs the most rigorous scholarly treatments of the Greek poet during the sixteenth and seventeenth centuries. Despite his reluctance to entertain allegorical interpretations in his 1583 Greek-Latin edition of Homer, the French Hellenist Jean de Sponde crams the margins of his commentary with several lengthy digressions concerning the French religious wars. In the margins of *Od.* 18.229, where Telemachus declares himself "aware of ... everything, the good and the bad" even though he once "thought as a child" [*d'eti nêpios êa*], Sponde relates his own fall from a similar state of childlike innocence, a disillusionment prompted by the Saint Bartholomew's Day massacre and the assassination of Peter Ramus. At *Il.* 9.63–4, where Nestor condemns those men who "love the horror of war among [their] own people," Sponde meditates in his commentary about how France lacks a Nestor capable of restraining those who "violate and destroy the bonds of human society" [*vincula societatis humanae violet & perfringat*].[11] In a chapter of his *Politica* devoted to the "miseries" [*miseriae*] of civil war, Lipsius cites the same lines from Book 9 of the *Iliad* as confirmation of Cicero's observation (*Philippicae* XIII.1) that those who "take pleasure in discord … and in civil war" [*quem discordiae … quem bellum civile delectat*] should be "expelled from humankind."[12] While some detect in Homeric epic a distaste for civil war that speaks to their own particular circumstances in sixteenth- or seventeenth-century Europe, other Renaissance readers of Homer interpret the *Iliad* and *Odyssey* as cautioning against more pervasive and universal forms of contentiousness. In lecture notes on the *Odyssey* transcribed by one of his students, the French scholar Jean Dorat (1508–88) allegorizes Antiphates, King of the Laestrygonians, as "a monstrous litigant and bringer of lawsuits" [*litium autor atque ingens litigator*] and interprets the episode in which he appears as a fable about the perils of lawyers who devour others with litigation, a reading reinforced, according to Dorat, by the size of Antiphates's wife: "mountain-high," she represents the immensity of protracted or delayed litigations.[13] If Dorat's interpretation smacks of Rabelaisian absurdity, it is likely because the French satirist, like many sixteenth-century readers of Homer, tends to mock and critique strife by transforming epic conflicts between heroic adversaries into the stuff of comedy – paltry controversies and ludicrous skirmishes both verbal and physical. If Homer shows his Renaissance readers how serious discord can be, he also shows them how utterly absurd it can be.

There are many ways to narrate the reception of Homer in the three centuries after Italian humanists recovered his poems in the middle of the fourteenth century. This study begins *in medias res*, skipping over the early labours undertaken by Petrarch, Boccaccio, and Greek scholars such as Leonzio Pilato to establish a reliable Greek text of Homer and translate the poems into Latin (which Pilato did in around 1363).[14] It also downplays the intertwined fortunes of Homer and Virgil, poets who were habitually compared and contrasted by Renaissance poets and scholars. Yet even as many sixteenth- and seventeenth-century readers of classical epic understood the "pathos and beauty" of the *Aeneid* as a product of Virgil's attempt to distance himself from his Homeric model, few readers saw Homer merely as Virgil's lesser Greek predecessor, and they tended to read the *Iliad* and *Odyssey* not just against Virgil's *Aeneid* but also against, or alongside, works by Hesiod and Aristotle, Lucian and Plutarch, Hippocrates and Athenaeus, and the Old and New Testaments.[15] As I pored through editions and translations of the Homeric poems, and as I refamiliarized myself with Homeric borrowings in later epic poems and other literary works, I realised that sixteenth- and seventeenth-century poets and scholars attentive to Homer were united above all by their recognition that his works were "about" strife – about the most injurious and alarming expressions of strife, such as civil war and religious sectarianism, but also about potentially beneficial forms of strife, such as intellectual rivalry, athletic competition, and spiritual trial. Readers of diverse political and religious allegiances approach Homer's poems as aetiologies of strife: narratives that identify the causes of discord, anatomize its dangers, and, in certain cases, justify its uses or benefits. They arrive at such interpretations with the assistance of Homer's ancient allegorists, who maintained that his poems illustrated, under diverse veils, the relationship between strife [*eris*] and love or concord [*philia*], forces central to pre-Socratic and to Platonic cosmology, as well as to many strands of Christian theology. But they also arrive at such interpretations by reading the dilemmas faced by Homeric heroes such as Achilles and Odysseus – heroes obliged to choose between tranquillity or love on the one hand and violence or strife on the other – according to the peculiarly contemporary political and spiritual problems they face as inhabitants of a post-Reformation culture of schism, controversy, and conflict.

This book argues that Renaissance interpretations of Homeric epic are shaped by diverse and conflictive responses to its representations of *eris* – of strife, conflict, or discord, as the Greek word has been variously translated. *Eris* pervades every aspect of the human and cosmic fabric in Homeric epic: martial and athletic contest, verbal argumentation, political debate, and the various conflicts that inhere between gods and mortals.[16] Bracketed on one end by early reformers such as Desiderius Erasmus and Philip Melanchthon, who read the works of Homer through the lens of contemporary religious controversy and factionalism, and on the other end by Milton and Hobbes, whose interpretations of Homeric epic are shaped by their experiences of the English Civil War, the book illustrates how the most compelling questions raised by Homer's poems for their Renaissance readers concern the nature of *eris*. Who is to blame, mortals or gods, for the existence of strife? To what extent might certain forms of discord be necessary or productive? Can and should eristic impulses be harnessed or directed so as to maximize their social, moral, or political benefits?

Homer and the Question of Strife argues that interpretations of Homeric epic are profoundly transformed during the sixteenth and seventeenth centuries by the religious and political debates of the Reformation. Greek editions, Latin translations, and scholarly commentaries on Homer suddenly abound north of the Alps after 1515.[17] Many of these works are shaped by particular controversies as well as by the *culture* of controversy that thrives during the Reformation, a culture whose vexed relationship towards debate and discord prompts a vigorous rethinking of the *eristic* not just as instantiated in classical literature and philosophy but also as manifested in the scriptures and in contemporary institutions, discourses, and practices.

My argument that the interpretation of Homeric epic during the period is best understood in the context of Reformation and post-Reformation debates about the value and danger of strife helps to justify what may appear a peculiar choice for my opening chapter. Desiderius Erasmus never edited or translated any of Homer's poems, and despite his significant scholarship on other ancient Greek writers, including Lucian, Euripides, and Libanius, he wrote no systematic commentary on the *Iliad* or the *Odyssey*. Yet Erasmus's inclusion of several hundred Homeric maxims in his *Adages* demands to be treated as an interpretation in its own right – one that had an enormous influence on Homer's reception for more than two centuries. In his *Adages*, as well as in other writings from the first two and a half decades of the sixteenth century, Erasmus labours to make Homer "fitted to things and times" – times defined, for Erasmus, by bitter theological disputes and petty academic skirmishes. As Erasmus's *Adages* transforms key passages from Homeric epic into weapons deployable in the contemporary arena of intellectual and religious debate, many of his fellow Dutch and German humanists, including Johannes Reuchlin, Philipp Melanchthon, and Joachim Camerarius, produce translations and editions of Homer that likewise mediate concerns about sectarian controversies.

Although Homer's two epics were read from beginning to end by serious scholars and poets, many sixteenth-century readers came to know his works through the pithy sayings collected by Erasmus. *The Adages* circulates many Homeric commonplaces then passed down by subsequent generations of readers, supplying what David Wilson-Okamura has called the "chitchat ... that could be exchanged over cocktails," or rather through letters, rhetorical treatises, and controversial writings.[18] The "clichés" into which Erasmus turns hundreds of lines from Homeric epic may appear less valuable, to the eyes of the intellectual or literary historian, than the philological labours evident in the margins of contemporary editions. Yet *The Adages* is a supremely important document for the reception of Homer during the Renaissance, both because the work establishes Homer as a tacit commentator on Reformation culture and also because it allows early sixteenth-century readers to construe Homer variously as a pacifist, a sceptic, an ironist, a beggar, and a mouthpiece for Christian piety.

As chapter 2 explores at length, the Erasmian tradition of interpreting Homer as an eirenic and fideistic sceptic acquires new implications in the hands of Melanchthon and François Rabelais. Each of these writers constructs a counter-epic Homer who exemplifies many of the rhetorical and philosophical habits – *copia*, dialogism, scepticism, and parodic self-critique – that serve contemporary writers as strategies for combating dogmatism and factionalism. Like Craig Kallendorf's "other" Renaissance Virgil, the "alternative" Homer of Melanchthon and Rabelais never entirely displaces the "dominant paradigm," and yet from the early sixteenth century until the rise of neoclassicism at the end of the seventeenth century, this eirenic, ironic, and irreverent Homer gives the *other* Homer – the high and serious poet who valorizes conflict and martial heroism – a run for his money.[19] In different ways, and for different reasons, each of the authors treated in this book is attracted to this "other" Homer, a poet defined by his *gioco*-seriousness, his repudiation of rhetorical and intellectual norms, and his satirical contempt for human ignorance and frailty.

Erasmus and his contemporaries read Homer for theological insight and guidance about effective or civil forms of conflict and debate. On the other side of the Alps, sixteenth-century Italian writers such as Baldassar Castiglione and Lodovico Dolce praise Homer for fashioning "a perfect Courtier" in the figures of Phoenix and Odysseus.[20] Inspired by contemporary debates over the moral and cultural chasm between classical epic and its sixteenth-century audience, Dolce's *L'Ulisse* (1573), a loose translation of the *Odyssey* written in *ottava rima*, transforms Odysseus into a *cortegiano* whose actions exemplify the "moral and military code of the Cinquecento" while the suitors, by contrast, violate the aesthetic and social norms of sixteenth-century court culture.[21] Edmund Spenser was heir to Italian as well as northern traditions, as well as to the classical and late antique allegorical interpretations of Homer that parse various episodes as illustrating cosmological or moral lessons about the interplay between strife [*eris*] and love or harmony [*philia*]. Spenser synthesizes various approaches to Homeric epic in his *Faerie Queene*, accommodating the virtues and trials of Homeric heroes such as Achilles and Odysseus to the chivalric codes of Arthurian romance as well as to the *Realpolitik* of the late Elizabethan court. Chapter 3 of this book considers *The Faerie Queene* not as a deliberate imitation of Homeric epic per se but rather as a text that incorporates into its own allegorical substructure a series of fables about the relationship between love and strife, fables modelled on the ones that Homer's ancient allegorists detect throughout the *Iliad* and *Odyssey*. Like Milton after him, Spenser labours to accommodate the Homeric pantheon to a Protestant theology that corroborates divine justice while simultaneously justifying the existence of strife in the sublunary world. But unlike Milton, Spenser grapples seriously with the allegorical traditions that construe various figures and episodes in Homer's poems – Zeus's golden chain, the wedding of Peleus and Thetis, the figure of Proteus, the union of Ares and Aphrodite, and Atê's fall from Olympus – as stories that explain the presence of strife in the cosmos and, in certain cases, demonstrate the necessity or productivity of conflict on both human and cosmic scales.

Chapters 4, 5, and 6 focus on three different seventeenth-century English writers, two of them translators of Homer (George Chapman and Thomas Hobbes) and one of them an epic poet (John Milton). Both Chapman and Hobbes contribute to the construction of an alternative, "counter-epic" Homer, a poet whose satirical bite and disdainful attitude towards conventional models of heroism are repurposed by each translator for different rhetorical, moral, and political ends. While Chapman regards Homer as a master ironist whose "scoptic" tone he labours to justify and emulate, Hobbes emphasizes the bathos of Homeric epic in order to to disenchant readers, thus making the Greek poet speak to Hobbesian assumptions about the nature of political power and human passion. Yet whereas Hobbes strips Homeric epic of its mysteriousness – his translations accentuate the political expediency of fear, display a contempt for superstition, and lay bare the seamy or self-interested motives for "heroic" actions – Chapman's ironic interpretation of Homer elevates the poet to a godly status and then claims for himself as translator a share in that status as the sole reader capable of grasping Homer's elusive ironies. And, whereas Chapman claims an intimacy with Homer that is predicated on the translator's uncanny ability to detect the poet's hitherto undetected ironies, Milton and Hobbes domesticate Homeric epic by making his poems espouse their respective political and theological beliefs. Hobbes turns Homer into an agnostic, Erastian defender of monarchy, while Milton's imitation of Homeric conventions and allusions in *Paradise Lost* turns the *Iliad* and *Odyssey* into epics about the vexing process of choice in a world defined by political and theological liberty – a world, much like Milton's own, in which heroes must engage in acts of moral deliberation that are both urgent and fraught with difficulty.

Each chapter of this book is attentive to the various ways in which Homeric epic provides a flexible and even encyclopedic rhetorical resource for its Renaissance readers. If Virgil is the great poet of praise for his Renaissance audience, then Homer is, conversely, the master of blame, a poet who instructs readers in effective methods of vituperation and other forms of verbal correction.[22] Chapters 1, 2, 4, 5, and 6 each address this dimension of Homer's Renaissance reception in different ways. While Erasmus's *Adages* stitches together a patchwork of Homeric lines that set down guidelines for decorous intellectual and theological debate, Chapman's translation and commentary anatomizes various satirical and ironic strategies in Homeric epic, a project that helps to justify some wildly deviant interpretations of the Homeric text while simultaneously assisting his own pursuit of a poetic voice grounded in the "just reproof" of human vice and ignorance. Whereas Rabelais takes delight in the dialogism and verbosity of Homeric epic, turning the rhetorical scuffles typical of the Homeric battlefield into his own joyous cacophony of "winged" and dynamic words, Milton and Hobbes are more suspicious of rhetorical prowess as a distinguishing feature of Homeric heroism, and each explores how rhetorical skill may be perverted or abused, particularly in speeches made in council or in the agora.

Other common themes unite the arguments of the book's individual chapters. Several of the authors studied in this book are devoted to the idea that Homer is, in some fundamental way, a comic poet – an ironist (as Chapman sees it), a parodist (as Rabelais seems to), or a master of paradox and serious play who infuses grave and tragic subjects with a spirit of levity and recreation (as Erasmus, Rabelais, Chapman, and Hobbes each do, in different ways). Chapters 1, 2, 4, and 6 explore the various motives driving these and other writers to prize the comic strains they detect in the Homeric corpus, an interpretive trend that at times works to ally the Renaissance Homer with sceptical or sophistic philosophical strategies, and at times casts him as a pious critic of the very epic values that his works (particularly the *Iliad*) appear to endorse. Each chapter is likewise attentive to the influence of classical and late antique allegorical traditions on Renaissance interpretations of Homer, traditions that some writers (Spenser, Dorat, Ronsard) absorb fully and systematically, while others (Rabelais, Sponde, Chapman, and Milton) engage more selectively and judiciously. Even those readers most suspicious of allegory, however, cleave to tradition in reading certain Homeric figures and episodes as veiled representations of the complementary forces of *philia* and *eris*. Yet these readings acquire diverse social, moral, and cosmological implications, in some cases serving to justify discord as a productive force and in other cases serving to imagine cosmic or political structures in which discord is contained or limited by harmony.

Despite the pervasiveness of the claim, discussed at length in chapters 3 and 4, that Homeric epic conceals the principles of pre-Socratic philosophy wrapped up in fables, Renaissance readers are equally interested in exploring Homeric epic as an antecedent of various other disciplines and philosophical discourses, from Hippocratic medicine to Epicureanism. They are also eager to explore the sympathies between Homeric epic and the scriptures, a project undertaken in a wide variety of texts including scholarly commentaries, concordances, theological treatises, and literary adaptations of Homer. It is hardly news that Homer was regarded as an honorary Christian by some of his Renaissance readers – so too were Orpheus, Pythagoras, and Virgil – but the perceived affinities between Homeric epic and the Greek and Hebrew scriptures are surprisingly flexible, varying according to the theological convictions of individual readers and according to the Homeric passage in question. Zeus, for instance, looks to some readers like the sardonic deity of Psalm 58 who derides his enemies, to others like the just God of Daniel, who weighs his subjects in a balance, and to still others like the merciful God the Father who sacrifices his only son for the good of humankind. As we have already seen, the desire to accommodate Homer's pagan wisdom to Christian ethics and soteriology makes for some inventive interpretations that diverge wildly from late antique and patristic allegorical traditions. Erasmus understands the *polumêtis* Odysseus as a pagan analogue to Saint Paul, whose rhetorical flexibility allows him to be "all things to all men," while Milton adapts Homeric narrative techniques such as the contrafactual into vehicles for articulating the theological liberty and contingency central to *Paradise Lost*.

The authors treated in this book have been selected out of a conscious effort to illustrate the various means through which a writer's work is "received" by later readers: translations of Homer (chapters 4 and 6), works of scholarship and philosophy (chapters 1 and 6), and works of literary fiction (chapters 2, 3, and 5), some of them (such as Erasmus's *Adages* and Spenser's *Faerie Queene*) not formerly acknowledged to possess significant debts to the *Iliad* or *Odyssey*. My research was guided by the premise that Renaissance interpretations of Homer can be found in some rather unlikely places. This book's attention to philosophical dialogues, rhetorical treatises, books of proverbs, scriptural commentaries, and the odd medical dissertation, among other genres, aims to provide a "record of interpretation" more compelling and more normative than what a more narrowly construed survey of editions, translations, and commentaries might have yielded.[23] My choice of material also reveals a broader scope than that indicated by the book's title: I frequently cite Italian texts, particularly mythographies, emblem books, epic poems, and works of literary criticism, with the recognition that northern Renaissance writers devoured these works, unimpeded by geographical boundaries or religious differences. Throughout the process of researching this book, I was helped immensely by reading recent Homeric scholarship – by "recent" I mean everything from F.A. Wolf to the latest edition of *Classical Quarterly*. Despite the gaping chasms between some Renaissance interpretations of Homer and those now accepted by scholars, I thought it worthwhile to account for a few of the sympathies, as well as some of the incongruities, between the Homeric scholarship of the Renaissance and its later permutations. My purpose is not to demonstrate that certain Renaissance interpretations turn out to be "right" according to contemporary standards, nor is it to shame contemporary Homeric scholars into the admission that some of their most innovative interpretations are not so new after all. At times, however, it seemed easier to figure out what early modern readers of Homer did and did not believe, or what they believed was worth arguing about, once I held their interpretations up against contemporary scholarship, a practice not intended to expose "errors" by either party so much as to demonstrate the remarkable instability of Homer's poems as objects of interpretation and to hold in suspicion the ideas that both sixteenth-century minds and twenty-first-century ones tend to embrace with particular fervour. I have therefore provided selective references to recent Homeric scholarship, in particular to works that contribute to a transhistorical understanding of key debates about especially problematic passages or about the history of Homeric texts themselves.

Homer's Two *Erides*

Set into motion by a series of quarrels stirred up by an apple of discord tossed by the goddess Eris into the crowd at the wedding of Peleus and Thetis, Homer's accounts of the Trojan War and of Odysseus's arduous journey home challenge Renaissance writers to consider both the utility and the danger of strife in their own political and intellectual culture, their natural philosophy, and their theodicy. Many read the *Iliad* as the product of an archaic Greek culture that valorizes rivalry and conflict. The *Odyssey*, by contrast, is interpreted by many readers of the period as a poem that privileges peace and self-restraint over conflict and disorder, a work that offers criticisms of, or solutions to, the eristic world of the *Iliad*.[24] Homer's Renaissance readers are both attracted to and troubled by the extent to which *agôn* – struggle or contest, either physical or psychological – shapes the rhetorical and political culture of Homeric epic and fuels the interactions between mortal and divine characters. As they struggle to understand the agonistic spirit of the Homeric cosmos or accommodate it to the demands of their own culture, Renaissance readers also weigh the merits and dangers of *philoneikia* [love of strife], an attraction to conflict that can be morally questionable, *aphrôn* [mindless], politically hazardous, or cosmically unsettling even as it may also foster positive ethical and social values such as *arête* [heroic excellence], *zêlos* [emulation], and *dikaiosunê* [justice].

Renaissance readers of Homer disagree on many things: whether it is decorous for Achaean princes to cook their own meat; whether Zeus retains primacy over his fellow Olympians; whether Odysseus's talent for deception and equivocation is admirable or despicable; whether Achilles's frequent crying jags strip him of heroic stature or endow him with a *pietas* that might befit the most devout Christian hero. But the subject on which they disagree most is the extent to which the strife dramatized in battle or verbal contest, among gods or among men, might have moral, political, or cosmological benefits. Although the disagreements that punctuate Homeric council scenes (both mortal and divine) are understandably disturbing to many readers, who tend to regard the censures of Calchas, Thersites, or Achilles as threats not just to Agamemnon's authority but also to Zeus's, these scenes appeal to readers with republican leanings, who find evidence in the council scenes of the *Iliad* that the poet intended to call the legitimacy of kings into doubt. The frequent conflicts and squabbles among Homer's Olympians, whom Vincenzo Cartari and other sixteenth-century mythographers interpret as the "counsellors of the celestial senate" [*conseilleurs du senat celeste*], strike some readers as impious and ridiculous.[25] But other readers understand these conflicts as allegories of elemental discord or as evidence of Homer's monotheism, in which one supreme god (Zeus) presides over a divine council with absolute authority. Although most Renaissance readers agree with ancient rhetoricians such as Hermogenes, Cicero, and Quintilian that Homeric epic is an encyclopedic repository of oratorical styles modelled by speakers as diverse as Nestor, Odysseus, Phoenix, Menelaus, and Ajax, there is much less consensus on the purpose and propriety of the verbal arguments that erupt periodically in council and on the battlefield. While some readers see these exchanges as models for effective and decorous verbal debate, others regard such flyting scenes as crude and disgraceful wrangling, foreshadowing the most debased polemical discourse of the day. And, even as his Renaissance readers recognize Homer's attentiveness to the brutality and caprice of war, they also recognize how war in Homer's world – as in their own – may exercise moral virtue, remedy injustice, and foster unity.

In the *Iliad*, the goddess Eris personifies love of conflict both for good and for ill. She nurtures the eristic impulses of Homer's warriors by reviving their flagging spirits and inciting them to battle. Sent by Zeus to the Achaeans at the beginning of Book 11 of the *Iliad* to "make war sweeter" [*polemos glukiôn genet*] to them than the prospect of returning home, Eris's intercession is not partisan, and it has "profound moral consequences" for both sides of the conflict (*Il.* 11.13). Only the *Iliad* features a personified Eris, and that poem contains no occurrence of the word that is "clearly positive in tone."[26] The *Odyssey*, by contrast, does not feature a personified Eris but offers up numerous positive examples of *eris*, often by transforming Iliadic strife into something that might be more productive, more controlled, or more reconciliable with harmony. In both poems, both the dangers posed by Eris and the profits reaped by her are collective rather than individual. While *polemos* [war] involves violence projected outside of a community, *eris* normally inheres "between members of a group or community" or in "group activities" such as councils, athletic contests, or verbal debates. Although there is no adjective in Homer meaning "eristic," a term favoured by later Greek writers such as Plato, all men are eristic in Homer's world, and *eris* exerts her greatest power upon communal institutions: upon the social dynamics of the agora and the battlefield, and upon various practices ranging from gift-exchange to conversation and feasting.[27] Yet early modern readers, influenced by theories of faculty psychology that post-date the Homeric poems by centuries, also discern an eristic strain in Homeric epic that resides within individual characters, in conflicts between *nous* [mind] and *thumos* [heart; gut] that to them dramatize the difficulty of making choices and of controlling impulses.

The goddess Eris and the eristic behaviours over which she prevails represent the starting point of a complex iconographic and intellectual tradition that runs from later classical epic and philosophy through the literature of the Renaissance. Homer's Eris possesses a large brood of descendants, creatures such as Atê, Discordia, Fama, and Litigium, who crop up in works ranging from Virgil's *Aeneid*, Quintus Smyrnaeus's *Fall of Troy*, and Statius's *Thebaid* to Boccaccio's *Genealogia Deorum*, Ariosto's *Orlando Furioso*, and an array of Elizabethan plays and masques.[28] Although frequently resuscitated as a stock figure of discord, Homer's Eris also helps Renaissance writers evaluate the role played by strife in the ancient world, interpreting her appearances in the *Iliad* in light of later Greek texts ranging from Plato's denunciation of eristic logic and Saint Paul's condemnations of strife to the analyses of civil war offered by Aristotle and Thucydides. In his copy of Eustathius, the twelfth-century

Byzantine commentator on Homer whose works were first printed, in four volumes, at Rome in 1542–50, the classical scholar Isaac Casaubon (1559–1614) glosses Homer's fullest description of Eris at *Il.* 4.440–4 by writing "Vide Arist: Politic: lib. 5, cap. 4," a chapter that opens with the observation that "factions arise not about but out of small matters [*ou peri mikrôn all'ek mikrôn*]; but they are carried on about great matters."[29] Martin Crusius, a sixteenth-century German classical scholar who left copious notes in his working copy of Homer, a 1541 Camerarius-Micyllus edition now held by Princeton University Library, cross-references *Il.* 4.440–4 in his copy of Homer with the same line from the *Politics*. Crusius evidently found Eris a significant enough player in the Homeric pantheon for him to add her name – twice – to the index in the back of his volume.[30] Both Crusius and Casaubon discern an implicit political lesson in Homer's description of the goddess who "first rears her crest just a little but then fixes her head in the heavens while her feet tread on earth" [*t'oligê men prôta korussetai, autar epeita, / ouranô estêrixe karê kai epi chthoni bainei*] (*Il.* 4.442–3). They interpret the passage, as Erasmus and Rabelais do before them, as a cautionary fable about the inexorable escalation of conflict, or the "mighty Quarrels" that rise from "trivial Things," to cite Alexander Pope's witty parody of epic *agôn* in the opening lines of his *Rape of the Lock*.[31]

In addition to Aristotle's *Politics*, Hesiod's *Works and Days* also plays an important role in helping Renaissance readers make sense of Homeric attitudes towards strife. The opening lines of Hesiod's poem describe two goddesses of strife: the blameworthy Eris who is contentious, fosters quarrels, and rejoices in adversity, and her benevolent twin, who is "wholesome for men," arousing healthy rivalries and eliminating idleness.[32] Although there is little to suggest that the Homeric poet conceived of Eris in the same way that Hesiod did, many Renaissance scholars believe the poets to be contemporaries and rivals, and they look to the passage in the *Works and Days* as a kind of gloss on the Homeric Eris, whom the first-century CE Homeric allegorist Heraclitus calls a Protean creature, "capable of incredible changes [*metabolas*] and reversals of form."[33]

Sixteenth- and seventeenth-century editors and commentators of Homer frequently invoke Hesiod's two *Erides* as a means of exploring when and to what extent Homeric *eris* might be ethically, politically, or spiritually advantageous. This question, which had already informed imitations of and responses to Homeric epic in antiquity, resurfaces in the sixteenth century and has continued to shape Homeric scholarship ever since. Particularly from the latter half of the nineteenth century onwards, classical scholars have debated how and to what extent the Homeric poems reflect an "agonistic" or "agonal" culture – a culture that privileges contestation or regards it as beneficial to the community. These debates have been shaped partly by the degree to which individual readers of Homer (or their cultures at large) value conflict. In an 1872 essay entitled *Homer's Contest*, Friedrich Nietzsche complains that Hesiod's "two Eris-goddesses," interpreted by him as a foundational myth of Greek ethical and political thought, have become "incomprehensible" to his own generation of scholars, who are only able to conceive of rivalry as the province of "the evil Eris."[34] Whereas classical Greek writers such as Aristotle "fin[d] no offense" in Hesiod's idea of a "good" Eris, according to Nietzsche, the ancients "thin[k] of spite and envy otherwise than we do," finding virtue in qualities such as *philotimia* [love of honour] and *philoneikia* [love of strife].[35] Renaissance culture inherits from antiquity and the Middle Ages an appreciation that conflict should be cultivated and might lead to the realization of ethical, political, or theological ideals. Scholars of the Renaissance have long testified to the various ways in which its courts, universities, and other institutions encourage forms of rivalry that aim to produce a "coincidence of struggle and assimilation" – in other words, to create harmony through strife.[36] Living in a culture that often employs verbal and physical competition more to "bond … than to distinguish," Homer's sixteenth- and seventeenth-century readers are in many respects better equipped than Nietzsche's contemporaries to grasp the concept of a "good" Eris.[37]

Yet many of Homer's Renaissance readers remain puzzled or disturbed by aspects of the Homeric ideal of "contest" [*agôn*] that Nietzsche would later call the "noblest Hellenic fundamental thought" and the one that most sharply divides the ancient world from the modern.[38] Jakob Burckhardt, Nietzsche's fellow professor at Basel, laboured to represent the Renaissance as the last and fullest expression of Greece's "agonal age," an epoch that transformed the *Iliad*'s "fundamental principle," "Always to be the best and to outdo others," into a "boundless ambition and thirst after greatness" that was satiated by athletic competitions, artistic contests, and skirmishes of "wit and sardonic malice" (*Il.* 6.208, 11.784).[39] Yet even as the educational, political, and legal institutions of the Renaissance encouraged rhetorical and intellectual athleticism, many of its writers and artists condemn disputation and striving as antithetical to Christian ethics or even to gentlemanly decorum. It is difficult to tell, for instance, whether to regard Giovanni Castello's rendition of the stone-throwing contest in Phaiakia in the Villa Pallavicino in Genoa, or Jan Muller's engraving of the

Figure 1. Jan Muller, after Cornelis Cornelisz van Haarlem. *The Fight between Ulysses and Irus*. 1589. Engraving. Courtesy of the National Gallery of Art, Washington, DC.

fight between Ulysses and Irus (see figure 1), as examples of the virtue-building competition typical of Castiglione's courtiers, as an instance of Greek barbarity in which athleticism thinly veils more hostile forms of aggression, or both at once.

In the wake of the Protestant Reformation, debates about religious tolerance and consensus, about the central message of the Gospels, and about the concept of a just war work to devalue adversarial behaviours in favour of cooperative values such as friendship, sympathy, and charity.[40] Yet no one would rightly call the first two centuries of the Reformation peaceful ones, and Homeric epic proves as useful to those wishing to valorize conflict as to those wishing to deprecate or condemn it.

The fortunes of Homer's reception during the sixteenth and seventeenth centuries are thus shaped by the culture's vigorous and multilayered rethinking of the moral, intellectual, political, and spiritual validity of *agôn*. While some readers understand how in Homeric epic, as perhaps in their own culture, violence may be displaced onto "ritualized conflict such as public speeches, gift exchange, and athletic competition," other readers offer radically different interpretations of Homer's attitude towards the social and political uses of strife.[41] In his 1675 *Traité du poëme épique*, translated in 1695 as *A Treatise of the Epick Poem*, René Le Bossu argues that "[a]ll the fables of the *Iliad*" convey the moral that "right understanding is the Preservation, and Discord the Destruction of States," a reading perhaps indebted to Hobbes's newly completed translation of the poem.[42] Although a few readers admire the eristic, glory-seeking forms of heroism embodied by Homeric epic, it is more common for Homer's sixteenth- and seventeenth-century readers to locate in the *Iliad* and *Odyssey* new kinds of heroism, characterized by patience, modesty, moderation, or ironic detachment.[43] This heroism is defined not by physical prowess or the pursuit of honour; rather, it is a "form of knowledge" – a knowledge of mortality, an awareness of the limits of human understanding, or the wisdom that ensues after delusion or error.[44] Such readings turn Odysseus into a sceptical hero attuned to the fleeting nature of mortal life, while Achilles, Menelaus, and Agamemnon become anti-heroes who fail to recognize the limits of human knowledge or the triviality or transitoriness of fame. The writers studied in this book challenge and transform conventional assessments of Homeric heroism in various ways. Erasmus celebrates Odysseus as the eloquent, pious ancestor of Saint Paul, while Chapman praises his ironic detachment. Milton finds a model of heroic spirituality in the acts of deliberation undertaken by Homer's protagonists, while Rabelais and Hobbes undercut the most heroic moments in Homer's poems at every turn, the former in order to tease out the sceptical and comic dimensions of Homeric epic and the latter to lend credence to his theory that "Nature hath made men so equall" that no one man may rightly claim pre-eminence over any other.[45]

To some degree, early modern disagreements over the nature of Homeric heroism anticipate modern scholarly debates about whether and to what extent Homer's poems display what Walter Burkert has called an "agonal spirit" – a cultural and social disposition towards "contest" that encourages and rewards "competitive struggle."[46] Although some scholars still maintain that Homeric Greece has an "agonistic conception of man" and is guided by "a spirit of struggle," Homeric scholarship in the last several decades has challenged the argument that "competitive values ... overwhelm gentler attitudes and cooperative ethics" in Homer's poems.[47] Refuting the work of A.W.H. Adkins, whose 1960 study *Merit and Responsibility* maintained that the "dominant values" of Homeric epic are "agonistic and individualistic," Douglas Cairns has proposed that the central conflict of the *Iliad* stems not from Achilles's love of conflict but rather from Agamemnon's "breach of the communal ethic of reciprocity in initiating the quarrel with Achilles," an act that violates the rules supposed to govern strife and contestation in the poem.[48] Rather than discern a sharp distinction between "competitive and cooperative values" in which the former prevail over the latter, Cairns instead finds in the *Iliad* "a wide range of behaviour, both competitive and cooperative" that may be deemed either "honourable" or "dishonourable" depending upon agent and context.[49] And, rather than regard competition and cooperation as contrary social impulses, scholars such as Cairns, Rutherford, and Martin have argued that even the most relentless expressions of strife in Homeric epic are in fact manifestations of ritualized competition that fosters social bonding.[50]

The Poet of Love and Strife

Recent scholarship has thus revived an "ideological contradiction" at the heart of the Homeric moral universe that many Renaissance readers, attuned to the nebulous boundaries between "the selfish and the social conception of *arête*," once took for granted.[51] The world of Homeric epic looks to its sixteenth- and seventeenth-century readers a world defined by its complex interplay between sympathy and antipathy, or *philia* and *eris*, but such an interpretation is rarely guided by the deep historical understanding of early Greek culture that Homeric scholarship now privileges. Rather, Renaissance interpretations of Homer are informed by classical and late antique allegorical traditions that gloss various episodes in the *Iliad* and *Odyssey* as illustrating a *coincidentia oppositorum* between love [*philia*] and strife [*eris*; *neikos*] that carries moral, political, spiritual, aesthetic, and cosmological implications. In order to explain or justify the value of strife in the Homeric poems and in the cosmos at large, Homer's ancient allegorists were especially eager to tackle episodes in which antagonism appeared either morally problematic (the desecration of Hector's corpse by Achilles; the fickleness and brutality of Ares and Poseidon) or ridiculous (the quarrels between Zeus and Hera or between Hephaestus and Aphrodite). Responding to the grievances of Xenophanes, Heraclitus, and above all Plato, Homeric allegorists rewrite these instances of conflict as manifestations of an underlying cosmic sympathy, an interpretive strategy that may, as Jean Seznec has argued, "cut both ways," either demolishing pagan polytheism or exalting it.[52] In his *Commentary on Plato's Republic*, Proclus interprets Hephaestus's enchaining of Ares and Aphrodite in Book 8 of the *Odyssey*, an episode often deemed ridiculous by ancient readers, as an allegory of the cosmic *desmoi*, or bonds, that Plato describes in the *Timaeus*. Similarly, the allegorist Heraclitus – not the pre-Socratic philosopher, but author of the *Homeric Problems*, widely available from the early sixteenth century onwards – interprets Zeus's binding of Hera at *Il.* 15.18–21 as an account of the creation of the four elements (air, fire, water, earth) through which "the harmony of the universe is secured by unbreakable bonds" [*tôn holôn harmonia desmois arragesi sunôchurôtai*].[53] The allegorical interpretation that proved most compelling to Homer's Renaissance readers is the one that regards various episodes in the *Iliad* and *Odyssey* as illustrations of the contrary yet complementary forces of *philia* and *eris* (or *neikos*), a concept central to the pre-Socratic cosmology of Heraclitus and Empedocles. This interpretation was commonplace in antiquity: Plato, Aristotle, and Plutarch all discuss episodes from Homeric epic that illustrate, allegorically, pre-Socratic cosmological principles. The approach receives sustained and systematic treatment in the two ancient commentaries of Homer that exerted the most influence on Renaissance readers: Heraclitus's *Homeric Problems*, first printed by Aldus Manutius in 1505, and the *Essay on the Life and Poetry of Homer*, a work attributed to Plutarch during the Renaissance, first printed in the 1488 *editio princeps* of Homer and translated into Latin in 1537.[54] The pseudo-Plutarchan *Life of Homer*, as I will refer to the work throughout, interprets several episodes in the *Iliad* and *Odyssey* as veiled illustrations of the Empedoclean doctrine that the cosmos is governed by the unifying and separating powers of *Philia* and *Neikos*, such that the elements "come together into one through love [*philotêti*] / and at another are polarized by the hostility of strife [*neikeos*]." These forces, the pseudo-Plutarchan *Life* explains, are symbolized, respectively, by Homer's Aphrodite and Ares: "she has the same force [*dunamenês*] as what Empedocles calls 'love' and Ares, what the philosopher calls 'strife' [*neikos*]. This is why they sometimes come together [*suneisin*] and are sometimes separated."[55]

Other classical, late antique, and Byzantine writers also detect submerged allusions to pre-Socratic doctrines of "love and strife" concealed in various passages of Homeric epic. In both the *Nicomachean Ethics* and the *Eudemian Ethics*, Aristotle compares lines from Homer to the philosophical doctrines of Heraclitus and Empedocles in an attempt to establish whether "opposition unites" [*antixoun sumpheron*], as the pre-Socratic Heraclitus holds, or whether "like aims at like" [*to gar homoion tou homoiou ephiesthai*], as Empedocles does.[56] Stobaeus, widely read throughout the Renaissance, finds pre-Socratic cosmological doctrines cryptically expressed by Hera's deception of Zeus in *Iliad* 14, by the union of Ares and Aphrodite, and by the theomachy of *Iliad* 20 and 21.[57] Heraclitus the allegorist interprets the conspiracy against Zeus at *Il.* 1.399–408 as a dramatization of the cosmological principle that "so long as uncontentious harmony [*aphiloneikos hê harmonia*] rules the four elements, and no one of them is especially predominant ... then everything will remain unmoved," while Proclus (here, in Gesner's Latin) argues that the war on Olympus adheres to a pre-Socratic model of the cosmos in which the "battles of the gods" [*pugnae deorum*] symbolize the "strife between similar and dissimilar, and between equal and unequal powers," thus yielding a "mutual opposition" [*oppositione mutua*] that acts as a creative and generative force in the cosmos.[58]

Sixteenth-century mythographers and other popularizers of classical philosophy and myth, eager to vindicate the violent exploits and amorous escapades of the Homeric gods, adopt these interpretive traditions by reading various episodes in Homeric epic as cosmological or moral allegories about harmony and strife. In his *Académie Françoise*, Pierre de la Primaudaye compares Empedocles's cosmological theory of "discord and disjunction" to the dim view of sedition voiced by Homer's Nestor, who argues in an oft-quoted line that "he which loveth civil war, is a most wretched, cruell, and detestable man."[59] In his *Oratio in expositione Homeri*, composed in 1486–7 and printed for the first time in 1498, Angelo Poliziano argues that Homer anticipates Empedocles's philosophy of concord and discord, a reading echoed by Ludovico Ricchieri, Natale Conti, Vincenzo Cartari, Henry Reynolds, and Mutio Pansa, the last of whose 1601 *De Osculo Ethnicae* points out that the Empedoclean principles of *odium* [strife] and *amor* [love] are not synonymous with the moral categories of evil and good, since, as Aristotle (*Metaphysics* 985a3–9) observes, "nothing bad can be the cause of something good" [*nullam malorum esse causam positiva[m]*].[60] Pansa is hardly the only Renaissance writer to ponder the implications of such Homeric allegories from the standpoint of Christian theodicy. If Homer's ancient readers deal with the misbehaviour of the Homeric gods by interpreting that misbehaviour according to cosmological theories that accord an essential role to *eris*, or strife, then Renaissance readers of Homer including Tasso, Spenser, Sponde, and Milton adopt these methods in order to justify the existence of discord in a

Christian universe, thus enlisting Homeric epic in some of the most pressing theological dilemmas of the Reformation and Counter-Reformation. If God generates strife in the mortal world, or if he permits it to thrive, how can he be a just God? And conversely, if strife is neither produced nor sanctioned by God, how can he be an omnipotent God?[61]

Homer's two epics and the allegorical traditions that grow up around them thus speak to one of the most cherished and pervasive paradoxes shaping early modern thought, namely, the paradox of *concordia discors*. The idea that harmony, beauty, or friendship depend upon or even arise out of discord, a principle that informs all manner of Renaissance thought ranging from courtly sprezzatura to musical composition, finds varied expression in Homeric epic as a cosmological principle, an aesthetic canon, a political rule, and a means of vindicating emotional or spiritual conflict. Eager to make sense of conflict and contrariety in their own lives, Renaissance readers of Homer locate the paradox at work in a wide array of Homeric episodes, ranging from the description of Achilles's shield and the war on Olympus to Demodocus's account of Hephaestus's entrapment of Ares and Aphrodite and Andromache "laughing through her tears" at the sight of her son.

Despite the commonplace early modern assumption that Homeric epic is animated by the complementary forces of sympathy and antipathy, readers disagree about whether *philia* or *eris* ultimately prevails. On one end of the spectrum, Poliziano interprets the *Iliad* and *Odyssey* as twin treatises on *amicitia* that exemplify the four chief kinds of love: "brotherly compassion" [*fratrum benevolentiae*] in Agamemnon and Menelaus, "friendship" [*amicorum*] in Achilles and Patroclus, the love of a "wife towards her husband" [*uxoris viriq[ue]*] in Penelope, and "love of country" [*amorem patriae*] in Odysseus.[62] On the other end of the spectrum, the Caroline essayist Edward Reynolds, who would later become one of the Westminster Assembly divines and then (under Charles II) Bishop of Norwich, verges on a Hobbesian interpretation when he proposes that Homeric epic illuminates the "secret antipathy" that resides "in the natures of some things one against another ... So *Homer* noteth of the *Lyon*, that hee feareth fire, and the Elephant nauseates his meat, if a mouse have touched it."[63] Between these two extremes are the many poets, scholars, and translators who appreciate Homer's ambivalent and complex attitude towards strife. In the royal dedication of his 1604 French translation of the *Odyssey*, for instance, Salomon Certon compares Henri IV to Odysseus in that both rulers are "nourished by Bellona, and rejecters of Mars," a distinction that elevates one model of war, circumscribed by the prudent wisdom of Athena, over another model, embodied by her fickle and hot-tempered brother.[64]

Thus, even within the confines of an interpretive framework that treats Homeric epic as a cosmological allegory about love and strife, there is a good deal of room in individual episodes to accommodate divergent attitudes towards the utility or inevitability of discord. One such episode, mentioned only briefly in the final book of the *Iliad* but nonetheless a crucial moment for readers eager to interpret the poem as an aetiology of strife, is the wedding of Peleus and Thetis. In *La Suite de Philostrate*, a French translation of Philostratus's *Imagines* first printed in 1578, Blaise de Vigenère explains that Eris was not invited to the wedding of Peleus and Thetis – the event that precipitates the Judgment of Paris and ultimately the Trojan War – because "in the generation of humankind, there must be no discord among the elements" [*en la generation de l'homme, il n'y doit point avoir de discorde des Elemens*].[65] But another interpretation of the wedding of Peleus and Thetis, one that appraises the actions of Eris as cosmologically beneficial, is espoused by the *Ovide Moralisé* tradition and by Jean Lemaire de Belges's *Illustrations de Gaule et Singularités de Troie*, which interprets Peleus and Thetis as "two contrary elements, the one active and the other passive, the one dry and the other humid" [*deux elemens contraires, lun actif et lautre passif: lun sec et lautre humide*].[66] The reading makes Eris's presence at the wedding essential and generative rather than disruptive.

When allegorizing the wedding of Peleus and Thetis in these and other ways, Renaissance readers are divided over whether to regard Eris's ultimate function as impeding the union or rather reinforcing the principle of *concordia discors* upon which that union is based.[67] They are equally divided over whether to understand the conflict and contrariety evident in Homeric episodes such as the war on Olympus, the union of Ares and Aphrodite, and Achilles's shield as antagonistic to harmony – or a necessary precondition of it. When Conti describes the union of Aphrodite and Ares as a "clash of opposites," he explains that the two gods "symbolize harmony and strife, both of whom are subdued by Hephaestus, or superfluous heat," a myth that conveys in veiled form "the balance that must be maintained in nature."[68] But when Dionysius Lambinus tackles the same allegorical tradition in a 1562 oration on Homer, he compares the bond between Ares and Aphrodite to the "incessant and implacable discord" between Apollo and Poseidon, a reading which makes the interplay between *eris* and *philia* symbolized by the union of the two Homeric gods appear dynamic and downright hostile:

> Empedocles believed that all things took their origin from the four elements ... but he added to this two other principles, love and strife ... Homer presents clearly this *concordia discors* of the four elements by the secret union of Mars and Venus ... And what is the meaning of the incessant and implacable discord between Apollo and Neptune if not the fact that heat and dryness are opposed to cold and humidity?[69]

Similar disagreements inflect other interpretations of Homeric episodes that are traditionally (but not exclusively) read as allegories of a cosmological *pas de deux* between love and strife. In a work heavily indebted to Conti and Cartari, the Elizabethan mythographer Richard Linche explains that the marital discord between Hera and Zeus, which reaches a climax when Zeus dangles his wife from Olympus by a chain, symbolizes the "distemperature and strugling contention of the elements," a reading that legitimates a petty spat between two gods by translating it into cosmological terms. In his *Mythomystes* (ca 1632), Henry Reynolds proposes that the war between Homer's Olympians represents the "naturall Contrariety of the Elements," an interpretation that makes its way onto the frontispiece of Sandys's translation of Ovid's *Metamorphoses*, which illustrates how all the "Opposites / That strove in Chaos" are united by "powrefull Love."[70] Although Renaissance mythographers tend to imitate Homer's ancient allegorists, diminishing both the pervasiveness and the strangeness of strife in his poems by accommodating it to recognized cosmological doctrines, other Renaissance writers interpret Homeric epic in ways that help legitimate discord in their own political or natural worlds. The early seventeenth-century French dramatist Isaac Benserade turns Achilles into a defender of strife: in his 1636 play *La Mort d'Achille et la Dispute de ses Armes*, Benserade's Achilles declares that "there is nothing so great as a just quarrel" [*Il n'est rien de si fort qu'une querelle juste*], a claim that explicitly justifies the clash between Achilles and Agamemnon whereas the narrator of the *Iliad* may in fact do just the opposite.[71] In his *De la Vicissitude*, a text which argues that "contrariety [is really] unity, and discord concord" [*la contrarieté, unité, et la discorde, concorde*], Louis Leroy offers up a lengthy catalogue of the crimes and misdemeanours of the Homeric gods, their "banquets, chuckles, lusts, laments, temper tantrums, rages, resentments, differences, discords, combats, wars, and battles" as evidence that discord and disharmony are – or at least appear to be – the ruling forces of the cosmos.[72] Yet as Leroy's treatise bears out, the discord celebrated by the Homeric gods is a positive rather than a negative force, since "nature relishes contraries" [*nature appete tant les contraires*] and the universe is "tempered and conserved by contraries" [*temperées et conservées par contraires*]. In order to lend credence to these doctrines with ancient examples, Leroy compares Heraclitus's doctrine that "war and peace are the father and mother of all things" [*la guerre et concorde estre pere et mere des choses*] to Homer's observation that "he who curses contention blames nature" [*qui mesdit de contention il blasme nature*].[73] Although there exists no line anywhere in the Homeric corpus that resembles, even faintly, Leroy's Homeric maxim, the misattribution is nonetheless repeated by later writers such as Louis Quattrehomme, who duplicates Leroy's imaginary adage in his 1604 *Discours ... sur les Vies de Moyse & d'Homere*, where it describes a Manichean conflict between two "genies" or spirits: "Our Homer wisely says that he who blames contention blames nature, which possesses in everything, big and small, two spirits which are continually in conflict with each other."[74]

Although not in fact derived from Homer, Leroy's and Quattrehomme's discussions of the above maxim do conform to a widespread Renaissance belief that various episodes in Homeric epic illustrate Heraclitus's doctrine that "[t]he attunement of the world is of opposite tensions [*palintonos*], as is that of the harp or bow" such that "what is at variance agrees with itself."[75] This perceived affinity between Homer and the pre-Socratic Heraclitus, which develops out of ancient interpretations of a passage in Book 21 of the *Odyssey* that compares Odysseus's "bent-back bow" [*toxon ... palintonon*] to the poet's lyre, holds that Heraclitus's doctrine of *palintonos harmoniê*, a harmony produced out of opposing tensions that resembles the two-way strain created by pulling back on a tautly strung bow or on the strings of a lyre, evolves out of Homer's implicit comparison between bow and lyre, respective symbols of the brutal strife of war and the civilizing harmony of the poet's song.[76]

Homeric epic thus dramatizes to its Renaissance readers a paradox by turns comforting and alarming: that strife is both the stubborn enemy of harmony and its inescapable partner. To read the Homeric poems in this manner allows them to speak to one of the most pressing theological questions of the period, namely, whether God permits, or encourages, conflict. If the battles among Homer's Olympians preserve a delicate equilibrium in the cosmos, and if Eris's ministrations to the Achaean troops participate in a larger and ultimately harmonious cosmic design, then war and bloodshed, at least when sanctioned by the immortals, may be seen as desirable and even pious. More so than Virgil, Lucan, or the ancient tragedians, Homer illustrates to his Renaissance readers that *eris* might be a properly godly force, not in the least inimical to the idea of a just and all-powerful God. This is precisely why Edward Stillingfleet, in his *Origines Sacrae*, rescues Homer from the potentially heretical implications of his goddess of strife by arguing that "all the *Heathen philosophers* were not so *gross* as to imagine two such *Anti-Gods* with infinitely active power," even if some of them were "driven to" this position "by consequence of their opinion concerning the *Origine of Evil* … Hence it was that Heraclitus as Plutarch tells us, attributed the *Origine* of all *things* to *discord* and *antipathy*, and was wont to say, that when *Homer* wished that all contention were banished out of the world, that he did secretly curse the Origine of things and wished the ruine of the world."[77] According to Stillingfleet, it is Heraclitus, rather than Homer's Achilles, who "wishe[s] the ruine of the world," and he does so by apotheosizing contention rather than by wishing for its banishment. Stillingfleet's reading places Eris – and other Homeric forces of contention – under the firm control of Zeus, a position that intervenes in some of the central dilemmas of reformation theodicy by asserting the omnipotence of Homer's chief deity and explaining that discord and antipathy are created by him rather than by a powerful "anti-God."

Another Homeric episode that raises similar theological problems for reformed readers of the sixteenth and seventeenth centuries is the "golden chain" speech of *Il.* 8.5–27, in which Zeus boasts that if the other gods try to pull him down from Olympus with a golden chain, they could not "drag [Zeus] to earth" and then threatens that if he should "pull with all my heart," Zeus could draw the whole earth up to Olympus with his chain (8.21–2). Examined without the rose-coloured glasses of Platonic and Neoplatonic exegetical traditions, which interpret this golden chain as a symbol of the concatenation between earth and heaven, of the divinely appointed order and harmony of the cosmos, or of the continuum between matter and spirit, it is a violent and threatening speech. Yet late antique and early Christian writers, including Prudentius, Macrobius, Proclus, and Martianus Capella, explicate the golden chain in terms of the "bond" [*desmos*] that unites the elements, a tradition that survives (even in the absence of the Homeric poems themselves) in later medieval texts such as Chaucer's *Knight's Tale* and the *Roman de la Rose*, the latter of which invokes the "beautiful golden chain / Which enlaces the four elements" [*bele chaeine dorée / Qui les quatre elemens enlace*].[78] From the late fifteenth century onwards, one finds Marsilio Ficino, Cristoforo Landino, Heinrich Cornelius Agrippa, Pierre Ronsard, and Guillaume des Autels each upholding this interpretation, turning Homer's terrifying image of a cosmic tug of war into a master metaphor for a cosmological system in which strife is circumscribed by concord or love. Written in the midst of the French religious wars, Des Autels's *Paix Venue du Ciel* reimagines Zeus's chain through the lens of Aristophanes's *Eirene*: Jupiter instructs Mercury to "take these six golden chains" [*pren ces six chains d'or*] and "attach them to the beautiful ivory cart of Peace" [*au beau char d'ivoire / De la Paix les attache*], and Mercury then gives the chain to the six deputies of Cateau-Cambrésis, who pull Peace to earth in a gesture that ratifies the peace treaties signed by Henri II of France, Elizabeth I, and Phillip II of Spain on 2–3 April 1559.[79] In readings that transform Homer's Olympian contest into a symbol of concord, the chain serves as a guarantor of natural law and divine omnipotence, representing "the order and arrangement of a universe that depends solely upon the power of a sovereign God" [*l'ordre et convenance de l'univers [qui] depend de la seulle puissance du souverain Dieu*].[80]

To interpret the golden chain as a symbol of God's sovereign power often involves reading it as a symbol of divine right monarchy. Yet not all of Homer's early modern readers interpret Zeus's golden chain as legitimating political absolutism. In his *De la Servitude Volontaire ou Contr'un* (1549), Etienne de la Boëtie interprets the golden chain as a symbol of tyranny. Perhaps in imitation of Lucian, who places the golden chain in various "unlikely" and parodic contexts, La Boëtie argues that the chain symbolizes the way in which many men "attach themselves to the tyrant by this chain, thus helping him, as in Homer, Jupiter, who boasts that, if he pulls the chain, he will pull all the gods towards him" [*par ceste corde se tiennent au tiran, s'aident d'icelle comme en Homere Jupiter, qui se vante, s'il tire la chesne, d'emmener vers soi tous les dieus*].[81] Although La Boëtie's interpretation is atypical in its refusal to affirm the image as a "golden cord, of Unitie" that suppresses "foule Discord" and bruises the "Cadmeian seede / Of strife," as the Jacobean poet Ralph Knevet puts it, early modern writers do recognize Homer's golden chain to be a capacious and flexible conceit, one variously interpreted by Homer's ancient readers and also potentially subject to abuse, as Spenser's Night and Milton's Satan each do when they manipulate it into an emblem of inextricable fate or boundless ambition.[82]

The Poet of War and Peace

Guided by ancient commentators who interpret various episodes in Homeric epic as allegories of the mutually constitutive relationship between *philia* and *eris*, Renaissance readers of Homer embrace the idea that the *Iliad* and *Odyssey* represent a "complete doctrine of life, divided into periods of peace and war," as Leonardo Bruni puts it in his 1424 *On the Study of Literature*.[83] The dedication to Giphanius's 1572 edition of the *Iliad* praises Homer for teaching both "civil law and military science" [*Iuris civilis & Rei militaris Scientia*], while Jean de Sponde, addressing the future king Henri IV of France, writes that "whether you are dealing with matters of war or of peace [*sive enim belli sive etia(m) pacis negotia administres*], your Majesty has here in these two volumes of Homer things not unfamiliar to your occupations."[84] Although claims of Homer's mastery of diverse disciplines of political philosophy are commonplace during the later fifteenth and sixteenth centuries, and although most writers agree that the *Iliad* and *Odyssey* represent the states of war and peace, there is substantial disagreement about how the poems, together or separately, represent the relationship between these modes of life or prioritize the one over the other. Praising Agamemnon as both a "good governour, and worthy warrior," Lipsius argues for the interdependence between martial skill and good government in what may constitute a response to Julius Caesar Scaliger, who argues in his *Poetices Libri Septem* that "Homer teaches the two forms of life we may follow, civil prudence [*civilem prudentiam*] in the *Odyssey* and military in the *Iliad*." According to Scaliger, however, whereas Homer has "shown these two types of life in two men" [*duas species in duobus viris ostendisset*], namely, Odysseus and Agamemnon, "Virgil has reunited them in one sole person, Aeneas" [*in uno utramque Aenea composuit Maro*].[85] Yet for Lipsius, Homer reconciles military virtue and civil prudence in a different manner than does Virgil, since while "military Courage outclasses all other virtues," Lipsius argues, Agamemnon's excellence as both a "good governor and a good commander" [*rector bonus, et bonus Induperator*] benefits his subjects both in war and at peace.[86]

The paradox that war produces peace, and discord concord, also shapes the variegated responses to the scenes of forgiveness and amnesty that conclude both the *Iliad* and *Odyssey*. Spenser adapts Athena's intervention at the end of the *Odyssey* into the truce that Cambina effects between Cambell and Triamond, while Milton reworks the poignant scenes of supplication between Achilles and Priam in the final book of the *Iliad* into a prayer that solicits the descent of prevenient grace after Adam and Eve have sinned. In readings alert to the rhetorical etiquette of Homer's verbal disputants, both Erasmus and Chapman look to Homer for guidance about when to deploy and when to desist from the kind of bitter or abusive speech that has the power either to create or to defuse strife depending upon the context in which it is used. Hobbes extracts a different set of lessons from Homer about how to convert strife into harmony, emphasizing throughout his translation the expediency of single rule and the utility of fear in maintaining political concord.

The passage that elicits the most diverse and fervent responses from Renaissance readers on these questions is the *ekphrasis* of Achilles's shield in Book 18 of the *Iliad*. The passage had long been read as exemplifying the contrary yet reciprocal relationship between war and peace, since the shield, in ancient allegorical traditions, depicts one city at peace [*tên men eirênes*] and another at war [*tên de polemou*]. Early modern writers frequently echo this reading, arguing that Achilles's shield, which represents "one [city] at peace and the other at war" [*l'une de paix et l'autre de guerre*], may be interpreted as an allegory of "the friendship and the dissension that are the foundation of things, according to the opinion of Empedocles."[87] For those readers disinclined to regard war as a productive form of strife, the two-sided shield provides a twin allegory, moralizing the consequences of good and bad government or of justice and injustice.[88] Lambinus offers a creative twist on this interpretation when he proposes in his 1562 oration on Homer that the "two cities" [*duarum civitatu[m]*] on Achilles's shield correspond to the "very different" [*inter se dissimiles*] cities of Ithaca and Phaiakia in the *Odyssey*: while Ithaca suffers under rapacious and unjust princes [*princeps rapaces, injustos*] who foster "*dissidiis, ac discordiis concitatum*," Phaiakia is ruled "by the consent of the people" [*populum consentientem*] and upholds the virtues of "modesty and shame" [*modestiam & pudorem*].[89]

Yet the relationship between the two sides of Achilles's shield (and between the shield and the *Iliad* as a whole) is variously construed: the scene of war may be interpreted as preceding the scene of peace or as following it, and the scene of peace may be read as a critique of martial conflict in the *Iliad*, as an alternative to it, or as an eventual outcome of war itself. Homer's Renaissance readers differ in their estimation of how best to assess the relationship between the two sides of the shield, which may represent war and peace as equally inevitable, equally ennobling, or even mutually constitutive. While some readers, such as Lambinus, interpret the shield as representing the moral and political superiority of peace, several of Homer's early modern readers instead stress the correspondence or moral equivalence between the two sides of Achilles's shield. In his 1666 *Armilogia Sive Ars Chromocritica ... Mythologized to the Heroical Theam of Homer on the Shield of Achilles*, Sylvanus Morgan argues that the peaceful city and the warring city represent, respectively, "Political Nobility" and "Martial ornament."[90] In his French translation of the *Iliad*, paraphrasing Homer's "two fair cities" [*poleis ...kalas*] at *Il.* 18.490–1, Sieur de Souhait

Figure 2. Pietro Testa, *Achilles Dragging the Body of Hector*. Circa 1648–50. Engraving. Courtesy of the National Gallery of Art, Washington, DC.

similarly suggests that the "two pleasant cities" [*deux agreables citez*] on either side of the shield both exercise valuable moral and political virtues. By underscoring the likeness as well as the difference between them, Souhait implicitly concedes that the *neikos* – the judicial dispute represented in the agora of the peaceful city – and the strife of war dramatized on the other side of the shield are, as it were, the recto and verso of a healthy and robust society.[91] The shield's depiction of war hardly exalts the heroics of the battlefield: an army stirred up by Strife and Tumult [*Eris en de Kudoimos*] slaughters some sheep and their herdsmen while Fate [*Kêr*] drags a bloody corpse off the battlefield in a scene that mirrors Achilles's dragging of Hector's corpse around the walls of Troy, matching the barbarity of the most horrific artistic renditions of that scene, such as Pietro Testa's engraving of ca 1648–50, which renders Hector's corpse with the vivid detail of an anatomical engraving by Vesalius (see figure 2).

Yet the peace and prosperity depicted on the other side of the shield, demonstrated by scenes of farming, dancing, a trial, a wedding, and a religious sacrifice, are linked together in the same "cosmic dance" on a shield encircled by the "great might of Oceanus" [*mega sthenos Okeanoio*], the father of the gods whose symbolic circumscription of the shield had long been read as an allegory of the *coincidentia oppositorum* dramatized by the poem as a whole (*Il.* 18.607). As Souhait explains, the "human condition always comprises two indissoluble aspects" [*la condition humaine comporte toujours deux aspects indissociables*]. Such a reading discerns the complementary forces of *philia* and *eris* at work on *both* sides of the shield, which "works to unify contraries" since both peace and war are a "permanent feature of man's condition, an eternal part of the cosmic design."[92] When Renaissance writers seek to describe the complex vision of the universe expressed by Achilles's shield, their language is redolent of cosmological allegory: as Ben Jonson and George Sandys each put it, the shield is a "spheare of heaven" and it contains "the whole world."[93]

Engendering "in one same air elation and agony" (*Il.* 4.450), war in Homeric epic is fraught with contradiction and paradox.[94] In both poems, conflict [*neikos*] is referred to repeatedly as *homoion* – common, shared, or unifying. For Renaissance readers, the epithet strengthens Homer's perceived affinities with the cosmology of the pre-Socratic Heraclitus, who holds that contraries are "set continually at variance" in a dynamic process that Nietzsche would later compare to a struggle between "two wrestlers of whom sometimes the one succeeds, sometimes the other."[95] In the *Iliad*, the concept of *neikos homoiion* and of related epithets such as *xunos Enualios* (*Il.* 18.309) suggests a counterbalance between opposing armies as well as between the adversarial forces of nature in order to convey how various forms of strife are governed by *dikê*, or distributive justice. Both epithets were much commented on in antiquity, and both were mined for their apparent cosmological undermeanings. Glossing the Homeric epithets *xunos Enualios* [Ares, or war, common to all] and *alloprosallos* [first on one side, then on the other], both applied to Ares, Heraclitus reads them as shorthand for the eristic processes of his natural philosophy, a philosophy that, as Aristotle explains in the *Nicomachean Ethics*, is founded upon the principle of *concordia discors*: "opposition brings things together [*to antixoun sumpheron*], and from tones at variance comes beautiful harmony, and all things come to pass through strife [*panta kat'erin ginesthai*]."[96] In part because these epithets were held by Homer's ancient commentators to contain veiled spiritual and cosmological truths, early modern readers are fascinated by the image of war as *xunos* and as *alloprosallos*, phrases that accrue various implications over the course of the sixteenth and seventeenth centuries.[97] In his *Adages*, Erasmus meditates on these epithets as sceptical expressions of vicissitude that convey the tragicomic nature of the human condition. Milton transforms them to work out the nature of divine impartiality, while Hobbes extracts a typically Hobbesian lesson about the fundamental equality between adversaries. For each of these writers, Homer's depiction of the process by which the vanquished may become the victor and vice versa – Ares "kills the killer" [*te ktaneonta katekta*], to cite Hector's prescient remark at *Il.* 18.309 – confirms their belief in the unerring sway of eternal laws or in the existence of an impartial God who effects topsy-turvy reversals of the "existing order" in order to preserve justice (1 Cor. 1:27).

Homer's Double Genius

Often read during the period as an emblem of the union of contraries, Achilles's shield is one of several episodes that demonstrate to Renaissance readers the "universality" of the *Iliad* and *Odyssey*, copious poems that "somehow imitat[e] the gigantic poem of the universe."[98] This way of reading Homeric epic often involves interpreting the poems as representing the plenitude of the natural world, a world in which discord and strife are seen to belong to and participate in a larger and more beneficent harmony. But many readers also understand Homer's universality – a universality that reflects the *copia* or variety of nature itself – as a product of the poems' multiple and conflictive perspectives on matters ranging from kingship and war to rhetoric. When fourteenth- and fifteenth-century Italian humanists inaugurate serious Homeric scholarship, they inherit from classical antiquity the commonplace that Homer's poems comprise a wide variety of literary genres and rhetorical styles. While this argument remains common in later Renaissance texts, it ceases to be conventional, instead carrying with it surprising implications for the status of Homeric epic vis-à-vis later imitations and adaptions. Moreover, while "two rival traditions of epic" may indeed shape the epic tradition after Homer, as David Quint has argued, these traditions are still inextricably linked in the *Iliad* and *Odyssey*, where they overlap and compete head on with each other.[99] This is because the two Homeric epics offer rival accounts of the same narratives, representing the same events from multiple points of view and thus casting doubt on the authority of any "correct" perspective in a manner that distinguishes Homer's narrative style from that of Latin imitators such as Virgil and Lucan. Like the ancient Greek tragedies to which Aristotle compared them, Homer's poems are dialogic and agonistic, presenting "two often irreconcilable sides to a central issue," and Homer's Renaissance readers are remarkably attuned to the ways in which both the *Iliad* and *Odyssey* dramatize moral and epistemological conflict.[100] Inheritors of an ancient commentary tradition that presents Homeric epic as full of "difficulties" [*aporêmata*] and "problems" [*problêmata*] of a philosophical nature, Renaissance readers not only seek out puzzles and questions [*zêtêmata*] as they study or imitate Homer but also accentuate the problematic in Homer – insoluble philological dilemmas, riddling prophecies, contradictions, sceptical aporias.[101] Erasmus, Rabelais, and Chapman each emphasize Homer's predilection for questioning and irony, though each finds different value in these philosophical and rhetorical strategies. Spenser, Milton, and Hobbes are each attentive to moments of hesitation or deliberation in Homeric epic, moments in which characters must, individually or collectively, choose between two competing positions, courses of action, or perceptions of truth. And readers of all stripes tackle the discontinuities and inconsistencies within and between the Homeric poems not by grappling with questions of authorship or textual history, as eighteenth- and nineteenth-century scholars would come to do, but rather by appreciating such textual "problems" as the deliberate product of a jocular and mischievous poetic mind.[102]

For many early modern readers, the dialogic and agonistic characteristics of the Homeric corpus are especially evident in its generic and stylistic range. Following Aristotle and Quintilian, sixteenth- and seventeenth-century commentaries and rhetorical treatises routinely identify Homer as the father both of tragedy and comedy, an argument that depends for them (as it did for Homer's ancient readers) on the belief that the author of the *Iliad* and *Odyssey* also composed several mock-epic works. Although the authorship of the *Batrachomyomachia* and the *Margites* was occasionally challenged during the Renaissance, most notably by Henri Estienne and Isaac Casaubon, the majority of Renaissance scholars resist the position embraced by the *chorizontes*, or separators, the name given to the Alexandrian editors who argued that the Homeric corpus was the product of multiple authors.[103] Sixteenth- and seventeenth-century readers are aware that the poems attributed to Homer came into existence through a messy and complex textual process and that they belonged to a larger body of rival narratives by other poets (now called the Epic Cycle). But the majority of Renaissance readers are nonetheless eager to believe that one poet wrote the *Iliad*, the *Odyssey*, and an assortment of hymns and epic parodies, and they are, for the most part, equally eager to argue for coherence both within and between these works even when it is difficult to discern. The appeal of the *Batrachomyomachia* during the Renaissance can be attributed in part to its brevity, which made the poem especially suitable for early printing and for elementary Greek training. But the poem also appealed to readers wishing to make sense of Homer's literary career in Virgilian terms, as well as to readers uncomfortable with the martial ethos of the *Iliad* and *Odyssey* or otherwise eager to regard Homer as a figure of humble piety rather than ostentatious grandeur. The oft-quoted lines from Book 10 of Quintilian ("*hunc nemo in magnis rebus sublimitate, in parvis proprietate superaverit*") offer early modern readers compelling testimony that Homer was equally skilled at high (or sublime) genres and at low ones. When Poliziano paraphrases Quintilian in his *Ambra* and his *Oration on Homer*, he offers up the line as proof that Homer is the source of all poetic genres and rhetorical forms, a copious nursery of all literary genres and styles.[104]

The idea that the Homeric corpus constituted a single, unified origin for all genres and rhetorical modes makes the study of Homer uniquely valuable for Renaissance readers interested in generic mixture and in the historical evolution of literary forms. In the preface to a 1531 commentary on Horace, Aulo Giano Parrasio praises Homer for "giving to poetry a single and definitive body" [*unum poeticae corpus perfectum fecit*] by "introducing into his works the subjects of comedies, tragedies, dithyrambs, and all kinds of poems."[105] Untroubled by the questions of authorial unity that later come to haunt Homeric scholarship, sixteenth-century scholars such as Parrasio instead regard the Homeric corpus as a vast repository of diverse genres, styles, and philosophical outlooks, its variant strains harmonized into a pristine unity. By the middle of the sixteenth century, it is common to find descriptions of Homer that praise him for generic multiplicity and mixture. In his 1554 *Discorsi intorno al comporre dei romanzi*, Giraldi Cinthio calls the *Odyssey* a "tragedia de fin lieto," a tragedy with a happy ending, while Gerhard Vossius argues in his 1647 *De Artis Poeticae Natura* that Homer's "double genius" [*utroque ingenio*] yields two poems, "one serious and honourable, the other humble and full of tender intercourse."[106] Playwrights and librettists follow suit as works such as Giovanni Falungi's *Ulixe Patiente* (ca 1535), Giambattista della Porta's *Penelope* (1591), J.G. Durval's *Les Travaux d'Ulysse, Tragi-Comédie tirée d'Homère* (1631), and Charles Boyer's *Ulysse dans l'Isle de Circe* (1649) fashion Odysseus's story into textbook examples of the mixing of kinds famously condemned by Philip Sidney.[107]

The desire to attribute mock-epic works to Homer often presupposes the idea of a poet adept at confounding jest and earnest. This is certainly the case for Aurelio Simmaco, whose 1456 Italian translation of the *Batrachomyomachia*, the first vernacular translation of the poem, argues for the work's authenticity by praising Homer's "wit at catching high and glorious things by low ones."[108] This common inclination to regard Homer as in possession of a Socratic wit accumulates new implications over the course of the sixteenth and seventeenth centuries. Whereas earlier Renaissance scholars embrace the authenticity of the *Batrachomyomachia* out of respect for ancient testimonies and in order to preserve authorial unity, later writers such as Erasmus, Rabelais, Nashe, and Chapman are more interested in the dissonance produced by the diverse generic modes and philosophical outlooks of a capacious Homeric corpus that contains – but does not necessarily reconcile – contrary visions of the world. In his *Adages* and other works, Erasmus presents a Homeric poet who embraces a tragicomic vision of human life that combines joy and sorrow, divine wisdom and mortal folly, thus concocting paradoxes similar to those generated by Erasmus's own *In Praise of Folly* and *Sileni Alcibiades*. Rabelais, by contrast, produces a serio-comic imitation of Homeric epic that refashions the heroic quests of the poems' protagonists into philosophical journeys whose crossroads are the pro-and-contra deliberation of various moral and epistemological questions, their answers remaining as elusive as Tiresias's prophecy. Responding to the "opposed and mutually conditioning voices" of the *Odyssey* as a text that parodies both the *Iliad* and itself, Rabelais's work exaggerates Homer's rhetorical *copia*, his dialogism, and his generic hybridity, the very stylistic virtues that made Homer so problematic, or even distasteful, for later generations of readers, particularly in the neoclassical era.[109]

Although Renaissance readers, like their classical forerunners, routinely condemn as indecorous the more ridiculous comic strains of Homer's poems, there were powerful and diverse motives for esteeming Homer as a comic (or rather a serio-comic) poet. His comic impulses, often understood as symptoms of a sceptical or cynical outlook, turn the Renaissance Homer into a figure who resembles beggar-philosophers such as Aesop, Diogenes the Cynic, and Socrates – models of involuted wisdom whose knowledge is hidden beneath a surface of poverty, humility, or absurdity. In his *Gynaikeion*, Thomas Heywood describes how during his "long peregrination through Greece," a blind Homer "groaping his way" meets a group of potters who "intreated him that hee would play them a fit of Myrth" in exchange for some pots and cups.[110] According to Heywood, the poem recited by Homer in return for this modest gift was the *Hymn to Athena*, one of more than a dozen hymns attributed to Homer during the Renaissance and a work that, alongside his epigrams and mock-epic poems, reinforces credence in Homer's generic range and flexibility.

These brief and nugatory works, subsequently deemed spurious, also reinforce Homer's image as a trenchant critic of strife. One of the reasons why Renaissance readers were reluctant to banish the *Batrachomyomachia* and the *Margites* from the Homeric canon was that these works were, or at least appeared to be, parodies of epic conflict, offering a mockery of the heroic strategies – boasting, acts of physical aggression, narrating genealogies – on display in the *Iliad*. Some of the most sophisticated and inventive early modern adaptations of Homeric mock-epic, including Luigi Pulci's *Morgante*, Teofilo Folengo's *Baldo*, and Samuel Butler's *Hudibras*, offer a bathetic view of strife by narrating the trivial causes of great conflicts. "It was about a wench," announces the opening line of a 1658 mock-epic entitled *The*

Innovation of Penelope and Ulysses, which then launches into an interpretation of the Trojan war that reduces Helen to a whore and recreates the *Iliad* in the seamy London districts of Smithfield, Hammersmith (the haunt of Hephaestus), and "Turne-mill street."[111] Even cruder is Ortuinus Gratius's *Dialogue between Mercury and a Potlicker*, one of a number of satirical dialogues written in the early years of the German Reformation and modelled on Lucian's Homeric parodies. In a scene that begins by mocking Zeus's golden chain speech, the plump and fatuous Potlicker enlists Mercury's help in hoisting him up to Olympus after consuming a giant meal; when their efforts are unsuccessful, Potlicker proposes that "[I] move my bowels, so I'll be lighter," but despite his boast that "one more leap and I'm in heaven," this plan also fails, and Potlicker tumbles down to Etna and finally into Vulcan's cesspool in a fall that resembles Hephaestus's slightly less comical plummet to Lemnos at the end of Book 1 of the *Iliad*.[112] However frivolous these texts may seem, they illustrate the centrality of mock-epic traditions to Homer's reception during the period. A.D. Nuttall is one of the few literary critics who has acknowledged how seriously the early moderns regarded Homer as a master of comedy, and he warns that although "[w]e commonly assume that Homer, the first and grandest of the epic poets, is also the most uniformly elevated … [t]he truth is that to early modern readers brought up on Virgil Homer himself, unaltered, could look very like burlesque."[113] This is not to say that Homer's Renaissance readers all admired the comic strains in Homeric epic – Marco Girolamo Vida and J.C. Scaliger both loathed this quality in Homer. But the Homeric penchant for comedy escaped the notice of very few Renaissance readers, and more often than not, his capacity for satire, burlesque, and mockery was seen as a literary virtue, rather than a fault.

For a culture that prized *gioco*-seriousness as a social, rhetorical, and philosophical strategy, the playful and ritualized aggression that pervades Homeric epic and mock-epic is easily assimilated to the early modern attraction to "rule-bound" or civil forms of conflict, which served to "domesticate" violence so as to mitigate it or put it to constructive use.[114] The Homeric corpus contains numerous examples of ludic strife capable of delaying, averting, or containing serious violence. Athletic competitions, witty disputations between combatants on the battlefield, and the comical brutality of gods, suitors, and beggars each provides a "pause from the tumult of combat" while at the same time nurturing the "agonistic spirit" required for victory in war.[115] For readers already predisposed to view the *Iliad* and *Odyssey* as vivid repositories of various rhetorical modes, both encomiastic and vituperative, the playfully aggressive speeches that fill both poems look to early modern readers like a "socially productive" form of strife, an eristic behaviour designed to convert "adversaries into allies" and thus help foster "social cohesion."[116] And, for a culture that so frequently sublimated rivalry and conflict through verbal wit, the rhetorical jousting typical of the Homeric poems offers a compelling model for the "playful resolutio[n]" of what would otherwise be serious disputes.[117]

Homer, Father of Everything

If Homer's generic and rhetorical range helps to enforce his universality as a poet, so too does his scope and suppleness when treating political and philosophical matters. Louis Leroy writes that Homeric epic represents "such great diversity of natures, multitude of disciplines, variety of actions, exercises, and works," and similar sentiments appear in many prefaces and dedications to sixteenth-century editions and translations of the *Iliad* and *Odyssey*.[118] Homer's association with universality and variety had already been ratified allegorically in antiquity through the figure of Okeanos, the primeval father of the cosmos who "gave birth to all things" (*Il.* 14.246). For some, Okeanos represents Homer's endorsement of the cosmological principle, associated with Thales by Virgil (*Georg.* 4.382), Cicero (*De Natura Deorum* 1.25), and other classical writers, that "water is the beginning of things" [*aquam...esse initium rerum*]; for others, his union with Tethys represents the generative interplay of "love and strife" [*philian kai to neikos*] among the elements. But Okeanos is also a figure of the poet himself, shorthand for Homer's oceanic abundance, or the profusion of ideas, doctrines, and styles that abound in, or derive from, his poems. Hadrianus Junius's 1558 edition of Eustathius's commentary on Homer – an abridged edition, ironically enough – is entitled *Copiae Cornu sive Oceanus enarrationum Homericarum* (Corncucopia, or an Ocean of Homeric commentaries), while Petrus Valens, in a 1621 oration in praise of Homer, writes that "Homer is the ocean of all knowledge and wisdom."[119] Similar metaphors course through the writings of Poliziano, who revives the ancient similes that liken the Homeric corpus to a "boundless and infinite sea" [*immensum quoddam atque infinitum pelages*] and to a pristine font from which "[a]ll things derive ... and in them are all things" [*Omnia ab his et in his sunt omnia*].[120] The idea that Homer is the origin of all literary models and intellectual disciplines is laid bare in Giovanni Battista Galestruzzi's 1658 engraving of *The Apotheosis of Homer*, which illustrates the Archelaos relief, excavated in Italy in the first half of the seventeenth century. In it, the poet is scaffolded by a train of female devotees representing the disciplines and genres to which he gave birth, including *Historia*, *Comœdia*, *Tragedia*, and *Physis*, or the study of natural philosophy (see figure 3).

Figure 3. Giovanni Battista Galestruzzi, *The Apotheosis of Homer* (engraving, 1658). Reproduced in Gisbert Cuper, *Apotheosis vel consecratio Homeri* (Amsterdam, 1683). Getty Images.

Imagined as the primordial, oceanic source of human wisdom, the Homeric corpus thus represents the possibility of a common and unified origin for disciplines of knowledge subsequently partitioned into schools and factions. As the poet who "flourish'd in the worlds first infancy," Homer promises to restore the unity of human knowledge, a fantasy evident throughout sixteenth- and seventeenth-century editions and translations as well as treatises of literary criticism.[121] In his *Epistre de Dame Poesie*, the versified preface to his French translation of the *Iliad*, Hugues Salel appoints Homer the "clear source" of human wisdom and argues that "there is no passage in philosophy, / howsoever diverse, which does not fortify itself / with some saying or notable sentence / of this poet."[122] According to Salel, every philosophical school, from the pre-Socratics and the Platonists to the Stoics and Epicureans, draws its doctrines from Homer: those who affirm that "harmony / and strife have created all things" [*l'Union / Et le debat, avoir fait toute chose*], those who believe in "the immortal soul" [*l'ame immortelle*], those who advocate "following virtue, and all honourable duties" [*Suivre vertu, and toute office honeste*], those who "think the only pleasure is virtue" [*pensoit la seule volupté / Estre le bien*], and those who "against truth assign all to chance" [*contre verité / Assignent tout à la temerité*].[123] What is not clear, however, is whether Salel understands this diversity of "opinions" that springs from Homeric epic as a virtue or as a dilemma – as a means of restoring a lost philosophical unity, or as a mark of the impossibility of intellectual concord. If Homer, according to Salel, is a poet "after whom are issued / Diversely received opinions" [*sont après issues / Opinions diversement recevues*], does that make him a poet who generates disagreement and dissent, or one who provides a solution to it?

The idea that all philosophical doctrines originate in the writings of Homer, already so commonplace in antiquity that it had become an object of satire, acquires new implications for the history of ideas in the sixteenth century as writers ponder whether and to what extent competing philosophical and religious sects can or should be reconciled to each other. Perhaps responding to the methods of Homer's ancient editors and glossators, who adhered to the principle that "Homer is his own best interpreter" [*ôs autos men eauton ta polla Homêros exêgeitai*], Seneca scoffs in one of his epistles that "if Homer is the master of many conflicting doctrines then he must really be the master of none," protesting that different philosophical sects attribute doctrines to Homer that are "irreconcilable with each other" [*enim inter se dissident*].[124] A few

Renaissance writers echo Seneca's complaint. In different ways, Rabelais and Montaigne each delight in pointing out the contradictions within and between Homer's poems, and one may detect equal parts admiration and contempt in the claim of one early seventeenth-century French writer that "Homer seems like a palace with many floors, where everybody may lodge themselves."[125] In an epigram entitled "On Homer," John Collop mocks the commonplace that Homeric epic is a vast repository of wise maxims, distilled into pithy morsels by his early modern readers:

> Some did his *Iliads* to a nutshell fit;
> A Cherystone might have confin'd the wit.
> The Gods know all; wise men sleep not all night,
> One man must govern; many can't do right.[126]

Despite Collop's apt mockery of the process by which Homer's vast and unruly poems were recycled into superficial, bite-size adages during the Renaissance, the majority of contemporary writers take seriously Homer's status as the "seedbed of all disciplines" [*omnium semina disciplinarum*], to use Poliziano's phrase, or the "father of all philosophy" [*père de toute philosophie*], to use Rabelais's.[127] Yet whereas Du Bartas praises "Sweet-numbred Homer … / Whose Schoole hath bred the many-differing sorts / Of ancient Sages," other writers express alarm at the fact that "after [Homer's] time, philosophy was divided into various sects" and that adherents to those various sects, such as Plato, use "the best passages extracted out of Homer to authorise his philosophical disputes."[128]

Homer's status as the father of philosophy thus cuts both ways. His works contain the seeds of intellectual discord but also provide an antidote to it. This ambivalence is already apparent in the ancient sources from which sixteenth-century writers such as Poliziano, Rabelais, and Du Bartas drew. In an oration entitled "Whether There Is a Homeric School of Philosophy," the second-century CE Greek philosopher and rhetorician Maximus of Tyre identifies Homer as "the first philosopher," a poet whose syncretic powers hold in tranquil suspension the conflicting doctrines of various philosophical sects. But since Homer's time, Maximus complains, "those warring camps of the philosophers" have divided themselves into "hostile factions" such that "the world [is] full of mumbled words, as sophists clash with sophists," an observation that makes Homer a kind of ground zero for intellectual conflict even as it also imagines Homeric epic to be capable of suppressing contention by illustrating the fundamental harmony of contrary philosophical outlooks.[129] Such a position agrees with the Platonic and Stoic allegorical traditions in which Maximus was steeped, traditions that interpret various episodes in Homeric epic as evidence of the "harmony out of opposites" [*harmonia ... ex enantiôn*] that is the governing principle of the cosmos.[130] Homer's Renaissance readers seize upon this paradox with equal parts delight and consternation. In a 1687 treatise entitled *Homeri Nepenthes*, Pierre Petit observes that if Homer is the source of all knowledge, then certain obscure passages are also a source of conflict, or rather the "occasion for all disagreement" [*occasio totius disputationis*].[131] Petit's remarks help to unravel the paradox that Homer's canonicity, far from ensuring interpretive stability, breeds "hermeneutical openness" for early modern and contemporary readers alike. The authority and familiarity of the *Iliad* and *Odyssey* are the very qualities that permit the poems' "increased flexibility" and even their abuse at the hands of readers eager to claim Homer as the forerunner of various philosophical and religious doctrines.[132] But Petit's observation also illustrates how thoroughly early modern interpretations of Homer are shaped by larger questions concerning the origin of strife in the universe at large. As the "father of poets and literature" [*Poetarum & literarum parentis*], Homer provides a means of appraising whether that foundation rests upon order and unity or upon conflict and discord.

Eris between Paganism and Christianity

This introduction began with an example of the ridiculous extremes to which some Renaissance writers are willing to go in their attempt to accommodate Homeric epic to Christian doctrine and history. The example of Jacobus Hugo is a far-fetched one, even by the standards of allegory. But his reading cannot be dismissed as a caprice, since the impulse to make Homeric epic intellectually and spiritually relevant is strong even among scholars who shun the fanciful flights of allegory for the firm ground of philology.[133] Scholars including Poliziano, Guillaume Budé, and Jean de Sponde frequently use passages from the *Iliad* and *Odyssey* in order to ponder contemporary theological and political disputes. While many Renaissance readers of Homer acknowledge their palpable cultural distance from his poems, this recognition does not mitigate the desire to make Homeric epic speak to present occasions. Filippo Sassetti remarks that since heroic deeds of the sort represented in ancient epic no longer occur, poets need "to adopt the actions" [*adoptare attioni*] of ancient heroes to the present age, and Giraldi Cinthio agrees, arguing that since all poets reflect the beliefs and customs of their times, many of a poet's "past virtues would be present vices, to be eschewed by the imitator."[134] There are a handful of vocal dissenters from this view, to be sure. Antonio Minturno argues in his 1563 *Arte Poetica* that "that which is true once must be true forever and in every age" such that Homer and Virgil provide timeless models of heroic virtue to be imitated rather than adapted to changing times.[135] But most of the editions, translations, and Homeric commentaries produced during the sixteenth and seventeenth centuries contend in one way or another with the problem that things "proper to [Homer's] times ... are now improper" and vice versa.[136] To study Homer's reception is thus valuable for broadening our understanding of more widespread early modern disputes concerning scholarly method and the relationship between antiquity and modernity. As Anthony Grafton has argued, the Homeric corpus plays a central role in early modern debates over whether "to make the ancient world live again, assuming its undimmed relevance" or whether to "put the ancient texts back into their own time, admitting that reconstruction of the past is difficult."[137] Despite R.R. Bolgar's claim that early Greek texts such as the *Iliad* were "too remote from civilized normality" to be deemed either useful or dangerous to their sixteenth-century readers, many scholars and translators of the period struggled over how to translate into modern parlance Homer's "habits, banquets, and manners of living" [*habitz, bancquetz, et manieres de vivre*] while at the same time preserving these "strange customs" [*usage estranges*] so that they reflect the "the naiveté of their antiquity" [*le naïf de l'ancienneté*].[138] Jacques Peletier (1517–82), one of Homer's first translators into French, appreciates that both strategies are necessary, even if they work at cross purposes to each other.

A full assessment of Homer's reception during the early modern period thus demands attention not only to the fortunes of the text itself – its editions, translations, commentaries, and scholarly paratexts – but also to the intersections and divergences between the practices, beliefs, and values of archaic Greece and those of the sixteenth- and seventeenth-century poets and scholars who read Homer. Renaissance readers puzzle over and sometimes condemn Homeric customs ranging from the ritual sacrifice of animals and the unashamed nakedness of Nausicaa to the pastimes of a hero who assembles his own bedroom furniture. But they also discern profound sympathies between their own culture and that of Homeric Greece, and they account for those sympathies in various ways. Homer may be Egyptian or Greek; the contemporary of Moses, or David, or Solomon; the rival of Orpheus or of Hesiod; an ancestor of the pre-Socratics, of Socrates, of the Epicureans or the Stoics. Charles Martindale has rightly argued that reception history always involves the "acknowledgement that past and present are always implicated in each other."[139] As Renaissance writers variously fashion Homer into a divinely inspired bard, a pacifist, a lowly beggar, a Socratic *eiron*, a Solomonic sage, a guardian of justice, or a defender of monarchy, they are also fashioning themselves, assessing the continuities and discontinuities between the ideals or customs they attribute to Homeric culture and the ones they value (or dislike) in their own. Both Martindale and Simon Goldhill have recently expressed the concern that "reception" may be "too passive a term for the dynamics of resistance and appropriation, recognition and self-aggrandisement" at work in the adaptation and transformation of classical texts by writers in later periods.[140] As Homer's Renaissance readers debate whether his poems are the product of an archaic sensibility or a modern one, they are simultaneously engaged in defining the dominant moral and spiritual values of their own culture, as well as ideas that may be vulnerable or eroding. Contrary to the assumption that "reception is fundamentally anti-historicist," this book is predicated upon the "historical contingency of the interpreter's position," and its readings treat Homer's Renaissance editors, translators, and imitators as "cultural and historical subject[s]" whose interpretations of the poet cannot be pried away from their cultural biases or from their most cherished political, theological, and aesthetic convictions.[141]

For the most part, Homer's Renaissance readers transvalue rather than reject wholesale the eristic aspects of Homeric epic they find disturbing or distasteful. Often, they do so by struggling to "assimilate, domesticate, and transcend the heroic tradition" by producing Christian heroic poems such as Vida's *Christiad* or Tasso's *Gerusalemme Liberata*.[142] But they also do so by searching for Homeric values and beliefs that continue to have ethical or spiritual merit in a Christian world, weighing the extent to which Christian theology and ethics might accommodate the eristic spirit of Homer's archaic Greek world. Homer was hardly "irredeemably pagan" to his early modern readers, as Robin Sowerby has claimed.[143] In fact, many Renaissance readers rely upon Homer's early Christian allegorists and upon patristic writers (especially Origen, Clement, and Jerome) for guidance about how best to accommodate Hellenic *eris* to Christian *agôn*. Origen in particular makes explicit the "analogy between the reading of Homer and the reading of the Gospels" such that later Christian readers are able to "acknowledge levels of meaning" within the Homeric poems and thus cull out "that which is entirely unacceptable without rejecting the rest."[144] Clement of Alexandria lends to early modern culture a distinctly Homeric metaphor for this process of accommodation. As Budé puts it, readers in search of the Christian pieties concealed in Homeric epic must have "circumcised ears" [*auribus circuncisis*], as do Odysseus's crew when they pass by the Sirens, or rather must tie themselves to the mast of Christian doctrine, as does Odysseus himself, in order to listen to the beautiful refrains of pagan antiquity without falling prey to its temptations.[145] Clement's lesson on the proper Christian method of reading Homer, a lesson embedded allegorically in a famous episode of the *Odyssey*, is taken to heart by the many Renaissance readers who regard Clement as an authority on what is and is not pious in Homeric epic. Sponde quotes a key passage from the *Stromata* at the beginning of his *De Poetica* to testify to the orthodoxy of his own theological interpretations of Homer, while Lipsius's many citations of Homer in his *Politica* are often passages either quoted or commented on by Clement.[146]

Homer's Renaissance readers disagree, however, about which aspects of his poems might most safely and productively be allowed to penetrate their sieve-like ears. Budé is one of a number of Renaissance scholars who attempt to redeem the theology of the *Odyssey*, arguing that its hero is "not the disciple of polytheism but rather of orthodoxy" [*non polytheiae quidem ipsi, sed orthodoxiae alumno*].[147] In the dedicatory epistle to his 1582 Italian translation of the *Odyssey*, addressed to Francesco de'Medici, Marco Girolamo Baccelli goes so far as to assert that the "injuries, deceptions, shameful acts, and other mortal things that Homer attributes to the gods are high mysteries of theology" as well as a means of accommodating divine truths to the limited understanding of the human intellect.[148] But other editors and translators are more guarded in their claims. In the preface to his edition of Homer, Sebastian Castellio confesses that when he began to read Homer, "I neglected to study Holy Scripture as carefully as I ought at that time," and he then admonishes his readers never to forget Christian doctrine when studying pagan texts, commenting that "the maid should not become the mistress, nor the mistress the maid" because "godly knowledge should rule over human knowledge and that the human should serve the godly."[149] That Homeric epic was regarded as a benign and legitimate object of study so long as it was interpreted in the service of Christian theology should come as little surprise to scholars familiar with the Renaissance reception of Lucretius, Lucian, or other classical authors whose ideas were most openly hostile to Christian orthodoxies. Yet no pagan writer apart from Homer managed to serve so many *different* Christian masters during the period. His poems lent support to Augustinian, Arminian, and Pelagian doctrines of the will, to Trinitarian and anti-Trinitarian theologies, to Hookerian defences of religious ceremony (in Chapman's translation of the *Odyssey*) but also to Milton's attacks on religious ceremony.

The impulse to seek out the correspondences between Homer and the scriptures is often motivated by the desire to trace the continuities and discontinuities between classical Greek and apostolic attitudes towards the eristic. In his *Lexicon Graecolatinum*, a dictionary first printed in 1579 that proved a popular resource for poets and scholars throughout the seventeenth century, Johannes Scapula fills the entries for *Eris* [strife], *Erizô* [to contend], and *Eridainô* [to contend with words] with examples from both classical Greek and New Testament literature, citing a line from Book 5 of the *Odyssey* next to passages from Xenophon's *Cyropaedia*, Plato's *Protagoras*, and several scriptural verses including 1 Cor. 12.25, where Paul condemns discord [*schisma*] between the members of Christ's body.[150] The seventeenth-century English theologian Henry Hammond, who quotes Homer liberally in his annotations and paraphrases on the New Testament, glosses Matt. 5.22 by noting that verbal abuse is proscribed by Christ but not by the *Iliad*: while "Minerva forbids Achilles striking Agamemnon," Hammond comments, she "gives leave to reproach him, and counsels to Contumelious words," which "here [are] most strictly prohibited by Christ."[151] In his annotations on Col. 3.21, however, Hammond discerns greater congruity between Homeric and New Testament attitudes towards verbal strife, observing that Paul's ban on verbal provocation has a Homeric legacy. Glossing the verse, "Fathers, do not provoke [*erethizete*] your children," Hammond explains that the word *erithizete*, a verb etymologically related to *eris*, "signifi[es] evil speaking in Homer," a remark that displays the theologian's recognition of the linguistic and ethical continuities between the archaic Greek world of Homer and the first-century CE Greek-speaking Mediterranean world through which the apostles moved. Several times in his paraphrases of the Pauline epistles, Hammond interprets Paul's diction, and his spiritual beliefs, as products of the "agonistical" behaviours and values of a much earlier Hellenic culture. Annotating Rom. 9.30, Hammond explains that the phrase "*diôkonta dikaiosunên katelaben dikaiosunên*" [pursuing righteousness and attained righteousness] contains verbs that "are all Agonistical, referring to the customes of the Grecian Exercises in their Olympian, Nemean, Isthmian, Pythian games, which are often alluded to in these Epistles," and he adds that the verb *diachein*, "pursuing, or striving to overtake, as any did in that exercise when he was behind another" might likewise be used to describe "swift-footed" [*podas ôkus*] Achilles and his excellence in running.[152] For Hammond, Paul is both heir to and reinventor of Homeric *agôn*. Glossing 2 Cor. 5.8, Hammond cites Eustathius to explain Paul's reference to "antient heathen customes in the agones," athletic practices and conventions apparently internalized and transformed by Paul's zealous spirituality, a reading borne out by another comment, at 1 Cor. 9.24, where Paul compares Christian "striving" [*agônizomenos*] for salvation to a race in which the prize is an "incorruptible crown" [*stephanon … aphtharton*] rather than a corruptible one. Puzzlingly oblivious to the distinction Paul is labouring to make between pagan competition for earthly fame and the Christian struggle for divine grace, Hammond remarks that "The discourse that here begins … is all perfectly Agonistical, no way to be explained but by observation of the customes in the Grecian games."[153]

Besides Hammond, a number of seventeenth-century English thinkers are eager to trace the correspondences between Homeric and Christian attitudes towards strife. In his *Mystagogus Poeticus*, Alexander Ross argues that Christians should "as earnestly strive for that whole Armor of God" as did "*Ajax* and *Ulysses*, about *Achilles* his Armor" and that "Christ is the true Achilles *achaluôn*, he that looseth us from all pains and diseases; who was tried in the fire of affliction, as gold in the furnace."[154] In a 1622 work entitled *Atheomastix*, Martin Fotherby attempts to prove the existence of divine grace by citing several Homeric passages, including a line from *Odyssey* 8 often used to such purpose during the period: "God hath not all his gifts bestow'd on all, or any one."[155] Although the line (as Fotherby admits) is spoken to "describe[e] the games of the Phaeacians, in Running, Wrestling, Leaping, Coyting," competitions in which "no man, could win in Two: much less, in all of them," the original context of the athletic contest only strengthens Fotherby's transvaluation of the line for theological purposes, since spiritual *agôn* is so often described by Paul (as well as by earlier Stoic and Jewish philosophers) as a contest or race. In the middle of the seventeenth century, English scholars are still catching up with their French, Dutch, and German counterparts as editors and commentators on ancient Greek literature and philosophy. The period between 1640 and 1670 in England witnesses an enormous rise in the printing of Homeric concordances, lexicons, and encyclopedias, many devoted to identifying correspondences between Homeric epic on the one hand and the Old and New Testaments on the other. It is probably no coincidence that the period in which Homeric scholarship began to flourish in England coincides, more or less, with the English Civil War, the Commonwealth and Protectorate, and the early Restoration, since many of the translations, commentaries, and concordances produced by scholars of the period – as well some of the most sophisticated and sensitive poetic imitations of the

Iliad and *Odyssey*, including Milton's *Paradise Lost* and Abraham Cowley's *Davideis* – value Homer for his wisdom on political and religious subjects dear to royalists and republicans alike during this turbulent period. As English writers weigh the merits of religious and political unity against liberty of conscience, and as they debate the legitimacy and effectiveness of their parliamentary government, works of scholarship appear that attempt to enlist the poet on various sides of contemporary debates or to adapt his works into forms that might speak to current problems.

One such work, James Duport's 1660 *Homeri Poetarum omnium seculorum facile Principis Gnomologia* [Homer, prince of poets for all ages, easily reduced to proverbs], lays bare its author's royalist sympathies by placing Homeric proverbs alongside classical and scriptural passages that praise kings as shepherds of their people, condemn rebellion, and exhort against the dangers of *hoi polloi*. Duport (1606–79), who was Milton's near-contemporary at Trinity College, Cambridge, also composed *Threnothriambos, sive, Liber Job Graeco carmine redditus* (1637), a Homeric paraphrase of the Book of Job, with a facing-page Latin translation, that earned Duport election to the Regius professorship of Greek. His Homeric "gnomology," which follows in the tradition of Erasmus's *Adages* and the many collections of Homeric epithets and maxims it spawned, compares Achilles's denunciation of strife at *Il.* 18.107 to several scriptural verses in which Paul forbids speaking or acting out of contention, including Rom. 13.13, "Not with contention or rivalry" [*Non in contentione & aemulatione*], and Phil. 2.3, "Do nothing with contention" [*nihil per contentionem facientes*].[156] But Duport also cites a number of instances where Homer and the scriptures are in agreement on the benefits of rivalry or discord. Among the classical and scriptural parallels he lists for *Od.* 24.514–15, where Laertes delights that his son and grandson are competing with each other honourably ("What a day this is for me, kind gods! Very glad am I: / My son and my son's son are vying with one another in valor" [*Quae mihi dies haec, Dii chari! Certè admodum gaudeo; / Filius neposque de virtute certamen ineunt*]) Duport cites Prov. 10.1 ("A wise son brings joy to his father" [*Filius sapiens laetisicat patrem*"], Hesiod's description of the good kind of strife from the opening of the *Works and Days*, Philostratus's praise of "honourable contention and splendid disputation" [*certamen honestum, & disputatio splendida*], and Cicero's commendation of *Agathê d'Eris* [good Eris] in Book 2 of his *De Finibus*.[157] Contained in the pages of Duport's collection is a literary and philosophical history of *agôn*, from its earliest incarnations in the athletic contests of Homeric heroes, to the spiritual struggles of Job, to more modern permutations in the clashes between seventeenth-century royalists and dissenters.

For the many readers who relied on such lexicons and concordances to navigate the *Iliad* and *Odyssey*, Homer's Greek language is presented not as a distinct dialect but rather as connected (albeit tenuously) to a continuous and complex linguistic and intellectual tradition. Particularly for those poets and scholars with adequate training in Greek – among whom we may safely include the six main writers analysed in this book – Homeric Greek is sufficiently related to later Greek literature, including the *koinê* Greek of the New Testament, and that of the Greek church fathers, to invite comparison between the authors of early Greek antiquity on the one hand and the authors of the Greek scriptures on the other. Such comparisons are sometimes made in the service of allegory, as is the case with Hugo's attempts to "translate" Homeric names into signs that narrate a symbolic history of the Catholic Church. But at times such comparisons or parallels reflect a desire to explore the linguistic affinities between poets believed to have lived during the same time period or to have shared certain cultural and spiritual values, as is the case with Duport's Homeric paraphrase of Job or Milton's translation of Psalm 114 into Homeric Greek, literary experiments both rooted in a recognition of the linguistic continuities between Hellenic and Hebraic antiquity. As the Reformation nurtured the desire to restore the spiritual values and ecclesiastical practices of the early church, it also nurtured a growing interest in reading the New Testament in Greek. Although the rediscovery of Homer in Western Europe took place two and a half centuries before Luther nailed his theses to the church door in Wittenberg, and although sixteenth-century classical scholars in the Protestant north rely heavily on the achievements of their Italian predecessors such as Leonardo Bruni, Lorenzo Valla, and Angelo Poliziano, the Reformation directs Homeric scholarship on a new path as scholars, poets, and theologians recalibrate the perceived relationship between the earliest forms of Christianity and the Hellenic and Hebraic cultures out of which Christianity grew. From Erasmus and Melanchthon to Milton and Duport, the interpretation of Homer participates in a larger scholarly project of the northern Renaissance: to trace the philosophical and literary debts that early Christianity owed to Greek antiquity and to discern between those aspects of Greek antiquity that might be, or might not be, ethically or spiritually useful for Protestant culture.

Homer *Agonistes*

Much recent scholarship on the afterlife of classical literature during the Renaissance – including studies by David Wilson-Okamura and Craig Kallendorf (on Virgil), Philip Ford and Marc Bizer (Homer), Stella Revard

(Pindar), Julia Gaisser (Catullus and Apuleius), Jonathan Bate and Raphael Lyne (Ovid), and David Marsh (Lucian) – focuses on the reception of a single classical author. This book is no exception. But it was written with the recognition that the conventional format of a single-author study does not adequately account for the various classical intermediaries who shape the interpretation of Homer and taught sixteenth- and seventeenth-century readers much about what they thought they knew about him.

This problem is particularly acute with respect to Homer. Unlike other classical poets, who may be temporarily "stranded" until they are "buoyed up once more on new tides, of new ideas and new institutions" in the Renaissance, there is no "original context" for Homer's poems to "outlive" but rather a long documentary history of frustration about the irretrievability of that original context.[158] Renaissance readers were all too familiar with the ancient stories about the assembly of the Homeric rhapsodies by Lycurgus or Peisistratus and about the later alterations made to the Homeric poems by their Alexandrian editors. These stories obliged Renaissance readers to confront the impossibility of recovering an "original" text of Homer – though some fantasized about it anyway, and a few, such as Henri Estienne, developed valuable new philological techniques as they tried. But for a culture in which many literary compositions were created collaboratively and orally, performed improvisationally, and then written down only later (if at all), as is the case with much Renaissance theatre and quite a bit of lyric poetry, these modes of literary production may have prepared sixteenth-century writers to surrender the impossible dream of an original or authoritative text in ways that later generations of Homeric scholars were less able to do.

The prospect of recovering an original text of Homer – or of recovering a robust understanding of archaic Greek customs and beliefs – may have seemed hopeless to some Renaissance scholars and useless to others, particularly to those eager to make Homer speak to contemporary debates and concerns. But to read Homer was to be inaugurated into the study of all of literary and intellectual history – to drink from the "fresh-flowing torrent," as Poliziano calls Homer, from which "the whole throng of poets imbibed their secret frenzies."[159] This was patently clear to Renaissance readers, even those with little or no training in Greek who learnt as much about Homer from his later classical and early Christian readers as they did from the texts of the *Iliad* and *Odyssey*. It is a rare classical text that does not imitate, parody, challenge, or critique some aspect of Homeric epic, and for Renaissance readers, expectations of what they might find once they cracked open the *Iliad* or the *Odyssey* were shaped by Plato and the ancient Stoics, rhetorical treatises by Aristotle, Cicero, Demetrius, and Longinus, the poetry of Pindar, Catullus, Horace, and Ovid, late antique and medieval allegories by Macrobius and Martianus Capella, the plays of Euripides and Aeschylus, the essays and dialogues of Lucian, Seneca, Cicero, Plutarch, and above all the epic poems of Apollonius, Quintus Smyrnaeus, Lucan, Statius, and Virgil.[160]

The copiousness of this list should indicate that the history of Homer's interpretation during the Renaissance is impossible to narrate in full. Moreover, for Renaissance scholars and poets who delighted in intertextual play and who often defined the chief stylistic characteristics of classical poets in contradistinction to other classical poets, Homer was challenging to situate within the neat dyads that often governed comparative literary criticism during the period; his relationships to later poets were too manifold and complex. Erasmus arrives at his understanding of Homer's Odysseus through the lens of the Pauline epistles and the Acts of the Apostles. Rabelais's interpretation of Homer is filtered through the writings of Lucian, Athenaeus, Pulci, and Folengo. Chapman and Sponde read Homer side by side with Hesiod, whose poems they also translated. Milton grapples with Homer's conception of divine justice by way of Solon, Euripides, and the Old Testament, while Hobbes turns to Thucydides and Aristotle to sharpen his understanding of Homer's politics and ethics. Even before late fourteenth- and fifteenth-century Italian humanists begin reading Homer in Greek and translating him into Latin, the *Iliad* and *Odyssey* were already the most thoroughly mediated works of classical antiquity. This quality would only have been felt more intensely by readers whose literary educations trained them to read for intertextual allusion. So, while this book is a single-author study, it is also a book that strives to trace Homer's wide-ranging influence on various literary genres and on various disciplines of thought ranging from medicine to rhetoric and from moral philosophy to theology.

Despite the breadth of Homer's influence on various disciplines of knowledge during the Renaissance, an influence partly accounted for by the fact that his poems were distilled and popularized in books of maxims, mythographies and emblem books, epitomes, and dramatic imitations, scholarship on the reception of Homer during the period has been unnecessarily preoccupied with the concern that few Renaissance writers were equipped to read his poems in the original Greek. As early as around 1515, in his *Letters of Obscure Men*, Ulrich Von Hutten mocks as idiotic a lack of familiarity with Homer through the caricature of a scholar who reports that he has just been apprised of a Greek writer named Homer while in Rome and, despite finding the story of the *Iliad* improbable, finds the book "very authentic" and begs for more information about it from his correspondent.[161] Around the same time, the emergence of printed mythographies, lexicons, and books of classical proverbs – Erasmus's *Adages* foremost among them – fosters a familiarity with Homer that might (unfairly) be deemed superficial, since while some of the Homeric "maxims" that circulate in the period are pat commonplaces, others are anything but. Admittedly, many Homeric allusions in the period crop up in the works of writers who may never have studied the *Iliad* or the *Odyssey* in Greek. Montaigne mocks this practice even as he owns up to it, admitting how "Some people quote Plato and Homer who have never looked at them. And I myself have taken enough passages elsewhere than at their sources."[162]

Particularly after around 1520, by which time the teaching of Greek had become common, if not universal, at universities across England, France, Germany, and the Low Countries, quite a few scholars, statesmen, and theologians could and did read Greek proficiently. The many abridged editions of Homer and commentaries on individual books printed during the early sixteenth century testify to the popularity of the *Iliad* and *Odyssey* as school texts. At many universities on both sides of the Alps, as well as in select grammar schools, students could expect instruction in several books of each poem; these usually included Books 1, 2, and 9 of the *Iliad*, which had been popular since the middle of the fifteenth century for their rhetorical and political content. University-educated scholars who did not benefit from the exemplary Greek training enjoyed by the likes of Rabelais, Budé, Spenser, or Milton could nonetheless make do with the many Greek-Latin editions of Homer printed during the period. In his popular Latin prose translation of Homer, first published at Venice in 1537, Andreas Divus explains that "those reading [Homer] in Greek may have at their disposal a Latin edition which allows them to see all at once, in a glance, both texts" such that readers with only elementary Greek might still consult the left hand side of the page – a practice borne out by the annotational habits of several late sixteenth-century readers, who circle keywords in Homer's Greek text and then provide transliterations (or translations into the Latin) in the opposite margin.[163]

Although it may be the case that many first encountered Homer's works in Latin translation rather than in the original Greek, it is not true, at least after the end of the fifteenth century, that "Homer tended to be judged, whether consciously or unconsciously, by the overriding standard of Virgil" during the period, or that Homer's Greek was regarded as inferior to Virgil's Latin in subtlety or complexity.[164] Although readers were keenly attuned to the many ways in which Virgil transformed Homeric epic – a subject that Wilson-Okamura's *Virgil in the Renaissance* addresses persuasively – other recent studies, by Tania Demetriou, Christopher Warner, Tobias Gregory, and Sarah Van Der Laan, have demonstrated that Renaissance poets such as Spenser, Tasso, and Milton could and did distinguish between Homer's ethical, spiritual, and political values and those of Virgil, at times preferring the Greek poet to his Latin imitator.[165] Although a handful of sixteenth-century literary critics, most notably Vida and J.C. Scaliger, are vehement in their preference for Virgil over Homer, the contrary position is equally common. Several times in the commentary to his translation of the *Iliad* and *Odyssey*, Chapman excoriates Scaliger for condemning Homer, tantrums for which Chapman was excoriated in turn by Ben Jonson in the margins of his personal copy of Chapman's Homer. An epigram by John Collop mocks the subtitle of Book 6 of Scaliger's *Poetics* by dubbing the scholar "not Hypercritick here but hypocrite" and then pointing out the contradictions in Scaliger's dislike of Homer and his reverence for Homer's best Roman pupil, Virgil, "[w]hose sprig was only gather'd at thy bayes."[166]

Treatises on rhetoric and literary criticism did make frequent comparisons between Homer and Virgil in order to acknowledge the respective strengths and weaknesses of each poet. These comparisons were often conceived as competitions – revivals of the ancient festivals at which bards and dramatists recited their works for prizes. Vida invites his readers to imagine that they are attending such an event when he invites them "compare our Aeneas with Aeacides, who flames in spirit, and with the wandering Ithacan, making the two bards compete [*concurrere*]" with each other.[167] Comparative analyses of Homer and Virgil, which became especially popular towards the end of the sixteenth century as debates over the relative merits of Ariosto and Tasso also reached a fever pitch, likewise pit the two poets against each other as rivals in an ongoing contest to be arbitrated by contemporary readers.[168]

Such contests not only reflect Homer's capacity to "compete" against Virgil; they also reflect the degree to which poetic excellence itself might be measured according to the perceived risks and rewards of literary rivalry. Although the imitation of ancient models was widely regarded as a means of cultivating poetic virtuosity – Virgil, his Renaissance admirers maintained, became a better poet than Homer by imitating and outdoing him – other referees of the contest between Homer and Virgil assert that Homer was the better poet precisely because *he had no models.* "Homer, who was the first poet," writes Giulio Del Bene in 1574, "had no master to teach him but was the most perfect poet."[169] As the only poet, save perhaps Orpheus, who possessed no teacher or forerunner, Homer supports what Andrew Ford has called the "divine model of strifeless transmission," a model of literary self-fashioning that imagines the poet outside of the dynamics of rivalry and imitation that shape all other literary genealogies.[170] This model is attractive to many Renaissance readers of Homer: in his *Ambra*, Poliziano melodramatically depicts Homer fleeing earth for the summit of Olympus, "where the horrid tempest of unjust Envy [*tempestas foeda Invidiae*] does not blow," and looking down "in perfect security … from afar upon the contending winds [*procul ventorum proelia tutus*]," an image that accords Homer a privileged place not *in* the literary canon but rather *above* it.[171] Particularly when considered through the lens of the bitter rivalries and the struggles for artistic self-determination that define so many Renaissance literary careers, Homer is a striking anomaly: a pre-eminent object of emulation and yet a poet who lacked models to emulate, a poet whose "firstness" both motivates and resists literary-historical narratives predicated on a dynamics of imitation and rivalry.

Every Renaissance schoolboy knew Donatus's story about how Virgil's detractors accused him of stealing his material from Homer, to which Virgil replied, "it is easier to steal the club of Hercules than a line from Homer."[172] The image of Hercules's club, however, is not original to Donatus, or even to Virgil: it is taken from one of Aesop's *Fables*, where it emblematizes the difficulty of conquering *eris*, or strife. In Aesop's version, Herakles spies an object lying on the ground and smashes it with his club; when he strikes it, the object "swell[s] up to twice its size," and when he strikes it again, "the thing then expand[s] to such a size that it blocked Herakles's way" until Athena advises him, "O Herakles, don't be so surprised! This thing that has brought about your confusion is *Aporia* [Contentiousness] and *Eris* [Strife]. If you just leave it alone, it stays small; but if you decide to fight it, then it swells from its small size and grows large.'"[173] The fable, and Donatus's subsequent manipulation of it, expands upon the description of Eris at *Il.* 4.440–4, turning Homer's personification of martial conflict and rivalry into a parable about the particular difficulties of striving with Homer, a poet who only grows more invincible as more adversaries do battle with him. For Renaissance readers who regard Homer as the principal object of literary emulation and rivalry, the fable speaks to an apparent paradox about the poet's reception: the more Homer is travestied, challenged, and revised by later writers, the greater his literary authority grows. Sixteenth- and seventeenth-century scholars are fascinated by the ancient parodies, centos, and sophistic declamations that playfully attempt to undermine

Homer's authority. For a few, such as Henri Estienne, these texts provide fruitful ground for philological investigation: Estienne used ancient quotations of Homer – including those cited or manipulated by parodists – to produce more accurate editions of the *Iliad* and *Odyssey*, ones that more closely resembled the texts before they were corrupted by the meddling of Alexandrian editors. For others, Homer's peculiar susceptibility to mischievous rewriting magnifies the conventional dynamics of "heuristic" imitation, the mixture of homage and critique created by imitations that "advertis[e] their derivation from the subtexts they carry with them" while at the same time "distanc[ing] themselves from the subtexts and forc[ing] us to recognize the poetic distance traversed."[174]

The Renaissance understanding of Homer's unique position in the literary canon was often framed in terms of his participation or non-participation in literary contest. Virgil's emulation of Homer could demonstrate the mutually beneficial effects of "eristic" imitation, but Homer was also seen as the victim (whether deserved or no) of "zealous imitation" [*megalôn … zêlôsis*] by another ancient rival, the philosopher who according to Longinus strove "with all his heart and soul to contest the prize with Homer, like a young antagonist [*antagonistês neos*]."[175] That philosopher is Plato, Homer's most notorious critic, but also one of his most gifted pupils. *The Republic*'s banishment of poets is often explained by sixteenth- and seventeenth-century writers as part and parcel of an intellectually productive rivalry between kindred thinkers – an excessive love of contention [*philoneikoteron*], as Longinus puts it, that confirms Hesiod's observation, "'Good is this strife [*eris*] for mankind'."[176] Defending Homer against the "reprehension of the divine Plato" in a 1577 work, Guillaume Paquelin explains that Homer is "the Plato of Poets, [and] that Plato is called the Homer of Philosophers," epithets also used by other sixteenth-century writers.[177] The logic that Plato's apparent hostility to Homer masks a deep indebtedness had informed Neoplatonic vindications of Homer by writers such as Proclus, who argues (here, in Gesner's 1542 Latin translation) that "In all his writings Plato emulated Homer in divine and in human things."[178] Such observations helped to attune Homer's Renaissance readers to the many sympathies between the two writers – their intermittent scepticism about the warrior ethic of archaic Greece, their shared preoccupation with mortality, their linguistic playfulness.[179]

Despite the perception that Homer was implicated in several different rivalries, these rivalries were often understood by Renaissance writers to exemplify a civility and productivity seen as lacking among "modern" poets. Lamenting the agonistic impulses of his own literary culture as a symptom of spiritual decay, Thomas Heywood observes that "[i]t was not so of old: Virgil, the best / Of Epicke Poets, never did contest / 'Gainst Homer."[180] Heywood's refusal to see Homer and Virgil as competitors is powerfully at odds with more recent critical tradition surrounding the Homeric poet: Nietzsche, Walter Ong, Andrew Ford, and Gregory Nagy each imagine the bards who recited the epic cycle as "contestant[s]" in an "agonistic" poetic world of "performance and struggle," not as "neutral, uncommitted" solitary poets.[181]

On one level, the poetry of Homer was very powerfully associated with contest by virtue of the ancient recitation of the Homeric poems at the Panathenaea, an athletic festival oddly revived in the 1612 Cotswold Games, where a man dressed up as Homer "did play / Admired raptures" during the games according to William Denny.[182] The idyllic, mirthful competition on display at the Cotswold Games may be hard to square with scenes of poetic competition depicted in Homeric epic, in particular *Il.* 2.594–600, which describes how the boastful, competitive poet Thamyris is punished by the Muses with blindness. It is also hard to square with another popular Renaissance legend about Homer that illustrates the "agonistic underpinnings" of his poems' composition and transmission through bardic contest.[183] That legend is narrated in the *Certamen Homeri et Hesiodi*, a later classical text that expands upon Hesiod's account (*WD*, 648–59) of a contest between the two poets; the story was also related, with some variations, by Plutarch and Stobaeus.[184] Although the *Certamen* is first and foremost a competition of poetic skill – Homer and Hesiod vie against each other in a stichomythia and then recite a passage from their respective poems – it also dramatizes a struggle between competing genres (epic and georgic) and between the competing ethical values embodied by each genre.[185] Although Homer's gory account of battlefield heroics (a rather unremarkable passage from *Iliad* 13) earns him the popular support of the audience, the king appointed to adjudicate the contest pronounces Hesiod the winner – peace triumphs over war, even if the better poet proves the loser.[186] The story, well known to many Renaissance readers, does not recount a poetic rivalry so much as a rivalry between two competing attitudes towards strife – the martial ethos of the Homeric battlefield versus Hesiod's georgic emphasis: "Work the work which the gods ordained for men," the latter poet's passage begins, celebrating the virtue-producing effects of adversity and humble labour. As Renaissance writers ponder the social, ethical, and spiritual merits of strife, Homer's poems at times model the most valuable forms of *eris*, but on other occasions, Homeric strife falls short.

Chapter One

Homer, Erasmus, and the Problem of Strife

"*Eris* is the last of the gods to finish an argument"

– Aeschylus, *Seven Against Thebes*

The *Adages* as a Latin *Iliad*

In a 1518 letter addressed to the University of Oxford, Thomas More expresses dismay at a quarrel that had recently erupted at Corpus Christi College between supporters and opponents of the study of Greek, the latter faction led by the Franciscan theologian Henry Standish. More complains in his letter that "certain scholars of your university, prompted either by hatred of Greek learning, by a misguided emulation of some other sort, or (as I think more likely) by a shameless addiction to joking and trifling [*improba ludendi nugandique libidine*], have formed a deliberate controversy to call themselves Trojans ... for the sole purpose of jokingly setting themselves up as a faction opposed to the greeks."[1] One of several controversies that erupts in the second decade of the sixteenth century over the teaching of Greek and Hebrew, including the protracted quarrel between the Hebraic scholar Johannes Reuchlin and members of the faculty of theology at the University of Louvain, the conflict between the "Trojan" Standish and his Greek adversaries is self-consciously modelled upon the Trojan War, so much so that members of Standish's faction assume the names of Trojan heroes, calling themselves Priam, Hector, and Paris.

The Oxford "Trojan War" of 1518 heralds a new era in the history of Homeric scholarship. Throughout the 1510s and early 1520s, the scholarly and theological quarrels of the early Reformation shape and in turn are shaped by interpretations of Homeric epic. This trend is nowhere more apparent than in the *Adages* of Desiderius Erasmus, a work that articulates its attitudes towards contemporary conflicts and disputes through interpretations of Homer's *Iliad* and *Odyssey* that foreground topical applications of ancient Greek lessons about conflict and its resolution. In *Esernius cum Pacidiano*, an adage added to the March 1518 edition of that work, Erasmus describes a public debate witnessed by him the previous year in London between Standish and another theologian, a "tireless Scotist" so pugnacious that, according to Erasmus, he might have been a "gladiator" instead of a theologian [*gladiator esse posset, ni theologus esset*].[2] The mock-heroic *Iliads* at Corpus Christi, Oxford, and at London reveal the extent to which the intellectual conflicts of the early sixteenth century are understood by their participants and spectators through the prism of Homeric epic. For writers such as Thomas More, Desiderius Erasmus, and the French Hellenist Guillaume Budé, who engage in contemporary disputes but also worry, to varying degrees, about the ethical and spiritual implications of engaging in them, Homer's complex treatment of the benefits and dangers of strife helps to establish a new decorum of conflict that informs intellectual arenas such as religious controversy and polemic.[3]

Presenting the evils of their time "*sub specie Homerica*," Erasmus, Budé, and their contemporaries imagine the central event of their age – the Reformation – as another Trojan War, one that Budé, in his 1535 *De Transitu Hellenismi ad Christianismum*, calls worse than the original one.[4] Homer's poems, which had already grown in popularity across northern Europe in the first decade and a half of the sixteenth century, acquire an immediate and pressing relevance for Erasmus and his generation, who bandy about Homeric allusions, proverbs, and epithets throughout letters and controversial writings as a running commentary on contemporary theological disputes and scholarly controversies. These allusions, often radically divorced from their original contexts, are offered up not as interpretations of Homer per se but rather as a means of critiquing the pernicious appetite for discord that dominates early sixteenth-century intellectual culture, fuelling controversies that at times appear to resemble an *Iliad* writ small. While Erasmus's *Adages* may seem an odd starting point to narrate the history of Homer's reception during the Renaissance, the collection does more than any other single text of the period to introduce passages from Homeric epic into the intellectual currency of sixteenth-century Europe. The *Adages* makes Homer familiar, not only by rendering thousands of lines from the *Iliad* and *Odyssey* into Latin but also by demonstrating the contemporary relevance of Homeric epic to an age both enthralled by and anxious about quarrel.

Homer occupies a special place in Erasmus's pantheon of ancient writers, a status evident in his placement, along with Plutarch and Solomon, in the highest niche on the frontispiece of the Froben editions of the *Adages*. Even before the perfection of his Greek allowed him to read Homer fluently, Erasmus expressed his special affection for the poet: in a letter to Augustine Vincent, written in September 1500, Erasmus writes that he is "so fired with love for [Homer] that though I am incapable of understanding the words, still I am refreshed and nourished by the very sight of them" [*Ego quidem ita huius autoris ardeo amore, ut cum intelligere nequeam, aspectu tamen ipso recreor ac pascar*].[5] Erasmus appears to have embarked on a translation of the *Odyssey* in late 1503 or 1504. Pyrrhus d'Angleberme, who studied Greek with Erasmus at Paris, refers in a letter to "the *Odyssey*, which my preceptor Desiderius has fortunately translated" [*Odyssea, quam preceptor meus Desiderius feliciter traduxit*], but the project either never saw completion or is no longer extant. Yet the vestiges of that translation make their way into the *Adages*, and more than four hundred of the adages in the book are based on lines from Homer's *Iliad* and *Odyssey*.[6]

In his revisions to the September 1508 Aldine edition of the *Adages*, Erasmus added 273 adages from Homer (III.viii.1 through III.x.75, with two exceptions), grouping them together with a brief preface, entitled "Some Proverbial Lines by Homer" [*Homerici Versus Aliquot Proverbiales*]. In the preface, Erasmus explains how "Homer was held in such high esteem by the ancients" [*Tantum honoris antiquitas habebat Homero*] that "almost every one of his verses was commonly celebrated as a proverb" [*singuli pene versus illius proverbii vice celebrarentur*] (*CWE* 35:281 [ASD II.6:481]). Separated from the rest of the work by this preface, Erasmus's Homeric adages are atypical of the *Adages* in several respects. In many cases, Erasmus proposes "figurative applications" for his Homeric proverbs that are quite "distant" from their original meanings or contexts – a process he refers to as *detorqueri* [torquing; perverting] – or cites Homeric verses in "ways that seem quite opposed to Homer's meanings" (*CWE* 35:281, editor's note). The preface to the Homeric adages explains how the special flexibility of Homeric epic encourages an interpretive licence that he "would not allow ... with other poets" [*(n)eque vero idem permiserim in reliquis poetis*], because a process of accommodation allows Homer's "words [to be] stretched [*detorseris*] to give a vastly different sense," and new meanings infused into the most familiar Homeric lines (*CWE* 35:282 [ASD II.6:482]). This practice of citing proverbial lines in surprising or incongruous contexts is largely responsible for producing the "novelty" that lends many of the adages their wit. According to Erasmus, an idea "launched like a javelin in proverbial form strikes with sharper point on the hearer's mind and leaves implanted barbs of thought" [*sententia proverbio quasi vibrata feriat acrius auditoris animum, et aculeos quosdam cogitationum relinquat infixos*] such that disputes which cannot be solved by arguments are "evaded by a jest" [*ioco eludi*] in the form of an aptly deployed adage (*CWE* 31:17 [ASD II.1:64]). This is precisely how Erasmus and many of his early sixteenth-century readers make use of his Homeric adages: as a vehicle for resolving, deflecting, or managing contention through wit.[7]

Although Erasmus periodically voices his contempt for Achilles and other "raging bandits" of classical antiquity, his heavy reliance on Homeric allusions in the *Adages* reflects his appreciation of the special applicability of Homer's wisdom to the resolution of contemporary disputes and conflicts.[8] Contrary to Lewis Spitz's claim that the works of Homer and Virgil "left [Erasmus] puzzled" and that he did not rely on their texts "except for minor borrowings, largely of myths and symbols," the *Adages* reveals Homer to be "Erasmus' most popular choice of literary source," and the patchwork of Homeric lines and allusions in the work have a profound influence on later sixteenth-century editors, translators, and readers of the *Iliad* and *Odyssey*.[9] An abridged, Latin edition of Erasmus's Homeric adages was printed at Antwerp in 1529, but as Rummel observes, the "clearest proof of the success of [the *Adages*] … is the use made of it by Erasmus' friends in their own compositions," an influence likewise evident in the margins of editions of Homer owned by Erasmus's friends and contemporaries.[10] In their copies of Homer, a number of sixteenth-century readers mark lines that appear in the *Adages*, sometimes collating the two works by jotting down Erasmus's Latin renditions of Homeric maxims next to the Homeric verse in question. Budé underlines and heavily annotates the line from the *Odyssey* that inspired the adage *Semper similem deus ducit ad simile*, while Christopher Comes, the German annotator of a 1535 edition of the *Iliad* published at Louvain, cross-references numerous lines from Homer's poem and notes their resemblance to adages including "Stubborn quarrelling" [*Pertinax contentio*] (Adage 3.8.19), "Absolutely hostile fortune" [*Fortuna prorsus adversa*] (Adage 3.8.26), and "Noisier than Stentor" [*Stentore clamosior*] (Adage 2.3.37).[11] In 1523, a former student of Philipp Melanchthon's named Achilles Pirminius Gasser annotates a 1520 edition of Books 1 and 2 of the *Odyssey* with several cross-references to Erasmus's *Adages*. In his handwritten transcription of Books 4 and 5 of the *Iliad*, Gasser frequently identifies the adage in which a given line appears, writing "Homo bulla" or "Vide adag. Bellerophontis ... Eras."[12] In his Latin translation of the *Iliad*, first printed in 1540, Eobanus Hessus includes marginal references to several of Erasmus's adages: "From here is born the adage, gold for bronze. Eras(mus)" [*Hinc natum adagium, chrusea chalcheiôn. Eras.*], he writes next to the exchange of armour between Diomedes and Glaucus in Book 6 of the *Iliad*, an episode that Erasmus invokes (*Adage* I.ii.1) to describe an unequal or imprudent deal.[13] These habits of annotation reveal the extent to which Erasmus's adages familiarize certain Homeric lines and, in some cases, transform the meaning of those lines. Early sixteenth-century readers of Homer encounter the texts of the *Iliad* and *Odyssey* through the lens of Erasmus, and they delight in noting the parallels between the writings of the Dutch humanist and one of his chief ancient resources for proverbial wisdom.

Capitalizing on the popularity of the *Adages*, several sixteenth-century scholars compile their own anthologies of Homeric *sententiae*. Boetius Epo's *Omnium Scriptorum Principis Homeri Sententiae*, printed at Louvain in 1555, includes a number of maxims also included in the *Adages*, including *Ex minimis initiis, maxima* (Adage III.viii.23), derived from *Il.* 4.442–3, and "God always leads like to like" [*Semper similem ducit deus ad similem*], (Adage I.ii.22), derived from *Od.* 17.218.[14] In a 1562 oration on Homer, Dionysius Lambinus cites an entire page of Homeric verses that are offered up as proverbs, and around the turn of the seventeenth century, Antoine Séguier compiled a lengthy manuscript, now at the Bibliothèque Nationale, that contains maxims and apophthegms from Homer.[15] Other collections of Greek maxims, many duplicating and supplementing Erasmus's long catalogue of Homeric adages, appear in works such as Michael Neander's *Gnomologicum Graecolatinum* (Basel, 1564), Johann Hartung's *Chilias Homericorum Locorum* (Basel, 1568), and Henri Estienne's *Homerici Centones* (1578), the last of which contains a section entitled "Proverbalium Homeri Versuum Libellus," a collection of Homeric sayings quoted by later writers such as Plutarch and Lucian.

The proliferation of such works secured Homer's status as an encyclopedic poet whose works contained morsels of pithy wisdom suitable for virtually any occasion or context. These *florilegia* also had more practical applications: by gathering up citations of Homer made by later ancient writers, scholars such as Estienne and Oporinus hoped to restore the "pristine" [*priscum*] Homer from the alterations to which he was subjected by ancient editors such as "Aristarchus, who swept away all the blots" [*Aristarchus maculas detergeret omnes*] in Homer's poems by obelizing lines deemed inconsistent, impious, or metrically substandard.[16]

For Erasmus, the dazzling variety and sheer size of the *Adages* may have been intended as a deliberate homage to the encyclopedic quality of the Homeric corpus. With the addition of 273 Homeric proverbs to the 1508 Aldine edition of the *Adages*, the work begins to assume palpably epic dimensions that reflect its possible role as a supplement to – or, perhaps, a substitute for – Erasmus's planned translation of the *Odyssey*. Writing to Cuthbert Tunstall in May 1517, Budé praises the *Adages* as "an *Iliad* ... of elegance in Greek and Latin" [*Iliadem ... illam leporum Graecorum iuxta Latinorumque*], a compliment that reflects the ever-increasing girth of the volume as well as its *poikilomuthos* display of rhetorical skill (Ep. 583, *CWE* 4:357 [Allen 2:566]).[17]

Not only is the *Adages* "As long-winded as the *Iliad*" [*Prolixius Iliade*], to cite one of Erasmus's own adages (IV.v.51, *CWE* 36:177), but it also reproduces the varied rhetorical styles and the polymorphic wit of Homer's most eloquent protagonists. A large number of Erasmus's Homeric adages derive from rebukes, insults, or wry witticisms swapped by Homer's speakers, utterances often intended to be used in a similar vein by Erasmus's readers. This function of the *Adages* does not escape Budé, who writes of the work that "I seem to see Minerva's own arsenal of language" [*logothecam Minervae videre mihi videor*] in it (Ep. 583, *CWE* 4:357 [Allen 2:566]). Budé avails himself of Erasmus's stockpile of Homeric javelins of verbal wit in numerous letters composed during the second decade of the sixteenth century, when the two men enter into a disagreement over Erasmus's handling of Jacques Lefèvre D'Etaples, a scholar with whom he had come to blows over competing interpretations of a verse in Paul's Epistle to the Hebrews. In a series of letters chock-full of witticisms, insults, and *sententiae* drawn from Homer, Budé and Erasmus engage in an epistolary skirmish that demonstrates the extent to which Homeric proverbs define and delimit rhetorical conflict in the era. In his letter to Tunstall, Budé recounts how, fearing that his debate with Erasmus might "break out into open conflict at any moment," he sought advice in "Homer's words, 'When two go together, one discerns before the other how profit may be had'" and resolves to play Diomedes to Erasmus's Ulysses – friends and allies, rather than enemies (Ep. 583, *CWE* 4:360–1 [Allen 2:569], citing *Il.* 10.224–5).[18]

Budé is one of several of Erasmus's friends and correspondents who trade Homeric lines and epithets, largely derived from the *Adages*, to add wit and erudition to discussions of contemporary disputes. In his preface to the *Adages*, Erasmus invites his readers to circulate its maxims, appealing to Varro's etymology of *adagio* (derived from "*ambagio*" or "*circumagium*") to explain that the adage is "something passed around" (*CWE* 31:5 [ASD II.1:46], citing Varro, *De Lingua Latina* 7.31). Many of Erasmus's contemporary readers follow his advice to "interweave [*intertexantur*] adages deftly and appropriately" in their writing, making use of proverbs from Homer and other ancient writers to fabricate cento-like accounts of academic quarrels and controversies (*CWE* 31:17 [ASD II.1:64]). Writing to Erasmus from Leipzig in January 1519, Petrus Mosellanus strings together a hodgepodge of Erasmus's adages and lines from Homer to describe the "sophisters" with whom he is currently at odds. Commenting that "Mars, who in battles of this kind is in no hurry to change sides, inclines to favour us" [*Ad nos tamen Mars in hoc bellorum genere non temere alloprosallos magis inclinat*], Mosellanus invokes one of Erasmus's favourite Homeric *topoi*, likens his conflict with Johann Eck and his fellow "Scotists" to the combat between Esernius and Pacidianus, two gladiators satirized by Adage II.v.98, and finally offers Erasmus some advice couched in two lines from the *Iliad* (Ep. 911, *CWE* 6:222–5 [Allen 3:468–70], citing *Il.* 6.112 and 4.447). Responding to Mosellanus several months later, Erasmus describes the "extraordinary turmoil" at Louvain in equally Homeric terms: "You would have thought some *Ate* was confounding the whole business of learning" [*Dixisses Aten quampiam turbare studiosorum negotium*], he writes, alluding to Jean Briart Atensis, one of the opponents of the Trilingual College at Louvain and a man whose name conveniently resembles that of *Atê*, the Homeric goddess of ruin or infatuation often conflated with Eris. Across the channel, Erasmus reports, another *Iliad* also rages, thanks to a faction of "Trojans" led by Henry Standish, whose opposition to the study of Greek at Oxford earns him the title of "barbarian" [*barbarus*] (Ep. 948, *CWE* 6:311, 6:316–17 [Allen 3:547]).

It was perhaps inevitable that humanist advocates of the study of Greek maligned their adversaries as *barbaroi* – non-speakers of Greek, and by extension uncivilized purveyors of gibberish, to the ancient Hellenic cultural imagination.[19] But the habits of Homeric citation adopted by Erasmus and his allies, in particular the frequent invocation of Homeric agents of discord including Atê, Eris, and Ares, provides a veiled commentary on the causes, symptoms, and the possible resolution of current disputes that is at once philologically subtle and ethically complex. By appealing repeatedly to code words and stock figures drawn from the *Iliad* and *Odyssey*, Erasmus and his intellectual circle create a Homeric idiom through which to articulate their own – and, at times, palpably un-Homeric – ethos of contention, one that defines itself both through and in contradistinction to the eristic culture of Homeric epic. Although Erasmus's profound distaste for war and its typical motives – honour and fame – makes him an unlikely fan of Homer, the *Adages* works to redeem those aspects of the *Iliad* and *Odyssey* most congenial to Erasmus's own ethics of friendship, cooperation, and non-retaliation. Excised and interpreted as texts that condemn strife instead of glorifying it, that prize unanimity and concord rather than dissent, the Homeric poems that emerge in the *Adages* prove sympathetic to Erasmus's Pythagorean-Platonic ethics as well as to his affection for Saint Paul, the apostle whose complex and vexed attitude towards *eris* most closely informs Erasmus's own attitudes towards the spiritual and intellectual benefits and dangers of discord.

Homer, Erasmus, and the Fine Art of Rebuke

Erasmus's decision to include so many Homeric proverbs in his *Adages* that address the legitimacy or effectiveness of contentious speech reflects the influence of fifteenth-century Italian scholarship on Homer. Fifteenth-century Italian readers of Homer view the *Iliad* and *Odyssey* as rhetorical manuals that exhibit a wide spectrum of rhetorical modes ranging from exhortation and blame to the soft and conciliatory modes of supplication and prayer. In the dedication to his Latin translation of Books 1 and 9 of the *Iliad*, two books notable for the number and variety of their speeches, Carlo Marsuppini paraphrases Quintilian's description of Homer as a rhetorical master of the sweet and the bitter [*dulcis et acer*].[20] Motivated by a similar desire to illustrate Homer's rhetorical range and the persuasive skill of his speakers in various contexts, the Florentine humanist Leonardo Bruni translates three speeches from Book 9 of the *Iliad* in the early fifteenth century as models of the three types of rhetoric (forensic, deliberative, and epideictic), all rendered into good Ciceronian Latin.[21] Bruni's *Homeric Orations* reveals how, in fifteenth-century Italy, "[e]ven nonoratorical works fed the humanist appetite for Greek oratory," and Homer's poems, with their numerous and rousing speeches made in council, on the battlefield, or on top of Olympus, promise to fashion skilled public speakers in a manner similar to the orations of Cicero or Demosthenes.[22] Fuelled by a keen interest in the complementary modes of epideictic rhetoric and invective, fifteenth-century translations of Homer by Erasmus's Italian predecessors showcase the Greek poet's twin mastery of praise and blame, as well as the prudence demonstrated by his speakers in choosing the most suitable rhetorical mode for the situation at hand.

Erasmus's youthful passion for Homer was nurtured by the fact that two of the fifteenth-century scholars he most admired, Lorenzo Valla and

Angelo Poliziano, both translated portions of the *Iliad.* Valla translated sixteen books of the *Iliad* into Latin between 1442 and 1444 at the behest of Pope Nicholas V; the translation was printed at Brescia in 1474. In the early 1470s, Poliziano translated Books 2 through 5 of the *Iliad* into Latin hexameters.[23] Valla and Poliziano both appreciated the rhetorical value of Homeric epic, in particular its skilful and apt use of invective and blame, an arena in which Valla, perhaps "the most argumentative" of the Italian humanists, excelled.[24] Erasmus clearly admired Valla's polemical stridency: in his dedicatory epistle to the Italian humanist's notes on the New Testament, the 1505 *In Latinam Novi Testamenti interpretationem ex collatione Graecorum exemplarium adnotationes*, Erasmus defends Valla from the charge that "he has hay on his horns and savages everyone" [*foenum … habet in cornu et neminem non lacerat*] (Ep. 182, *CWE* 2:90 [Allen 1:408]). For Erasmus, who regarded the saccharine sweetness of flattery as a "sword smeared with honey" [*Melle litus gladius*, Adage I.viii.57] that does more harm than the blunt weapon of candour, Valla's censures of his fellow scholars are "necessary rather than insolent," a defence that echoes Paul's condemnation of "smooth speech and flattery" [*chrêstologias kai eulogias*] at Rom. 16.18.[25] Erasmus argues in the dedicatory epistle to his edition of Valla that "compliments are nearly always harmful, while reprehension is always beneficial" [*Nam ut nunquam fere non nocet laudator, ita semper prodest repraehensor*], a lesson also contained in several adages that condemn the "mutual back-scratching" of flattering speech (Ep. 182, *CWE* 2:91–2 [Allen 1:408]).

Much like Valla, Erasmus takes his principal cue in rhetorical matters from the kindred advice of Homer and Saint Paul, figures who sanction verbal rebuke when it is necessary for moral and spiritual improvement but condemn it when used to incite discord. In the many Homeric adages addressing verbal contention, Erasmus often selects lines from the *Iliad* and *Odyssey* that have clear parallels in Acts or in the Pauline epistles, a technique perhaps intended to compensate for the fact that, as Erasmus admits, the *Adages* includes very few proverbs from scripture even though "Christ … used expressions as familiar as possible in order to raise our humble understanding by every means to his sublimity" [*Christo … ita sermonibus quam maxime familiaribus uteretur, quo nostram humilitatem modis omnibus ad suam proveheret sublimitatem*] (Adage III.x.91, *CWE* 35:392 [ASD II.6:582]). Nestor's observation that "the exhortation [*paraiphasis*] of a companion is a good thing" [*Bonus est afflatus amici / Admonitoris*], which Erasmus adapts into the adage *Amicorum est admonere mutuum* [It is the duty of friends to admonish each other] (III.viii.52), provides a pagan counterpart to Paul's praise for his fellow apostles' ability to "admonish each other" [*allêlous nouthetein*] as well as to the Pauline injunction to "rebuke, reprove, exhort, in season, out of season" [*eukairôs akairôs, elenxon, epitimêson, parakaleson*], a verse that Erasmus repeatedly invokes to justify his own satirical writings (Adage III.viii.52, *CWE* 35:301 [ASD II.6:500], citing *Il.* 11.793).[26] In adages such as *Iubentis aperte loqui* [Speak it out] and *Modis omnibus incitat* [By every means he urges], Erasmus turns lines from the *Iliad* into proverbs commending frank or bold speech, a move that reflects his appreciation that certain of Homer's characters, particularly Nestor and Odysseus, possess a Pauline capacity to adapt their rhetorical style to the situation at hand in order to reprove their companions effectively and without the taint of excessive adversarialness (Adages III.viii.4; III.viii.98, *CWE* 35:283, 35:317).

If some Homeric proverbs supply Erasmus with ammunition for justifying rebuke and invective, others help restrain the impulse towards verbal conflict typical of so many humanist gladiators of letters. One of Erasmus's favourite Homeric phrases, adopted from Petrarch via Poliziano, is *herkos odontôn* [the barrier of the teeth], a phrase useful for censuring unrestrained speech or verbal aggression.[27] The phrase, which appears twice in the *Iliad* and six times in the *Odyssey*, is loosely adapted by Erasmus into the adage *In absurde locutum* [Against one who has spoken out of place], a proverb he derives from *Od.* 1.64, where Zeus chastises Athena, "what a word has escaped the barrier of your teeth" [*poion se epos phugen herkos odontôn*]. As Erasmus notes, the Homeric verse, which he translates as "*Dentis claustra tui quae vox elapsa reliquit,*" is praised by Aulus Gellius as a lesson about checking "wanton words" [*petulantiae verborum*], a moral also extracted by Poliziano, whose gloss on the phrase explains that "the teeth restrain rash speech".[28]

In the *Noctes Atticae*, Erasmus's most immediate source for the adage, Aulus Gellius contrasts the loquacity of "empty-headed, vain, and tiresome babblers" to the judicious and sparing speech of Odysseus, "a man gifted with sagacious eloquence" [*virum sapienti facundia praeditum*].[29] Erasmus follows Gellius in treating Odysseus as the model of Homer's prudent advice to restrain "reckless speech" [*loquendi temeritas*].[30] In his *Lingua*, a treatise on the proper government of the tongue first printed in 1525 but composed somewhat earlier, Erasmus commends Homer for depicting his heroes as "firm keepers of silence" [*facit et silentii tenaces*]. He singles out Odysseus's exemplary reticence when the hero "persevere[s] in concealing his true identity" [*constanter tamen dissimulat quis esset*] (*CWE* 29:304 [ASD IV.1:278]). By contrast, the "clamorous and rabidly loquacious" [*clamosam ... ac rabiosam loquacitatem*] Thersites provides Erasmus with evidence that "no failing has ever been more loathed even by the pagans" than garrulity (*CWE* 29:269, 29:271 [ASD IV.1:246–7]). Perhaps not surprisingly, Thersites's name becomes synonymous during the early decades of the sixteenth century with the contentious scholars whom Erasmus and his intellectual allies brand as "sophists" or "Scotists." In a letter from August 1520, written at the height of Erasmus's dispute with Edward Lee, Wolfgang Capito compares the English scholar to Homer's Thersites on account of the severity of his rebukes, and he praises Erasmus for having "many men like Ulysses enrolled among his troops," men who exercise verbal restraint when faced with rude admonition.[31]

Erasmus was both attracted to and repelled by verbal aggression, and he sees in Homeric epic a kindred ambivalence about the ethical and political legitimacy of contentious or blameful speech. Recent Homeric scholars including Gregory Nagy, Richard Martin, Deborah Beck, John Heath, and Hilary Mackie have studied the complex role accorded to blame and rebuke in the Homeric poems, arguing that while the *Iliad* is characterized by "outspoken [verbal] strife" and by numerous "episodes of public wrangling," some of the poems' harshest rebukes demonstrate how blame may alleviate social tensions or "defus[e]" conflict "in an orderly and productive manner."[32] Uncertain whether to regard polemical and controversial discourse as a catalyst for more violent expressions of conflict or as a possible remedy for them, Erasmus relies on the Homeric poems to work out a complex decorum of verbal strife, one able to accommodate Paul's seemingly contrary injunctions to rebuke and exhort in season and out of season and yet to shun "contentions, envyings, animosities, dissensions, [and] detractions" [*contentiones, aemulationes, animositates, dissensiones, detractiones*].[33]

If Erasmus's writings acknowledge the kindred challenges posed by the rhetorical culture of the Homeric poems and his own rhetorical culture, they also testify to his recognition of a kinship between Homeric epic and the writings of Paul. Particularly in his *Paraphrases* and *Annotations on the Acts of the Apostles*, the book of the New Testament containing the greatest quantity and variety of speeches, Erasmus displays his awareness that "the biblical text is shaped into a form determined by the rules of rhetoric derived from antiquity" (*CWE* 50:xiv, xvi), and he seeks out affinities between Homer's most effective speakers and the great apostolic orators of Acts, namely, Paul, Barnabas, and Peter.[34]

In particular, Erasmus delights in collating pagan and Christian versions of the paradox that the tongue may prove helpful or harmful depending on the uses to which it is put. In his *Lingua*, Erasmus cites some verses from

Hesiod's *Works and Days* which observe that the tongue can produce a "whole world of evils" [*Mundus malorum est mala lingua*] even as the sparing tongue is "the best treasure," lines that bear a close resemblance to James 3.8–9, which calls the tongue as "an unstable evil" [*akatastaton kakon*] because it both blesses and curses (*CWE* 29:365 [ASD IV.1:330], citing Hesiod, *WD*, ls. 719–20). In his paraphrase on Acts 2.4, in the middle of a description of how the apostles "sow the seeds of heavenly doctrine," Erasmus comments that "[n]o member of the human body is more destructive than a wicked tongue, none more beneficial than a good tongue" [*Nullum hominis membrum pestilentius mala lingua, nullum salubrius bona*], an interjection intended to defend the apostles' reliance on frank and harsh speech (*CWE* 50:14 [LB VII:667B]).

Throughout his career, Erasmus is fascinated by the paradox that strong words may both harm and cure, a dilemma explored in the *Parabolae* through the metaphor that "Telephus' wound was healed by the same spear that inflicted it, and the wound of reproof [*obiurgationis*] will be healed by him that gave it" (*CWE* 23:180 [ASD I.5:166], citing Plutarch, *De Auditu* 16, *Moralia* 46f).[35] The apostles similarly wound in order to heal, and Erasmus regards them as physicians whose tongues are their *pharmakoi*, both poison and remedy. Paraphrasing Acts 5.5, which recounts how Ananias is "smitten by so severe a rebuke" that he drops dead, Erasmus explains that while we might "wonder at Peter's harshness [*austeritatem*] towards Ananias," the apostle did not intend to harm him but rather "poured upon Ananias the acrimony of rebuke to heal him" [*sed obiurgationis infudit acrimoniam, ut sanaret*] (*CWE* 50:39 [LB VII:684F, VII:685B]).[36] Such medical metaphors abound in Erasmus's *Paraphrases on the Acts of the Apostles*; in his dedication to the work, Erasmus testifies to the medicinal power of reproof by citing "Homer's saying that 'a physician is a man worth many men,'" a line that links the curative power of apostolic rhetoric with the harsh but morally instructive speeches of Homeric heroes, since both groups of men use their tongues to "heal disorders [rather] than to suppress them" (*CWE* 50:3 [LB VII:651], citing *Il.* 11.514).

Homeric and New Testament analogues often motivate Erasmus's discussions of rhetorical matters, particularly those concerning the importance of restrained or measured speech on the one hand, and frank or honest speech on the other. In the adage *Ne quid nimis* [Nothing to excess], Erasmus argues that this rhetorical virtue may be "trace[d] back to Homer as the fountainhead" [*ad Homerum veluti fontem referant*].[37] *Ne Quid Nimis* cites two Homeric sources for the adage: Menelaus's statement to Telemachus that "due measure is better in all things" [*sint mediocria cuncta*] and Odysseus's command to Diomedes to "praise me not too much, nor blame me [too much]" [*Ne nimis aut laudes, Tytida, aut vituperes me*], a line that Erasmus adapts elsewhere as one of his chief guidelines for good and honest friendship (*CWE* 32:64 [ASD II.2:120], citing *Od.* 15.71 and *Il.* 10.249). But Erasmus also looks to Homer to develop or explicate adages that commend frank speech, a habit that situates the Greek poet as the illustrious ancestor of those apostles whose *parrhêsia* (frank or bold speech) is repeatedly praised in Acts.[38] In the adage *Iubentis aperte loqui* [Of one who commends frank speech], Erasmus creates a Homeric genealogy for apostolic *parrhêsia* by deriving the proverb from a line spoken in which Thetis tells her son Achilles to "speak out" his grief (Adage III.viii.4, *CWE* 35:283 [ASD II.6:485], citing *Il.* 1.363). Although the line, in its Homeric context, has little to do with the importance of candour between friends, Erasmus seems to delight in its close resemblance to the command received by Paul from the Holy Spirit at Acts 18.9: "Do not fear, but speak and do not keep silent" [*Noli timere, sed loquere, et ne taceas*] (ASD VI.2:394). Despite the occasional objections of scholars such as Joseph Scaliger, who mocks Jean Dorat for "seeking the whole Bible in Homer," the Erasmian strategy of collating Homeric and scriptural parallels is common among Reformed and Catholic scholars alike.[39] Annotating his 1535 edition of the *Iliad*, for instance, Christopher Comes glosses 2.196, a verse that reads "proud is the heart of kings" [*thumos de megas ... basilêôn*], by writing "apud Paul ad Rom. 13," an allusion to the verse in which Paul urges his audience to "submit to the supreme authorities."[40] Hugo grants Saint Paul a different sort of Homeric genealogy when he argues for an etymological connection between the apostle's birthplace (Tarsus) and the name of the *Iliad*'s uppity Thersites, a correspondence strengthened by Hugo's perception that both men are "always adversarial" [*semper adversantem*].[41]

Erasmus's appreciation for candour and bluntness helps to explain his perplexing admiration for Menelaus, a character whom he repeatedly praises for his "plainness and outspokenness in speech" [*dicendo simplicitatem libertatemque*] (Ep. 177, *CWE* 2:73 [Allen 1:392]). Glossing the adage *Pauciloquus, sed eruditus* [Sparing of words, but learned], a phrase fit "for someone whose words are few but worth hearing" [*qui pauca quidem, sed tamen auditu digna loquitur*], Erasmus cites Homer's description of the "*breviloquo*" Menelaus at *Il.* 3.213–14 in order to celebrate the virtue of spare and direct speech (Adage III.viii.77, *CWE* 35:310 [ASD II.6:508]).[42] Erasmus invokes Menelaus as a model speaker elsewhere in his writings. In the dedicatory epistle to his *Aliquot Declamatinculae*

Graecae, a Latin translation of three declamations by Libanius first printed in 1519 but composed as early as 1503, Erasmus explains his special esteem for the speech that Libanius composes for Menelaus because it captures his "breviloquence" as a speaker (Ep. 177 [Allen 1:392]).[43] Menelaus's characteristically "laconic" style also gives rise to the adage *Laconicus*, which extols his "pointed economy" [*argutam breviloquentiam*] and argues that "Lacedaemonian brevity of speech and honesty" [*frugalitas et integritas Lacedaemoniorum*] are interrelated (Adage II.x.49, *CWE* 34:146 [ASD II.4:308]). Erasmus's high regard for Menelaus's rhetorical skill is inseparable from the character's conciliatory temperament, a disposition that at times appears to reflect the ideals to which Erasmus aspires in his conduct with scholarly adversaries. A modest speaker and, according to Erasmus, a man of "enormous self-control and good humour" [*summa cum moderatione neque non animi iucunditate coniunctam*] who does not utter "ill-natured or vindictive" [*atrocios aut rabiosius*] words against Paris even when merited, Menelaus possesses the perfect temperament for resolving disputes (Ep. 177, *CWE* 2:74 [Allen 1:392]).

Erasmus accordingly adapts Menelaus's anti-war speech from Book 13 of the *Iliad* as a means of appeasing his own opponents. In a 1520 letter that attempts to assuage a member of Louvain's faculty of theology, Erasmus paraphrases Menelaus's speech condemning those never satiated with battle: "Homer expresses surprise that mortal men can never have enough of war, although of all other things they soon have more than they want; but I think it is still astonishing that we never have enough of this civil strife" (Ep. 1059, *CWE* 7:169 [Allen 4:156]). One of Erasmus's favourite speeches from the *Iliad* – he also cites it in the *Querela Pacis* to testify to the human insatiability for war – Menelaus's powerful criticism of those who never have their fill of war helps explain the role in which he is cast in the *Adages*, often playing the part of peacemaker by arguing for an end to the Trojan War or by chastising the interests and passions that fuel war.[44] In the adage *Turpis iactantia* [Boasting is ignoble], Erasmus condemns braggarts with a line spoken by Menelaus at *Il.* 17.19, "It does not look well to boast [*huperbion*] proudly of oneself," while in *Sero Sapiunt Phryges* [The Phrygians learn wisdom too late] he argues that the Trojans "would have saved themselves from innumerable calamities" [*innumerabilibus sese calamitatibus subduxissent*] had they returned Helen much earlier, precisely the argument presented by Libanius's declamation, in which "Menelaus argues that Helen should be given back to the Greeks" in order to end the war (Adage III.ix.46, *CWE* 35:336; Adage I.i.28, *CWE* 31:76–7 [ASD II.1:142]).[45] In 1517, Erasmus expands the second of these adages so as to make it speak to contemporary conflicts in Europe, commenting that "[n]ot even the misfortunes of so many years have taught us to hate war, nor do we even now at long last begin to think about peace, which ought to be perpetual between Christians" (*CWE* 31:77 [ASD II.1:142]). Ventriloquizing Menelaus's anti-war diatribe as his own, Erasmus's affection for the speech blinds him to its ironies. Menelaus and his wayward wife are, at very least, the indirect causes of the war, and Menelaus is the poem's exemplary coward, a timid fighter who is compared at various points to a fly, a child, and a watermelon.[46]

As the *Adages* transforms Homeric epic into a rich storehouse of proverbial wisdom by turning lines exchanged on the battlefield into artful *skômmata*, or mocking sayings, useful for targeting ineffective, imprudent, or overly loquacious speakers, they perform an accommodation similar to that effected by the Pauline Epistles and by early church fathers such as Justin Martyr and Clement of Alexandria, who translate a pagan idiom of combat into the discourse of Christian *agôn* by adapting military and athletic metaphors for spiritual ends.[47] As Erasmus points out in one of his adages, proverbs achieve their greatest wit when "derived from the combat of gladiators in the arena" [*a gladiatoria item harena translatum*] but then "transferred to things of the mind" [*ad rem animi transferantur*] (Adage I.ix.83, *In arenam descendere*, *CWE* 32:224 [ASD II.2:396]), a process of adaptation fraught with difficulty, since, as Paul routinely points out, Christian contests do not – or ought not to – resemble pagan ones.[48]

Erasmus's transculturation of Homeric lines into Christian proverbs that instruct in spiritual combat relies on a wit that profits from the incongruity between the proverb's original context and its adapted usage. A line spoken in the midst of combat at *Il.* 10.135 ("A spear he seized, stout and sharp-tipped" [*Hastam corripuit robustam cuspide acuta*]) can thus be repurposed to describe someone "who when challenged proceeds to shout insults" [*qui iam provocatus aggreditur conviciis agere*], a strategy that manages to recuperate Homer while simultaneously demeaning Iliadic aggression by yoking it to the most spiteful and petty-minded kind of scholarly wrangling (*Litem incipere* [To start a dispute], Adage III.viii.41, *CWE* 35:297 [ASD II.6:496]). In another adage of Homeric origin, *Magna de re disceptatur* [A great matter being debated], Erasmus hints at the satirical potential of the saying by demonstrating how Lucian accommodated it to mock-heroic purposes and proposing that Homer's description of the combat between Achilles and Hector at *Il.* 22.159–60 might prove useful to "mock philosophers quarrelling disgracefully before the judges about their fees" [*cum ridet philosophos turpiter apud iudices de salario contendentes*] (Adage III.ix.29, *CWE* 35:329 [ASD II.6:526]). Other adages borrow lines from Homer to lend a sardonic mock-grandeur to ignoble verbal squabbles between adversaries: *Et meum telum cuspidem habet acuminatam* [My weapon too has a sharpened point] notes that a line first uttered by Hector at *Il.* 20.437 might likewise come in handy "whenever we admit that we are indeed the weaker, but nevertheless do not lack the power to hurt" (Adage I.ii.88, *CWE* 31:219 [ASD II.1:294]).

Yet even as many of the adages derived from Homeric battle scenes provide witty retorts for the participants of early sixteenth-century word wars, others provide veiled criticism of the act of swapping insults, a behaviour often denigrated as unmanly in the *Iliad* and criticized by the poem's sixteenth-century readers as absurd and indecorous. Erasmus concocts the adage *Ne quid moveare verborum strepitu* [Don't be put off by loud words] from a line spoken by Apollo to Aeneas at *Il.* 20.108–9, while Aeneas's chastisement of Achilles later in the same book yields the adage *Verbis pugnans, non re* [You are fighting with words, not facts], a proverb that insults the art of insult itself by suggesting that "It is easy to exchange insults, but difficult to convince by the facts" [*Facile est conviciis altercari, verum re vincere difficile*] (Adage III.ix.17 and Adage III.ix.16, *CWE* 35:324).

As a work that aspires to exhaustiveness rather than consistency, the *Adages* displays a spectrum of attitudes towards the moral and spiritual legitimacy of rhetorical combat that reflects Erasmus's ambivalence about verbal contention as well as the flexibility of Homeric epic to accommodate competing attitudes towards it. In the adage *Lingua bellare* [To fight with the tongue; *glôssê polemizein*], Erasmus cites four different sources from the *Iliad* whose attitudes towards tongue warfare range from extremely positive to extremely negative (Adage II.x.47, *CWE* 34:145 [ASD II.4:305–6]). Explaining the principal source for the adage, Erasmus cites Menelaus's use of "reviling words" [*neikei oneidizôn*] when he chastises his fellow Trojans for cowardice at *Il.* 7.96, a scene that Erasmus clearly regards as one of the poem's more noble expressions of verbal combat. But other possible sources for the adage identified by Erasmus, including *Il.* 20.367 and 3.8–9, offer a less redemptive view of *glossaspidas*, or men who "bear in their tongues the poison of an asp" [*aspidis venenum in lingua circunferunt*] – a vice that correlates with Paul's indictment of venom-mouthed deceivers and blasphemers at Rom. 3:13.[49] The Homeric and New Testament parallel is especially evident in Erasmus's derivation of the adage from Hector's admission at 20.367–8 that "I too with words would even fight [*contendere*] the immortals, but with the spear it is hard [*durum*], for they are mightier far" (ASD II.4:306, II.4:304), lines striking for their close resemblance to the divine message heard by Paul on the road to Damascus at Acts 9.4, which Erasmus paraphrases as "It is hard for you to kick against the goad, for you are struggling not against human beings but against God, whose will no one can resist" [*Durum est enim tibi adversus stimulum iactare calces. Non enim reluctaris hominibus, sed Deo, cuius voluntati nemo potest resistere*] (*CWE* 50:64 [LB VII:703A]).

One of the other Homeric sources identified by Erasmus for the adage *Lingua bellare* also has a close parallel in the New Testament. Establishing a possible derivation for the proverb from Homer's contrast between the "evil strife" [*kakên erida*] of the Trojans and the orderly Achaeans, Erasmus appreciates that Homer's Trojans are thrice associated with "clamour" [*klangê*] in the space of eight lines (*Il.* 3.1–8), a close relative of the Greek term used by Paul at Eph. 4.31 to criticize men who neglect charity because of their "bitterness and anger and wrath and clamor" [*pikria kai thumos kai orgê kai kraugê*].[50] Reshaping Homer's frequent contrast between the noisy clamour of the Trojan troops and the disciplined silence of their adversaries, Erasmus casts his own enemies as noisy barbarians and correspondingly depicts himself and his allies as the descendants of Homer's Greeks, who march into battle silently, "eager at heart to come assist each other" (*Il.* 3.8–9).[51] The contrast, which Erasmus invokes once again in his *Lingua*, helps to explain one of his favourite Homeric allusions for conveying the evils of an undisciplined tongue: the character of Stentor, the "brazen-voiced" Trojan who appears only once in the *Iliad* but crops up frequently in Erasmus's writings as an emblem of academic noise pollution (*Il.* 5.785).[52] Unlike Homer's Stentor, a "great-hearted" [*megalêtori*] man whose "brazen voice" [*chalkeophônô*] is used to rebuke his fellow Trojans for cowardice, Erasmus's Stentors are loud-mouthed nonsense-peddlers, clamorous dialecticians and sophists who act boisterously in academic disputes (*CWE* 23:43 [ASD I.1:68]). With adages such as *Stentore clamosior* [Noisier than Stentor], *Absit clamor in colloquio aut lusu* [Against brawling in conversation or in games], and *In clamosos* [Against people who shout], the last drawn from a line in the *Iliad* that describes how Poseidon "shouts as loudly as nine / or ten thousand men as they join battle," Erasmus enlists Homer as an unlikely ally in his condemnation of "*megalophônoi*" – big-mouthed or boisterous men (Adage II.iii.37, *CWE* 33:150; Adage III.ix.37, *CWE* 35:332; Adage III.viii.91, *CWE* 35:315 [ASD II.6:512], citing *Il.* 14.148–9).[53] For Erasmus, Stentor's "brazen" voice resonates with Paul's observation at 1 Cor. 13.1 that men who speak without love sound like a "noisy brass gong" [*chalkos êchôn*] or a "clanging cymbal" [*kumbalon alalazon*], images that transform Homer's aural contrast between Greeks and Trojans into Paul's more spiritually urgent distinction between Christian concord and Gentile schism.

Erasmus's Homeric adages thus offer a variety of lessons about Christian eloquence and obloquy. The range of rhetorical situations in which Erasmus deploys lines from Homeric epic reflects the commonplace Renaissance belief that Homer's poems achieve their rhetorical brilliance through frequent modulation between different rhetorical registers. Erasmus would have encountered this idea in the works of ancient rhetoricians such as Aristotle, Longinus, and Quintilian, and he would have been convinced of the humanistic utility of the idea by Poliziano, whose commentaries and orations on Homer treat him as the source of all rhetorical styles, a "boundless and infinite sea" of rhetorical models.[54] Poliziano's observations on Homeric rhetoric are deeply indebted to pseudo-Plutarch's *Life of Homer*, a work first printed in the 1488 *editio princeps* of Homer that outlines how the *Iliad* and *Odyssey* give each of their speakers "the appropriate form of speech" [*to prepon eidos tôn logôn*] and give "each orator a particular character" [*oude charaktêrisai tous rhêtoras*], making Nestor sweet and pleasing, Menelaus "brief and winning" [*brachulogon kai eucharin*], and Odysseus a master of "many complex ingenuities of language" [*pollê kai puknê plêktikê tê deinotêti tôn logôn*].[55]

In the long section of the pseudo-Plutarchan *Life* devoted to rhetoric, Odysseus emerges as the most sophisticated and supple speaker, an orator who speaks "with appropriate directness" [*parrhêsia tê prepousê*] when necessary but also a speaker capable of winning over his audience "with gentle words" [*logois prosênesi peithôn*] and for "rebuking them with moderation" [*metriôs men oneidisas*].[56] Poliziano echoes these sentiments in his *Ambra*, which commends the "salutary intervention" of Odysseus as orator when he "mixes sweet words with harsh ones, [and] represses the abusive language of an uncontrolled tongue" [*cum dulcibus aspera miscet, / cum vaga clamosae reprimit convicia linguae*].[57] This well-tempered mixture of sweet and harsh words is one of the key rhetorical principles of the *Adages*. Erasmus repeatedly extols the rhetorical flexibility of Homer's Odysseus by associating him with that most accommodating of apostolic rhetoricians, Paul, a man who according to Erasmus's *Paraphrase* on Acts 17.22 "knew how to become all things to all people, and how to accommodate his eloquence to the character of any listener" [*noverat omnia fieri omnibus, [et] eloquentiam suam ad omnium mores attemperare*] (*CWE* 50:108 [LB VII:736A]).[58] Glossing the adage *Polypi mentem obtine* [Adopt the outlook of the polyp], Erasmus argues that Odysseus and Paul both exemplify the most positive connotations of the saying, the former in his polytropic cunning and the latter in his ability to "become all things to all men [*tois pasin gegona panta*] so that I might save some" (Adage I.i.43, *CWE* 31:133–5, citing I Cor. 9.22). The chameleon-like flexibility of Odysseus and Paul is principally a rhetorical virtue: as Erasmus explains in a related adage, *Omnem vocem mittere* [To use every kind of tone], Paul's wish to be able to "change [his] tone" [*allaxai tên phonên mou*] at Galatians 4.20 stems from the basic principles of classical decorum, since "the man who employs at different times rebukes, flattery, preaching, humility, threats, and consolation" [*nunc obiurgat, nunc blanditur, nunc se praedicat, nunc semet demittit, nunc territat, nunc consolatur*] and is capable of "changing his tone [*mutat vocem suam*] all the time, like a skilled precentor, in order to persuade in some way or other" (Adage IV.vi.57, *CWE* 36:253 [ASD II.8:54]).[59] As Erasmus understands it, the apostle who is dubbed "Hermes" on account of his eloquence derives the skill "to know how to answer everyone" from the same set of rhetorical principles guiding Homer's most accommodating and flexible speakers.[60]

In several adages, including *Modis omnibus incitat* [By every means he urges] and *Cothurno versatilior* [More versatile than a buskin], Erasmus testifies to the Homeric origins of this "mobility of intellect" and its accompanying virtue of rhetorical flexibility, characteristics he repeatedly associates with Odysseus, "called a man of many turnings" [*polutropon dixit*] because he can "play any part to perfection – the general, the beggar, the head of the house" [*quod quamvis personam apte gereret, ducis, mendici, patrisfamilias*] (Adage I.i.94: *Cothurno versatilior*, *CWE* 31:136–7 [ASD II.1:204]). Paul's capacity to season his speech with equal parts "grace and salt" [*chariti halati*] at Col. 4.6 is modelled throughout the *Adages* by various Homeric speakers who are equally adept at tempering praise and blame. In *Modis omnibus incitat*, a maxim which applies to "someone [who] uses every means to persuade someone else, prayers, flattery, censure, threats" [*quis modis omnibus animum alterius sollicitat, nunc precibus, nunc blanditiis, nunc iurgiis, nunc minis*], Erasmus identifies a paradigm for this behaviour in a line from the *Iliad* that describes how Automedon instils courage into Achilles's horses after the death of Patroclus: "Again and again he commanded them with lashes of his whip, / Again and again he coaxed them with soft words, again and again he threatened" [*Multum ille scuticaque cita celerare iubebat, / Multum idem blande afflatus multumque minatus*] (Adage III.viii.98, *CWE* 35:317 [ASD II.6:514–15], citing *Il.* 17.430–1). Erasmus discerns a powerful correspondence between the rhetorical principle enacted by these verses from the *Iliad* and those observed by the apostles, as his *Paraphrases on Acts* reveals. Paraphrasing Acts 4.1, which describes how Peter and John begin addressing their audience, Erasmus elaborates admiringly on how the "divine orator" and his companion urge the people to embrace the gospel: "They flattered no one; rather, they persuaded [*suadentes*] with the testimony of the prophets, striking terror through fear of the future judgment, then again soothing and enticing [*lenientes ac pellicientes*] with an easily available and a ready pardon" (*CWE* 50:30 [LB VII:678E]). Again, at Acts 4.13, Erasmus's paraphrase embellishes a description of "Peter's boldness" [*Petrou parrêsian*] to emphasize his "forthright" [*loquutus*] speech and to praise his rhetorical subtlety and flexibility. In Erasmus's rather circumlocutory paraphrase upon the verse, Peter speaks "bravely and extemporaneously [*libertate constantiaque*], moderating his speech with admirable prudence so that freedom should not end in abuse, or softness smack of adulation or fear" (*CWE* 50:32 [LB VII:680E]).[61] By cultivating the virtuous mean between excessive blame and flattery, Peter inherits and even improves upon the Homeric virtue of rhetorical moderation, applying his Odyssean capacity to "change his tone" [*omnibus loquitur*] so as to preach the gospel with greater efficacy and to address his audience "that he might gain them all" [*omnes lucrifaciat*] (*Paraphrase on Acts* 10.29, *CWE* 50:73, 50:232, note 42 [LB VII:709E]).

Erasmus's recognition of the rhetorical and ethical kinship between Homeric epic and the New Testament – and especially between Odysseus and Paul – is less surprising than it might seem given his repeated endorsement of allegorical interpretation as a means of accommodating pagan myth to Christian doctrine. In the *Enchiridion*, Erasmus observes that the "poetry of Homer and Virgil is of no little profit if you remember that it is entirely allegorical" [*Ita non parum utilis est Homerica, Virgilianaque Poesis, si memineris eam totam est allegoricam*] (*CWE* 66:33 [LB V:7F]). Erasmus understands the adage as a form closely related to "poetic allegories," dislocatable scraps of pagan wisdom that conceal Christian truths (Ep. 211, *CWE* 2:141). As is evident in adages such as *Silenus Alcibiades*, which celebrates the involuted nature of philosophical and spiritual knowledge, ancient proverbs and maxims may be regarded as secret storehouses of Christian wisdom, wisdom revealed only when their cloaked meanings are accommodated to new spiritual contexts and demands. In *Sui dissimilis* [A different face], Erasmus invokes Odysseus's description of Athena's capacity for disguise at *Od.* 13.313 – "you change your shape at will" – as a synecdoche for the "wisdom that is concealed with different wrappings [*variis involucris*] in the ancient writers and is presented in ever-changing images, especially in holy scripture" (Adage III.x.32, *CWE* 35:368 [ASD II.6:562]). According to Erasmus, Athena "put[s] on now one face, now another" [*Nunc alio, nunc rursum alio fis obvia vultu*] in a manner similar to ancient adages themselves, which "adopt all kinds of figurative variations" [*schematum species ... varietur*] in order to make the wisdom they contain "fitted to things and times" [*accommodatum rebus temporibusque*] (*CWE* 35:368 [ASD II.6:562]; *CWE* 31:6, 31:3 [ASD II.1:48, II.1:45]). This technique of fitting ancient wisdom to modern contexts, practised throughout the *Adages*, becomes a hermeneutic model for many of Erasmus's friends and followers. In his 1535 *De Transitu*, Budé argues that Christianity must not be "reluctant to borrow something from Homer's philosophy," a technique modelled on Erasmus's representations of Pauline accommodation.[62] By developing adages from lines in the *Iliad* and *Odyssey* that bear an obvious likeness to verses from Acts and from the Pauline epistles, Erasmus emulates Paul's willingness to adapt certain gentile customs to Christian doctrine. As he points out in his *Paraphrases on Acts*, "in citing their poets [Paul] sometimes accommodated himself to them" [*in citandis illorum Poetis, nonnunquam est obsequutus*].[63]

Strengthened by his perception of a strong continuity between classical and Christian rhetoric, Erasmus's understanding of the affinity between Odysseus and Paul is reinforced by the many biographical and temperamental similarities between the apostle and the Homeric hero: their journeys and shipwrecks, their eloquence, their capacity for conversion and metamorphosis, and even their willingness to resort to cunning in adverse situations.[64] But for Erasmus, the most compelling connection between the two men – and the one that links both of them to the intellectual and rhetorical techniques espoused by the adages themselves – is their capacity to accommodate themselves rhetorically to the demands of their audience, a skill that includes (but is not limited to) the ability to temper praise and rebuke and to evaluate the circumstances in which verbal strife might prove a legitimate and effective means of persuasion. Mediated through the lens of the New Testament, Erasmus's interpretation of Homeric epic in the *Adages* assists him in constructing a complex ethics of verbal contention that in turn guides his involvement in polemical debates and theological controversies, in which Erasmus appears by turns a reluctant and a fervent participant. Although Erasmus rejects certain expressions of pagan contentiousness in Homer as irreconcilable with Christian concord and amity, many of the eristic rhetorical behaviours exhibited by Homer's most vehement speakers may be adapted for Christian purposes in order to support the virtues – charity, humility, communalism – most prized by Erasmus.

Eris and the Causes of Quarrel

As he enlists Homeric epic in his enterprise of establishing a Christian decorum of scholarly contention, Erasmus adapts Homer's representations of strife and conflict to his own ethics of friendship and *homonoia* [concord] as well as to his distinctive understanding of Pauline spiritual *agôn.*[65] Culminating in *In Praise of Folly*, the *Querela Pacis*, the *Adages* of 1515 and 1517, and various controversial writings, Erasmus's writings during the second decade of the sixteenth century offer a subtle yet coherent interpretation of Homeric epic that revolves around how the Greek poet establishes rules and limits for contention and rivalry. Although cognizant of the fact that the intensely eristic world of Homeric epic makes the *Iliad* and *Odyssey* difficult to accommodate to the Christian Platonism of works such as the *Adages*, with its emphasis upon friendship and communalism, Erasmus regards Homer as a poet sensitive to the benefits and the liabilities of conflict and rivalry, and thus a useful model in establishing a new etiquette for intellectual and theological disputation.[66] Despite repeated protestations to the contrary, Erasmus is a frequent and virtuoso contributor to controversies during the 1510s and early 1520s. As he becomes embroiled in disputes with men such as Jacques Lefèvre, Martin Dorp, Edward Lee, Martin Luther, and Guillaume Budé, Homeric epic proves a key resource for Erasmus to articulate what he finds most distasteful or alarming about the controversies in which he is involved, as well as to articulate new principles and ideals of contention that might mitigate rancour and turn bitter animosities into intellectually productive rivalries.

Erasmus assesses the uses and dangers of verbal contention during this period by calling upon a pantheon of Homeric deities associated with conflict, including Ares, Atê, and Eris. Invoked repeatedly by Erasmus and his contemporaries and correspondents throughout the 1510s and early 1520s, these divnities help Erasmus construct a complex mythography of discord that helps him mediate his own, ambivalent attitude towards disputation and offers psychological and spiritual insight into the origins of conflict. Erasmus's allusions to Eris and Atê – goddesses often confused or conflated with each other – are often symptomatic of his discomfort with quarrel and controversy. In several polemical works, Erasmus identifies one or both of Homer's goddesses of strife as a *casus belli* in order to resolve a dispute by blaming its cause on external and supernatural forces. In the *Apologia ad Fabrum*, Erasmus twice appeals to Atê, asking Lefèvre to "do what Homer's Agamemnon does and fall back upon some madness [*Aten aliquam*] as the cause of this unfortunate occurrence" (*CWE* 83:91 [ASD IX.3:174]). By calling upon his adversary to lay the cause of their quarrel upon "the Fates, or the goddess Strife, or Homer's Atê" [*vel fatis vel Eridi vel Atae Homericae*], Erasmus hopes to placate Lefèvre by assigning blame elsewhere – in this case, to the deity responsible for instigating the "*Iliad* of troubles" born out of the rivalry between Agamemnon and Achilles over Briseïs (*CWE* 83:107 [ASD IX.3:196], paraphrasing *Il.* 9.505 and 19.91).

In the *Querela Pacis*, written one year before the *Ad Fabrum*, Erasmus explains how the practice of invoking Atê can have a conciliatory effect, for "just as in Homer the causes of the quarrel which arose between Agamemnon and Achilles are blamed on the goddess Atê by those who appeal for a reconciliation [*apud Homerum dissidii causas, quod inter Agamemnonem et Achillem intercesserat, in Atem deam reiiciunt qui vocant ad concordiam*], so anything excusable must sometimes be blamed on fate or on some evil genius" so that "your anger [may be] transferred to these from the persons involved" [*in haec odium ab ipsis hominibus transferatur*] (*CWE* 27:316 [ASD IV.2:92]). In other words, casting blame upon Atê soothes tensions between adversaries by reassigning culpability to external forces: once a conflict is understood by both parties as governed by impulses imposed from above, the "*Litae* will follow after *Atê* on their slow feet, reconciling men and seeking to heal their injuries," as Erasmus explains, paraphrasing Phoenix's fable from Book 9 of the *Iliad* (Adage I.vii.13, *CWE* 32:73 [ASD II.2:136]; paraphrasing *Il.* 9.505–7). As it provides Erasmus with a mythological foundation that explains the origins of human conflict, the Homeric fable also offers some strikingly Christian wisdom about how strife may be alleviated through prayer and forgiveness. Erasmus was captivated by Phoenix's fable of the *Litae*, the "prayers" who "turn [men] from wrath to supplication" [*knisê te paratrôpôs'anthrôpoi / lissomenoi*] and thus ensure forgiveness of transgressions and the restoration of harmony between enemies.[67] The Homeric parable has obvious appeal for Erasmus's eirenic Christian sensibilities. In the adage *Ira omnium tardissime senescit* [Anger is the last thing to grow old], Erasmus even ventures that Atê is "thought by some people to be close to the Christian belief that Lucifer was hurled down from heaven" (Adage I.vii.13, *CWE* 32:73 [ASD II.2:137]).

In his 1523 *Spongia*, addressed to Ulrich von Hutten, Erasmus once again impugns "Homer's Atê" as the root cause of the acrimonious treatise to which he is responding.[68] In his *Expostulation*, printed earlier that same year, von Hutten had accused Erasmus of depicting Martin Luther as a reincarnation of Eris who has tossed an "apple of discord" into the otherwise convivial banquet of early sixteenth-century religious culture.[69] When Erasmus takes up his pen against Luther several years later in his 1527 *Hyperaspites*, he insults the German reformer with a barrage of Homeric epithets, calling him "an Achilles leading flies for troops" [*armis submovet Achillem muscarum*] and comparing his "extraordinary impudence" [*insigni impudentia*] to that of Homer's petulant hero (*CWE* 77:420, 77:616 [LB X:1378D, X:1474D]). The vast fund of verbal abuse unleashed by Luther in his polemical writings only strengthens his Homeric associations for Erasmus, who protests that Achilles, Ajax, and Agamemnon engage in the same sort of "quarrels, jeers, and insults" [*obtestationes, expostulationes, obiurgationes*] for which he finds fault in Luther (*CWE* 77:401 [LB X:1369C]). Erasmus's introduction of Homeric epithets and phrases into his polemical writings grows out of the *Adages*, where, as we have seen, proverbs about abusive language and vituperation often have Homeric genealogies: *Naves onustae convitiis* [Shiploads of abuse] derives from an image at *Il.* 20.246–7, while *Domesticum dissidium* [Discord in the home], a maxim suitable for describing "abominable domestic quarreling" [*detestandam seditionem domesticam*], derives from *Od.* 16.423 (Adages I.viii.67, IIIx.44; *CWE* 32:163, 35: 372 [ASD II.6:565]). In works such as the *Antibarbarorum Liber*, the "gladiatorial fury" of opponents of humanistic learning is granted a Homeric legacy in Erasmus's parodic accounts of the Reuchlin affair, a dispute whose combination of visciousness and pettiness exemplifies for Erasmus the way in which small conflicts can quickly grow out of control. In the revisions to the *Antibarbarorum Liber* made shortly before its publication in 1520, as well as in adages and letters composed during the same period, Erasmus teasingly refers to one of Reuchlin's most vociferous opponents – a certain Jean Briart Atensis, then vice-chancellor of the University of Louvain – as Atê.[70] In the *Antibarbarorum Liber*, Briart's opposition to Reuchlin reincarnates Atê as a "scourge of studies" rather than of Achaean kings (*CWE* 23:39). Used repeatedly throughout the late 1510s, Briart's Homeric nickname stuck, in part because it allowed Erasmus to cast aspersions on his adversary in a subtle and indirect way. Reporting to Petrus Mosellanus about the turmoil at the University of Louvain in spring 1519, Erasmus suggests that Homer's Atê – Atensis – is to blame for the conflict. Writing to Willibald Pirckheimer several months earlier, he blames the "riots and cabals" [*tumultus et conspirationes*] over the Reuchlin affair upon infernal powers, commenting that "Homer puts the blame for turmoil of this sort on Atê" [*Homerus huiusmodi perturbationum causam in Aten reiicit*] (Ep. 856, *CWE* 6:66 [Allen 3:358]).

In addition to supplying a witty, coded allusion to Briart, Erasmus's frequent references to Homer's Atê also offer an opportunity to meditate on the underlying causes of intellectual quarrel. Writing to Erasmus in April 1518 about his recent controversy with Lefèvre, Guillaume Budé invokes the "*noxae Homericae*" – an apparent conflation of Eris and Atê – to lament how scholars "let themselves be tempted and seduced by discord, parent of Eris [*parens illa discordiae contentio*], who once, they say, tossed into the middle of a feast of the gods a golden apple inscribed with the words 'to the fairest'" [*quae in deorum olim convivio aureum illud malum inscriptum 'ê kalê labétô provoluisse in medium dicitur*] (Ep. 810, *CWE* 5:373–5 [Allen 3:273–5, 3:270]). Budé's allusion to Eris's intrusion into the wedding of Peleus and Thetis grants a Homeric ancestry to the polemical dispute between Lefèvre and Erasmus, an event he blames on "Homer's Atê, who 'with madness fraught strides over the heads of men'" [*casum noxae Homericae tribuis, êge, ut inquit ille, kat'andrôn kraata bainei Blaptous'anthrôpous*] (Ep. 810, *CWE* 5:373 [Allen 3:273], citing *Il.* 19.93–4]).[71] Budé's deft interweaving of Homeric allusions into his accounts of contemporary controversies treats the *Iliad* as the archetypal poem of contention, a work whose deities of discord may still be invoked to explain how quarrels, altercations, and wars begin over two thousand years later.

Yet as Budé explains to Erasmus, Homeric epic provides a remedy for the infectious discord it diagnoses, since the poet "left for posterity an antidote for the cholerous and quarrelous humour" [*velut iracundiae et contentionis antidotum posteritati reliquit*] in the form of a speech made by Achilles in Book 18 of the *Iliad*. According to Budé's synopsis of that speech, which he cites in Greek, "Achilles regrets that he has obeyed the anger in his heart" and "at length sees that he is in the wrong and curses strife" (Ep. 810, *CWE* 5:376 [Allen 3:275], paraphrasing *Il.* 18.107–10). But Budé misidentifies the location of the speech in the *Iliad*, placing it in the twenty-second book and not in the eighteenth – a crucial difference, since Achilles's indictment of strife precedes, rather than succeeds, his triumphant return into battle and his ignominious treatment of Hector's corpse. Whether by accident or design, Budé misreads Achilles's speech as an unambiguous censure of violence, not a passing cloud of doubt about the glories of war dispelled by his mother's consolation and by the replacement of his shield.

None of these contextual problems prevents Erasmus or Budé from seizing upon Achilles's condemnation of strife at *Il.* 18.107–10 in order to articulate their own distaste for controversy and discord. In another letter to Erasmus, written in June 1519, Budé repudiates the controversies he has been waging against the "barbarophiles" [*philobarbárois*] by citing Achilles at *Il.* 18.104, who calls himself "a useless burden on the earth" [*etôsion achthos arourês*] (Ep. 987, *CWE* 6:402 [Allen 3:616–17]).[72] Whereas Budé invokes the line to bewail his entanglement in bitter and fruitless scholarly disputes, Achilles's motive in calling himself a "profitless burden" stems from precisely the opposite sentiment: he is lamenting not the futility of strife but rather his inaction – his failure to assist his fellow Achaeans at war.

Despite their repeated appropriation of these lines to voice an aversion to controversy, both Erasmus and Budé are able to discern Achilles's faults and to comprehend the profound differences between Iliadic values and their own. Erasmus criticizes Achilles several times for his *philoneikia* [love of strife] and his *philotimia* [ambition or love of honour], qualities also repudiated by Plato's Phaedrus in the *Symposium*. Yet while Phaedrus singles out Achilles and Patroclus as exemplary friends capable of "refrain[ing] from all that is base in mutual rivalry for honour [*philotimoumeoi*]," Erasmus regards this Homeric paragon of male friendship in quite a different light.[73] In several works, including the preface to his edition of Quintus Curtius, printed at Strasbourg in June 1518, Erasmus places Achilles in the same unflattering category as Alexander the Great, Xerxes, and the heroes of chivalric romance, "shocking examples for a good prince" [*pessimum uterque boni principis exemplar*] by dint of their excessive ambition, their lust for honour, and their irascibility.[74] In the *Institutio Principis Christiani*, first printed in 1516, Erasmus's distaste for aggression and honour-seeking prompts him to issue a blanket condemnation of pagan heroism, arguing that young and impressionable readers will be incited to violence if, "without being equipped with an antidote, he reads about Achilles or Alexander the Great or Xerxes or Julius Caesar" [*si non praemunitus antidoto Achillem aut Alexandrum Magnum aut Xersem aut Iulium legerit*] (*CWE* 27:250–1 [ASD IV.1:179–80]). One must be on guard against the "enormous prestige" of these heroic figures, Erasmus argues, for they are not heroes but "raging bandits" [*furiosos latrones*].[75] As for so many Renaissance readers of Homer, Erasmus's admiration for the poems depends upon selective and creative rereading. The *Iliad* may contain moments that celebrate friendship, communalism, and nonviolence, but it also depicts the "passions of foolish kings" and revolves around an "idiotic" [*ineptius*] conflict over the possession of a "barbarous slut" [*barbara puellula*].[76]

This last point – that the *Iliad* narrates the escalation of a massive conflict out of a matter so trifling as the ownership of a woman – is one of

Erasmus's most frequent refrains when he enlists passages of Homeric epic to voice his disdain for conflict. Elevated to proverbial status in adages such as *Haec Helena* [This is the Helen] and *Ex minimis initiis maxima* [From little things grow great ones], the futility and triviality of the Trojan War are central themes for Erasmus, who sees the nugatory quibbles of sophists and theologians as stemming from the same "terrible and fatal contention of sorts" [*diram [et] capitalem animorum contentionem*] that he and Budé depict as fuelling petty disputes over Helen and Briseïs.[77] This argument is rehearsed in adages such as *Inanus conatus* [Useless effort], which enlists a line spoken by Agamemnon – "to fight a fruitless fight and a useless war" [*pugnam infrugiferamque et inutile ducere bellum (aprêkton polemon polemizein êde machesthai)*] – to testify to the vanity of strife (Adage III.viii.8, *CWE* 35:285 [ASD II.6:486], citing *Il.* 2.121). Yet as is so often the case in the *Adages*, Erasmus's citation diverges from Agamemnon's intended meaning: the Greek king ends the speech in which the line is contained by rousing the *thumos* of his soldiers and arousing their renewed enthusiasm for battle.

Erasmus's most protracted and sophisticated misreading of a Homeric passage in the *Adages* grows out of his effort to accommodate Homer's description of Eris at *Il.* 4.440–4 to a palpably un-eristic, Christian ethos of pacifistic non-retaliation. In *Dulce bellum inexpertis* [War is sweet only to the inexperienced], an adage first developed in a 1514 letter to Antoon Van Bergen and then printed in the 1515 Froben edition, Erasmus reworks several lines that describe how Eris "first rears her crest only a little, but then her head is fixed in the heavens while her feet tread on earth" (*Il.* 4.441–3). Whatever this Homeric fable might mean in its original context – that strife pervades both divine and mortal realms, or that petty human disputes have grave celestial consequences when they ascend to the heavens – to Erasmus, the lines contain a moral lesson about "how rashly, for what trivial reasons war is begun," an interpretation perhaps indebted to the Homeric allegorist Heraclitus, who observes of the verses that this is "what always happens to quarrelsome [*philoneikousi*] people: strife begins with a trivial cause, but once stirred up it swells up into what is indeed a great evil" (Adage IV.i.1, *CWE* 35:401 [ASD II.7:12]).[78] The dilemma that small quarrels breed larger ones profoundly shapes Erasmus's understanding of the dire consequences of engaging in even the most trivial scholarly contests over grammar or philology. It resurfaces as the central axiom of adages such as *Litem paret lis, noxa item noxam parit* [Quarrel follows quarrel and hurt follows hurt], *Lis litem serit* [Quarrel comes from quarrel], and *Ex minimis initiis maxima* [From little things grow great ones], the last two of which invoke Homer's Eris in order to explain how strife grows usuriously if left unchecked (Adage I.viii.98, *CWE* 32:178; Adage II.x.41, *CWE* 34:143; Adage III.viii.23, *CWE* 35:291). In the last of these adages, Erasmus calls Homer's description of Eris "wonderfully apt," since her ability to span heaven and earth demonstrates how "very serious fires are ignited by very tiny sparks" [*ex minutissima scintillula gravissimum incendium*], a moral that Erasmus may recognize as a pagan analogue to James 3.5: "How great a forest is set ablaze by a small fire" [*Idou hêlikon pur hêlikên hulên anaptei*] (Adage III.viii.23 [ASD II.6:491]).[79]

The verse in James is not the only place in the New Testament that confirms the lessons Erasmus discerns in Homer's account of Eris, a scene rendered vivdly by Vincenzo Cartari, whose buoyant *Discordia* floats in a nimbus of clouds, the most light-footed of bad angels (see figure 4). Kindled by the smallest of sparks, the goddess of strife becomes, in Erasmus's handling, a personification of the trivial and petty disputes that Paul, in the epistles to Timothy and Titus, calls *mataiologia*, or "fighting endlessly about frivolous nonsense" [*insanit circa frivolas quaestiones*].[80] In his *Annotations* and *Paraphrases*, Erasmus dwells at length upon Paul's criticism of "*mataiologoi*," peddlers of trivial arguments or men who have a "morbid craving for controversies and disputes over words" [*zêtêseis kai logomachias*].[81] Erasmus's concern that even the most trivial instances of verbal disputation can intensify into serious conflict may appear to sit ill at ease with the ludic stance cultivated by works such as *In Praise of Folly* and the *Colloquies*, literary recreations founded upon the principle that jesting rebuke is an effective means of persuading, confounding, or critiquing adversaries. Although often held up as the *homo ludens* of his age, Erasmus struggles to divorce playful intellectual scrimmage from its potentially deadly consequences. In the adage *Dulce bellum inexpertis*, he observes that "war is born from war, and a real war from a counterfeit one, and a huge war grows from a tiny one" [*quin etiam bellum e bello seritur, e simulato verum, e pusillo maximum exoritur*], a loose paraphrase of Homer's description of Eris that reveals keen anxieties about the precariously intimate relationship between physical violence and its various rehearsal spaces in the rhetorical and scholarly arena (Adage IV.i.1, *CWE* 35:404 [ASD II.7:16]).

Erasmus's assertion that "simulated" warfare leads to real war reflects his doubts about the productive interplay between *philia* and *eris* that was and still is widely held to animate Homeric epic and other archaic Greek texts. For certain modern Homeric scholars, as well as for some of his ancient allegorists, *agôn* has a binding power, such that certain forms of

De gli Antichi. 357

Imagine della Discordia secondo Aristide, laquale per li suoi mali effetti fù caciata dal Cielo, ne fù inuitata con li altri Dei alle nozze di Peleo e Tetide genitori d'Achille, acciò con suoi veneni non le turbasse; e pur le turbò co'l gettar del pomo d'oro significante, che alli machinatori non mancano occasioni di discordie.

Z 3

Figure 4. Vincenzo Cartari, *Le vere e nove imagini de gli dei delli antichi* (Padua: Pietro Paolo Tozzi, 1615), p. 357: “Imagine della Discordia secondo Aristide.” Courtesy Rubenstein Rare Book and Manuscript Library, Duke University. Durham, NC.

strife, including ritualized competition and rivalry, may forge friendship and community.[82] As the spectrum of meanings for terms such as *agôn*, *neikos*, and *machê* suggests, recreational and serious forms of conflict are closely intertwined in early Greek literature and philosophy.[83] Erasmus's blindness to the function of ludic contest in Homeric epic is especially apparent in the strong distaste he voices for pagan athleticism, an arena of activity long recognized both as preparation for violent conflict and as a means of neutralizing potentially threatening tensions and hostilities.[84] Sensitive to the evolution of Greek terms such as *agôn* and *athlos*, which shed their physical meanings for spiritual ones in the Hellenistic and New Testament idioms of Philo and Saint Paul, Erasmus frequently contrasts the physical struggles of classical heroes with the spiritual trials of Christian "athletes" and "soldiers," contestants bound by different rules who compete for altogether different prizes.[85] Erasmus's work as a translator and annotator of the New Testament nurtures in him a profound recognition of how early Christianity transvalues the pagan Greek vocabulary of combat. Moreover, as a scholar who understands language as the "inevitable medium and mediator of all human experience," Erasmus's scriptural annotations reveal an acute awareness of the complex process through which early Christian writers appropriate Greek terms such as *zêlos* [rivalry, emulation] and *athliotês* [struggling, suffering], in the process transforming them into something quite different from what these terms mean in the context of an Archaic Greek heroic poem.[86]

Particularly in the Pauline epistles and in Acts, scriptural language is saturated with athletic metaphors that Erasmus appreciates as markers of the ethical and spiritual gulf between pagan and Christian culture.[87] In the *Enchiridion*, Erasmus contrasts the spiritual warfare waged by the Christian soldier to the mere bodily violence inflicted by "the cruel victor Achilles … upon Hector" [*in Hectorem potuit crudelissimus victor Achilles*] and he explains how the system of reward and punishment in the "contests" [*certaminibus*] of the classical world is irrelevant to Christians, who should be motivated neither by the "reproach incurred by cowardice [n]or by the desire for reward" [*nos contra, neque pudore, neque praemio accendimur*] [(*CWE* 66:27 [LB V:4A, V:3E]). Although the inception of the most famous ancient Greek athletic competitions post-dates the composition of Homeric epic by several centuries, Erasmus frequently imagines the competitive impulses at work in ancient Greek culture as fundamentally Homeric, an association probably encouraged by Plutarch, who issues frequent condemnations of the aggressively adversarial behaviour of Homeric heroes in his *Moralia*, a work that in turn shapes Erasmus's interpretation of Homer in the *Adages*.[88] Contrasting the Christian and pagan ethics of reward and punishment in the *Enchiridion*, Erasmus asks, "What prizes [*praemia*] has our director of the games set before us? Surely not tripods or mules as Achilles offered in Homer" (*Enchiridion*, *CWE* 66:27 [LB V:3F]). Protected by the arsenal of Holy Scripture rather than by the arms of "Pallas Minerva" [*Palladi … arma*] or those of Vulcan, Erasmus's Christian militant rejects the weapons of paganism in favour of the word of God, even as the Greek words used to describe both arsenals are identical (*Enchiridion*, *CWE* 66: 36 [LB V:9D–E]).

In his polemical and controversial writings, Erasmus's Pauline idiom of spiritual *agôn* helps to distance him from the gladiatorial combativeness of his adversaries and to establish a Christian decorum for intellectual contest. In the *Ad Fabrum*, Erasmus selects two Greek verbs as proof that it is "indecorous" for scholars to "compete for love of honour or or to behave insolently" [*sit indecorum philotimeisthai aut neaneuein*] (*CWE* 83:6 [ASD IX.3:82]), an instance of Erasmian bilingualism that ultimately seeks to dissociate Greek from Latin rather than yoke them together.[89] In his attempt to separate polemic from its etymological origins in *polemos*, however, Erasmus launches two very different sets of arguments about the relationship between rhetorical and physical combat, both of them grounded in his interpretations of Homeric epic. At certain times, Erasmus condemns verbal altercation on account of its likeness to martial combat; at other times, he commends rhetorical contest by distinguishing it from acts of physical violence. In order to lend credence to the first of these positions, Erasmus looks to the *Iliad*'s frequent depiction of verbal contention as unproductive, shameful, or effeminate, singling out a speech made by Aeneas to Achilles in Book 20 of the *Iliad* that was fodder for sixteenth-century humanists looking for Homeric testimonials to the perils of scholarly quarrel.[90] In that passage, cited in no fewer than three adages, Aeneas scolds his adversary: "let us talk like children no longer ... what need have we two to exchange strifes and wranglings [*eridas kai neikia*] with each other like women, who when they have grown angry in soul-devouring strife [*cholôsamenai eridos peri thumoboroio*] go out into the middle of the road and wrangle with each other with many words [*neikeus'allêlêsi*]" (*Il.* 20.251–4). In the adage *Verbis pugnans, non re* [You are fighting with words, not facts, Erasmus quotes several verses from the scene (*Il.* 20.201–2, 20.247–50) as an admonishment for *logemporoi*, men who "exchange insults" rather than "convince by the facts," while in *Qui quae vult dicit, quae non vult audet* [He who says what he would will hear what he would not] Aeneas's speech serves to caution the reader that verbal abuse rebounds to its utterer "such that the word you speak is the word you will hear back" [*hoc est ut tua fuerit oratio, ita tibi respondebitur*], a saying whose "first begetter appears to have been Homer" [*primus huius adagii pater Homerus fuisse*] (Adage III.ix.16, *CWE* 35:324; Adage I.i.27, *CWE* 31:74 [ASD II.1:140], citing *Il.* 20.250). The prominent role accorded to the speech in the *Adages* may account for why Budé marks it so enthusiastically in his copy of Homer, writing "*volubilis versatilis*" next to Homer's "*Streptô … glossê*," a phrase used by Erasmus to lament the way in intellectual controversies degenerate into the kind of flyting matches performed by Homeric warriors (III.ix.16, ASD II.6:522).[91]

Whereas Homer's Aeneas dissociates verbal from physical combat in order to discredit his opponent's weapon as effeminate, Erasmus endeavours to dissociate verbal from martial combat so as to establish intellectual quarrel, rather than brute violence, as the only truly masculine, and ennobling, form of conflict. In the adage *Bellum haud quaquam lachrymosum* [War without tears], a phrase suitable for describing how quarrelsome people wage a "wordy battle" [*conflictatione literaria*] without any "risk of them coming to blows," Erasmus comments that like the related proverb "a war without weapons," the moral lesson contained in the adage is that only contests fought with words are "worthy of wise men; anything else is fit for beasts and gladiators" [*nam id demum viris sapientibus dignum; alioqui ferro congredi ferarum est et gladiatorum*] (Adage II.vi.23, *CWE* 33:303 [ASD II.4:36]). In an effort to enforce this moral distinction between verbal and physical combat, Erasmus dwells elsewhere in the *Adages* upon two Greek words used in the *Scholia* to Theocritus: *erizein*, or "*verbis certant*" [fighting with words] and *eridein* [fighting in deed].[92] Like Plato's distinctions between *dialogomenos* [conversing] and *agonizomenos* [competing] and between *amphisbêtein* [to dispute as friends] and *erizein* [to dispute as adversaries], the subtle difference between the two terms assists Erasmus in maintaining a crucial yet precarious distinction between the civilized disagreement that thrives among true lovers of learning and the bestial wrangling of barbarous sophists.[93]

In order to bolster his position that intellectual debate is a more humane, mature form of combat, Erasmus must devise creative misreadings of various Homeric verses. In an adage based on the Greek proverb "Battles depend on hands, but deliberations upon words," Erasmus locates the sentiment in several Homeric verses, including a line from the *Iliad* that portrays Nestor as "foremost in councils, but useless in battles" because of his advanced age. Yet in his gloss to that adage, *Facta iuvenum, consilia mediocrium, vota senum* [Deeds of the young, advice of the middle-aged, prayers of the old], one of the Homeric sources that supposedly testifies to the superiority of words over deeds carries no such significance. In it, Aeneas tells Meriones that the Trojans "must not multiply harsh words, but must fight" [*Illic pugnandum est neque prosunt aspera dicta*] (Adage III.v.2, *CWE* 35:68 [ASD II.5:298], citing *Il.* 16.631). By manipulating Aeneas's speech into a defence of verbal strife, Erasmus enlists the *Iliad* in his own very un-Iliadic condemnation of physical force.

Yet Homeric ideals of contest may only be accommodated so far to Erasmus's own ethos of contention. In his *Lingua*, Erasmus capitulates to the fact that Christians must not indulge in the "verbal abuse" typical of Homer's heroes. Whereas Homer's Pallas Athena holds back Achilles from fighting and "limits his resentment to verbal abuse," Erasmus reasons, "our Pallas Athene does not allow us even to vent our passion against a man in abuse, even if we do keep our hands clean" [*Ad nostra Pallas ne id quidem permittit, ut convitiis in quenquam debacchemur, etiamsi temperetur a manibus*] (*CWE* 29:390 [ASD IV.1:351]). Whereas Achilles is permitted to revile Agamemnon verbally, Erasmus's Christian soldiers must "heed the spirit of Christ" [*auscultare spiritui Christi*] and "return blessings for curses" [*pro maledictis referenda sunt benedicta*] even when they find themselves at the receiving end of verbal abuse (*CWE* 29:390 [ASD IV.1:351], citing Rom. 12.14).

Erasmus's Two *Erides*

The *Adages* repeatedly invokes Hesiod's account of the two *Erides* – the blameworthy goddess of strife who fosters war and discord, and her more beneficient twin, who nurtures productive competition and rivalry. Erasmus struggles to accept Hesiod's conviction that the rivalry or *zêlos* that inheres between men of the same profession is a positive intellectual and spiritual influence. In the first Chiliad of the *Adages*, a portion of the work largely devoted to the subject of social harmony and discord, Erasmus probes Hesiod's assertion that the "good" Eris presides over mutually beneficial rivalry between friends and equals, often challenging Hesiod's claim that *eris* and *philia* are cooperative social impulses.[94] In part by setting Hesiodic and Homeric notions of friendship and rivalry at odds with each other, Erasmus posits Homeric origins for the virtues of friendship and fellowship – virtues such as *homophrosunê* [like-mindedness] and *homonoia* [likeness; concord] that might prove antithetical to Hesiod's praiseworthy rivalry. In the adage *Amicitia aequalitas* [Friendship is equality], Erasmus argues that there is "no dissension where the mind is one and the same" [*neque dissensio, ubi idem animus*], a sentiment he derives in part from Achilles's declaration that he honoured Patroclus "above all my comrades and equally with myself" [*Aeque atque meum ipsius caput*] (Adage I.i.2, *CWE* 31:37 [ASD II.1:86], citing *Il.* 18.82). Several other proverbs also provide a Homeric foundation for the virtues of concord and like-mindedness that animate the intellectual communalism at the heart of the *Adages*. *Concordia fulciuntur opes etiam exiguae* [With unanimity even slender resources are strengthened] hails from Poseidon's words to Idomeneus at *Il.* 13.237 (Adage III.viii.63), while *Concordia* [Concord] is inspired by Nestor's description of himself and Odysseus as "always of the same mind, having the same ideas and coming to the same conclusions" [*animo sed semper eodem / Et sentire eadem atque eadem decernere vidit*] (Adage III.ix.52, *CWE* 35:338 [ASD II.6:535], citing *Od.* 3.127–8). Although the *Odyssey* chiefly celebrates *homophrosunê* as a virtue that inheres between husband and wife, the perennial bachelor Erasmus instead defines like-mindedness as the cultivation of intellectual and spiritual harmony among men, a form of fellowship exemplified by the apostles, who are knit together by the Holy Spirit "in the same mind and in the same thought" [*en tô autô noi kai en tê autê gnômê*] at 1 Cor. 1.10.[95]

In a series of adages that explore whether likeness is a guarantor of friendship, Erasmus establishes a Homeric genealogy for the Pythagorean-Christian virtue of *homonoia* as he examines the extent to which social and spiritual harmony might tolerate or even thrive upon diversity and conflict. An adage "born out of Homer" [*ex Homero natum*], *Semper similem ducit deus ad similem* [God always leads like to like] derives from a line in the *Odyssey* that enjoys an illustrious afterlife in the writings of Plato and Aristotle as a maxim concerning the virtue of friendship.[96] In Plato's handling, Melantheus's sardonic comment about "the vile leading the vile" [*kakos kakon hêgêlazei*] acquires a newfound seriousness as it comes to exemplify the binding power of attraction as a social and cosmological force. The principle that *homonoia* – a similarity that assures friendship – is guaranteed by cosmic laws is clearly attractive to Erasmus, who asserts in several adages that equality or likeness ensures harmony while "inequality … is the mother of discord" [*inaequalitas discordiarum est mater*] (Adage IV.ii.96, *CWE* 35:550 [ASD II.7:138]).[97]

Erasmus's extended meditation upon these questions in the *Adages* arises out of his uncertainty about the extent to which disagreement and rivalry should be tolerated or even encouraged between scholars, practitioners of the same profession whose differences of opinion may produce hostile antagonism but also may result in mutual intellectual advancement.

In a series of adages concerning friendship (I.ii.20 through I.ii.25), Erasmus tests out the Homeric principle that likeness attracts against the contrary principle (as represented by Hesiod) that similarity breeds envy and contempt. In *Simile gaudet simili* [Like rejoices in like], *Semper similem ducit deus ad similem* [God always leads like to like], *Semper graculus assidet graculo* [Jackdaw always sits by jackdaw] and *Cicada cicadae chara, formica formicae* [Cicada loves cicada, ant is dear to ant], Erasmus retraces the logic of Socrates in *Lysis*, who cites the Homeric maxim that "like and like together God doth draw" [*Ad simile deus adducit similemque paremque*] in order to lend credence to his ideals of intellectual communalism (ASD II.1:240–1, citing *Od.* 17.218].[98]

In Plato's *Lysis*, however, Socrates also proposes the antithesis of this principle: "likest things [are] filled with envy [*phthonou*], contention [*philonikias*], and hatred against each other."[99] Erasmus follows suit, temporarily displacing his own ideals of *homonoia* in the adage that follows by questioning the extent to which friendship may thrive between similar creatures. In that adage, *Figulus figulo invidet, faber fabro* [Potter envies potter, and smith envies smith], Erasmus appeals to Hesiod's distinction between the two *Erides*. Yet in contradistinction to Hesiod, who distinguishes between "two kinds of emulation" [*duplex aemulationis genus*], Erasmus proposes that similar occupations arouse "mean-spirited competition" [*damnans ... concertationem*] more than they arouse "honourable contestation" [*honorumque certamina*], and he expresses surprise that Hesiod approves of competition between peers (Adage I.ii.25, *CWE* 31:170–1 [ASD II.1:242], paraphrasing *WD*, ls. 24–6). In the expanded 1515 version of the adage, Erasmus paraphrases Hesiod's distinction between the two *Erides*, the one honourable and the other "nasty and pernicious" [*foedum ac perniciosum*], yet in his discussion of the passage from the *Works and Days*, he gives examples only of the latter variety, the bad Eris who provokes the "warlike and pugnacious spirit" [*bellacem ac pugnacem*] condemned by Plutarch's *Table-Talk*: "roosters have it," Erasmus comments, "and sophists, mendicants, poets, singers" [*qualis est gallorum gallinaceorum qualisque est inter sophistas, mendicos, poetas, cantores*] (*CWE* 31:170 [ASD II.1:242, II.1:244]).[100]

Erasmus's ambivalence towards Hesiod's endorsement of virtuous emulation reflects his doubts about whether human relationships founded upon likeness – friends, neighbours, scholars – are strengthened and enriched by rivalry, and whether like-mindedness might lead not to amity but rather to an antipathy that may not prove intellectually productive. At stake in such questions is Erasmus's perplexity about the relationship between *philia* and *eris*, the cosmological and social forces whose interplay animates allegorical interpretations of Homeric epic throughout antiquity and prompts many of Homer's classical and early modern commentators to align his poems with the doctrines of pre-Socratic philosophers such as Empedocles and Heraclitus. Throughout the *Adages*, Erasmus alternates between depicting *philia* and *eris* as hostile forces and conceiving of them as a reconcilable coincidence of opposites. Despite his repeated claim that "similarity is the mother of good will" or the means of achieving conciliation between friends [*similitudo mater est benevolentiae consuetudinisque et familiaritatis conciliatrix*], Erasmus also testifies to the limits of likeness and equality as guarantors of amity (Adage I.ii.20: *Aequalis aequalem delectate* [Everyone loves his own age] *CWE* 31:165 [ASD II.1:236]). In *Amicitia aequalitas*, Erasmus observes that "equality pushed to extremes becomes extreme inequality" [*ita summa aequalitas summa fit inaequalitas*], thus producing discord rather than harmony.

This paradox helps to explain Erasmus's preoccupation with the dilemma posed by "equal contests" – with fights or disputes between evenly matched contestants that end either in a mutually constructive struggle or in mutual defeat (Adage I.i.2, *CWE* 31:31 [ASD II.1:86]). The peculiar nature of conflicts between "equally matched contestants" [*aequalium ... contentionem*] is explored in several Homeric adages including *Pertinax contentio* [Stubborn quarrelling] and *Aequa concertatio* [Contest between equals] (Adages III.viii.18 and III.viii.31, *CWE* 35:289, 35:293 [ASD II.6:490]). Derived from passages in Books 4 and 5 of the *Iliad*, these adages describe what transpires when "two parties [are] equally matched to debate or to fight" [*duos ex aequo paratos ad disceptandum rixamue*], a situation dramatized throughout Homeric epic by the formulaic phrases "*neikos homoiion*" and "*homoiiou ptolemoio*" [common, or shared, war].[101] For reasons explored at the end of this chapter, Erasmus is fascinated by the coincidence of harmony and strife conveyed by both of these Homeric phrases, which capture both the intimacy of discord and the precarious counterbalance achieved by contests between equals. In *Pertinax contentio*, Erasmus offers a pessimistic gloss on the concept of a well-matched contest, citing Hera's chastisement of Zeus at *Il.* 4.58 as evidence that "it is perverse and unmanly for people of equal standing [*aequalium*] to carry on quarrelling [*contentionem*] because neither one wants to appear inferior to the other" (*CWE* 35:289 [ASD II.6:490]). In other adages, contests between equals reveal the futility of war or the collective stubbornness that leads to war; Erasmus delights in the poetic justice achieved through the mutual destruction of well-matched opponents such as Esernius and

Pacidianus (II.v.98) or Bithius and Bacchius (II.v.97), proverbial gladiators who are so "well-matched in strength and courage" [*pares arte, pares audacia*] that contests between them reach an impasse in which "neither will yield to the other" [*neuter alteri velit concedere*] (Adage II.v.97, *CWE* 33:285–6 [ASD II.3:472]). Although Erasmus idealizes intellectual conflict as exemplifying the best kind of equal contest, he also savours the grim irony of conflicts between adversaries so equally matched that the battle either ends badly for both or, perhaps worse still, fails to end at all.

Throughout the *Adages*, the threat of futile, unresolved, or never-ending conflict is identified with the Trojan War. *Inanis conatus* [Vain effort] is illustrated by Agamemnon's assessment at *Il.* 2.121 that the Achaean troops have "vainly fought a fruitless war" [*Pugnam infrugiferamque et inutile ducere bellum*], while the adage *Frustratus conatus* [Vain attempt] takes its inspiration from another scene in the *Iliad* in which an arrow shot at Hector misses him and hits Gorgythion, another of Priam's sons, instead (Adage III.viii.8; Adage III.viii.36, *CWE* 35:285, 35: 295 [ASD II.6:486, 6:495], the latter citing *Il.* 8.301–2). In what may well be Erasmus's bleakest treatment of the subject, *Flet victus, victor interiit* [The loser weeps, the winner's dead] invokes Hesiod's "two Erides, the one pestilent to mortals, the other fruitful" [*duas facit Eridas, quarum altera pestifera sit mortalibus, altera frugifera*] and proceeds to argue that the *Iliad*, a "totally insane war [*insanissimum bellum*] waged for all those years about a worthless young woman," exemplifies the more destructive form of strife (Adage II.vi.24, *CWE* 33:303–4 [ASD II.4:37–8]).[102]

Erasmus weighs his own ideals of scholarly contest against this grim depiction of the Trojan War, an event that terminates with a Cadmean victory in which "both sides have suffered ... the winner in character, and the loser in circumstances" [*qui vicerit, discedit improbior, qui victus sit, infelicior*]. *Flet victus, victor interiit* does, however, acknowledge the possibility of a more constructive sort of conflict, one in which "the winner gains distinction" [*qui superior evaserit, discedit clarior*] and the "defeated party goes home a better man" [*qui superatus fuerit, discedit seipso melior*]. In the first decade and a half of his career, Erasmus appears confident in the possibility of this kind of productive disagreement. But over the course of the 1510s, he begins to capitulate to the idea that hostility between scholars is a law of nature: "just as wild animals are at war with other kinds that eat the same food," he writes in the *Parabolae*, paraphrasing Plutarch, "so there is envy and rivalry between men who practice the same skill" [*Ut feris bellum est cum iis quae iisdem aluntur ... sic invidia et aemulatio inter eiusdem artis professores*] (*CWE* 23:155 [ASD I.5:130], citing *Moralia*

486b).[103] This analogy between man and beast proves problematic elsewhere in Erasmus's writings, however, since human antagonists are not necessarily bound by the same natural laws that bind the rest of God's creatures. In his two chief anti-war manifestos – the *Querela Pacis* and the *Dulce bellum inexpertis* – Erasmus waffles on this issue, arguing in the first work that "Only men are not reconciled to each other by Nature" and cannot be "bound together by the many advantages of agreement" but in the latter work stating that humans are "born entirely for friendship, which is formed and cemented most effectively by mutual assistance [*amicitiae nasci, quae mutuis officiis et coit et cohaeret potissimum*] (*CWE* 27:294–5 [ASD IV.2:63]; Adage IV.i.1, *CWE* 35:402 [ASD II.7:14]). This rosy view of humanity bound together by "chains of friendship," a metaphor that grants amity a cosmic inevitability, is hard to reconcile with the spirit of adages such as *Homo semper contradicens* [It is human never to stop arguing] or *Amicitias immortales esse oportet* [Friendships should last forever], in which Erasmus cynically remarks that "feuds last forever and friendships are more fragile than glass, and one *Atê* is more powerful than a hundred Prayers" [*simultates sint immortales, amicitiae plus quam vitreae, plusque posit una Ate quam centum Litae*] (Adage IV.vii.13, *CWE* 35:288; Adage IV.v.26, *CWE* 36:157–8 [ASD II.7:257]).

Erasmus finds a solution to this problem in his theory of religious toleration, which allows for the articulation of diversity of opinion as a means of advancing divergent truth claims without jeopardizing social and spiritual harmony. In the *Adages*, these principles of toleration are taught jointly through Odysseus and Paul, whose acceptance of diverse opinions provides the inspiration for *Quot homines, tot sententiae* [So many men, so many opinions]. Erasmus derives the maxim from Odysseus's observation at *Od.* 14.228 that "different men take joy in different works" [*Nanque aliis aliae res arridentque placentque*] as well as from Rom. 14.5, in which "St Paul the Apostle ... says that for the putting aside of strife [*ad praecludendam aemulationem*], we should allow every man to have his own convictions" (Adage I.iii.7, *CWE* 31:240–1 [ASD II.1:320]). Elsewhere in the *Adages*, Odysseus is a pagan prototype not just for the rhetorical flexibility displayed by Paul but also for this different facet of Pauline accommodation, which encourages indifference to variations in opinion and custom inessential to salvation.

As Erasmus recognizes, neither Odysseus nor Paul retreat from valid and productive disputes, but both choose their quarrels carefully, a prudence instructed in the adage *Cum amico non certandum aemulatione* [Do not compete in rivalry with a friend], adapted from Odysseus's observation that it is "foolish ... and worthless to strive in a contest [*erida propherêtai aethlôn*] with [one's] host" (Adage III.x.24, *CWE* 35:365[ASD II.6:559], citing *Od.* 8.209–10). Erasmus translates Odysseus's refusal to compete against his host ("*Quis namque benigno cum hospite pugnet?*") as a proscription against rivalry between friends, though Faustus-like, he omits the boastful challenge that concludes Odysseus's speech: "But of all the rest I refuse none ... but rather wish to know their skill and compete [*atherizô*] against them."[104] The omission is telling. Erasmus paints Odysseus as a peacemaker who shuns rivalry and competition, and his annotations on the Pauline epistles reflect a similar effort to sanitize some of Paul's pronouncements on the spiritual urgency and legitimacy of quarrels and disputes.[105]

Such misreadings arise in part out of Erasmus's justifiable confusion over the meaning of the Greek term *zêlos*, a word that denotes both destructive, ungodly rivalry and pious zeal or a devout emulation of Christ.[106] Erasmus's grasp of the term as it used in the New Testament is shaped by his interpretations of Hesiod's distinction between honourable and pernicious expressions of *zêlos*, as well as by the diverse and subtle idiom of rivalry and contestation in Homeric epic and in later Greek writers such as Aristotle and Plutarch. In his *Paraphrases* and *Annotations*, Erasmus is eager to distinguish between godly and ungodly forms of *zêlos* – the former exemplified principally by the apostles and the latter by their Jewish adversaries, whom Paul describes at Rom. 11.11 as "provoked to jealousy" [*parazêlôsai*] by the followers of Christ. In his annotations on the verse, Erasmus objects to the Vulgate translation of *parazêloô* as *aemulari*, since while the Greek verb can mean "to provoke to emulation," it can also mean to provoke to anger, and only the latter reading accords with Erasmus's dim view of the Jews as willing to embrace Christ only if Paul arouses in them "a kind of jealousy [*aemulatione*]" (*CWE* 56:302 [LB VI:642A]; *CWE* 42:64 [LB VII: 814B]). Yet in other verses, such as Rom. 11.13, Paul uses the verb *parazêloô* in a positive sense when he challenges the Jews "to emulate your piety, even by a kind of envy and jealousy" [*ad aemulandum pietatem vestram, vel invidia quapiam ac livore*], a form of emulation that Erasmus terms "*zelotypum*" in order to distinguish it from the negative *zêlos* of Rom. 11.11 (LB VII:814D).[107] Other annotations and paraphrases on the Pauline epistles reflect Erasmus's effort to resolve the "confused continuum" represented by the Greek *zêlos* into a sharper opposition that diminishes the ambiguity of the word.[108] At 1 Cor. 14.1, Paul commands his audience to "pursue love and eagerly desire the spiritual things" [*diôkete tên agapên zêloute de ta pneumatika*], and

Erasmus renders the Greek *zêloute* as *aemulamini*. But one chapter earlier (1 Cor. 13.4), when Paul observes that "love is not jealous" [*agapê ou zêloi*], the qualification befuddles Erasmus, who translates *zêloi* as *invidet* in one place and as *aemulatur* in another, his indecisiveness reflecting an underlying uncertainty about whether *zêlos* and *agapê* – rivalry/zeal and charity – are reconcilable for Christians.[109]

Fuelling Erasmus's decisions about how to translate these key terms in the Pauline epistles is his doubt about the social and spiritual function of rivalry in the apostolic community and, by extension, its function in Erasmus's own community of scholars. At times, Erasmus defends the piety of the disputes that periodically erupt in Acts between Paul and the other apostles, quarrels he views as invigorated by the most virtuous kind of *zêlos* even if they appear to threaten the apostolic ideals of fellowship and concord. In his paraphrase of Acts 15.39, Erasmus justifies the "sharp disagreement" [*paroxusmos*] between Paul and Barnabas, arguing that each "strove [*contendebat*] to get what he thought was the best for the work of the gospel" (*CWE* 50:100 [LB VII:729E]). Although Erasmus apologizes for the behaviour of Paul and Barnabas in his annotation of the passage, writing that "They were apostles, but they were also men" [*Apostoli erant, sed tamen homines erant*], his *Paraphrases* defend the dispute as spiritually productive, arguing that "[d]ifference of opinion [*sententiae varietatis*] does not harm, provided hearts are united in their purpose to advance the gospel" (ASD VI.6:274; *CWE* 50:100 [LB VII:729E]).[110] Erasmus's defences of apostolic dissent and reproof at verses such as Acts 15.39 and Galatians 2.11 (where Paul opposes Peter "publicly and to his face") are animated by the belief that verbal rebuke, when intended to encourage greater piety, can be a form of charity, an interpretation that accords with the pedagogical principles laid out in rhetorical works such as *De Conscribendis Epistolis*, which advocates the "honourable kind [of rivalry] implanted in our minds by wise nature, so that through the desire to excel our rivals [*aemulatione contra certantium*] we might be incited as by a sharp goad to act vigorously" (*CWE* 42:104 [LB VII:949E]; *CWE* 25:82 [ASD I.2:328]).

As an interpreter of the New Testament, Erasmus is acutely aware of the process of transculturation by which the apostles accommodate the spirit of pagan rivalry (and its accompanying idiom) for nobler spiritual ends. That process of accommodation must, for Erasmus, continue in the intellectual community of early sixteenth-century Europe, an era in which factionalism and schism demand reassessing what forms of competition might promote or threaten the sort of "harmonious agreement" [*ex concordi consensu*] once cultivated by the apostles (Paraphrase on Acts 1.15,

CWE 50:10 [LB VII:664C]).[111] As the opening proverb of the *Adages* makes clear, sixteenth-century scholarly culture should ideally emulate the apostolic community, a community that according to Erasmus "holds all things in common" and yet also engages in mutual admonition and exhortation, forms of sharp speech that enhance rather than diminish the apostolic spirit of charity (*CWE* 31:30; *Paraphrase* on Acts 4.32–3, *CWE* 50:37 [LB VII:683C]).

Yet Erasmus's efforts to encourage productive forms of rivalry are complicated by his involvement in polemical disputes such as the controversy with Lefèvre, which self-consciously implicates the two scholars in a Hesiodic rivalry between *faber* and *faber*, a pun on the French theologian's Latin name. Concerned that some members of their readership will "infer that we have been spurred on by rivalry [*aemulationis stimulos*]," Erasmus writes to Lefèvre that "they may hurl against us Hesiod's observation that 'craftsman envies craftsman [*fabrum invidere fabro*],' the more so since we have chanced to light upon the same topic" (*CWE* 83:5 [ASD IX.3:82]). With equal parts irony and arrogance, Erasmus protests that unlike the emulous *fabers* described by Hesiod, he has "not acted out of love of strife" in his criticisms of Lefèvre, a thinly disguised insult inasmuch as it implies that there is nothing about his opponent that Erasmus might wish to emulate (*CWE* 83:7 [ASD IX.3:84]).

The controversy with Lefèvre grew sufficiently nasty that it prompted Budé, in a letter to Erasmus, to express concern that "excessive competition between friends" [*philoin ... philoneikias*] may stir up "a whole *Iliad* of unfortunate contention" [*Ilias tis kakês*].[112] Erasmus at times appears eager to defuse the hostilities by inviting Lefèvre to "join in conflict [*conflictatione*] with each other and either teach or learn something," portraying their polemical dispute as the kind of cooperative and mutually beneficial exchange celebrated by adages such as *Pari iugo*, or "Matched in double harness," which describes how friends, like yoked oxen, may "reap a double harvest" [*conduplicatio lucro ditescere*] once they overcome their reluctance to work together and instead cooperate "with equal devotion and equal effort" [*pari studio parique conatu*] (*CWE* 83:97–8 [ASD IX.3:182]; Adage I.vi.8, *CWE* 32:9 [ASD II.2:32]). This cooperative ideal cannot be achieved between Erasmus and Lefèvre, however, because as Erasmus is wont to remind his audience, the two men are hardly equals. In a rhetorical tour-de-force, the *Ad Fabrum* dramatizes the disparity between them through the lopsided and rivalrous model of male friendship symbolized by Homer's Diomedes and Glaucus, whose exchange of weapons at *Il.* 6.234–6 symbolizes "unequal exchange" [*inaequalem commutationem*] for Erasmus in adages such as *Amicitia aequalitas* (I.i.2, *CWE* 31:31) and

Diomedis et Glauci permutatio (Exchange between Diomedes and Glaucus, I.ii.1, *CWE* 31:144). This episode, in which Diomedes dupes Glaucus, at least according to some classical and Renaissance commentators, into trading his golden armour for bronze by promising that the exchange of gifts will cement their familial bond, is a perversion of the communalism celebrated by adages such as *Amicorum communia omnia* (*CWE* 31:29–30).[113]

Throughout the *Adages*, the gift-exchanges and gestures of hospitality that bind together friends and competitors in Homeric epic are offered up as corrupt or imperfect versions of Erasmian *communitas*. In addition to Diomedes and Glaucus, whose exchange of weapons lends credence to the lesson that "A bad gift is as good as a loss" [*kakon ge dôron ison esti zêmia*] in the adage *Malum munus* (Adage IV.iii.4, *CWE* 36:6), the similarly infelicitous exchange of weapons between Hector and Ajax provides material for *Hostium munera non munera* [The gifts of enemies are no gifts], an adage that circulates widely during the sixteenth century thanks to the emblem by Andrea Alciati ("In Dona Hostium"), based on Erasmus's adage.[114] In that adage, Erasmus warns that both Hector and Ajax "came to grief through the gift he had received," a consequence quite different from the one anticipated by Hector, who promises that the exchange will diffuse the "soul-devouring strife" [*eridos ... thumoboroio*] between the two men and allow them to part in friendship (Adage I.iii.35, *CWE* 31:263 [ASD II.1:346]; *Il.* 7.301–2). In other adages of Homeric origin concerning gift-giving, including *Cyclopis donum* [Gift of the Cyclops] and *Alybantis hospitis munera* [Gifts of an Alybantian host], Erasmus similarly misconstrues or cynically misreads Homeric gestures of reciprocity and mutual assistance, interpreting scenes of gift-exchange in Homeric epic as marked by insincerity or motivated by self-interest.[115] In Homeric epic, the exchange of gifts may indeed conceal a hostile intent, but Erasmus consistently reads more antagonism into such exchanges than is actually there, interpreting the practice of "dueling through gifts" as a distortion of the ideals of scholarly communalism celebrated by the *Adages*. In *Diomedis et Glauci permutatio*, an adage whose location in the collection (I.ii.1) suggests that it may have been intended as an answer to the opening adage of the collection, *Amicorum communia omnia* (I.i.1), Erasmus exaggerates "the vanity of Glaucus and his boastful swaggering," traits that make it easy for Diomedes to take advantage of the situation and trade his golden armour for Glaucus's bronze, the "unequal exchange" [*inequalem commutationem*] that gives the adage its title (*CWE* 31:144 [ASD II.1:213]).[116]

The controversy with Lefèvre aggravates many of the concerns already evident in Erasmus's writings about scholarly disputation: in what spirit should scholars exchange their "gifts" of learning, and how best should scholars exchange the oft-beneficial yet unappreciated gift of criticism? As Erasmus recognizes, the exchange of gifts is all too easily co-opted by self-interest, as illustrated by adages such as *Manus manum fricat* [One hand rubs another], *Gratia gratiam parit* [One favour begets another], and *Par pari referre* [To render like for like], each of which laments the human inability to bestow gifts or favours without expecting them to be returned in kind (Adages I.i.33, I.i.34, and I.i.35, *CWE* 31:82–4). As a means of articulating his ideal of charitable gift-giving among scholars, Erasmus adapts the Homeric phrase "bronze for gold," invoking the parable of Diomedes and Glaucus to model both the self-sacrificing generosity of the charitable scholar and his modesty in depreciating the gifts he has to offer.[117] Writing to Andrea Ammonio in October 1511, Erasmus explains that in exchange for a shipment of wine, "you are to receive verses of the worst kind – precisely, in Homer's famous phrase, 'bronze in return for gold'" [*Tu pro optimo vino versiculos accipies pessimos, hoc est plane kata to Homêrikon ekeino, chalkea chruseiôn*], and Ammonio invokes the same phrase when he responds a month later (Eps. 234 and 243, *CWE* 2:177, 2:197 [Allen 1:473, 1:486]). In their epistolary tango of mutual deference, Erasmus and Ammonio each imply that their gifts are bestowed with charity and humility, and are in no way intended to rival the gift received by the other. In a 1517 letter to Budé, Erasmus again uses the phrase to distance himself from the potentially competitive impulses that motivate scholarly transactions, thanking his fellow scholar for having "repaid my ill-educated letter with one of such exquisite learning, giving me like Glaucus in Homer more than gold for what was hardly bronze" [*pro tam indocta epistola tam eruditam, hoc est iuxta Glaucum Homericum pro vix aerea reddideris plusquam auream*] (Ep. 531, *CWE* 4:223 [Allen 2:459]). While the unequal bartering of brazen for golden learning may reflect underlying hostilities, as it does with Lefèvre, the *topos* of unreciprocated generosity between scholars may also replicate the incommensurability of divine grace. Demurring that he is "matched against Budé, the champion of scholars, like some Thersites against Achilles," Erasmus's letter implicitly reminds its recipient that giving gifts that cannot be reciprocated is a means of imitating the gratuitous generosity of God himself, whose grace Clement of Alexandria compares to that of Homer's Glaucus, willing to trade "gold in exchange for brass."[118]

Erasmus's Homeric Folly

The *Adages* constitutes a monumental effort to accommodate pagan to Christian wisdom, a project in which Homer plays a central yet vexing part.

While Erasmus is attuned throughout to the rhetorical and ethical continuities between archaic Greek literature and the New Testament, as well as to the sympathies between certain sentiments and values of Homeric epic and the Christian Platonism of the *Adages* itself, he also uses certain Homeric episodes and phrases in order to enforce distinctions between pagan and Christian standards for intellectual conflict. Animated by Hesiod's distinction between the good and bad Eris, Erasmus's transvaluation of classical into Christian *agôn* seeks to dissociate those aspects of pagan contestation – from athleticism to rivalrous gift-giving – he deems irreconcilable with Christian charity and fellowship while at the same time preserving for Christianity in general, and for scholarly culture in particular, specific forms of the "good" Eris who encourages cooperation and mutual assistance.

Erasmus's efforts to synthesize certain eristic impulses of classical Greece with Christian ideals of toleration and charity produces a different set of results in his *In Praise of Folly*, a work as biting as it is eirenic. Granted a distinctly Homeric genealogy by her creator, Folly is kin to the Homeric and Hesiodic goddesses of strife who serve Erasmus as mythological shorthand for the kinds of conflict he wishes to condemn. Yet she is also an antidote to conflict, an anti-Eris who, like Erasmus himself, repeatedly enlists Homeric allusions and commonplaces as remedies for the *philoneikia* that has gripped the intellectual and religious culture of Erasmus's age. As a reflection of Erasmus's efforts to regulate conflict while simultaneously preserving a certain licence to participate in verbal dispute and contestation, Folly constitutes Erasmus's creative revision of Homer's goddess of strife. Her speech peppered with Homeric allusions and epithets such as "mighty-fathered Pallas" [*obrimopatrês ... Palladis*] and "cloud-gathering Jupiter" [*nephelêgeretou Iovis*], Folly appropriates Homeric speech patterns, much as many of Lucian's interlocutors do, in order to valorize the counter-epic, Erasmian values of love, harmony, pleasure, and ease (ASD IV.3:80, IV:18, citing *Il.* 5.747 and 5.736).

Folly accomplishes this, in part, by banishing the divinities that preside over conflict in the *Iliad* and *Odyssey*. She recounts how her fellow gods "lost their tempers and threw [Momus] together with Atê headlong down to earth because he disturbed the gods' carefree happiness with his wisdom" [*hunc nuper irati una cum Ate in terras praecipitem dederunt, quod sapientia sua felicitati deorum importunus obstreperet*], and she distinguishes herself from Eris, proclaiming that, unlike Homer's goddess of strife, she does not "confound heaven and earth if someone has sent out invitations to all the other gods and left me out" [*Nec coelum terrae misceo, si quis reliquis invitatis diis me domi relinquat*] (*CWE* 27:94, 27:119–20

[ASD IV.3:88, IV.3:132]). Dissociating herself from the more discordant aspects of the Homeric pantheon, the "underworld Plutos, Atês, Punishments, Fevers" [*Plutones, Atas, Poenas, Febres*] that wreak havoc on the mortal world, Folly aligns herself instead with Sound Sleep [*Nêgreton Hypnon*] and Oblivion [*Lêthê*], two key salves for conflict in *The Odyssey* (*CWE* 27:119, 27:89, 27:91 [ASD IV.3:132 IV.3:78, IV.3:82]). Her native landscape abounds in Nepenthe, Lotus, Ambrosia, and Moly, Homeric concoctions that cultivate *amnesia* and *amnestia*, the forgetting and forgiving of past wrongs associated with the Litae as well as (in the *Odyssey*) with Helen and Athena.[119] The deep draughts of forgetfulness that Folly supplies from "our fountain of Lêthe" [*Lethes nostrae fontem*] bring "oblivion" and "was[h] away the cares of the soul" [*potarint oblivia ... dilutis animi curis*], making her followers "tipsy with nectar like the Homeric gods, with a dash of nepenthe too" [*pariter deorum Homericorum nectare non sine nepenthe temulenti*] (*CWE* 27:91, 27:86 [ASD IV.3:82, IV.3:71]). In the *Adages*, too, Erasmus identifies oblivion as a specifically Homeric antidote to conflict: both *Ne malorum memineris* [Remember no wrongs] and *Malorum oblivio* [Forgetting wrongs] cite lines from the *Iliad* that address the crucial role of forgetting as a means of establishing peace (Adage II.i.94, *CWE* 33:72–3; Adage III.viii.22, *CWE* 35:291).

In certain respects, Folly takes to an extreme the accommodation of Homeric epic to Christian Epicureanism that characterizes many of Erasmus's own interpretations of Homer in the *Adages*. At times her method indulges in an interpretive licence that verges on downright error: when Folly praises the Homeric gods for their ability to "have their fun with much more gaiety and freedom, 'living an easy life,' in fact, as Homer says" [*iam multo licentius ac suavius nugantur dii, vere rhaon agontes, ut inquit Homerus*], she misquotes a well-known Homeric epithet for the gods (*rheia zôontes*, living at ease), a blunder that inverts the meaning of the original Greek.[120] And when she claims for herself the title "true bestower of all good things" [*vera illa largitrix eaôn*], an epithet awarded to the Homeric gods at *Od.* 8.325, Folly takes what was for many readers one of the most objectionable passages in the poem, a scene in which the gods unleash their "unquenchable laughter" on Hephaestus, Ares, and Aphrodite, and strips from it all its negative associations with laughter and ridicule (*CWE* 27:87 [ASD IV.3:74].

Folly's revisionist interpretations of Homeric epic both echo and parody Erasmus's own efforts to accommodate pagan wisdom to Christian doctrine, a process that, as he argues in the *Adages*, is especially suited to Homer, whose words may be "stretched to give a vastly different sense" [*ad longe diversam sententiam verba detorseris*] (ASD II.6:482). As they demonstrate what is both perilous and salvific about Christian attempts to transvalue classical wisdom, Folly's misreadings of Homer reveal moments of authorial self-scrutiny in which Erasmus exposes the vulnerabilities of some of the hermeneutic techniques he uses elsewhere to "stretch" pagan texts in a manner that may, as Folly points out, "turn everything topsy turvy, the sacred and the profane" [*sacra prophanaque omnia sursum ... miscentur*] (*CWE* 27:88 [ASD IV.3:76]). Her misreadings also reclaim some of the most ethically precarious images of Homeric epic. Recounting her birth, Folly uses the Homeric phrase "lay with her in love" [*en philotêti michtheis*], a formula used to describe illicit or lascivious sexual intercourse, and her praise of Hephaestus as he "plays the buffoon at the assembly of the gods" [*in deorum conviviis gelôtopoion agere*] likewise salvages a word that normally has "coarse and scurrilous connotations" in antiquity.[121] Taking his cue from Lucian, Erasmus packs into Folly's oration a dense tissue of Homeric allusions that subvert many of the core values of the Homeric poems themselves and turn them into a mouthpiece for Erasmus's Socratic and Pauline morosophy. As in the *Adages*, the principal goal of this process of accommodation is to reconcile Homer with Paul: by associating the Homeric gods with the domain of Folly, Erasmus satirizes their irreverent antics while at the same time resolving their comic invulnerability with the theology of 1 Corinthians: "if anyone cares to ask Homer and the other poets about the lives even of the sterner gods, he'll find folly everywhere [*reperiet stulticiae plena omnia*]" (*CWE* 27:94 [ASD IV.3:86–8]).

Folly identifies not one but two kinds of Homeric folly in her oration, the first ventriloquized through a question posed by Horace: "what is the subject of that divine poem the *Iliad* if not the passions of foolish kings and peoples?" [*Quid autem sacrum Iliadis Carmen nisi stultorum regum et populorum continet aestus*?].[122] The second kind of Homeric folly resides in the ludic technique of "treat[ing] serious subjects in a trivial manner" [*seria nugatorie tractare*], a form of literary recreation to which Erasmus grants an explicitly Homeric legacy in his dedication to More (*CWE* 27:84 [ASD IV.3:68]). Appealing to the example of Homer, who "amused himself [*luserit*] ages ago with all his Battle of the Frogs and the Mice," Erasmus defends himself against his critics by allying himself with those writers who have enjoyed the "freedom to exercise [their] wit on the common life of man, and with impunity" [*ingeniis libertas permissa fuit, ut in communem hominum vitam salibus luderent impune*] (*CWE* 27:83–4 [ASD IV.3:68]). Homer is the eldest in this distinguished lineage, the pristine source of ludic reproach and, it turns out, the pagan counterpart to that great defender of Christian Folly, Saint Paul. When Folly parrots the Homeric-Platonic-Apostolic refrain of the *Adages*, "God always brings like to like" [*hôs aiei ton homoion agei theos hôs ton homoion*], her syncretic logic hangs together by the fact that Homer and Paul both use the word *nêpios* [child, fool] in order to articulate their paradoxical ideals of foolish wisdom (*CWE* 27:92 [ASD IV.3:84]). Explaining that the "Greek word for a child, *nêpios*, means 'foolish,' and is the opposite of *sophos*, 'wise,'" Folly anchors Paul's claim that "when I was a child [*nêpios*] I used to speak like a child" to Homer's description of Telemachus at *Od.* 11.449: "In Homer, too, Telemachus wins the poet's praise in every way, but is now and then called *nêpios*" [*Iam apud Homerum Telemachus, quem modis omnibus laudat poeta, subinde nêpios appellatur*] (*CWE* 27:148, 27:142 [ASD IV.3:186, IV.3:178]).

The comparison is self-consciously disingenuous: while Paul regularly uses the term *nêpios* in a positive sense, Homer almost never does. In twenty-seven out of the thirty-eight uses of the word in the *Iliad* and *Odyssey*, the person referred to as *nêpios* perishes soon afterwards, and the epithet is often bestowed with grim irony by the narrator.[123] This detail, however, does not prevent Folly from appealing once again to Homer when called upon to explicate the proverb that "[t]he fool tries everything, meets his dangers at first hand, and thereby acquires what is genuine prudence ... which is why Homer says, 'even the fool is wise after the event'" [*Stultus adeundis cominusque periclitandis rebus veram, ni fallor, prudentiam colligit. Id quod vidisse videtur Homerus, etiamsi caecus, cum ait rhechthen de te nêpios egnô*] (*CWE* 27:102 [ASD IV.3:104]). Although she puts the verse to a different and rather more specious use, Folly's quotation of *Il.* 17.32 – "when [harm] is done, even a fool [*nêpios*] can recognize it" – is the very same line quoted by Erasmus in *Sero sapiunt Phryges* [The Phrygians learn wisdom too late], an adage that yokes Homeric to scriptural wisdom by virtue of a striking parallel between Homer's *Odyssey* and a scene in Acts. After suffering through a storm at sea, according to Erasmus's paraphrase of the verse, the prudent Paul tells his fellow sailors that although they might have avoided their current distress, "it remains for you to be wise, though belatedly" [*Oportebat, ô viri, prius obtemperare consilio meo, quo monui vos*] (Paraphrase on Acts 27.21, *CWE* 50:146 [LB VII:766B]).

The "*sapientia praepostera*" – a belated wisdom, but also a preposterous or foolish wisdom – that Folly identifies with Homeric epic, and which reachest its fullest expression in Paul, has the potential to effect a "radical reversal" of "scales of values" in the manner of 1 Cor. 3.18, the paradoxical assertion that one must become a fool in order to become wise ("*môros genesthô, hina genêtai sophos*") that lies at the heart of Erasmus's *In Praise of Folly*.[124] In Folly's hands, the verse helps to establish Homer and Paul as twin patrons of morosophy, a tradition of interpreting Homer that would shape the responses of later sixteenth-century writers including Melanchthon, Rabelais, and Montaigne, who each detect in Homer a different aspect of foolish wisdom, and accommodate it to a distinctly Pauline brand of wise folly.

The Tug of War: Erasmus's Homeric Neutralities

In the adage *Filum contentionis tunc erat* This, then, was the thread of the dispute], a proverb suitable for describing "two obstinate disputants, when each is so stubborn that neither will yield" [*Dici solitum in pertinaces, cum uterque pervicax est neuterque concedit alteri*], Erasmus cites a phrase used by Saint Jerome – "funiculum contentiosum ducere" [to tug the rope of contention] – to explain the central metaphor of the adage (Adage III.iii.77, *CWE* 34:307 [ASD II.5:227], citing Jerome, *Epistle* 62.3). Explaining that he has never seen the phrase except in Tertullian's *Adversos Judaeos*, Erasmus proposes that both Jerome's phrase and his own adage derive from a "game in which two men stand, one at either end of a rope, and each tries to pull the other over to him" [*ludo, quo duobus hinc atque hinc funem tenentibus uterque conatur alterum ad se trahere*]. In other words, a tug of war.

The metaphor, if not the game, derives from the *Iliad*, in which the image of a rope or chain of contention dominates one of the most well-known passages in the poem. Zeus's speech at the beginning of Book 8 of the *Iliad* presents a hypothetical tug of war in which he challenges his fellow deities to "make fast … a chain of gold [*seirên chruseiên*], and lay hold of it, all you gods and goddesses; yet you could not drag [*erussait*] Zeus to earth … But whenever I might want to pull [*erussai*] with all my heart, then with earth itself I would pull it up [*erussai*] and bind the rope around the peak of Olympus so that all those things would hang in space" (*Il.* 8.19–26). The key verb in the passage – *eruô*, to drag, pull, or fasten together, as in a chain – conveys both tension and cohesion as each side pulls in an opposing direction, thus creating a *stasis*, a word that means stand or position but also, in later classical Greek, sedition or civil war. Homer's conceit of a tug of war between Zeus and the subaltern gods posits a hostile cosmos ruled by contrary forces. But the dominant sixteenth-century interpretation of the passage, indebted to Plato's *Theaetetus* and to many subsequent Homeric allegorists and commentators, treats the golden chain as a master metaphor for the harmonious concatenation of a divinely ordered cosmos. Even Erasmus's Folly perpetuates this reading, calling the "golden chain" [*torquem auream*] a symbol of the "concord between all the virtues" [*omnium virtutum cohaerentium consensum*], a reading adapted to various ends by later sixteenth-century writers such as Rabelais, Ronsard, and Spenser (*CWE* 27:136 [ASD IV.3:169]).

Folly's allusion to the golden chain is not without its ironies; the phrase graces the costume of an ignorant and self-interested prince more interested in displaying the trappings of concord than in cultivating the virtue itself. In the *Iliad*, too, Zeus's golden chain by no means upholds the ideal of harmony discerned in it by later allegorists. Rather, it is one of several passages in the *Iliad* in which, as in Jerome's metaphor, strife is likened to the action of tugging threads, chains, cords, or hides in two opposing directions at once. During the one of the battle scenes of the middle books of the *Iliad*, Zeus "stretches evenly the line of battle" [*isa machên etanusse*] and "stretches taut the cords of mighty strife" [*erida kraterên etanusse Kroniôn*] until the "cords of war's strife" are "strained" [*erida ptolemoio tanussan*] to their limits, a metaphor grimly literalized over the dead body of Patroclus, who is "dragged" [*eruein*] by Trojan and Greek soldiers in a tug of war that the narrator compares to the stretching [*tanuein*] of the skin of a fatty bull until its "hide is stretched [*tanutai*] to the utmost."[125] Such metaphors convey the stress of war, "as if intensity were expressed by extension," and they also convey the equilibrium of battle – those moments of suspense in which the equal and opposing exertion of two antagonists creates a counterbalance or even an impasse.[126]

Although he does not acknowledge the possible connections between Jerome's metaphor and its Homeric counterparts, Erasmus does show great interest in another group of Homeric terms and phrases concerned with the equilibrium or counterbalance of conflict, namely, the characterization of war, or Ares, as "*alloprosallos*" – leaning first to one side and then to the other – and the related characterization of strife [*neikos*] as "*homoiion*," a word that means evenly balanced, impartial, or shared in common.[127] In the adage *Cothurno versatilior*, the *polutropos* Odysseus is not the only example of Protean versatility drawn from Homer, for Erasmus also mentions how Homer "speaks of Mars suddenly changing sides, and uses a new word, *alloprosallos*" [*Homerus Martem, ni fallor, subinde mutantem parteis novo verbo alloprosallon*], a term that conveys the unpredictability of war as well as the whimsy of the god who presides over it (Adage I.i.94, *CWE* 31:137 [ASD II.1:204], citing *Il.* 5.831 and 5.888). In Book 5 of the

Iliad, Zeus and Athena both call Ares "*alloprosallon*" within the space of sixty lines (*Il.* 5.831–4, 5.873), accusing him of ficklnessness and commenting that "strife is always dear to [him], and wars and fighting" [*eris te philê polemoi to machai te*] (*Il.* 5.890). As Ares's defence against these accusations suggests, *alloprosallos* is a complex, and not entirely a negative, attribute akin to neutrality. At its worst, it is associated with capriciousness, treachery, and aloofness. At its best, it is associated with impartiality and even with the proper distribution of *dikê*, or justice.

For Erasmus, the term's ambivalance dramatizes some key questions of Christian theodicy and also helps to mediate conflicting attitudes towards neutrality in political or spiritual disputes, a characteristic for which Erasmus was eventually excoriated by Reformers and Catholics alike. In the adage *Duabus sedere sellis* [To sit on two stools], a phrase suitable for those who "belong for certain to neither party," Erasmus teases out the negative implications of the term, elaborating on his previous observation that "Homer coins a new word, *alloprosallos*, double-faced, and applies it to Mars, because he favors one side and then the other" [*quo verbo nove composito alloprosallon Homerus appellat Martem, id est nunc his, nunc illis partibus faventem*] (I.vii.2, *CWE* 32:68 [ASD II.2:128–9]).[128] In this adage, the lesson is clear: "to intrigue with both sides is most dishonourable" [*turpissimum cum utraque parte colludere*]. Yet in other adages, Erasmus invokes Homer's representation of the unpredictability and impartiality of war in more positive terms, even interpreting the *Iliad*'s common tropes of victory as a "turncoat" and of war (or Ares) as "*alloprosallos*" as concepts congenial to his theology as well as to his ideals of moderation and religious toleration. In *Omnium rerum vicissitudo est* [All things do change], Erasmus supports the titular maxim by citing two descriptions of *Ares alloprosallos*: Paris's observation to Hector that "Victory changes sides from man to man" [*nikê d'epameibetai andras; nunc his, nunc illis contingit vincere*] and Hector's later remark that "The God of War / Impartial slays the slayer in his turn" [*Xunos Enualios, kai te ktaneonta katekta; Communis Mars inque vicem perimit perimentem*] (Adage I.vii.63, *CWE* 32:104 [ASD II.2:188], citing *Il.* 6.339 and 18.309). Although the more ominous implications of these lines do not escape Erasmus's attention, they also serve his anti-war stance, if only because the unpredictability of battle makes war a rather undesirable activity in which to engage. In *Mars communis* [*Arês Koinos*], an adage added in 1528 and taken from a line in the *Iliad* describing how "Alike to all is the god of war, and slays the slayer in turn" [*Communis Mars inque vicem perimit perimentem*], Erasmus explains that the expression, which had already achieved the status of a maxim in antiquity, conveys "how uncertain and varied the outcome of a war could be" [*incertum ac varium belli eventum*], a lesson somewhat different from its source at *Iliad* 18.309, where Hector states that "Ares is impartial" [*Xunos Enualios*] in order to drum up hope that the Trojans might win the war after all (IV.vii.49, *CWE* 36:309–10 [ASD II.8:95]).[129] As Erasmus notes, Aristotle uses the expression at *Rhetoric* II.xxi.11 ("*Nunc his, nunc illis contingit vincere*") but as in Homer, Aristotle invokes the phrase as an example of how to exhort an army to bravery when it is inferior in number, rather than to caution against war altogether.[130]

In *Omnium rerum vicissitudo est* [All things do change], Erasmus discusses several other Homeric *topoi* for vicissitude that help to explain his attraction to the theological implications of the Homeric concept of *allosprosallos* and related depictions of divine impartiality or neutrality. The most famous of these is the account (at *Il.* 8.69–72) of Zeus's two scales, in which the god lifts up his "golden balance" [*chruseia … talanta*], places in it "two fates of grievous death," grasps the balance by the middle and raises it, watching as the "day of doom" sinks down one side or the other. For Erasmus, Zeus's weighing of the fates of the Greeks and Trojans [*Jupiter aureis lancibus expendit Troianorum ac Graecorum fata*] is a testimony to Homer's sound theodicy, proof of Zeus's enforcement of a distributive justice that might appear to wreak vicissitude in the mortal world but in fact remedies injustice by ensuring a balanced dispensation of good and evil (ASD II.2:190). As such, the *Iliad* presents Erasmus with a pious, redemptive twist on the proverb that "all things do change," since while the Homeric gods may permit "victory to turn the tide of battle" [*machês heteralkea nikên*] towards one side and then the other (a phrase Erasmus translates as "*victoriam alternatim nunc his, nunc illis obtingentem*"), this alternation of sides also ensures a certain "*koinos*" [common, shared] aspect to mortal life (Adage I.vii.63, ASD II.2:190, citing *Il.* 7.26).

Erasmus detects a similar principle at work in Achilles's account of Zeus's two jars, likewise cited in *Omnium rerum vicissitudo est*. In that passage, Achilles explains that Zeus has two urns, "the one of ills, the other of blessings" [*in hoc mala sunt, bona in illo*], and to whomever Zeus gives a "mixed lot" [*miscens dispensat*] drawn from both urns "meets now with evil, now with good" [*Nunc mala distribuens ac tristia, nunc bona rursum*] (ASD II.2:189, translating *Il.* 24.527–30). This "mixed" lot of human life – an idea conveyed by the common Homeric verb *anamignêmi* [to mix up, interchange, alternate] – reminds Erasmus of the "answer given by Aesop" when, in an anecdote related by Diogenes Laertius, he is asked what Zeus is doing as he doles out the contents of his two urns. Aesop's chiastic reply,

"Bringing down high things and exalting things of low degree" [*Ta men hupsêla tapeinôn, ta de tapeina hupsôn*], helps to shed light on the correspondence Erasmus must have seen between Homer's Zeus and the God of 1 Cor. 1.27–28, who shames the strong by raising up "what is low and contemptible of the world, things that are not" (Adage I.vii.63, ASD II.2:189, citing Diogenes Laertius, *Lives*, I.69). The striking similarity between Aesop's gloss on Zeus's two jars and these verses from 1 Corinthians helps to explain why Erasmus returns again and again in his *Adages* to Homeric terms that convey the neutrality of divine forces or the capacity of those forces to intermix or overturn the established order of things. Often, Erasmus takes solace in Homer's conception of the gods as *alloprosallos* or *enualios*, with the admixture of good and bad fortune, and happiness and grief, which those ideas convey. Glossing the adage *Plus aloes quam mellis habet* [More aloes than honey in it], Erasmus identifies its source in Homer's acknowledgment of the "alternation in human affairs, this mixture of sorrow and joy in man's lot ... in the image of the two jars which stand, he said, on Jove's threshold, one full of sad things and the other of gay ones" [*rerum humanarum vices ac tristium laetorumque mixturam Homerus ... figmento duorum doliorum, quae scribit in Jovis limine sita esse, quorum alterum sit plenum tristibus, alterum laetis*] (I.viii.66, *CWE* 32:162 [ASD II.2:290]).

This mixed lot of mortal existence is, for Erasmus, a condition to which humans must respond with corresponding versatility. The *polutropos* Odysseus accommodates himself to changing circumstances as a means of responding to, or even resisting, the *alloprosallos* Ares, Homeric figures who appear alongside the versatile [*strophaios*] Hermes in a passage of the *De Duplici Copia* devoted to the virtues of rhetorical and intellectual flexibility (*CWE* 24:642–6). Such versatility involves a Stoic indifference to adverse fortune – a common enough interpretation of Odysseus during the Renaissance, and one that Erasmus appears to endorse in *Omnium rerum vicissitudo est* by reworking two lines spoken by Helen as she prepares to administer Nepenthe to Menelaus and his visitors at *Od.* 4.236–7: "Now to this one, now to that, / Jupiter sends now joy, now grief" [*Nunc huic, nunc Juppiter illi / Nunc laeta immittit, nunc tristia*] (Adage III.ix.72, *CWE* 35:345 [ASD II.6:541]). In addition to permitting a flexible response to the vicissitudes of fortune, the polytropic cunning of Homer's characters also reflects their liberty of choice in what Erasmus, like Milton a century and a half later, recognizes to be a contingent cosmos, one that presents its inhabitants with competing choices and grants them the freedom to choose correctly. Erasmus's interpretation of Zeus's two jars as an expression of free-will theology may reflect the influence of the pseudo-Plutarchan *Life*, which argues that Homer's conception of human experience as composed of "mixtures of good and evil" helps to "generate multiple possibilities and a multitude of situations," a liberty intimately connected to the exercise of free will: "Since this material has things of the worse mixed into it, the recognition and choice of the better becomes easier."[131] Erasmus adopts this reading in several adages that focus on the Homeric term *heteralkês*, a word whose prefix, derived from *heteros* (the other, one of two) is defined by the adage *Vir fugiens et denuo pugnabit* [He that fights and runs away may live to fight another day] as meaning "that which sides in turn now with one party and now with the other" [*vicissim nunc apud hos, nunc apud illos pollentem*] (Adage I.x.40, *CWE* 32:252 [ASD II.2:446]). Although *heteralkês* is a term principally used to describe the power of the Homeric gods to reverse the fortunes of war – Apollo accuses Athena at *Il.* 7.26 of granting the Achaeans "victory to turn the tide of battle" [*machês heteralkea nikên*] – Erasmus compares the sentiment to Paris's remark to Hector at *Il.* 3.439–40 that "victory shifts [*epameibetai*] from man to man" [*alterna viris victoria cedit*] as well as to a similar observation made by Paris at *Il.* 6.339 (*CWE* 32:252 [ASD II.2:446]). Paris's naive optimism notwithstanding – the tide of victory does not, ultimately, shift back to the Trojan side – Erasmus finds truth in these Homeric formulae by virtue of the support they lend to his doctrines of theological liberty as well as to his ideal of an impartial and just God.

The contingency of the Homeric cosmos can also prove unsettlingly precarious to Erasmus, however, as revealed by adages such as *In acie novaculae*, a phrase derived from Nestor's observation that "we all stand on the razor's edge, / Whether for the Achaeans it be life / or sore destruction" [*Nunc etenim cunctis sita res in cuspide ferri est, / Vivantne an tristi exitio absumantur Achivi*] (Adage I.i.18, *CWE* 31:66 [ASD II.1:130], citing *Il.* 10.173–4). This Homeric phrase and related ones, as the penultimate chapter of this book argues, will help Milton develop his own distinct epic vocabulary for theological liberty and for the processes of deliberation that exercise said liberty. Yet for Erasmus, the unpredictable outcome of war in the *Iliad* also helps to buttress his scepticism and to convey the challenge of remaining impartial in contemporary disputes. If, as Erasmus observes in the *Parabolae*, a "doubtful mind [*dubius animus*] is like the tongue of a balance, disposed equally towards either side [*in utramque partem*] and tilted towards neither," a sceptical suspension of judgment is a suitable response to the vagaries of a world in which good and bad fortune are measured out variably and unpredictably (*CWE* 23:165 [ASD I.5:146]). Erasmus's treatment of Homeric representations of vicissitude elucidates the ways in which his sceptical outlook and his theological commitment to the freedom of the will are symbiotic, each predicated on the other. In the adage *Anceps eventus rei* [Two possible outcomes], Erasmus attempts to establish the Homeric foundations of free will by testifying to the poet's representation of multiple possible outcomes for the same event. When describing situations that have "two possible outcomes or [when] it is uncertain which way victory inclines" [*cum anceps rei discrimen significamus et incertum, utro vergat Victoria*], Erasmus explains, "we may cite *Iliad* 22.209 or 8.69, 'Then the father balanced the two pans of his golden scales'" [*Tum pater auratas librabat utrinque bilances*] (Adage III.ix.28, *CWE* 35:328 [ASD II.6:526]).

By recuperating Homer's conception of the gods as *alloprosallos* and *heteralkês* – impartial and disinterested in their dispensation of good and ill – Erasmus implicitly aligns Homer's theodicy to that of the New Testament, whose God is "no respecter of persons" [*ouk estin prosôpolêmptês; non sit personarum respectus apud deum*] (Acts 10.34; ASD VI.2:316).[132] For Erasmus, the mixed lot of joy and sorrow meted out by Homer's Zeus reveals a serio-comic and paradoxical vision of mortal existence. In the adage *Gaudium dolori iunctum* [Joy is linked to pain], a phrase suitable for describing "when something happens at which we rejoice and grieve equally" [*cum partier accidit, quod et gaudeamus et doleamus*], Erasmus comments on the mixture of contrary emotions that defines Eurycleia's reaction as she recognizes Odysseus's scar: "Joy and grief came together upon her heart" [*Laetitia huic moerorque simul praecordia cepit*] (III.x.61, *CWE* 35:378 [ASD II.6:570], citing *Od.* 19.471). Erasmus is so moved by this scene that he cites the line once again in his *Panegyricus* to the Archduke of Austria, one of three Homeric episodes singled out in that work in which Homeric characters experience "mixed emotions" of joy and sorrow simultaneously.[133] In his *De Duplici Copia*, in the midst of a discussion of the difference between *pathê* and *ethê*, Erasmus explains that tragic and comic modes are "often interspersed [*miscentur*] in the *Iliad* and Greek tragedy," and the example he provides, one long favoured by the scholiasts, is *Il.* 6.484, where Andromache "smiles through her tears" [*lachrymabile ridens*] as she sees how the fierce plumes of Hector's helmet scare their infant son (*CWE* 24:654–5 [ASD I.6:276–8]). But whereas Homeric scholiasts praise the scene for its "vividness" [*enargeias*], Erasmus appears to admire this and other instances of mixed emotion in Homeric epic as a proleptic anticipation of Acts 4.24, a verse that demonstrates for Erasmus how God ensures that human life consists of a dappled mixture of joy and sorrow. "God blends everything for his servants," Erasmus writes, "he mixes the happy with the sad, so that they might be able to endure, while they in turn give thanks for the happy things and supplicate the Lord for the sad" [*Sic Deus omnia temperat suis famulis, ut laeta tristibus misceat, quo possint sustinere, utque vicissim pro laetis agant gratias, pro tristibus Dominum deprecentur*] (*CWE* 50:36 [LB VII:682C]).[134] This intermingling of grief and joy shapes Erasmus's theology and also informs the dazzling variety that characterizes the *Adages*'s cornucopian vision of human wisdom, an all-embracing panorama of mortal experience ranging from the most tragic heights to the most absurdly comic depths.

Scaliger would later single out Homer's description of Eris at *Il.* 4.440–4 as "ridiculous," holding up the passage as a prime example of Homer's inferiority to Virgil.[135] Erasmus's reliance upon a Homeric mythography of discord as a means of condemning petty spats between fatuous scholars may likewise reflect his recognition that there is something essentially comic, or even ridiculous, about Homer's goddess of strife, but unlike Scaliger, Erasmus also discerns the tragic consequences implicit in Homer's depiction of strife as a force that grows exponentially as it feeds off of itself. To Erasmus, this eristic spirit is at once deeply tragic and profoundly comic. His devotion to a spirit of serious play in both the *Adages* and *In Praise of Folly* originates in large part from his recognition of Homer's serio-comic vision of the world, a vision described by the pseudo-Plutarchan *Life of Homer* in language that sounds strikingly similar to that used by Erasmus in his dedicatory epistle to *In Praise of Folly*: "we cannot live in a constant state of alertness and tension but need also to be relaxed at times in order to be equal to the toils of life. The amusing parts of Homer will be found to be aimed toward this goal."[136] In the dedicatory epistle to his translation of Lucian's *Dialogues*, printed in June 1514, Erasmus advises that even the most serious scholars should "refresh [their] care-wearied minds with laughter," an activity in which Lucian proves especially instructive. "[E]ven Jupiter laughs," Erasmus writes, "the father of gods and men" [*rideat et maximus ille patêr andrôn te theôn te Juppiter*], a comment that identifies Homer's morosophic deity as source of the serio-ludic wisdom so prized by Erasmus: the fount of Lucianic *spoudaiogeloion*, of Socratic irony, and above all, of Pauline folly (Ep. 293, *CWE* 2:291 [Allen 1:562]). As the next chapter explores, Erasmus's *gioco*-serious conception of Homer is adapted in various ways by two sixteenth-century writers deeply indebted to the Dutch humanist, Philipp Melanchthon and François Rabelais, who interpret Homeric epic as supportive of a *concordia discors* that possesses complex social, spiritual, and cosmological implications.

Chapter Two

The Remedy of Contraries: Melanchthon, Rabelais, and Epic Parody

"Is it possible that eminent Homeric scholars have found so much seriousness in the more humorous parts of the *Odyssey* because they brought it there? To the serious all things are serious."

– Samuel Butler, *The Authoress of the Odyssey*

Homeric Mockery and the Legacy of Erasmus in Early Reformation Germany

In his 1869 lecture "Homer and Classical Philology," Friedrich Nietzsche remarks that the Homeric scholars of nineteenth-century Germany are guided by "a certain standard of inner harmony" such that "whatever is seen to be below this standard and opposed to this inner harmony is at once swept aside as un-Homeric."[1] Yet as Nietzsche goes on to point out, Homer's readers of previous generations were not necessarily motivated by similar expectations. Aristotle, for instance, was capable of believing that Homer was "the author of the original of all comic epics, the *Margites*," a fact that strengthens Nietzsche's larger claim that during antiquity, the prevailing idea of the Homeric poet "comprehended an abundance of dissimularities."[2] A century before Nietzsche, in his *Prolegomena to Homer*, Friedrich Wolf voices similar objections to the ancient Greek scholiasts who laboured to make Homer appear "nowhere inconsistent or unworthy of himself, often removing many verses" in order to bring the poet into agreement with himself.[3] Wolf's and Nietzsche's complaints are hardly new: in his *Discourse on Homer*, a late first-century CE text frequently printed in sixteenth-century editions of the *Iliad* and *Odyssey*, Dio Chrysostom describes how the Stoic allegorists struggled in their commentaries to "save Homer from appearing to be at war with himself [*autos autô machomenos*] in certain matters that were held to be contrary [*enantiôs*] to each other as narrated by Homer."[4]

In the centuries before Wolf posed his "Homeric Question," thus casting doubt on the authorial unity of the Homeric corpus, the vast majority of Homer's readers did not look for consistency between or among his poems, nor did they prize the coherence or harmony cherished by later scholars. While most sixteenth-century readers of Homer believed that a single poet authored the *Iliad* and *Odyssey* as well as a motley jumble of hymns, epigrams, and mock-epic works such as the *Margites* and the *Batrachomyomachia*, they did not expect or even desire to find congruity of style or outlook among these works, and some even delighted in the very dissonance and contradictoriness that came to vex subsequent Homeric scholars. Particularly during the first several decades of the sixteenth century, when reformers and humanists came to find political and philosophical value in the comic elements of the Homeric corpus, interpretations of Homer are often guided by the conviction that his works display a rich generic spectrum. They are likewise guided by the conviction that those comic elements, far from being indecorous, are the very moments where the Homeric poet is at his most eirenic, providing solutions to conflict or criticizing the eristic values of heroic poetry.

Homer's talent as a comic poet was widely acknowledged during antiquity, above all by Lucian but also by earlier Greek writers such as Hipponax, Hegemon, and Timon of Phlius, the authors of *silloi* or mock-heroic hexameters who took parodic aim at Homer by rearranging verses from his poems or dislocating them from their original context.[5] Used as an elementary text for the teaching of Greek during the Renaissance, the pseudo-Homeric *Batrachomyomachia* (*The Battle of the Frogs and the Mice*) enjoyed enormous popularity during the late fifteenth and early sixteenth centuries. Between 1472 and 1551, the poem was printed in Greek or in Greek-Latin editions no fewer than twenty-three times, and it was translated early and often into vernacular languages across Europe. Particularly in the decade after the appearance of *In Praise of Folly*, whose preface aligns Erasmus's work with the *Batrachomyomachia* and other mock-epic and mock-encomiastic works, a number of writers take up Folly's project of identifying Homer as the progenitor of a pacifistic, ironic, counter-epic attitude that passes, via Socrates and Lucian, down to Erasmus himself.

In Wittenberg, which enjoyed a strong tradition of Greek studies since the founding of its university in 1502, three Latin translations of the *Batrachomyomachia* appeared within the space of a decade: Johannes

Reuchlin's 1510 translation into Latin hexameters, Tilman Conradi's 1513 Latin verse translation, and Philipp Melanchthon's Greek-Latin edition of the poem, complete with a preface and commentary, which was probably composed around the time of Melanchthon's arrival in Wittenberg in 1518.[6] Melanchthon's interest in the *Batrachomyomachia* was almost certainly aroused by Reuchlin, his great-uncle and teacher of Greek. For Reuchlin, Melanchthon, and their allies, the *Batrachomyomachia* was a useful weapon in the academic and religious controversies of the era. Not only does the poem provide a suitable introductory text that might entice young boys to learn Greek, thus combating the intellectual conservatism that reigned at Reuchlin's Louvain, but it also offers a trenchant parody of Iliadic strife in which an attentive and caring Zeus intervenes to save the frogs from utter destruction at the hands of their arrogant and aggressive adversaries, the mice. Interpreted through the lens of the contentious early years of the Reformation, the poem's *casus belli* – the incompatibility between different species of animals – conceals an ominous and urgent lesson for contemporary readers, such as Melanchthon, who value concord and toleration. While the frogs – in particular their leader, King Puff-Jaw – are kindly and hospitable, the mice repudiate the friendly overtures of their amphibious neighbours by arguing that frogs and mice are "altogether different in nature" [*ton eis phusin ouden homoion*], a difference that erupts into open war after one of the mice is drowned while being ferried across a river by a well-meaning but not entirely altruistic frog who dives under the water to avoid a snake.[7]

Although Reuchlin's spare translation of the poem has neither preface nor scholarly apparatus, later sixteenth-century editions and translations of the *Batrachomyomachia* by German scholars including Melanchthon and Martin Crusius reveal how the poem serves to satirize contemporary academic disputes and theological controversies. Crusius, a professor of Greek at the University of Tübingen during the latter half of the sixteenth century, studied at Strasbourg under Joachim Camerarius, a fellow Homeric scholar and friend of Melanchthon who produced commentaries on the first two books of the *Iliad* as well as (with Jacob Micyllus) a Greek edition of Homer that also included the Didymus *Scholia*, in addition to Porphyry's *Homericarum Quaestionum liber* and his *De Antro Nympharum*.[8] In an oration delivered at Tübingen on 3 April 1581 that later formed the preface to his Latin translation of the poem, Crusius praises the *Batrachomyomachia* as "honourable, useful, and sweet" [*honesto, utili, and suavi*], and he dwells on the work as a resource for avoiding or assuaging disputes.[9] For Crusius, Homer's fable illustrates the tensions and difficulties that inhere in "friendship between unequals" [*inaequalium amicitias*], a lesson he also locates in Achilles's pessimistic maxim that "between lions and men there are no oaths of faith" [*ouk esti leousi kai andrasin horkia pista*]. According to Crusius, the *Batrachomyomachia* also teaches the wisdom of "sometimes ignoring injuries received" [*interdum dissimulare injurias acceptas*] and of the "private and public benefit of patience and an eagerness for peace" [*privatim & publicè utile, patientiam, & pacis studium*].[10] Crusius even discerns moral lessons about verbal and intellectual conflict in the proper names of the poem's characters: Poluphêmus (literally, many voices) represents the vice of garrulity, Hupsiboas (literally, loud shouter) is too clamorous, and Kraugasidês (from *kraugê*, clamour or shrieking) symbolizes the threat of tumult or sedition.[11]

Crusius praises the *Batrachomyomachia* for its blending of "sententiae" and "[i]ucunditas," concluding his oration by calling the mock-epic "child's play, but serious play" [*lusus puerorum, sed spoudaion paignion, serius lusus*].[12] Such an interpretation is in keeping with the prolegomenon to Crusius's *Commentationes in I Lib. Iliad. Homeri*, published posthumously in 1612, which identifies Homer as the source not just of tragedy but also of comedy, epigram, and satire.[13] In Crusius's hands, the *Batrachomyomachia*'s jovial account of inter-species strife conceals a serious condemnation of wars fanned by pride and contentiousness, thus offering up an apt, sardonic commentary on the warring intellectual and theological camps of sixteenth-century academic culture. For the two generations of northern European scholars active before Crusius, between around 1510 and 1550, enthusiasm for the *Batrachomyomachia* in scholarly circles is motivated by the work's palliative dimension as a text that might offer antidotes to the prevailing culture of controversy and factionalism. Along with the mock-epic and sophistic works of late antique Greek writers such as Lucian, Libanius, and Dio Chrysostom, Homer's counter-epic fable exerts a powerful sway over works of Reformation satire in the 1510s and 1520s: its influence can be discerned in Willibald Pirckheimer's *Apologia seu podagrae laus*, a mock-Iliadic work based on Lucian's *Tragopodagra*, Ortuinus Gratius's *Dialogue between Mercury and Pot-Licker*, and Crotus Rubianus's *Theologists in Council*, the last of which convenes its characters at a suspiciously Homeric-looking council in order to satirize the boisterous disputations of academics at a faculty meeting.[14]

Although Lucian and other Greek writers of the Second Sophistic are often regarded as turning topsy-turvy Homer's epic values and motifs, the popularity of these authors in early sixteenth-century northern Europe is intimately related to the equal enthusiasm for Homer's *Odyssey*, *Batrachomyomachia*, and the *Hymns* and *Epigrams*, works widely understood during the period to undermine or critique the heroic ethos of the *Iliad*. Like Lucian's dialogues, which were rendered into Latin by an enormous number of northern humanists in the first half of the sixteenth century (Agricola, Reuchlin, Mosellanus, Erasmus, More, and Melanchthon), contemporary editions, translations, and imitations of the *Batrachomyomachia* provide a similar venue for lampooning academic quibbles and criticizing the frivolity of intellectual and theological disputes.[15] And, like Lucianic dialogue, the *gioco*-serious tone of the *Batrachomyomachia* mixes gravity and levity in a manner that highlights the oft-trivial causes of serious disputes, a lesson encapsulated by Erasmus's Homeric adage that "greatest things [come] from the smallest beginnings" [*ex minimis initiis maxima*].[16] If the horrors of war arise out of the pettiest of causes, the diminutive heroes of the *Batrachomyomachia* dramatize this principle with absurd literalness for many of the poem's sixteenth-century readers.

In the preface to his *Scholia* on the *Batrachomyomachia*, first printed in 1541 but probably composed significantly earlier, Melanchthon extracts precisely such a lesson from the poem, writing that it "implants in young boys a hatred of disorder and sedition" [*adolescentibus odium turbarum & seditionum inserere*].[17] Melanchthon voices a similar sentiment in a 1526 oration entitled *On the Usefulness of Fables* (*De Utilitate Fabularum*), delivered in his capacity as Professor of Greek and Rhetoric at Wittenberg. Melanchthon shows his true Erasmian colours in the oration, interpreting the poem as a pacifistic, proto-Christian parable about the miseries of war and the importance of forgiveness: the work "teaches how much better it is to ignore a wrong than to avenge it, how uncertain is the outcome of all quarrels and wars, and that it happens not infrequently that the stronger are defeated by the weaker ... implanting in children's minds a hatred of war and strife, [and] a zeal for tolerance" [*doceret quantum praestaret dissimulare quam ulcisci iniuriam, quam sint incerti turbarum ac bellorum omnium exitus, nec raro accidere, ut ab inferioribus potentiores vincantur ... puerilibus animis inseri, atque odium bellorum ac turbarum, tolerantiae studium*].[18] By locating in Homer's mock-epic values consonant with the Sermon on the Mount, Melanchthon's interpretation of the *Batrachomyomachia* assimilates the ethically dubious Odyssean virtue of *mêtis*, or cunning intelligence, to a New Testament ethos of humility and non-retaliation, a strategy resembling Erasmus's repeated "collation" of Odysseus and Saint Paul in *The Adages*. By condemning the mice as too easily provoked by the accidental drowning of one of their own, and by regarding the frogs as meek underdogs who owe their victory to divine intervention, Melanchthon's interpretation of the poem as a fable about "how the stronger are defeated by the weaker" helps to explain why the *Batrachomyomachia* was sometimes printed with Aesop's *Fables* during the sixteenth century: both works moralize the eventual victory of Christ-like values such as patience and humility over aggression and brute force.[19]

After studying Greek at Pforzheim with Reuchlin and Georg Simler, Melanchthon took up a professorship at the University of Wittenberg in 1518 and began lecturing on Homer in that same year.[20] Over the course of the next four decades, Melanchthon had a profound impact on the course of Homeric scholarship in Northern Europe as well as on Hellenic studies more generally. His lectures on Homer inspired Martin Luther to study Greek and may have inspired a similar reaction in William Tyndale, who matriculated at Wittenberg in May 1524. Many of the scholars who studied or came into contact with Melanchthon, including Melchior Lotther, Johann Lonitzer, Vincent Opsopoeus, Joachim Camerarius, Eobanus Hessus, Wolfgang Capito, and Simon Lemnius, went on to produce editions or translations of Homer.[21] Lonitzer's edition, a two-volume Greek text of the *Iliad* and *Odyssey* printed at Strasbourg in 1525, is dedicated to Melanchthon, as is the 1542 Strasbourg edition of the *Iliad* compiled by Capito and Richard Gerbel. The anonymous *Compendiosa explicatio in errores Ulyssis*, appended to an edition of Xenophon's *Symposium* and printed at Hagenau in 1531, contains Melanchthon's versified summary of the work. Achilles Pirminius Gasser, who studied with Melanchthon, copiously annotated his copies of Camerarius's commentaries on the *Iliad* and of Andreas Cratander's 1520 edition of Books 1 and 2 of the *Odyssey*; these notes reflect the rigours of his Wittenberg Greek training as well as the pervasive influence of the *Adages*.[22]

For the two generations of northern humanists who studied under him or were educated through his grammars, lectures, and orations, Melanchthon was instrumental in shaping interpretations of Homeric epic that highlighted the poet's distaste for war and represented him as a pagan champion of Christian peace and piety. In his 1518 *On Correcting the Studies of Youth* (*De corrigendis adolescentiae studiis*), the inaugural lecture at Wittenberg that helped cement his reputation as an advocate for educational reform, Melanchthon invokes Homer's depiction of the conflict between Ares and Athena as evidence that war and wisdom do not mix, and he interprets the squabbles of the Olympian gods in light of his own aversion to academic disputes and controversies.[23] It is perhaps for this reason that Melanchthon began his career at Wittenberg by lecturing on Homer and on Paul's Epistle to Titus, one of several Pauline epistles that vehemently condemn "quarrels and fights" [*ereis kai machas*] as "unprofitable and pointless" [*anôpheleis kai mataioi*]. As Melanchthon surely knew, Titus 1.15 also contains one of the New Testament's most compelling justifications of pagan wisdom: Paul's claim that "To the pure all things are pure" [*panta kathara tois katharois*] was widely interpreted during the sixteenth century as an argument for the potential wholesomeness of classical texts if piously interpreted by judicious and charitable readers.[24] As with Erasmus, Melanchthon enlists Homer and Paul as allies in his struggles against contemporary *barbaroi* who oppose humanistic learning or devalue tolerance and peace.

Influenced, no doubt, by Erasmus's heavy reliance on Homer in the *Adages*, Melanchthon reads Homeric epic as a series of commonplaces, proverbs to be deployed in a variety of different contexts. In his *Preface to Homer*, written in 1538 for his fellow Wittenberg scholar and former pupil Veit Winsheim, Melanchthon criticizes those who "read Homer in such a way that they seek nothing but pleasure from it, and aphorisms collected like little flowers" [*evolvunt Homerum, ut nihil hinc nisi voluptatem venentur, et sententiolas quasdam ceu flosculos hinc inde collectas*], although he goes on to argue that Homer's wisdom is second only to Holy Scripture, his poems full of "common and most useful rules and precepts for morals, life, and civil duties" [*communibus et utilissimis regulis ac praeceptis morum, vitaeque et civilium officiorum*].[25] This method of reading Homer is evident in the annotations of Gasser, who underlines or otherwise marks the many *sententiae* of the *Iliad* and cross-references several lines in his handwritten transcription of Book 6 of the *Iliad*, dated 1523, with corresponding Erasmian adages. Next to Glaucus's famous comparison between the passing generations of men and autumn leaves scattered by the wind, Gasser writes in his margins, "*Adag. Homo bulla*," a proverb whose origins Erasmus traces back to the same passage in the *Iliad* and describes as having been a "favorite with Pyrrho, the Academic philosopher."[26] On the following page, next to Glaucus's account of his illustrious ancestor, Gasser writes "*Vide Adag. Bellerophontis*," and he marks two additional parallels to Erasmus's *Adages* in his margins to Book 6 alone.[27] In his copy of Cratander's Basel 1520 edition of Books 1 and 2 of the *Odyssey*, also annotated in 1523, Gasser takes special note of the remark in Poliziano's *Oratio*, which serves as preface to the edition, that Homeric epic contains numerous "*locis sententiā*."[28]

In addition to collating Homeric passages with scriptural proverbs through the mediating influence of Erasmus's *Adages*, Melanchthon and his students interpret various passages in Homer's epic and mock-epic poems as supportive of the kind of eirenic, sceptical outlook that reveals the scholar's temperamental sympathies with Erasmus despite his unwavering theological commitment to Lutheranism. In various writings, Melanchthon interprets the *Iliad* as a poem concerned with the disciplining of anger and with the dangers of false pride or the human tendency to "extol our own wisdom and power" above that of God.[29] The *Batrachomyomachia*, for example, demonstrates that neither of the warring parties is strong on its own merit, and neither can hope for victory without the assistance of Zeus, who in the final moments of the poem sends in an army of crabs, *deus ex karkina*, to help the frogs defeat the mice in what might otherwise have been a "boundless conflict" [*dêrin apeiresiên*]. Melanchthon also discerns in Homeric epic and mock-epic alike sceptical lessons concerning the limitations of the human intellect and the unknowability of the divine. He commences his *Preface to Homer* by stressing the "dense darkness" [*prodigiosis … tenebris*] of human reason, "blind in things that are divine and beyond human understanding" [*in rebus divinis et supra captum humanum positis caecutiunt homines*], and his annotations to the *Iliad* credit a similarly pessimistic view of human nature to the Homeric narrator.[30] Writing "[*f*]*oliis similes homines*" twice in his margins, paraphrasing the famous simile comparing autumn leaves to the passing generations of mortal men, Melanchthon dwells upon Apollo's observation at *Il.* 21.464–6 that mortals are "pitiful creatures, who like leaves are now full of flaming life ... and now waste again and perish." His interest is equally aroused by a passage addressing how the fallible intellect subjects mortals to discord and delusion. During the battlefield debate between Achilles and Aeneas in Book 20, Melanchthon heavily annotates the exchange with moralizing tags such as "tongue" [*lingua*] and "many true, many false" [*multa ver[a], multa u[e] falsa*], a cynical riff on Aeneas's observation that "glib is the tongue of mortals" and that he and his adversary "wrangle against each other with many words – some true, some false."[31]

Yet even as Melanchthon detects in the *Iliad* a pessimism about the capacity of its human characters to grasp truth or achieve concord, he nonetheless argues that Homer's poems inculcate both civility and concord, since they teach "grace and gentleness of manners" [*venustas et suavitas morum*] and thus make readers' "minds ... become more humane and peaceful" [*ingenia … humaniora et magis placida*].[32] Such an interpretation helps to explain Melanchthon's preference for the *Odyssey* (as well as the *Batrachomyomachia*) above the *Iliad*, for while the *Iliad* teaches "the arts of the military and of war" [*militiae bellique artes*], the *Odyssey* "paints a picture of civil and peaceful life" [*civilis et togatae vitae*] in which the hero's conflicts with Polyphemus and the suitors represent, respectively, his struggle "with tyrants and with quarrelsome and vicious men" [*cum tyrannis, et cum seditiosis pravisque hominibus*].[33] Melanchthon paints Homer as a pacifist even when glossing passages that seem to present a direct affront to that interpretation. In another Wittenberg oration, the 1523 *In Praise of Eloquence* (*Encomium Eloquentiae*), he reads the contrast between the two cities on Achilles's shield as evidence of Homer's eirenic nature: "how better could [Homer] have shown how hateful – as I believe – war is most destructive for all that is excellent ... the laws are silent, the forum mute, and the destruction of all civil things is to be pitied" [*quo magis invisum, opinor, bellum rem perniciossimam optimo cuique faceret ... silent leges, mutum est forum, postremo miseranda est omnium civilium rerum vastitas*].[34] For Melanchthon, Homer's hatred of war is inseparable from the proto-Christian values of poverty and humility that his poems implicitly support. In his *Preface to Homer*, Melanchthon describes the Homeric poet as "destitute," a biographical detail that he may have culled from Dio Chrysostom's Fifty-Third *Discourse* or from either of the *Lives* of Homer attributed to Plutarch and Herodotus, the latter printed, with a Latin translation, in Melanchthon's 1531 *Grammatica Graeca*.[35] Melanchthon sees Homer's beggarly and contemptible way of living [*contemptus ... viveret*] as evidence that true wisdom often resides under a "poor roof" [*pauper tecto*], a sentiment that echoes Dio's comparison between Homer and the lowly Socrates.[36]

By emphasizing the canonicity and the ethical importance of the *Batrachomyomachia* in Homer's poetic career, Melanchthon establishes an Erasmian set of analogies between Homer and Socrates as well as between Homer and Christ, figures united by their Silenus-like concealment of pious wisdom beneath a seemingly worthless or foolish exterior. By imagining Homer as an indigent poet who preaches the destructiveness of war and anticipates the ultimate triumph of the weak and powerless over the strong and worldly, Melanchthon fleshes out Erasmus's submerged interpretation of Homer in his *Adages* by making him a supporter of the counter-epic values of the Gospels and of Paul's refrain that "you should become foolish [*môros*] so that you may become wise [*sophos*]," a verse whose perceived Homeric antecedents were made all the more compelling by the hijinks of the Homeric gods and the lowly comic scenes of the *Odyssey* and the mock-epic works.[37]

Rabelais and Homeric Mock-Epic

Influenced by Erasmus's *Adages* and by the scholarly controversies in which they were engaged, early sixteenth-century reformers and humanists such as Melanchthon, Camerarius, and Crusius favour counter-epic interpretations of Homer that privilege the apostolic values of peace, cooperation, fellowship, humility, moderation, and self-restraint. Often, though not always, their interpretations valorize the *Odyssey* and the *Batrachomyomachia* over the *Iliad* as texts that promise to resolve conflict or subdue excessive adversarialness. Perhaps echoing Nietzsche's complaint that late nineteenth-century Homeric scholars were unable or unwilling to embrace the contrarieties and contradictions inherent in the Homeric corpus, Mikhail Bakhtin observes in his *Dialogic Imagination* that "it did not bother the Greeks to think that Homer himself wrote a parody of Homeric style," and it did not bother the majority of Homer's sixteenth-century readers, either.[38] The epic parodies attributed to Homer during the period made his poems easier to assimilate to the ethics of the New Testament, and they also helped to identify in the Homeric poet an eclectic and cornucopian philosophical outlook that comprises sceptical, Platonic, and Epicurean strains.

According to Bakhtin's definition, parody permits the creation of a "contradictory reality" by "combining opposites" such as the sacred and the profane in order to adjudicate between conflicting values or beliefs.[39] As a literary mode capable of sustaining contradiction, parody does not merely aim to debase "high" or "classic" works of literature but also functions "to reduce the very distinctions between high and low upon which such canonisations are based."[40] As a means of harmonizing contrary ethical values or arenas of human experience, parody is not merely an oppositional strategy but rather a form that may be both "critical of and sympathetic to" its object, often assuming "an ambivalent, or ambiguous, relationship" towards a text that is both source and satirical target.[41]

The writings of François Rabelais offer the most sustained and complex Homeric parody in sixteenth-century Europe. From the comic invulnerability of Epistémon in *Pantagruel*, a text dedicated to Hugh Salel, Homer's first serious French translator, to Panurge's parodic exposition of Zeus's "golden chain" in his praise of debtors (*TL*, chapters 3–5), Rabelais stitches together a pastiche of Homeric lines and episodes in order to favour palpably counter-epic values, some of which are vices inverted (cowardice, hunger, self-interest) while others (fellowship, peace) align with the spirit of Christian humanism. The remainder of this chapter is devoted to Rabelais's Homeric parody – his parodic treatment *of* Homer but also his imitation of Homer *as* parodist, as a poet who repeatedly challenges, inverts, and critiques his own epic impulses. Despite the significant critical disagreement about how best to define the generic identity of the four books attributed to Rabelais, most critics acknowledge that

Rabelais's work is characterized by a "dialectic of opposites" or a "bipolar structure" fostered in part by the juxtaposition of seemingly antithetical genres.[42] As Rabelais's Trouillogan, the non-committal Pyrrhonist of the *Tiers Livre*, might say, his writings are "Tous les deux" [both/and]: simultaneously epic and counter-epic.[43] As a poet believed to work across these generic divides, Homer exerts a strong influence on the dialogic, generically hybrid strategies of Rabelais's work, often serving as the principal model for his serio-comic vision of the world.

Generations of scholars have noted Rabelais's frequent allusions to Homer as well as Homer's more diffuse influence on the narrative structure of his work. Yet many dismiss the influence as superficial, stopping short of asserting that Rabelais is engaged in any serious or protracted imitation of Homer if only because such an assertion would seem to cast Rabelais as supportive, rather than critical, of the rhetorical conventions and ethical norms associated with heroic poetry. The vast majority of Rabelais's modern readers agree that the narrative structure of his text is modelled loosely on Homer's two epics – the first two books imitating the battle scenes of the *Iliad* and the latter two (or three, for proponents of Rabelais's authorship of the *Cinquième Livre*) imitating the voyages recounted in the central books of the *Odyssey*. But Rabelais's other debts to Homer are often dismissed as trivial: Gérard Defaux, for instance, is willing to argue that the *Iliad* and *Odyssey* shape Rabelais's "strategy of form" [*strategie de la forme*] but then remarks that most of Rabelais's Homeric allusions are "anecdotal."[44]

Critical discussions of Homer's influence on Rabelais emphasize the latter writer's parodic inversion of the former into what is variously termed a "comic epic" (Duval), a "parody of epic" (Tetel), or a "burlesque *Iliad*" (Demerson).[45] Such a reading makes sense if we regard the Homeric poet as the purveyor of all things heroic and serious. But the Homer of the early sixteenth century is rather different from ours: distinguished by a capacity for sophistic verbal play and sceptical self-parody, a master of comic modes who adeptly mingles jocularity and serious grandeur. The prevailing belief that Homer was a comic as well as a tragic poet renders it unnecessary for Rabelais to separate the "manifestly heroic" dimensions of his works from their satirical and burlesque elements. As a pacifistic, *gioco*-serious poet who valorizes humility and moderation over conventionally heroic values such as honour, force, and courage – precisely how Melanchthon interprets him, and often how Erasmus does – Homer emerges as a profound and complex influence on Rabelais, a poet who has deep sympathies with some of Rabelais's favourite classical thinkers, including Lucian, Diogenes the Cynic, and Socrates.[46]

The Homeric poet emulated by Rabelais is a poet who takes parodic aim at himself. If the *Odyssey* "consistently asserts its views and its claim to greatness at the expense of the *Iliad*," an argument sometimes made by sixteenth-century readers about the mock-epic works ascribed to Homer during the period, then one might usefully regard Rabelais's topsy-turvy renditions of epic conventions and attitudes as parodies of Homer, but also as earnest and affectionate imitations of Homer's own *gioco*-serious tendency to undercut the norms and values of his own poems.[47] Such a reading posits an alternate lineage for Homer, one which downplays his position as the forefather of heroic poetry and instead identifies him as the progenitor of a sceptical, comedic, and eirenic tradition that later descends through Socrates, Aristophanes, Lucian, Erasmus, and Rabelais himself.

For many Renaissance readers, Homer's predilection for levity and self-mockery helps to harmonize the seeming "dissimularities" of his poetic corpus into a concordant whole, reconciling the contrary generic and rhetorical registers of high and low so as to privilege a more flexible conception of decorum and one that better accommodates Christian doctrine according to the arguments of Augustine.[48] In his *L'Art Poétique*, published in 1605 but composed several decades earlier, Vauquelin de la Fresnaye praises "Le Margite d'Homere" for representing "the middling sort and humble citizens, in which one sees the nature and customs of the bourgeois life" [*des hommes moyens ... [et] ... des humbles citoyens, / Se voyoit la nature et la facon bourgeoise*], even though the poem is written in a high or heroic style.[49] Such an interpretation testifies to Homer's latent pacifism and also provides compelling evidence of his capacity for self-criticism, an idea likewise supported by Martial's oft-cited description of Homer as a poet able to "relax" – to joke, to indulge in *prolixitas*, to wilfully undermine the seriousness of his own work. In Book 14 of his *Epigrams*, Martial justifies the nugatory quality of his own poems by instructing his readers to "Read through the frogs sung in Maeonian song [i.e., the *Batrachomyomachia*] and learn to relax your brow with my trifles" [*Perlege Maeonio cantatas carmine ranas / et frontem nugis solvere disce meis*], an argument echoed by Erasmus's *In Praise of Folly*, which legitimates its own jocularity by providing a catalogue of normally serious-minded writers, headed up by Homer, who occasionally indulge in frivolous literary recreations.[50]

Like Erasmus, many sixteenth-century readers of Homeric mock-epic regard these works as containing, in involuted and ludic form, a high and serious wisdom. Echoing Socrates's claim that the *Margites* reflects Homer's "enigmatic" tendency to "conceal rather than exhibit his wisdom," Guillaume Royhier defends his 1544 French translation of the

Batrachomyomachia by arguing that his "little work" [*petit ouvrage*] covertly critiques the "warlike acts of earthly princes" [*les belliqueux actes des princes de la terre*] "under the shadow of a trivial pretext" [*sous l'ombre de petit cas*].[51] Translating Virgil's assessment of the arduous yet thankless task of writing poems that fall short of epic dimensions, Royhier observes: "In small forms there is labour, / But not much honour" [*En petit cas [il] y a labeur, / Mais il n y a [que] petit honneur*].[52] Yet while Virgil is commonly understood by sixteenth-century writers to progress from the diminutive genres of eclogue and georgic towards the higher and more glorious genre of epic, the relationship between the epic and mock-epic works ascribed to Homer during the sixteenth century is far less clear-cut. While most of his ancient biographers identify the *Batrachomyomachia* and similar works as having been written during Homer's youth, rather than in his old age, none of the ancient biographical paratexts on Homer argue for the kind of coherent generic progression evident in Virgil's literary *cursus*. Instead, they stress the ways in which the riddles, hymns, epigrams, and above all the mock-epic works attributed to Homer offer up competing, self-mocking, or otherwise deflationary treatments of epic values and norms.[53]

Homer's perceived capacity to work across epic and mock-epic genres is understood by some Renaissance readers as a reflection of his *copia* and his scepticism. This view, already evident in the Homeric *Scholia* and in the pseudo-Plutarchan *Life*, as well as in the writings of Aristotle, Quintilian, and Aulus Gellius, also dominates the Homeric scholarship of Poliziano, who greatly admired the poet's generic flexibility and rhetorical abundance.[54] Homer's ability to negotiate between competing genres and outlooks is often linked by classical and Renaissance readers to his sceptical weighing of competing perspectives and values. This interpretive tradition, which identifies Homer as the father of both scepticism and sophistry, is a genealogy essential for understanding Rabelais's manipulation of Homeric allusions and motifs into vehicles for embracing the multiple or two-sided nature of truth as a means of emulating typically Homeric rhetorical and logical techniques such as irony, dialectic, and antilogic.[55]

Although Plato's comparison between the rhetorical virtuosity of Odysseus and Nestor and that of the sophists is hardly intended as a compliment, ancient sceptics and sophists both claim Homer proudly as their forerunner, praising him for the eristic or oppositional argumentation [*agôn logon*] that Plato condemns in the *Phaedrus*.[56] Dio Chrysostom claims a Homeric foundation for both philosophical outlooks, arguing that Homer was Socrates's "mentor" and also crediting him with the first paradoxical encomium, since the *Iliad* turns "all the events [of the

Trojan War] topsy-turvy and reverse[s] them."[57] Sophists showcased the Homeric origins of their signature rhetorical techniques by composing mock-encomiastic works based on episodes or characters from Homeric epic; satirical revisions of Homer's account of the Trojan War were a "popular game" throughout antiquity.[58] In addition to Gorgias's *Encomium of Helen* and his *Defence of Palamedes*, works that challenge the *Iliad* by rewriting portions of the poem from competing standpoints, a number of late antique works, including the imaginary "Homeric" speeches of Libanius, several of Dio's *Discourses*, Philostratus's *Heroikos*, and many of Lucian's *Dialogues* offer fictionalized declamations or dialogues that aim at the "correction or emendation" of Homeric texts.[59] On the one hand, these paradoxical encomia and mock-declamations challenge Homer's literary authority by legitimating his most marginalized or maligned characters, by mocking the Homeric gods, or by recounting well-known episodes from a peripheral perspective. Yet on the other hand, the ancient Sophists embrace Homer as their predecessor, and "in a sense rightly so" given their compulsive use of Homeric motifs and allusions.[60]

During the first several decades of the Reformation, mock-encomia and other sophistic genres, adapted to topical use as vehicles for attacking ignorance and contentiousness, playfully manipulate and decontextualize passages from Homer, transforming the Olympian gods into squabbling academics, battlefields into lecture halls, and Trojan and Greek forces into competing theological sects. Like Erasmus before him, Rabelais puts these Homeric conventions to satirical use, enlisting various passages from both the *Iliad* and *Odyssey* in order to inveigh against discord or to envision harmonious (if not also preposterous) solutions to that discord. In so doing, Rabelais exploits the Homeric foundations of the paradoxical encomium, a genre both indebted to and in rivalry with Homeric epic. From Gorgias's *Praise of Helen* to Synesius of Cyrene's *In Praise of Baldness*, classical and late antique mock-encomiasts turn Homeric narratives topsy-turvy and make mischievous use of Homeric material in order to demonstrate, with equal parts affection and derision, his authority as well as his unreliability as a poet. Although Rabelais at times represents sophistry as a threatening or unproductive mode of philosophical discourse, he relies heavily on some stock sophistic techniques, including paradox, antithesis, and parodic quotation or cento-making, in order to represent "two contradictory faces of the same phenomenon" [*deux faces contradictoires d'un même phenomène*].[61]

Rabelais's most immediate source for many of these techniques is Lucian, whose dialogues are a "patchwork of Homeric lines and formulae" put to comic and eristic use: interlocutors swap Homeric allusions in a "slinging match" (as in *The Dead Come to Life*) or they summon up "as many contradictory references as possible out of Homer, Hesiod, and the Homeric hymns" in order to entrap the Olympian gods in inconsistencies and lies (as in *Zeus Catechized*).[62] Lucian's techniques are best understood as a travesty not of Homer per se but rather of his ancient readers, editors, and commentators, who labour to prove (as Porphyry puts it in his *Quaestiones Homericae*) that "Homer explains himself" [*autos men eauton … Homêros exêgeitai*] – in other words, that any unclear or obscure passage in the Homeric poems may be clarified through the proper interpretation of another, clearer passage.[63] This technique was central to the editorial methods of Aristarchus, the Alexandrian grammarian who sought to "clarify Homer with Homer" [*Homêron ex Homêrou saphênizein*] in order to minimize the contradictions inherent in the Homeric corpus and thus produce a coherent and internally consistent text. Lucian, by contrast, places Homeric lines at odds with each other, or cites them out of context, in order to underscore the tensions and incongruities of the texts as a whole and to generate a skirmish of contradictory references that anticipate the "ricochet song" [*chanson du ricochet*] played by Rabelais's Pantagruel and Panurge in chapter 10 of the *Tiers Livre*.[64] Lucian's parodic revisions of Homer also tease out the "unofficial" aspects of his poetry, those suppressed or disparaged by his Alexandrian editors. When Lucian's narrator meets Homer in the *Vera Historia*, he asks the poet whether "the bracketed lines" – the ones obelized by his Alexandrian editors – had been written by him. When Homer takes credit for the passages, the narrator resolves to hold "the grammarians Zenodotus and Aristarchus guilty of pedantry in the highest degree," thus entertaining a fantasized recovery of the "true" Homer – a poet liberated from the erroneous "corrections" made by editors eager to purge inconsistent passages, and a poet whose works sustain rather than foreclose conflict and contradiction.[65]

Rabelais learns from Lucian how to endow the Homeric corpus with a comic spirit of absurdity, contradiction, and disproportion. By incorporating radically decontextualized, inconsistent Homeric lines and episodes into texts that sustain contradiction and dissent, Rabelais transforms Homer into a sceptical instrument able to mediate between contrary opinions and thus support both toleration and dissent. Two of Rabelais's most sustained and complex allusions to Homer are contained within paradoxical encomia: Panurge's encomium on debts (*TL*, 3–5) and his speech in praise of the herb Pantagruelion (*TL*, chaps. 49–52). Flanking the *Tiers Livre*, these episodes are inspired by passages of Homeric epic that were fodder for some of the most far-fetched allegorical exegeses of Homer: Zeus's golden chain speech in Book 8 of the *Iliad* and Hermes's gift of the herb Moly to protect Odysseus from Circe's magic. In the first of these episodes, Panurge engages in a sophistic rhetorical exercise by praising something normally considered unworthy (debt) while simultaneously offering a virtuoso parody of the Neoplatonic allegoresis of Homer's golden chain, a method of reading Homer that Rabelais had already derided in the Prologue to *Gargantua*.[66] In Panurge's mock-allegorical exegesis, the economic bonds of borrowing and lending replace Zeus's cosmic *desmoi* as the ties that bind together the disparate parts of the cosmos. Whereas Ficino's *Commentary on Plato's Symposium* makes "the whole world cohere in mutual love," Panurge perverts this Platonic ideal by applying it to "self-loving, one-way debts, never to be repayed."[67] As an ironic inversion of the kind of cosmic harmony located in Homeric epic by its ancient allegorists, Panurge's "chain of borrowing" travesties the tradition of interpreting the golden chain of Book 8 of the *Iliad* as a master metaphor for concord while simultaneously offering an affectionate parody of Rabelais's own Senecan-Erasmian ideals of gratuitous benefit and mutual fellowship.[68] Thomas Greene has rightly detected the influence of Erasmus upon the episode: taking his cue from adages such as *Amicorum Communia Omnia* and *Dulce Bellum Inexpertis*, Panurge celebrates the network of "mutual bonds linking humanity and all creation in proper spontaneous obligations" but also debases that ideal by illustrating how it may be realized through the "*hexis* of a world bound together by mutual debt."[69]

By imagining a chain of debt that fosters "a connection and colligation between heaven and earth, uniquely preserving the lineage of Man" [*une connexion et colligence des cieulx et terre, un entretenement unicque de l'humain lignaige*], Panurge ironically returns us to an interpretation of Zeus's chain that more closely resembles the logic of the Homeric cosmos, animated by a tug of war that produces harmony out of discord (*TL* 3:383).[70] As he reshapes Homer's golden chain into the *enchaînement* of debt, Rabelais is acutely aware of the fact that Homer's texts are long-suffering victims of such distortive and perverse interpretations. Panurge's speech is a powerful piece of socio-economic satire, but it also travesties the allegorical tendency to excavate cosmological and moral undermeanings in the most unlikely of Homeric passages: if an image of conflict may be remade into a symbol of harmony, then symbols of harmony may likewise be misappropriated by specious or uncharitable interpreters in the service of tyranny, fancy, or self-interest.

Many sixteenth-century readers of Homer read Zeus's speech through the lens of Lucianic satire rather than Platonic allegory. In the margins of his copy of Eustathius, Isaac Casaubon writes in his margins next to the opening lines of the commentary on Book 8 that "this is the fable about the gods enchained [*seiras*], a speech very elegantly expressed by Lucian in his dialogue Mars and Mercury."[71] Panurge's speech likewise takes its cue from Lucian's travesties of the golden chain: in *Zeus Catechized*, Cyniscus undermines the legitimacy of the Homeric gods when he tells Zeus that "your cord and your threats hang by a slender thread," while in *Zeus Rants*, Hermes likewise mocks Zeus's threat to "pull up the earth and the sea from their foundations with ... that cord of gold" as an idle boast that Hermes assesses as bathetic rather than heroic.[72] One of several instances in the *Iliad* in which an Olympian god makes a menacing but unconsummated threat against his adversaries, Zeus's speech is treated by Lucian as an example of *bômolochia*, the "stylized" verbal abuse that links Homeric epic to iambic blame poetry, Old Comedy, and Lucianic dialogue.[73] If the plot of the *Iliad* is "initiated and repeatedly refueled by insult and humiliation," it is especially fitting that Panurge delivers Rabelais's send-up of Zeus's speech, since he is the character most intimately associated with the ritualistic language of insult that functions through a system of "reciprocal exchange."[74] Through Panurge's tour de force of ironic blame-by-praise, Rabelais transforms a prime instance of Homeric blame speech into an extended meditation upon the cosmic *karma* of reciprocity as forged by the *liens* of borrowing and lending, by the mutual exchange of praise and blame, and above all by the ties of mutual fellowship and charity. Like debt, insult is an act that involves more than one person: according to the logic of Rabelaisian insult, "one gives offense and another takes offense or returns it with a counter-offense" in order to foster an atmosphere of "fearless, free ... truth."[75] The reciprocity of insult at times makes it "therapeutic" for Rabelais's characters, whose frequent mutual exchange of insults takes on a healthfully "ludic" dimension.[76]

By creating a network of mutual alliances in which "all are debtors, all are lenders" [*tous soient debteurs, [et] tous soient presteurs*], Panurge's "Homeric chain" [*chaîne homéricque*] provides an intriguing gloss upon the adage that prefaces and governs the *Tiers Livre*: "war is the Father of all that is good" [*guerre estre de tous biens père*] (*TL* 4:386, 3:383, Prologue:366). The maxim, attributed by Rabelais to the pre-Socratic philosopher Heraclitus but probably derived from Erasmus's adage III.v.36 [*Bellum omnium pater*] [War is the father of all things], accrues multiple meanings, both serious and ironic, across the *Tiers Livre*.[77] On the surface,

Rabelais's praise of the beauty and goodness of war is an ironic attack upon France's current state of political and military affairs. But Heraclitus's paradox that "in war all the species of the fair and the good do appear" [*en guerre apparoisse toute espèce de bien et beau*] also illustrates the oxymoronic logic of the *Tiers Livre* itself, a world governed by antiphrasis, antilogic, and antithesis (*TL* Prologue:366).[78] In fragments cited frequently by sixteenth-century scholars, Heraclitus repeatedly finds fault with Homer for his inability to grasp that "unity underlies ... opposition" and thus to recognize that war, despite its horrors, nonetheless plays an essential role in preserving the harmony of the universe.[79] While Rabelais does not intend to endorse the virtues of war in a literal sense, his invocation of Heraclitus's criticism of Homer signals his conviction that discord may be productive of harmony, rather than its simple contrary.

If discord can yield to harmony, tragedy likewise yields to comedy in Rabelais's parodic cosmos. In *Pantagruel*, this comic transvaluation of Homeric epic takes place through the creation of two different versions of Odysseus in the figures of Panurge and Epistémon. Epistémon's journey to the Champs Elysées in chapter 30 of *Pantagruel* is a "radical version of an underworld visit" that David Marsh finds deeply indebted to Lucian's *Menippus* even as the episode also "caricatures the *Odyssey*" and Plato's myth of Er.[80] Epistémon's parodic *nekyia* adheres closely to the underworld experiences of Homer's Odysseus, a figure with whom Epistémon has already earned comparison for his crooked wisdom: in chapter 24, we learn that Epistémon belongs to "the lineage of Sinon" [*la lignée de Sinon*] and knows "all the feints and subterfuges of the art of war" [*toutes les ruses et finesses de discipline militaire*] (*P* 24:312). Inasmuch as it turns the Iliadic values of honour and fame topsy-turvy, Odysseus's descent to Hades in Book 11 of the *Odyssey* is itself somewhat parodic of Iliadic values, and the underworld visited by Epistémon follows suit, a place where the values and hierarchies of the mortal world are "altered in an outlandish fashion" [*changé en estrange façon*] (*P* 30:335). In his pseudo-epic catalogue of Homeric worthies stripped of their heroic stature, Rabelais does not mock Homer so much as channel a profoundly counter-epic impulse already latent in the *Odyssey*. In Rabelais's underworld, Achilles is turned into a "dyer, Agamemnon a licker-out of dishes, Ulysses a scyther, Nestor, a rag-and-bone man ... Priam traded in rags and tatters ... Hector a stir-sauce, Paris a tattered beggar, Achilles, a baler-up of hay" [*Achilles, teigneux, Agamenon, liche casse, Ulysses, faucheur, Nestor, harpailleur ... Priam vendoit les vieulx drapeaulx ... Hector estoit fripe saulce, Paris estoit pauvre loqueteux, Achilles, boteleur de foin*] (*P* 30:335–6).[81] By effacing the marks of honour and virtue that distinguish Homer's heroes from their sub-heroic counterparts, Rabelais's counter-epic underworld generates an "an ironic reworking" of the *Iliad* that resembles Homer's "complex mode of comedy" in the *Odyssey*, a comedy that turns on the profound physical and moral transformation to which the *Iliad*'s heroes are subjected after death.[82] In voicing his preference to be a slave – or, in Rabelais's version, a hay baler – on earth rather than be lord over his fellow shades in Hades, Achilles rejects the honour-seeking heroic ethos of the *Iliad* in favour of the *Odyssey*'s sceptical undermining of it. Although a number of critics, including Duval, have claimed that chapter 30 of *Pantagruel* is "highly unorthodox" in its "moralizing version of the epic underworld," the changes of fortune that Rabelais's Homeric worthies undergo bear a striking similarity to those experienced in the *Odyssey*'s own, carnivalesque underworld, a place that challenges the false or outmoded forms of heroism that dominate the *Iliad*.[83]

Parallel Burlesques: Comedy, Copia, and Consumption

Early modern readers of Homer and Rabelais are alert to their shared predilection for irony, bathos, linguistic play, exaggeration, and the use of various textual strategies that support "opposed and mutually conditioning voices or viewpoints."[84] In a 1711 treatise entitled the *Parallele Burlesque, ou Dissertation, ou Discours qu'on nommera comme on voudra, sur Homere et Rabelais* (Parallel Burlesque, or Dissertation, or Discourse-call-it-what-you-will, on Homer and Rabelais), Charles Rivière Dufresny argues that one of the chief parallels between Rabelais and his Greek predecessor is their tendency to mix high and low styles and subjects. Moving back and forth between "the small and the large, and the high and the low" [*du petit and du grand, du haut and du bas*], both Homer and Rabelais collapse the "sublime" and the ridiculous by using "badinage" in the service of "grandeur."[85]

Dufresny's admiration for Homer and Rabelais's shared capacity for badinage – joking or play – deviates from the canons of neoclassical literary criticism, which was for the most part quick to condemn the frivolity and levity of Homeric epic. In his 1664 *Comparaison des Poëmes d'Homere et de Virgile*, René Rapin voices an objection common to his era when, following Horace (*Ars Poetica* 359), he criticizes Homer as a poet who "forgets himself sometimes" [*s'oublie quelquefois*] but then qualifies that Homer does not nod off but rather "plays the jester from time to time in degenerating into the familiar and turning things around with a joking attitude" [*devient badin de temps en temps, en degenerant dans le familier, and tournant les choses d'un air de plaisanterie*].[86] While Rapin finds Homer's jocular attitude distastefully vulgar, his contemporary René Le Bossu praises Homer's lowly and humble qualities in his *Traité du poëme epique* (1675), translated into English as *A Treatise of the Epick Poem*. Invoking Horace's condemnation of epic bombast from the *Ars Poetica* – "the mountains labour, and a mouse is born" – Le Bossu proceeds to praise the *Odyssey* as "simple and modest," since it proposes no "great actions" for its hero.[87] In chapter 24 of the *Tiers Livre*, Epistémon paraphrases the very same line from Horace, a phrase that gained common currency as one of Erasmus's *Adages*, *Parturiunt montes*, where it serves to condemn braggarts who promise great things but produce only (as Screech brilliantly translates the phrase) "amousing trifles" [*une petite souriz*] (*TL* 24:456).[88] In typically Rabelaisian style, Epistémon misconstrues the phrase, suggesting that it refers to a woman in the throes of childbirth who, despite "cries and lamentation" that suggest the imminent arrival of a monstrously large child, delivers only a "trifling mouse/smile" [*A son cris et lamentation accourut tout le voisinaige, en expectation de veoir quelque admirable et monstrueux enfantement; mais enfin ne nasquit d'elle qu'une petite souriz*] (*TL* 24:456). In the *Ars Poetica*, however, the phrase is directed against poets who slavishly imitate Homer by using hackneyed and hyperbolic invocations such as, "as the Cyclic poet of old: / 'Of Priam's fate and famous men I'll sing'" [*ut scriptor cyclicus olim: / 'fortunam Priami cantabo et nobile bellum'*].[89] Instead of pursuing the "foolish effort" [*molitur inepte*] of imitating the *Iliad*, Horace recommends that poets open with invocations such as the one that begins the *Odyssey*: "Sing, Muse ..." [*dic mihi, Musa*].[90] According to Horace, the proper stance of the epic poet should be humility, not boastfulness: he should aim at all times to undercut expectation with a self-deprecating modesty that approaches irony. Panurge's French rendition of the Horatian passage hints at precisely this principle as he ekes out a pun on *souriz* [mouse] and *soubrys* [smile], a near-homonym which suggests that the poet who wishes to imitate Homer effectively must shun the grand style of the *Iliad* in favour of the modest and homely tone of the *Odyssey* or even *The Battle of the Frogs and the Mice*.

Rabelais's adaptation of Horace's lesson on how not to become a Homeric poet contributes to his larger project of mocking epic hyperbole – the kind of exaggeration that makes "an elephant out of a fly" [*elephantum ex musca facis*], to cite the adage that Erasmus derives, via Lucian, from Homer.[91] Only one chapter earlier in the *Tiers Livre*, Panurge paraphrases the description of Ares's resounding cry at *Il.* 5.859 when, injured by Diomedes, "Homer says that he yelled at a higher pitch and with more terrifying shrieks than ten thousand men put together" [*Homère dict avoir crié en plus hault ton et plus horrificque effroy que ne feroient dix mille hommes ensemble*] (*TL* 23:454). The passage demonstrates the hyperbolic pitch of many Homeric allusions in Rabelais's work, particularly in *Gargantua*, where the young giant's outrageously long gestation is backed up by the authority of "Homer, who says that the child with whom Neptune impregnated the nymph was delivered after one year had gone by" [*Homère [dit] que l'enfant duquel Neptune engroissa la nymphe nasquit l'an après révolu*], his booming voice is compared to that of "Stentor ... at the battle of Troy" [*Stentor ... à la bataille de Troye*], and the long lists of countries and wildfowl in chapters 33 and 37 approach the gigantic dimensions of the *Iliad*'s epic catalogues (*G* 3:47, *G* 23:114). In contradistinction to the mountain-labouring epic of Horace's bad imitators of Homer, the hyperboles of *Gargantua* instead emulate Homer's gargantuan exceeding of rhetorical and logical norms, a habit that produces not grandeur but copious extravagance.[92]

Like *In Praise of Folly*, which authorizes its *gioco*-serious tone by appealing to the "Homeric method of leaving the heavens in order to return to earth" [*la façon Homerique de quitter les cieux pour revenir sur terre*], Rabelais invokes Homeric lines, episodes, and conventions in order to legitimate his own debasement or distortion of epic norms.[93] Often, these allusions fix upon the most sub-heroic and (to some Renaissance readers) the most indecorous aspects of the Homeric poems, in particular scenes of laughter, eating, drinking, and other bodily urges, all cornerstones of the Rabelaisian carnivalesque. In chapter 11 of the *Quart Livre*, Pantagruel recounts a story related by Plutarch, Dio Chrysostom, and Erasmus that provides an implicit defence of Homeric and Rabelaisian indecorum. The story relates how Antigonus, King of Macedonia, discovers the poet Antagoras in his kitchen frying eels. "Was Homer frying conger-eels when he described the prowesses of Agamemnon?" [*Homère fricassoit-il congres, lorsqu'il descripvoit les prouesses de Agamennon*], the king asks the poet indignantly, to which the poet answers, "do you think that when Agamemnon was performing those prowesses, he ever thought of asking whether anyone in his camp was frying up eels?" [*estimes-tu que Agamennon, lorsque telles prouesses faisoit, feust curieux de sçavoir si personne en son camp fricassoit congres*] (*QL* 11:612). As a poet imagined as cooking up a plate of eels while singing about the great deeds of Agamemnon, the Homer of Pantagruel's anecdote is allowed to traverse social and rhetorical boundaries in a manner that erodes the distinction between epic and mock-epic by conflating the dignified art of poetry with the very undignified *technê* of cooking.[94]

In Rabelais's hands, the story serves to defend the fricassee-like admixture of high and low subjects and styles typical of the Homeric corpus as he understands it. It also provides a riposte to the myriad complaints about dietary indecorum in Homeric epic voiced as far back as Plato, who protests that soldiers should not "convey pots and pans along" to battle.[95] Similar objections surface periodically during the early modern period, reaching a fever pitch at the beginning of the eighteenth century. The Italian humanist Angelus Decembrius (ca 1415–66) exalts Virgil above Homer because the Roman poet does not depict "everything that happens privately or is said publicly, as did Homer, the most copious in the Greek manner of speaking, who brought even housewives' salted fish and porridge together with the deeds of heroes" [*ita non de omnibus quae vel privatim fiunt, seu publice dicuntur, poeta noster recensendum excogitavit: ut Homerus graecorum more dicendi copiosissimus, qui mulierum etiam salsamenta et pultes in heroum gesta contulerit*].[96] Similar objections punctuate neoclassical literary-critical treatises by Houdar De La Motte, Claude Fleury, and Anne Dacier, who protest the inappropriateness of representing "kings cook[ing] meat."[97] But for Rabelais, the poet who sautées a meal while reciting a heroic battle scene marks him as resistant to the generic and social conventions that falsely divide heroic action from baser impulses and appetites, a lesson repeatedly enforced by the hunger-driven exploits of Gargantua and Panurge.

Pantagruel's anecdote places the Homeric poet in the humble surroundings of a kitchen in order to overturn the distinctions between high and low likewise upset by *Pantagruel*'s topsy-turvy underworld, where Homeric heroes, divested of their heroic stature, are engaged in menial culinary tasks. Hector acts as a "fripesauce," or saucier, while Agamemnon becomes a "lichecasse," or dish-licker, jobs that evoke the names of the creatures in the *Batrachomyomachia*, known by epithets such as "Lick-platter" [*Leichopinax*] and "Crumb-snatcher" [*Psicharpax*].[98] By imagining Hades as a kitchen and Iliadic heroes as its line cooks, Rabelais not only dramatizes Menippus's observation that the pagan underworld effaces social distinctions but also enlists Homer as a chief resource in what Dorothy Coleman has aptly termed Rabelais's "epic treatment of appetite."[99] As he adapts various episodes and passages from the *Odyssey*, Rabelais expands upon Homer's own reflections upon the exigencies of hunger – and upon the pleasure of its satisfaction – in order to craft a text that makes "fear of hunger" a key motive for heroic action.[100]

Food is a prime source of comic tension in the *Odyssey*.[101] Through Panurge, the appetite-driven beggar whose continual quest to satisfy his hunger inspires his cunning, Rabelais turns a pastiche of Homeric maxims concerning the belly and its demands into the motive power of his narrative: the procurement and enjoyment of food. In chapter 9 of *Pantagruel*, a scene acknowledged by many critics to be deeply and complexly indebted to Homer, Rabelais assembles a veritable cento of Homeric allusions to establish Panurge's associations with Odysseus and, by extension, to posit a causal link between hunger and verbal wit or cleverness.[102] Like Odysseus, Panurge is reduced to beggary; like Odysseus, moreover, Panurge relies upon feats of rhetorical virtuosity in order to secure food from Pantagruel and Epistémon, even comparing himself to his Homeric prototype in a speech that echoes Odysseus's observation that "nothing is more shameless than one's hateful belly [*gasteri*]." "Just now," Panurge pleads, "I have a more pressing necessity: to feed! Everything is ready: sharp teeth, empty belly, dry throat and screaming appetite" [*pour ceste heure j'ay nécessité bien urgente de repaistre: dentz agues, ventre vuyde, gorge seiche, appétit strident*] (*Od.* 7.216–17; *P* 9:256).

Panurge's repeated requests for food in thirteen different languages (four of them imaginary) demonstrate hunger to be a powerful rhetorician, a forceful persuader whose pleas cannot be denied. Panurge's argument that hunger speaks louder than words is aptly expressed in the Greek of his Homeric model: "talk and words are superfluous when the facts are clear to everyone. Discussion is required only when the facts discussed are not evident" [*tote logus te ce rhemata peritta hurparchin, opote pragma asto pasi delon esti. Entha gar anancei monon logi isin, hina pragmata (hon peri amphisbetumen) me prosphoros epiphenete*] (*P* 9:254–5). Inspired partly by Eumaeus's punning remark to the disguised Odysseus that "wanderers [*alêtai*] in need of sustenance tell lies at random and have no desire to speak the truth [*alêthea*]," Panurge's Greek plea for food during his first appearance in *Pantagruel* magnifies the appetite-driven motives of Odysseus's own epic return, a reading already lurking in ancient burlesques such as Cratinus's *The Odysseuses*, which depicts Polyphemus as an expert cook.[103] When Panurge (in intelligible Latin) begs for food by citing "that old adage which says a hungry belly has no ears," a maxim cited once again in the *Tiers Livre* ["*Le ventre affamé n'a poinct d'aureilles*"], he echoes several adages of Erasmus that capture the mutually constitutive relationship between hunger and rhetorical ingenuity (*P*9:255; *TL*15: 424). In *Ventres* (Bellies), *Venter auribus caret* (The belly has no ears), *Glôssogastores* (Bellytalkers), and *Necessitas magistra* (Necessity is a teacher), Erasmus describes hunger as a persuasive rhetorician who "admits no counter-argument."[104] Although Erasmus condemns *gastrimargoi* as men who are slaves to their stomachs and resort to unscrupulous rhetoric in order to satiate their appetites, Rabelais strikes a much more positive stance towards the stomach as "master of art and bestower of wit" [*Magister artis ingenique largitor*], a phrase that Erasmus adapts from Persius in order to testify to the way that hunger may stimulate inventiveness and mental acuity.[105] Unlike Erasmus, who criticizes "bellytalkers" for "hav[ing] a tongue that can be bought and say only what profits their belly" [*Qui linguam habent venalem, ea loquentes quae ventri conducunt*], Rabelais transforms the *Adages* into a celebration of the rhetorical skills nurtured by hunger, a quality nowhere more evident than in the writer's own lengthy catalogues of foodstuffs, virtuoso performances of linguistic *copia* that supplement the cornucopia of the table.[106]

Rabelais thus transforms the hunger that is "an accursed plague" for Homer's Odysseus into a source of *jouissance*.[107] "Homer never wrote fasting" [*Homère jamais n'escrivit à jeun*], observes the Prologue to the *Tiers Livre*, and his satiety ensures a "living spring, an everlasting stream" [*source vive et veine perpétuelle*] of poetry, a "real cornucopia of joy and merriment" [*vraye Cornucopie de joyeuseté et raillerie*] (*TL* Prologue:367, Prologue:371). Taking his cue from the many classical and late antique commentators who interpret the *Odyssey* as anticipating Epicurean attitudes towards the satisfaction of hunger as a natural and virtuous pleasure, Rabelais models Pantagruel and Panurge on an Odyssean spirit of gustatory pleasure but also on the voracious gluttons of pseudo-Homeric mock-epic poems such as *Margites*.[108] In chapter 13 of the *Tiers Livre*, Pantagruel challenges the health benefits of fasting by citing "the authority of Homer, the Father of all philosophy, who says that the Greeks stopped weeping out of grief for Patroclus, the great friend of Achilles, when, and only when, hunger showed itself and their bellies swore to supply no more tears" [*l'auctorité de Homère, pere de toute philosophie, qui dict les Grègeoys lors, non plus tost, avoir mis à leurs larmes fin du dueil de Patroclus le grand amy de Achilles, quand la faim se déclaira et leurs ventres protestèrent plus de larmes ne les fournir*] (*TL* 13:417). Unlike Homer's Achilles, who refuses to eat until he has slaked his appetite for grief and only reluctantly participates in the "loathsome banquet" [*stugerê ...daiti*] held in the dead Patroclus's honour, Rabelais's Pantagruel emulates the gastronomic prudence of Odysseus, who persuades his fellow Achaeans that "food and wine" [*sitou kai oinoio*] will give them "courage and strength" [*menos ... kai alkê*] for the battle that lies ahead (*Il.* 23.48, 19.161).

For Odysseus, as for Pantagruel and Panurge, food and wine are therapeutic, antidotes that nurture peace, fellowship, and sweet sleep.[109] In Phaiakia, Odysseus resolves to eat even though he is "laden with grief" [*phresi penthos echonta*], reasoning that eating will make him "forget [*lêthanei*] all that I have suffered" (*Od.* 7.218–21). Yet Rabelais also follows Homer in cautioning against gastronomic excess: just after Pantagruel appeals to Homer's endorsement of mid-war snacks, he observes that "in all cases the mean is to be praised" [*Mediocrité est en tous cas louée*], echoing a piece of wisdom voiced by the Delphic oracle but also by Homer's Alkinous, the Phaiakian king who twice repeats the maxim that "moderation is best in all things" [*ameinô d'aisima panta*] (*TL* 13:417; *Od.* 7.310). Even so, the temperate Alkinous is descended from the same lineage as the cannibalistic Polyphemus, a genealogy that according to Jenny Strauss Clay complicates the *Odyssey*'s "opposition between civilization and barbarism" and between restraint and excess.[110] Homer's Polyphemus may at first appear to resemble Rabelais's voracious protagonists inasmuch as the "only authority" the Cyclops recognizes is his own "*thumos*" or appetite.[111] But the immoderate appetites of Rabelais's giants redeem voracious hunger by partnering it with more spiritually legitimate expressions of abundance such as linguistic *copia* and charity. In *Gargantua and Pantagruel*, hunger has the power to distort, making small things great and great things small, but it also has the power to rectify the spiritual deformations to which mortals are subject.[112]

In Phaiakia, Odysseus learns to appreciate the intertwined pleasures of food and poetry and to satisfy his appetite without abusing it through excessive food or drink. Yet Odysseus's cunning or *panourgos* nature places him in situations that demand the periodic suspension of moderation and civility in order to secure food.[113] Rabelais exaggerates this Odyssean narrative, motivated by the appetites of its hero, his crew, and the suitors, by writing a series of Odyssean journeys that culminate in the *nostos* of a mouth or a belly. At the end of *Pantagruel*, we are transported to the world inside Pantagruel's mouth (*P* 32), while in the *Quart Livre*, the protagonists embark upon what Alice Berry calls an "*Odyssey* of the stomach" [*Odyssée du Ventre*] that leads its characters through a digestive track even more ambagious than the Homeric journey upon which it is modelled.[114] This second journey may be viewed as an allegory of digestion that mimics or parodies an epic *nekyia*: the coils of the intestines are so many circles of a Rabelaisian inferno whose lowest level symbolizes "the fleshly appetite that absorbs all" [*la consommation charnelle [qui] absorbe tout*].[115]

Such a reading accords with Rabelais's emphasis on the tyranny of hunger, a motif likewise grounded in Homeric allusions and narrative strategies. At the beginning of the *Tiers Livre*, Rabelais reminds us that when Achilles accuses Agamemnon of tyranny, he calls him "Demoboros, that is, Devourer of his people" [*demovore, c'est à dire mangeur du peuple*], an allusion pilfered from Erasmus, who twice cites the Homeric phrase "people-devouring king" [*dêmoboros basileus*] as an epithet for tyrants who figuratively cannibalize their subjects (*TL* 1:374–75, citing *Il.* 1.231).[116] The metaphor of the tyrant hunger is literalized by the Gastrolastres of *Quart Livre*, chapters 57–62, who exercise a "ventripotent" form of tyranny through the idolatrous worship of their bellies such that their stomach becomes their God: "le Ventre est le Dieu" (*QL* 60:743, 58:739). Although the Gastrolastres, like Euripides's Polyphemus, worship their bellies as "the greatest of all the gods" [*le plus grand de tous les Dieux*], their leader, Master Gaster, possesses a remarkable inventiveness stimulated by appetite even as his followers are rendered "lazy" [*ocieux*] by overeating, becoming "a useless load and burden on the world" [*poys et charge inutile de la terre*] (*QL* 58:738, 62:748, 58:739). This last passage transforms a well-known line from the *Iliad* (18.104), spoken by Achilles as he laments his inaction as a soldier, into a condemnation of gluttony.[117] Yet the desperate search for sustenance may also incite heroic action, as it does in the final two books of Rabelais's work, driven by a quest for the "dive bouteille," an oracular bottle of wine that leads to "knowledge of the divine" [*la congnoissance divine*] and "flood[s] the mind with all truth" [*remplir l'âme de toute vérité*] (*CL* 47:917, 45:909). When Panurge and Pantagruel at last receive their oracular command – "Trinch!" – at the end of the *Cinquième Livre*, Bacbuc sends them on their way by urging them to cultivate the virtue that Homer and Herodotus call "*alphestes*, that is to say researchers and inventors" [*alphestes, c'est à dire rechercheurs et inventeurs*] (*CL* 47:916n). The lesson elaborates on the ways in which Odyssean *mêtis* – the cunning intelligence that unites the hungry beggar and the poet – makes use of appetite in the service of poetic inspiration.

If food, in the Rabelaisian vision of the Homeric cosmos, stimulates heroic action and poetic wit, Rabelais's figure of the "vinosus" Homer also generates a theory of *copia* that unites gastronomic with linguistic superabundance. Rabelais repeatedly emulates what might best be termed the "overstuffed" style of the Homeric poems.[118] In the *Quart Livre*, Master Gaster teases out the double meaning of the word *farci* – farcical, but also a term that refers to any food stuffed with another kind of food – in order to establish a far-reaching set of correspondences between linguistic *copia* and gastronomic excess.[119] Rabelais plays with these correspondences in his repeated invocations of the Trojan horse, an object whose "stuffed" or *farci* nature is transformed into a symbol of culinary extravagance in Erasmus's *Porcus Trojanus*, an adage that describes the Roman custom of serving up a large animal, such as an ox or a camel, with smaller, edible dainties inside of it.[120] In Rabelais's handling, the Trojan horse is a consummate metaphor for linguistic and culinary excess that is generative rather than decadent. When Pantagruel is cured of a stubborn "mound of ordure" [*montjoye d'ordure*] by men descending into his belly with pickaxes, he vomits them back up and they emerge from their capsules like "the Greeks emerging from the Trojan horse" [*les Grégeoys sortirent du cheval en Troye*] (*P* 33:349–50). In the *Quart Livre*, Rabelais profts from a pun on Troie and Truye (the French word for sow) as he describes how some engineers fashion a sort of *porcus Trojanus* in order to combat the Andouilles: they fit up a pig [*truye*] that fires cannonballs and also conceals more than two hundred men inside it. Before launching into an epic catalogue of the men who enter the sow – figures whose names run the culinary gamut from "Bellardon" (pretty bacon) to "Leschevin" (lick-wine) – the narrator praises these "doughty and valiant cooks who entered the sow as into the Trojan horse" [*des preux et vaillans cuisiniers, lesquelz, comme dedans le cheval de Troye, entrèrent dedans la Truye*] (*QL* 40:690).

In both scenes, the Trojan horse symbolizes a plenitude that is at once rhetorical and gastronomic. Classical parodies of Homer often use similar strategies to transform heroic quests into culinary ones while simultaneously demonstrating the abundance and flexibility latent in the language of Homeric epic, transmuted easily by the parodist into a menu or a description of a feast. In addition to the pseudo-Homeric *Margites*, the fragmentary remains of poets such as Hegemon and Matro of Pitane feature hungry, comical anti-heroes goaded by their appetites through landscapes that take satirical aim at the ethical and rhetorical conventions of Homeric epic.[121] Although the fragments of Hegemon and Matro were not printed until Estienne's editions of 1573 and 1575, Rabelais would have encountered their extant writings in Athenaeus's *Deipnosophists*, first edited by Marcus Musurus (Venice: Aldus, 1514); the work appears as one of the ancient texts recommended by Gargantua to his son.[122] In a section drawn from the treatise "The Life of the Heroes in Homer," Athenaeus praises the poet for inculcating moderate and disciplined appetites, and his symposiasts interpret the *Iliad* and *Odyssey* as dietary treatises, quoting at length from various *parodoi* whose improvised imitations of Homer distort familiar verses into mock-epic accounts of feasts.[123] The work of one such parodist, Hipponax, stars a glutton named Eurymedontiades, its invocation riffing on the *Odyssey* as it introduces the defining characteristic of its protagonist: "Tell me, Muse, of that maelstrom wide as the sea, that belly-knife, son of Eurymedon, who eats indecently."[124]

Other Homer parodies preserved in Athenaeus, including the *Egyptian Iliad* (*Aigyptiakê Ilias*) and Archestratus of Gela's *The Life of Pleasure* (*Hedupatheia*), also narrate gastronomic quests, cultivating a "decidedly sub-heroic" tone by reassembling "scattered bits and pieces of verse from Homer and Hesiod" into mock-epic "gastrologies" that send their heroes travelling over land and sea for tasty delicacies.[125] These Homer parodies – including the outrageous 142-line *Deipnon* (*Dinner*) of Matro of Pitane (fourth century BCE), whose gluttonous hero wanders across an enormous buffet of cuttlefish and conger eel – are all constructed through a cento-like pastiche of Homeric lines and epithets that turn stock Homeric phrases such as the "white-armed goddess Hera" [*thea leukôlenos Herê*] into exotic dishes such as a "divinely tasty white fish" [*thea leukôlenos Ichthus*].[126] Despite the seeming abuse to which these parodies subject Homer's texts, the poems of Hegemon, Hipponax, and Matro also seize upon Homer's own preoccupation with food and drink in a manner likewise typical of one of Rabelais's more immediate sources, Teofilo Folengo's *Baldus*, first printed at Venice in 1517 and enlarged (as the *Opus Macaronicorum*) in 1521. A mock-heroic quest for the "many odd components required for concocting treacle," Folengo's poem transforms the Elysian fields into an all-you-can-eat paradise while Parnassus, home to the narrator's "paunchy Muses," metamorphoses into a sea of gravy in which goddesses, seated in boats of pastry, "fish for gnocchi, fritters, and golden meatballs" [*piscantes gnoccos, fritolas gialdasque tomaclas*].[127]

In Folengo, as in Rabelais, gastronomic and linguistic copiousness go hand in hand. The titular pasta of the *Opus Macaronicorum* comes to be synonymous with the poem's coarse and motley dialect. As a form "inseparably linked to a carnival sense of the world," parody generates an excess that is intrinsically linked to the world of food and drink, perhaps explaining why even the most serious scholars of the period, such as J.C. Scaliger, thought it fitting to compose parodies of Virgil that turn the poet's heroic subject matter into a series of poems on the "subject of drink."[128] By travestying epic conventions and imagining mock-epic food fights wielded with weapons such as game-puddings, dumplings, and sausages (*QL* 35 and 36), Folengo and Rabelais build a series of associations between parody and gastronomic satiety, a connection strengthened by the false but common etymology of the word *parôdia*, whose suffix Henri Estienne traces either to *ôdê*, meaning "poetic tribute" [*poetis tribuatur*] or to *adên* (to one's fill, to satiety). Estienne's second derivation of the term makes parody a species of *copia*, a generic form that distorts through overstuffing much like Rabelais's Trojan horses, crammed full of Homeric matter that is transmuted into a "mound of ordure."

Margites, or, Death by Laughter

In his *Poetics*, Aristotle identifies the pseudo-Homeric *Margites* as the first paradoxical encomium, a poem that demonstrates his exemplary skill as a comic poet. While Homer is the "supreme poet of elevated subjects" according to Aristotle, he is also "the first to delineate the forms of comedy, by dramatizing not invective but the laughable: thus the *Margites* stands in the same relation to comedy as do the *Iliad* and *Odyssey* to tragedy."[129] The pseudo-Homeric *Batrachomyomachia* was, as we have seen, extremely popular during the late fifteenth and early sixteenth centuries, its brevity lending itself to frequent printings and to classroom use. The *Margites* also attracted its fair share of attention during the period, in spite of the fact that it was, and still is, extant only in a few brief fragments. One of these fragments is preserved in the pseudo-Platonic *Second Alcibiades*, where Socrates makes a derisive remark about the poem's eponymous hero as a man who "knew many things but knew all of them badly" [*Polla men êpistato erga, kakôs de phêsin, êpistato panta*].[130] Like the *Kerkôpes*, another mock-epic formerly attributed to Homer about two knavish brothers – literally, "tail-men" or "dick-faces" – who travel around the world deceiving people, the hero of the *Margites*, whose name (from the Greek *margos*) means reckless, ravenous, or greedy, is also characterized by his *panourgia*, or mischief, as well as by his insatiable appetite. In one of the only remaining fragments of the work, Margites gets his penis caught in a narrow-necked chamber pot while attempting to evacuate in an inconspicuous place in the middle of the night.[131]

The pseudo-Homeric *Margites* was resuscitated at the end of the fifteenth century from the oblivion that condemns most non-extant texts by way of Margutte, Morgante's short-lived but memorable companion in Luigi Pulci's 1483 *Morgante Maggiore*. Pulci's lively parody of chivalric romance influenced the mock-epic adventures of Rabelais's equally gigantic and gluttonous protagonists, shaping the latter writer's appreciation of the parodic potential latent in Homeric narratives. Driven by persistent hunger, self-interest, and curiosity, Pulci's Margutte is a wandering musician who dreams that he will "someday / Troy, Hector, and Achilles sing in rhyme," a fantasy that casts him as a Homeric bard who, like the disguised Odysseus, must rely upon his *mêtis* to survive in an adverse world.[132] In a scene that anticipates chapter 9 of *Pantragruel*, when Margutte meets Morgante, he declares himself to be neither Christian nor Saracen but instead an adherent to the religion of capon, butter, beer, and cake, a creed to which he remains faithful by partaking, along with Pulci's hero, in several exotic feasts featuring a buffalo, an elephant, and even a unicorn. But the gastronomic adventures of the two giants come to a premature and bizarre end when Margutte becomes the victim of his companion's practical joke. While Margutte is asleep, Morgante hides his shoes, and he awakes just in time to see that "a little monkey had got hold of them, and had already tried them on and off." Margutte begins to laugh and cannot stop:

> he kept on laughing, and his laughter grew
> so loud, his chest, which needed some relief,
> could not at all some respite ever find,
> so much impeded and constrained and blocked.
> The little monkey tried them on again;
> Margutte's laughter reached such a commotion,
> there was right in the end a great explosion.[133]

Despite the apparent disparity between Pulci's ill-fated giant, felled by excessive laughter, and the gravitas with which most Homeric heroes meet their deaths, the scene draws its inspiration from a collage of Homeric and para-Homeric sources. Margutte falls prey to the *asbestos gelos*, or inextinguishable laughter, associated with the Olympian gods as well as with the suitors of the *Odyssey*, whose laughter inspires the "proverbial hyperbole" *emori risu* (to die laughing), an adage that Erasmus derives from *Od.* 18.99–100.[134] But Margutte's end also resembles that of Homer himself: according to a widely circulated anecdote, the poet died at the hand of a riddle. In a story recounted in both ancient *Lives* of Homer and repeated by a number of early sixteenth-century writers including Melanchthon, Francesco Berni, and Ravisius Textor, some young fishermen tell Homer an "intricate and perplexing enigma" [*intricatum & perplexum aenigma*] that, in Textor's Latin version, reads, "what we caught, we left behind; what we did not catch we took away with us" [*se quaecumque cepissent, reliquisse: quae vero non cepissent habere*].[135] Either because he is unable to come up with the solution to the riddle – the boys have left what they caught (their fish) behind but they have nonetheless departed with some lice (what they did not catch but still took away) – or because the answer sends the poet into a fit of hilarity, Homer succumbs to the same kind of fatally bad humour that finishes off Pulci's Margutte as well as Thomas Urquhart, Rabelais's English translator, who was reputed to have dropped dead from a fit of hilarity upon hearing of the Restoration of the Stuart monarchy.

Why did so many late fifteenth- and sixteenth-century writers find this account of Homer's death-by-riddle so compelling? In part, the anecdote's appeal resides in its depiction of Homer as a shabby, low-life character; in part, it plays into a tradition of interpreting the Homeric corpus as a philosophical and medical resource on laughter, particularly the sort of morbid laughter associated with physiological intemperance and even death. From the cruel chuckling of the Olympian gods at Hephaestus's deformities to the suitors' scornful howls at the beggars in their midst, Homeric laughter is cruel and savage, a symptom of the poet's tragic irony and pessimism rather than a diversion from it. Renaissance writers are attentive to dark and sinister laughter in Homeric texts and paratexts, and contemporary treatises on laughter often cite Homer alongside Galen and Hippocrates as an authority on the physical processes and effects of laughter. In a manuscript notebook culled from Eustathius's commentary on the *Odyssey*, the seventeenth-century French writer Pierre de Marcassus reveals a keen interest in the poem's many scenes of excessive, demented, or otherwise discomfiting laughter. Marcassus paraphrases an anecdote about the Tyrinthians, an ancient Greek civilization afflicted with persistent laughter who fall into a "very amusing raillery" [*raillerie fort plaisante*] when they sacrifice a bull to Neptune in order to rid themselves of the condition that also afflicts Pulci's Margutte, cursed with such incessant laughter that he cannot desist from chuckling even in the afterworld and thus supplies "the only fun allowed in hell."[136]

A number of Renaissance writers look to Homer to anatomize different species of laughter and to explore its physiological causes and effects. Laurent Joubert, whose theories of laughter often provide a contemporary medical context for Rabelais thanks to their shared medical training in sixteenth-century Montpellier, cites several Homeric examples in his discussion of Sardonian, or sardonic, laughter, a "feigned and simulated laughter" that emanates from people who delight in "cover[ing] their malevolence."[137] According to Joubert, Odysseus smiles "a most sardanian and bitter smile" when Ctesippus throws an ox-hoof at him but misses; Joubert cites Eustathius's interpretation of the passage (*Od.* 20.302) as well as several other passages in Homer that depict characters as laughing or smiling out of "rage, felony, or ill-will," including the mean-spirited grin emitted by Hera as she plots the seduction of her husband (*Il.* 14.222–3) and the grim smirk that comes over Ajax's face as he arms himself for battle with Hector (*Il.* 7.212).[138] For Joubert, these passages exemplify the Hippocratic physiological principle that laughter is "born of two contraries" rather than out of one single emotion or physiological mechanism.[139] Produced by a "contrariety or battle of two feelings," such as joy and sorrow, laughter is the result of two conflicting physical impulses, the alternating contraction and dilation of the chest.[140] While these contrary impulses, as well as the heat and cold that produce them, ought to counterbalance each other in order to temper the body's humours, it is possible, argues Joubert, that when these alternating contractions and dilations are too quick or extreme, laughter may "extinguis[h] and suffocat[e]" its victim, causing loss of consciousness or even death.[141]

Brought about by excessive heat in the extremities produced by an overactive spleen, lethal or inextinguishable laughter – what Homer calls *asbestos gelôs* – is evidence for Joubert of the intemperance of the Homeric gods.[142] Ludovico Ricchieri espouses a similar theory in his oft-reprinted *Lectionum Antiquarum libri* of 1517, which cites the "*gelôta asbestos*" of the Homeric gods as proof that an excessively splenetic humour produces copious and "inextinguishable" [*inextinguibilem*] laughter, while a 1566 commentary on the opening book of the *Iliad* explains that Hephaestus excites laughter among his fellow gods because he symbolizes the excessive heat generated by their spleens.[143] By marrying the traditions of Homeric allegory – in which divine and human conflicts are interpreted in terms of cosmological and physiological processes – to Hippocratic and Galenic medical theory, Renaissance writers produce compelling explanations for epic strife as well as for the generic hybridity of the Homeric poems, composed as they are of a mixture of joy and sorrow. In a 1613 work addressing the scientific undermeanings of the *Odyssey*, an interlocutor named Providus, identified as a Galenic physician, proposes that both tears and laughter arise out of a combination of joy and grief, since both responses result from the interaction between "contrary elements" [*elementa contraria*].[144] By interpreting the laughter of the gods as reflective of the *coincidentia oppositorum* that characterizes many different aspects of Homeric epic, Renaissance writers counter Plato's charge that divine laughter is dissolute or impious. Guillaume Paquelin, for one, argues that the laughter of the gods is "sweetly [expressed] and without excess" [*suavement & sans excez*] and that it is a "pharmakon" that drives away anger and sadness.[145] As Joubert also demonstrates, laughter can cure as well as kill: in one particularly Pulci-esque anecdote, he relates how a patient who witnessed a monkey trying on the red fur robe of his doctor laughed so violently that he recovered his health.[146]

The attention paid by early modern physicians and natural philosophers to the physiology of Homeric laughter is reflective of a more widespread tendency during the period to glean medical knowledge from Homeric epic. Ancient readers already regarded Homer as a valuable medical resource. Pseudo-Plutarch praises Homer's knowledge of "dietetics" [*diaitêtikon*]; the interlocutors of Athenaeus's *Deipnosophists* debate the healthfulness of the regimens followed by the heroes of the *Iliad* and *Odyssey*; other ancient writers cite Homer as an authority on the medicinal uses of wine, exercise, sleep, and various drugs.[147] Poliziano spends three pages discussing Homer's medical knowledge in his *Oratio*, and sixteenth-century medical scholars frequently cite Homer in the company of Hippocrates, Galen, and Dioscorides in discussions of physiological ailments and mechanisms including grief, loss of appetite, laughter, farting, and sneezing. Although early modern medical treatises are steeped in humanist learning, Homer stands out among ancient poets for the wealth of information he offers natural philosophers and physicians such as Antoine Valet, the author of a 1570 oration on ancient medicine whose observations are extracted out of allegorical interpretations of Homer, a method perhaps indebted to Valet's former teachers, the French Hellenists Jean Dorat and Adrien Turnèbe.[148]

For his *cour de stage* at Montpellier in 1531, Rabelais explicated Hippocrates's *Aphorisms* and Galen's *Ars Parva*; in 1532, he published a Greek edition of the *Aphorisms*; and in 1537, when he returned to Montpellier for his *license*, Rabelais explicated the Greek text of Hippocrates's *Prognostics*.[149] This substantial medical training helped Rabelais recognize the Hippocratic and Galenic doctrines embedded in Homeric epic, in particular the Hippocratic principle that "opposites are cured by opposites" [*ta enantia tôn enantiôn estin iemata*]. Derived via the sophists from the cosmological theories of Heraclitus, this central principle of the Hippocratic corpus applies to human physiology the pre-Socratic doctrine that harmony is the result of oppositional tensions in which, like two men sawing a log, "the one pulls, and the other pushes, [and] herein they do the same thing ... Such is the nature of man."[150] For the authors of the Hippocratic corpus, the body is subject to the same *palintonos harmoniê* – literally, counter-stretched harmony, or the harmony produced out of opposing tension (*tonos*) –that Heraclitus discerns at work in the cosmos at large and often explains in terms of the Homeric simile that likens the"stretched-back bowstring" [*toxon ... palintonon*] to the plucked string of a lyre

(*Od.* 21.11, 406–8), an image that comes to symbolize, for the pre-Socratic philosopher, the unity of opposites as the governing force of the cosmos.[151] By joining two seemingly contrary arenas of human experience, the strife of war and the harmony of the poet's song, Homer's bow and lyre testify to the *concordia discors* that in turn ensures the attunement of the cosmos: physical forces, Heraclitus explains, are "at variance" but also "agree" such that "there is a connection working in both directions, as in the bow and the lyre [*toxou kai lûrês*]."[152]

Early modern readers steeped in ancient medical and philosophical learning would thus be familiar with these Homeric images of tension – the *palintonos* of the bent-back bow, the lyre whose strings are stretched around a new peg, or the tautness of an evenly strained battle [*isa machê tetato*] – that were subsequently adapted for scientific ends by Heraclitus and Hippocrates.[153] In its Homeric usage, as well as in its later applications for cosmology, *tonos* implies both tension and bond, a double meaning that informs the Stoic doctrine of *pneuma*, in which the tonic (or tension-producing) qualities of air combine with fire and thus ensure the stability or *hexis* of the cosmos.[154]

Steeped in a Stoic-Hippocratic-Galenic tradition that interprets both cosmological and physiological processes as animated by a *tonos*, or tension, that generates attunement, Rabelais repeatedly invokes relevant Homeric tropes in contexts that reveal his perception of the underlying sympathies between Homeric epic and these traditions of natural philosophy. In its mocking celebration of a "push-me-pull-you" model of cosmic order, Panurge's speech in praise of debt uncovers the Homeric logic behind the Hippocratic principle that "contraries are cured by contraries" [*contraria contrariis curantur*], a concept both exemplified and distorted by Panurge's sophistical methods of pro-and-contra argumentation. By superimposing upon a monistic and pneumatic cosmos – a cosmos united by the *hexis* of debt – Christian ideals of charity and reciprocity, Panurge's speech emphasizes how the interconnectedness of a society bound by *tonos* permits the forces of strife and disorder to be turned to good. This premise informs Rabelais's writings throughout and often serves to validate certain forms of conflict as natural and productive: in the Prologue to the *Tiers Livre*, Rabelais's narrator admits that "only a little holds me back from adopting the opinion of that good man Heraclitus that war is the Father of all that is good, and from believing that in Latin war is called *bellum* ... because in warfare appear all species of the fair and good" [*peu de chose me retient que je n'entre en l'opinion du bon Heraclite, affermant guerre estre de tous biens père, et croye que guerre soit en latin dicte belle ... parce qu'en guerre apparoisse toute espèce de bien et beau*] (*TL* Prologue:366). This tentative endorsement of Heraclitus's maxim, made familiar by Erasmus's *Adages*, is itself a model of *antiphrasis* that turns on two false etymologies: between *guerre* [war] and *guère* [hardly] and between *bellum* [war] and *belle* [beautiful]. Although it should not be read as a sincere endorsement of war, the Prologue does establish *palintonos harmoniê* as a guiding principle of Rabelais's cosmology, ethics, medicine, and hermeneutics, a principle likewise articulated in one of Rabelais's favourite maxims, "opposites placed against each other shine more clearly" [*opposita juxta se posita magis elucescunt*], a tenet taken to absurd limits by Panurge and Bridoye even as it also finds serious expression in the ethical and narrative structure of Rabelais's work.

The Remedy of Contraries: Rabelais's Homeric Scepticism

Although the writings of Rabelais are marked by a "constant play of oppositions and antitheses" [*jeu constant d'oppositions et d'antithèses*], the rhetorical, legal, and medical principles of contrariety that animate his work are repeatedly subject to distortion and abuse by Panurge and his adversaries in the *Tiers Livre*.[155] When Bridoye, the dice-rolling judge, invokes the principle that opposites placed next to each other elucidate each other, he does so to justify his arbitrary legal judgments (*TL* 3:513).[156] Despite the specious use to which it is put, Bridoye's purloined maxim reflects an earnest endorsement of contrariety as the "principal and unifying structure of the Pantagruelian universe" [*le principe structural unique de l'univers pantagruélien*], a universe in which harmony or attunement depends upon tension.[157] This is the lesson contained in the fable of Physis and Antiphysis in the *Quart Livre*, in which Antiphysis, who "has ever been the party hostile to Nature" [*de tout temps est partie adverse de Nature*], produces two "topsy-turvy" [*au rebours*] offspring, Amodunt and Discord, in order to rival Physis's children, Beauty and Harmony (*QL* 32:671). Like the myth of Eros and Anteros, Rabelais's fable of nature and counter-nature naturalizes and legitimates the agonistic impulses intrinsic to nature itself. But Rabelais takes his version of the myth one step further by turning Antiphysis into a sophist whose "rhetoric of reversal" convinces fools and madmen that her children are more beautiful than those of Physis, a conclusion that testifies to the way in which the "coexistence of contraries" may, as Defaux puts it, transcend the "law of contradiction."[158]

Arguably, all ancient Greek thinkers understood cosmic and microcosmic processes alike as animated by what Jan Huizinga has called an "eternal conflict of opposites."[159] But this tendency is especially pronounced among the pre-Socratic, Hippocratic, and Stoic philosophers whose doctrines grew out of allegorical and euhemeristic interpretations of Homeric epic. Rabelais interprets Homeric epic in light of this legacy, as the copious nursery of an eclectic assortment of philosophical outlooks united by their shared endorsement of the constructive or curative nature of contrariety. Like the fable of Physis and Antiphysis, the story of Bringuenarilles in chapter 44 of the *Quart Livre* provides a jocular demonstration of the allopathic theories of Hippocrates when his indigestive state – brought on by the consumption of too many hens – is cured by the ingestion of a fox, a treatment that in turn requires further treatment in the form of greyhounds (*QL* 44:699–701). Although the episode mocks the Hippocratic principle that contraries cure contraries, Rabelais elsewhere illustrates the principle to be sound both medically and rhetorically. Despite his scorn for sophists who "in their disputations seek not the truth but wrangling and controversy" [*en leurs disputations ne cherchent vérité, mais contradiction et débat*], Rabelais nonetheless entertains the idea that pro-and-contra argumentation can be curative, and that the kind of verbal sparring beloved by Panurge can be an antidote to conflict rather than simply an occasion for it (*P* 18:294).[160] Verbal disagreements may, in certain instances, achieve harmonious resolution through *epochê* or the counterbalance of opposing tensions. Such is the case at the end of chapter 13 of *Pantagruel*, where a legal dispute between Humevesne and Baisecul is put to rest and the "two parties, contending in contradictory judgements, [are] equally contented with a definitive verdict" [*deux parties, contendentes en jugement contradictories, soient égualement contentez d'un arrest diffinitif*] (*P* 13:270). At its worst, Rabelaisian sophistry threatens to destroy the sacred correspondence between words and things, using language to seduce or dominate rather than to cultivate "exchange and mutual comprehension" [*l'échange et la comprehension mutuelle*].[161] But at its best, the sophistic antilogic of Rabelais's most belligerent interlocutors duplicates the *palintonos harmoniê* of a cosmos whose equilibrium is preserved through *tonos*, or tension.

Critics interested in analysing Rabelais's adaptation of his epic and mock-epic sources rarely pay attention to his preoccupation with sceptical and sophistic philosophical strategies, or vice versa. Yet the two inheritances are intimately related to each other, yoked together by the intertwined classical legacies that represent Homer as the founder of one or both schools of philosophy. Many of his ancient interpreters, including Dio Chrysostom, Plato, and pseudo-Plutarch, identify Homer as the father of sophistry, a dubious honorific bestowed upon him on account of his rhetorical skill, his multiple and conflictive retellings of Trojan legend, and his characters' frequent recourse to *logon agônas* and other forms of verbal contest. Although no compliment is intended by Plato's claim (at *Protagoras* 316d–e) that Homer and Hesiod are both "sophists in disguise," other classical writers, including pseudo-Plutarch, praise Homer's mastery of "rhetorical antithesis [*tên antithesin tôn logôn*], a form of discourse that introduces the opposite [*enantiôn*] of everything said, simultaneously proving and disproving the same thing."[162] This Homeric mode of sophistry, which closely resembles Panurge's *chanson du Ricochet*, rests upon the perception that paradox, irony, and reversal are the poet's signature rhetorical techniques, techniques emulated by later sophists such as Gorgias, Lucian, Maximus of Tyre, and Dio, who write mock-declamations and paradoxical encomia on Homeric themes.[163]

For Rabelais, the sophistic techniques of antilogic, antithesis, and two-sided argumentation [*dissoi logoi*] may be productive of both truth and harmony when embedded in and contained by the larger structure of epic, a polyphonic genre capable of generating a plenistic and copious view of truth by allowing readers to "see in the same reality now one aspect and now another" or by calling attention to what "the prevailing account of the world leaves out."[164] Irony, above all other techniques, is the argumentative strategy that links Homeric epic to later medical and philosophical theories predicated upon the curative power of contrariety. Often defined during the Renaissance as the reversal of a word or phrase "from contrary to contrary" [*ex oppositis ad opposita*], irony replicates the allopathic principles of Hippocrates by offering what Thomas Nashe, in his 1589 preface to Robert Greene's *Menaphon*, calls a "remedie of contraries" that cures through opposition.[165]

The two paradoxical encomia delivered by Panurge in the *Tiers Livre*, both steeped in Homeric allusions, demonstrate how this curative power of ironic contrariety works. Although Screech calls Panurge a sophistical master of "perverted ingenuity" who can "make black seem white," his praise of Pantagruelion deploys that ingenuity to more fruitful ends, since it "properly reveals ... the vast and varied uses to which [the] humble plant can be put."[166] Pantagruelion has a strange set of Homeric origins and associations: the ships that Pantagruel is preparing for sail (the event that is the occasion for the speech) are likened to those of Ajax of Salamis, whose vessels brought the Greeks to Troy, and a series of allusions to Circe, Penelope, and Odysseus remind us that like Homer's Moly, with its tough, black root and its delicate white blooms, the "peculiar properties" [*vertus et singularitez*] of the similarly bi-coloured Pantagruelion,"green outside, white inside" [*verd au dehors, blanchissant au dedans*], form a coincidence of opposites (*TL* 49:542–3, 50:545, 51:549).[167] In its various uses, Pantagruelion can cure as well as kill: it supplies the material for hangmen's ropes, catapults, and crossbows but also provides remedies for colic, burns, and gout (*TL* 51:550). Although its woody stem is useless, its fibres are so powerful that they provoke the Olympian gods to call a council to discuss the threat posed by the plant (*TL* 52:553–4). Its virtues hidden inside a seemingly worthless exterior, Pantagruelion is a Silenus, at once banal and divine. Hemp, or Pantagruelion, is a symbol of the curative nature of paradox, celebrated by a speech that itself uses paradox in order to demonstrate contrariety as curative.

Panurge's two paradoxical encomia in the *Tiers Livre* represent the world "in reverse" [*au rebours*] in order to lay claim to an alternative genealogy for Homeric epic that identifies it with the sophists but also with scepticism.[168] From the Prologue to *Gargantua* onwards, Rabelais pairs Homer and Socrates as the twin purveyors of a scepticism characterized by an involuted, *gioco*-serious, and ironic wisdom. In that prologue, the description of Socrates as a Silenus, a "little box" [*petite boite*] whose undistinguished and ridiculous appearance conceals the "celestial and invaluable drug" [*céleste et impréciable drogue*] of his philosophy, yields to the more complex image of the "substantificial marrow" [*sustantificque mouelle*] hidden within Homer, a poet whose beggarly appearance and appetite for drink make him a different sort of Silenus, "ever laughing, ever matching drink for drink with all comers, ever joking, ever hiding his God-sent wisdom" [*tousjours riant, tousjours beuvant d'autant à un chascun, tousjours se guabelant, tousjours dissimulant son divin sçavoir*] (*G* Prologue: 38–9). This depiction of Homer may derive from Lucian's *Dionysius*, which compares the eloquence of Odysseus to the "splendid voice" of men under the influence of Silenus – that is, to drunks.[169] United by their shared love of wine, Rabelais's Homer and Socrates both conceal the profoundest truths in the humblest and most unassuming containers: the comic antics of the Olympian gods, the sardonic humour of the battlefield, the diminutive protagonists of mock-epic works all conspire to make Homer the forefather of the philosopher who confounds earnest with jest and jest with earnest (*G* Prologue:40).[170] At the end of the prologue, Alcofribas invokes this *vinosus Homerus* whose "verse whiffed more of wine than of midnight oil" [*ses carmes sentoyent plus le vin que l'huille*], a characterization inspired by Horace, *Epistles* I.XIX, who writes that poems written by "water-drinkers" do not endure, while "the wino Homer" [*vinosus Homerus*] will last forever, and Rabelais transforms this epithet into his "Homère biberon," the Maeonian poet whose taste for wine connects him to Bacchic mysteries and accounts for his verbal fluency and copiousness.[171] As the *bien yvres* observe in chapter 5 of *Gargantua*, "Whom did overflowing cups not fluent make?" [*Foecundi calices quem non fecere disertum*]: drunkenness is a guarantor of poetic skill and longevity (*G* 5:50).[172]

If Rabelais makes Homer into a Silenus, he is a rather different sort of Silenus than that of Erasmus, who interprets the figure as a symbol of textual involution or *huponoia* that illustrates how human beings, like texts, contain both a "literal sense and a mysterious sense."[173] Homer may, like Alcibiades's depiction of Socrates, conceal "unadulterated divinity under a lowly and almost ludicrous external appearance," but Rabelais invokes the Silenus, and then yokes it to the figure of Homer, in order to call into question allegorical interpretation rather than to endorse it. For Rabelais, the Silenus is a synecdoche for the logic of hermeneutic reversal demanded by complexly ironic texts, for texts that may appear "worthless and absurd" on the surface and "yet [are] admirable when seen from a closer and less superficial view."[174] Offering his own work as "easy at the first approach, and harder at close hand" [*legiers au prochaz et hardiz a la rencontre*], Rabelais both dramatizes this hermeneutic principle in his writing and also relies upon that principle (rather than allegory) to interpret Homer as a poet who conceals his substantial marrow of wisdom inside the ridiculous husk of comedy (*G* Prologue:39).

Rabelais's pairing of Homer and Socrates in the Prologue to *Gargantua* is indebted to a long tradition of interpreting Homeric epic – particularly the *Odyssey* and the spurious mock-epic works – as foundational texts of scepticism. Dio Chrysostom identifies Homer as Socrates's "mentor," while Diogenes Laertius characterizes him as the originator of Pyrrhonian scepticism because he gives "different answers at different times ... to the same questions" in a manner similar to Trouillogan, the Pyrrhonist of the *Tiers Livre* whose "opposed and contradictory responses" [*répugnantes et contradictories responses*] frustrate Panurge (*TL* 35:499). Not all Renaissance readers of Homer are fond of his sceptical tendencies: Poliziano sounds alarmed when he asserts that Homer is the founder of the "Pyrrhonian heresy that asserts nothing" [*Pyrrhonia haeresis, quae definiat nihil*].[175] But Rabelais finds in Homeric scepticism a strategy useful for solving the problem that arises when one is presented with "two simultaneous contradictions" [*deux contradictions ensemble*] of the same text, as well as a method that instructs in both the benefits and the dangers that arise when texts are interpreted in multiple and contradictory ways (*QL* Prologue:574).

Rabelais wields Homeric scepticism as an instrument to combat boastfulness, a project taken up full force in the *Tiers Livre*, where the lineaments of an epic quest are interwoven with a sceptical mission to defeat the dogmatism, arrogance, and contentiousness of characters such as Herr Trippa and Hippothadée.[176] Panurge alternately plays the parts of *eiron* and boaster: while he indirectly allies himself with Odysseus by comparing Herr Trippa to Irus, the verbally aggressive and obnoxious mendicant with whom Odysseus comes to blows upon his return to Ithaca, the mock-humility of Rabelais's beggarly hero falls short of its Homeric model. Calling Her Trippa "poorer than Irus ever was" [*paouvre plus que ne feut Irus*] and more *ptôchalazôn*, or beggarly-boastful, than his Homeric counterpart, Panurge aligns himself with the "polypragmon" Odysseus as he invokes Aristotle's two contrary extremes of truth: *alazoneia*, or boastfulness, and *eironeia*, concealed or dissimulated wisdom (*TL* 25:462).[177] Yet as Aristotle points out, these excessive and defective extremes of truth can prove difficult to distinguish from each other, and so too are Herr Trippa and Panurge, since the latter's mock-humility often constitutes a form of boastfulness. Although Panurge parrots both the Socratic maxim that "I know nothing" [*je ne sçay rien*] and the Delphic injunction to "Know thyself" [*Cognois-Toy*] that served as the "first line of philosophy" [*le premier traict de philosophie*] for the ancient sceptics, both adages fall on Panurge's own deaf ears, thus further enforcing his distance from Homer's Odysseus (*TL* 25:460, 25:462). As an epic journey that takes the form of a "skeptical inquiry into the nature of marriage and the possibility of fidelity," the *Tiers Livre* leads its protagonists through an Odyssean landscape whose obstacles are not rocks and whirlpools but rather the variable and perplexing nature of human judgments.[178] Whenever Rabelais is contemplating the interpretive dilemmas posed by texts, the uncertainty of human judgment, the ambiguity or pliancy of language, Homeric allusions lurk, speaking to the question of whether it is desirable or even possible to reconcile "inconsistency" and "contradiction" (*TL* 35:545) and thus to make "every truth … consonant with all other truths" [*tout vray à tout vray consone*], the elusive hermeneutic and epistemological fantasy that drives the *Tiers Livre* (*TL* 20:444).

Homer's classical and Renaissance readers discern two strains of scepticism in his poems, one deeply pessimistic and the other more playful and joyous. The first surfaces in Homer's attention to the weakness and vulnerability of mortal life, a sentiment expressed through frequent similes that "liken men to wasps, flies, and birds."[179] The second is seen as residing in Homer's predilection for linguistic ambiguity and for representing the flux of human judgments, an outlook evident in the poet's tendency to "giv[e] different answers at different times ... to the same questions" such that, according to Diogenes Laertius, many "call Homer the founder of this [the Pyrrhonian] school."[180] Arguing that Homer is "never definite or dogmatic about the answer" to the questions raised by his poems, Diogenes Laertius cites Aeneas's speech to Achilles in Book 20 of the *Iliad*, "Pliant [*streptê*] is the tongue of mortals," as proof of Homer's recognition of the "equal value of contradictory sayings" (*Il.* 20.248).[181] The passage arouses the interest of many sixteenth-century readers of Homer, including Erasmus, Budé, and Montaigne, who cites the speech in the essay *On the Uncertainty of Our Judgment* as evidence of the variability of human opinions and beliefs, since it conveys that "there is much to be said on all matters, both for and against."[182] When he broaches the subject of Homer's scepticism once again in the *Apology for Raymond Sebond*, Montaigne argues that Pyrrho and his fellow "Epechists" derive their doctrines from Homer, a poet whose outlook resembles that of Socrates in that both were "doubters ... never concluding, never satisfying ... and never [claiming any] other knowledge than that of opposing."[183]

For Rabelais, as for Montaigne, Homer's texts do not merely endorse a sceptical attitude towards flux and volubility; the texts themselves, or their interpretive history, also *dramatize* sceptical dilemmas by illustrating how certain texts may, to their detriment, be construed in diverse and conflicting ways. When Montaigne questions whether "it is possible that Homer meant to say all they make him say, and that he lent himself to so many and such different interpretations," he echoes a problem that Rabelais tackles over and over again with respect to his own works as well as the writings of Homer.[184] This dilemma is spelled out explicitly by the Prologue to *Gargantua* when Alcofribas asks whether we may really believe that Homer, in writing the *Iliad* and *Odyssey*, "was thinking of the allegories dreamt up by Plutarch, Heraclides Ponticus, Eustathius, and Phornutus" [*pensast es allegories lesquelles de luy ont calfreté Plutarche, Heraclides Ponticus, Eustatie, Phornute*], a reflection that cautions against the perils of allegory as well as against the more general error of assigning any fixed or stable meaning to Homer's pliant range of words (G *Prologue*:40). Philip Ford has identified a source for this passage in Melanchthon's *Encomium Eloquentiae*, which mocks that "mob of Greek grammarians who interpret all of Homer's poetry in terms of natural philosophy, and who are extremely pleased with themselves when, by a new metamorphosis, these pretty triflers make Jupiter into ether and Juno into air, things which Homer never even dreamt of even when he had a fever."[185] But the specious manipulation of the Homeric corpus was already a cause for complaint in antiquity:

while some readers, pseudo-Plutarch explains, laboured to turn his poems into scripture, using them "for divination, just like the oracles of God," others profaned the sacred font of Greek learning by "put[ting] forth entirely different subjects and ideas and fitting [*harmozousin*] the verses to them, transposing them and stringing them together [*metatithentes kai suneirontes*] in new ways."[186]

Yet pseudo-Plutarch, who voices these complaints, also justifies his own effort to "attribute every virtue to Homer" on the grounds that many readers have already "found in his poetry things he did not himself think to include," and Rabelais similarly alternates between the impulse to limit the interpretive licence he associates with Homer's allegorists and the contrary impulse to invite readers to mine his works for a "doctrine ... absconce" that may not have been put there by the author. As Jerome Schwartz points out, the attack on allegory in the Prologue to *Gargantua* is "not a denial but a paradox" in that it simultaneously "contest[s] and affirm[s] the reader's privilege to allegorize."[187] Inasmuch as the *Prologue* offers us "two ways of reading the book" and then "invites us to choose the second, but without canceling the first," it supports two alternative methods of interpreting both Rabelais and his hermeneutic twin, Homer, a poet who likewise both invites and refuses the "metamorphoses" that his works undergo at the hands of readers.[188] This paradox is further elaborated at the end of *Gargantua,* when Gargantua and Friar Jean disagree over the meaning of a prophetic riddle: the former asserts that it signifies the "course and upholding of divine Truth" [*le décours et maintien de vérité divine*] while the latter dissents, claiming that "it has no other hidden meaning than the description of a tennis-match" [*je n'y pense aultre sens enclous q'une description du jeu de paulme*] in which the "'round globe' is the ball; the 'guts' and the 'innards' of the 'innocent beasts' are the rackets; and the folk who are het up and wrangling are the players" [*la machine ronde est l'esteuf, et ces nerfs et boyaulx de bestes innocentes sont les racquestes, et ces gentz eschauffez et desbatans sont les joueurs*] (*G* 58:206–7n24). As a "parody of allegory," Friar Jean's reading "deflates the whole idea of an *altior sensus*" and instead leaves the reader to puzzle over two conflicting interpretations of the riddle, each founded on opposing ideas about the origin and purpose of strife.[189] Whereas Gargantua interprets the "discordz, venues, et allées" represented by the poem as reflective of divine order, Friar Jean understands these same "noises et debatz" as the product of frivolous human sport, a form of *agôn* that despite its to-and-fro movement bears no analogical correspondence to the *palintonos harmoniê* of the cosmos (*G* 58:204).

Framed by these twin burlesques of allegory, each of which "explicitly alerts us to the dangers of ascribing ... any particular significance" to the text under interpretation, *Gargantua* uses allusions to Homeric epic to draw attention to the hermeneutic problems raised by Rabelais's own text, a text that invests in the selfsame allegorical methods it travesties.[190] This feint of employing the techniques of allegory against itself arises out of a hermeneutics of suspicion generated by the multiple and conflicting interpretive traditions that attach themselves to the Homeric corpus. It culminates, in seventeenth-century France, with the post-Rabelaisian tradition of "libertine allegory" exemplified by works such as François de La Mothe Le Vayer's *Explication de l'antre des Nymphes.* Written around 1630, La Mothe Le Vayer's work is a learned satire of Neoplatonic exegesis that parodies Porphyry's *De Antro Nympharum* by "explicating" the famous double-doored cave of Book 13 of the *Odyssey* as an allegory of the female genitals, both fore and aft.[191] The work takes aim at the allegorical interpretations to which Homeric epic has been subjected by using those same interpretive methods to deflate and discredit the lofty metaphysical and cosmological claims made by Homer's ancient allegorists. Protesting that "it is not from Homer that we must look for philosophy" [*ce n'est pas dans Homère que nous devons chercher la philosophie*], La Mothe Le Vayer proposes an interpretation of the relevant lines in the *Odyssey* whose sense is "much less constrained, more natural, and more accommodated to the letter" [*beaucoup moins constraint, plus naturel et plus accommodé à la lettre*].[192] This naive reading liberates Homer from the province of learned Hellenists, renders him a "real glutton, or some jolly rascal" [*vrai goulu, or quelque bon fripon*], and delivers him into the hands of the libertine, the epicure, the anatomist, and the sceptic to interpret him aright.[193] It is a Rabelaisian reading of Homer, through and through.

The premise of La Mothe Le Vayer's allegory – that the two entrances of Homer's cave represent two alternate routes to sexual satisfaction – creates the occasion for a mock-debate between *con* and *cul* that reiterates in a playfully obscene manner the author's claim (from his *Dialogues*) that Homer was "the founder of scepticism" [*fondateur de la Sceptique*]. La Mothe Le Vayer's *Explication* does not hesitate "in good skeptical ironic form to underline the inadequacies, contradictions, and extravagances" [*en bon sceptique ironiste, à souligner les insuffisances, les contradictions et les extravagances*] of the *Odyssey*, and the work repeatedly criticizes readers of Homer who dismiss the sensual, jocular, or contradictory aspects of his poems in an effort to preserve either a dignity or a unity that is not really there.[194] Although La Mothe Le Vayer does not go so far as to suggest that Homer intentionally laid traps for the unwary reader, he does imagine Socrates as Homer's ironic co-conspirator, "laughing" at Plato for making him "say what [Homer] never thought" such that "Homer would have really been inclined to mock him with the many different meanings [*sens differents*] given to him."[195]

This conception of the Homeric poet who derides and thwarts his readers' efforts to attribute various meanings to his works takes to a playful yet disturbing extreme the commonplace Renaissance belief that the textual and philological history of the Homeric poems has rendered them vexingly unstable for later readers. Particularly after the publication of Estienne's 1567 edition of Homer, whose Greek text was collated from eighteen earlier editions of the poems and from various ancient citations of Homeric verses later altered or obelized, early modern scholars resign themselves to the problem that (in the words of Isaac Casaubon) "we can hardly hope for a sound text of Homer, no matter how old our manuscripts may be."[196] This is a very different state of affairs from the common ancient account of the stitching together of the Homeric rhapsodies, "previously disordered" [*confusos antea*] according to Cicero's version of the account, until they were assembled by Peisistratus into what was, almost always, deemed a more coherent and orderly set of texts.[197] Exacerbated in the sixteenth century by debates over scriptural hermeneutics, by nominalist and sceptical impulses, and by the emergence of philological methods that privilege the oldest and most "original" texts, the problems posed by the textual history of Homer provide opportunities for some early modern readers to meditate on larger problems of language and interpretation. For these readers, the Homeric poems are not simply texts to be interpreted but rather works that narrate the history of interpretation in miniature, not a "finite text," as Jorge Luis Borges would later observe, but rather a medium for exploring the "incalculable repercussions of texts."[198] Five centuries before Borges acknowledges that the textual history of Homer constitutes a "long experimental lottery of omissions and emphases" that renders the text into a "mutable fact," Rabelais and Montaigne ascribe to Homer the idea that "all things are in perpetual flux, change, and variation" and also interpret his poems accordingly, acutely aware that the multiple and conflicting interpretations to which the Homeric poems have been subject throws into doubt the very techniques and assumptions that make persuasive interpretation possible in the first place.[199]

Scattered Leaves: Hermeneutic Disordering in Rabelais

The hermeneutic conflicts that flank *Gargantua* take centre stage in the *Tiers Livre*, in which possible interpretations of texts or signs are repeatedly debated but not resolved. In several of these episodes, the debate revolves around the interpretation of texts that are, in one way or another, "Homeric" – the Homeric and Virgilian lots, a dream whose veracity is weighed according to Penelope's exposition of the two gates of sleep, and a Sibylline prophecy rearranged, cento-style, to form an obscene ditty. The recurrence of Homeric allusions and motifs in these episodes reflects Rabelais's understanding of the strong correspondence between the interpretive challenges posed by Homeric epic and those posed by his own works – works which in spite of their "hidden instruction" [*doctrine ... absconce*] employ rhetorical techniques such as irony and antilogic so as to resist the imposition of a single, monolithic interpretation (*G* Prologue:39). Philip Ford has rightly argued that Rabelais often invokes Homer "as a symbol of the author in general" [*comme symbole de l'auteur en général*].[200] But Rabelais also situates many of his work's most pressing hermeneutic dilemmas within this symbolic Homeric ur-author in order to address how best to interpret texts at odds with themselves and how to grapple with the elasticity of certain interpretive methods, in particular allegory, which endeavours to make Homer's texts consistent and harmonious, and parody, which deliberately misappropriates Homeric texts so as to invert their intended meanings. The former method, for Rabelais, is more perverse than the latter, because it is more discomfited by contradiction and by the plurality of meanings: to allegorize Homer is to try and stabilize meaning by resolving those cruxes where (as Dio Chrysostom describes the methods of Zeno) Homer appears to be *enantios*, or contrary to, himself. Rabelais corrects this impulse to sanitize contradiction by reintroducing interpretive cruxes back into our field of vision as readers of Homer, a strategy that accords with his more widespread tendency to "sport with signs."[201]

In the Prologue to *Gargantua*, Rabelais dubs Homer the "paragon of all the word-lovers" [*paragon de tous philologes*], an epithet that acknowledges the Greek poet's predilection for puns and etymological wordplay as well as his propensity for probing the vicissitudes of language (*G* Prologue:40). Alcofribas's remark may have been inspired by Guillaume Budé, whose 1532 *De Philologia* identifies Homer as the inventor of philology – the first word-lover, but also, perhaps, the first nominalist, a poet who questions the relationship between words and things and exploits the ambiguity of language for both comic and tragic effect.[202] Rabelais's interest in these questions is mediated through Homer in four interrelated episodes of the *Tiers Livre* and the *Quart Livre*: the casting of the Homeric and Virgilian lots (*TL*, chapters 10–12), Panurge's explication of Homer's two gates of sleep (*TL*, chapters 13–14), Panurge and Pantagruel's consultation of the Sibyl of Panzoust (*TL*, chapters 17–18), and their encounter with the "thawing words" [*parolles dégelées*] (*QL*, chapters 55–6). Each of these scenes employs lines or leitmotifs from Homer as avenues for exploring how best to sustain multiple and contrary interpretations of a given text, how to mediate between those contrary interpretations, and how to remedy the reductive or unsympathetic interpretations of uncharitable readers, those unable to embrace the "abundance of dissimularities" contained within a given text. Particularly in the *Tiers Livre*, which is obsessed with such interpretive dilemmas, Homer is the key to Rabelais's map of misreading: snippets of his poems are repeatedly scattered, rearranged, quoted out of context, "caulked up" [*calfreté*], or otherwise misconstrued, reflecting Rabelais's predilection for hermeneutic play but also his acute sensitivity to the threat of "abusive interpretations" (*G* Prologue:40).[203]

While Panurge emerges in the *Tiers Livre* as a perverse, uncharitable reader who insistently imposes singular and dogmatic meanings upon ambiguous, opaque, or ironic texts, Pantagruel emerges as Rabelais's charitable reader, one capable of admitting ambiguity and resisting the desire to impose textual coherence or unity where it does not exist. In his effort to "license to an interpretive approach which ... stresses the indeterminate character of its products," Rabelais repeatedly fosters correspondences between the act of reading (or rather misreading) Homer and the act of misreading his own texts, correspondences that reflect his perception of the two writers' shared vulnerability to the reductive interpretations of "laughless" [*agelastes*] readers who refuse to adhere to the moral and hermeneutic norms of a "common language" [*langage commun*].[204] The 1552 dedication to the *Quart Livre* focuses on precisely this sort of hermeneutic error, contrasting those readers who interpret texts "perversely ... [and] against all rational and routine linguistic usage" [*perversement et contre tout usaige de raison et de langage commun*] with the "faithful and unknowing reader" [*fidèle Anagnoste*] whose interpretations are guided by a willingness to embrace the "joyous follies" [*folastries joyeuses*] of the text (*QL* Ded.:564–5). His parodic handling of Homeric epic might seem an odd corrective to what Rabelais saw as the perverse and deadening effects of allegory. But if allegory overreaches in its attempt to enforce unity and conformity both within and between texts, then parody permits contradiction and inconsistency to flourish by teasing out the submerged counter-arguments concealed within a text and thus fostering "an ambivalent, or ambiguous relationship" to that text in order to remain at once "critical of and sympathetic" to it.[205]

The *Tiers Livre* repeatedly subjects both Homer and Virgil to "comic quotation and textual rearrangement" as well as to outlandish, profane, or otherwise absurd interpretations that provide a hermeneutic model for the *folastrie joyeuse* of the good reader while simultaneously cautioning against the dangers of misreading.[206] In chapters 10–12 of the *Tiers Livre*, Pantagruel and Panurge resort to the *sortes Homericae* and *Virgilianae*, the Homeric and Virgilian lots, in order to predict whether or not Panurge will be cuckolded. As Pantagruel's ironic understatement suggests – "I have no wish to imply that such lots are infallible in every case" [*je ne veulx toutefoys inférer que ce sort universellement soit infaillible*] – the selection of random passages from the *Iliad* and *Aeneid* is an exercise in wishful reading as Panurge interprets each randomly selected passage "in reverse" [*au rebours*] in order to forecast a happy marriage in even the bleakest and most ominous lines (*TL* 10:405, 12:411). Mocking the belief in divination as well as the radical decontextualization of epic verses associated with the cento tradition, Rabelais's long disquisition on the casting of Homeric and Virgilian lots demonstrates how the practice, howsoever dubious as a predictive tool, turns topsy-turvy in a quintessentially parodic manner the oppositional categories of the sacred and profane and the serious and trivial.

Although a few Renaissance writers, including André Tiraqueau and Girolamo Cardano, take the practice seriously – the Scottish scholar George Crichton even wrote a 1597 treatise devoted to the casting of Homeric lots entitled *De Sortibus Homericis Oratio* – most sixteenth-century scholars had disdain for the casting of lots using epic verses.[207] Perhaps following Cicero, who attacks the casting of lots as a superstitious and ineffectual form of divination, Agrippa's *De incertitudine et vanitate scientiarum* explains how the *Sortes Homericae* and *Virgilianae* turn pagan poets into "Prophets" by licensing their "trifling verses" to be "transferr'd and apply'd to Sacred Text" and "us'd as Oracles and Answers of Divination."[208] Agrippa's complaint that the casting of lots conflates pagan with Christian, and trifling with sacred, is as much a virtue as a vice for Rabelais. As represented in the *Tiers Livre*, the casting of the Homeric lots creates an ironic dissonance between the selected lines and Panurge's absurdly optimistic interpretations of them, thus producing a kind of *coincidentia oppositorum* by transforming stately descriptions of Venus and Dido into projections of Panurge's adulterously lusty wife-to-be. The effect is similar to that of the "*chanson du Ricochet*" discussed by Panurge at the beginning of chapter 10, in which two speakers engage in an endless exchange of "contrary repetitions" [*redictes contradictories*] such that "one cancels out the other" [*les unes destruisent les aultres*] (*TL* 10:403). In their stichomythic contest over the meaning of the lots, Pantagruel and Panurge continue to engage in a similar kind of *ritournelle*, the former insisting that the passages provide evidence of Panurge's inevitable cuckolding while the latter reverses each line, "*au rebours*," so that he may "take the ... lots to be in my favor" [*prens ces ... sorts à mon grand advantaige*] (*TL* 12:413).

Panurge's sophistic talent for turning the most self-evident meaning of a given text to the contrary duplicates the process of assembling centos – poems composed of various scraps of Homeric or Virgilian verses artfully rearranged so as to create a new, and often an utterly contrary, sense. Chapter 9 of *Pantagruel* is, in effect, a Homeric cento: Panurge's first appearance is fashioned out of a "pastiche and transposition of Homeric elements," and Pantagruel probes his identity by adapting a line from the *Odyssey* – "Who are you? Where do you come from? ... What is your name?" [*Qui estes-vous? Dont venez-vous? ... Et quel est vostre nom?*] – that already had a long interpretive legacy among Homeric allegorists and Homeric parodists alike.[209] It may be significant that the verse also appears in the *Batrachomyomachia*: in the *Histoire Facetieuse des Rats contre les Grenouilles*, Jean Sara's 1609 French translation of that poem, the frog asks the mouse who meets him at the river's edge, "Strange friend, who are you, where do you come from, and who brought you here to this river bank?" [*Amy estranger, qui es-tu, d'où viens-tu, & qui t'a icy amené sur ce rivage?*].[210] But the verse had also been long recognized, and prized, for its scriptural parallels: Clement of Alexandria compares the verse (which he holds to be infused with the divine *Logos*) to Isa. 40.3, John 1.20–3, and Matt. 3.3, where a voice in the wilderness cries out to announce the arrival of the Lord.[211] Rabelais manipulates his own allusion to the verse so as to highlight his departure from the Homeric source as well as from its purported scriptural parallels. Whereas Pantagruel does share certain features in common with Telemachus, the first speaker of the line at *Od.* 1.170, Panurge is hardly a substitute for Pallas Athena, to whom the verse is addressed, and he is certainly no Christ. Rather than use the verse to build a set of allegorical correspondences, Rabelais instead invokes it as a meditation on the profits and dangers of extracting meanings out of texts or (as Clement puts it) of selecting "ambiguous expressions" from them in order to "wrest them to their own opinions" [*ta amphibolôs eirômenai eis tas idias metalousi doxas*].[212]

Panurge is a master of wringing specious interpretations out of the many texts that he and Pantagruel encounter on their journey. In the *Tiers Livre*, this practice often involves the rearrangement or manipulation of passages from Homer in order to forge interpretations that invert the normative meanings or values of the Homeric text.[213] In antiquity, Homer was the pre-eminent target of textual "distortions and mischievous rewriting" by parodists who subjected his poems to a dazzling array of self-consciously fallacious or unsound interpretations through the composition of *silloi* and *centones*.[214] Some of these works, such as Nestor of Lycia's *Iliad Omitting Letters* and Triphiodorus's *Odyssey Omitting Letters*, were designed to showcase the rhetorical virtuosity of their authors, while other works excised passages from Homeric epic for satirical or moral ends, shuffling around lines in order to form prayers, psalms, or other spiritual works.[215] Composed by several Byzantine writers including Patricius and Eudocia (the wife of Emperor Theodosius II), the Homeric *Centos* rely on a particularly aggressive form of allegory in order to establish correspondences between Homeric epic and the scriptures, in particular between Odysseus (or Achilles) and Christ.[216] These methods and aims make the Homeric centos a frequent target of mockery by patristic writers: Irenaeus inveighs against those poets who "propose themes which they chance upon and then try to put them to verse from [the] Homeric poems, so that the inexperienced think that Homer composed the poems with that theme," while Tertullian calls cento-writers "poetasters" and "collectors of Homeric odds and ends, who stitch into one piece, patchwork fashion, works of their own from the lines of Homer."[217]

When the Homeric centos first appear in print, edited by Aldus Manutius in 1502 (rpt. Frankfurt, 1541 and 1554) and then again by Henri Estienne (as the *Homerici Centones*) in 1578, they revive an old debate as to whether the cento constitutes a perverse form of reading or a resourceful method of transvaluing and redeeming pagan literature for Christian purposes. Particularly for theologians and scholars involved in the hermeneutic debates of the Reformation, questions concerning the intellectual and spiritual legitimacy of the cento form become entangled in larger disputes over the proper methods of interpreting scripture and of reconciling pagan with Christian wisdom. Anticipating a common complaint of Erasmus, his sixteenth-century editor, Jerome compares those readers who "force the scriptures reluctantly to do their will" to the techniques of the cento-writer, who "adapts conflicting passages to suit his own meaning," forgetting (as Jerome continues) that "we have read centos from Homer and Virgil; but we never think of calling the Christless Maro a Christian because of his lines 'now comes the virgin back,'" an allusion to the supposed prophecy at *Eclogues* 4.6.[218] Erasmus adapts Jerome's critique of the cento into a master metaphor for hermeneutic perversity and disingenuousness: his adage *Farcire centones* [To stuff a patchwork coat] rebukes "boastful men who have a habit of stitching together a whole string of lies [*consarcinatis fabulamentis expleas*]," while in the *Ciceronianus*, one of Erasmus's interlocutors satirizes those "who have collected snippets of verses [*fragmentis … versuum*] from here, there, and everywhere in the Homeric or Virgilian corpus, and strung them together into a patchwork poem [*in centonem consarcinatis*] on the life of Christ."[219] The example selected by Erasmus is unusually preposterous: the process of assembling a cento, he argues, is tantamount to "breaking up" [*dissolvat*] a mosaic that depicts the rape of Ganymede and rearranging it to represent the Annunciation, in which "the angel Gabriel brings the celestial message to the maiden of Nazareth," a metamorphosis that either exemplifies or burlesques the syncretism at the heart of Renaissance humanism, depending on one's point of view.[220] But Erasmus's example is no more preposterous than the Homeric interpretations of Pierre Le Loyer (1550–1634), the French demonologist who claimed to have discovered in a line from the *Odyssey* a rebus conveying his name, nationality, and birthplace: "Pierre Le Loyer, Angevin, Gaulois, à Huillé."[221]

Pantagruel takes aim at such hermeneutic practices when he summarizes the findings of those scholars who conclude that "the kneeling Achilles was wounded by the arrow of Paris in the right heel [because] his name is an odd number of syllables" [*Achilles, estant à genoulx, feut par la fleiche de Pâris blessé on talon dextre: car son nom est de syllables impares*] or that "Venus was wounded by Diomedes before Troy in her left hand, since her name in Greek has four syllables" [*Venus par Diomedes, davant Troie, blessée en la main guausche, car son nom en grec est de quatre syllables*] (*QL* 37:685). Although based on pseudo-Plutarch's discussion of Pythagorean number theory in chapter 145 of his *Life of Homer*, which demonstrates Homer's belief in the principle that even numbers are imperfect while odd numbers are perfect, Pantagruel's version of Homeric numerology casts doubt on Pythagoras's conviction that "numbers have enormous power" [*tous arithmous megistên dunamin*].[222]

Despite the derision voiced by Erasmus, a few sixteenth-century scholars, including Henri Estienne and Justus Lipsius, regard the Homeric cento tradition as a serious literary form, one valuable for modern philologists. In his 1575 *Parodiae Morales*, whose preface contains a long discussion of the "type of poem made out of fragments of Homeric verses" [*genus carminis ex Homericorum versuum fragmentis*], Estienne praises a specimen of the genre by Stratonicus that makes "Homer's words contend with Homer" [*Homeri verbis cum Homero contendat*].[223] Unlike allegory, which strives at all costs to preserve textual unity and coherence, the cento tradition accentuates the incongruities and dissonances of the Homeric poems, qualities that prove valuable for Estienne's philological methods as an editor of Homer. In order to produce his edition of the *Iliad*, *Odyssey*, and *Batrachomyomachia*, Estienne collated eighteen different editions and a "very old [*vetustissimus*] codex," later identified as Codex Genevensis 44, the Geneva *Scholia* to the *Iliad*, in order to study their textual variants, a process that highlights the degree to which Homer's texts might be, as it were, contending with each other. By placing Homer's words in conflict with each other, the cento genre as Estienne understands it highlights the diverse and discordant strains within the Homeric corpus and thus illustrates the "many uses" [*multos usus*] to which his poems may be put, an adaptability likewise evident in what Estienne calls the "*proverbalium Homeri versuum Erasmica synagoge*," the several hundred adages culled by Erasmus out of Homeric epic and "accommodated to [many] uses" [*accommodare usum*].[224]

As Estienne recognizes, the cento form is intimately related to parody.[225] The Homeric centos composed by Lucian's Charon, for instance, rearrange lines from Homeric epic in order to make the text contradict itself, and a similar principle of reversal animates Nicolas Prustus's 1610 collection of Homeric centos or "antigraphi," as he calls them.[226] In a treatise on ancient parody printed in his 1573 edition of the *Homêrou kai Hesiodou Agôn*, Estienne explains that parody employs "*katachresi*[*s*]," the deliberate misuse or abuse of another text, in order to effect its distinctive mixture of admiration and contempt or to "turn tragedy into the comic" [*ex tragoediis mutuatur comica*].[227] Like parody, the cento both profits from and heightens the intrinsic flexibility of the Homeric corpus, perhaps explaining why Estienne saw fit to include the Homeric centos in his revised, 1588 edition of Homer, the *Homeri Poemata Duo*. As Lipsius explains in his *Politica*, a collection of political aphorisms that he likens to centos woven together from various sources, "departures from the original meaning are always allowed and even praised" in the cento genre. Such licence – Lipsius speaks of "playing" [*luserunt*] centos as if they were a game – is undergirded by a sceptical recognition of the pliancy of language and the variability of human judgments, conditions that exercise the intellectual virtues of prudence and versatility so prized by Lipsius.[228]

Panurge's inclination to privilege univocality and textual coherence over the ambiguity and textual conflict prized by Pantagruel and Rabelais himself is again in evidence when he "commends himself to the two gates of

Homer" [*me recommende aux deux portes de Homère*] and resolves to interpret his dreams as portents of future marital happiness (*TL* 13:417). Before Panurge beds down for the night, Pantagruel offers the commonplace sixteenth-century gloss on the two gates of sleep described by Penelope at *Od.* 19.562–7, and imitated by Virgil (*Aen.* 6.893–6). Through the ivory gate "enter confused, fallacious, and uncertain dreams" [*entrent les songes confus, fallaces et incertains*] while "certain, true and infallible dreams" [*les songes certains, vrays et infallibles*] pass through the gate of horn, whose "shining gloss and diaphaneity" allow "all species [to] appear certainly and distinctly" [*sa resplendeur et diaphaneïté apparoissent toutes espèces, certainement et distinctement*] (*TL* 13:418). Yet the subsequent punning on the word "*corne*" [horn] collapses Penelope's distinction between true and false dreams, since the very substance (horn) that supposedly represents clarity and transparency also provides occasion for ambiguity. After Panurge recounts his dream, in which a young woman tickles him and caresses the "two pretty little horns over my forehead" [*deux belles petites cornes au dessus du front*], Pantagruel interprets the dream to mean that Panurge's wife will be unfaithful (*TL* 14:419). But Panurge interprets the dream "*au rebours*," asserting that "in my marriage I'll have goods in plenty together with the horn of abundance" [*en mon mariage j'auray planté du tous biens avecques la corne d'abondance*], a gloss that confirms Friar Jean's assertion that "the dreams of horned cuckolds ... are always true and infallible" [*les songes des coqus cornuz ... sont tousjours vrays et infallibles*] (*TL* 14:420, 13:418). Over the course of chapters 13 and 14 of the *Tiers Livre*, the word "*corne*" accumulates three very different meanings: the clarity or transparency associated with the substance of horn, the signature emblem of the cuckold, and *cornu*copian abundance. Rabelais's recurrent punning is a nod to its Homeric source: when Penelope observes that dreams passing through the ivory [*elephantos*] gate deceive [*elephairontai*] men, while dreams passing through the gate of horn [*keraôn*] will come to fulfilment [*krainousi*], she, too, puns on the Greek *keras* [horn] and *krainô* [to fulfil] as well as on *elephas* [ivory] and *elephairomai* [to deceive].[229] Although Odysseus protests that it is not possible to "bend this dream aside and give it another meaning" [*hupokrinasthai oneiron / allê apoklinant'*], Penelope embraces the ambiguity of dreams by arguing that they are "*akritomuthoi*" – babbling, confused, disorderly, and thus hard to interpret (*Od.* 19.565–8). Playing Penelope to Panurge's Odysseus, Pantagruel invokes a familiar Homeric simile – the falling and scattering of leaves – to describe the unreliability and ambiguity of dreams: "the ancient prophets and poets mystically teach us that vain and fallacious dreams lie hidden beneath the leaves carpeting the ground, for it is in the autumn that the leaves fall from trees [*les anciens prophètes et poëtes mysticquement nous enseignent, disans les vains et fallacieux songes gésir et estre cachez soubs les fueilles cheutes en terre, par ce qu'en automne les fueilles tombent des arbres*] (13:417).[230]

From Virgil to Dante, poets had imitated this Homeric simile, which likens falling leaves to the passing generations of men, to express the vanity or transitoriness of the mortal condition. Rabelais transforms the simile into a sceptical meditation on the limitations of human knowledge. That the "scattered leaves" described by Glaucus at *Il.* 6.146 serve some Renaissance readers as a master metaphor for the flux of human judgment should come as no surprise given that Diogenes Laertius, in a passage cited by Erasmus's adage *Homo bulla* [Man is a bubble], identifies Glaucus's speech as a "particular favourite with Pyrrho the Academic philosopher" [*Pyrrhonem Academicum peculiariter delectatum*].[231] For Rabelais, reticulated in this image of scattered leaves is the disjointed and dispersive nature of Homer's texts – texts that began as a diffuse, confused jumble of *folii* to be stitched together by later editors. Hopeful that the Homeric text he has in front of him has been stitched together properly, the sixteenth-century Dutch scholar Guillaume Canter argues that the Homeric poet moved from one myth to another not by hazard but with order and care, and "so regularly that all the parts are attached together with the greatest harmony" [*tantoque cum ordine persecutus est, ut eius singulae partes aptissime inter se cohaereant*].[232] Other contemporary scholars are less confident, however: in the preface to his 1572 edition of the *Iliad*, printed at Strasbourg, Giphanius agrees with the ancient assessment that Homer's works, once "scattered" [*confusos*], are now in order, but then adds (paraphrasing Josephus's *Contra Apion*) that "there are still certain vestiges of this former confusion ... such that there remain places in Homer in conflict with each other" [*confusionis quoque prioris vestigia quaedam esse reliqua ... quod quaedam in Homero reperiantur, inter se pugnantia*].[233] For Giphanius, the confused state of the Homeric text is a problem to be overcome with the assistance of philology. For Rabelais, the confusion is a *folastrie joyeuse* to be embraced rather than resolved.

When the *rime sparse* of the Sibyl's prophecy are scattered to the wind in chapter 17 of the *Tiers Livre*, the resulting textual diaspora dramatizes the instability of literary history and the precarious transmission of ancient poems to modern readers. Pantagruel and Panurge rearrange the scattered leaves of their Sibyl to form an obscene ditty about getting a woman pregnant, thus profaning a sacred prophecy through an act of misreading. The consultation of the Sibyl of Panzoust is an episode more obviously indebted to Virgil than to Homer. Yet while the *Aeneid* strives to enforce a single, orderly text by obliging its Sibyl to read her oracle aloud rather than present it as a written, unbound text whose leaves might be dispersed by the wind, Rabelais's Sibyl is a Homeric and not a Virgilian figure, a "true Sibyl and a true portrait, naturally represented by the *tê kaminoi* [old charwoman] of Homer" [*vraye sibylle et vray protraict naïfvement repraesenté par tê kaminoi de Homère*] (*TL* 17:431). By comparing the Sibyl of Panzoust to Homer's old charwoman, an allusion to an insult that Irus delivers to the disguised Odysseus at *Od.* 18.27, Epistémon underscores the Homeric foundations of the flexible, diasporic language of Sibylline prophecy. The obscure and unreliable prophets of Homeric epic testify to the "fallibility" of prophecy rather than to the certainty of its meaning or outcome.[234] By yoking together Odysseus and the Sibyl as Silenus figures, Epistémon's reference holds up both figures as emblems of involuted and ironic knowledge that "enclose unadulterated divinity under a lowly and almost ludicrous external appearance."[235] The entire scene ultimately reads like an obscene parody of Virgil: the Sibyl's grotto becomes her *trou* [arsehole], and her oracular utterances a dirty broadside ballad. Moreover, the process of "sifting and sieving" [*le grabeau et belutement*] required by the Sibyl's windborne prophecy resembles the kind of interpretive problems posed by Rabelais's own mock-Prognostications of 1533, opaque and malleable predictions that may "be sifted this way and that through my coarse riddle and perhaps may happen and perhaps may not" (*TL* 16:428).[236] Rabelais's teasing refusal, derived most immediately from Erasmus's adage *A Sign good or bad*, is a saying attributed to Tiresias, Homer's ambiguous soothsayer who qualifies his prophecies by claiming, "Whatever I say, either will be or will not be."[237] Panurge is unable to sustain the ambiguity of Tiresias, however: signs for him must be either good or bad, true or false, and one reading of a text must prevail over all other possible interpretations.

As a meditation on the instability and manipulability of the written word, Rabelais's Sibylline prophecy demonstrates, with equal parts gusto and anxiety, the ease with which texts may be altered or deformed by readers who (in the words of Saint Irenaeus) "gather together sayings and names from scattered places and transfer them ... from their natural meaning to an unnatural one."[238] After they leave the Sibyl's cave, Pantagruel tells Panurge that on account of the "amphibologies, equivocations, and obscurities in the words" [*amphibologies, équivocques et obscuritez des motz*] of her oracle, they might profit more by consulting a mute, because "languages," as Pantagruel observes, "arise from arbitrary impositions and conventions amongst peoples: vocables, as the dialecticians put it, do not signify naturally but at pleasure" [*les languaiges sont par institutions arbitraries et convenences des peuples; les voix, comme disent les dialecticiens, ne signifient naturellement, mais à plaisir*] (*TL* 19:437–8). Panurge profits from the pliancy of the Sibyl's prophecy, "perversely expounding" [*perversement exposant*] it so that it foretells a happy marriage to a woman who will "suck my sweet tip" [*me sugsera le bon bout*] (*TL* 18:435–6). But at the heart of the episode is the recognition that such pliancy makes texts vulnerable to the self-interested motives of readers who wilfully remake texts so as to confirm the beliefs and values to which they are already predisposed. As Montaigne observes, "whoever has needed oracles and predictions has found enough in [Homer] for his purpose," since his poems may "be made to say whatever you want, like the sibyls."[239]

Rabelais and Montaigne are each responding, somewhat sardonically, to the widespread Renaissance tendency to syncretize the pristine wisdom of Homer with that of the Sibylline Oracles and the Orphic Mysteries. Couching his praise in strikingly Virgilian language, Poliziano calls Homer an oracular poet whose arcane verses "emerge out of the sacred inner recess of the gods" [*sacrisque deorum adytis emugiverit*], while in his 1586 edition of the Sibylline Oracles, Jean Dorat argues that the Delphic Sibyl lived before the fall of Troy and that "Homer stole some of her verses and mixed them in with his own" [*cuius versus furatus Homerus / Versibus inservit propriis*], a theory elaborated by Dorat's *Mythologicon*, which likewise claims that much of the *Odyssey* "appears to have been taken from the Sibylline oracles" [*Plurima quae in hoc libro sunt desumpta esse videntur e Sybillinis oraculis eaque praesertim*].[240] This belief in Homer's Sibylline ancestry helps to explain why various writers of the period are so attentive to the poet's ambiguity and predilection for linguistic play.[241] Yet while ancient writers such as Cicero and Plutarch deride the Sibylline oracles as "intricate and obscure," criticizing their uninterpretability as the "throwing and scattering [*diaspeîrai*] of words into the infinite," the prophecy delivered by the Sibyl of Panzoust celebrates the dynamic nature of language, words endowed with power at the very moment that they take to the wind.[242]

Winged Words

Rabelais transforms the Homeric motif of scattered leaves in order to illustrate the pliancy and energy of language, of words that move and are exchanged in a vitalistic, kinetically active universe. The Sibyl's scattered leaves dramatize the arbitrariness of language but also its vivacity and vigour, qualities that Rabelais explores in further depth in the "*paroles dégelées*" episode of the *Quart Livre*. As Terence Cave has argued, the leitmotif of "moving words" [*paroles mouvantes*] is one of the primary ways that sixteenth-century texts "manifest their own problems," and Rabelais explores both the appeals and the perils of linguistic mobility through the "winged" words of Homer, which he describes as "fluttering, flying, moving, and thus animated" [*voltigeantes, volantes, moventes, et par conséquent animées*] (*QL* 55:730).[243] Whereas other Renaissance readers of Homer express concern at the volubility of his speakers or the verbosity of their narrator, even arguing that Homer was the "first author of that fable" of the Tower of Babel and the "confounding of tongues," Rabelais emulates Homer's untethered, flighty, and "wide range of words" [*epeôn de polus nomos*] (*Il.* 20.249).[244]

Tolerance for linguistic *copia* was much greater during the sixteenth century than in the three centuries that followed. Even so, the verbal superabundance associated with Homeric epic was not universally regarded as a virtue. Paolo Beni comments that "Homer [is] reputed to be verbose and noted for garrulity," an attitude very much in evidence in Guillaume Budé's copy of Homer.[245] In the margins next to Aeneas's observation that "the tongue of mortals is pliant [*streptê*] and full of many and various words" [*polees d'eni muthoi / pantoioi*], Budé writes the phrase "*volubilis versatilis*," a rather severe assessment of the speech that Diogenes Laertius identifies as encapsulating the core doctrines of Pyrrhonian scepticism.[246] A few lines later, Budé glosses the phrase "*polus nomos entha kai entha*" [wide is the range of words on this side and that] by writing "*phora [kai] xusis*" [rushing and flooding] in the margin; the latter word, which literally means a flood or stream, is also one of the terms that Cicero and Longinus use to denote fluency or copiousness of speech.[247] Classical readers understood the liquidity, redundancy, and copiousness of Homeric language as the consequence of oral composition, whose products are typically "bloated with amplification."[248] For many of Homer's Renaissance readers, the strangeness of this style is compounded by the profuse chatter of characters who not only violate Ciceronian canons of decorum but also constitute a threat to the social or political order of the poems. In his *Grammatica Graeca*, which prints Thersites's sole speech from Book 2 of the *Iliad*, as well as a Latin translation of it, Melanchthon characterizes the character as "loquacious, empty, rude, and prodigious with his tongue" [*loquax, vanus, ac importunus [et] linguae prodigus*].[249] Melanchthon's objections to the voluble Thersites foreshadow the condemnations issued by late seventeenth-century critics such as Rapin, who faults Homer for "verbal intemperance" [*intemperance de paroles*] and for a "linguistic flux" [*flux de langue*] inferior to the brevity and solidity of Virgil, a poet whose words are firmly fixed to the things they represent: "everything is anchored," Rapin writes of the *Aeneid*, "and his words are things" [*tout y est fondé, and ses paroles sont des choses*].[250]

Yet even Rapin acknowledges that Homer possesses greater verbal energy or "*vivacité*" than Virgil, a quality likewise noted by many of Homer's ancient readers, who use the terms *energeia* and *enargeia* to describe, respectively, the vividness and the dynamism of Homeric epic. In the sixteenth century, these terms give way to a new idiom for describing the vivid realism of Homer's language, that of *naïveté*. Some readers find his rough, copious, and disorderly style inferior to the practised and elegant language of Virgil: Scaliger remarks that "Homer scatters; [Virgil] connects; the one disperses; the other collects" [*Fudit Homerus, hic collegit: ille sparsit, hic composuit*].[251] But other readers prize the primitive naturalism of Homeric Greek, a mixed dialect whose lack of refinement tethers it more closely to the humble simplicity of a golden age. In his *Art Poétique*, Jacques Peletier favours the "natural felicity" [*naive felicité*] of Homer over Virgilian styles that he deems "*appelées et recherchées.*"[252] In his own translation of Homer, Peletier goes to great pains to capture this "*naiveté Homerique*" in French, rendering into his own vernacular what his editor Paul Laumonier describes as "the awkwardness of a language in formation" [*la gaucherie d'une langue en formation*].[253] Ronsard similarly emulates the raw, unrefined qualities of Homeric diction and style, writing in the preface to his *Franciade* that his own epic has "imitated the natural facility of Homer more than the curious diligence of Virgil" [*patronné … plustost sur la naive facilité d'Homère que sur la curieuse diligence de Virgile*].[254] For these and other sixteenth-century French readers, the naive and natural language of Homer is a less mediated language, one closer to the material world but also closer to the word of God.

These literary-critical debates about the relative merits of Homeric and Virgilian language – the former naive, dynamic, and diffusive and the latter sophisticated, stately, and compact – inform Rabelais's account of the airborne shards of frozen words encountered by Pantagruel and Panurge in chapters 55 and 56 of the *Quart Livre*. The episode may usefully be read as an extended gloss on the Homeric epithet *epea pteroenta* [winged words], a phrase that appears more than 120 times in the *Iliad* and *Odyssey* and whose precise meaning has puzzled readers for centuries. To some readers, the epithet evokes the flight of a feathered bird or the fletched feathers of an arrow; to others, it conveys the "inherent spontaneity of speech" or speech animated by virtue of its emotional intensity or urgency; to others still, Homer's "winged words" convey the transitory nature of speech or its irrevocability, since words, especially those spoken spontaneously or without restraint, cannot be retracted once uttered.[255] This last interpretation of the epithet conforms best to those proposed by sixteenth-century scholars such as Erasmus and Nicolaus Girardus, who explain that the phrase denotes "words that are winged, because they take flight easily but do not know how to fly back" [*Verba alata ... quod facile evolent ac revolare nesciant*], an interpretation likely indebted to one of Horace's *Epistles*: "Once sent, the word irrevocably flies" [*semel emissum volat irrevocabile verbum*].[256] Although this irretrievability may prove epistemologically disturbing and socially perilous, the transitoriness of Homer's winged words also offers a moral lesson about the value of forgiving and forgetting in the adage *Ne malorum memineris* [Remember no wrongs], which Erasmus derives from *Od.* 8.408–9: "'But if a harsh word has been uttered, let the wind seize it and bear it away'" [*Si dictum est verbum durius ullum, / Id procul abripiant venti per inane procellae*].[257]

For Rabelais, however, Homer's *paroles mouvantes* convey the reciprocity of speech, the way in which words of praise or blame, when transmitted or exchanged, return to their speaker through a sort of discursive *karma* that is implied in the Homeric verb *ameibomai* [to answer, to exchange], a term that shows the degree to which oral communication is governed by an "ethic of reciprocity."[258] In Rabelais's writings, similar processes of verbal exchange are exercised through debate, through *chansons du ricochet*, and through other rhetorical interchanges that sustain the circulation of verbal energy. "Giving words is what lovers do" [*donner parolles estoit acte des amoureux*], observes Pantagruel as the frozen words melt in his hands (*QL* 56:732). When Panurge asks to buy some words from him, Pantagruel responds, "Selling words is what lawyers do" [*C'est acte de advocatz ... vendre parolles*], a comment that contrasts the gratuitous reciprocity of Pantagrueline lingua franca with the linguistic exchanges that govern the meretricious world of the law. Once thawed – once allowed, that is, to participate in the fluid economy of a living language – Rabelais's frozen words supply a well that never runs dry. This is why, when Panurge wishes to preserve a few "gullet-words" [*motz de gueule*] by wrapping them up in straw, "Pantagruel would not allow it, saying that it was madness to pickle something which was never lacking and always to hand as are gullet-words amongst all good and merry

Pantagruelists" [*Pantagruel ne le voulut, disant estre follie faire réserve de ce dont jamais l'on n'a faulte et que toujours on a en main, comme sont motz de gueule entre tous bons et joyeulx Pantagruelistes*] (*QL* 56:732–3). The episode is the culmination of a contrast between the natural abundance of a living language and the meagre economy of a deadened one that has been building since *Gargantua* and *Pantagruel*, where the exchange of *motz de gueule* or "rather sharp words" [*parolles bien picquantes*] turns into an "excellent sport" [*du passetemps beaucoup*] when it achieves the dynamic, reciprocal quality of Homer's winged words (*QL* 56:732). As Thomas Greene has argued, Rabelais's conception of therapeutic power of abusive language is rooted in his understanding of the "animate" quality of Homeric rhetoric.[259] Words that melt are words that accommodate themselves to the ears of their audience. They possess a persuasive force akin to Odysseus, who speaks "words like snowflakes on a winter's day" [*epea niphadessin eoikota cheimeriêsin*], a simile that conveys the power of a speech that silences its listeners, but also the delicacy of a speech that melts as it reaches its goal (*Il.* 3.222).

Rabelais's fable of the frozen words in chapters 55 and 56 of the *Quart Livre* is shaped by a rich tissue of classical discussions concerning the dynamic, animated quality of language in Homeric epic. In *The Art of Rhetoric*, Aristotle commends Homer for "speak[ing] of inanimate things as if they were animate" [*apsucha empsucha legein*] and for "giv[ing] movement and life to all" [*kinoumena gar kai zônta poiei panta*]. Plutarch similarly praises Homer as "the only poet who wrote words possessing movement because of their vigour" [*Homêron elege kinoumena poien onomata dia tên energeian*], adding that only the utterances delivered by the Delphic Oracle possess a similar "movement ... [and] are filled with the divine spirit" [*sunkineisthai ... alla peplêsthai panta theiotêtos*].[260] For many classical and early modern readers, these qualities are defined by the terms *energeia* and *enargeia*, which translate roughly to dynamism and vividness.[261] But Rabelais turns these commonplace tributes to Homer's rhetorical mastery into an exposition on the materialism of the *logos* in order to illustrate how speech is an invisible yet material substance made of atoms and that sounds are created when particles of voice or noise mingle with similar particles in the air and form acoustic images, or *eidola*, which enter the ear.[262] Democritus, Gorgias, and the ancient Stoics, the philosophers from whom Rabelais adopts these doctrines, likewise mediate their discussions of the materiality of language through Homeric epic. In his *Encomium of Helen*, Gorgias asserts that the *logos* is a "*dunastês*" or power that has a "miniscule and invisible body" but still accomplishes divine things, while Democritus, in a fragment of a lost work entitled *On the Proper Use of Words and Glosses* or *Of Homer* and quoted by Poliziano in his *Oratio*, observes that "Homer, chancing to get a divinely acting nature, constructed a universe of all sorts of words" [*Homêros phuseôs lachôn theazousês epeôn kosmon etektênato pantoiôn*], a comment that secures the vividness and etymological richness of Homeric epic to Democritus's materialist cosmology.[263]

Like the ancient Stoics, who turn to etymological interpretations of Homeric epic in order to correct the "divergence of human language from its natural foundation," Rabelais regards Homer's winged words as an antidote to the "deadening" of language, a means of restoring its "full and perfect relation" to the world of things.[264] From Plato's *Cratylus* onwards, ancient and Renaissance debates over whether language is natural or artificial often centre on the language of Homeric epic, in particular on the Homeric custom of having gods and mortals using different words for the same things.[265] As their initial fear at the sight of the frozen words gives way to an aural *jouissance* at the sound of their thawing, Pantagruel and Panurge participate in a Rabelaisian fantasy of communicating by means of a language that is at once immediate and transitory, visceral and fleeting. Casting "fistfuls of frozen words" onto the deck of their boat that "look like sweets of many colors" [*jecta sus le tillac plenes mains de parolles gelées, et sembloient dragée perlée de diverses couleurs*], Panurge comments that "at the foot of the mountain on which Moses received the Jewish Law, the people actually *saw* the voices" [*l'orée de la Montaigne en laquelle Moses receut la loy des Juifz, le people voyoit les voix sensiblement*] (*QL* 56:731–2). By pairing Homer and Moses (as well as Homer and Plato) as twin "logotherapists" who promise to heal the breach between *verba* and *res*, the episode of the *parolles dégelées* entertains the dream of a language "animated or inflated by some authentic wind" – by the *pneuma* that fills and shapes Rabelais's vitalistic and plenistic cosmos.[266]

Homer, Father of Farts

The *paroles dégelées* episode develops out of Rabelais's manipulation of the Homeric foundations of Stoic cosmology, which holds that all matter exists along a "dynamic continuum" differentiated only by "degrees of tension" or *tonos* that generate an ongoing process of "expansion and contraction."[267] This particular Stoic dimension of Homeric epic is widely acknowledged in antiquity: the pseudo-Plutarchan *Life* devotes four chapters to the Stoic dimensions of Homer's ethics and physics, and

Heraclitus's entire treatise is steeped in Stoic allegories of the Homeric gods and etymological interpretations of their names.[268] The Homeric undercurrents of the Stoic concept of *pneuma* are all the more persuasive to sixteenth-century writers given the close and mutually animating relationship between the pneumatic plenum of Stoic physics and ancient doctrines of poetic enthusiasm or *hierou pneumatos*, to use the phrase favoured by Democritus.[269] In his *Preface to Homer*, Melanchthon draws upon this connection when he asserts that Homer "fills, adorns, and endows the wind ... with enormous, and far more noble, and eternal riches," a model of poetic inspiration that is rooted in the vitalistic, plenistic cosmos often discerned in Homeric epic.[270] Widely acknowledged for his deep commitment to monistic vitalism, Rabelais finds the affinity between Homeric epic and Stoic physics appealing on several levels. In episodes such as Panurge's encomium to debt (*TL* 3–5), Homeric motifs assist in dramatizing a "pneumatic hexis" that produces cohesion out of tension, and, throughout his writing, Rabelais teases out Homer's ironies and incongruities so that his poems "ac[t] simultaneously in opposite directions" like the tonic motion of *pneuma*.[271]

There are plenty of serious motives for Rabelais's plenistic reading of Homer, which helps to valorize universality, communality, and mutuality on rhetorical, ethical, and spiritual levels. Yet Rabelais also manipulates the pneumatic elements of the Homeric cosmos – wind, air, breath, and flatulence – into vehicles for the comic deflation of epic grandeur. In chapter 5 of *Gargantua*, one of the drunken interlocutors justifies his lusty appetite by asserting, "Nature abhors a vacuum" [*Natura abhorret vacuum*], a maxim that promises a "remedy against thirst" [*remède contre la soif*] and also establishes a rhetorical and cosmological principle to which Rabelais adheres throughout his work (*G* 5:53–4). By placing all manner of terrestrial and bodily wind along a single continuum – an idea adapted from the Hippocratic treatise *Peri Phusôn* [On Wind; On Farts] – Rabelais promotes flatulence as a vital cosmic force, elevating it to the same height as the *Ruach*, or divine spirit, that nurtures the creation and continuation of the cosmos. He mentions the Hippocratic "*lib[er] de Flatibus*" in chapter 43 of the *Quart Livre*, a scene that transforms the Aeolus episode in the *Odyssey* – an episode frequently moralized by Homer's ancient allegorists – into a disquisition on flatulence, observing that "all maladies are born and proceed from wind" [*toute maladie naist et procède de ventosité*] (*QL* 43:698). The inhabitants of the Isle of Ruach "live on nothing but wind" [*ne vivent que de vent*] and "copiously break wind, fizzle, and fart" [*ilz vesnent, ilz pètent, ilz rottent copieusement*] (QL 43:697–8), their bodies becoming the "vast subterranean prison" into which both Virgil (*Aen.* 1.50–123) and Lucretius (*DRN* 6.189–203) transform Aeolus's cave of the winds from Book 10 of the *Odyssey*.[272] Unlike "Aeolus, that good snorer" [*le bon ronfleur Aeolus*], who gave his bag of wind to Odysseus "to direct the course of his ship in a calm" [*pour guider sa nauf en temps calme*], Rabelais's islanders guard theirs religiously "like another *sangréal*, curing several serious illnesses with it merely by releasing and delivering just enough for the patients to produce a virginal fart (the kind which nuns call a *son net*) [*comme un autre Sangréal, et en guérissoyt plusieurs énormes maladies, seulement en laschant et eslargissant ès malades autant qu'en fauldroit pour forger un pet virginal: c'est que les sanctimoniales appellant* sonnet] (*QL* 43:699). The conflation of celestial, terrestrial, and bodily wind on the isle of Ruach – all three are the same kind of "flowing and undulating air" [*air flottant et undoyant*] – creates a plenum that is at once cosmological and generic: divine afflatus and fart, inspired poet and coarse parodist, are infused with the same spirit (*QL* 43:698). If Homer's "magic wind-bag" provides Rabelais with a master metaphor for the "fallen text," it also provides an occasion to explore some of the paradoxes at the heart of his habits of mind.[273] Inhabiting "both medical and theological vocabularies," wind conflates high and low such that Aeolus's bag serves as an "epic bladder or codpiece," a wineskin, and a container to hold the winds, the "immortal, animate beings" that guarantee the continuance and equilibrium of world and body alike.[274]

Rabelais's travesties of Aeolus participate in a mock-epic tradition of great popularity and long duration in European literary culture. In Charles Cotton's *Scarronides* (1664–5), Aeolus whips up a storm by "withdrawing a peg from his anus and releasing a huge fart."[275] The mock-epic preoccupation with flatulence may take its origins from the *Homeric Hymn to Hermes*, where the infant god issues a fart, "an omen, menial servant of the belly, rude messenger" [*tlêmona gastros erithon, atasthalon angeliôtês*] that Apollo interprets as a divine sign.[276] Even in antiquity, mock-epic treatments of Aeolus existed, often serving to attack vanity and triviality, especially of the verbal variety. Aulus Gellius describes a Homeric parody by Timon of Phlius that satirizes sophists and "babblers" by comparing their heads to "the bags in which Aeolus deposited all his winds: balloons inflated with empty ideas."[277] This is certainly one of the undermeanings in *Pantagruel*'s debate by signs, in which Thaumaste "exhales" [*soufflait*] and "puffs up his cheeks" [*enfler les deux joues*] and then lets out a "great [lumberjack's] fart"[278] [*un gros pet de bûcheron*] in order to refute his adversary, a gesture that may take its cue from the adage *Subventanea parit* (III.vii.21), a phrase useful for describing empty utterances or "airy nothings" [*anemophorêta*] that Erasmus traces back to the Homeric expression "to speak words of wind" [*kakon d'anemôlia bazein*] (*P* 19:297).[279]

The pervasiveness of such mock-epic interpretations of Homeric epic during the Renaissance contribute to the image of Homer as poetic master of the nugatory, a counter-epic writer who relies heavily upon antithesis and paradox, but also a "whorson hungrie begger" and a "poore, blind, riming rascall," to cite Ben Jonson's two epithets from *Poetaster*, both indebted to Rabelaisian representations of the poet.[280] While Spenser and the poets of the *Pléiade* remain attentive to the serious moral and spiritual undermeanings of Homeric epic, other Elizabethan and Jacobean writers turn their eye to the *Batrachomyomachia*, a work already championed by two generations of northern reformers for its capacity to offer up trenchant criticisms of tyranny, factionalism, and religious strife in its witty and diminutive container. Even before Chapman tackles his English translation of the mock-epic, published in 1624, the *Batrachomyomachia* was rendered into English by William Fowldes (1603) and into Latin by Christopher Jonson (1580) and by William Gager, the latter also the author of *Ulysses Redux*, a tragicomic adaptation of the *Odyssey* that was performed at Christ Church College, Oxford, in February 1592.[281] While Gager appears intermittently uncomfortable with the low, ridiculous elements of the Homeric corpus, even inventing a speech in which Momus condemns Irus as "hungry, cowardly, and covered in rags," other Elizabethan writers embrace the comic dimensions of Homeric epic and mock-epic alike.[282] Retracing the literary genealogy laid out by the preface to Erasmus's *In Praise of Folly*, Thomas Nashe defends his *Lenten Stuffe* by protesting that "Homer of rats and frogs hath heroiqut it" and that "other oaten pipers" have followed suit by praising creatures as inconsequential as gnats, fleas, grasshoppers, butterflies, and even "Phillip Sparrow."[283] By identifying Homer as the father of the paradoxical encomium – a defender of all things petty and lowly – Nashe presents a rather different picture of a poet conventionally lauded as the favourite bedtime reading of military leaders such as Alexander the Great. Protesting in *Quaternio* against the attitude that "*Homer* [was] ... a Poet, that writ of warres and nothing els," a different Thomas Nash (1588–1648) explains that we should instead esteem Homer "and that which he had written *vt quisquiliae volantes, and venti spolia*, as dust and chaffe which the winde drives to and fro. *Erasmus* likewise after that he had written his *enchômion môrias*, knowing the dispositio[n] of the giddie *vnstable multitude*, to be prone to ranke him among mad-men and fooles, for that he had written in the prayse of *folly*, desires them whom the lightnesse of the subiect should any way offend ... he was not the first that had written of toyes and trifles."[284]

For Nashe, as well as for Nash, Homer's status as the original purveyor of the "toyes and trifles" later disbursed by Erasmian morosophy is inseparable from the poet's overturning of normative heroic values and conventions. This habit of debasing Iliadic heroism of *biê*, or force, in favour of an Odyssean heroism of *mêtis*, or cunning, emulates Homer's mock-epic inversion of norms, as does the parodic *Odyssey* narrated by Thomas Coryate's *Coryats Crudities* (1611), which fashions its protagonist into a "mad Greeke" and riffs on the opening lines of the *Odyssey* as it narrates sordid and outlandish adventures involving a famously enormous "Heidelbergian barrel" and a Venetian courtesan.[285] The numerous parallels between Coryate and Odysseus that crop up in the prefaces and dedicatory epistles of the *Crudities* may appear little more than an ongoing exercise in ironic debasement: a giant beer barrel bears little resemblance to the Trojan horse, except in its large capacity, and Coryate's "Venetian puncke" resembles Circe even less. Although his adventures are hardly the stuff of epic, the identification of Coryate as "our Britaine-Ulysses" demonstrates the extent to which Odysseus – and with him, Homer – assist Elizabethan and Jacobean writers in elevating an emergent cluster of intellectual virtues, including cunning, prudence, curiosity, and wit, that were beginning to challenge older forms of heroism.[286] Although he proves to be a very different kind of "English Homer" from Coryate or Nashe, Edmund Spenser likewise relies upon Homeric epic in order to expand and complicate his repertoire of heroic virtues in *The Faerie Queene*, a poem modelled on Homeric epic as well as on the allegorical commentary tradition that grew up around it.

Chapter Three

Spenser, Homer, and the Mythography of Strife

"he reckoned himself deceived and betrayed by faithless Discord, to whom he had entrusted the duty of sparking quarrels among the pagans: she had done this task poorly – indeed, if he looked at his intended goal, she seemed to have done the very opposite of what he designed."

– Ariosto, *Orlando Furioso*, XXVII.35

Part 1. The Concatenation of Virtue

Preparing to narrate his "chronicle of Briton kings" at the beginning of Book 2, canto 10, of *The Faerie Queene*, Edmund Spenser asks his muse for assistance in the "haughtie enterprise" in order to launch an "[a]rgument worthy of *Maeonian* quill."[1] It may seem odd that Spenser invokes Homer, and not Virgil, at this moment: the Roman poet is certainly the more logical patron of the dynastic epic about to unfold inside the castle of Alma. The allusion is a revealing moment for Spenser, a poet praised by contemporaries as "the only Homer living," a writer "whose hart inharbours Homers soule."[2] What makes the chronicle a Maeonian, rather than a Maronian, argument is that it presents an aetiology of discord, a narrative whose aim, much like that of *The Faerie Queene* as a whole, is to explain the origin and nature of strife.

Spenser's invocation of Homer reveals a profound debt to the Greek poet. Governed throughout by the idea of *concordia discors*, *The Faerie Queene* incorporates into its narrative and ethical structure one of the foremost principles of ancient and Renaissance Homeric allegorists, who interpret various episodes in the *Iliad* and *Odyssey* as dramatizing the oppositional yet complementary forces of *philia* and *eris*. This complex interplay between love and strife, which animates the interpretive tradition familiar to Spenser and other sixteenth-century readers of Homer, exerts itself on every level of Spenser's poem, from its treatment of psychological, social, and political discord to its representation of theological and cosmological conflict.

This is not to say that Spenser's most important or deliberate influence was Homer. So much of Spenser's knowledge of Homeric epic was mediated by Virgil and Statius, by Tasso and Ariosto, and by various philosophical and mythographic works that it is often difficult to distinguish Homer's influence from the influence of virtually every other writer at Spenser's disposal. He could and did read Homer in the original language, first at the Merchant Taylors' School, which from its founding in 1561 required Greek training in the upper forms, and then at Cambridge. While Spenser's Cambridge was no longer the centre of Greek studies it had been during the late 1530s and 1540s under the influence of John Cheke and Roger Ascham, its curriculum nonetheless included the study of Greek poetry and drama, and judging from Mulcaster's fellow students during the period, Spenser would have arrived there already proficient in Greek.[3] Henry Hutchinson, who attended the Merchant Taylors' school several years ahead of Spenser, left a probate inventory of his books in 1573 that includes two editions of Homer, one a Greek-only edition, as well as a "greake lexicon in two volumes" and several other Greek-Latin texts including works by Diogenes Laertius and Lucian. One of his contemporaries described Spenser as "perfect in the Greek tongue," praise that, even if hyperbolic, suggests sufficient skill to read the 1488 *editio princeps* of Homer and the 1517 Lascaris edition of the Homeric *Scholia* given to Cambridge University Library by Cuthbert Tunstall earlier in the sixteenth century, as well as manuscripts of Eustathius's and Tzetzes's Homeric commentaries, both donated from the same source.[4] At Cambridge and afterwards, Spenser would have had easy access to various Latin translations of Homer, including the 1573 abridged Latin *Iliad*, translated by Eobanus Hessus and owned by Gabriel Harvey, Spenser's friend and fellow member of Pembroke Hall.[5]

None of this means that Spenser was, or even wished to be, an expert scholar of Greek after the manner of Pierre de Ronsard or Jean Dorat, though he does share with these two *Pléaide* poets the tendency to imitate not Homer per se but rather those motifs and commonplaces teased out by Neoplatonic allegorical interpretations of Homeric epic. In the absence of an extant book collection or library catalogue such as we possess for Harvey, we cannot be certain that Spenser read any or all of the central texts of the Homeric commentary tradition, but contemporary English scholars certainly did. As early as 1531, a full decade before the *editio princeps* of the Byzantine commentary was printed at Rome, Thomas Elyot is already quoting Eustathius, "the expositour of Homere," in his *Boke of the Governour*. In the 1591 preface to his translation of *Orlando Furioso*, John Harington mentions the "treatise of the praise of Homers works," almost certainly a reference to the *Life of Homer* then attributed to Plutarch, printed in several sixteenth-century editions of the *Moralia* as well as in numerous contemporary editions of Homer.[6]

Spenser relies on these Homeric paratexts, as well as on para-Homeric myths such as the wedding of Peleus and Thetis and the Judgment of Paris, in order to fashion an epic whose underlying narrative is shaped by the allegorical traditions through which Homeric epic was interpreted by sixteenth-century poets and mythographers. Such an epic might not appear Homeric to our eyes, but it certainly does to Spenser, since the motif of elemental strife that dominates *The Faerie Queene*, and which "defin[es] the terms by which [he understood] harmony and conflict, stability and change," is pervasive in the allegorical paratexts that accompany the reintroduction of Homeric epic into Western Europe during the fourteenth and fifteenth centuries.[7] Readers of *The Faerie Queene* from S.K. Heninger and Robert Durling to David Quint and Jon Quitslund have persuasively demonstrated how the interplay between love and strife – the dynamic animating allegorical interpretations of the *Iliad* and *Odyssey* – shapes Spenser's representation of social and political interactions, of human passions, and of cosmological processes. But no critic yet has taken seriously the possibility that Spenser's persistent reliance on elements of Homeric allegory constitutes a protracted imitation of Homeric epic.

Spenser's renditions of Homeric episodes and motifs are often represented in the form of a *krisis*, a situation or event that requires judging or distinguishing between competing values such as harmony and discord, ease and toil, or contemplation and action.[8] As Spenser's characters come into contact with Homeric objects and landscapes – the houses of Morpheus and Ate; Phaedria's Phaiakian dystopia; Mammon's Hephaestian forge; Acrasia's Circeian bower; Florimell's Aphroditean girdle; Cambina's Nepenthe; Artegall's Achillean shield – they are obliged to confront the conflictive values embedded in an allegorized Homeric landscape animated persistently and variously by the forces of love and strife.

The first half of this chapter explores a key trope of *The Faerie Queene*'s Homeric mythography of strife: the golden chain. Spenser refashions Homer's golden chain into a master metaphor for his own narrative – a narrative that links his titular virtues "in lovely wize" (1.ix.1, 2) – and as a flexible conceit capable of embodying both correct and erroneous theological, cosmological, and ethical beliefs about the relationship between harmony and strife. Aware that the golden chain had already been marshalled by dozens of classical, patristic, and medieval writers in the service of various philosophical ideas and theological arguments, Spenser permits the Homeric conceit to be repeatedly misunderstood or misappropriated by the villains of *The Faerie Queene*. Night, Despair, Philotime, and Ate all invoke the chain to support doctrines that err by overemphasizing the appeals of ease or tranquillity, or by attributing to the chain mistaken ideas about the virtues of toil, rivalry, or strife.[9] The golden chain allows Spenser to imagine how contention might be both integral and subservient to a larger cosmic harmony, thus offering him a deeply attractive, conciliatory vision of a cosmic and theological order capable of embracing but also of controlling strife. Yet *The Faerie Queene* also dramatizes concerns that the metaphor might be deployed towards morally or theologically dangerous ends – towards the unabashed encouragement of rivalry in Philotime's court, or towards the contrary but equally perilous defence of tranquil inaction justified by Night's and Despair's misreadings of the chain. By demonstrating how the golden chain might encapsulate the two most dangerous extremes of contemporary Protestant theology – the view that fate fetters even the will of God, and the contrary belief in the limitless potential of the human will – Spenser's applications of the conceit assist him in steering through the Scyllas and Charybdises of his own theological landscape while at the same time helping him explore whether rivalry and ambition, as figured by the chain, support or erode the political stability of the Elizabethan court.

Spenser's Brazen Chains

Of the various incarnations of the golden chain in Spenser's *Faerie Queene*, the one that most eerily resembles its Homeric source is the "great gold chain ylincked well" that Philotime dangles, Zeus-like, from her throne in Book 2 (2.vii.46, 2). Like many of Spenser's representations of the conceit, as well as the vast majority of sixteenth-century allegorical interpretations of the golden chain, Philotime's *aurea catena* of ambition, its "upper end to highest heaven" knit and its lower part reaching "to lowest Hell," symbolizes "a certain correspondence and concatenation between elemental and celestial things" [*une certaine correspondence & concatenation des choses elementaires aux celestes*] (2.vii.46, 3–4).[10] While Mammon's regal daughter sits above the fray, her subjects struggle to heave themselves aloft while striving to keep their competitors from rising by the same means:

> And all that preace did round about her swell,
> To catchen hold of that long chaine, thereby
> To clime aloft, and others to excell:
> That was *Ambition*, rash desire to sty,
> And every lincke thereof a step of dignity. (2.vii.46, 5–9)

Tugged upon by rival courtiers each hoping to advance themselves through "unrighteous reward," "close shouldring," or "flateree," Philotime's chain of ambition exposes the seamy underbelly of political rivalry at the court of Elizabeth I, providing a stark contrast with the cooperative spirit embodied by the "goodly golden chaine" of Book 1, canto 9, which knits together Arthur and Redcrosse Knight in mutual friendship and assistance (2.vii.47, 2–3). Together, the two chains dramatize the poem's deep ambivalence about courtly rivalries capable of generating either cohesion or tension through rituals of male bonding that demand competition and cooperation at once. While Philotime's chain testifies to the ominous moral and spiritual consequences of rivalry, envy, and ambition, these vices are corrected by the chain binding Arthur and Redcrosse, a chain that represents the courtly virtues of cooperation, friendship, and chivalry.

The hostility inherent in Philotime's chain approximates Homer's two accounts of the golden chain in the *Iliad*, the first describing Zeus's boast that the subaltern gods cannot pull him down from Olympus by means of his "golden chain" [*seirên chruseiên*], and the second depicting an equally omnipotent and threatening Zeus as he suspends Hera from Olympus by a golden bond or chain [*desmon ... chruseon*] that cannot be loosened by any of the other gods (*Il.* 8.19–27, 15.18–28). As in Book 8 of the *Iliad*, where the resistance of the subaltern gods to Zeus's strength produces a *stasis* – a conflict marked not by turbulent dynamism but by stagnation between adversaries – Philotime's chain ensures her continued authority by hindering the mobility of those who try to ascend it; as Mammon points out to Guyon, "Honour and dignitie" are awarded solely by her (2.vii.48, 7). This is how George Chapman interprets the "golden chaine of Homers high device" in his *Shadow of Night*, glossing it as "Ambition ... or cursed avarice, / Which all Gods hailing being tyed to Jove, / Him from his settled height could never move."[11] Whether or not one interprets Spenser's Philotime as an indictment of what Wallace MacCaffrey has called the "frenetic atmosphere of pushing competition" in Queen Elizabeth's court, the courtly rivalries instigated by Philotime inhibit, rather than encourage, the virtuous emulation fostered in competition between the *Faerie Queene*'s more amicable rivals such as Cambell and Triamond or Calidore and Coridon.[12] The problem is not that Philotime's courtiers compete for attention and favour, but rather that, in a complaint already voiced by Erasmus in explicitly Homeric terms, their competition serves only to improve themselves and not each other.[13] Because Spenser understands rivalry and emulation as potentially beneficial forces, he is obliged to distinguish between wholesome and spiteful rivalry, a task in which he enlists Homer's golden chain as a symbol of both virtuous and vicious rivalry.

Sixteenth-century writers frequently look to Homeric epic for models of a virtuous rivalry that is binding rather than divisive, socially productive rather than corrosive. Pierre de La Primaudaye praises Nestor for rehearsing his own "prowes and valiant acts, to incourage Patroclus and the other nine knights to undertake the combat against *Hector* man to man" in a speech that uses "examples joined with the pricke of emulation." For Spenser, like La Primaudaye, the rivalry between *homotimi*, or men equal in honour, helps to strengthen and confirm the cosmological doctrine that "all things that moove within this generall globe are maintained by agreeing discords."[14] In other words, emulation is a social adhesive that helps to hold together the cosmos and its human inhabitants in a state of *concordia discors*, a principle especially evident in the rivalries that erupt in Books 4 and 6 of *The Faerie Queene*, only to be resolved into firm friendships. In the Sidney-Leicester circle during the 1580s, there is a particularly strong interest in studying classical texts that demonstrate the moral and political benefits of emulation. Works such as Xenophon's *Cyropaedia*, the text whose hero informs Sidney's theories of poetic imitation, show how martial and athletic competition may "kindle and stirre up in mens minds a strife" such that "games and exercises ... imprin[t] in the best sort contentions and emulations one with another."[15] Scenes of competition in *The Faerie Queene*, such as Book 4's Tournament of Maidenhead, exemplify this sort of emulation while simultaneously exercising the moral faculties of Spenser's readers, encouraging us to distinguish between the kind of strife that imprints virtue, and the kind of strife that does not.

Arthur and Redcrosse, Redcrosse and Guyon, and Cambell and Triamond each practise an idealized form of competition that strengthens their social bonds with each other while also exercising the physical and ethical virtues of both contestants. As friends who demonstrate the social benefits of competition, Cambell and Triamond resemble John Davies's praiseworthy description of two friends who become an "undevided One" through a mutually virtue-enhancing form of rivalry:

> In love contending who, for Vertues sake,
> (O blessed Strife excelling Unitie!)
> Shall do most good, & most men bounden make
> To you, to whom the World it selfe would tye.[16]

Invoking a chain that symbolizes the binding power of rivalrous energies, Davies's metaphor demonstrates how "blessed strife" (and not "unitie") is the force that "tye[s]" virtuous men to one another.

Philotime's golden chain, by contrast, condemns the political rivalry aroused by *philotimia*, or love of honour. This reading accords with the one offered by Natale Conti, who interprets the golden chain of Homer as an allegory of "ambition," which "drag[s] many men away from God's true religion and in the direction of false belief."[17] Both Conti and Spenser base their interpretations of the chain on Plutarch's and Aristotle's discussions of *philotimoi* – ambitious men, those stricken with an excessive love of honour, or those plagued with *kataphronêsis*, or contempt, the ailment afflicting Philotime's golden guard, Disdaine.[18] Yet, as is evident in the many examples of virtuous honour-seeking in the 1590 *Faerie Queene*, including Arthur, his squire Timias, and the Castle of Alma's Prays-Desire, *philotimia* is regarded by Aristotle and other classical writers not simply as a vice but also as a positive, virtuous mean between excessive and defective ambition; rather confusingly, perhaps, Aristotle refers to both the virtuous mean and its vicious excess by the same term, *philotimia*.[19]

The subtlety of the difference poses a central problem for Spenser as well as for the characters of Book 2, since it is not always clear how much unknightly railing, righteous indignation, and violence is appropriate to Guyon as he combats the enemies of temperance. With its failure to inculcate the benevolent, friendly rivalry implicit in the "goodly golden chaine" that links Arthur and Redcrosse in Book 1, Philotime's chain helps set into relief Spenser's vexations as he labours to distinguish virtuous from vicious *philotimia* and to condemn the more dangerous consequences of honour-seeking while still valorizing its benefits. Read side by side, the two allusions to the golden chain in Books 1 and 2 of *The Faerie Queene* reveal the profound ambivalence of the symbol as an allegorical vehicle for virtuous emulation and also for threats to it, depending on the context in which it is used.

Like Ate, Book 4's rendition of Homer's goddess of strife who longs "that great golden chaine quite to divide" in order to unravel the bonds of Concord, Philotime is an agent of discord who suffers a similar fall from aloft (4.i.30, 8). Formerly "worthy of heaven," Philotime is thrust down by the gods "for envy," a fate which calls into question her political authority by stripping away her powers of concatenation between earthly and celestial realms (2.vii.49, 5–6). Rather than justify her supremacy by naturalizing the hierarchical structure upon which her authority rests, Philotime's chain draws attention to its status as an artificial instrument of rule. Her effort to imitate Homer's Zeus, the original wielder of the chain, also illustrates how the image of a concatenated universe, a scale, ladder, or chain that reaches from heaven down to earth, may be abused – used to mythologize and legitimate an authority that is false or precarious. We are never far in spirit from Philotime's chain in the genealogies spun by Spenser's demonic monarchs and giants, figures such as Orgoglio, Mutability, and Lucifera, whose accounts of their own theogonies reveal their envious and rivalrous affections towards the Homeric gods from which they spring.[20]

Philotime's golden chain also breeds the kind of will-worshipping encouraged by a mistaken belief in unimpeded upward mobility across social and cosmic hierarchies. But Spenser shows how the golden chain may be used to support precisely the opposite theological affliction, namely, belief in an excessively fixed view of fate that equates a concatenated cosmos with one governed by an adamantine chain (or "spindle," to use Plato's metaphor) of Necessity.[21] If Philotime's chain of ambition highlights the ways in which political and natural philosophies founded upon a belief in the concatenation and coherence of celestial and terrestrial realms might foster rivalry or an excessive love of honour, Book 1's two master manipulators of the golden chain – Night and Despair – demonstrate the conceit to be equally dangerous when deployed in the service of a theology that errs by arguing for the fixity of fate and by regarding such fatalism as an antidote to spiritual strife. While Ate yearns to break the golden chain in order to unleash discord on the world of Book 4, Night and Despair misappropriate the golden chain in order to mitigate strife rather than to arouse it. A flexible tool in the hands of Spenser's characters, the golden chain may either justify or condemn discord by modifying the ways in which the purpose and value of that discord is understood.

The first incarnation of Homer's golden chain to appear in *The Faerie Queene*, Night's invocation of the "chayne of strong necessitee, / Which fast is tyde to Joves eternall seat," misconstrues the conceit as proof of the inextricability of fate, a belief which permits Night to abnegate responsibility for her sins and to advocate a philosophy of moral and spiritual indifference that perverts both Calvinistic and Stoic ideals of patience and *apatheia* (1.v.25, 5–6). It is possible to read Night's gloss on the chain as Spenser's condemnation of Homer's view of Fate, or *moira*, a reading strengthened by the fact that Calvin's *Institutes* cites the *Iliad* in order to criticize the misconception, commonly noted by English theologians of the 1590s, that divine providence releases us from responsibility for our sins, an error evident in Agamemnon's demurral that "I am not the cause, but Zeus and Fate."[22] Like many of Homer's classical and early Christian allegorists, Calvin detects a proto-Stoic doctrine of fate in Agamemnon's account of Ate, who "blinds" [*aatai*] men and "brings all things to their end" [*theos dia panta teleuta*], as well as in Hector's observation that "no man, whether good or bad, has ever escaped his fate [*moiran*]" (*Il.* 19.90–1, 6.488–9). But other Homeric commentators, including pseudo-Plutarch, argue that far from endorsing the belief that everything comes about through fate, Homer demonstrates how "a certain amount falls under the control of men, who have freedom of will, though an element of necessity is somehow attached to this."[23] Interpreted in this context, Night's error duplicates the misreading of the golden chain perpetrated by certain Stoics, who, according to Du Bartas, "tie / With Iron Chaines of strong Necessitie / Th'Eternals hands, and his free feet enstocke / In *Destinies* hard Diamantin Rocke."[24] As a means of explaining why the gods have favoured the "sonnes of Day" over her own children, Night's chain of necessity also fails to take into account a crucial aspect of Plato's explanation of the Fates in the myth of Er, whose adamantine spindle of necessity in no way cancels out either free will or the human responsibility for sin. "The blame is his who chooses," Plato's prophet explains, and "God is blameless," a statement that echoes Zeus's speech at the beginning of the *Odyssey*, which justifies the fate suffered by "blameless [*amumonos*] Aegisthus" by arguing that mortals blame their ills on the gods: "It is from us, they say, that evils come, but they themselves, through their own blind folly, bring upon them sorrows beyond those which are ordained" (*Od.* 1.29, 1.33–4).

By depicting necessity as chained to Zeus's seat, Spenser's Night refuses to acknowledge the compatibilist theology detected in Homeric epic by classical and Renaissance readers alike. Although "Spenser's own thinking [is] not so bound by the 'chayne of strong necessitie,'" as Quitslund rightly points out, the poet's urgency in pointing out Night's error does not necessarily constitute an attack on Homer's theology in the manner of Calvin, but may instead signal his efforts to ensure a sounder interpretation of that theology by privileging a Platonic exegetical tradition of Homer over a Stoic one.[25]

Night's misappropriation of the golden chain is all the more blatant given that several theological treatises of the 1590s allude to Homer's chain as an allegory of divine providence. Influenced by Thomas Aquinas's *Catena Aurea*, the title given to his Latin edition and concordance of the Gospels, late Elizabethan Calvinists make especially frequent recourse to the metaphor. William Perkins's *Golden Chaine*, first printed in 1591, invokes the concept even in its title to illustrate the "frame of the doctrine of Providence," and the treatise provides an elaborate flow chart depicting the first link in the chain as "Gods eternall decree" and the final link as the "manifestation of Gods glorie."[26] Although Night's chain of necessity posits a theology hostile to both Perkins and Calvin, Spenser opts to refine the metaphor of the golden chain rather than abandon it, offering a series of tutorials throughout the first two books of *The Faerie Queene* on how to interpret the chain. These lessons are modelled in part on the teachings of Boethius's Lady Philosophy, who explains that providence "binds" the actions and destinies of men in "an unbreakable chain of causes" [*indissolubili causarum conexione constringit*] but then qualifies this assertion by demonstrating that a "close-linked series of causes" does not negate the freedom of the will, since even a "fatal chain" [*fatalis catena*] does not bind men's minds.[27] *The Faerie Queene* follows a similar pattern of emendation: first, Night errs in conceiving the golden chain as a manifestation of Stoic *Heimarmenê* [fate or the orderly succession of causes and effects] that fetters both God and man, then Arthur intervenes at two later points in Book 1 to correct her account of the relationship between providence and human will, first to Una in canto 7, and then again to Redcrosse Knight two cantos later (1.vii.33, 1.ix.6).

Arthur's two accounts of the concatenatory power of providence complicate the standard Elizabethan gloss on Homer's golden chain by refusing either to assert or to deny the existence of a "fatal chain" that binds men's minds and actions. Unlike Abraham Fraunce, who interprets Jupiter's binding of Juno with a "golden chayne" as an allegory of the "cohoerent concatenation and depending of things united so in order, as none but the almightly Jupiter can dissolve the same," Arthur invokes the chain in order to meditate on our human incapacity to comprehend divine providence.[28] Spenser's interpretation of the golden chain thus anticipates Francis Bacon's 1605 *Advancement of Learning*, which reflects upon it as an allegory of divine accommodation: "That men and Gods were not able to draw Jupiter down to the Earth, but contrariwise, Jupiter was able to draw them up to Heaven. So as wee ought not to attempt to drawe downe or submitte the Mysteries of GOD to our Reason: but contrarywise, to raise and advance our Reason to the Divine Truthe."[29] Night's golden chain fetters God by positing a fate that circumscribes even His will, while Philotime's chain fetters God by inflating the capacity of human will into something so powerful that it may comprehend and even rival things divine. Like Bacon, Arthur recognizes that in order to support a theology that does not err towards either of these dangerous extremes, the golden chain must be interpreted as an allegory of accommodation. Tugging on the chain does not raise us up to God but instead pulls God down by reducing Him to our own limited capacity: "[i]f any strength we have, it is to ill, / But all the good is Gods, both power and eke will" (1.x.1, 8–9).

As the principal means by which divine truth is accommodated to the human intellect, language is at the heart of Spenser's understanding of the Homeric conceit. In the first episode that casts Arthur as glossator of the chain of providence, he allays Una's grief by teaching her how to reconcile will and grace, faith and despair, and flesh and reason: "Despaire breedes not (quoth he) where faith is staid. / No faith so fast (quoth she) but flesh does paire. / Flesh may empaire (quoth he) but reason can repaire" (1.vii.41, 7–9). While no chain is explicitly mentioned in Arthur's "well guided speach," it lurks rhetorically in the very structure of the exchange that, like the speech patterns of many of Spenser's most persuasive speakers, uses a rhetorical device called *concatenatio*. In other words, the dialogue between Arthur and Una *is* a golden chain, and its reliance upon repetition to link one line to the next creates ligatures that are cosmological and social as well as rhetorical. Throughout *The Faerie Queene*, tongues are bound and linked to one another by chains: both Malfont's tongue and that of the Blatant Beast are muzzled by chains "made with many a lincke," an image which constitutes the *in malo* version of Arthur's concatenatory eloquence, since both are linked emblematically to the Gallic Hercules, the figure whose rhetorical virtuosity is represented by his ability to draw a crowd of people towards him with a golden chain attached to his tongue (6.xii.34, 3). Hercules persuades his audience by the "force of that chayne fastned to his tong," according to George Puttenham's paraphrase of Lucian, and Arthur's "well guided speach" draws Una in a similar fashion.[30]

Other Spenserian orators frequently resort to similar rhetorical devices, including *synathrismus* (the stringing together of related terms), *anaphora* (the repetition of a word or phrase at the beginning of successive clauses or lines), and *epanalepsis* (the repetition of a word or phrase at the beginning and the end of a line or stanza). Such rhetorical devices often appear in passages that explicate the nature of cosmic or social bonds or that emphasize the conciliatory interlacement of opposites – the mutual yielding of victory between Cambell and Triamond (4.iv.36, 4–6), the account of Love and Hate bound together by Concord (4.x.32, 6–9), or the description of the intertwined triad of Book 6's Graces, whose postures and rhythm, according to Edgar Wind, create a "dialectic" that moves from concord to opposition and finally to "concord in opposition."[31] But Spenser's demonic masters of persuasion such as Despair and Phaedria use similar rhetorical patterns to devastating effect, suggesting that for Spenser, the *adamantis catenis* of eloquent persuasion may be as dangerous as it is salutary, capable of exacerbating spiritual conflicts and tensions as well as of solving them.

The greatest threat posed by Night's misconstrual of the golden chain is the melancholy fatalism she shares with Duessa, Sansjoy, and Despair.[32] Her belief in a "fatal chain" that binds the human will fuels a hopelessness that discourages both the active pursuit of virtue and the avowal of personal responsibility for sin. The Homeric and Hesiodic foundations of Spenser's Night contribute to her role as a cautionary emblem for the spiritual indifference and false tranquillity that prove so tempting throughout *The Faerie Queene*.[33] Despair tempts Redcrosse into spiritual apathy with his offer of "Sleepe after toyle, port after stormie seas," while Spenser's Night and her kin expose as false and spiritually hazardous the ease and resignation that arise out of hopelessness (1.ix.40, 8). When Duessa, Night's granddaughter, descends to Hades to persuade Aesculapius to cure Sansjoy, her arguments prey upon a similarly illusory belief that, already "[e]mprisond ... in chaines remedilesse" and forever "in the powre of everlasting Night," Æsculapius "canst not hope for thing" and might as well compound his former sins by helping her out (1.v.36, 8, 1.v.43, 5, 1.v.43, 3).

The second malevolent invocation of the golden chain in Book 1 of *The Faerie Queene* shows the danger posed by the conceit when it is used to argue for the spiritual value of *stasis* and immobility – a danger far greater, it turns out, than the tension and strife inherent in Homer's depiction of the chain or in the narrator's adaptation of it at 1.ix.1. Echoing Night, Despair calls into doubt Redcrosse Knight's ability to "strive with strong necessitie, / That holds the world in his still-changing state, / Or shunne the death ordayned by destinie?" (1.ix.42, 6–8). By placing an excessive emphasis on cosmic fixity, as exemplified by a chain that links but also binds the "still-changing" cosmos, Despair offers a theology that complements and supports his false representation of death as sleep or peaceful ease – precisely the kind of tranquillity that Arthur describes himself as having repudiated at the beginning of canto 9. In the episode with Despair, Spenser represents sleep as a spiritually deadening *elisio* or as a malevolent fantasy of *Elysium*, a reading shaped by his reading of Book 14 of the *Iliad*, in which Hera enlists Sleep, Night, and the *cestus* of Aphrodite – that discord-provoking girdle which appears in Book 4 of *The Faerie Queene* – to entice her husband Zeus into a post-coital stupor in order to distract him from her intended aim of rekindling the conflict between the Greeks and the Trojans while he sleeps. The "sound sleep" [*hupnos … nêgretos*] so often associated in Homeric epic with tranquillity and mental release in fact produces the opposite effect when manipulated by Hera, and Spenser repeatedly warns his readers that the "eternall rest / And happie ease" promised by Despair is no way to escape strife (*Od.* 13.79–80; *FQ* 1.ix.40, 1–2). Even as sixteenth-century mythographers routinely gloss the Homeric personification of sleep as "the giver of ease & quiet, & the mittigater and allaier of great and heavie labors," Spenser's confidence in the moral and spiritual value of labour and adversity complicates his ability to endorse the values that underpin the Homeric epithets of sweet sleep and sound sleep.[34]

Spenser's heroes are repeatedly tempted by ominous fantasies of retreat, resignation, and the "carelesse Quiet" of sleep and death, twinned states presented as opportunities for liberation from "repining strife" that, in the words of Sansloy, permits us "In peace [to pass] over *Lethe* lake" (1.i.41, 8, 1.iii.36, 5–6). The first two books of *The Faerie Queene* repeatedly present their heroes as facing a difficult choice between ease and adversity or between tranquillity and strife. The lessons taught by Belphoebe and the Palmer, or those learnt by Redcrosse Knight in his exchange with Heavenly Contemplation, all reveal the correct choice to be the turbulent and "loathsome life" dismissed, wrongly, by Despair as consisting of nothing but "Feare, sicknesse, age, losse, labour, sorrow, strife" (1.ix.44, 6, 1.ix.44, 9). If sleep and ease fail to deliver the tranquillity they seem to promise, instead signalling a fatalistic capitulation to destiny or spiritual indifference, Spenser is less interested in identifying the best means of arriving at such tranquillity than he is in exposing the falsity of choosing tranquillity over the spiritually productive conditions of adversity and conflict.

Greeks Giving Gifts

The Faerie Queene's "correct" version of the golden chain is the "Goodly golden chaine" praised by the narrator in the invocation to Book 1, canto

9, an image that celebrates neither divine providence nor the correspondence between celestial and terrestrial realms but rather the concatenation of virtue and, by extension, the triumph of cooperative over competitive values that Spenser identifies as the essence of true chivalry:

> O Goodly golden chaine, wherewith yfere
> The vertues linked are in lovely wize:
> And noble minds of yore allyed were,
> In brave poursuit of chevalrous emprize,
> That none did others safety despize,
> Nor aid envy to him, in need that stands,
> But friendly each did others prayse devize. (I.ix.1, 1–8)

As a device that connects one knight to another, Spenser's golden chain should be read in the context of the argument to canto 9, which recounts how the "knights knit friendly bands" in order to exorcise the contentiousness and envy that so often motivate feats of chivalric virtue elsewhere in *The Faerie Queene*. On one level of Spenser's text, Arthur appears to be the chief link in a chain that unites all of Spenser's titular virtues by interweaving each of their narratives with his own. On another level, however, the chief link is Redcrosse Knight, whose binding power as Spenser's allegorical instantiation of holiness confirms Clement of Alexandria's observation in the *Stromata* that all virtues are connected to each other by way of the central virtue of faith.[35] Archimago's primary aim (and that of Ate, his Homeric sidekick in Book 4) is to destroy this chain of virtues: when he spies Redcrosse Knight at the beginning of Book 2, he plots to "stirre up enmitye / Of such, as vertues like mote unto him allye," thus dividing faith from temperance until their connection is reaffirmed by the arrival of the "blessed Angels" who come to Guyon's assistance at the beginning of Book 2, canto 8 (2.i.23, 8–9, 2.viii.1, 8).

In order to underscore his careful revision of Homer's golden chain, a revision that translates a symbol of internecine strife among the Olympian gods into a metaphor for social concord, Spenser binds Arthur and Redcrosse by adapting a Homeric scene of gift-giving. When the two knights exchange "goodly gifts" and join hands "fast friendship for to bind," they participate in but also improve upon a typically Homeric vehicle for social bonding, translating the Homeric custom into a practice congenial to the Elizabethan custom of exchanging gifts (1.ix.18, 6, 1.ix.18, 8).[36] Inasmuch as the scene both imitates and revises this Homeric *topos*, the exchange of gifts between Arthur and Redcrosse endorses cooperative values such as friendship and charity – values that Spenser labours to uphold throughout *The Faerie Queene* by sifting them out from potentially contrary impulses, such as rivalry or love of honour, that motivate the heroic deeds of the Homeric warriors upon whom Arthur's and Redcrosse's exchange is partially modelled. Both of the gift exchanges in the *Iliad* – Diomedes's disingenuous gesture of friendship, designed to persuade Glaucus to swap his own golden armour for the bronze weapons of his Greek adversary (*Il.* 6.232–6), and the subsequent exchange of arms between Hector and Ajax (7.299–302), in which the two soldiers swap weapons that ultimately bring about the destruction of both men – produce violence and discord rather than allaying it. The tokens of friendship exchanged in the *Iliad* often become *echthistos* – hostile gifts that confirm the Greek proverb, popularized by Erasmus's *Adages* and Alciati's *Emblemata*, that the gifts of enemies are no gifts. But the objects exchanged between Arthur and Redcrosse Knight do not backfire against their recipients. Instead, the gifts knit together the two knights and also help to reconcile their respective virtues of magnificence (or magnanimity) and faith.[37]

As a trope that assists in transforming the Homeric gift exchange between Arthur and Redcrosse into a celebration of charity and mutual assistance, the golden chain of Book 1, canto 9 is one of several efforts by Spenser to improve upon epic scenes of hospitality and gift-giving, particularly those depicted in the *Iliad* and *Odyssey*, where the exchange of gifts, howsoever crucial it may be to the social fabric of the poems, often fails to cement social bonds. At various moments in *The Faerie Queene*, scenes of gift-giving and related expressions of hospitality turn against their Homeric sources, alerting the reader to the limitations of an ethical framework that valorizes guest-host relations at the expense of other, more valuable, moral virtues such as temperance. Hospitality, a virtue especially prized in the *Odyssey*, is explicitly repudiated by Guyon, who despite his resemblance to Homer's wandering hero finds himself in situations where he must resist false gestures of hospitality offered by Mammon and by the inhabitants of the Bower of Bliss. Guyon's antagonists adhere slavishly to a Homeric decorum of guest-host relations, but their gifts, much like the weapons exchanged between Hector and Ajax, underscore that the gifts of enemies are no gifts. In the Cave of Mammon, Guyon refuses to accept "Thing offred, till I know it well be got," turning down Mammon's offers of money, his daughter's hand in marriage, and an apple resembling the one tossed by Atê at the wedding of Peleus and Thetis (2.vii.19, 2). The allusion hints at the fact that the Trojan War was set into motion by a hostile and self-interested gesture of generosity, a gift that was no gift at all.

Mammon offers Guyon two quintessentially Homeric "gifts of discord" that disrupt rather than strengthen social bonds: the apple tossed by "false Ate," an allusion to Eris's contribution to the wedding of Peleus and Thetis, and a "silver stoole / To rest thy wearie person" (2.vii.54, 5, 2.vii.63, 8–9).[38] James Nohrnberg has speculated that the stool is an allusion either to the "Lethaea," or chair of forgetfulness, described by Horace (*Odes* IV.7) or to *Il.* 14.239–42, where Hera promises Sleep a "fair throne" and a "stool for the feet, on which you may rest your shining feet."[39] Stools are common enough resting places for the feet of classical heroes, but Spenser may also have in mind another Homeric stool, this one (like his own) a silver one. In Book 18 of the *Iliad*, Charis welcomes "silver-footed Thetis" to Hephaestus's cave and displays the "hospitality" [*xeinia*] that befits her name by offering Achilles's mother a silver-studded chair and stool on which to rest her feet while the god of the forge toils away at her son's shield. Particularly given Mammon's strong associations with Hephaestus, the Greek god of the forge, the correspondence between the two silver stools is persuasive, even as it is also deceptive: Guyon must figure out whether the stool is a genuine offer of hospitality (as it is in *Iliad* 18) or a perilously Lotos-like narcotic that induces oblivion (as do the stools in *Iliad* 14 and Horace). Since no Charis attends upon Spenser's Mammon – the money God is hardly inclined to give away his money for free – the silver stool instead represents the disingenuous hospitality that abounds in Mammon's cave, a false Charis corrected and redeemed by "th'exceeding grace / Of highest God" that is given to Guyon at the beginning of the following canto in order to rouse him from the lethaean stupor into which he slips after emerging from Hades (2.viii.1, 5–6).

The episode in Mammon's cave indicts Homeric *philoxenia*, the hospitality that, counter to Spenser's comprehension of divine grace, is not performed "all for love, and nothing for reward" but rather is motivated by enlightened self-interest: in Homeric epic, for the most part, gifts are given so that gifts will be received (2.viii.2, 8). But Guyon's trial in the cave of Mammon also reflects a hermeneutic dilemma faced by all Renaissance readers of pagan texts: whether to follow selectively or to abstain wholly from the ethical principles and ideals endorsed by Homer and other classical writers. Evoking a metaphor used by Christian readers of pagan texts from Clement of Alexandria to Guillaume Budé, Arthur Golding advises in the preface to his 1567 translation of Ovid's *Metamorphoses* that those readers unable or unwilling to cull "wholesome hests and precepts" from Ovid's text should instead "abstain until he be more strong, / And for to use Ulysses' feat against the mermaids' song."[40] This interpretive strategy informs Guyon's movements through the palpably Odyssean landscapes of Book 2 of *The Faerie Queene*. The most Odyssean of Spenser's heroes, Guyon exercises his virtue of temperance – a virtue founded upon, yet also distinct from, the moderation of Homer's Odysseus – by learning to discern between the *Odyssey*'s more wholesome values and its dangerous ones (2.vii.1, 7).[41]

Despite the "impeccable politeness" detected in him by some readers, Homer's Odysseus does not accept every gift offered to him. He refuses Calypso's offer of immortality in favour of "great suffering and toil" [*polla pathon kai polla mogêsa*] and the aging wife who awaits him in Ithaca (*Od.* 5.220–4), a choice that Milton will render ironic and tragic as he narrates Adam's fall in *Paradise Lost*.[42] Whereas Plato interprets Odysseus's rejection of immortality as a rejection of honour in favour of the "life of an ordinary citizen who minded his own business," Guyon's refusal to accept the gifts offered by his Homeric hosts does not simply duplicate Odysseus's rejection of immortality and fame for the contentment of *mediocritas*.[43] Guyon's temperance is different from the moderation of Odysseus, though both forms of *mediocritas* do allow for sudden outbreaks of intense violence fuelled by indignation, and both allow for heroes eager to pursue "honour vertues meed" (2.iii.10, 8). Even so, Guyon has a strained relationship with his Homeric counterpart, since his reluctance to indebt himself to strangers distances him from Odyssean models of gift-giving.

The Odyssean model of *philia*, in which reciprocal bonds between friends or between guest and host are established through the giving and receiving of gifts, is explicitly challenged at the beginning of Book 2, canto 8. Arthur has just rescued Guyon from Pyrochles: when Guyon declares himself eternally bound to his rescuer, he is corrected by his fellow knight for misconstruing the golden chain of chivalric friendship as an endorsement of the tit-for-tat mentality that binds Paridell and Blandamour, albeit temporarily, in Book 4. Arthur asks Guyon, "what need / Good turnes be counted, as a servile bond, / To bind their doers, to receive their meede?" (2.viii.56, 1–3). Yet twice more, in the Bower of Bliss, Guyon is tested for his continued vulnerability to a Homeric model of reciprocal gift-giving in scenes that interrogate whether the Odyssean ideals of courtesy and hospitality are really consonant with the canons of Elizabethan chivalry. In both instances, Guyon passes the test by deviating from the *politesse* that defines Odysseus's behaviour in similar circumstances: first he spurns Genius's "idle curtesie" by dashing his bowl of wine violently to the ground; then, he similarly rebuffs Excesse, overturning her cup of nectar despite the seeming kindness of the gesture: "It was her guise, all

Straungers goodly so to greet" (2.xii.49, 7, 2.xii.56, 9). Unlike Odysseus, who protects himself with Hermes's Moly – an herb alternately interpreted by the allegorists as a symbol of temperance or of right reason – so that he may partake safely of the contents of Circe's cup, Guyon has no compunction about offending his hosts. Instead, he uses the Palmer's rod – Spenser's version of the *Odyssey*'s Hermetic *rhabdos* – to beat them off.

Elizabethan readers of Homer often acknowledge that the moral values and social codes of ancient Ithaca, Mycenae, and Pylos were far different from those prevalent at Nonsuch and Hampton Court. In the 1591 preface to his English translation of Ariosto's *Orlando Furioso*, John Harington excuses the barbarity of certain scenes in the *Iliad* and *Odyssey* when he observes that what was "commendable in [Homer] to write in that age, the times being changed, would be thought otherwise now."[44] Spenser appears to agree, demonstrating that the decorum governing Odysseus's behaviour during his travels does not apply to Guyon, and thus preventing his readers from confusing the virtue of temperance with civility or (worse still) with the superficial veneer of good manners.

Guyon's deviations from Odyssean decorum not only preserve and defend the culturally contingent values of the *Odyssey* as distinct from those celebrated by Spenser's poem but also help to explain his destruction of the Bower of Bliss, an act often misconstrued by readers as excessively violent. As he tears down Acrasia's palace with "rigour pitilesse," Guyon transforms a specifically Odyssean conception of the virtue of moderation [*metrios*]. At the end of the *Odyssey*, Odysseus's restraint gives way to a spectacular frenzy of violence with the massacre of the suitors, a scene represented in the sixteenth-century fresco cycles of Giovanni Castello (Villa Pallavicino, Genoa) and Francesco Primaticcio (Palais de Fontainebleau, France, now destroyed). But at various other junctures in the poem, Odysseus totters on the brink of committing acts of violence only to stop short of bloodshed: Pellegrino Tibaldi (see figure 5) depicts one such moment, when Odysseus, as instructed by Hermes, pulls his sword against Circe in order that she might submit to him and swear an oath, a scene that both imitates and corrects Achilles's near-murder of Agamemnon in the opening book of the *Iliad*.

Guyon destroys what Odysseus only threatens to destroy. While Book 2 of *The Faerie Queene* opens by grounding Guyon's virtue in Peripatetic ideals of moderation, those ideals grow more complicated as the book unfolds, eventually giving way to a brand of temperance that works hand in hand with the righteous indignation, or Nemesis, with which temperance was often associated in sixteenth-century emblem books and

Figure 5. Pellegrino Tibaldi, *Ulysses and the Sorceress Circe*. Circa 1550. Fresco, Sala di Ulisse, Palazzo Poggi, Bologna, Italy. Courtesy Bridgeman Images.

mythographies.[45] In Homeric epic, Nemesis is a form of distributive justice – to each his due reward or punishment – that involves the moderation of emotional excess and of cosmic or social imbalances, often achieving that moderation through dynamic and often violent means.[46] Defined by his temperance but also by his shamefastness and his susceptibility to indignation, Guyon's affective range is neatly circumscribed by the Homeric meanings of the verb *nemesaô*: to feel just resentment or properly directed shame.

Many Renaissance readers condemn the irate outbursts of Homeric heroes as marks of their vulnerability to unruly affections. Spenser, like Tasso before him and Milton after, attempts to recuperate Homeric wrath as a species of righteous indignation or pious scorn. Guyon's anger is modelled not on Achilles but rather on Odysseus, and Spenser is careful to distance Guyon's moderate anger from the uncrontrollable wrath of Pyrochles and Huddibras, Book 2's versions of Achilles and Ajax, whose anger is kindled by a rabble of quasi-Homeric deities including Atin, Furor, and the "fell Erinnys" whose "hellish brond" rouses the "strifull" minds of Medina's sisters and their suitors (2.ii.29, 2–3; 2.ii.13, 5). Charles Lemmi has pointed out that Spenser deviates from the usual Homeric conception of the Erinnys as "ministers of retribution," which is how Phoenix invokes them, along with Atê, in Book 9 of the *Iliad*. Instead, Spenser invokes these furies as "spirits of discord or furious anger," externalizations of debased and irrational passion rather than instruments for carrying out a divinely ordained curse.[47]

Spenser's heuristic imitation of Homeric scenes of gift-giving, which reaches a climax at the end of Book 2, drives home the structural and functional difference between pagan virtues of generosity and hospitality and Christian ideals of charity or grace. Like Erasmus, who interprets Homeric proverbs about gift-giving through the lens of Clement of Alexandria, Spenser transforms the epic convention of armourial exchange into an allegory of divine grace – a gift for which there is no adequate recompense.[48] Both Arthur's gift to Redcrosse, a diamond-encrusted box containing a liquor of "wondrous worth, and vertue excellent," and Redcrosse's gift to Arthur, a copy of the New Testament and a "worke of wondrous grace, and able soules to save," are divine gifts; neither really belongs to each knight to give away, since, as Spenser is keen to remind us in the invocation to Book 1, canto 10, whatever virtue mortals possess derives from the gratuitous gift of God's grace (1.ix.19, 4; 1.ix.19, 9). As symbols of divine grace whose bestowal is made without regard to merit and cannot be reciprocated, the gifts exchanged by Arthur and Redcrosse complicate the role played by gift-giving in the culture of pagan epic, where the mutual exchange of objects creates reciprocal bonds of *philia* by establishing debts that can and will be paid back in turn.

The Muse of Love and Strife

The golden chain of Book 1, canto 9 at first appears to repudiate the spirit of rivalry and strife that shapes the social and cosmic superstructures of its Homeric source. Yet a mere ten stanzas after Spenser's narrator introduces the Homeric conceit of a chain linking the two knights in a palpably un-Homeric bond of mutual cooperation and friendship, Arthur confesses his own youthful attraction to contention, relating how he once scorned the "idle name of love, and lovers life" and instead "joyd to stirre up strife" (1.ix.10, 1–3). Although Arthur's contentious spirit is soothed, to some degree, by Gloriana's night-time visitation, the remainder of Book 1, canto 9 redirects and corrects Redcrosse Knight's similar struggle to reject what might be regarded as an excessive love of contention. In the cave of Despair, Redcrosse demonstrates himself to be perilously vulnerable to the erroneous logic that he must relinquish "All those great battels, which thou boasts to win, / Through strife, and bloud-shed, and avengement" (1.ix.43, 3–4). The subsequent trial, in which Redcrosse struggles to resist the promise of tranquillity and return to a life of strife and martial conflict, underscores the difficulty of discerning whether the desire for rest and ease is dangerous, virtuous, or both at once. By reiterating some of Despair's criticisms of the warrior life in the previous canto ("For bloud can nought but sinne, & wars but sorrowes yield"), Heavenly Contemplation provokes in Redcrosse yet another fit of *contemptu mundi*, telling him that once he has won his "famous victorie," the knight must "turne againe / Backe to the world, whose joyes so fruitlesse are" (1.x.60, 5; 1.x.60, 7–9). In light of Redcrosse's desire to "wash [my] hands from guilt of bloudy field," the instructions provided by Heavenly Contemplation make for a rather bittersweet victory over the dragon, one in which little sense of triumph or honour accrues to the victor. This ambivalence is echoed by the narrator's equally half-hearted resignation to the "unfitter taske" of writing heroic poetry as he reluctantly trades in his "Oaten reeds" for "trumpets sterne" in the Proem to Book 1. One of the commendatory verses to *The Faerie Queene*, written by W.L., grants Spenser's initial unwillingness to enter into the domain of epic a Homeric origin – Homeric by way of Statius's *Achilleid*, anyway. Like Achilles disguising himself in "womans weedes" in the hope that he might "by sleight the fatall warres to scape," a ruse which works only until Odysseus discovers the masquerade and forceably conscripts his comrade, Spenser had to be coaxed by Sidney into the role of epic poet: just as Odysseus "brought faire *Thetis* sonne / From his retired life to menage armes: / So *Spencer* was by *Sidneys* speaches wonne, / To blaze her fame not fearing future harmes."[49]

Throughout Book 1, Spenser's narrator represents his decision to follow the Virgilian poetic *cursus* laid out by the pseudepigraphic prooemium to the *Aeneid* – from the "slender pipe" to the "eager husbandman" and finally to the "shuddering arms of Mars" – as a choice fraught with the trade-offs and perils also faced by Homer's Achilles, who casts off his "shepheardes weedes" for armour in an exchange later inverted by Book 6's Calidore, who downsizes from "steelehead speare" to "shepheards hooke" (6.ix.36, 5).[50] Spenser's narrator depicts his transformation from pastoral to epic poet not as the ascent traced by the pseudo-epigraph to the *Aeneid* but rather as the Achillean dilemma of choosing between the serenity of a long but obscure life and a brief life marred by conflict but memorialized by fame. The narrator thus aligns the vexations of his own poetic career with a series of Homeric and para-Homeric episodes that concern the difficulty of choosing between strife, fame, and immortality on the one hand and the tranquil pleasures of rusticity and retreat on the other. Portions of Spenser's narrative appear to follow the counter-epic, homeward route of Odysseus, the "long wandring Greeke, / That for his love refused deitie" (1.iii.21, 4–5). Both Redcrosse and Guyon are repeatedly lured away from heroic quests and towards an Odyssean *nostos*, a narrative entangled throughout *The Faerie Queene* with the misdirected desire to remain "in peace" in the New Jerusalem, that "last long voyage" that promises sleep after toil (1.x.63, 3–4). Elsewhere, Spenser's narrator depicts himself at the crossroads of a heroic *krisis* in which he must negotiate between strife and love or between martial conflict and pastoral ease (1.iii.21, 4–5).[51] In the *Proem* to Book 1, this conflict is dramatized by a triadic muse that promises to reconcile love and strife, uniting the sensual pleasure and heroic fame that prove mutually exclusive for Homer's Achilles but not necessarily for the heroes of Spenser's poem. Invoking Venus, the disarmed Cupid, and "triumphant *Mart*, / In loves and gentle iollities arrayd, / After his murderous spoiles and bloudy rage allayd," Spenser's narrator represents the guiding force of the poem not as an epic muse but rather as a *post-epic* muse, one who enjoys the renown gained from former triumphs but basks in an enervating serenity that (disturbingly) resembles the lethargy of Cymochles and Verdant, figures cast as a disarmed Mars who has succumbed to the powers of an Acrasian Venus (1.Proem.3, 7–9).

By invoking this poetic trinity, Spenser draws upon an established tradition of interpreting the union of Venus and Mars, a myth first recounted by the bard Demodocus in Book 8 of the *Odyssey*, as an allegory for the oppositional yet complementary powers of *eris* and *philia*. The muse of the Proem to Book 1 seeks to achieve a similar *concordia discors* between the oaten reeds of love and the stern trumpets of strife, announcing that it is not "the time for the horrors of Mars" ("*nunc horrentia Martis*") but rather past that time as Spenser's post-epic muse introduces a Mars enjoying the "jollity" and serenity that come after his military triumphs. In the invocation to Book 1, canto 11, Spenser imagines his muse as animated by a similar coincidence of opposites. This time, however, inspiration comes from a pre-epic muse who proclaims that the time for war has not yet arrived. Invoking his muse to "gently come into my feeble brest," Spenser's narrator declares his desire to temper his heroic wrath and postpone its full expression until a later date:

> Come gently, but not with that mighty rage,
> Wherewith the martiall troupes thou dost infest,
> And harts of great Heroes doest enrage,
> That nought their kindled courage may aswage,
> Soone as thy dreadfull trompe begins to sownd. (1.xi.6, 1–6)

Reserving the "furious fit" of his epic muse "Till I of warres and bloudy Mars do sing," an event that presumably would have taken place in the final book of *The Faerie Queene*, Spenser banishes the *thumos*-rousing trumpet associated throughout Homer's *Iliad* with Ares, the god of war, and his sister Eris, the goddess of strife (1.xi.7, 1–2; see *Il.* 11.11–14). If Homer's Eris helps to clarify the choice between a heroic death in battle and an ignoble homeward retreat – the choice faced by Spenser himself according to W.L.'s commendatory verse –the invocation to Book 1, canto 11 of *The Faerie Queene* delays and questions the urgency of making such a choice, instead seeking out a *via media*, a "second tenor" that moderates and reserves the poet's more "haughtie string" (1.xi.7, 7–8).

Spenser's plea for a muse gentler and less courage-kindling than the one imagined as governing the poem's projected final battle scene is often interpreted as a moment of self-doubt in which the narrator questions his epic project.[52] However, like the epic convention of "non-encounter" between two adversaries, such as the combat between Aeneas and Achilles cut short by a blinding mist issued from Zeus, Spenser's "second tenor" is designed not to banish the warring spirit of epic but rather to perfect it through delay, a technique, called "keeping in store" [*phulattein*], that is identified by Homer's ancient scholiasts at several critical junctures of the *Iliad*.[53] While the invocation to Book 1, canto 11 has been interpreted as evidence of *The Faerie Queene*'s Virgilian (and thus counter-Homeric) design in that it anticipates the turn away from Odyssean romance and towards Iliadic epic made by the *Aeneid*, the invocation also delays the poem's promised (but unfulfilled) turn from one mode to the other.

The two invocations of Book 1 present two of the poem's many configurations of the union of Venus and Mars that serve as iconographic shorthand for one of *The Faerie Queene*'s dominant poetic, moral, and cosmic principles: the *coincidentia oppositorum* of love and strife. This motif dominates the various dyads of Books 3 and 4 – Venus and Diana, Amoret and Belphoebe, Concord and Ate, Love and Hate – who dramatize the oppositional yet complementary relationship between forces that were widely regarded during antiquity and in the sixteenth century as the building blocks of an allegorized Homeric cosmos. At times, the forces of love and strife manifest themselves as internal tensions within a single character such as Cupid, the god of love who is also the "enimy of peace, and author of all strife," or Britomart, whose combination of "manly terrour" and "amiable grace" marks her as a *Venus Victrix* and as a descendant of Athena, the goddess who favours peace yet sports a shield adorned with images of Phobos, Eris, Alkê, and Iôkê – terror, strife, valour, and assault (3.vi.14, 9; 3.i.46, 1–2).[54] At other times, Spenser's allegorical interplay of love and strife refracts these cosmic principles of self-contrariety upon the landscape of such places as Garden of Adonis and the Temple of Venus.[55]

As Quitslund has argued, the narrative and ethical structure of *The Faerie Queene* is founded upon the idea that the perpetuation of order depends upon two antipathetic but equally necessary forces, the firm grasp of love and the divisive power of strife. Yet Quitslund argues that Spenser ultimately "devalues strife" and does not "glorify heroic striving per se," an argument hard to reconcile with the position that, for Spenser, strife "is intrinsic to the dynamics of its antithesis, love."[56] Even as the forces of *philia* may ultimately have emerged victorious at the non-existent end of the poem, strife often acts as a productive and generative force in *The Faerie Queene*, and it is not true that Spenser has "little use ... for striving" until that final moment arrives.[57] On the contrary, whenever the forces of *philia* in *The Faerie Queene* threaten wholly to dominate the forces of strife – as they do in the Bower of Bliss – we are right to be alarmed that such a conquest inhibits both creative energy and virtuous action.

Spenser's most persuasive advocate of love's triumph over strife is Phaedria, whose bower, like those of Ariosto's Alcina and Tasso's Armida, is an Epicurean perversion of a Homeric *locus amoenus*.[58] Much like Homer's Phaiakia, which enjoys eternal spring, Phaedria's bower is an oasis of pleasurable calm. Yet unlike Homer's pristine paradise, Spenser's lacks the healthy spirit of rivalry and active virtue instilled in the *Odyssey* by poetic and athletic competition. Intervening in the conflict between Cymochles and Guyon, Phaedria persuades them to put off their "Debatefull strife, and cruell enmitie" by appealing to the union of Venus and Mars, the myth recounted by Demodocus in Phaiakia: "*Mars* is *Cupidoes* frend, / And is for *Venus* loves renowmed more, / Than all his wars and spoiles, the which he did of yore" (2.vi.35, 1, 2.vi.35, 7–9). Yet the lesson that Phaedria extracts from the myth is quite different from the meanings teased out by Spenser's invocation, which interprets Demodocus's song about the union of the two gods (as did many Homeric allegorists) as a veiled exposition of the antipathetic forces of *Philia* and *Neikos* in the pre-Socratic cosmos. Rather than establish the happy coexistence of love and strife necessary for the preservation and perpetuation of cosmological and social order, Phaedria errs by banishing strife from her realm completely.[59] Moreover, while Alkinous, Homer's Phaiakian king, advocates "balance in all things" [*ameinô d'aisima panta*], Phaedria encourages intemperance by favouring love and peace over discord and toil, an ethics that sits ill at ease with Guyon's delight in "armes and cruell warre" (*Od.* 7.310, 2.vi.37, 6; 2.vi.37, 8).

A prime example of what Thomas Greene has called "heuristic imitation," Spenser's Phaedria is a figure constructed to combat the Epicurean philosophy of pleasure that was often detected at the heart of the *Odyssey*'s odd earthly paradise.[60] Both Eustathius and pseudo-Plutarch depict Homer as a closet Epicurean, while Heraclitus's *Homeric Problems* argues that Epicurus stole his philosophy of pleasure from the Phaiakian episodes in the *Odyssey*, a position echoed by Pico Della Mirandola and other Renaissance humanists.[61] An advocate for excessive or misdirected tranquillity, Phaedria devalues conflict and debate in a manner that is difficult to reconcile with Book 2 of *The Faerie Queene*'s persistent dramatization of the spiritual and moral benefits of strife.[62] Even paradises, for Spenser, may include and depend upon discord: the garden of Adonis suffers seasonal change, decay, and death, and the Temple of Venus must cope with the persistent, if circumscribed, presence of hate, concessions that foreshadow Dame Nature yielding to Mutability's enormous power over the sublunary world.

The Faerie Queene's precarious counterbalance of love and strife, of tranquillity and conflict, is also conveyed through its manipulation of the master metaphor of the golden chain. Spenser departs from the

Neoplatonic interpretation of the golden chain as a pagan analogue to Jacob's ladder, a *scala naturae* that guarantees the continuum between celestial and terrestrial realms. This conventional interpretation of the golden chain is found throughout sixteenth-century mythographies and emblem books: Cesare Ripa's *Iconologia*, for instance, depicts a man grabbing hold of "a golden chain hanging from heaven" [*una catena d'oro pendente dal Cielo*] in order to illustrate the "conjunction of Human and Divine Things" [*congiungimento delle Cose Humane con le Divine*]. The Spenserian characters who interpret the chain in this manner do so as a means of usurping divine authority: Philotime, but also Argante, whose family of Titans "heaped hils on hight, / To scale the skyes, and put *Jove* from his right," and Lucifera, who "strove to match ... / Great *Junoes* golden chaire ... / ... when she does ride / To *Joves* high house," and Mutability, who wishes "T'attempt th'empire of the heavens hight, / And *Jove* himselfe to shoulder from his right" (3.vii.47, 4–5; 1.iv.17, 4–7; *CM* vi.7, 4–5). These aspirants to the top of Zeus's chain appear to have neglected to read the second half of Ripa's emblem, which reminds its readers that the man who grasps the chain must do so "humbly" [*humilmente*] and warns us that "God may, whenever he pleases, draw the chain towards him and raise our minds up to Heaven, from whence all our own forces and all our own power will not enable us to leave" [*il quale Iddio quando gli piace ci tira a se, & leva le menti nostre al Cielo dove noi con le proprie forze, & tutto il poter nostro non potemo salire*].[63]

In Ripa's explication, the golden chain is both a metaphor for divine omnipotence and a symbol of the threats posed to that omnipotence. This interpretation is as much indebted to satirical and parodic treatments of the scene in Book 8 of the *Iliad* as it is to the Homeric episode itself. In Lucian's *Dialogues of the Gods*, Ares jokes to Hermes that they should attempt a coup on Mount Olympus, since while Zeus might be "more than a match and too strong for any one of us," the war god refuses to believe "that he's too much for all of us put together."[64] Although some Renaissance readers do recognize, along with Lucian, the potentially subversive implications of a scene that Arthur Hall calls a "threat and surly speech," Spenser does not, instead driving home how the repeated failure of his Titans to raise themselves up to Zeus's seat illustrates the potential hazards of a political theology founded on the principle that there is a concatenation between divine and earthly beings.[65]

Spenser also deviates from the standard Neoplatonic interpretation of the golden chain as a symbol of the invisible bonds that guarantee cosmic harmony or the "regulated order of the universal world, and the joining and compacting of celestial bodies" [*Diakosmos universi mundi, & coagmentatio atque compactio orbium coelestium*], creating a structure so firmly bound, according to Joachim Camerarius the Younger, that "Zeus' agitation and pulling of that chain in no way impedes or retards that process" [*ut Jovis agitatio & ductus neutiquam impediatur aut retardetur*].[66] By contrast, Spenser's conception of the chain appears to take its cue from Socrates's gloss in the *Theaetetus*, which argues that it represents the sun "and means that so long as the heavens and the sun go round everything exists and is preserved, among both gods and men, but if the motion should stop, as if bound fast, everything would be destroyed."[67] Rather than interpret the golden chain as a symbol of cosmic fixity or coagmentation, Socrates understands the Homeric image as evidence of the stability produced out of, but not in opposition to, ceaseless motion. Particularly in Book 4, whose cast of characters includes a Homeric pantheon of discord, Spenser tests out Socrates's hypothesis in the *Theaetetus* that "stillness causes decay and destruction and that the opposite brings preservation" by showing how concord is forged out of, and is to some degree dependent upon, the continual agitations of Ate, Hate, Duessa, and other forces of strife.[68] In so doing, Spenser exposes the dangers or insufficiencies of the belief that cosmic and social harmony depends upon the total elimination of dynamic or adversarial relationships, whether between man and God, among the elements of nature, or across social networks. As a symbol of the cooperative rivalry between Arthur and Redcrosse, or as employed by Book 4's Concord to bind Love and Hate, Spenser's golden chains establish dyadic partnerships between oppositional forces in order to depict conflict as binding rather than divisive.

Spenser's interpretation of the Homeric-Socratic conceit runs counter to those of contemporary English poets, who tend to invoke the golden chain as a symbol of peace, friendship, or concord. In Ben Jonson's 1606 *Hymenaei*, as the masquers complete a dance "in manner of a chaine," Reason compares their motions to "the Golden Chaine let downe from Heaven," since the links they forge in their dance eliminate "*contention, envy, griefe, deceit*" in favour of "*peace*, and *love*, and *faith*, and *blisse*."[69] In his 1628 *Stratiotikon: or a Discourse of Military Discipline*, Ralph Knevet advises his soldier-courtier readers to be "joyned all together" by a "Golden cord, of Unitie," one whose "well order'd linkes," forged out of friendship and mutual "respect," enable men to "banish all debate, and strife" in order to ensure the concord essential for military strength.[70] Despite the clearly negative implications of Philotime's chain of ambition and the endless series of petty rivalries it nurtures among its hangers-on,

Spenser in no way intends to banish all debate and strife from Faerie land, instead looking to the golden chain and related images to explore the extent to which conflict might be both necessary and productive as a social and cosmic force.

In particular, Spenser adopts a Homeric idiom of the knots, chains, and bonds of conflict as a means of articulating his vision of *concordia discors* in which hostile cosmological energies are bound together by contrary forces. In his *Hymne in Honour of Love*, Spenser describes how the elements strive against each other until "Love relented their rebellious yre," and God, "tempering goodly well / Their contrary dislikes with loved means, / Did place them all in order," an order preserved by means of "Adamantine chaines" (*An Hymne in Honour of Love*, 80, 84–9).[71] James Hutton has called the passage an "untraditional" articulation of the Platonic bond of the elements – untraditional because, unlike Plato's account of the "adamantine spindle of necessity" in the *Republic*, Spenser sidesteps the issue of the relationship between necessity and human agency that is paramount to Plato's discussion and instead stresses how the conceit illustrates the reconciliation of oppositional forces.[72] Moreover, unlike Plato's account of God bringing the elements into order in the *Timaeus*, which emphasizes the providentially inspired beauty of nature, Spenser's adamantine chains illustrate how the "contrary forces" of love and strife may be united through a twofold, and paradoxical, process.[73] The result is that even the forces of strife participate in harmony: in Book 4 of *The Faerie Queene*, when Ate tries to "divide" that which "Concord hath together tide" (4.i.30, 8–9), she becomes an unwitting player in a larger harmonious plan that depends upon her participation. This is not to say that Spenser intends to apotheosize Ate's delight in disorder, but rather that, like Mutability, her discordant powers are ultimately revealed to be instruments of a larger harmonious plan.

Accounts of the process by which discord helps to produce a harmony to which it then yields dominate Spenser's cosmology in both *The Faerie Queene* and his lyric poems. *Colin Clouts Come Home Againe* (1595) explains how order in the natural world results from strife among the four elements, at first "great enemies" until they are "drawne together into one, / And taught in such accordance to agree" so that "they wexed friends, / And gan by litle learne to love each other" (*Colin Clout*, 844–6, 851–2). This pattern is mirrored in the interactions among Spenser's titular virtues, whose initial conflicts and rivalries are eventually resolved into friendships or romantic bonds.[74] At the beginning of Book 3, Guyon and Britomart engage in a strenuous combat before "reconcilement was betweene them knit, / Through goodly temperance, and affection chaste," a resolution that Spenser's narrator compares to the ligatures of a "golden chaine of concord" (3.i.12, 1–2; 3.i.12, 8). But the chain knitting together Guyon and Britomart must be actively forged out of a primal instinct for discord, suggesting that temperance and chastity, while ultimately reconcilable to each other, must first engage in some some ethical wrestling before the two virtues may achieve full cooperation. This is in part because, concocted out of a mixture of "terrour" and "grace," Britomart's chastity consists of two competing aspects that alternately attract and repel each other like half of an elemental tetrad (3.i.46, 1–2). These discordant elements do not form a "perfect complement" as they do in Belphoebe but rather generate a "confused strife" that makes Britomart stand apart from the poem's various couples, in particular the "sweet countervayle" of Scudamour and Amoret at the end of the 1590 text (3.v.55; 3.ii.32, 9; 3.xii.47a, 1). While Spenser's text appeals repeatedly to the idea that, as La Primaudaye puts it in his *French Academie*, all virtues are "knit together and depend one of another," the process of interlacement by which Spenser's virtues are knit together is protracted and filled with struggle.[75]

Similar patterns of discord yielding to concord dominate the initial encounters between Britomart and several other knights, including her future husband. At the beginning of Book 4, Britomart jousts with a fellow knight over Amoret, but once she defeats her competitor, their "former strife" is turned into "accord," a fitting prelude to the book in which debates stirred up by Ate are quieted by the forceful bands of Concord (4.i.15, 5). Throughout Book 4 in particular, images of chains, links, and bonds illustrate the disturbingly intimate relationship between conflict and harmony, marking the establishment of virtuous friendships but also the falsification of that virtue. Although we later learn that they begin as adversaries, Cambell and Triamond first appear as "two knights, that lincked rode in lovely wise," while their respective ladies, Cambina and Canacee, are likewise "linckt in lovely bond," the four figures constituting a perfect elemental tetrad yoked together by adamantine chains (4.ii.30, 3; 4.ii.32, 9). Yet because Book 4's specimens of discord and self-serving friendship – Paridell and Blandamour, Ate and Duessa – are so good at falsifying these golden chains of *philia*, Spenser must interrupt his description of the insincere and temporary reconciliation between his two "faire weather" friends in order to remind us that "vertue is the band, that bindeth harts most sure" (4.ii.29, 9). But if Spenser's virtues are enchained, so too are the poem's forces of disorder, who put on a persuasive show of unity during orderly processions in Lucifera's palace, in Busirane's masque, at Duessa's trial, and finally in *The Two Cantos of Mutabilitie*, where Order, Nature's sergeant, ensures that the witnesses testifying on behalf of Spenser's goddess of discord do not engage in the kind of disorderly conduct that would lend credence to their case.

The kinship and cooperation among Spenser's forces of discord demonstrate how sins and vices may be "enchained" – interlocking and mutually constitutive – as well as virtues. Du Bartas imagines Adam's transgression as "a chaine where all the greatest sinnes / Were one in other linked fast," a metaphor dramatized by Jonson's *Masque of Queenes*, whose antimasque depicts Atê trailed by a parade of vices "as if one lincke produc'd another, and the Dame were borne out of them all."[76] Spenser's Ate is likewise capable of simulating the "inviolable bands" wrought by Concord, forming chains of conflict that rival or mimic the "faire workmanship" of her opponent (4.x.35, 4; 4.i.30, 6). That the same language describes the work of both characters illustrates how harmony in *The Faerie Queene* is not simply the antagonist of discord but also its product.

Concatenation shapes the moral, rhetorical, and narrative structure of *The Faerie Queene*, synthesizing the poem's discordant forces into a projected, if not fully realized, vision of order and harmony. Despite the firm allegiances established between the titular heroes of each book, Spenser highlights the potential for conflict among his protagonists, and their harmonious enchainment is never a foregone conclusion. While it may be tempting to imagine that the concluding canto of *The Faerie Queene* would have looked something like the final chorus of a comic opera by Mozart, with multiple couplings of titular virtues singing in harmony at the wedding of Arthur and Gloriana, the process by which Spenser's titular virtues work to achieve concord is fraught with conflict. This is partly because the poem dramatizes the tense relationship between the means and the ends of particular virtues: Redcrosse Knight and Artegall must commit acts of bloodshed to uphold faith and justice, while Britomart, Calidore, and Guyon are obliged by their "long experiment" in the woods and seas of experience to modify their own understanding of how best to act upon the virtues they embody (2.vii.1, 7). It is also because the discord that springs up between the poem's titular virtues often takes the form of a mutually educative and beneficial emulation: the altercations between Guyon and Britomart, and between Artegall and Britomart, create resolutions that tighten the bonds between each pair of knights (3.v.55, 6).

If the golden chain illustrates conflict to be binding rather than divisive in Spenser's *Faerie Queene*, the conceit also operates as a double motif for the poem's narrative structure, one that seeks to reconcile the underlying tensions between the competing modes of epic and romance. As a narrative trope, Spenser's golden chain operates on both sides of the generic boundary that *The Faerie Queene* so persistently tests and complicates: it symbolizes the haphazardly interlocking, episodic narratives typical of Ariosto or Boiardo but also the tidier, chain-like narrative structure exemplified by Tasso's *Gerusalemme Liberata.* Thrown together in the house of Lust in Book 4, Amoret and Aemylia each understand their situation as "haplesse," or governed by apparently random forces beyond their control, but also ordered by those forces in the manner of a chain. Upon hearing Aemylia's tale, so similar to her own, Amoret asks her, "But what are you, whom like unlucky lot / Hath linckt with me in the same chaine attone?" a question which implicates the chain in the narrator's impulse (particularly prevalent in Book 4) to imitate the dilatory and fortuitous narrative style of Ariostan romance (4.vii.14, 7). In a 1596 work entitled *Della Poesia romanzesca*, Gioseppe Malatesta defends the *Orlando Furioso* as a poem whose narrative is "well disposed and ordered" [*bene disposto, & ordinato*] by comparing Ariosto's romance to a suspiciously Homeric-sounding *catena*: "I also think that by virtue of the chain which attaches all human things to each other, it is almost impossible to separate any one of them from the others enough so that it would be, as it were, divided and sundered from them or so that it would have no involvement or mixture with any nearby or contiguous action separate from itself."[77] Yet while Spenser's narrative conforms to and defines itself in terms of Malatesta's Ariostan chain of romance, it also exemplifies the more unitary, causally deliberate narrative praised by Tasso's *Discorsi del Poema Heroico* and by contemporary defenders of Tasso such as Orazio Lombardelli, whose 1586 *Discorso Intorno a i contrasti che si fanno sopra la Gerusalemme Liberata* praises the unified, teleological narrative of the *Gerusalemme* by comparing it to a "marvellous chain" [*maravigliosa catena*] capable of linking all the poem's actions back to its principal plot at the end:

> all the parts of his poem have been so well knotted and tied together ... his promise to sing of the glorious reconquest, and then to delay it, to put so many blocks in its way, to interrupt it and bring it almost to the point of desperation ... and with so much interweaving and correspondence between one part and another that there is never any doubt that every part is important nor such disturbance to the memory that it would fail to reattach quickly one part to another, until finally all the obstacles are eliminated.[78]

Even as they also refract the knotty entanglements of episodic romance, the ties, chains, and bonds that shape the allegorical landscape of *The Faerie Queene* gesture towards a similar interconnectedness, an "interweaving and correspondence" in which Arthur plays a starring role. Nohrnberg has argued that Arthur is the poem's emblem of "multiple unity," both because he makes cameo appearances in all six books and also because he is the allegorical instantiation of the poem's impulse towards union and resolution.[79] Arthur's partially unrealized capacity to knot and tie together the work's titular virtues suggests that his character might have developed more fully into a personification of the "goodly golden chain" invoked in Book 1, canto 9 to describe the friendly bands he knits with Redcrosse. The image exalts Arthur – and, perhaps, the narrator of the poem – for reconciling the tensions inherent in its chivalric ideals, in which the pursuit of honour, encouraged by competition between knights, so often comes into conflict with the cooperative values of friendship, charity, and mutual assistance.

Part 2. The Two Faces of Atê

This chapter has argued thus far that *The Faerie Queene* models its narrative and ethical structure on Homer's golden chain, an image transformed by Spenser from a Neoplatonic metaphor for cosmic harmony into a symbol of the *coincidentia oppositorum* between love and strife. This idea pervades the poem's cosmic and moral design as well as its depiction of social and political interactions that demonstrate an ongoing struggle to validate rivalry, contest, and competition as ethically and socially constructive. *The Faerie Queene* is, it must be admitted, full of instances in which heroes err by embracing physical or verbal strife when they should not. Guyon is aroused by the sight of the Bower of Bliss's wrestling sirens, while Artegall, Britomart, and Arthur each struggle to restrain their indignation against adversaries best resisted through non-violent means. Yet while conflict does prove dangerously enticing for certain of his characters, Spenser nonetheless labours to distinguish wholesome from unwholesome expressions of strife, often by adapting motifs derived from Homeric epic or from para-Homeric texts and myths. The striving mermaids of the Bower of Bliss, for instance, who "fondly striv'd / With th'*Heliconian* maides for maistery," are mythological figures original to Spenser, but ones also synthesized out of Homer's myth of Thamyris, Hesiod's fable of the hawk and the nightingale, a parable about shunning the bad Eris (*WD*, 203–11), and Ovid's account of the Pierides, turned into magpies after challenging the Muses to a singing match (*Metam.* 5.372–433, 812–30). All three fables are conventionally read during the Renaissance as cautionary tales about the perils of poetic rivalry: Homer's Thamyris is punished by the Muses when he "declare[s] with boasting that he would win even if the Muses themselves were to sing [*aeidoien*] against him" (*Il.* 2.596–8).[80] Spenser's mermaids meet a similar punishment, but when they moralize their fate by tempting Guyon to abandon his "troublous toyle," the poet reverses the usual moral: Guyon is certainly not meant to repudiate contention and struggle but rather to recognize their song as a morally flawed defence of the dangerously false harmony that pervades Acrasia's bower (2.xii.32, 8).[81]

In order to affirm the cosmological and ethical value of discord in his poem, Spenser frames various sections of his narrative with the para-Homeric myths of the wedding of Peleus and Thetis and the Judgment of Paris, intertwined stories that precede the *Iliad* chronologically and (in the epic cycle to which Homer's *Iliad* and *Odyssey* belong) offer aetiologies of discord that recount the origins of the Trojan war. In *The Faerie Queene*'s various retellings of the wedding-Judgment plot, an episode alluded to only in passing in the final book of the *Iliad*, Spenser errs along with George Peele and a number of other Elizabethan poets and mythographers in conflating Eris and Atê, the chief Homeric deities of strife. Hesiod identifies Atê as one of Eris's daughters; in Homeric epic their relationship is never explained. But sixteenth-century Latin translators of the *Iliad* follow the cues of the medieval Troy Book tradition, conflating the two goddesses and renaming her Discordia, Lis, or Contentio, names that help to establish her kinship with a monstrous brood of strife-provoking deities, including Virgil's Fama, the Discordias of Statius's Thebaid and of Prudentius's Psychomachia, Silvestris's Noys, Boccaccio's Litigium, Lydgate's Dyscord, who disrupts the feast in his *Assembly of Gods*, and Phineas Fletcher's Erithius. Spenser not only fuses the two deities into one but also imitates his epic predecessors in spawning a pantheon of discordant figures including Atin, Ate, Duessa, Furor, Philotime and Mammon, Envy and Sclaunder, Hate, the Blatant Beast, and Mutability.

Several of Spenser's personifications of discord, including Atin, Ate, Hate, Duessa, and Mutability, are either contained as threats or redeemed by their moral or social utility such that the danger they pose to the narrative and ethical order of the poem is limited or put into perspective by Spenser's larger allegorical framework. This is particularly the case with *The Faerie Queene*'s six different invocations of the wedding of Peleus and Thetis, the intrusion of Eris, and the Judgment of Paris, myths whose chronologies and contexts are rearranged so as to dramatize the *coincidentia oppositorum* of love and strife that animates Spenser's poem as a whole and informs its interpretation of Trojan legend. Each of Spenser's allusions to these narratives functions as an aetiology of strife that legitimates the existence of discord by tracing it back to its origins or by showing it to participate in a larger harmony. Particularly from Book 3 onwards, Spenser reverses the normal chronology of these para-Homeric narratives: his own poem recedes ever further from the fall of Troy as it moves backwards to the Judgment of Paris, the wedding of Peleus and Thetis, and finally, in *The Two Cantos of Mutabilitie*, to an Olympian conflict that both precedes and prefigures the banishment of strife (or Atê) to the sublunary world.

Discordant Paradise: Book 2

The Faerie Queene's first allusion to the wedding-Judgment plot appears in the Garden of Proserpina, visited by Guyon during his tour through the bowels of Mammon's cave in the middle of Book 2. There, the "famous golden Apple" thrown by "false *Ate*" and "For which th'*Idaean* ladies disagreed, / Till partial *Paris* dempt it *Venus* dew" grows in the same orchard with various fruits symbolic of concord – the apples of the Hesperides and the apples that Hippomenes and Acontius use, respectively, to woo Atalanta and Cydippe (2.vii.55, 4–7). Like his daughter Philotime, Mammon's association with strife is expressed through his kinship with various Homeric deities of discord. Guyon's suspicion that Mammon's promise of money will yield nothing but "Strife, and debate" is confirmed by the figures flanking the gates of Pluto's kingdom, "infernall Payne" and "tumultuous Strife," a pair whose long literary ancestry turns Guyon's *nekyia* into a grand tour of Spenser's epic models.[82] As it develops throughout Book 2, however, Spenser's mythography of strife is more complex than it appears either in Phaedria's bower or in Mammon's cave, allegorical landscapes that respectively devalue and overvalue the moral benefits of conflict. Guyon's chief task in these middle cantos of Book 2 is to negotiate between Phaedria's total repudiation of "[d]ebatefull strife" and the futile or destructive manifestations of *eris* exhibited by Philotime's courtiers or by the vain travails of Mammon's metalworkers (2.vi.35, 1). As he negotiates whether and to what extent the virtue of temperance may be reconciled with conflict and violence, Spenser reaches a tentative compromise between the two in "stryfull Atin," the "light-foot Page" who "breathe[s] strife and troublous enmitie" into Pyrochles and wreaks havoc by stirring "[c]oles of contention" but also serves more constructive uses, rescuing Cymochles from his bucolic torpor and pricking various characters, Guyon included, with "spurs of shame and wrong" (2.viii.10, 4–5; 2.viii.11, 4–5; 2.v.38, 9). His soft step a nod to Homer's Eris, whose "head is fixed in the heavens while her feet tread on earth," Spenser's Atin also shares the moral neutrality of his Homeric analogue: introducing himself as a servant to Pyrochles "in wrong or right," Atin reminds us that he is an instrument capable of being used wisely as well as rashly, able to rouse virtuous affections such as courage, righteous indignation, and shame, but also capable of provoking dangerous passions that must be moderated by Spenser's hero of temperance (*Il.* 4.442–3; *FQ* 2.iv.42, 5).

Yet Guyon's task of distinguishing between wholesome and unwholesome strife in the middle cantos of Book 2 is made more difficult by the fact that both the torpid ease induced by the Bower of Bliss and the sweaty toil valorized by Mammon's forge masquerade as the complement and the antidote to each other. The "swincke" and "sweat" of Mammon's Hephaestian labourers tempt Guyon by promising to counterbalance the ersatz harmony of Phaedria's venal pleasures (2.vii.36, 9). By appearing as though they might have a tempering effect upon each other, both locations appeal to Guyon's quest for moderation and, read together, simulate the poem's master trope of *concordia discors* by pretending to reconcile the moral, aesthetic, and cosmic contraries – ugliness and beauty, labour and ease, strife and love, fire and water – symbolized by the mismatched couple of Vulcan and Venus. In this respect, the Bower of Bliss duplicates the dissimulatory powers of Archimago, an adversary who works by stifling the eristic inclinations of his adversaries, plotting at the beginning of Book 2 to draw virtuous knights from "pursuit of praise and fame" by tempting them to "slug in slouth and sensuall delights" (2.i.23, 2–3).

Unlike Tasso's Armida, whose garden appeals to Rinaldo precisely because it promises to "soothe conflict and care," the Bower of Bliss is artfully designed to allure a hero who, though "demure and temperate," is also "sterne and terrible" and inclined towards earnest competition: "Well could [Guyon] turney and in lists debate" (2.i.6, 2–3; 2.i.6, 7).[83] The first clue that the Bower of Bliss is designed to prey upon Guyon's love of wholesome strife is the rivalry it precipitates between art and nature. The arbor in canto 5 shows "art striving to compaire / With nature," a motif enlarged in canto 12 through the "painted flowres" and other *paragone* that disguise themselves as models of virtuous emulation:

One would have thought ...
... That nature had for wantonesse ensude
Art, and that Art at nature did repine;
So striving each th'other to undermine,
Each did the others worke more beautifie. (2.v.29, 1–2; 2.xii.58, 5, 2.xii.59, 1–6)

The pretence of a morally productive rivalry at work in these landscapes provides a fitting backdrop for the pagan deities worshipped there, "Olympicke Jove" and his son Hercules, "whenas hee / Gaynd in *Nemea* goodly victorie," each god represented as successful contestants of an *agôn* (2.v.31, 3; 2.v.31, 5). Framed by a "sweet consort" of birds who produce a "chearfull harmonie," Jove and Hercules appeal to the morally upright kind of contestation already validated by Belphoebe's eloquent defence of toil as well as by Guyon's own adversarial temperament (2.v.31, 7–8). Quitslund observes that the "artfully contrived harmony of the elements, especially fire and water, is part of the fascination exercised by Acrasia in her Bower of Bliss."[84] By portraying harmony as natural and strife as a product of the human artifice that threatens the pacific instincts of the natural world, Acrasia's Bower attempts to validate the former over the latter by enforcing a strict distinction between concord and discord. But this distinction has already been challenged by Medina, whose oxymoronic praise of the "brave ... warres" of concord gives the lie to the Bower's too-simple antithesis between concord and discord as well as to Phaedria's false contrast between "nothing envious nature" and the "carefull paines" of human artifice (2.ii.26, 6; 2.ii.26, 8; 2.ii.31, 5; 2.vi.15, 4; 2.vi.15, 9).

The Odyssean landscape through which Guyon navigates in the final canto of Book 2 revises some of the lessons about decorous contention embedded in Homer's description of Phaiakia, a paradise in which tranquillity and contestation happily coexist. The Bower of Bliss, by contrast, persuades its visitors into the erroneous conviction that they must choose between pleasure and toil, between Epicurean *ataraxia* and a life of virtuous action. Phaedria and Acrasia are sirens who arouse a longing for ease designed to quench the desire for heroic fame, and both urge their victims to "chuse" between pleasure and "fruitlesse toile" (2.vi.17, 9). Guyon must exercise his virtue not by choosing but rather by detecting the fallacy of the choice: pleasure and heroic action are not simple opposites in *The Faerie Queene* any more than they are in the *Odyssey*, where the Phaiakians' appetite for food and drink is counterbalanced by an emphasis on *arête* or heroic excellence. Guyon's trial is complicated, however, by the fact that the false paradises of Book 2 create the illusion that they foster a healthy synthesis between harmonious pleasure and virtuous strife, an insincere promise of reconciliation nowhere more apparent than its wrestling maidens, half-naked ladies who "strove ... / ... to aggrate" Cymochles by participating in a competitive striptease: each participant peels off her garments, boasting of her superiority as she "all for tryall strips" (2.v.33, 1–2; 2.v.33, 9). The ladies who "seemed to contend,

/ And wrestle wantonly" in front of Guyon in the final canto of Book 2 likewise appeal to his modesty as well as to his belief in the spiritual and moral utility of trial, a concept often represented in the scriptures as a literal or metaphorical wrestling match: the *agôn* of Job, Jacob wrestling with the angel, Satan's temptation of Christ, or even Rachel's "excelle[n]t wrastlings" with her sister Leah (2.xii.63, 7–8).[85]

When he enters the Bower in canto 12, Guyon discovers a pseudo-Odyssean landscape replete with warnings that exercise his ability to distinguish between virtuous and unwholesome strife. Reaching the quicksand of Unthriftyhed, Guyon and the Palmer spy a merchant ship stuck in the mire, and "[n]either toile nor travell" prove effective in extricating the vessel (2.xii.19, 9). The quicksand is an allegory for futile or imprudent conflict. As Spenser's imitation of Scylla, the creature whom Homer's Circe advises "is not to be fought with" and whom Francis Bacon interprets as a symbol of "contentious learning" and "monstrous altercations," the quicksand exposes the vulnerable underside of Guyon's love of toil, teaching a lesson similar to that espoused by Homer's Circe when she chastises Odysseus for his eagerness in taking on Scylla by cautioning him that his heart is "set on the labour of war and toil" [*polemêia erga ... kai ponos*] (*Od.* 12.119, 116–17).[86] While Homer's Circe teaches Odysseus to moderate, rather than eliminate, his impulse towards strife, the inhabitants of Acrasia's pseudo-Circean bower persist in a total demonization of strife. Condemned for striving with the muses, Spenser's Sirens sing a tune that moralizes their punishment by inviting Guyon to abandon his own "paine and wearisome turmoyle" (2.xii.32, 9), a message that directly contradicts the *Odyssey*'s valorization of Odysseus as a model of heroic endurance, a figure who "suffers ... woes" [*pathen algea*] rather than circumventing them.

It is fitting that Guyon's heroic quest comes to its conclusion in a bower that both imitates and subverts the landscape inhabited by Homer's Circe. Circe and her four handmaidens are frequently allegorized by sixteenth-century mythographers as symbols of the elements or the seasons, the dynamic and conflictive forces that are "tempered" through a process of "commixtion and composition."[87] Elsewhere in the bower, we are reminded of another Homeric allegory about the production of harmony out of strife as the Palmer re-enacts Hephaestus's entrapment of Aphrodite and Ares from Book 8 of the *Odyssey*, ensnaring Acrasia and Verdant in his net and thus (at least according to the standard allegorical interpretation of the Homeric episode) reconciling the oppositional forces of *philia* and *eris*.[88] Whereas Spenser's Palmer is a Hephaestus figure whose actions preserve the value of strife as an ethical principle and a cosmic force, Mammon, Book 2's other Hephaestus figure, applies his skills as a virtuoso forger to counterfeit the sincere and earnest toil defended by Belphoebe. By contrast to the "darke obscuritee" and "oblivion" that buries those who pursue a life of ease, Belphoebe argues that those who embrace "painfull toile" are rewarded with both earthly and heavenly honour: "Before her gate high God did sweat ordaine" (2.iii.40, 3–4; 2.iii.40, 9; 2.iii.41, 5). Mammon's cave simulates this godly toil right down to the beads of sweat on its workers' foreheads, and it is only when we finally penetrate the darkest recesses of Pluto's Dis that we are fully able to appreciate the difference between the toil praised by Belphoebe and the "labour vaine" of Pilate and Tantalus, the latter "vainely swinck[ing]" for an apple he cannot reach in a scene that sums up, with almost parodic literalness, the fruitless toil Mammon's cave (2.vii.61, 9; 2.vii.58, 7).

The Two Faces of Atê: Book 4

Ate's brief appearance in Book 2, canto 7 as the goddess responsible for tossing the apple of discord at the wedding of Peleus and Thetis initiates Spenser's reworking of a para-Homeric narrative that grows in complexity as *The Faerie Queene* unfolds and achieves an increasingly wide-angle perspective on the double plot of the wedding-Judgment.[89] When the apple of discord appears again in the opening canto of Book 4, it is as a memento of Ate's destruction of Troy, the "cause of all their wrong, / For which the three faire Goddesses did strive" (4.i.22, 5–6). Although Ate is bent on deconcatenating the golden chain upon which the narrative and ethical design of *The Faerie Queene* depends, Spenser undercuts her power in the latter half of his epic by panning out from the initiating act of discord – the jettisoned apple – and by recounting the fall of Troy in reverse.

Medieval Troy legends identify the "goddesse Discord" as the "seed of strife and root of all offense," often beginning their narratives with the wedding of Peleus and Thetis, an event that explains the origin of variance or discord in the world.[90] Spenser does precisely the opposite. Beginning with Paridell's account of the destruction of Troy in Book 3, canto 9, Spenser moves ever backwards to the abduction of Helen (Book 3, canto 10), the allusion to the Judgment of Paris at the opening of Book 4, the wedding of Peleus and Thetis (the marriage of Thames and Medway in Book 4, canto 11), and Calidore's return to the pastoral state of "*Phrygian Paris* by *Plexippus* brooke," before the Trojan shepherd's abandonment of Oenone at the "time the golden apple was unto him brought" (6.ix.36,

7; 6.ix.36, 9). This narrative-in-reverse is completed by *The Two Cantos of Mutabilitie*, which begin in imitation of an Olympian council and end by limiting the power of the aspiring Mutability to the sublunary world, a conclusion that duplicates Zeus's banishment of Atê to earth in Book 19 of the *Iliad* while at the same time reversing and correcting the self-inflating nature of Homer's Eris, whose "head is fixed in the heavens while her feet tread on earth" (*Il.* 4.442–3).

As a tale of Troy told in reverse, the 1596 *Faerie Queene* does not simply aim to replicate the *Aeneid*'s topsy-turvy imitation of Homer's two poems, in which Aeneas's Odyssean travels precede the Iliadic battles of the latter six books and finally lead to the founding of Rome, the first *Troynovant*. Spenser reverses the narrative so that, Theseus-like, he might find his way out of the labyrinthine passageways of Discord's house, which has "many waies to enter" yet "none to issue forth when one is in: / For discord harder is to end then to begin" (4.i.20, 7–9). Whereas the first three books aim to demonstrate the potentially productive aspects of strife, the latter three books of *The Faerie Queene* lead us out of Ate's house by dramatizing the ways in which strife may be controlled or counterbalanced by the forces of concord.[91] The description of Ate in the opening canto of Book 4 captures the escalative, infectious power of Homer's Eris, who provokes small conflicts that threaten to grow "dayly more offensive unto each degree" (4.i.18, 9). In an image indebted to Ariosto, who twice describes Discordia as sowing "seedes of strife," Ate's garden is full of "wicked weedes" sown from the "little seedes" of conflicts,

> evill wordes, and factious deedes;
> Which when to ripenesse due they growen arre,
> Bring foorth an infinite increase, that breedes
> Tumultuous trouble and contentious jarre. (4.i.25, 4–8)[92]

Yet far from illustrating Ate's ever-growing power, the remainder of Book 4 and the two subsequent books increasingly circumscribe her authority. Not only is Ate one of the least violent villains of *The Faerie Queene*, preferring to wreak havoc through "debate" and "dissention" rather than physical force, but she is also patently incapable of dissimulation ("such as she was, she plaine did shew"), a characteristic that distinguishes her from the poem's more pernicious villains such as Duessa and Archimago (4.i.19, 1–2; 4.i.18, 7). Like Book 2's Atin, her kin and namesake, Ate also proves rather useful on a number of occasions, most notably as a key witness for the prosecution in Duessa's trial in Book 5. Ate's motives for testifying are not entirely noble – her fondness for legal wrangling betrays her affiliation with Boccaccio's Litigium and Fletcher's Erithius, the latter a lawyerly lover of "fond contention" from whose belt hang "sheaths of his paper-swords; / Fill'd up with Writs, Sub-poena's, Triall-cases."[93] But she is nonetheless an instrument capable of being put to good use by forces such as Zele, Mercilla's righteous defender of the realm who calls her to the bar to testify against Duessa (5.ix.47).

The limits of Ate's power are evident from the opening canto of Book 4, when Britomart resolves her "former strife" with a rival knight into "accord," a hopeful reminder that Spenser's goddess of strife and her discordant kin – Detraction and Slander, Duessa and Mutability – ultimately have little effect on the "faire workmanship" of Concord (4.i.15, 5; 4.i.30, 6). Consecrated to the virtues of friendship and harmony, Book 4 of *The Faerie Queene* represents strife not so much as the enemy of friendship but as its constant and necessary companion, an idea adapted from Homeric and para-Homeric sources. In the *Iliad* and *Odyssey*, Atê produces a "temporary clouding" of reason, and sixteenth-century mythographers such as Charles Estienne define her as the "goddess who entangles men in evil, seducing their minds" [*dea homines malis implicans, mentesque seducens*].[94] Five of the two dozen allusions to Atê in Homeric epic refer to her interference in the Paris-Helen affair, which might explain why she is so persistently confused with Eris, whose apple-throwing sets into motion the Judgment of Paris and the subsequent abduction of Helen. Homer's Atê also seduces her victims by arousing in them an excessive love of conflict.[95] Spenser's Ate conforms to the behaviour of her Homeric antecedent: described as "most fit to trouble noble knights, / Which hunt for honor, raised from below," she is a kindred spirit to Book 2's Philotime, who preys upon courtiers' excessive love of honour and their passion for competition (4.i.19, 5–6). Yet in *The Faerie Queene*, as in Homeric epic, *philotimia* and *philoneikia* can be instruments of virtuous action, thus explaining why, as Quitslund puts it, "Spenser does not indulge in the fantasy of destroying [Ate] and all her works," instead concentrating on the ways in which his poem might coax "harmony out of discord" and thus preserve the wholesome strife that is exercised "within the bounds of civility."[96]

Spenser's Ate is insistently twofold: her cross-eyed stare glances in "contrarie wayes," her feet and hands move in opposite directions, the two parts of her "divided" tongue "conten[d]" with each other, and her heart is similarly "discided, / That never thought one thing, but doubly still was guided" (4.i.27, 2; 4.i.27, 7–9). Her doubleness dramatizes the paradox that strife is not merely the adversary of harmony but also its inescapable partner, much like the figure of Discordia in Lillio Geraldi's *De Deis Gentium*, who is married to Concordia, a *bello-brutto* pairing that symbolizes the union of opposites animating the cosmos.[97] Although Spenser's Ate strives to heap "confusion" upon the binding powers of "blessed Concord," the fact that she is "divided" and "discided" in both heart and tongue ensures that she does not simply function in opposition to Concord but also in opposition to herself, a paradox that would no doubt have delighted a poet whose principal representatives of spiritual or cosmic disorder, from Error and Despair to Mutability, each testifies to the self-consuming nature of discord (4.i.27, 6; 4.i.27, 8). With feet that "contrarie trode" and "unequall" hands that pull and push in opposing directions at the same time, Spenser's Ate is animated by a principle of self-contrariety (or *discordia concors*) that resembles the "to and fro" of cosmic processes at work in the Garden of Adonis, or the dyadic Dame Nature, who is at once young and old, male and female, and "mooving, yet unmoved" (4.i.28, 9; 4.i.29, 1–2; 3.vi.42, 1–2; *CM* VII, 13, 2–3).

As a "symbolic statement of [Spenser's] metaphysics of *discordia concors*," Ate assists in mediating between two opposing social and cosmological principles of friendship, the principle that like is attracted to like and the contrary principle that opposites attract.[98] These contrasting doctrines of friendship had, as chapter 1 of this book argues, been granted a Homeric foundation in Erasmus's *Adages*, which adapts the Odyssean axiom that "God always brings together like [*homoion*] and like" into a central principle of its own ideals of fellowship and communalism.[99] Homeric epic provides its Renaissance readers with a number of compelling models for male friendship, including the cooperative partnership between Diomedes and Odysseus (*Il.* 10.224) and Achilles's reverence for his "friend Patroclus above all other comrades and as equal [*ison*] to himself" (18.81–2). But friendships in Homeric epic may be animated by difference and contrariety as well as by likeness, a principle that Plato uses to establish the correspondence between Homer and Empedocles, whose cosmology is founded upon the law that "what is dissimilar craves and loves dissimilar things."[100] Book 4 of *The Faerie Queene* favours the latter model of friendship over the former, since the bonds of true amity grow out of hostility. Cambell and Triamond begin as enemies, and Cambell even kills Triamond's two brothers before the two men are "[a] llide with bands of mutuall couplement" (4.iii.52, 3). Roche has pointed out that Cambell's name represents the "warring elements of the *bellum intestinum*," while his mate Canacee represents the "human elements that sustain man in his battle against himself and the world," etymologies that confirm the central principle of the legend of friendship: that cosmic and social harmony is the product of contrariety rather than similarity.[101] The competitions and tournaments of Book 4 demonstrate rivalry and contention to be generative, morally edifying forces, while the turbulence of amorous affection reveals the way in which love is tested and strengthened through strife. Although Spenser does differentiate between the "deare debate" of lovers and Ate's perverse desire to stir up "mischievous debate," Book 4 nonetheless highlights the difficulty of distinguishing between the bittersweet pleasure of erotic tension – the "unquiet thoughts" that haunt Scudamour in the House of Care, for instance – and the more threatening adversarial impulses of Ate or Lust (4.*Proem*.1, 5; 4.i.26, 4; 4.v.35, 9).

In the middle books of *The Faerie Queene*, romantic love is born out of conflict. The amorous liaisons of Britomart and Artegall, Florimell and Marinell, and Amoret and Scudamour are each shaped by Cupid, a god whom Spenser depicts as the "enimy of peace, and author of all strife" (3.vi.14, 9). Whereas figures such as Canacee provoke "unquiet strife … / Among her lovers, and great quarrels wrought," the exemplary friendship between Cambell and Triamond is knit by a more productive form of strife, namely, emulation (4.ii.37, 3–4). When Ate fuels the antagonism between Blandamour and Paridell, she attempts to "stirre up strife, twixt love and spight and ire" (4.ii.11, 7–8). If the bonds of friendship are weakened when love is divided from spite, then true friendship in Book 4 depends upon a harmonious synthesis of contrary affections, a mixture of love and hate, or *philia* and *eris*, exemplified by Cambell and Triamond. Repeatedly pitted against each other by Ate, Blandamour and Paridell subscribe to a perilously literalistic version of the Homeric-Erasmian adage that God draws like to like. Through them, Spenser devalues likeness and equality as guarantors of friendship. Blandamour and Paridell are so eager to achieve parity with each other that they pledge a covenant dictating that "every spoyle or pray / Should equally be shard betwixt us tway" (4.ii.13, 4–5). Such deal-making travesties the poem's communalistic ideals of friendship: their failed attempt to share all things in common reflects their misunderstanding of the spirit of cooperation and mutuality exemplified by Cambell and Triamond or by Triamond's brothers, who share one soul three ways.[102] The superficial similarity of Spenser's fair-weather friends is dramatized with hilarious results in canto 9, when in the midst of an altercation over Florimell, four "skirmishing" knights, Druon, Claribell, Blandamour, and Paridell, "gan they change their sides, and new parts take," and the ease with which they change sides effects a parodic reprisal of an earlier scene in which Cambell assumes Triamond's identity in battle (4.ix.20, 2; 4.ix.26, 1). Their "unruliment" compared to the elemental strife that "From all foure parts of heaven doe rage full sore," the discordant quartet perverts the mutual interplay of *philia* and *eris* that informs both Spenser's cosmology and his theory of friendship (4.ix.23, 5–6).

Blandamour and Paridell's friendship is made fragile not by conflict or aggression but rather through their shared predilection for blandishment. Explaining the danger of flatterers at court, Stefano Guazzo observes that flattery is a "way to make friends" among those who wish to "avoide contention," a fault diametrically opposed to those who "fall to contention continually."[103] By contrast, the friendship between Cambell and Triamond is established through the controlled strife of morally edifying competition. Like Eros and Anteros, the sparring cupids whose fraternal rivalry is deemed by Ben Jonson's Hymen to be "a strife, wherein you both winne," Cambell and Triamond compete in order to improve both themselves and each other.[104] Their insistence upon sharing the prizes and the honour that accrue to each competitor confirms Frank Whigham's argument that, rightly used, tilts and other chivalric combats in late sixteenth-century England achieve a "display of parity through emulation," thus turning competition into a "coincidence of struggle and assimilation" that allows for the "carefully regulated release of aggressive energies" and aims to "bond rather than to distinguish."[105] Advocating "emulation to the letter" in his *Positions*, Mulcaster justifies this bond of conflict by quoting Melantheus's observation in the *Odyssey*: "The greeke poet saith, that God draweth allway the like to the like, and therefore men may well follow the president [*sic*]."[106] Like the push and pull of Ate's contrarious hands, the emulous affection between Cambell and Triamond yokes them together by pitting them against each other, creating a friendly tug of war along the golden chain of concord that ultimately cements social and cosmic bonds.

Book 4 of *The Faerie Queene* thus demonstrates how the aggressively competitive masculine culture of the Elizabethan court knits the bands of *amicitia* through the controlled and productive "enmity" of rivalry (4.iv.11, 9). As his name suggests, Cambell is the book's spokesperson for decorous contestation.[107] When a group of knights and ladies provoke Braggadochio in canto 4, Cambell tells them that they "doe wrong / To stirre up strife, when most us needeth rest" for the Tournament of Maidenhead, but when the time is right, "who so list to fight, may fight his fill," a deferral reminiscent of Spenser's own postponement of the "furious fit" of his epic muse

(4.iv.12, 3; 4.iv.12, 6). When Cambell later assumes Triamond's armour so as to "purchase honour in his friends behalve," a gesture that duplicates Patroclus's assumption of Achilles's arms with happier results, he must be rescued by Triamond, who is dressed in turn like Cambell (4.iv.27, 3). The scene illustrates how victory in war depends upon the cultivation of friendship and the related virtues of cooperation and mutual exchange. It culminates in a preposterous dramatization of Alciati's emblem *Concordia Insuperabilis* (see figure 6), whose motto, "One can do nothing, two can do much" [*Unum nihil, duos plurimum posse*], is based on Diomedes's observation at *Il.* 10.224–6 that "when two go together ... profit may be had; alone, if one perceives [*noêsê*] anything, his perception is less sharp, and his cunning [*mêtis*] weaker."[108] After Cambell and Triamond manage to fight off a hundred knights, the battle ends with the unanimous verdict that the two knights have won the field equally, a fitting conclusion but one that satisfies neither of them:

> all with one consent did yeeld the prize
> To *Triamond* and *Cambell* as the best.
> But *Triamond* to *Cambell* it relest.
> And *Cambell* it to *Triamond* transferd;
> Each labouring t'advance the others gest,
> And make his praise before his owne preferd:
> So that the doome was to another day differd. (4.iv.36, 3–9)

While a tie might appear to be the perfect solution to a competition instigated by Spenser's divine and human agents of discord, neither knight of friendship is satisfied with an even draw. By competing against each other in a contest where victory can paradoxically be won only by ceding to the adversary, Cambell and Triamond supply a corrective to the vainglorious Braggadochio, who earlier refuses to fight in a tournament whose stakes include the dubious prize of the goddess of strife.

The competition between Cambell and Triamond, a contest whose "doome" is deferred, is one of a number of instances in *The Faerie Queene* where characters bond through conflict, a paradox that Spenser develops out of the Homeric concept of *homoiios polemos* – literally, the likeness or harmony of war. An epithet used throughout Homeric epic to denote the equalizing or levelling power of war or strife, the phrase is of particular interest to Homer's sixteenth-century readers. Citing the phrase from *Od.* 18.264, where Eurymachus suggests to Penelope that Odysseus may have died in the "great strife of equal

Emblemata. 83

Vnum nihil, duos plurimum poſſe.

EMBLEMA XLI.

LAERTÆ genitum, genitum quoque Tydeos unà.
Hac cera expreßit Zenalis apta manus.
Viribus hic pręſtat, hic pollet acumine mentis,
Nec tamen alterius non eget alter ope.
Cùm duo coniuncti veniunt, victoria certa eſt.
Solum mens hominem, dextrave deſtituit.

EXPLICAT. CLAVD. MIN.

CHARACTER huius Emblematis duci mihi videtur ex Iliad. Homericę κ. quo loco Diomedes, cum mittitur exploraturus Troiana caſtra, petit aliquē ſocium ſibi adiungi, ſed in primis Vlyſſem, vt ſit ei à conſilijs, ipſe viribus vtatur corporis. Ex quo intelligimus. ad res quaſque graues, vt militares, & quæ pertinent ad

F 2 Reipub,

Figure 6. Andrea Alciati, *Emblemata* (Padua: Pietro Paolo Tozzi, 1618), p. 83: Emblem 41: "*Unum nihil, duos plurimum posse.*" Courtesy Rubenstein Rare Book and Manuscript Library, Duke University, Durham, NC.

war" [*mega neikos homoiiou polemoio*], Nicolas Prustus explains in a 1594 volume of Homeric epithets that to call war *homoios* does not mean that war is "evil, serious, difficult" [*noxium, grave, difficile*] but rather denotes "a fight which because of the similitude and equality of warlike exploits on both sides, ends with uncertainty" [*propter similitudinem & aequalitatem pugnantium in re strenuè gerenda, exitusque incertitudinem*].[109] In the marginal notes of his copy of Eustathius, Isaac Casaubon marks a similar phrase in Book 4 of the *Iliad*, where Eris is described as creating "*neikos homoiion*" – literally, *homonoia*, or harmony, through strife.[110] Adversarialness, in these similes, is figured as union, and union as adversarialness. Homer's knots and cords of war, ties that bind as they divide, reverberate in the conjoined antagonists of *The Faerie Queene*: Artegall and Radigund, Pyrochles and Cymochles, Cambell and Triamond, Love and Hate, Dame Nature and Mutability all enter into conflicts that illustrate the *concordia discors* implicit in the Homeric epithet.

In Homeric epic, the phrase *neikos homoiion polemoio* also describes the way in which a balanced conflict between evenly matched antagonists produces an inextricable *stasis* or knot. The final appearance of the phrase occurs five lines before the end of the *Odyssey*.[111] In the final moments of the poem, Athena descends from Olympus and directs Odysseus to "stop the strife of war, common to all," at which point the warring factions swear a truce and both the fighting and the *Odyssey* end (24.543). Spenser adapts this scene in Book 4, canto 3, when the "doubtfull ballance" that hangs over the weary heads of Cambell and Triamond creates an impasse resolved by the appearance of Cambina, whose descent closely resembles that of Homer's Athena as well as of Aristophanes's *Eirene*, a figure frequently invoked by sixteenth-century poets as a goddess of peace (4.iii.37, 1). Even as the scene replicates the conclusion of the *Odyssey*, Spenser's imitation of it questions Athena's means of producing concord out of discord. Unlike the *Odyssey*, in which oaths sworn between warring parties lead to an enduring and conclusive peace, the oaths sworn by characters in Book 4 are ineffective, perpetuating strife rather than ending it. Although Blandamour and Paridell swear an oath of friendship in the opening canto – "my selfe will for you fight, / As ye have done for me: the left hand rubs the right" – they proceed to break it only one canto later (4.i.40, 8–9). By contrast, when Cambina binds together Cambell and Triamond with her dose of Nepenthe in the following canto, they are bound by heart and hand, and not by word. As if forewarned by the sad relics of "sworne friends, that did their faith forgoe" decorating the walls of Ate's house, Cambell and Triamond do not stake their friendship upon the tenuous bonds of a spoken oath (4.i.24, 3).

In another set of Homeric allusions that raise questions about the legitimate means of producing concord, Spenser provides Cambina with various peace-making instruments: "tears immixing prayers meeke," a cup of Nepenthe, and a "rod of peace" to "pacifie the strife" between Cambell and Triamond (4.iii.47, 6; 4.iii.42, 1; 4.iii.40, 9). The latter two objects both have an Odyssean ancestry: Nepenthe is the drug that Helen administers to Menelaus and his guests in order to alleviate the grief they feel at the loss of fellow Achaeans, while the rod, a caduceus crowned by an olive garland, resembles Hermes's *rhabdos* as well as Circe's wand. Maurice Evans has argued that Cambina's entry is cause for "confusion and disquiet" among "th'unruly preace" witnessing the spectacle, not simply because her power is "beyond human understanding," but also because the "rude confusion" she provokes both links and opposes her to Ate, a figure who delights in the "seditious trouble, / Bred in assemblies of the vulgar sort" (4.iii.41, 1; 4.iii.41, 6; 4.i.28, 3–4).[112] When persuasion fails and Cambina is obliged to use her rod of peace as a weapon, smiting the two warring knights "lightly with her powrefull wand," her actions dramatize a paradox earlier voiced by Book 2's Medina, who oxymoronically praises the "brave ... warres" of "lovely concord" (4.iii.48, 2; 2.ii.31, 5). Throughout *The Faerie Queene*, peace must at times be achieved through conflict, a lesson first introduced to Redcrosse Knight when he realizes, with the help of Heavenly Contemplation, that the surest route to the New Jerusalem passes through the bloody field.

Cambina's various attempts to resolve the conflict between Triamond and Cambell unravel a potential conflict between the ends and means of peace that has its roots in the closing books of Homer's *Odyssey*, where Odysseus's deceptions and his spectacular violence against the suitors strike some Renaissance readers as deeply problematic ways of resolving the poem's conflicts. The tension between Cambina's goal and the means she uses to achieve that goal is particularly evident in the decisive weapon in her arsenal of peace, a Homeric opiate that chases away "bitter gall" and washes away "all cares forepast ... / ... quite from their memorie," thus threatening the value of memory, a faculty that Spenser usually holds in a positive light (4.iii.43, 3–4; 4.iii.44, 6–7). Although Roche notes that Spenser "christianizes" Nepenthe in a manner similar to Milton's *Comus*, the latter poet never calls the drug a "drinck of soverayne grace" as does Spenser: rather, the evil Comus praises the intoxicating powers of his "cordial Julep" in a speech that imitates Spenser's Despair both rhetorically and spiritually in its promise of "Refreshment after toil, ease after pain."[113] Spenser is more confident in allegorizing Nepenthe as a symbol of *eleusis* or divine grace, a reading supported by Clement of Alexandria, who cites *Od.* 4.221 – "soother of grief and wrath, that bids all ills be forgotten" [*nêpenthes t'acholon te, kakôn epilêthon apantôn*] – in order to exhort his audience to heed the "new song" of the gospel.[114]

Despite its Christian associations with forgiveness and grace, Cambina's Homeric amnesiac poses a grave danger in a poem filled with warnings about the perils of forgetting, warnings often expressed by way of allusions to ancient Greek herbs or drugs. Pluto's deadly garden contains a dementia-inducing mixture of Hellebore, Coloquintida, and Hemlock, while the stream coursing through the Bower of Bliss makes its Odyssean visitor "forget / His former paine," an allusion to the repast of "deep forgetfulness" set out by Tasso's Armida as well as to the *Odyssey*'s various agents of amnesia and lethargy (2.v.30, 8–9). Homer's Odysseus prudently inoculates himself against these substances – the Lotos that induces forgetfulness of one's homeland, and the potions of "Circe's pharmacopeia" [*Kirkês ... polupharmakou*] that banish grief only by disarming Odysseus's crew, weakening their faculties of memory and reason (*Od.* 10.276).[115] For a poem that so greatly reveres the "immortal scrine" of memory, it is puzzling that the characters of Book 4 of *The Faerie Queene* are not more careful in emulating their Homeric counterparts and protecting themselves against the threat of oblivion (2.ix.56, 1).

Cambina's reliance on an amnesia-inducing drug to effect the amnesty between Triamond and Cambell is all the more troubling given that the greatest admirers of Nepenthe during the sixteenth century are neo-Stoic philosophers such as Lipsius, who interprets the substance as a symbol of the power of right reason and constancy to induce *apatheia*, or freedom from "cares and sorrowes."[116] The Proem to Book 4 assails the "Stoicke censours" who wish to excise "naturall affection" from the hearts of virtuous men, and throughout *The Faerie Queene*, but especially in Book 4, Spenser rejects *apatheia* in favour of the peculiarly ennobling passions of grief and pain (4.Proem.3, 9; 4.Proem.2, 4). Although the emotional wounds of sorrow and lovesickness ultimately heal in several of its key characters, Book 4 still insists upon both the unavoidability and the moral utility of pain, and the poem as a whole stresses the spiritual urgency of feeling and expressing grief: "unfold the anguish of your hart," Arthur advises Una, for "counsell mitigates the greatest smart" (1.vii.40, 6; 1.vii.40, 8). The Homeric wisdom of speaking one's grief, popularized by Erasmus's adage *Iubentis aperte loqui*, is construed by some sixteenth-century readers as a direct assault on Stoic *apatheia*: Jean de Sponde addresses the poet's imaginary Stoic adversaries when he insists that "Homeric men are not made of stone or horn, but are human beings" [*illi homines Homericos non esse saxeos aut fibris corneis, nec in rebus humanis humanam naturam exuere*].[117] To make a similar point, Spenser often models scenes of complaint in *The Faerie Queene* on Homeric episodes featuring characters engaged in the histrionic expression of intense passion, a tendency that reflects the more widespread habit during the 1590s to adapt scenes from the *Iliad* into works of poetic lament and complaint such as *Hecubaes Mishaps* (1590) and *The Lamentation of Troy for the Death of Hector* (1594).[118]

By the turn of the seventeenth century, Nepenthe had become a philosophical shorthand for the Stoic ideal of *apatheia*: advocates and critics of Stoicism alike invoke the Homeric drug as a means of weighing the benefits and the risks of abolishing passions such as grief and anger. Early seventeenth-century natural philosophers such as Giovanni Battista Persona (*Noctes Solitariae*, 1613) and Pietro La Sena (*Homeri Nepenthes; Seu, De Abolendo Luctu Liber*, 1624) attack Stoic ethics by interpreting Nepenthe as an endorsement of the philosophy that demands an impossible or undesirable "stupor [et] inhumanitas." As La Sena argues, there are numerous examples of praiseworthy and virtuous grief [*luctus*] in Homeric epic, from Andromache's lament for Hector to Zeus's mourning over the death of Sarpedon.[119] Persona similarly expresses puzzlement at Helen's administration of Nepenthe only a hundred or so lines after Nestor's son validates Telemachus's urge to "mourn" [*oduromai*] for his father and describes how "I ease [*terpomai*] my mind with weeping" (*Od.* 4.102), a line that Persona proposes to change to *tleromai* or *tlesomai* (to suffer or torment) so that it might better convey the anguish, rather than the pleasure, of grief.[120] Spenser likewise invokes Nepenthe at a moment when the narrator acknowledges the pleasure of emotional distress while at the same time stressing the importance of tempering one's affections in order to achieve tranquillity and social concord.

Other Elizabethan writers describe Homer's Nepenthe as a "purgative of care" (George Chapman) or as a "drinke which gladness brings, / Harts griefe expels, and doth the wits Refine" (Sir John Davies).[121] But those properties prove problematic in a poem that valorizes the experience and expression of grief as much as does *The Faerie Queene*. In Spenser's epic, Nepenthe is not (or ought not to be) a remedy for all human feeling but rather a social lubricant, a catalyst for friendship and civil conversation. Eustathius, in his commentary on the *Odyssey*, calls Nepenthe a "*pharmakon*," an antidote to strife that has some toxic side effects, since it causes men "not only to cast off all sorts of ills [*kakôn epilêthon apantôn*], but also to lose their memory."[122] Similarly, the harmful cancellation of memory induced by Cambina's Nepenthe cannot be pried away from its beneficial ability to produce amnesty. That Cambell and Triamond enjoy the benefits of Nepenthe while other of Book 4's characters endure "hard distresse" (4.x.28, 9) and long-suffering fits of melancholy can be explained by the fact that, as Spenser's narrator explains, "few men, but such as sober are and sage" are allowed to taste it (4.iii.43, 7). By reserving the drink as a privilege "assynd" by the gods to "famous men," heroes of "great dignitie," and other luminaries, the narrator implies that Nepenthe may legitimately be used to put a stop to strife but not to prevent it altogether, a reading confirmed by La Sena, whose treatise on the drug identifies it as suitable for those who are "*post infelices*" or "*post bellum*," designed to cure post-war trauma rather than to prevent the misery of war altogether.[123] This interpretation makes Nepenthe an ideal antidote for the lingering grief that clings to the post-war setting of Homer's *Odyssey* as well as for the similarly exhausted emotional state reached by Cambell and Triamond after their long combat, a battle that leaves both of them "[s]o wearie ... of fighting ..., / That life it selfe seemd loathsome, and long safetie ill" (4.iii.36, 8–9).[124]

As a means of resolving the "doubtfull ballance" that hangs over the weary heads of Cambell and Triamond, Cambina's Nepenthe reproduces the effects of Athena's truce in the final moments of the *Odyssey*, when she descends from the heavens and directs Odysseus to "stop the strife of war, common to all" (4.iii.37, 1; *Od.* 24.543). As he adapts this scene for Book 4 of *The Faerie Queene*, Spenser transforms the Homeric concept of *homoiios polemos* by yoking it to the spirit of *discordia concors* that animates his poem. Throughout *The Faerie Queene*, oppositional forces such as Love and Hate, brothers "of contrarie natures to each other," achieve concord when they are "forced hand to joyne in hand" (4.x.32, 5; 4.x.33, 2).[125] Although more immediately indebted to the Temple of Venus in Book 7 of Boccaccio's *Teseida*, Spenser's Temple of Concord also reflects the influence of the late antique and medieval allegorical tradition that holds Discordia to be the parent (or, at times, the partner) of Concordia, Amor, or Harmonia. In his *De Planctu Naturae*, Alanis Insulis argues that "Love is peace joined with hatred," while Boethius's Lady Philosophy describes how Concordia holds the "striving seeds" [*pugnantia semina*] of matter in balance with the assistance of natural law and of *Amor*.[126] In Spenser's handling, these medieval allegories of *discordia concors* join forces with Homeric allegories that locate in various episodes and conflicts of the *Iliad* and *Odyssey* illustrations of the double process by which the striving elements "come together by love into one" while simultaneously remaining separated by the "hostility of strife" [*neikeos echthei*], who holds them "dicha," or divided.[127] Reworking the Empedoclean philosophy that many ancient and Renaissance readers discerned in Homer's two epics, Concord's binding of Love and Hate stages an ambivalent triumph of Love over Strife in which the latter force holds certain elements "suspended aloft" in perpetual conflict [*neikos eruke metarsion*].[128] If Hate's persistent "despight" for Concord and Love illustrates that strife will never yield entirely to its opposite, his contempt for the "lovely band" with which Concord restrains him nonetheless makes Hate an inevitable, if reluctant, participant in cosmic harmony (4.x.31, 4). As he "turn[s] his face away" from the rest of the party, Hate inadvertently recreates Spenser's favourite triangular configuration of *discordia concors*, the three Graces: according to E.K.'s gloss on the subject in *The Shepheardes Calender*, two graces turn towards the viewer while the third turns "fromwarde."[129] The more powerfully Hate pulls against his two adversaries, the more taut become the bonds of Concord, a tug of war that dramatizes the Homeric principle of *homoiios polemos* while also accommodating it to Spenser's Senecan-Christian ideals of concord and friendship.

Ocean, Father of All Things

The reconcilement of Love and Hate in the Temple of Concord is one of several lessons in the 1596 *Faerie Queene* concerning the containment of discord by harmony. From the marriage of Thames and Medway to Dame Nature's verdict at the end of the *Mutabilitie Cantos*, the forces of strife exert their powers only to be incorporated into, or assimilated by, the forces of harmony. Yet the process of producing concord out of discord is a vexed one in *The Faerie Queene*, fraught with ethical as well as practical difficulties. The program of Homeric allusions in the 1596 and 1609 editions of the poem draws attention to those difficulties by casting doubt on the extent to which discord can be – and should be – fully contained by concord.

In addition to Ate's apple of discord, Book 4 of *The Faerie Queene* contains another object whose Homeric origins conceal another aetiology of strife: Florimell's girdle. Both Roche and Nohrnberg have observed that the girdle is a persistent source of conflict in Book 4, a "comparable provoking object" to the apple of discord in that it manages to arouse both the virtuous *zêlos* of Britomart and the "strifull stoure" stirred up among Blandamour, Paridell, Satyrane, and Erivan (4.v.24, 5).[130] Spenser's true and false Florimells are conventionally interpreted as an adaptation of the myth of the "two Helens," a counter-narrative to the *Iliad* recounted by Stesichorus, Euripides, Plato, and various Homeric allegorists.[131] While the false Florimell, like the phantom Helen who was supposedly sent to Troy with Paris, allegorically symbolizes the "generated and material place ... in which there is war and sedition," the true Florimell, like the authentic Helen who remains with the Greeks, symbolizes the purity and stability of form, thus turning the Greek victory over the Trojans into an allegory of the primacy of form over matter and the triumph of truth over illusion.[132] Whereas the false Florimell entices her admirers with "shadowes" of "vaine delight" (3.viii.10, 7–8), the true Florimell represents the resistance to false beauty and worldly vanity also embodied by Britomart, whose victory at the Tournament of Maidenhead appears to confirm Spenser's initial explanation of the girdle's symbolism. Wrought by Hephaestus for Aphrodite in order to guarantee his wife's fidelity, the girdle possesses the power to "bind lascivious desire, / And loose affection streightly to restraine," an apt prize for *The Faerie Queene*'s chief defender of feminine chastity (4.v.4, 7–8). Yet far from ensuring "*legitimos coitus*," as Boccaccio's *Genealogia Deorum* would have it, Aphrodite's girdle does the opposite. As the fable unfolds both in Homer's *Iliad* and in Spenser's rendition of it, the girdle does not restrain desire but rather arouses it, thus exacerbating the marital, social, and cosmic discord that it falsely promises to bind and control.[133]

In Book 14 of the *Iliad*, Aphrodite relinquishes her girdle not in the heat of adulterous passion, but because she is tricked into giving it away. Hera tells the goddess of love that she would like to use the *cestus* to patch up the marriage between Oceanus and Tethys, parents of all the gods: to "loose for them their unresolved strife [*akrita neikia lusô*], since for a long time they have remained aloof from one another, from the marriage bed and from love, since wrath [*cholos*] has fallen on their hearts" (*Il.* 14.205–7). But this is a lie: Hera in fact plans to use the girdle in order to seduce her own, equally estranged husband and then lend aid to the Greeks as a post-coital Zeus nods off unawares. Homer's girdle thus symbolizes the "cajolery that cheats even the wisest," as Aristotle remarks when he cites *Il.* 14.217 in the *Nicomachean Ethics*.[134] For Spenser, however, the girdle also symbolizes those powers of seduction through which the agents of strife – from Despair and Acrasia to Ate and the false Florimell herself – are able to masquerade as representatives of love or harmony.

When Alexander Pope contrasts the nature of Florimell's girdle with its Homeric source, he points out that Homer's girdle has "the power to raise up loose desires" while Spenser's possesses "the more wonderful faculty to suppress [desires] in the person that wore it." Yet Pope overlooks the fact that Hera uses the girdle to play a clever and divisive trick upon her own spouse when he jokingly remarks that "Homer's Cestus would be a peace-maker to reconcile man and wife; but Spenser's would probably destroy the good agreement of many a happy couple."[135] Spenser in fact follows Homer in representing the girdle, and Florimell herself, as a *casus belli.* He also incorporates into his own poem the philosophical and cosmological undermeanings of the *cestus* as interpreted by Plato and Stobaeus, who interpret the Homeric episode as an allegory of cosmic flux. In the *Theaetetus*, Socrates equates Homer's identification of Oceanus and Tethys as the parents of all the gods with the philosophical doctrine that "nothing ever is, but is always becoming," an argument reiterated by Montaigne and other sixteenth-century sceptics, who are fond of observing how Homer "made the Ocean father of the gods, and Thetis [*sic*] mother, to show us that all things are in perpetual flux, change, and variation."[136]

Describing the Tournament of Maidenhead as a "doutfull case" that concludes with the flight of its victor and the renewed bickering of its remaining participants, Spenser dramatizes the insoluble, or *akritos*, cosmic tensions at the symbolic heart of the dispute over Florimell and her girdle (4.v.6, 9). While Montaigne interprets the girdle episode in the *Iliad* as evidence that "changing man cannot know unchanging God," Spenser uses it to suggest that changing matter cannot fully be fixed or stabilized by unchanging form, an idea first cultivated in the Garden of Adonis and expressed once again through the relationship between Florimell and Proteus, the god associated by the Homeric allegorists with unformed (or preformed) matter.[137] As the symbolic instantiation of *hulê*, or prime matter, Proteus imprisons Florimell in a subterranean enclosure reminiscent of Homer's cave of the nymphs, the double-doored structure that Heraclitus the allegorist interprets as symbolizing the ceaslessly moving, chaotic nature of the *prima materia* before it is ordered by the imposition of form.[138]

If the aim of Book 4's heroes is to impose "the harmony of form upon chaos," Proteus is a central yet ambivalent figure in this process.[139] According to Giambattista Della Porta, who interprets the figure of Proteus as an allegory of how "form" descends to matter from the "highest heavens," the allegory "agrees fitly with the rings of Plato['s *Ion*], and with Homers golden chain" by demonstrating how form and matter are interconnected "like as it were a cord platted together, and stretched along from heaven to earth, in such sort as if either end of this cord be touched, it will wag the whole; therefore we may rightly call this knitting together of things a chain."[140] A key link in the golden chain that informs the poem's narrative and cosmic structure, Spenser's Proteus similarly functions as a symbol of the interconnectedness of form and matter. This is why the "great banquet of the watry Gods" takes place in Proteus's den, and why the marriage of Thames and Medway, in which contrary elements are united in wedlock, is framed by the larger narrative of Proteus's imprisonment of Florimell and her subsequent release: both episodes narrate the imposition of orderly form upon disorderly matter (4.xi.10, 8).

Marinell's wounding in the cave of Proteus and his subsequent cure at the hands of Apollo has been interpreted as Spenser's "free rendition and reversal of the fate of Achilles" as recounted in Book 24 of the *Iliad* and in Book 12 of Ovid's *Metamorphoses*, where Apollo assumes the shape of Paris to slay Achilles. Other events in Book 4 likewise produce a "reversal" of corresponding episodes in the *Iliad*: while Homer's poem ends (in its final book) with a brief glance back at the wedding of Peleus and Thetis, Spenser's legend of Friendship begins with Ate and her golden apple, ending with a more perfect union – a wedding, unlike that of Peleus and Thetis, that is relatively undisturbed by the intrusion of discord.[141] As a mirror image of the wedding between Achilles's parents, the marriage of Thames and Medway returns Spenser's readers to the source of epic, the first step in a chain of events that proceeds to the Judgment of Paris, the Trojan War, and finally Achilles's death. During the nuptials, we get a glimpse at this sequence of events through Nereus's prophecy, which predicts that after Paris's abduction of Helen, "her all *Greece* with many a champion bold / Should fetch againe, and finally destroy / Proud *Priams* towne" (4.xi.19, 5–7). Yet the thrust of Book 4 is not forward but *fromward*, towards the origins of the Iliadic strife rather than its destructive climax. Its bride and groom descended from Oceanus and Tethys, "th'oldest two" (4.xi.18, 2) of all the gods according to Spenser's narrator, the wedding's regressive movement dramatizes the Homeric epithet "backward-flowing Oceanus" [*apsorroou Okeanoio*] by returning us to the embryonic origins of epic conflict.

In the *Iliad*, Oceanus and Tethys are never explicitly reconciled. As if concerned that these two primal cosmic forces have still not patched up their differences, Spenser stages a marriage between two analogous bodies of water in order to rectify Hera's failure to deploy the girdle's conciliatory powers towards a useful end. As we move from Florimell's girdle to the marriage of Thames and Medway, Book 4 rewrites the allegorical substructure of Book 14 of the *Iliad* with a happy ending that realizes the potential concord in a Homeric episode that ends without resolving the tensions between two bickering deities. Spenser's river wedding is also indebted to the allegorical marriages of Martianus Capella and Alanis Insulis: the *De Nuptiis Philologiae et Mercurii* begins with a sacred wedding attended by Homer and Orpheus, while *De Planctu Naturae* depicts a wedding between Nereus and a virgin that, according to Insulis, represents the "concordant discord, the single plurality, the dissonant consonance, the dissenting agreement" produced by *Natura*.[142] By grafting the undermeanings of these two allegorical unions onto a wedding whose roots lie in the prehistory of the *Iliad*, Spenser's narrative moves from Iliadic strife to the triumph of *concordia discors* at the end of Book 4.

The Homeric poet identifies Oceanus as the source "from which the gods are sprung" [*Okeanon te, theôn genesin*], a genealogy that makes water "the first principle and beginning of all things" and, according to pseudo-Plutarch and Eustathius, anticipates or even gives rise to the philosophy of Thales (*Il.* 14.302).[143] Spenser need not have dug deep into the ancient *Scholia* to find similar testimonies: for Virgil and other Roman poets of the Augustan period, the "classic expression" of Homer's status as the "cultural wellspring of Greece is … the ancient equation of the poet with Ocean, the divine source of all waters," an image famously invoked at *Georg.* 4.380–3, where Cyrene pours a libation to "Ocean, the father of all things" [*Oceanumque patrem rerum*].[144] The idea that Homer's Oceanus is the origin of all things, as well as the related idea that the Homeric poet narrates the origin of all things from the *prima materia* of water, thrives in sixteenth-century scholarship: Philippe de Mornay compares Homer to Moses in that both writers "reduceth all things to Water and to a certeyne Mud as to their original," and Lambinus's commentary on Book 1 of the *Iliad* identifies Homer as the source of Thales's doctrine that water is the first principle, the element from which all else originates, an idea that likewise motivates Giulio Romano's striking depiction of Oceanus (see figure 7), a preparatory sketch for a bowl or dish that depicts the god's mouth as the eye of a whirpool out of which emanates all the creatures of the deep.[145] As the climactic elemental allegory of Book 4, the marriage of Thames and Medway is shaped not just by the allegorized union of Oceanus and Tethys but also by another Homeric wedding, that of Peleus and Thetis, which was conventionally interpreted as the union of earth (represented by Peleus) and water (Thetis) or as an allegory for the "natural forces of generation."[146] In the *Ovide Moralisé* tradition, this elemental wedding is hailed as stable and harmonious because its two participants embody "two contrary elements, one active and the other passive, one dry and the other moist" [*deux elements contraires, lun actif et lautre passif, lun sec et lautre humide*].[147] This allegorical tradition survives in literary and artistic depictions of the wedding in the late sixteenth- and early seventeenth-century Dutch and Flemish paintings of Cornelis Van Haarlem, Jacob Jordaens, and Joachim Wtewael, who render the event as an energetic, even chaotic bacchanal that suggests an underlying cosmological dynamism.

Figure 7. Giulio Romano, *The Stream Oceanus*. Early sixteenth century. Pen and brown ink with wash on paper. Chatsworth House, Devonshire, UK. Courtesy Devonshire Collection, Chatsworth. Reproduced by permission of the Chatsworth Settlement Trustees / Bridgeman Images.

In order to depict the wedding as an active, generative natural process, Spenser describes the rivers in attendance as "flowing," "glistring," "tempestuous," "swift," "unquiet," and "troublous," qualities that highlight the dynamic flux of nature's elements (4.xi.20–1; 4.xi.37, 7). The dominant silver imagery evokes the figure of Thetis, whose own wedding is similarly allegorized: Amphitrite's diadem of "silver haire," the grey beard of the Thames, "Deawed with silver drops," and the vestments of Medua "that seem'd like silver, sprinckled here and theare / With glittering spangs" all evoke the glittering appearance of "silver-footed" [*arguropeza*] Thetis as she appears throughout the *Iliad* (4.xi.11, 8: 4.xi.25, 8–9; 4.xi.45, 4–5). This descriptive language reveals Thetis's resemblance to her "swift-footed" [*podargos*, *podarkês*] son Achilles; the epithets are virtually synonymous in Greek, since *argos* means silver or glistening but also swift, flickering, or glimmering, like a shiny surface that reflects the quick motions around it. The swiftly flowing rivers who attend the marriage of Thames and Medway signal the liberation of Spenser's twin pools of mental and cosmic *stasis*: Cymochles (literally, shut-wave), whose swelling spirit is constricted by Phaedria in Book 2, and Cymodoce/Cymoent (literally, wave-receptacle or wave-limiter), who ends Book 4 by helping to cure her son Marinell of the melancholy that renders him a stagnant swamp, "unable once to stirre or move" (4.xii.20, 9).[148]

The final two books of the *Faerie Queene* provide two additional accounts of the wedding-Judgment double plot that further modify and put into perspective the power exerted by Eris in Spenser's epic. The first of these allusions appears during Book 6's pastoral interlude, when Spenser likens Calidore to Paris before the Judgment, "[w]hen he the love of fayre *Oenone* sought, / What time the golden apple was unto him brought" (6.ix.36, 8–9). While Calidore's condition at Meliboee's house returns him to a state of relative innocence and tranquillity, the wedding of Peleus and Thetis (and the intrusion of Eris and her apple) has nonetheless already taken place, since Colin Clout's account of the Graces at the beginning of the next canto explains that the triad is descended from Jove and Eurynome, the daughter of Ocean, as the gods meet upon Jove's return from "*Thetis* wedding with *Aeacidee*" (6.x.22, 5). As befits the beneficence of the Graces and the "pleasant grove" in which they are conceived, no goddess of strife appears to have presided over Spenser's version of that wedding, since the event is characterized only by "feastfull glee" (6.x.22, 3–4). Yet the intrusive effects of strife are felt in the description of the Graces as well as in the pastoral episode of Book 6 at large. As Donald Cheney points out, the apparition of the Graces illustrates how harmony may be "built again ... out of discord's ravages," and this argument is nowhere more evident than in their genealogy, since their birth results from the event that also precipitates the Judgment of Paris and the Trojan War.[149] As Stanley Stewart has shown, Spenser's conjoining of the wedding of Peleus and Thetis and the Judgment of Paris into one continuous episode mirrors the conventions of late sixteenth-century iconography, which tends to depict how the wedding, "Ate's retribution, and the Judgment of Paris are inextricably intertwined."[150] If Spenser's Graces present a "double vision of strife and concord," so too do his repeated allusions to the wedding of Peleus and Thetis and to the Judgment of Paris, events that symbolize the unavoidable intrusion of strife into a pastoral, golden world.[151]

The fleeting allusion to the wedding of Peleus and Thetis in the final book of the *Iliad* reflects a profound sense of loss, a nostalgic glance back at "a time – perhaps the last time – when gods and men joined together in feasting."[152] In late sixteenth- and early seventeenth-century paintings of the myth, the wedding is often a pastoral affair that signals the imminent end of pastoral itself: the early seventeenth-century Flemish painter Jan Van Balen represents the event as part bacchanal, part *fête champêtre*, disturbed only by the arrival of a portentous black bird in the upper left-hand corner (see figure 8). Spenser's narrator evokes a similar nostalgia when, as the Olympic pantheon assembles for the trial at the beginning of the final canto of Mutability, the assembly of gods is compared to the time

That all the gods whylome assembled were,
On *Hoaemus* hill in their divine array,
To celebrate the solemne bridall cheare,
Twixt *Peleus* and dame *Thetis* pointed there;
Where *Phoebus* self, that god of Poets hight,
They say did sing the spousall hymne full cleere,
That all the gods were ravisht with delight
Of his celestiall song, and Musicks wondrous might. (*CM* vii.12, 2–9)

Spenser's comparison between Mutability's trial and the wedding of Peleus and Thetis revises the aetiology of Eris offered up in the opening lines of the *Iliad*, where the Homeric narrator invokes his muse to recount how Agamemnon and Achilles "first parted in strife" [*prôta diastêtên erisante*] (*Il.* 1.6). The correspondence between the wedding of Peleus and Thetis and Mutability's trial also works to construct Spenser's narrator as an Apollonian-Homeric bard, a poet whose subject is theomachy and whose task is to explain and legitimate the underlying beneficience and justice of discord in the cosmos. In Book 2, canto 10, as we have already seen, the narrator invokes Homer and Phoebus Apollo, two poets who shed light upon the divine origins of strife (2.x.1, 2). Presenting the poem as an account of how the gods came to bring Agamemnon and Achilles "together to contend" [*eridi xuneêke machesthai*], the opening passage of the *Iliad* (1.8) promises an aetiology of strife, the very task that Spenser's narrator has in mind when he compares Arthur's history of Britain first to an argument "worthy of Maeonian quill" and then to Apollo's account of Jove's victory over the Titans (2.x.3, 1–5). Based on Statius's account of the poet Apollo, who "recounts the deeds of the gods ... and then reveals what spirit drives the thunderbolt or guides the stars, whence comes the fury of the rivers, what feeds the winds," Spenser's invocation of Phoebus Apollo places him in a family of poets devoted to clarifying and vindicating conflict in the sublunary world.[153]

Elsewhere in *The Faerie Queene*, Spenser assumes the role of Orphic bard, the "godlike man" whose harp quenches the fire of "wicked discord," but in the *Two Cantos of Mutabilitie*, the narrator alters his poetic identity as his task shifts to the justification of discord in the cosmos (4.ii.1, 5–6). Yet the narrator lays claim to this literary genealogy relucantly and nervously, chastising his "greater Muse" for removing him from the "woods and pleasing forrests" of Arlo Hill and lifting up his "fraile spirit (that dooth oft refuse / This too high flight" (*CM* vii.1, 1–5). The "furious fit" that Spenser's narrator restrains at the end of Book 1 is kept in reserve not for a climactic, earthly battle fought in defence of Gloriana, but rather for the "heavenly things" narrated, in imitation of a Homeric war in heaven, in the *Two Cantos of Mutabilitie* (*CM* vii.2, 6).

As a reunion of the gods present on Mount Pelion when Eris tossed her apple, Mutability's trial returns us to the pre-Homeric scene of the crime but delivers a verdict that ultimately differs from and improves upon the original proceeding.[154] Like Atê, whom Zeus flings down to earth because of her divisive and ruinous effects (*Il.* 19.132–3), Mutability is consigned to the mortal world, cast down from the "high authority" to which she aspires (*CM* vi.3, 2). Yet Spenser leaves unresolved the question of whether the exile of his goddess of discord constitutes a punishment for humankind (as the exile of Homer's Atê is understood by Zeus) or whether her banishment participates in a larger and more benevolent providential design. This question, central to the *Mutabilitie Cantos*, also informs Sperone Speroni's 1542 *Dialogo della Discordia*, a work that influenced Giordano Bruno's representation of the Titanomachy in his *Spaccio*, one of Spenser's

Figure 8. Jan Van Balen I (1575–1632), *The Marriage Feast of Peleus and Thetis.* Circa 1630. Oil on panel. Courtesy Kelvingrove Museum, Glasgow, UK.

possible models for his unfinished seventh book. In Speroni's work, Jove informs the goddess Discordia that she has a double rather than a single nature: "one of you is a good and natural thing, and has come to be called divine, while the other is totally the opposite" [*l'una di voi è buona, e natural cosa, la quale vien appellata divina, et l'altra in tutto co[n]traria*].[155] With the help of Dame Nature, who does not so much undercut Mutability's power as demonstrate that power to work towards a beneficent end, the *Two Cantos of Mutabilitie* envision the ultimate displacement of the "harmful" [*dannosi*] goddess in favour of her "healthful" [*salubri*] twin who helps to create and conserve the world.

Spenser tests out Speroni's assertion that the cosmos is produced and "conserved by contention" [*con lite conserva*] by dramatizing his theomachy not as a violent conflict but rather as a "well disposed" trial whose decorum is preserved by Order, "*Natures* Sergant" (*CM* vii.4, 6–7). The cosmic justice responsible for the creation and perpetuation of Mutability's power is reinforced by the non-violent means through which her quarrel is resolved: a "counsell close" attended by Olympian gods who are "quite unarm'd" and a subsequent trial that testifies to the due process of nature itself (*CM* vi.24, 2–3).

Spenser's Jove would "rather talk than fight," and so too would Mutability. Particularly in contradistinction to Dame Nature, who gives "her doome in speeches few," Mutability's loquaciousness has invited comparison to Momus in Lucian's *Parliament of the Gods*, to an "ironic" rendition of Alanis of Insulis's "Natura querellis," and to similar personifications of discord that emphasize the goddess's garrulity rather than her recourse to force (*CM* vii.57, 9).[156] Spenser's emphasis on the rhetorical dimensions of Mutability's dispute does not, however, guarantee that the resolution of *The Faerie Queene*'s theomachy is more just or orderly than its classical and medieval antecedents. Like her compatriots Sclaunder, Envy, and Detraction, Mutability's verbal arsenal reveals her kinship with Litigium, the goddess of discord as imagined by Boccaccio, Leone Ebreo, and Abraham Fraunce, who emerges from the womb of chaos to "bre[e]d brabbles, ma[k]e a foule stirre, sti[r] up contentions, and str[i]ve to mount up toward heaven."[157] Late sixteenth- and early seventeenth-century texts frequently envision classical deities of discord as goddesses of litigiousness: in Peele's *Arraignment of Paris*, for instance, Atê's "fatal fruit" wreaks havoc through a palpably unjust trial, and Robert Baron's 1649 *Apologie for Paris* represents "Dame Ate" as a "Barretter" or barrister.[158] In the *Two Cantos of Mutabilitie*, by contrast, Spenser is guarded in his attack on the eristic nature of legal institutions and discourses. When "bold Alteration" appears at "Natur's Bar" to "plea[d] / Large Evidence," the trial defends the adversarialness of nature even as it simultaneously arraigns the love of contention typical of lawyers and legal proceedings (*CM* vii.arg.1–3).

In his account of the first day of creation in *Les Sepmaines*, Guillaume Salluste Du Bartas justifies the contrariety of nature as divinely ordained by summoning up a parade of cosmic opposites who closely resemble the witnesses at Mutability's trial: day and night, summer and winter were created by God, Du Bartas argues, because "none can right discerne the sweets of Peace, / That have not felt Warres irksome bitternes."[159] Appealing to this principle of alternation in nature, Spenser's Mutability makes a similar plea for the necessity and utility of discord, but Dame Nature's verdict reveals how the conflict wreaked by Mutability in the sublunary world is, though legitimate, also restricted and unnecessary: the state of nature adheres to a *coincidentia oppositorum*, but it need not, a solution that prevents the episode from endorsing a Manichean view of the cosmos. In *The City of God*, Augustine facetiously derides the ancient Romans for building a temple to Concord on the site of several seditions and massacres, demanding to know whether there is "a reason for Concord being a goddesse while Discord is none." Augustine resolves this contradiction by asserting that discord depends upon the existence of concord, but not vice versa, for there may be "peace without any warre or contention: but contention, cannot be without some peace."[160] Contraries may coexist and even come to rely upon each other, according to Spenser's Augustinian logic in the *Two Cantos of Mutabilitie*, but this does not make them equal in power.

Spenser's Cosmic Process: The Shield of Achilles

As the latter half of this chapter has argued, the 1596 and 1609 texts of *The Faerie Queene* are built upon the same allegorical substructure used to interpret key episodes of the *Iliad* and *Odyssey* in terms of the union of the contrary forces of love (or concord) and strife. Such a reading helps to explain the puzzling Homeric armour carried by Spenser's knight of Justice in Book 5 of the poem: "Achilles armes, which Arthegall did win" (3.ii.25, 6). It is an understatement to say that "critical comment on this line has been confused."[161] But the solution proposed by Michael Leslie, among others – that Artegall is an Achilles-figure who learns to temper his wrath – is correct but inadequate, since Homer's ekphrasis in Book 18 of the *Iliad* was widely understood during the Renaissance to represent in miniature the distinction between a just society and an unjust one. Seen in this light, it makes perfect sense that Artegall should inherit the object that S.K. Heninger interprets as a Renaissance symbol of the "cosmic dance" of Justice.[162] Spenser's decision to bequeath Achilles's shield to Artegall reveals a deft transformation of the allegorical traditions surrounding the shield, traditions that acknowledge its paradoxical status as a catalyst for strife (because it is the occasion for the contest between Ajax and Odysseus) and also as a symbol of justice and concord.

In addition to his sword, Chrysaor, whose Greek name derives from the weapon used by Zeus to defeat the Titans at *Il.* 5.509, Artegall's Achillean shield helps to establish the complex relationship between justice and strife – between the "[p]eace universall" that thrived before Astraea's flight, when "Justice sate high ador'd with solemne feasts," and the discord that marks the "stonie" age that follows (5.Proem.9, 6–8; 5.Proem.2, 2). In the epic cycle, the wedding of Peleus and Thetis – the union that produces Achilles – results in the displacement of strife from the divine to the human plane. A gift to Peleus upon his marriage to Thetis, Achilles's original shield "reifies the displacement of immortal *eris* to earth" in a manner similar to the bequests made by Spenser's Astraea to her disciple Artegall, while his replacement shield, crafted by Hephaestus in Book 18 of the *Iliad*, attempts to remedy the intrusion of strife into the world with its double vision of the world before the appearance of Eris, and of that same world after her arrival on earth.[163] As a kind of anamorphic device that slips back and forth between an idyllic (and perhaps unattainable) vision of peace and a brutal panorama of the horrors of war, Achilles's two-sided shield was often interpreted during antiquity as a dramatization of the pre-Socratic cosmologies of Heraclitus and Empedocles, cosmologies that accord Eris an essential role in the preservation of order and justice. In one of his fragments, Heraclitus cites several lines from Homer's description of the shield to support the argument that "war is shared and Strife is Justice, and that all things come to pass in accordance with Strife."[164] By asserting that "Justice is Strife" [*dikên erin*], Heraclitus extends the concept of *Dikê* – judgment or balance – to the elemental counterbalance between *philia* and *eris* that perpetuates cosmological order: inasmuch as *Dikê* guarantees a due proportion between crime and punishment, it duplicates the "cosmic system of opposition and 'reversals' [*tropai*]" that Heraclitus understands as preserving the equilibrium and fitness of nature.[165] Imbued with a similar allegorical significance, Artegall's shield establishes a set of correspondences between cosmological and juridical processes that together depend upon the exertion of eristic forces.[166]

Yet Book 5 struggles to make sense of Heraclitus's doctrine (here paraphrased by Aristotle) that "all things come to pass through strife" [*kai panta kat'erin ginesthai*]. In the Proem to Book 5, the peaceful and warring cities of Achilles's shield, which may be interpreted as coexisting simultaneously, are rewritten so as to introduce a temporal gap between the peace that formerly reigned during the Golden Age and the "contrarie constitution" of the present time (5.Proem.4, 8). Although much of Book 5 seems pessimistic about the possibility of returning to this lost age of peace, there is one episode that recreates the peaceful side of Achilles's shield as if to suggest that its revival is possible after all. When Artegall and Arthur arrive at Mercilla's court, the queen is participating in a trial that resembles the one taking place on the peaceful *recto* of Achilles's shield:

Dealing of Iustice with indifferent grace,
And hearing pleas of people meane and base.
Mongst which as then, there was for to be heard
The tryall of a great and weightie case,
Which on both sides was then debating hard. (5.ix.36, 4–8)

This is, we are meant to assume, good government in action: a juridical resolution to conflict that is presided over by a judge who is at once merciful and "indifferent" to each party. The trial of Duessa may appear to challenge this harmonious vision of due process when the floor is yielded to Ate, a witness for the prosecution who, as a "survivor from Homer's heroic world," might be expected to erode the virtue of justice in the "barren and conflictual world of Book V."[167] Yet as I have already suggested earlier in this chapter, Ate's role in the trial does not threaten Book 5's ideals of justice, for she acts during the trial as the instrument of Zele, or righteous indignation, a figure who turns the dangerous passion of wrath to godly ends.

Inasmuch as Spenser's Ate serves as a legitimate minister of justice, rather than the sort of demonic figure of litigiousness we find in the works of Peele and other contemporary writers, the scene demonstrates how justice *is* strife, or rather that justice *depends* upon strife. It also depends, however, on the presence of the Litae, the daughters of Jove and Themis who wait upon Mercilla and symbolize her ability to season justice with mercy (5.ix.31, 4–6).[168] While Homer's account of the Litae in Book 9 of the *Iliad* depicts them as following in Atê's footsteps and "healing the hurt" she creates in men's hearts, thus turning their wrath into pity, Spenser's Litae provide a corrective not to his Ate but to the rigorous and uncompromising justice of a vengeful God: they wait upon "*Joves* judgement seat" so that "when in wrath he threats the worlds decay, / They doe his anger calme, and cruell vengeance stay" (*Il.* 9.502–7; *FQ* 5.ix.31, 7–9).[169] In the *Iliad*, Phoenix's fable of the Litae is offered as proof that "even the very gods can bend," an argument designed to persuade Achilles to master his *thumos* and soften his "pitiless heart" (9.496–7). Artegall is taught this same lesson again and again throughout Book 5: Guyon urges him not to "wreake [his] wrath" on Braggadochio (5.iii.36, 8), Britomart teaches him equity, and Mercilla exhibits a "piteous ruth" (5.ix.50, 2) at Duessa's trial that serves as example for Artegall.

This tissue of Homeric allusions to Atê and the Litae helps to pose two of Book 5's most pressing ethical questions: what kind of anger, and directed to what end, is supportive of a just cosmos, and whether the peaceful resolution of conflict is a tenable ideal in a corrupt and unjust world. Book 5 of *The Faerie Queene* mediates between contrary answers to both questions: while we are taught that even the most rigorous execution of justice demands the restraint of anger and brute violence, as Artegall repeatedly restrains Talus, we also learn that the avoidance of strife and violence is at best an impractical ideal and at worst a means of compromising justice, as it is when Burbon, a thinly disguised Henri de Navarre, abandons his shield in battle in order to "stint all [the] strife and troublous enmitie" it provokes (5.xi.54, 3). Burbon errs in thinking that the two visions of society represented on the two sides of Achilles's shield are mutually exclusive – that the strife roused by Eris on the one side will never lead to the establishment of the harmonious and just government on the other. Arguing that "truth is one in all" (5.xi.56, 8), Artegall persuades Burbon otherwise. The end of Book 5 anticipates a future time when strife will be the handmaiden of justice, and the two sides of the shield reconciled to each other:

> It often fals in course of common life,
> That right long time is overborne of wrong,
> Through avarice, or powre, or guile, or strife,
> That weakens her, and makes her party strong:
> But Justice, though her doome she doe prolong,
> Yet at the last she will her own cause right. (5.xi.1, 1–6)

Homeric scholars have long held that the trial on the peaceful side of Achilles's shield "put[s] the *Iliad* itself into perspective" by allowing us to "think about war and see it in relation to peace."[170] Arguing that the ambush of the herd described at *Il.* 18.520–32 reflects the destruction of an innocent, pastoral existence by war, Oliver Taplin interprets the scenes of social and juridical harmony on the peaceful side of Achilles's shield as a nostalgic glance back at a harmony that no longer exists. Spenser's Achillean shield likewise glances back to a time when Astraea still inhabited the earth, but it also presents an optimistic vision of the future, betokening the greater justice and peace that lie ahead for Spenser's Christian heroes.

By giving Achilles's shield to Artegall, Book 5 of *The Faerie Queene* justifies the strife that drives Homeric and Spenserian epic alike by shifting our perspective so that we are able to discern the tranquillity and concord that might arise out of conflict. By contrast to Book 3's Paridell, who blames the fall of Troy upon the "direfull destinie" of "angry Gods, and cruell skye" (3.ix.33, 4–5), Spenser's narrator draws attention to the justice that undergirds the Homeric episodes of conflict imitated by his own epic. By enfolding his Homeric deities of discord (Ate, Atin, Mutability, and Duessa) into a set of cosmic processes presided over by divinities (Dame Nature; Astraea; Venus and Concord; the Horae, the Litae, and the Graces) who safeguard due process, Spenser reinvents the Homeric mythography of strife so as to ensure that justice ultimately triumphs. In an emblem entitled "Finally, finally Justice prevails" [*Tandem, tandem Justitia obtinet*], Alciati allegorizes Achilles's shield as a symbol of the slow progress and ultimate triumph of justice, and the accompanying engraving shows how the shield is carried to Ajax's tomb after the death of Achilles, restored, at long last, to its rightful owner.[171] As inheritor of the shield, Artegall is a reminder that, despite the present inescapability of discord and conflict, justice will finally prevail, at which point the tensions between the recto and verso of the shield will yield to a union of contraries that makes truth "one in all." When that time comes, Spenser's post-epic muse, guided by a unified Venus and Mars, will be at the ready.

Chapter Four

Chapman's Ironic Homer

Homer used jests for sharpness's sake, and his jests may prove terrifying, like that of the Cyclops: "No Man will I eat last."

– Torquato Tasso, *Discourses*

In Act 3 of Thomas Randolph's *The Muses looking-glasse*, published posthumously in 1643, Alazon and Eiron – two characters who personify the excessive and defective "extreames of Truth" – have a conversation about Homer. Alazon claims both for himself and his interlocutor a Homeric genealogy, boastfully dubbing himself "the Hector of the age" and calling Eiron "Achilles," a label that Eiron rejects with characteristic mock-humility: "No, I am not Achilles: I confesse / I am no coward."[1] In the conversation that follows, both Alazon and Eiron claim Homeric origins for the opposing rhetorical vices they embody. As they discuss their favourite authors, Eiron proclaims, "There is no Poetry but Homers *Iliads*," an assertion difficult to accept at face value since, as we are cautioned at the beginning of the scene, Eiron is apt to "dissemble his qualities" and to deny the truth. As might be expected from a character wont to "arrogat[e] that to himself which is not his," the braggart Alazon protests that he, and not Eiron, is Homer's true heir.[2] Yet Alazon's claim that Homer's *Iliad* is the cradle of boastful, rather than ironic, speech is complicated by his own predilection for false boasts, as well as by the fact that – as Aristotle points out in his treatment of alazony and irony in the *Nicomachean Ethics* – boastful speech and and the mock-humble dissimulations of ironic speakers are, at times, quite difficult to differentiate from each other.[3] Since Randolph's Alazon and Eiron are both distinguished by the untrustworthiness of their claims – one deviates from the virtuous mean of truth by making false boasts, while the other "offend[s] in denying a truth" – the scene ends without any resolution to the question of whether Homeric epic gives birth to boastful speech, ironic speech, both, or neither.[4]

The competing claims to a Homeric heritage made by Randolph's personifications of alazony and irony read like an abridgment of George Chapman's translations of Homer. Throughout his prefaces and commentaries to the *Iliad* and *Odyssey*, Chapman frequently notes passages where the Homeric narrator or the poems' various speakers use two rhetorical tropes: ironic and scoptic speech. In his efforts to label various passages *ironicè* and *scopticè* – the latter term, used by Homer's ancient scholiasts, means scoffing, derisory, or sarcastic – Chapman endeavours in his Homeric commentaries to establish an ironic interpretation of Homeric epic that serves several purposes. First, Chapman's location of irony in Homer identifies in the epics a model for rhetorically effective and ethically valid means of moral correction. Second, Chapman's recognition of Homeric irony legitimates the obscurity that characterizes much of Chapman's own poetic corpus and likewise validates his hermeneutic authority as a translator of Homer. Third, Chapman's ironic readings of Homeric epic help to smooth out some of the most disturbing theological and ethical problems in the poems, namely, the grim sense of humour ascribed to the gods and the narrator's associated scorn for mortal ignorance and arrogance.[5]

In certain respects, Chapman's attentiveness to the range of rhetorical models exemplified by Homer's speakers – from the bluntness of Achilles to the wry obliquity of Odysseus – reflects the era's more widespread preoccupation with the rhetorical dimensions of Homeric epic, a preoccupation evident in numerous sixteenth-century grammar books and Homeric commentaries including several (such as Poliziano's *Oration on Homer*) that Chapman relied on heavily for his own commentary. Yet in other respects, Chapman's Homeric commentaries are the product of a stubbornly eccentric mind, one determined to establish an interpretation of Homer's *Iliad* and *Odyssey* that might confirm Chapman not only as an authoritative critic but also as Homer's most genuine and intimate poetic heir.

Many contemporary Homeric scholars would express little surprise at Chapman's insistence that Homer is a master ironist.[6] Yet Chapman's interest in ironic and scoptic speech has received little critical attention from scholars devoted to his Homeric translations, and for the few critics who have remarked upon it, Chapman's ironic interpretations of Homer prove puzzling. Millar MacLure admits that he is "unable to determine" where Chapman got the idea that Homer was such a "superb ironist," while George De Forest Lord's *Homeric Renaissance*, the classic study of Chapman's translation of the *Odyssey*, does not once mention the translator's interest in ironic epithets and speeches.[7] Chapman produced the bulk of his Homeric translations from the late 1590s through the first decade of the seventeenth century, and his sustained investigation into the use of ironic and scoptic speech in the *Iliad* and *Odyssey* resonates with the urgent renegotiation of satirical discourse in the wake of the Bishops' Ban and the War of the Theatres, two events that shape Chapman's conception of irony and sarcasm as more justifiable or permissible means of expressing scorn than the biting and misanthropic satires of Marston, Nashe, and other late Elizabethan writers censored by the Bishops' Ban.

After the official proscription of verse satire and epigram in 1599, satirical discourse in England needed to be reconfigured, and the involutions of irony provided a number of early seventeenth-century writers with an effective yet safe means of expressing scorn and disdain. In his 1615 *Essays and Characters, Ironicall and Invective*, John Stephens explains that he will make his essays "prove an Ironie" by cloaking his "extreme derision" under a "shadow of reproofe."[8] Like Stephens, Chapman's *Andromeda Liberata* and its subsequent *Justification* make use of an irony that announces itself through the conventional language of allegory – the veil, mantle, or shadow that conceals meaning. The prevailing fashion for satire that obscures itself as satire is not admired by all: John Hoskyns complains that *katachrêsis*, or verbal abuse, has grown into fashion along with "the figure *Ironia*," while Joseph Hall condemns poets whose verse is "riddle-like, obscuring their intent."[9] But for many early seventeenth-century writers, the obfuscations of irony act as a protective shield, a veiled satirical mode suitable for dangerous times.[10] In his Homeric commentaries, as well as in the dedications and prefaces of his lyric poems, Chapman establishes a kinship between irony and other "dark conceits" such as allegory and enigma. Yet while his ironic interpretations of Homeric epic at times look indistinguishable from those of sixteenth-century Homeric allegorists such as Conrad Gesner or Jean Dorat, Chapman diverges from conventional allegorical interpretations of Homer by dedicating himself to the reconstruction of Homer's authorial intent, a goal normally at odds with the hermeneutic methods and presuppositions of the allegorist.

Chapman's preoccupation with the variety of satirical modes in Homeric epic, from railing and "insultation" to ironic and scoptic speech, is fuelled by many of the same concerns that animate poems such as *The Shadow of Night*, *Euthymiae Raptus*, and *Andromeda Liberata*, works that fervently defend the moral and poetic legitimacy of their own satirical strategies. Versed in classical treatments of the trope by Aristotle, Plato, Cicero, and Quintilian, Chapman understands irony as a technique of concealing blame, a subtler means of reprehension, and consequently a more charitable or prudent one, than overt rebuke. Even as the obscurity of irony holds an appeal for Chapman, the trope can prove so difficult to detect that it fails to serve a morally corrective use. Renaissance writers often grapple with the problem that the targets of their ironic attacks often "escaped unashamed while the ironist remains the sole and sterile audience to his own cleverness," and contemporary rhetoricians such as Henry Peacham caution against an irony that is so cleverly concealed that readers who lack "subtlety of wit" cannot perceive this "privie kind of mocke."[11] This problem is summed up neatly by the epigraph to Chapman's *Ovids Banquet of Sence*, which adapts a question posed in the opening lines of Persius's First Satire: "who will read stuff like this? / Not a soul, by Hercules, / One or two perhaps, or nobody" [*Quis leget haec? / Nemo Hercule Nemo. / Vel duo vel nemo*].[12] Given Chapman's repeated claim that he is misunderstood by the vast majority of his readers, the epigraph proves a fitting motto for his career as a poet and translator.

Yet the perception that he is the frequent victim of misreading also serves to align Chapman with a poetic tradition that reaches back to the neglected and misjudged narrator of Persius's *Satires* and, ultimately, to Homer. According to Chapman's familiar refrain, prior translators and editors of the *Iliad* and *Odyssey* have consistently overlooked, misinterpreted, or wrongly condemned the ironic and scoptic aspects of his poems. Chapman's frequent claim that he has discovered hitherto undetected ironies in Homeric epic helps fashion him into the only reader capable of interpreting Homer correctly. Such a motive often lurks behind readerly claims of irony. Chapman employs many of the critical techniques of self-legitimation evident in more recent literary critics who tend to bandy about the term irony "in a self-serving manner and often in bad faith" in order to reappropriate "poetic authority" for themselves.[13] By depicting himself as the sole possessor of the ironic key that unlocks Homeric epic, Chapman constructs a literary genealogy that links him to his Greek predecessor by establishing himself not simply as Homer's heir but also as his ideal reader.

Despite his frequent assertions that only he is sufficiently attuned to Homer's satirical and ironic tones to translate him accurately, Chapman is by no means the only Renaissance reader or translator of the *Iliad* and *Odyssey* to notice the ironic and scoptic tone of various speeches in both poems. In his lectures on Homer, written in 1594 and published in 1612,

Martin Crusius notes Agamemnon's irony in calling Achilles "*agathos*" at *Iliad* 1.131, the same term of praise that Chapman interprets ironically when it is later applied to Menelaus. In the preface to his unfinished translation of the *Iliad*, Arthur Hall contrasts Thomas Phaer's "Heroicall Virgil" with his own "Satiricall Homer," although what, exactly, he means by calling Homer *satirical* is unclear, since the only evidence of satire in Hall's translation is his rendition of Thersites in Book 2, who takes "delight to mocke and scorne" his fellow Achaeans.[14] Among other English contemporaries, Abraham Fraunce shares Chapman's keen appreciation for the ironic and scoptic speeches of the *Iliad*'s battle scenes. In his 1588 *Arcadian Rhetorike*, Fraunce cites numerous Homeric passages as examples of ironic or derisory speech. Defining irony as a rhetorical trope that "by naming one contrarie intendeth another," Fraunce praises the "speciall grace" of irony evident in the "jesting and merie conceipted speaches" made by Patroclus to Cebriones when the latter soldier falls off his chariot to his death in Book 16 of the *Iliad*.[15] Like Chapman, who glosses the passage with the marginal note, "Patroclus jests at the fall of Cebriones," Fraunce regards Patroclus's speech as an example of "indignation" and "derision," citing the speech once again in a later chapter devoted to scorn and rebuke.[16]

Chapman and Fraunce's attention to instances of irony in Homeric epic reflects the influence of ancient Greek and Byzantine rhetorical learning, for it was the Greek, and not the Latin, critics of Homer – including Demetrius, Hermogenes, Longinus, pseudo-Plutarch, Tzetzes, and Eustathius – who developed a complex rhetorical idiom to describe the varieties of Homeric wit. Hermogenes and Eustathius are especially careful to distinguish the various species of irony, reproach, and scornful speech in Homeric epic, using terms such as *drimutês* (bitter or abusive speech that contains a "hidden sting" or that is used to launch an argumentative attack); *barutês* (blameful, reproachful, or scornful speech); and *gorgotês* (hasty or agitated speech).[17] Although he does not preserve the specificity of this rhetorical idiom, Chapman adopts two of Eustathius's key rhetorical terms – *ironicè* and *scopticè* – for his own Homeric commentaries. Although he may well have pilfered these terms from the commentary to Jean de Sponde's 1583 Greek-Latin edition of Homer, a text he borrows from intermittently but also attacks in his marginal notes, Chapman also cites the Greek text of Eustathius's commentary directly at several points, perhaps in an effort to refute the allegation that he translated Homer "out of the Latine onely."[18]

Chapman also relies heavily on the *De Vita et Poesi Homeris*, the pseudo-Plutarchan biography he cites from Xylander's Latin edition of the Greek essayist. According to Dilwyn Knox, the pseudo-Plutarchan

Life helped to introduce into the sixteenth-century literary-critical vocabulary a number of terms pertaining to irony and related rhetorical devices, terms that the author of the *Life* probably adopted from Hermogenes.[19] Yet unlike Fraunce, whose principal aim is to classify the different rhetorical tropes and strategies used in Homeric epic, Chapman draws attention to ironic and scoptic passages in order to legitimate Homeric episodes deemed ridiculous or indecorous by earlier readers as well as to persuade us that these ironies have not been detected or properly analysed by earlier editors, thus turning his capacity to construe ironic texts into the mark of his superior, and even divine, wisdom.[20]

Chapman's Ironic Homer

In a marginal note glossing the boastful vaunt delivered by Epeus, one of the competitors at Patroclus's funeral games in Book 23 of the *Iliad*, Chapman alerts the readers of his translation of the *Iliad* to the poet's acerbic wit: "Note the sharpnes of wit in our Homer, if where you looke not for it, you can find it."[21] According to Chapman, Homer's readers can only hope to recognize the pungency of Epeus's speech if they "looke not for it," an act that demands a kind of readerly *sprezzatura* whose methods of attainment are puzzling if not downright contradictory. The gloss on Epeus's speech is one of several places where Chapman proves remarkably attentive to the tonal range of Homer's speakers. In a speech that is at once arrogant and full of ironic mock-humility, Homer's Epeus rises to volunteer for a fist-fighting match proposed by Achilles, a contest in which the winner is to be awarded a mule and the loser a cup. Predicting his own victory even before another contestant rises to the challenge, Epeus claims the mule as his and mockingly concedes the cup to his imaginary adversary. The whole speech is a fine illustration of Aristotle's argument that irony and alazony, though apparent opposites, can at times coincide such that "mock humility does really seem to be boastfulness."[22] The dominant tone of the speech is jocular self-deprecation: Epeus demurs at line 584, "I am no souldier," and yet he manages to triumph over Euryalus, an adversary described as a "man god-like."[23] Epeus's speech uses just the sort of rhetoric that the pseudo-Plutarchan *Life* has in mind when it praises Homer for creating the irony that arises when a speaker "underrates himself to create just the opposite impression" or when that speaker "pretends to praise someone else but is in fact censuring him."[24]

The character Chapman interprets as drawn with Homer's most ironic brushstrokes is Menelaus. Throughout his commentaries, Chapman repeatedly presents Menelaus as the target of scornful and mocking speech issued from various characters as well as from the narrator himself. The first suggestion that Chapman regards Homer's treatment of Menelaus as ironic appears in his commentary to Book 2 of the *Iliad*, where he glosses the lines "And uncalled came Menelaus, good at the war-cry" [*automatos de' oi elthe Boên agathos Menelaus*].[25] Chapman challenges previous scholars who have translated the epithet *Boên agathos* as "good-voiced" [*voce bonus*] or as "*bello strenuus*," neither of which captures the "mind of our Homer" according to Chapman, since *boê* does not mean voice but rather "*vociferatio* or clamor." His ironic interpretation of the passage is a two-part process: after establishing the precise and literal meaning of the epithet, Chapman unravels that meaning by proposing that Homer's description of Menelaus's voice, translated by him at *Il.* 2.355 as "at-a-martiall-crie," is in fact intended as a piece of irony. To read the epithet seriously, as denoting Menelaus's loud or powerful voice, demands reading Homer in a manner "straind beyond sufferance" according to Chapman, "unlesse it be ironically taken," since elsewhere in the *Iliad*, Homer describes Menelaus's voice as "*mala ligeôs, valde stridulè or arguto cum stridore*, *ligeôs* being commonly and most properlie taken in the worse part, and signifieth shrillie, or noisefullie, squeaking."[26] Chapman concludes that the epithet is intended to describe Menelaus as "small, and shrill-voiced (not sweet or eloquent, as some most against the haire would have him)," an interpretation that preserves the coherence of Menelaus's character by "reading against the hair," deviating from more literal renderings of the phrase offered by previous translators.

Chapman elaborates upon this interpretation of Menelaus's voice in his gloss on Book 3's more familiar contrast between the oratorical skills of Menelaus and of Odysseus, a passage that for many Renaissance readers exemplifies Homer's wide range of rhetorical styles. In Chapman's translation of the passage, Menelaus's voice is described as "passing lowd, small, fast, yet did not reach / To much, being naturally borne Laconicall, nor would / His humor lie for any thing."[27] By contrast to Odysseus, out of whose "ample breast" pours a "great voice ... / And words that flew about our ears like drifts of winter snow," Menelaus is a terse, simple, and honest speaker whose chief rhetorical characteristic is his *parrhêsia*, or forthrightness.[28] Justifying his translation of the phrase "*Menelaos epitrochadên agoreue*," Chapman protests in his commentary that "*epitrochadên*" does not mean succinctly, but rather "*velociter*, properly, *modo eorum qui currunt*" such that Homer intended to depict Menelaus as a figure who "spake fast, or thicke."[29] Chapman also objects to his predecessors' renderings of "*alla mala ligeôs*," a phrase wrongly assumed to convey Menelaus's supposed clarity of speech and thus translated by Sponde as "*sed valdè acute*." Arguing for a reading that better captures Homer's dim opinion of Menelaus, Chapman instead proposes to translate the phrase as "*valde stridulè*, shrilly, smally, or alowd," a reading that "maketh even with his simple character at all parts – his utterance being noisefull, small or squeaking, an excellent pipe for a foole."[30]

In his interpretation of both passages describing Menelaus's voice, Chapman's paramount concern is to translate Homer's poem in a manner that preserves the coherence of the Homeric text. According to Chapman's logic, Menelaus's voice, howsoever variously described, must always remain in agreement with the lineaments of his character. If he speaks in a glib, squawking, or foolish manner in Book 3 of the *Iliad*, then he must speak in a similar manner throughout the poem, no matter which epithets the poet uses. In order to bring the apparent inconsistencies of Homeric epic into agreement, Chapman interprets various passages as ironic or mocking in tone. Far from producing ambiguity, the irony that Chapman detects in Homer's delineation of Menelaus's character aims to stabilize meaning by bringing the *Iliad* into harmony with itself, a goal more in keeping with the philological investigations of eighteenth-century Homeric scholars such as F.A. Wolf than with the flights of interpretive fancy typical of sixteenth-century allegory. Accordingly, Chapman boasts in his commentary to Book 1 of the *Iliad* that "where all others find discords and dissonances [in Homer] I prove him entirely harmonious and proportionate," poetic virtues that Chapman establishes, above all, by reading Homer ironically.[31] While it is a Renaissance commonplace that various episodes of Homeric epic demonstrate the "opposition of contraries as a principle derived from nature," Chapman is perhaps unique in conceiving of Homer's irony as fostering this *concordia discors*, since irony creates the "opposition" necessary to create convincing characters whose "contrarieties are simultaneous and all necessary to a portrait of a full man."[32] Homer's readers had long praised his poems for the realism of his characterizations. Chapman understands this realism as the product of irony and contradiction: a character such as Menelaus is believable because he is represented alternately as fool and sage, shrill-voiced and booming, coward and hero, oppositions that contribute to, rather than detract from, his vivid lifelikeness.[33]

In keeping with his aim to prove Menelaus's character consistent and harmonious with itself, Chapman mocks previous efforts to translate the phrase "*Oud'aphamartoepês*" (literally, not random-talking) as "*Neque in verbis peccans*" (not erring in words), a reading that wrongly suggests that "a foole were perfectly spoken; when the word here hath another sence and our Homer a farre other meaning."[34] Chapman probably has in mind a definition for *aphamartoepês* (random-talking, babbling) that is closer to its root verb *aphamartanô* – to err or miss one's mark – and thus proposes translating the phrase as "*neque mendax erat* – he would not lie by any meanes, for that affectedly he stands upon hereafter." Unlike the evasive Odysseus, Menelaus is – or at least thinks he is – a straight-talking speaker who prizes his bluntness. For Chapman, Homer's assessment of Menelaus's speech as "never missing the mark" does not describe the character's actual rhetorical skill but rather his affectation of honest simplicity and plain speaking. A correct translation of the passage must take as its starting point the nature of Menelaus's character: "You see, then, to how extreme a difference and contrarietie the word and sence lie subject, and that without first finding the true figures of persons in this kind presented it is impossible for the best linguist living to expresse an Author trulie."[35]

Despite his acknowledgment that Homer's intended "sence" is often at odds with his "word," Chapman's translation of the *Iliad* is motivated by the idea that speech reveals character: as Ben Jonson puts it, "[l]anguage most shewes a man: speake that I may see thee."[36] Chapman similarly explains in his commentary that the "voice or manner of utterance" of each character provides a "key that discovereth his wisdome or folly."[37] Such an insight helps to explain why Chapman is so assiduous to translate and explicate accurately the tone of Homer's speakers as well as the narrator's descriptions of their voices. It also explains Chapman's concern to capture the ever-shifting tone of the narrator, whose voice is variously ironic, sweet, vehement, or mocking, depending upon the object of its attention. In his explication of *Il.* 2.355, Chapman rests his interpretation on the premise that the Homeric narrator is "speaking scoptically" in the verses describing Menelaus: the poet "breakes open the fountaine of his ridiculous humour" in a manner that (as Chapman boasts) has "never by anie interpreter [been] understood, or touched at" until his own commentary brought to light the "ingenious conceited person" of the narrator.[38] This is not to say that Chapman finds the Homeric narrator to be consistently "ridiculous" or "conceited" throughout his poems – elsewhere in his commentary, he chides other translators for assuming too much consistency in the poet's narrative voice. Yet Chapman repeatedly acknowledges that the principal challenge facing Homer's translators and readers is the fine art of distinguishing levity from gravity and jest from earnest, stances often difficult to distinguish because of Homer's ironic wit.

Chapman's attentiveness to the ironic and scoffing passages in Homer is also motivated by his desire to demonstrate how the perceived "dissonances" of Homeric epic conceal the meaning of a text that, properly interpreted, is in fact "harmonious" with itself at all points. The coherence that Chapman posits in Homeric epic paradoxically depends upon creating an appearance of contrariety by building characters such as Menelaus out of a jumble of "crosse and deformed parts."[39] According to Chapman, prior translators have erred not only in neglecting to detect Homer's ironic treatment of the Spartan king, but also in adhering to a false notion of decorum that demands unity of character. In order properly to understand the complexity of Menelaus's character, Chapman argues that Homer's readers must abandon the conviction that "fooles [are] alwaies foolish, cowards at all times cowardly, &c," since such a uniform view of human behaviour is "farre from the variant order of nature, whose principles being contrary, her productions must needes containe the like opposition."[40] Menelaus may be a fool and a coward, but even so, he is – or at least may appear to be – wise and brave on occasion. Sometimes understood during the sixteenth century as a species of *copia*, irony becomes, for Chapman, a means for the Homeric poet to represent the heterogeneous and discordant elements of a "variant" nature.[41]

Chapman supports his argument that Homer's treatment of Menelaus is deliberately ironic by highlighting the disparity between the Spartan king's perception of himself – courageous, manly, and wise – and the Homeric narrator's rather different perception of him as cowardly and foolish. By clarifying as ironic the derisory praise that intermittently interrupts Homer's predominantly anti-heroic handling of Menelaus, Chapman's interpretation helps to make sense of a character who might otherwise appear to be a "motley and confused man," heroic and ridiculous, and aggressive and cowering, by turns.[42] Commenting on the narrator's use of the epithet "*Arêiphilos*" [Ares-loving, or war-loving] to describe Menelaus in Book 3 of the *Iliad*, Chapman chastises those scholars who have "untrulie" translated the phrase as "*bellicosus*," an error inasmuch as the Latin term means both martial skill and mere enthusiasm for war, only the latter of which is characteristic of Menelaus. If Menelaus is "he who loves Mars" [*cui Mars est carus*], according to Chapman's corrected Latin rendering of the phrase, it does not necessarily follow that Mars returns the favour: Menelaus "might love the warre, and yet be no good warriour, as many love manly exercises at which they will never be good."[43] In giving Menelaus this epithet, Homer intends to describe a "vainglorious affectation in him rather than a solid affection," for while he may well think himself to be *bellicosus*, Menelaus is "Ares-loving" only inasmuch as he fancies himself a formidable warrior.[44]

Either by chance or by design, Chapman proceeds according to an interpretive principle that resembles the "solution from the character" [*lusis ek tou prosôpou*] proposed by Homer's ancient scholiasts, who observed that because different Homeric speakers, including the narrator, have various perceptions of themselves and the world around them, contradictions in the Homeric poems may be resolved by taking into account who is speaking. Porphyry explains away the "self-contradictions" [*enantia heautô*] in Homer's poems by arguing that although inconsistent and even "contrary" [*enantia*] claims are made by different characters, "all that [Homer] said himself from his own person" is "consistent and not mutually contradictory."[45] Much of the irony that Chapman detects in Homer's treatment of Menelaus arises out this problem of two competing perspectives: Menelaus's belief in his military prowess and other characters' recognition of his cowardice. As the Trojan Pisander runs at Menelaus in the heat of battle in Book 13 of the *Iliad*, Chapman marks as "*Scopticè*" the narrator's derisory apostrophe to Menelaus as he anticipates the shame of Pisander's defeat at the hands of such an unimpressive adversary: "O Menelaus, that he might by thee in dangerous warre / Be done to death."[46] Menelaus does in fact manage to kill Pisander a few lines later – even a vainglorious fool has his valorous moments – yet in Chapman's reading, Menelaus's victory in battle merely offers the Homeric narrator another opportunity for ridicule. Standing over Pisander's corpse, Menelaus delivers what Chapman calls his "most ridiculous insultation," an unintentionally parodic version of the boastful vaunts made by other Homeric heroes in battle, which are often noted as "insultations" in Chapman's margins.[47] Unlike the bitter reproaches and acerbic jests uttered by other warriors over the dead and dying bodies of their enemies, however, Menelaus's speech is "ridiculous" precisely because it lacks the sharp wit of the rhetorical model he is trying to emulate. Instead, Menelaus delivers an earnest, sombre speech indicting the Trojans for their insatiable love of war:

> Satietie of state,
> Satietie of sleepe and love, satietie of ease,
> Of musicke, dancing, can find place, yet harsh warre still must please
> Past all these pleasures, even past these. They will be cloyd with these
> Before their warre joyes: never warre gives Troy satieties.[48]

Out of context, there is nothing intrinsically "ridiculous" about the speech, and a number of other sixteenth- and seventeenth-century writers, including Erasmus, cite the passage as proof of Homer's sincere hatred of war.

Yet Chapman sees Menelaus's "lame reproofe" as evidence of the "continuance" of his "ridiculous character," both because he fails to duplicate the testosterone-laden flyting matches typical of the *Iliad*'s battle scenes and also because there is something singularly inappropriate about Menelaus – the vainglorious, Ares-loving cuckold whose wayward wife was the prime catalyst for the Trojan War – complaining about the Trojans' unslakeable appetite for war.[49]

The absurd humour of Menelaus's speech is compounded for Chapman by its accompanying threat to the Trojans that Zeus will destroy them for "ravishing my goods and wife, in flowre of all her yeares."[50] Calling Helen his "*kouridiên alochon*" – a phrase translated by Sponde as "*virginem uxorem*" [virginal wife] – Menelaus is "ingeniously" revealed to be a fool by the Homeric narrator when he voices his belief that "he married a virgin." Answering the objections of previous translators that Helen was not, in fact, a virgin when she married Menelaus – according to several post-Homeric myths, Helen was raped by Theseus before Menelaus married her – Chapman scoffs at those readers who are "so simple to thinke that the Poet thinketh alwaies as he maketh others speake," especially since it is "no verie strange or rare credulitie in men to beleeve they marrie maids when they do not."[51] Yet instead of recognizing the passage as a jibe at Menelaus's "good husbandly imagination of his wive's maidenhead," prior editors and commentators twist "ropes of sand" as they debate whether Homer was familiar with the story of Theseus's ravishment of Helen, or whether the poet should be "taxed with ignorance" for calling Helen a virgin when she was not. In contradistinction to the excessively erudite and complicated glosses provided by his predecessors, Chapman's solution is deliciously simple: Menelaus believes that he married a virgin, while Homer – and his readers – laugh at the cuckold in their superior knowledge that he did not.

The label of irony allows Chapman to clarify a number of obscure passages whose meanings have been obscured by the tortuous "intelligencing knowledge" of scholars who rely too much on arcane learning and not enough on the common sense required to grasp the "true simplicitie" of Menelaus's character, a technique that Chapman may have learnt from the ancient scholiasts, who rejected certain verses based on the premise that they did not reflect common sense or experience. Yet common sense at times seems an insufficient guarantor of interpretive accuracy for Chapman, for despite his protests that Homer could not have made "plainer this good King's simplicity," he also argues that the poet's ironic treatment of Menelaus is a ruse to trap unwary readers, "mists" that "our Homer casteth before the eyes of his Readers, that hindereth their prospects to his [i.e., Menelaus's] more constant and predominant softnesse and simplicitie."[52] When analysing the use of the epithet *agathos* [good] in reference to Menelaus, Chapman praises how "ingeniously Homer giveth him [Menelaus] still some colour of reason for his senselesnesse, which colour yet is enough to deceive our Commentors," but he quickly becomes exasperated with his self-appointed task to "make clear a thing plaine" for those readers who fail to detect the irony of the epithet. Declaring that "I am weary with beating this thin thicket for a woodcocke," Chapman's metaphor suggests that the *Iliad* is – at least relative to his own, "strange Poems" – a "perviall" or transparent text whose meanings can be unravelled with ease even by a "Simplician."[53] The idea that irony is obvious – or, rather, that it is obvious to those few readers capable of discerning it – likewise informs Chapman's gloss on Epeus's speech in Book 23 of the *Iliad*, a speech whose irony is evident only to those readers who "looke not" for it. Unlike allegory, which submerges deep meanings under a veil or *transenna*, irony hides in plain sight: either wholly visible or completely invisible to its audience, irony demands none of the "deepe searching" required by readers of poems such as *Ovids Banquet of Sence*. As Wayne Booth has argued, there is a great difference between "the traps laid by stable irony and the invitations offered by allegory," since the naive reader who fails to detect irony "will totally misunderstand what is going on."[54] Howsoever cloudily enwrapped, allegorical texts are by definition inclusive, whereas ironic texts are exclusive: they presuppose victims and address themselves only to a portion of their audience. Witness the titles of Chapman's poetic prefaces: to the "Understander," to the "trulie learned," to "you [who] are not every bodie."

In his Homeric commentaries, Chapman distinguishes between two kinds of readers: the "understanding" reader whose "eyes [are] more sharpe than not to see pervially" through Homer's mists, and the "prophaned ... Traducers" of Homer, for whom his poems remain a "darke and perplext ... riddle."[55] Animated by his dissatisfaction with these "prejudicate" and "peremptory" readers, Chapman's commentaries speak to his most pressing frustrations as a poet, particularly as expressed in his early dedications to Mathew Roydon, which declare Chapman's contempt for the "prophane multitude" and instead "consecrate[s]" his "strange Poems" to those "serching spirits" in possession of "the iudiciall perspective."[56] Yet Chapman's translations of Homer differentiate the pure from the profane reader rather differently from the dedications to *Ovids Banquet* and *The Shadow of Night*, which call for the reader's "Herculean labor" in undertaking the "deepe search of knowledge" required to read his poems correctly. In his early poetic dedications, the reader's efforts at deep reading are rewarded because the riches of a text are "digd out of the bowels of the earth, not found in the superficies of it."[57] Yet in his Homeric commentaries, Chapman argues that the "blindnes" of prior commentators such as Scaliger and Sponde is the result of too *much* digging, rather than not enough, for these and other scholars make the mistake of trying to "wrest and racke out of [Homer]" a hidden sense even when the simplest and most obvious interpretation is often the correct one.[58] Such an error, according to Chapman, is particularly common among Homer's "prozers," or prose translators, who fail to rely on common sense, producing "affected expositions" rather than interpretations based on an intuitive understanding of human character.[59]

In certain respects, Chapman's hermeneutic methods as a translator of Homer conform to the poetical credo laid out by the dedications to *Ovids Banquet* and *The Shadow of Night*. Both sets of works distinguish between artificial and natural obscurity, condemning the former as "pedanticall and childish" while praising the latter as necessary rather than gratuitous, derived from a poet's complex handling of the dark and variant truths of nature.[60] Obscure passages in Chapman's own poems, as well as in Homer's, cannot be elucidated merely by the instruments of philology. Instead, readers must establish meaning by ceasing to look for it – precisely the advice given by Chapman's gloss on Epeus's speech. Yet as he protests that even the obscurest passages of Homeric epic are easily clarified by his translation, Chapman nonetheless appeals to that obscurity as a guarantor of Homer's poetic genius as well as of his own rare critical insight. As he puts it rather bluntly in the preface to his 1611 *Iliads*, there is "nothing in all respects perfect but what is perceived by few."[61]

Two hundred years later, in his own commentary on the *Iliad*, Alexander Pope interprets Chapman's "ironical" interpretation of Menelaus as a shameless attempt to bolster the translator's intellectual authority: "This is one of the mysteries which that translator boasts to have found in Homer," Pope scoffs, arguing that "we must endeavor to rescue [Menelaus] from this misinterpretation."[62] This is not to say that Pope detects no irony in the *Iliad*: in the "Poetical Index" at the end of his translation, he divides the poem's speeches into six categories, including "In the Vituperative Kind" and "speeches to horses," and he provides a lengthy list of speeches punctuated by irony or sarcasm, many of which are likewise deemed ironic by Chapman.[63] Yet Pope nonetheless wishes to recuperate the dignity of Menelaus's character from Chapman's "ironical" interpretation, an interpretation fuelled partly by the earlier translator's enthusiasm for the anti-heroic strain he discerns coursing through Homeric epic. Chapman repeatedly seizes upon images and epithets that lend themselves to a satirical and even bathetic reading. This is particularly apparent in his gloss on *Il.* 17.488–9, a simile in which the Homeric narrator describes how Athena, rousing the Achaean troops in battle, fills Menelaus's knees "liberally / With swiftnesse, breathing in his breast the courage of a flie."[64] In a gloss half stolen from Sponde, Chapman mocks prior translators for assuming the metaphor to be in earnest, and thus incompetent: "all his interpreters ridiculously laugh at [this simile] in Homer, as if he heartily intended to praise Menelaus by it, not understanding his Ironie here, agreeing with all the other sillinesse noted in his character."[65]

Like many of Chapman's glosses, this one ends with a snotty outburst against the mob of of "great Clerks" who "are perplext and abuse Homer," falling into errors that Chapman unearths with equal parts contempt and glee.[66] Possibly in an effort to imitate the irony he discerns in the Homeric narrator, Chapman adopts an intermittently ironic tone towards his own readers, lavishing upon them an insincere praise that thinly veils his contempt. In a verse preface to the reader first printed in the 1608 edition of the *Iliad*, Chapman praises the "great Clarkes" who have preceded him but then annotates the passage in his margins with the word "*Ironicè*," the same term that alerts readers to the ironic passages in the poem.[67] This mocking critical voice serves a double purpose: it emulates the sardonic tone of the Homeric narrator and also trains his readers – or at least his more judicious readers – to practise their methods of reading ironically at the margins of the Homeric text. At *Il.* 17.70 and following, for instance, Chapman's marginal comment to "Note the manly and wise discourse of Menelaus with himselfe" is clearly intended as ironic praise of Menelaus's purported courage in a scene that depicts his flight from battle.[68] Yet rather than make explicit the ironic dimensions of Menelaus's speech and his subsequent escape, Chapman assimilates Homeric techniques of ironic praise into his marginal notes in order to tempt us into the error of believing that the poet "heartily intended to praise Menelaus" by comparing him to a lion when he in fact makes a "Lionlike retreate."[69]

Despite its value as a means of reinforcing his own critical authority, Chapman's ironic interpretation of Homer also reflects his recognition that one of the greatest challenges faced by the translator is to render accurately the crucial subtleties of tone that convey meaning implicitly rather than explicitly. In one of his prefaces and again in his commentary to Book 1 of the *Iliad*, Chapman justifies the "paraphrasis or circumlocution" of his translation as the most effective means of preserving the spirit in which Homer's speeches are delivered. According to Chapman, the translator's task is not to turn Homer "word for word," but rather to "follow ... the materiall things themselves," to weigh the meaning of the lines and then "to clothe and adorne them with words and such a stile and forme of Oration as are most apt for the language into which they are converted."[70] Chapman defends this method by arguing that speech is the primary means through which we may understand the nature of character in Homeric epic: the poet has inspired his "chiefe persons with different spirits," and those persons are distinguishable from each other by "their speeches, being one by another as conveniently and necessarily knowne as the instrument by the sound."[71] Like a chorus in which Menelaus's squeaky voice assumes a soprano role while Odysseus and Nestor take up the alto and bass lines, Homeric epic is a symphony of different vocal registers that must carefully be distinguished by the translator. "If a Translator or Interpreter of a ridiculous and cowardly described person" fails to understand these key characteristics, Chapman remarks in his commentary, and if that translator "violates and vitiates the originall to make his speech grave and him valiant," then the essence of Homer is "abused."[72] Consequently, Chapman devotes a great deal of attention in his marginal notes to the tones of speeches, especially those he perceives to be admonitory, caustic, or scoffing. He notes, for example, the "sharpe invective" of Hera, the "railing" of Thersites, Helen's "chid[ing]" of Venus and her "bitter reproofe" of Paris, the "rough speech" that Sthenelus delivers to Agamemnon and the "rebuke" that he receives in return from Diomedes, and the "sharpe jest" made by Pallas to Zeus.[73]

Chapman also argues at several places that passages confusing to previous translators might be clarified by a translation attentive to the diction or tone of a speech rather than its apparent meaning. He objects, for instance, to previous translations of a simile that compares the voices of several Trojan elders to the "chirping" sound of grasshoppers, challenging the rendering of the Greek *leirioessan* [lily-like] as the Latin *suavem* [sweetly, softly] in a passage describing how the old men "softly speak winged words to each other while sitting on the wall" [*êka pros allêlous epea pteroent' agoreuon*].[74] Rather than translate the "weake faint sounds" of the men as *vocem suavem*, as Sponde does at 3.152, Chapman instead proposes "*vocem teneram* ... for Grasshoppers sing not sweetly, but harshly and faintly, wherein the weake and tender voices of the Old Counsellors is to admiration exprest."[75] Since the faintness of this sound presumably counterbalances its harshness, Chapman chastises Sponde for translating the word as "garrulous." Although Chapman concedes that grasshoppers can indeed sound "stridulous," Sponde's translation cannot be reconciled with Homer's description of the men as "*Esthloi agorêtai*," or good speakers, since "the word *esthlos* signif[ies] ... temperate or full of al moderation, and, so, farre from intimating any touch of garrulitie."[76] A similar attentiveness to the "forme and stile of Oration" informs Chapman's gloss on the sound made by "whuling Scylla" [*Skullê ... deinon lelakuia*], whose voice is "terrible" [*deinon*] not because of its "gravitie or greatnesse" but rather on account of the "monstrous disproportion" between the "vast frame" of her body" and her voice, which sounds like a "newly kitn'd kitling."[77]

Chapman's consideration of the broad spectrum of voices and tones in Homeric epic reflects his awareness that Homer was an oral poet whose verse, originally intended for the ear and not the eye, possesses an aural dimension difficult to reproduce in the silent medium of print. The ear of the Homeric translator must be finely attuned to the intonations of ironic and scoffing speech, as well as to the rich array of similes that compare human voices to grasshoppers, trumpets, or the cry of a newborn lion cub. But Chapman also recognizes the potential for humour in the fact that certain Homeric characters are unable to discern the tonal distinctions that divide sincere from insincere (or ironic) praise. This humour is directed primarily at Menelaus, whom Chapman interprets at various points as the oblivious target of ironic or scoffing remarks made by the narrator or by his fellow characters. After he rails against Antilochus in what Chapman calls a "ridiculous speech for conclusion of his character," Menelaus becomes the unwitting victim of Antilochus's sharp wit, although Chapman helpfully marks the "ironicall reply" of Nestor's son in his margins so that readers might recognize what Menelaus does not.[78] Scolded by Menelaus for cheating in the chariot race and knocking him into the dust, Antilochus responds to the accusation with eloquent but disingenuous praise as he begs Menelaus's forgiveness:

> You more in age
> And more in excellence, know well the outraies that engage
> All yong men's actions; sharper wits but duller wisdomes still
> From us flow than from you.[79]

Concerned that readers might misconstrue Antilochus's "ironicall reply" as an earnest apology, Chapman marks two additional places in the ensuing fifteen lines where he detects irony, first when Antilochus, in mock-deference, offers to give Menelaus his prize, and again when the narrator compares the stirrings of Menelaus's heart to ears of corn waving in the breeze:

> it rejoyc't him so
> That, as corne-eares shine with the dew, yet having time to grow
> When fields set all their bristles up, in such a ruffle wert thou,
> O Menelaus.[80]

Blissfully unaware of Antilochus's insincerity, Menelaus is the equally unwitting victim of the poet's ridiculous and "meerly Ironicall" simile, one of several such comparisons noted in Chapman's commentary as an example of blame disguised as praise. At *Il.* 17.588 and following, Chapman interprets ironically a simile comparing Menelaus to an eagle, an image intended to capture not his "magnanimitie and valor" but rather the ridiculous way he "looks about, leering."[81] It is for similar reasons, Chapman adds, that Homer calls Menelaus "*malakos aichmêtês, mollis bellator*" [soft spearman, soft warrior], an epithet no doubt intended to cast aspersions on his sexual prowess as well as his martial skill.

To Compare Great Things to Small: Chapman's Bathetic Homer

Chapman's appreciation of Homer's use of similes and epithets for satirical, ironic, or otherwise humorous use reflects his understanding of the Homeric simile as an oxymoronic structure, a syntactic unit that juxtaposes the high and the low or unites jarringly different arenas of human experience. Many Homeric similes bring together heroic and pastoral elements, or martial and domestic scenes, in a manner that generates irony by throwing into relief the contrary values or perspectives of the poem as a whole.[82] This ironic potential of the Homeric simile appeals immensely to Chapman, who singles out for the highest praise one particular comparison, from Book 12 of the *Iliad*, in which the narrator likens two enemies locked in an even fight to the movements of a spinster weaving a web, balancing in her hand the "weights and wooll, till both in just paise stand."[83] In his margins, Chapman celebrates the simile as a means of "comparing mightiest things with meanest, and the meanest illustrating the mightiest," and he explains how the simile permits seeming contraries to "mee[t] in one end" and thus produce that *concordia discors* for which "our Homer is beyond comparison and admiration."[84] Irony is often understood by Renaissance writers as a "remedie of contraries," a device that reconciles opposing beliefs or perspectives in order to "expell the infection of Absurditie," as Thomas Nashe puts it.[85] Chapman grasps the Homeric simile, with its latent irony, as a means of uniting the contrary styles and attitudes – high and low, sublime and bathetic, serious and trivial – at play in the *Iliad* and *Odyssey*.

Chapman's observation that the simile in Book 12 of the *Iliad* compares "mightiest things with meanest" intervenes in an ancient literary-critical dispute concerning the decorum – or rather the indecorum – of the Homeric simile. In *On Style*, Demetrius observes that metaphors and other tropes of comparison ought to "compare the smaller [*mikra*] to the greater [*meizonôn*], not the reverse," citing as a negative example *Il.* 13.388, which compares "heaven resounding" to a "resounding trumpet," as an example of a simile that produces "triviality [*mikrotêtos*] rather than grandeur [*megethos*]."[86] Yet Longinus cites the very same verse from the *Iliad* as an example of the terror-producing imagery that makes Homer a master of poetic sublimity.[87] In his eagerness to prove that such Homeric similes do not "breach the canons of propriety [*to prepon*]" so long as they are interpreted correctly, Chapman clearly sides with Longinus, even finding evidence of Homer's sublimity in the topsy-turvy juxtapositions of triviality and grandeur condemned by other readers as indecorous.[88]

The irony that Chapman discerns in Homeric epic is a species of *inversio*, a type of irony in which, as Quintilian defines it, the "meaning is contrary to that suggested."[89] In other words, the power of the Homeric simile to yoke together the "meanest" with the "mightiest" derives from the topsy-turvy effects of irony, a trope often defined in Renaissance rhetorical treatises as the "turning upside down of a thing, or contrary to the right form."[90] The involutions detected by Chapman at the structural and thematic core of the *Odyssey* constitute an attenuated form of ironic inversion in which the "magnificent" (as Chapman labels the *Iliad*) is replaced by the "low" or "jejune," terms Chapman associates with the *Odyssey*. Preferring the latter poem to the former, Chapman rejects Longinus's "Censure" of the *Odyssey*, which compares the *Iliad* to "the Sunne rising" and the *Odyssey* to its "descent or setting."[91] In his dedication, Chapman challenges Longinus's distinction between *hupsous* [height, sublimity] and *bathos* [depth, ridiculousness] by testifying to the various ways in which Homeric epic complicates and conflates the categories of the sublime and the bathetic. To Steven Shankman, this makes Chapman look like a writer who "subvert[s] ... the criteria of Longinian elevation" rather than fulfilling it, as Pope would later do.[92] Yet while Chapman's debts to Longinus are sparser and less conventional than those of Pope, whose translation of the *Iliad* was produced under the shadow of Boileau's *Art Poétique* and similar neoclassical manifestos of sublimity, Chapman's reliance on the *Peri Hupsous* in his translation of the *Odyssey* reveals a subtle and strikingly original conception of *hupsous*, or sublimity, as the inescapable counterpart of bathos and irony rather than its simple opposite. More elevated than the *Iliad* by virtue of its "low" or "jejune" subject matter, the *Odyssey* attains its own peculiar form of sublimity, for Chapman, through its most scoptical and ridiculous moments.

Chapman's understanding of the differences between the *Iliad* and *Odyssey* are shaped by a familiar argument first voiced by Aristotle and revitalized by fifteenth- and sixteenth-century writers such as Poliziano, Erasmus, and Rabelais, that Homeric epic is at once tragic and comic in that it combines the "serious" [*spoudaia*] and the "laughable" [*to geloion*].[93] Poliziano, from whom Chapman borrows heavily in the prefaces and notes to his own Homeric translations, describes Homer as the font of both tragic sublimity and comic bathos, a poet who tempers the "grandiloquent language" [*magniloquis voces*] of tragedy with the "lascivious laughter of the comic socks" [*lasciva datos riserunt compita soccos*].[94] Yet in spite of his almost parasitical dependence upon Poliziano in some of his prefaces, Chapman takes the Italian humanist's discussions of Homer's rhetorical and generic range in a different direction by arguing that it is in the most trifling or ridiculous episodes of Homeric epic that one finds concealed the most serious truths about human nature.

Capable of representing "all things spher'd in Nature," Homer's poetry is "circular" according to Chapman, an image that suggests the poems' encyclopedic range, and their copious mixture of subjects and styles that bring the dissonant forces of the cosmos, and of human experience, into harmony.[95] A century before Chapman began his translation, Poliziano's *Ambra* had celebrated Homer's "fecund opulence" [*felix opulentia*], praising his poetry as the unified origin of all philosophical doctrines – a *prisca scientia* that illustrates how "natural causes conspire together in an aggressive alliance [of] discordant accords" [*conspirantes pugnaci foedere causas / discordemque fidem*].[96] Yet Chapman diverges from Poliziano in pursuing the cosmological allegories generated by such an interpretation, refraining almost completely in his prefaces and commentaries from explicating the poems in terms of the pre-Socratic and Platonic doctrines that feature so prominently in Poliziano's interpretations as well as in the pseudo-Plutarchan *Life of Homer*, an important resource for both translators.

Instead, Chapman adopts Poliziano's idea of Homeric epic as a union of "discordant accords" in order to explicate and defend the *gioco*-seriousness of the *Iliad* and *Odyssey*. In the margins of his translation of Book 8 of the *Odyssey*, Chapman cites, almost verbatim, a passage from Plato's *Phaedrus* as a gloss on Demodocus's account of Hephaestus's entrapment of Aphrodite and Ares, an episode whose comic dimensions had prompted ancient and earlier Renaissance commentators to "rescue" the passage by interpreting it as an allegory about the union of love and strife. As Hephaestus loosens the net binding the adulterous couple and they flee, laughing, Chapman remarks, "This is *to ta mikra megalôs*, &c. *Parva magne dicere*; grave sentence out of lightest vapor."[97] In his speech on love in Plato's *Symposium*, Agathon offers a similar comment after recounting the amorous follies of the Olympian gods, concluding his account of the entrapment of Ares and Aphrodite by stating that "I have done my best to mingle amusement [*paidias*] with a decent gravity [*spoudês*]."[98] Yet in citing the *Phaedrus* rather than the *Symposium*, Chapman invokes the Platonic concept of mingling jest and earnest from a rather odd context, since in the *Phaedrus*, the phrase in question appears as part of Socrates's condemnation of the sophists Gorgias and Tisias, who "make small things seem great and great things small by the power of their words" [*smikra megala kai ta megala smikra phainesthai poiousin dia rhômên logou*].[99] As Chapman interprets the passage, the rhetorical technique of making great things seem small and small things seem great characterizes sophistic logic but also Homeric *spoudaiogeloion* – serious laughter, or "speaking the truth under a jest."[100]

Chapman's invocation of Socrates's assessment of sophistry in the *Phaedrus* to describe the mingling of jest and earnest he detects in Homer's *Odyssey* may reflect his awareness that Gorgias and other Greek sophists regarded Homer as their literary ancestor.[101] Chapman need have looked no further than the *Phaedrus* to learn about the Homeric origins of Greek sophistry, since in that dialogue, Socrates mentions that Nestor and Odysseus composed two oratorical manuals during their leisure hours at Troy and compares the rhetorical skill of these Homeric heroes to "the work of Palamedes," the hero purportedly betrayed by Odysseus, suppressed by Homer, and finally resuscitated and defended by Gorgias's mock-encomium.[102] Chapman adapts Socrates's "*to ta mikra megalôs*" into a kind of motto for his translation of Homer, one that links the *gioco*-serious attitude of Homer's Olympian gods with the poet's own ironic habits of mind. When the phrase from the *Phaedrus* appears once again, with slight alterations, in one of Chapman's dedications to the *Odyssey*, it serves to align Homer with the Silenus to whom Alcibiades compares Socrates at *Symposium* 216d–e, the sculpted satyr whose ridiculous exterior conceals a hidden wisdom.[103] In his dedicatory epistle, Chapman proposes that the essential spirit of the *Odyssey* may be summed up by Socrates's tag from the *Phaedrus*: "*to ta mikra, megalôs; kai to koina kainôs*," a phrase he translates into Latin ("*Parva magnè dicere; pervulgata novè, jejuna plenè*,") and then, loosely, into English: "To speake things litle, greatly; things commune, rarely; things barren and emptie, fruitfully and fully."[104] Despite its resemblance to a passage in Plato's *Sophist* that criticizes sophists for a "shadowy play of discourse" that makes "what seem[s] important" appear "trifling" and "what seem[s] easy difficult," Chapman's repeated allusions to the *Phaedrus* recuperate this sophistic technique by revealing its sympathies with Socratic and Homeric irony, both of which conceal profound wisdom in the most trivial or vulgar containers.[105] Chapman takes seriously this alliance between Homer and Socrates: in one of his prefatory essays, he cites Dio Chrysostom's assertion that "Socrates was Homer's scholler," a claim that helps to rebut some of the most common imprecations against Homer during the Renaissance, namely, that his poems are crude, indecorous, or – according to J.C. Scaliger's especially vehement condemnation – "ridiculous."[106]

Chapman, by contrast, is insistent in his attempt to reclaim the poetic merits of the ridiculous, refuting "Scaliger and all Homer's ... ridiculous detractors" by turning the "commune" and "jejune" aspects of the *Odyssey* into the poem's chiefest virtues.[107] While the *Odyssey* lacks the "feastfull" and "magnificent" grandeur of the *Iliad*, it is "for this," Chapman goes on to remark – for the meagre, low, and contemptible subject of the *Odyssey* – that "this Poeme [is] preferred to his *Iliads*."[108] Although the "whole scope and object" of the *Odyssey* is the humble tale of "[t]he returne of a man into his Countrie," the poem is nevertheless "vast, illustrous, and of miraculous composure" for Chapman, achieving on a figurative level the sublimity that it might appear to lack on the literal level. Other Renaissance readers who prefer the *Odyssey* to the *Iliad* tend to do so because they find it a more peaceful poem, and a more pious one. But Chapman is unusual in valuing the *Odyssey* on the grounds that it is the more trivial and vulgar poem, an attitude that also may explain his decision to present his 1624 translation of the *Batrachomyomachia* under the subtitle, "Crowne of all Homers Worckes."[109] Although the title might be intended ironically, Chapman's claim does, if taken in earnest, testify to his enduring admiration for Homer's inversion of rhetorical and generic norms.

In the century and a half before the appearance of Chapman's translation of the *Batrachomyomachia*, printed with his translation of the *Homeric Hymns* and *Epigrams*, it had become commonplace to print

Homer's apocrypha alongside the works of Greek lyric poets such as Orpheus, Musaeus, and Hesiod. All three were among Chapman's chief poetic models from the early 1590s onwards, models suitable for legitimating his own, rather nugatory, lyric poems. In his 1598 continuation of Marlowe's *Hero and Leander*, Chapman prefaces his work with an apology for writing on "so trifeling a subject," a demurral undercut by his subsequent quip that "he that shuns trifles must shun the world."[110] More than two decades later, in his dedication to the Earl of Somerset, Chapman defends Homeric mock-epic on similar grounds, calling the *Batrachomyomachia* a "ridiculous Poem of Vermin" written "in contempt of men."[111] If Chapman's kinship with Homer arises partly out of his aspiration to be a divinely inspired and gnomic poet who conceals sacred truths from the vulgar multitude "under diverse vailes of *Hieroglyphickes*," it also arises out of his perception that the low and contemptible genres in which they both work, such as mock-epic and epigram, are those best able to conceal hidden wisdom.[112] Chapman repeatedly describes his "sleight labors" as a lyric poet in these very terms, deprecating a poem such as *The Shadow of Night* as a "poore and strange trifle" but then asserting that the text demands a "deepe search of knowledge" by its readers.[113]

For Chapman, the briefest texts, including lyric, mock-epic, and epigram, demand the deepest search because they best conform to the rhetorical principle of *multum in parvo*. The paradox that less is more, and that smaller is greater, informs Chapman's interpretations of Homer as well as his original verse, in which he self-consciously reproduces the greatness in little he associates with the Homeric corpus.[114] In the dedication to his 1598 *Seaven Bookes of the Iliads*, Chapman defends his decision to publish only a small portion of the poem, claiming that there is "so much quintessence to be drawne from so little a project, it will aske as much judgement to peruse worthily as whole volumes of more perviall inventions."[115] While translating seven books of the *Iliad* hardly constitutes a "little" project in terms of length or scope of subject, Chapman's contrast between the "quintessence" of Homeric epic and other, "more perviall" works reflects his appreciation that the excellence of Homer's poems resides not in their length but rather in their *depth*.

Guided by the conviction that Homeric epic derives its ethical and rhetorical potency from *enargeia* or vivid description, Chapman describes his own lyric poems in a similar manner, fixing on terms such as shadow and heightening, *schêma*, "materiall Oration," digging and searching, and *enargeia*, which he defines as the "cleerenes of representation, requird in absolute Poems."[116] Distinguishing *enargeia* from the "perspicuous delivery of a lowe invention," Chapman follows Quintilian in defining it as the rhetorical technique involved in bringing a vivid image in front of the reader's eyes "openly" [*aperte*], and yet concisely and rapidly, thus producing a density or brevity that may obscure or clarify the image in question.[117] In other words, *enargeia* produces a selective clarity that requires the reader to fill in the missing parts of an image, thus making explicit what is merely implicit in a process of "omition" that Chapman likens to the painterly technique of foreshortening.[118] Like irony, *enargeia* requires the reader to assume a "iudiciall perspective," and the affinity between the two tropes is further strengthened in Chapman's mind by virtue of their shared exclusivity. Unlike the "perviall" or superficial clarity that Chapman denigrates as "the plaine way to barbarisme," the "cleerenes" produced by irony and *enargeia* is not equally clear to all readers. For Chapman, this selective clarity is superior to the "pedanticall and childish" obscurity cultivated by poets who indulge in the gratuitous "affection of words, & indigested concets."[119] By contrasting this superficial obscurity with the more admirable kind of poetical darkness that "shroudeth it selfe in the hart of his subject," Chapman justifies his poems as "shadowed" in a "darknes" created by the crevices of nature itself.[120]

The Shadow of Night and *Ovids Banquet of Sence* were printed a half-decade before the 1598 publication of Chapman's first instalment of the *Iliad*, and Chapman's two dedications to Mathew Roydon contain the seedlings of poetic theories that would come to shape his interpretation of Homer. As early as the early 1590s, Chapman derives a number of key terms in his poetic idiom from the Homeric commentary tradition. His conception of *enargeia*, for instance, derives from Quintilian's and Erasmus's discussion of the exemplary vividness of Homeric epic, and his conception of several other rhetorical terms, including *enigma*, *emphasis*, *schêma*, and irony, derives from the Homeric paratexts that probably occupied prime shelf space in Chapman's library during the 1590s.[121] Chapman's understanding of *schêma*, a term used in the dedication to *Ovids Banquet* to denote the poet's method of "varying in some rare fiction, from popular custome" in his "materiall Oration," is adopted almost verbatim from the pseudo-Plutarchan *Life*, which praises Homer's use of *schêmata*, or figures, defined as any "turn of phrase that departs from the usual rules, for the sake of ornament or utility" [*to de schêma esti logos exêllagmenos tou en ethei kata tina plasin kosmou ê chreias charin*].[122] Homer was frequently praised by his ancient readers for his skilled and varied use of *eschêmatismenos logos*, a form of figured speech from "which one stands back," or which remains "incomplete until the audience completes the meaning."[123]

The rhetorical figures of *schêma* and *emphasis*, in particular, are understood as creating an impression of "omition": we see, or think we see, what is not there in Homer's poems, or we see clearly things that are only implied.[124] The *Iliad* and *Odyssey*, as ancient commentators often note, are filled with gaps and omissions – events that take place only implicitly (*siôpômenon*), *paraleipses* in which details at first omitted are later mentioned explicitly, and other techniques that create a "lacunose" narrative, one that demands a reader who "actively participates in the rather complex process of making meaning."[125] Chapman's poetic theory rests upon a similarly oxymoronic kind of darkness visible, and his poems cultivate a rhetorical *chiaroscuro* of "shaddow" and "heightening" in order to yield a "luster" or vividness that results from obscurity. Grounding his conception of these tropes and figures in analogies to the art of perspective, Chapman's early poems explore the possibility that a certain kind of figured language allows the poet to omit certain elements of the narrative, thereby encouraging the reader to attain a certain distance from the text and attain a "iudiciall perspective."[126] In his Homeric translations, Chapman comes to understand irony as demanding a similar distance between reader and text: only from "a farre of[f]" can the reader look past the "dissonances" and "discords" of Homer's poems in order to discern the true lineaments of its "variant" nature.[127]

Homer Misconstrued: Chapman's Map of Misreading

As Chapman labours to justify his poetic obscurity in the prefaces to his early lyric poems, he develops a hermeneutic that ultimately serves to legitimate his ironic interpretation of Homer. By fostering what Booth has called a "double vision," Chapman's ironic interpretations also work to divide Homer's readership into two distinct camps.[128] Chapman enforces this distinction through frequent contrasts between pure and impure readers, a nod to Titus 1.15 ("To the pure all things are pure; but nothing is pure to the tainted minds of disbelievers"), a verse invoked frequently by Elizabethan poets and translators to describe how allegorical reading may purify the indecorous, impious, or impenetrable portions of pagan texts.[129] Responding to those readers who find the dedicatory epistle to his 1598 *Seaven Bookes of the Iliad* to be "darke and too much laboured," Chapman protests in an epistle, "To the Understander," printed with his 1598 translation of *Achilles' Shield*, that "there is nothing good or bad, hard or softe, darke or perspicuous but in respect," and he casts aspersions on those readers with such "loose capacities" that "any worke worthily composde is knit with a riddle."[130]

Chapman may have been alerted to the ironies of the *Odyssey* from his reading of Eustathius, the Didymus *Scholia*, or the pseudo-Plutarchan *Life*, each of which dwells upon Homer's varied and skilful use of irony, emphasis, and related tropes discussed above. But Chapman understands the moral and theological implications of Homeric irony differently from Homer's classical Greek and Byzantine exegetes, since he reads the *Iliad* and *Odyssey* through the Christian Neoplatonism of Ficino and Pico as well as through Plato's dialogues, whose descriptions of Socratic irony provide a foundation for Chapman's hermeneutic methods as both a reader and a translator of Homer. This is not to say that Chapman's interpretation of Homer is Neoplatonic in the usual sense of the term. Quite the contrary: his commentaries downplay the metaphysical and cosmological allegories that dominate Neoplatonic exegetical traditions from Porphyry and Proclus down through sixteenth-century Homeric allegorists. Instead, Chapman relies on Plato to launch an epistemological and theological defence of Homeric irony, grounding this defence in the model of pious and concealed wisdom embodied by Socrates, the philosopher who "spends his whole life ironizing [*eirôneuomenos*]" and who uses irony as a tool of sceptical enquiry and moral correction.[131]

This perceived genealogy between Homer and Socrates fosters some of the most vexingly ironic moments in Chapman's own poems. In one of his most bizarre prefaces, to the *Free and Offenceles Justification of a lately publisht and most maliciously misinterpreted Poeme, Entituled. Andromeda Liberata*, Chapman vindicates the poet's "priviledg'd licence" to "conceale ... some sappe of hidden Truth" under "divers vailes of *Hieroglyphickes*, Fables, and the like," hiding his learning "from the base and prophane *Vulgare*" by wrapping it in "Misteries and allegorical fictions."[132] The work was primarily designed to defend Chapman's ill-received and misunderstood *Andromeda Liberata*, published in 1614 in honour of the marriage between Robert, Earl of Somerset, and the Lady Frances, daughter of Thomas Howard, Earl of Suffolk, and former wife of the Earl of Essex. Despite its reliance on the language of allegory, the *Justification* makes it clear that the "vailes" poets drape over the truth are not simply "allegorical fictions" but rather various tropes of concealment, including enigma, amphibology, and irony. Chapman argues that his fable of Andromeda is "darkened" by his "ambiguous and different construction," an ambiguity he elaborates upon and also compounds by citing a phrase uttered by Socrates at *Second Alcibiades* 147a: "*Esti te phusei poiêtikê ê sumpasa ainigmatôdês* &c. *Est enim ipsa Natura universa Poesis aenigmatum plena, nec quiuis eam dignoscit.*"[133] His loose English translation of the passage turns Socrates's observation – literally, "it is the nature of all poetry to be enigmatic" – into an implicit defence of irony: "This Ambiguity in the sence, hath given scope to the varietie of expositions; while Poets in al ages ... have ever beene allowed to fashion both, *pro & contra*, to their owne offencelesse, and iudicious occasions."[134] Chapman's paraphrase of the passage from *Second Alcibiades* also contains an implicit celebration of Homeric irony, for Socrates's pronouncement about the enigmatic nature of poetry follows closely on the heels of his discussion of the pseudo-Homeric *Margites*, a mock-epic so ridiculous that Socrates interprets it as proof that Homer, above all other poets, "wishe[d] so far as possible to conceal rather than exhibit his wisdom."[135] Chapman's licence to "fashion both, *pro and contra*" in his own poems thus finds validation in the authority of the pseudo-Homeric *Margites*, as well as the Socratic Silenus, to "conceal" their wisdom by shrouding it in the veil of irony.

Chapman's *Andromeda Liberata* was printed in the same year as his initial, twelve-book instalment of the *Odyssey* and dedicated to the same Earl of Somerset. The poem invites its readers to interpret the poem much as Chapman interprets Homeric epic – as a work that is alternately, and at times simultaneously, bathetic and sublime, jocular and serious, obvious and obscure. According to the *Justification*, *Andromeda Liberata* poses many of the same hermeneutic questions with which Chapman struggles as a reader and translator of Homer. Foremost among these is the problem that, while poets enjoy the privilege to conceal the truth in fables and mysteries, some readers "strai[n] the Allegorie past his intentionall limits" and thus make the text "give blood, where it yeeldes naturally milke" – in other words, readers' "overcurious wits" prompt them to look for "a sting in a flie" and think a poem satirical when it is not.[136] According to Chapman, who may be protesting his immunity from the Bishops' Ban and his distance from conventional verse satire, no satirical undermeanings lurk behind the folds of *Andromeda Liberata*'s allegorical veil: the poem is a "spleenelesse flie" whose intended meaning is open and obvious. "*Hic Rhodus, hic saltus*" [Here is Rhodes; here, jump], Chapman quips, adapting one of Erasmus's adages into a vexing riddle of straightforwardness: "as I said of my life, so of my lines; heere is the Poeme," a work whose meaning is simple and clear except to those "partiall and prejudicate" readers who insist that "everie sillable of it be tortured" until it yield a deeper sense.[137]

In his Homeric commentaries, Chapman sets up a similar contrast between readers who "torture" obscure passages with excessively complex and arcane interpretations, and readers such as Chapman himself, who find Homer's meaning plain and obvious. Ideally, the true meaning of Homer's lines will dawn upon their readers "like eastern light, / Showing to every comprehensive eye," the image invoked by Chapman to describe how Thomas Hariot reads his 1598 translation of *Achilles' Shield*, an episode that promises to reveal "Nature made all transparent" to the keen-eyed reader.[138] Such clarity can, however, be illusory, as Chapman suggests in his verse epilogue to the *Odyssey*, which laments how the "inestimable Pearle" of Homer's poem will all "Our Dunghil Chanticheres but obvious call."[139] Chapman chooses his words carefully, since the *Odyssey* is "obvious" in two very different ways: to the judicious reader, the poem is open, accessible, and easy, but to "prejudicate" readers, it presents obstacles and difficulties, the Latin *obvius* signifying readily seen or understood but also obtrusive or in the way.

The *Andromeda Liberata* aims to cultivate precisely this twofold and ambivalent kind of obviousness, and Chapman makes seemingly competing claims for the poem's mysterious opacity and its benign transparency. *Seemingly* competing, that is, because, as in his Homeric commentaries, Chapman's protestations of poetic obviousness in his *Justification* are themselves often ironic. His teasingly straightforward offer – "heere is my Poeme" – subtly mocks those "overcurious" readers who find abstruseness even where none exists, even as it also contains a self-mocking admission of the obscurity that Chapman so frequently and triumphantly claims for his poems. His directive that readers not "strain" the poem's allegory past its "intentionall limits" complicates the hermeneutic principles of earlier works such as *The Shadow of Night* and *Ovids Banquet*, in which Chapman instructs his readers to "mine" and "dig" and "search" in order to strike deep veins of hidden sense. By contrast, the "iudiciall" reader imagined by Chapman's 1614 *Odyssey* and his *Andromeda Liberata* need not – indeed, must not – undertake this kind of deep search for meaning. The interpretive shift reflects Chapman's increasingly sophisticated understanding of irony as a trope that permits obscurity and clarity to coexist: unlike allegory, irony hides in plain sight, obvious to some readers while completely obviated from others.[140]

Among the appeals of irony for Chapman, then, is that it fosters a selective and even elective kind of obviousness, a rhetorical skill at which Homer excelled. In his commentary on the *Iliad*, while remarking upon how prior translators such as Valla and Hessus have misconstrued a line in Book 14, Chapman defends Homer against the charge that he ought to make himself clear to "every vulgar reader's understanding" and instead praises him as a "great master of all elocution [who] hath written so darkly that almost three thousand sunnes have not discovered him, no more in five hundred places than here – and all perviall enough (you may well say) which such a one as I comprehend them."[141] In his mock-humble boast that even the most obscure passages of the *Iliad* are "perviall" – that is, not impervious to – him, Chapman bolsters his interpretive authority not by claiming a special exegetical gift for unfolding the mysteries revealed in Homer but rather by claiming to have discovered that there are no such mysteries to unfold. Chapman makes little effort to conceal the underlying motives for making such a claim, writing that "where a man is understood," it is by virtue of "a proportion betwixt the writer's wit and the writee's."[142] If a work is misunderstood, the responsibility for error lies with the reader and not with the writer, a line of argumentation that echoes Erasmus's defence of his *In Praise of Folly* against uncharitable readers such as Dorp while simultaneously echoing Lucretius's condemnation of "those dolts who admire and love everything more which they see hidden amid distorted words."[143]

By identifying the overlooked ironies of Homeric epic and then arguing for the "perviall" quality of its most perplexing passages, Chapman might appear to undermine the very critical authority cemented by his claims of irony. It may seem odd that Chapman so frequently assists his readers in recognizing ironic and scoptic passages in Homer that they might otherwise fail to notice. But as Dilwyn Knox has shown, the practice of glossing passages with the tag "*ironicè*" was commonplace during the sixteenth century, and the practice demonstrates "how remote ideas of ambiguity were from contemporary notions of *ironia*."[144] Even so, Thomas More mocks Germain de Brie for marking the ironic passages in his *Antimorus* with marginal notes such as "*ironia*" and "*per ironiam*," since from More's perspective, irony is effective only if it remains unidentified by a portion of a text's readers. While Chapman might seem to abandon this principle in his Homeric commentaries, his careful identification of Homer's irony allows a second strain of irony to emerge, an irony embedded in his repeated claim that Homer's irony is obvious.[145]

Chapman's self-proclaimed status as a "knowing and judiciall interpreter" of Homer rests largely upon his alleged capacity to distinguish the ironic and scoptic elements of Homeric epic from its more serious or straightforward strains. In order better to capture the scoffing and derisory spirit of particular speeches and episodes, Chapman deviates from the "literal interpretation" favoured by earlier translators and (as he explains) justifies the resulting "circumlocution" in a vocabulary normally associated with allegory, not irony. By translating according to the (ironic) spirit and not the (earnest) letter, Chapman claims to uncover the "mysteries / Reveal'd in Homer," mysteries that the "Clerkes" and "Grammarians" so often maligned by Chapman cannot solve because they insist upon adhering to word-for-word translations that fail to "search" Homer's "deepe and treasurous hart."[146] Yet for all his boasts to reveal Homeric mysteries, Chapman shows little interest in the kind of sustained allegorical interpretations generated by many sixteenth-century readers of Homer. Nowhere in his commentary does Chapman fault another scholar for failing to notice, or to interpret correctly, the allegorical meaning of a given passage. The chief distinction between Homer's "iudiciall" and his more "perviall" readers is not that the latter group misinterprets or overlooks allegorical undermeanings in Homer but rather that they lack the capacity to discern Homer's pervasive irony, a trope that exercises a very different set of intellectual faculties on the part of the reader, and that reflects a very different philosophical and spiritual orientation on the part of the poet.

By emphasizing Chapman's devotion to uncovering Homeric irony, my reading challenges the prevailing critical assumption that Chapman's translations of Homer endorse, in wholehearted or uncomplicated fashion, the tradition of interpreting the poems as moral allegories. Chapman does absorb and employ a literary-critical idiom associated with this exegetical tradition, at times even parroting the claim (here voiced by Fortunio Liceti) that "The letter kills, and the spirit gives life in Homer" [*Litera occidit, sensus vivificat in Homero*].[147] But Chapman's efforts to uncover the "spirit" of Homeric epic are inspired by a different hermeneutic model from the one guiding allegorical readers of Homer; at times, Chapman even voices alarm that the transcendent system of symbolic meanings assumed by allegorical readers strains the Homeric texts beyond their intended meaning. Chapman is dedicated to reconstructing Homer's authorial intent, an interpretive strategy fundamentally at odds with the methods of the allegorist.[148] He spells out this distinction rather explicitly in the verse epilogue to the *Odyssey*, which contrasts Homer's true interpreters, compared to "stars" because they "retaine" the "radiance and cleere right" of the poet's intended meaning, with those false readers whom Chapman compares to "Cloudes [who] would faine / Obscure the Stars" when they impose "selfe-blowne additions" upon Homer's text.[149] Fixed in place by the unchanging intent of the poet, the interpretations of Chapman's stars "shall shine ever," while the hermeneutic edifices constructed by nebulous readers are nowhere tethered to the anchor of the text, such that "one blast" of error's strong wind "teares down th'Impostor's Mast, / His Tops, and Tacklings."[150]

Chapman's image of this *Narrenschiff* of scholars who sink to the depths of "the Fishy Monarchy" when their complex yet fragile interpretive apparatus fails them provides an ironic commentary on the commonplace Homeric image for the hermeneutics of the pure reader, namely, Odysseus lashing himself to the mast of his ship so that he might listen safely to the song of the Sirens without succumbing to temptation. In the preface to his translation of the *Metamorphoses*, Arthur Golding advises his readers to "use Ulysses feat ageinst the Meremayds song," binding themselves to the mast of Christian doctrine when reading pagan poetry and thereby supporting their interpretations upon a foundation of piety.[151] For Chapman, however, the mast to which the pure reader must bind himself is Homer's original intent. The reader must anchor his interpretations to the intrinsic meaning of the text, the one put there by its author, rather than to the extrinsic spiritual value of a text imposed upon it after the fact by allegory.

By contrast to the prefaces and poems of the 1590s, which are dominated by images of night and shadow designed to valorize Chapman's obscurity, the clouds and mists that feature in the apparatus of his Homeric translations represent the perilous obfuscations of readers whose interpretations dim rather than enlighten the text. In the 1598 verse dedication to Thomas Hariot, Chapman likens Homer's text to a "beame of light" that breaks "through a chink" as well as to a sunbeam that "breake[s] forth like easterne light" through the "mistes" of error.[152] Sixteen years later, in his 1614 dedication of the *Odyssey* to the Earl of Somerset, Chapman uses similar metaphors to praise the singular clarity of his own translation when, reversing the analogy employed by Longinus, he compares the *Odyssey* to the rays of a dawning sun: at first Homer's verses are "all hid in clouds" but they "at length got free / Through some forc't covert" by beaming their "vented rayes / Farre off," presumably into the distant and shady woods of Chapman's own head.[153] The metaphor of Homer's guiding light shining obliquely through a thick cumulus of misreaders, finally beaming down on a poet far distant from the text he is translating, legitimates Chapman's authority by virtue of his remoteness from, rather than his proximity to, the text he is translating.

If the "iudiciall perspective" of Homer's ideal reader requires distance from his object of study, then it also depends upon a different sort of distance, namely the translator's departure from the literal meaning of the Homeric text. Inveighing against the "superfluitie" of translators whose "innovations" to Homer's text render its meaning "utterly false," Chapman understands the resulting "overplus" of meaning to be the product of literal, rather than "paraphrasticall," translation.[154] By contrast,

Chapman's own circumlocutory method offers a more effective means of preserving the tone, if not the actual words, of specific passages, a claim which suggests that the accuracy of a translation is, paradoxically, dependent upon the willingness of the translator to deviate from his source. This is the principle motivating Chapman's interpretation of Helen's speech to Aphrodite in Book 3 of the *Iliad*, in which "Helen ... bids her renounce heaven and come live with Paris till he make her his wife or servant."[155] Chapman judges the speech to be "scoptically or scornefully" spoken, even though "Valla, Eobanus [Hessus], and all other interpreters (but these *ad verbum*) have utterly mist."[156] Since irony, sarcasm, and other forms of scoptic speech are evident in the tone, rather than in the literal meaning, of the words, the translator who strives for a literal rendering of each line runs the risk of letting the poet's irony slip away. Only the translator who adheres to the ironic spirit, rather than the earnest letter, of the poems will be able to preserve Homer's intended meaning.

The Laughter of the Gods: Homer's Divine Irony

Chapman understands Homer's capacity for irony as a divine gift, one akin to the *enthousiasmos* of the inspired poet. This attitude is especially evident in Chapman's translation of the *Odyssey*, where his ironic reading of the poem develops out of Odysseus's observation in Book 18 that "*Of all things breathing, or that creepe on earth, / Nought is more wretched than a humane Birth.*"[157] Rendered by Chapman's printer as an italicized couplet so as to identify it as one of the many sententious proverbs punctuating the *Odyssey*, Odysseus's remark also fuels Chapman's conception of Homeric irony as the product of an insurmountable gulf between divine and mortal points of view. Sponde's gloss on these lines occasions a deeply pessimistic, Calvinistic meditation on the "miserable and fragile condition" [*misera & fragili conditione*] of humanity. In it, he cites a line from Sophocles describing how mortal vision affords "only a breath or a shadow" [*pneuma kai skia monon*] of divine truth.[158] Chapman adopts the same verse from Sophocles in his dedicatory epistle to the *Homeric Hymns* to convey how human knowledge is "lighter than the shadow of a corke," and he cites the line again in *Eugenia*, calling mortal life a "dreame," a "Spiders web ... lighter than the shadow of a corke," the message underscored by a marginal note transcribing the verse in Greek: "*phellou skias kouphoteron.*"[159]

Several episodes in the *Odyssey* provide an opportunity for Chapman to expound on the ways in which Homeric irony is produced out of the conflict between disparate perspectives – the gulf between the poet's perspective and that of his characters, or the gap between divine and mortal points of view.[160] In the *Odyssey*, as in the *Iliad*, it is Menelaus who is most frequently identified by Chapman's glosses as the victim of textual ironies that envelop and yet remain invisible to him. This reading of the Spartan king acknowledges the grim humour generated out of the schism between "human and divine perspective[s]," a gap that produces "irony and pathos" by illustrating the "unbridgeable alienation of the gods from human beings" dramatized by the poems' most anxiously comic moments.[161] This brand of dramatic irony, in which the "detachment" of the Homeric gods "affords a sort of double perspective" on human action in the epics, was widely recognized by English Renaissance rhetoricians such as Henry Peacham, who explains that the ironist scolds vice "with the sharpe edge of contrarie comparison" in order to provoke his audience to recognize the "great difference between what he is, and what he ought to be."[162] Chapman's Homeric commentaries conceptualize irony in precisely this manner, as a trope that sets into opposition clashing perspectives in order to produce a double and divided perspective on human experience. When Chapman recounts how the spirit of Homer visits him in his 1609 *Euthymiae Raptus*, a poem accompanying the translation of the *Iliad* that Chapman presented to Henry, Prince of Wales, the Greek poet teaches his acolyte to see humankind as simultaneously "divine, / And horrid ... as hee should shine, / And as he doth."[163] Homer's apparition acknowledges the grim, terrible humour generated out of the radical disparity between gods and mortals, an "opposition" between "tragically serious mortals and frivolous divinities" that Richard Rutherford has called "one of the most brilliant creative strokes of the epic tradition."[164]

In both the *Iliad* and *Odyssey*, Chapman marks as ironic several passages in which one of the Homeric gods – or the Homeric narrator, who arrogates a godly perspective – voices his superiority, invulnerability, or bemused indifference to the suffering of mortals below. Menelaus is twice identified by Chapman as the unwitting target of the narrator's irony, a vulnerability that underscores the character's spiritual blindness or his inability to grasp divine truths. As Menelaus recounts his homeward voyage from Troy and his encounter with Proteus in book 4 of the *Odyssey*, Chapman marks as "*ironicè*" a passage in which Menelaus describes the "huge exploit" he is obliged to undertake by Eidothea before she allows him to entrap her shape-shifting father. It is easy to see how Chapman might have found the ensuing adventure humorous: Menelaus and his crew are forced to disguise themselves by donning the smelly skins of seals, not exactly a labour of the order of Hercules. When he finally receives his prophecy from Proteus, Menelaus is loathe to return to Egypt to make a sacrifice, and his persistent questioning annoys the sea god, who scolds Menelaus for trying to exceed the "proper limits" of human knowledge: "Men's knowledges have proper limits set, / And should not prease into the mind of God."[165] In the brief exchange that follows, Menelaus learns virtually nothing from Proteus, who commands him to stop whining, desist from asking questions, and get on with his sacrifice. The whole episode reflects rather poorly on Menelaus, particularly since he prefaces the account of his malodorous exploit by promising to "impart" to Telemachus all the "oracles ... / Disclosde to me" by Proteus.[166] But Menelaus fails to appreciate that, while Proteus tells the truth, he tells it slant. Unlike Odysseus's later encounter with Tiresias, Menelaus does not recognize the prophecy delivered to him as partial, ambiguous, and subject to his own, foolish misinterpretation.[167]

Chapman interprets the task assigned to Menelaus by Eidothea and Proteus – to cloak himself in a smelly sealskin and retrace his steps back to Egypt – as fit humiliation for a character regarded as a simpleton by the Homeric narrator. Chapman's classification of the episode as ironic also casts Menelaus's misinterpretation of Proteus's prophecy as an allegory of misreading, a parable about the traps laid by Homeric irony and the difficulty involved in seizing control of its shape-shifting meanings. In his hand-signed dedication of a copy of his 1624 *Crowne of all Homers Worckes* presented to Henry Reynolds, the author of *Mythomystes*, Chapman advises Reynolds that "if at first sighte he [Homer] seme darcke or too fierie," the reader must "hold him fast (like Proteus) till he appears in his proper similitude and he will then shewe himself," at least to the judicial reader.[168] Although Menelaus does manage to grasp hold of Proteus until the god assumes his proper shape, a feat Chapman compares to the methods required to grasp Homer's own "darcke" and Protean text, Menelaus then misconstrues Proteus's prophecy in a manner similar to those readers who fail to detect the ironies of the poem he inhabits.

Menelaus's inability to interpret divine prophecy again makes him the unwitting victim of irony in Book 15 of the *Odyssey*, when, in the middle of a feast honouring Telemachus's departure from Sparta, a portent appears in the form of an eagle soaring through the air while carrying a goose in its claws. Nestor's son Antilochus asks Menelaus to venture an interpretation of the omen, and although Menelaus "put[s] to study" to solve the puzzling omen, he is unable to "give fit answer," only to be rescued by Helen, who takes it upon herself to "play the Prophet's part" and provide "[t]h'ostent's solution."[169] Chapman glosses the lines, "Nestor's sonne to Menelaus – his Ironicall question continuing still Homer's Character of Menelaus," a reading that draws attention to Antilochus's thinly veiled insult that caricatures Menelaus, the "Jove-kept king" of the omen, as an overfed, trussed-up goose, helpless in the talons of Antilochus's cunning wit. Menelaus, once again, is cast as the consummate misreader, blind to the multiple senses of an ambiguous portent and of Antilochus's "Ironicall question," both of which elude his simple-minded nature. By contrast to Penelope, who later interprets a similar omen as subject to multiple and competing interpretations and acknowledges that "dreams exceede / The art of man t'interpret," Menelaus is unable to parse ambiguity in divine signs.[170]

The divine irony that Chapman detects throughout the *Odyssey* is shaped by his interpretation of the poem's opening scene, in which Zeus aims his cruel sense of humour against the mortal vulnerability to illusion and self-deception. As he presides over the Olympian council, Zeus mentions "blameless [*amumonos*] Ægisthus," the lover of Clytemnestra who is killed by Orestes upon his father Agamemnon's return from the Trojan War.[171] Deliberately mistranslating the epithet "Faultfull Ægisthus," Chapman turns the literal meaning of Zeus's speech inside out, peeling away its veneer of seeming praise and revealing the intended blame lurking beneath. In his marginal note, Chapman explains that he has decided not to translate the Greek *amumonos* [blameless] as "not culpable" [*inculpabilis*] because Zeus's usage of the term deviates "from the true sence of the word as it is here to be understood – which is quite contrary."[172] In other words, Zeus's invocation of "blameless Ægisthus" is a moment of irony, the first of many such moments in the *Odyssey* noted by Chapman, whose reading of the passage is borne out by Zeus's subsequent condemnation of mortals who fault the gods, rather than themselves, for their evil actions:

O how falsly men
Accuse us Gods as authors of their ill,
When by the bane their owne bad lives instill
They suffer all the miseries of their states –
Past our inflictions and beyond their fates.[173]

Ægisthus is only "blameless" according to his own, delusional perspective, and Zeus calls him *amumonos* in order to mock the erroneous assumption that mortals do not see themselves to blame for the ills they inflict and suffer.[174] In the same marginal note, Chapman also observes that Homer uses epithets elsewhere to similarly ironic effect: both "*antitheos*" and "*oloop-hrônos*" may denote cunning but also the destructive nature of a crafty mind, since the epithet means those who are "*Divinus*, or *Deo similis*" in one place, "but in another (soone after) *contrarius Deo*," and the poet thus profits from the intrinsic ambiguity of the word: *oloophrôn* means mindful of everything, but it may also mean malevolent, a problem that had vexed Homer's readers since the time of Cleanthes.[175] The reader can only hope to "distinguish" between the contrary meanings of these and other epithets by paying close attention to context, and Chapman stresses the importance of noting "the person to whom the Epithete is given" as well as the spirit in which the passage as a whole is spoken.

The ability to make such distinctions, and thus to recognize Homer's irony, depends upon acknowledging the circumscribed and limited nature of human wisdom.[176] Chapman understands Odysseus's heroism as residing in his prudent and humble scepticism, and yet he labours to wrest the cunning wisdom of the *polytropos* Odysseus from the problematically crooked wisdom of Atlas and Prometheus, the latter represented in Chapman's translation of Hesiod's *Works and Days* as "wisdome-wresting," his rendering of the Greek "*ankulomêtês*," or crooked of counsel. In the margins of Chapman's translation of the *Works and Days*, Prometheus's epithet merits the following moralizing gloss: "*qui obliqua agitat consilia*; who wrests that wisdome which God hath given him to use to his glorie, To his owne ends; which is cause to all the miseries men suffer."[177] This interpretation of Prometheus is, as Chapman himself admits, indebted to Francis Bacon's *De Sapientia Veterum*, in which (according to Chapman's summary of the fable) Prometheus represents "learned Mens over-subtile abuse of divine knowledge; wresting it in false expositions to their own objects. Thereby to inspire, and puffe up their owne prophane earth."[178] Bacon's account of Prometheus's attempt to "bring the divine wisdom itself under the dominion of sense and reason" offers Chapman a cautionary tale about the danger of trying to grasp divine truths with a limited mortal intellect, a form of pride to which Prometheus falls prey while Odysseus does not.[179]

Perhaps inspired by Bacon's observation in the preface to his *De Sapientia Veterum* that fables are "pliant stuff" that "freely ... follow any way you please to draw" them, Chapman interprets Prometheus's "wresting" of divine knowledge as an aetiological fable about the danger of misreading.[180] The pliancy of myth is a dominant concern of Chapman's Homeric commentaries, in which "learned Criticks" are assailed for wresting the wrong meanings out of Homer's texts, twisting "ropes of sand" in order to impose "selfe-blowne additions" onto Homer's poems.[181] Whereas the reader who grasps Homer's ironies possesses the polytropic, flexible wisdom of Odysseus, Homer's misreaders lack the sceptical humility necessary to bring the *Odyssey* into agreement with the moral of Bacon's Prometheus: "all things are hidden away from us," Bacon writes, and "we know nothing," because "the true and the false are strangely joined and twisted together," a condition both reflected and exacerbated by irony itself.[182]

The ability to read ironically, for Chapman, is dependent not only on polytropic wisdom but also upon the reader's initiation into a sacred mystery. In his commentary, Chapman regards the scoffing and ironic speeches made by the Olympian gods as a mark of Homer's divine inspiration, an inspiration that affords the poet – and, by extension, his knowing translator – a godly perspective on human affairs. Adapting an image from Poliziano's *Ambra*, one of Chapman's dedicatory epistles to the *Odyssey* imagines Homer gazing down scornfully at his readers and critics from above: "He sits and laughs, to see the jaded Rabble, / Toile to his hard heights."[183] This attitude of mocking superiority fuels Chapman's disdain towards readers who fail to discern the ironies of the *Iliad* and *Odyssey*, and it also informs his tendency to depict himself as Homer's true interpreter in explicitly Eleusinian terms. A select group of readers – perhaps so select as to include only Chapman himself – are chosen, purified through ritual, and then finally allowed to enter the innermost sanctum of Homeric epic, an *adytum* that contains the poems' secret, and secretly ironic, meanings. At the beginning of his commentary on the *Iliad*, Chapman explains that he "dissent[s] from all other Translators and Interpreters" of Homer, especially in those places where the poet's "divine rapture" eludes the "capacitie" of those "Grammatical Criticks" unable to discern "the inward sense or soule of the Sacred Muse" visible only to a kindred "Poeticall spirit" such as Chapman himself.[184] Scholarly learning affords no advantage in this system, in which translators learn their art as if inducted into a mystery cult.

In a series of prefatory verses first printed in his 1608 *Iliad*, Chapman makes this initiation mystery explicit, likening the act of translating Homer to a purification ritual akin to the "Holy Rites" administered by the Delphic priests of Apollo. Again echoing Poliziano, whose *Manto* cautions that "no prophane persons invade the sacred precincts" [*Ad haec nulli perrumpant sacra profani*] of Virgil's poetry, Chapman instructs his readers to "[w]ash here," at the sanitizing font of his preface, "[l]est with foule hands you touch these Holy Rites" before completing the initiation required to enter the "Porch to [Homer's] numerous Phane" and to "[h]eare ancient Oracles speake" through his poetry.[185] Late antique allegorists such as Porphyry and Iamblichus had represented the hermeneutic techniques used to interpret Homer in terms of an initiation into sacred mysteries, an idea reworked by Poliziano's *Oratio in Expositione Homeri*, which imagines Homer's poems as "flow[ing] out of the sacred inmost recess of the gods" [*sacrisque deorum adytis emugiverit*].[186] Chapman's *Teares of Peace*, a poem modelled partly on the appearance of the divine Pimander to Hermes Trismegistus in Book 1 of the *Pimander*, adapts this language in order to describe Chapman's own initiation into Homeric mysteries.[187] Echoing Poliziano's assertion that Homeric epic contains a "kernell" of divinity that lies "obscur'd" in its deepest recesses, and modelling his divine rapture on Ennius's dream of Homer in his *Annales*, Chapman imagines himself transported by the ghost of Homer from a hill near Hitchin to a hidden shrine dedicated to sacred and recondite wisdom.[188]

Terrible Jests

In an age that embraced the idea that the scriptures use ironic and scoffing speech for pious and corrective purposes, it is natural for Chapman to yoke Homer's predilection for irony to his status as a divinely inspired poet.[189] In Homeric epic, as in scripture, irony and sarcasm are understood as tropes appropriate to heroic poetry, forms of humour that befit the grand style. In his *Observations on Orlando Furioso*, printed in a 1584 Venetian edition of Ariosto's poem, Alberto Lavezola praises both Homer and Virgil for observing the precept "that jokes little become serious poetry" [*che i ridicoli non si convengano ne'Poemi gravi*], yet he also concedes that these poets rightly allow their characters to "us[e] bitter quips against their enemies, called sarcasm" [*usano i poeti quei motti amari, che si dicono contra i nemici, chiamati Sarcasmus*].[190] Even as Chapman couches his ironic interpretations of Homer in the arcane symbolism of sacred mysteries, he also recognizes that Homer's mortal characters are often punished for arrogating the godly weapons of sarcasm and verbal abuse. In the *Odyssey*, Athena afflicts the suitors with a case of uncontrollable laughter as fit punishment for their scoffing ways. Similarly, in Book 5 of the *Iliad*, Chapman highlights the danger of mortal laughter and scorn through Apollo's lesson to Diomedes after the Greek soldier wounds Aphrodite and rebukes Sthenelus: "What? Not yeeld to Gods? Thy equals learne to know: / The race of Gods is farre above men creeping here below."[191] Laughter in Homeric epic can be a sign of "presumed eminence," as is the case with Penelope's suitors, but it can also denote a "real ... physical or moral superiority," as is the case with the gods, whose superior strength and wisdom entitles them to gestures of smiling or laughing often described as *blosurôtis* – terrible or threatening.[192] The Olympian gods enjoy greater licence than mortals to censure and rebuke each other with the kind of "sharpe jest" that Athena and Hera, angered by Paeon's healing of Aphrodite, make at their fellow goddess's expense. In a passage marked "*Scopticè*" by Chapman, Athena and Hera "quit [Zeus's] late-made mirth" by teasing Aphrodite that her wound was inflicted not by Diomedes but rather by the "golden claspe" of a girdle worn by "those Grecian Dames," a joke that provokes a smile in Zeus before he resorts to a little teasing of his own, telling Aphrodite to steer clear of "those rough workes of warre."[193]

Throughout his translation of the *Iliad*, Chapman emphasizes the laughter and smiles of the gods as the visible signs of their superiority. During the *Iliad*'s theomachy, Athena "insults over Mars," according to Chapman's marginal note, when she defeats him in battle. As he tumbles to earth, his dusty body landing on "seven Acres land," she "laugh[s]" and taunts him with a scoffing speech before Aphrodite helps the god of war to his feet: "'O thou foole," Athena cries out, "yet hast thou not bene taught / To know mine eminence? Thy strength opposest thou to mine?"[194] Accompanied by the kind of ironic barbs also exchanged between Homer's mortal combatants, the cartoon-like violence of the Homeric gods reveals a grim jocularity that would become more widely recognized and revered in the two centuries after Chapman's translation: the sardonic flyting of Milton's war in heaven, the bathetic diction favoured by Hobbes in his English translations of Homer, and the mock-epic anatomy of trivial conflict in Pope's *Rape of the Lock* each make explicit, in different ways, the implicitly comic dimensions of Homeric battle scenes.

Like Milton after him, Chapman is attracted to Zeus's tendency to exert his supremacy through scoffing and threatening language, a habit that displays the potential piety of satirical discourse while simultaneously legitimating Homer's supreme god as an omnipotent deity akin to Chapman's own. At the end of Zeus's "dreadfull speech" at the beginning of Book 8 of the *Iliad*, in which he threatens to cast his fellow gods down to the depths of Barathrum, Zeus smiles at Athena and tells her to "[b]e confident," since "I speake not this with serious thoughts, but will be kind to thee."[195] Yet after Zeus's command is ignored by Pallas and Hera, who promptly intervene on the Greek side only to be met by the threat of his thunderbolt, he taunts his wife and daughter in a speech marked "*Scopticè*" by Chapman, teasing them that "thunder would have smit you both" had they "held [their] glorious course" against the Trojans.[196] Zeus's reliance upon ironic debasement as a means of asserting his authority is often marked by a smile, a gesture that Homer's ancient commentators associate with *sarkasmos*, a "form of irony" [*eidos eirôneias*] expressed when "someone, with a feigned smile, reviles another by saying the contrary."[197] In a gloss on *Od.* 20.302, a scene in which Odysseus passively resists the verbal and physical provocation of the suitor Ctesippus by "smiling in his heart a most grim and bitter smile" [*meidêse de thumô / sardanion mala toion*], Eustathius explains that this Sardonian (or Sardanian) smile is distinguished by a stiffness or affectation in the lips, a gesture also in evidence when Hera laughs at Zeus at *Il.* 15.103, her lips tensely pursed and her forehead furrowed with indignation.[198]

Chapman's attentiveness to the sounds and gestures associated with scorn and mockery reflect the culture's more widespread fascination with the physiological and affective dimensions of Homeric laughter, a subject discussed at greater length in chapter 2 of this book. Erasmus's adage *Risus Sardonicus*, Joubert's *Traité du Ris*, and a number of later medical works and treatises on the passions gloss the tense-lipped laughter of various Homeric characters as a sign of bitterness, mockery, arrogance, or derision, passions that result from an "opposition of contraries" [*oppositoru[m] contrariu[m]qu[e]*] within the body.[199] This principle is evident in Chapman's translation of a passage describing Hera's laugh at the beginning of Book 15 of the *Iliad*. As she takes her place "displeasedly" in the Olympian council, Hera joins the other gods in "[b]ewraying privie splenes at Jove," sublimating her anger into a spiteful, partially submerged chuckle:

> and then (to colour all)
> She laught, but meerly from her lips, for over her blacke browes
> Her still-bent forehead was not cleer'd; yet this her passion's throwes
> Brought forth in spight, being lately school'd.[200]

Traces of anger still evident in her furrowed brow, Hera then delivers a scoffing speech that simultaneously praises and undermines Zeus's power (15.101–8), following it up with a speech "of purpose to incense Mars *Scopticè*" that provokes the war god by praising him for bearing so patiently the death of his son Ascalaphus, a wartime casualty of "Jove's high grace to Troy."[201] In so doing, Hera manages to enrage Ares as well as Poseidon, who according to Chapman's marginal note at line 173 becomes "incenst with Jupiter" when Iris delivers a message from Zeus that warns the sea god not to "vaunt equalitie" with his elder brother, whose "powre is farre superior" to his own.[202] By exposing Zeus's attempt to arrogate the authority of his two brothers, Poseidon confirms the submerged message of Hera's earlier speech, and Chapman draws attention in both speeches to the scoffing anger of the gods, an anger which remains playful on Olympus but which has serious consequences for the mortals beneath.

Sixteenth-century readers of Homer often recognize the feigned smiles and the derisory laughter of his characters as the visible evidence of irony, in particular a species of irony termed *Mycterismus*, or "counterfayted laughter."[203] In the *Odyssey*, the frequent laughter of the suitors is aroused by their erroneous perception of invulnerability, thus creating a dramatic irony fulfilled when they – quite literally – "die laughing" [*gelô ekthanon*].[204] In the *Iliad*, too, scoffing words and gestures often hint at the eventual downfall of the deliverer, as Abraham Fraunce points out in his interpretation of the "jesting and merie conceipted" speech that Patroclus delivers to Cebriones as the latter falls off his chariot to his death in Book 16. Fraunce mentions the speech in two different chapters of his *Arcadian Rhetorike*, first citing it as an example of "Exclamation," or the kind of speech that expresses "indignation" or "derision," and then quoting it once again in his chapter on irony as an example of a rhetorical device in which "the manner of utterance quite differ[s] from the sense of the wordes."[205] A marginal gloss next to Chapman's rendering of the speech observes how "Patroclus jests at the fall of Cebriones," and the translation itself underscores the way in which Patroclus's words rebound ironically back to the utterer: as he scoffs at Cebriones, Patroclus "jested ... so neare / His owne grave death."[206] In Homer's Greek text, the narrator makes no such comment. Chapman's addition alerts the reader to the irony that Patroclus meets the same fate as his adversary only a hundred lines later when, mortally wounded by Hector, he finds himself on the receiving end of a barrage of verbal abuse glossed in Chapman's margins as "Hector's insultation over Patroclus." In that latter scene, Chapman shows how Homer turns the ironic screw once again as Patroclus delivers his final speech, predicting in a "prophetique rage" that his slayer "shalt not long survive thy selfe."[207]

These marginal embellishments are typical of Chapman's tendency to highlight the grimly comic aspects of Homeric violence. When Diomedes decapitates Dolon in Book 10 of the *Iliad*, for instance, his head tumbles off but continues "speaking on the ground," a gruesome sight that provides Chapman with an occasion for some grisly humour: in the marginal note glossing Diomedes's murder of the Trojan spy, he quips: "Diomed's sterne reply to Dolon."[208] In these and other marginal comments, Chapman adopts the sharp and biting wit he so admires in the Homeric narrator as well as in the Olympian gods, a wit that often accompanies a cruelly ludic stance towards the poems' mortal characters. This attitude is acutely evident in a passage from Book 15 of the *Iliad* that describes how Apollo assists the Trojans by helping to build and then destroying a wall constructed by their adversaries. Just as a "boy upon the sea-ebd shore / Makes with a litle sand a toy and cares for it no more," the simile begins, Apollo raises and then topples the retaining wall "childishly, so in his wanton vaine / Both with his hands and feete he puls and spurnes it downe againe."[209] In an image that anticipates Gloucester's assessment of the gods in *King Lear*, who kill men "for their sport" like boys swatting flies, Apollo's playful destruction of the wall masks a callous indifference towards creatures who appear to him no larger than motes from his scoptic heights. In keeping with his admiration for the Homeric simile as a means of comparing the "meanest" with the "mightiest" and vice versa, Chapman praises the comparison for demonstrating "from how low things it may be taken, to expresse the highest."[210] By uniting the apparent opposites of earnest and jest, the bathetic and the sublime, and the mortal and the divine, the simile illustrates that the difference between these pairs of contraries is only a matter of perspective.

Chapman's Scoptic Homer

Chapman's defence of ironic and scoptic speech in the *Iliad* and *Odyssey* is shaped by his concern to identify prudent and effective modes of satirical discourse that might prove ethically and politically viable after the Bishops' Ban, issued on 1 June 1599. With the censorship of "Satyres and Epigrammes," as well as "all nasshes bookes" and the verse satires of John Marston and Joseph Hall, Chapman – already hard at work on his translation of the *Iliad* – comes to recognize Homeric epic as an alternative to verse satire, a genre equally capable of providing moral correction without arousing the suspicion of the ecclesiastical authorities. Used to mock weakness and folly, the blameful speeches exchanged between Homer's interlocutors are regarded by Chapman as akin to the biting satires of Juvenal, one of which he translated towards the end of his career in 1629. Although often criticized by other sixteenth-century readers for their indecorum or cruelty, Homer's scoptic speeches appeal to Chapman for their righteous indignation, a legitimate and even pious anger that drives speeches such as Poseidon's vituperation of the Greeks in Book 13 of the *Iliad*, which concludes with the god's wish that "reprehension" and "just shame" – Chapman's rendering of *nemesis* and *aidôs* – will strike the hearts of his audience.[211] Throughout his commentaries, Chapman reads Homeric epic as a rhetorical handbook on verbal abuse or "insultation," often emphasizing in his margins the degree to which Homeric blame speech resembles the "biting" satires of Chapman's most vituperative contemporaries.[212]

As a satirist concerned to identify the bounds of legitimate reproof, Chapman's glosses often recuperate Homer's acerbic wit as a valid and even heroic vehicle of shame and mockery. He is remarkably attentive to the variety of satirical modes in Homeric epic, frequently marking specimens of skilful "insultation" in a manner reminiscent of Puttenham's *Arte of English Poesie*, with its colourful anatomy of abuse illustrated by terms such as "Insultatio," "the Disdainfull," and "the Repochfull or scorner."[213] It is rare for Chapman to pass silently by the *Iliad*'s more explosive episodes of verbal combat. In the margins of a three-way flyting match of Book 11, for instance, Chapman highlights the riveting volley of abusive epithets by noting how "Diomed insults on Hector" and "Paris insults on Diomed" in an exchange so vehement that it has prompted recent Homeric scholars to argue for a generic kinship between Homeric epic and Greek iambic, invective poems associated with the Dionysian rituals of archaic Greece.[214]

At times it appears as though the satirical modes represented by Homeric epic might provide Chapman with a more palatable outlet for his own indignation than those associated with Roman verse satirists such as Juvenal and Persius, who both enjoyed enormous popularity during the late 1590s when Chapman began translating Homer. Juvenal in particular was a problematic satirical model for late Elizabethan writers on a number of counts. From the subtitle of his first satire onwards, Juvenal arouses doubt about the motives and the efficacy of his satirical project, since his titular claim that "It is difficult not to write satire" [*Difficile est Saturam non Scribere*] depicts the poet's vituperative impulses as the product of a wayward and excessive passion. Moreover, while Juvenalian satire (particularly *Satire 10*) tends to undercut epic heroism, the *Iliad* and *Odyssey* support it, offering Chapman and his contemporaries several different models of heroic raillery in its cast of characters both mortal and immortal.

Yet Chapman only defends scoptic speech in Homeric epic when it is used in suitable contexts and for suitable ends. Similarly, Robin Sowerby has argued that Chapman's treatment of Achilles is motivated by a preoccupation with the "pathology of anger" and with a concern to distinguish between ethically legitimate and illegitimate expressions of that passion.[215] Although Chapman certainly believes that vituperation and invective have their proper place in Homer's rhetorical arsenal, and although he recognizes the moral potency of these rhetorical modes when deployed in their proper context, he also praises the prudence with which Homer's characters temporarily soften or repress scoffing or blameful speech.[216] Commenting on a speech in Book 14 of the *Iliad* in which Odysseus calls Agamemnon "prince of men," Chapman's commentary challenges Sponde's assumption that the epithet "*princeps populorum*" (as Chapman cites Sponde's Latin) is intended "to be given in scorne and that all Ulysses' speech is *scôptiche*, or scoffing," instead proposing that while Odysseus does speak "altogether seriously and bitterly to this title at the end," the epithet is in fact "spoken *êpios*, *molliter* or *benigne*, of purpose to make Agamemnon beare the better the justice of his other austeritie."[217]

Groping for new satirical models after 1599, Chapman pays particular attention to speeches that mitigate the most "biting" elements of satire by mixing the *barus* [bitter, scoffing] and the *glukês* [sweet] so as to ensure that praise – whether sincere or feigned – follows and mollifies verbal blame or abuse.[218] Chapman makes several remarks about speeches whose moral efficacy depends upon cloaking, softening, or delaying blame. In a marginal note to *Il.* 9.32–5, Chapman praises Diomedes's self-discipline in postponing his response to Agamemnon's earlier rebuke of him, noting how he "takes fit time to answer his wrong done to Agamemnon in the fourth booke" as Diomedes himself reveals, explaining to the Achaean general that he "was silent, knowing the time, loth any rites to breake / That appertaind thy publicke rule."[219] The virtue exhibited by Diomedes here is *euphêmia*, a term which denotes either silence or the prudent control of one's tongue.[220] As a means of avoiding direct insult or open violence, *euphêmia* is a key rhetorical virtue in Homeric epic, especially in the *Odyssey*, where Odysseus proves extremely adept at maintaining silence under pressure, a quality often noted by Homer's ancient commentators and his Renaissance readers alike.[221] Yet in antiquity, there is disagreement over whether Odysseus's reticence is a deceptive tactic (as Euripides and Sophocles represent it) or whether (as Plato argues) it is a mark of moral endurance.[222] Chapman sides with Plato in regarding Homeric silence as a sign of admirable self-restraint, and he understands this form of silence, like irony, circumlocution, preterition, and emphasis, as a rhetorical technique useful for avoiding conflict or for delivering insults surreptitiously.

In Homeric epic, silence may be a sign of self-control, but it is also a sign of hostility – a veiled threat that functions like irony.[223] Chapman's admiration for Diomedes's restraint in Book 4 of the *Iliad* reveals his recognition that silence, like other forms of verbal restraint such as delay and obliquity, is an effective means of expressing scorn precisely because it is so carefully regulated. When Hector "right cunningly" chides his brother Paris for his defeat at the hands of Menelaus, Chapman explains in a marginal note how Hector cleverly conceals his primary motive for the speech – disgust at his brother's "effeminacie" – and instead "dissembles the cowardise he finds in Paris, turning it as if he chid him for his anger at the Troyans for hating him being conquerd by Menelaus."[224] This skill at deflecting or "turning" blame mirrors a rhetorical technique used by the Homeric narrator, one frequently noted by Homer's ancient Greek and Byzantine commentators. Eustathius praises Homer's ability to cloak his disdain for various characters by ventriloquizing that disdain through the reproofs and insults exchanged between those characters: when Homer wishes to deride [*skôpsai*] Paris, for instance, he does not express his contempt directly but rather shifts the responsibility to Hector, who censures his brother "freely and boldly" [*parrêsiazesthai*].[225]

Chapman likewise recognizes that in Homeric epic, the most effective scoptic speech must be restrained or redirected, even as a number of characters have difficulty keeping their insulting language in check. In a marginal note to *Od.* 22.360–1, Chapman remarks upon the Greek term *philokertomos*, or reproach-loving, a word he translates in the text of the poem as a lover of "bitter taunts" and of "wound[ing] / The heart of any with a jest."[226] The word is used by Philoetius, who kills Ctesippus with a dart while simultaneously accusing him of being *philokertomos*, a man whose wit "never yeild[s] / To fooles in folly" and who revels in "putting downe" his adversaries by "spitting forth / Puft words at all sorts."[227] In the *Odyssey*, this predilection for scoffing achieves its most demonic expression in characters such as Ctesippus and Melantheus, both punished with death for their mocking ways. Yet as Chapman recognizes, Odysseus is also at times *philokertomos*, and his gusto for insultation is hard to square with Chapman's assertion that Odysseus is a figure of "over-ruling Wisedome" whose mind remains "unbroken, unalterd with any most insolent and tyrannous infliction."[228] At certain moments in Chapman's commentary, Odysseus hardly appears to be the exemplary Stoic sage he is held up to be in the dedication to the Earl of Somerset. In Book 9 of the *Odyssey*, just as Odysseus and his sailors manage to escape from the cave of Polyphemus, Homer's hero cannot resist "insulting" the Cyclops as his ship pulls away from shore, provoking the blinded giant to lob a huge boulder at their craft. In his marginal note on the passage, Chapman remarks upon "Ulysses' continued insolence" as he reveals his identity to his adversary, explaining that Odysseus bellows out his true name not simply "to repeate what he said to the Cyclop" but rather "to let his hearers know his Epithetes, and estimation in the world."[229] The entire episode demonstrates how Odysseus, a character elsewhere capable of remarkable verbal restraint, is not always able to preserve a mind "unalterd" by the "continuall aesture and vexation" of mortal life.[230]

If Odysseus is indeed a Stoic hero for Chapman – a frequent critical claim whose limitations are addressed later in this chapter – his virtue is not defined by the *parrhêsia* or forthrightness of the typically "honest" Stoic sage but rather by the verbal skills associated with *mêtis* – the dissimulation, joking, and ironic speech that allows Odysseus to trick or elude his adversaries. This skilful mixture of insult and jest, often praised by Homer's ancient commentators, can lessen blame by mitigating terror [*deinos*] with grace or wit [*charites*], a common rhetorical tactic in both poems.[231] Demetrius, for instance, declares Homer to have been "the first to invent the grim joke" [*prôtos te eurêkenai dokei phoberas charitas*], since "jesting adds to the fear" [*paizôn phoberôteros esti*] in speeches such as Polyphemus's ironic promise that "No-man I will eat last."[232] Like Tasso, who admires Homer's ability to "use jests for sharpness' sake," Chapman reveres Odysseus's reliance upon sardonic quips, hidden stings, and subtle smiles to vent his anger while at the same time preserving the "self-sufficient strength of virtue" that characterizes the Stoic sage.[233]

Yet Chapman also admires the licence enjoyed by Homer's characters to engage freely in blame and vituperation, a characteristic of Homeric heroism also praised by sixteenth-century Continental scholars such as Crusius and Sponde. Commenting on Achilles's invitation to Calchas to speak his mind freely at *Il.* 1.85, Sponde remarks that "this is not how they conduct themselves nowadays, those who would rather drive away innumerable Calchases [*Calchantas innumeros potius repellunt*] than suffer that their free speech offends the delicate little ears of kings [*quam ut eorum libera oratione delicatulas regum aures offendi patiantur*]."[234] Homer never uses the word *parrhêsia*, a term first used by Euripides, adopted as a fundamental principle of Athenian democracy, and later transformed by the Cynics and the apostles to defend bold speech as a guarantor of spiritual and philosophical liberty. But the term is frequently linked to Homeric epic by readers such as Crusius, whose heavily annotated edition of Homer marks the "*parrhêsia modestu*" of Nestor's bluntly critical speech to Agamemnon (*Il.* 9.107–8) as well as the "*parrhêsia*" of Polydamas's speech to Hector (*Il.* 13.725–30), the latter speech cross-referenced by Crusius with "1 Corinth. 12," presumably the verse in which Paul asserts that the Holy Spirit reveals itself in certain men through wise and frank words.[235] Chapman likewise regards Homer as a defender of the spiritual and moral prerogative to speak brazenly, an interpretation which, like that of Crusius, may have been shaped by Erasmus's habit of reading Homeric epic through the lens of the Pauline scriptures. Homer's Calchas is, after all, a prophet, thus explaining why he enjoys a privilege to speak his mind. In his *Quaestiones*, appended to the 1564 edition of Melanchthon's *Elementorum Rhetorices*, Crusius defines *parrhêsia* as "audacious and free speech" [*audacia et libertus loquendi*] and cites as a key example Calchas's speech to Agamemnon in the opening book of the *Iliad*.[236] In his own translation of the speech, Chapman describes Calchas as inspired by a "Prophetique rage," a divinely appointed, righteous indignation that takes deserved aim at the pride and folly of Agamemnon. For Calchas, as well as for Patroclus, whom Chapman describes as motivated by a similar "prophetique rage" when he delivers his dying speech to Hector, prophetic inspiration undergirds the spiritual and moral legitimacy of Homer's most vituperative speakers.[237]

Perhaps following Eustathius, who frequently praises hostile verbal exchanges in the *Iliad* for their "heroic recklessness" and their "merriment," Chapman pauses twice in his own commentary on the *Iliad* to defend verbal strife between Homeric warriors as decorous and heroic.[238] In the first of these glosses, Chapman defends the lengthy exchange between Diomedes and Glaucus (*Il.* 6.145–231) against the criticisms of prior critics such as Marco Girolamo Vida who "taxe [the passage] as untimely, being (as they take it) in the heate of fight."[239] Chapman's gloss takes issue with a passage in the *De Arte Poetica* in which Vida questions the plausibility of the scene, writing that "I can scarcely believe that when savage Tydides met Glaucus in the full flow of battle, with slaughter raging all about, they whiled away so much time in lengthy conversations with each other."[240] By contrast, Chapman is unruffled by the scene's lack of verisimilitude, and he praises the exchange as "full of decorum," a "gallant shew and speech" that befits its context and also displays Homer's ability "to vary and quicken his Poem with these episods."[241] Yet Chapman's defence of such verbal skirmishes in the *Iliad* is odd, at least inasmuch as various characters in the poem assail each other for verbal skirmishes that make soldiers appear – as Chapman's Aeneas puts it to Achilles – "like women that will wear / Their tongues out."[242] While verbal strife is often depicted in the *Iliad* as effeminate or childish – Nestor reproaches his fellow Achaeans for "talk[ing] / Like children all, that know not warre" instead of "command[ing] / In active field" – Chapman regards the *Iliad*'s flyting matches as a means of producing the *aidôs*, or shame, that supports and heightens the heroic ethos of the poem.[243]

Accordingly, Chapman defends the inclusion of four lines spoken by Achilles to Patroclus at the beginning of Book 16 of the *Iliad*, lines rejected in the recensions of Zenodotus and Aristarchus because, as Chapman explains, they were deemed "unworthy the mouth of an Heroe."[244] His gloss argues that Achilles's speech provides evidence of the character's "frolicke and delightsome humour, being merry with his friend in private" after having chastised Patroclus for shedding "unseemely teares" a few lines earlier. Far from being inconsistent with his character, the final, obelized lines of that speech – in which Achilles voices the hope that he and Patroclus will be the only two survivors at the conclusion of the war – are not spoken "out of his heart" according to Chapman, but instead evince a jocularity that is "as poorely conceipted of the expungers as the rest of the places in Homer that have groned or laughed under their castigations."[245] This is precisely the kind of claim for which Pope will later mock Chapman, even as both translators display a debt to Eustathius by defending scornful and sarcastic speech as compatible with the sublimity of epic, speech that, in Pope's words, "becomes a hero" rather than "raising laughter."[246]

Even as he recognizes that certain forms of invective and satire may attain the grand style, Chapman also understands that both the *Iliad* and *Odyssey* contain some less-than-exemplary models of blameful rhetoric in figures such as Thersites and Irus.[247] Neither character was especially beloved by the majority of Homer's sixteenth- and seventeenth-century readers, who tend to regard the former as a slanderous political subversive and the latter as a vulgar, ridiculous character whose earthy language ill befits an epic poem. The Elizabethan scholar William Gager, who also translated (into Latin) the pseudo-Homeric *Batrachomyomachia*, apologizes in the epilogue of his *Ulysses Redux*, a Latin play based on the *Odyssey* performed at Christ Church, Oxford in 1581–2 and again in 1584–5, for allowing the figure of Irus to debase the tragic dignity of the play, an objection to which Gager also responds in his preface to the printed edition of the play, which argues that *Ulysses Redux*, like its Homeric source, falls short of both tragedy and epic because of the "beggarliness of its material" [*materiae ... mendicitate peccat*] and because the scenes with Irus move the audience to laughter rather than pity.[248]

Apart from dubbing Irus a "rogue" in the argument to Book 18 of the *Odyssey*, an epithet that aligns him with the knavish characters populating late Elizabethan drama and prose fiction, Chapman is silent on his character. Arguably, however, Chapman models the buffoons and railers of his comedies, plays such as *The Blind Beggar of Alexandria*, *A Humorous Day's Mirth*, and *Sir Giles Goosecap*, on the beggar who reviles and taunts Odysseus upon his return to Ithaca.[249] But Chapman takes a much more particular interest in Thersites, and the revisions he makes to Thersites's speech between the 1598 and 1611 editions of his *Iliad* reveal a conflicted attitude towards Homer's most notorious railer.[250] In the earliest version of the text, Chapman teases out Thersites's lack of rhetorical and emotive control: his voice makes a "tuneles jarring," and the narrator accuses him of being a "foole" who makes "barbarous tauntes," chiding Achilles and Odysseus "eagerlie" with a mischievous, undisciplined gusto for vituperation. In his 1611 translation, Chapman's Thersites grows both more eloquent and more menacing. Described with terms such as "railing," "vehement," and "bitter checke," Thersites is transformed from a toothless into a biting satirist akin to Marston's Kinsayder, a figure unable to contain his spleen but able to vent it through artful and pungent invective.

At stake in Chapman's two very different depictions of Thersites is the question of whether to regard Thersites as heroic or cowardly in his boldness. Courage, as Aristotle argues in the *Nicomachean Ethics*, is the midpoint between the extremes of rashness [*thrasus*] and cowardice or fear [*phobos*], but these excessive and defective expressions of courage may appear the same, since "most rash men are really cowards at heart."[251] Such is Thersites, according to the standard reading of his character: a rash man who is "an impostor" [*alazôn*] since he pretends to a courage that he only acquires by imitating [*mimeîtai*] the truly courageous man, namely Achilles. Although Achilles and Thersites are united by their *parrhêsia*, Chapman works to distinguish ever more sharply between Homer's heroic and anti-heroic incarnations of alazony in the post-1598 revisions to his translation of Books 1 and 2 of the *Iliad*. As his Thersites devolves into the sort of railing satirist proscribed by the Bishops' Ban, Chapman's characterization of Achilles moves in the opposite direction, growing less prone to scoff or to exchange what the Homeric narrator calls "wrangling words" [*antibiosis epeessi*].[252] As John Channing Briggs has pointed out, Chapman's 1598 translation of *Il.* 1.154–60 grants Achilles "more license to revile Agamemnon" than does the 1608 revision of the same passage; the latter version diminishes both the length and the intensity of Achilles's rebuke by removing several of its "vindictive phrases," including the comparison between Agamemnon and the "brute mind of a Fox" that Chapman had concocted for his 1598 Achilles.[253] Chapman's increasing discomfort with what his 1598 Agamemnon calls "contumelious wordes" is likewise reflected in his modifications to another passage in Book 1 of the *Iliad*, the speech in which Pallas Athena seizes Achilles's sword in mid-air and tells him to "ceasse contention" with his adversary and instead use "words" to attack Agamemnon, "and such as may / Be bitter to his pride, but just."[254] In the 1598 version of the speech, Athena tells Achilles to curb his "violent furie" and "rule that part that strives, / Reprooving him with words more safe," but only in the revised version of the passage does Athena's advice make clear that Achilles should choose his words carefully, since while rhetorical combat might be preferable to physical combat, some bitter and reproving speeches are nonetheless more prudent and decorous than others.[255] By 1611, Chapman's translation of the passage reveals a poet grown hesitant about whether verbal strife is in fact more heroic – or, for that matter, more effective – than physical violence. Chapman's 1598 Achilles explains his internal conflict in the opening book of the *Iliad* in terms of a "strife" between his "rationall and angrie parts," the former faculty urging him to "restraine his froward mind and calme his anger's heat" while the latter stirs him to "draw his wreakefull sword" against Agamemnon.[256] In the 1611 translation, the discord raging within Achilles's "devided selfe" diminishes into a somewhat murkier opposition between the "two waies" of his "discursive part," such that his internal debate about whether to kill Agamemnon or to "sit his anger out" is no longer reducible to a simple *psychomachia* between reason and passion or between the corresponding weapons of verbal and physical force.[257]

Chapman's alterations to Achilles's speeches in Book 1 of the *Iliad* reflect his larger concern to identify whether and to what extent vituperative speech arises out of an irrepressible, undisciplined passion, and when it may instead be the product of a heroic "perturbation" sanctioned by right reason. Other Elizabethan readers of Homer, such as Fraunce, attribute the "sharpe voice" that Achilles uses towards Agamemnon to his "bitter, angrie, cholerike, and furious" character, yet Chapman comes to possess a subtler and more redemptive understanding of Achilles's wrath.[258] His effort to fashion Achilles into a character who engages mainly in the most ennobling form of verbal strife is evident not only in his revisions to several scenes featuring Achilles but also in a series of glosses on the word *arizêlos*. According to Chapman, the term – which means extremely worthy of emulation or zeal-provoking – has suffered "strange abuse" at the hands of Homer's Latin translators, who have erred in emending the word to *aridêlos* [very distinct or clear] and then translating it "*clarus* or *illustris*."[259] In the first of several discussions of the word in his commentary, Chapman follows Scapula in deriving the term from "a compound of *ari*, which is *valde*, and *zêlos*," or emulation, such that the word as a whole "signifies *quem valde aemulamur*, or *valde aemulandus*" – that which inspires, or is very worthy of, zeal or emulation. In the Homeric passage in question, Zeus sends a portent to the Greeks: a dragon appears at their altar, massacres a group of sparrows, and then (in a line obelized by Aristarchus) turns to stone. Interpreted by Calchas as a "powerfull meane / To stirre our zeales up," the omen sent by Chapman's Zeus is neither *aridêlos* [very clear] nor *aidêlos* [annihilated, made unseen], as many modern editors emend the phrase, but rather *arizêlos*: it arouses wonder among the Greek troops and provokes from them an "unmeasur'd shout" of enthusiasm at the prospect of remaining in Troy.[260] Chapman's concern to interpret the above passage as a manifestation of how divine portents may inspire their audience is clarified by another discussion of the term at *Il.* 18.184–9, where Achilles calls his Myrmidons to battle with an *arizêlê phônê*, a "voice ... heard / With emulous affection" whose pitch, amplified by Pallas Athena, "[w]on emulously th'eares of all." In his commentary, Chapman justifies his translation of the passage by arguing that Homer's intention in describing Achilles's voice as *arizêlê* was "not to expresse the clearnesse or shrilnesse of his voice in it self, but the envious terror it wrought in the Troyans – *arizêlê phônê* not signifying in this place *clara*, or *cognitu facilis vox*, but *emulanda vox*, *arizêlos* signifying *quem valde aemulamur, aut valde aemulandus*," a voice that "works a terror" in its hearers such that Homer compares it to the way a "trumpet of a dreadfull and mind-destroying enemie" sounds to a "citie besieged."[261]

By translating Achilles's *arizêlê phônê* as an "emulous voice" capable of producing "terror" in its auditors and thus inspiring them to battle, Chapman aligns his voice with a number of other horror- and zeal-producing sounds and voices heard throughout the *Iliad*. Chapman's translations often amplify the profoundly *noisy* quality of Homeric epic. His rendering of the *Iliad* is deafeningly loud, filled with the ireful threats and "insultations" exchanged between gods and mortals, the "showts and clamors" of the Trojans that resemble the "baaing" of sheep, the cries of wounded soldiers and the "shrieking" of the kin who mourn their death. Above all, Chapman's *Iliad* thunders with the personified sounds of strife and war: the tumultuous din of "Clamor [who] flew so high / Her wings strook heaven and drownd all voice," the roar of wounded Ares, whose voice sounded "[a]s if nine or ten thousand men had bray'd out all their breaths / In one confusion," and finally the war cry of Eris, whose "Orthian" song "thunderd ... / High and with horror through the eares of all the Grecian throng."[262] For Chapman, as for Demetrius and Longinus before him, the ugly and harsh sounds that fill the *Iliad* elevate the poem by inspiring "terror" and "horror" in its audience, and Chapman's near-obsessive use of these two words preserves the strongly aural dimension to Homer's sublimity even in the silent medium of print.[263] As Chapman explains in a marginal note, Homer calls Zeus "the god of sounds for the chiefe sound his thunder," a sound echoed by the voices of various minor deities, such as Clamour, Terror, and Eris, who augment the cacophonous din of war. The voice of Eris has a special zeal-provoking power, and Chapman notes at the beginning of Book 11 how "Eris (contention) sings and excites the Grecians."[264] Like the zeal-provoking voice of Achilles, Eris can "inflame" and "inspire" her hearers with her "verse," which sets the hearts of the Greek troops "on fire" and makes "bitter warre more sweet a thousand times" than the prospect of returning to their "native climes."[265]

Chapman's interpretation of the inspiring voice of Homer's Eris, a voice that provokes its audience to heroic action, is shaped by his reading of Hesiod's *Works and Days*, a poem he translates in 1618 and quotes intermittently in various earlier works. Glossing Hesiod's description of the two *Erides*, Chapman puzzles over the poet's distinction between "harmefull discord" and "virtuous contention," the latter characterized by "Artizans aemulations for riches" and similar instances of professional rivalry.[266] In his Homeric commentaries, too, Chapman attempts to distinguish between good and bad incarnations of Eris, even referring to her, when she appears in the midst of battle on Achilles's shield, as "perverse Contention," an epithet that appears to interpret Homer's goddess of strife through the lens of Hesiod's twin deities by casting this Eris as one and not the other.[267]

Chapman's understanding that Homer, like Hesiod, aims to distinguish between virtuous and harmful manifestations of strife rests largely upon his complex interpretation of Homer's representation of human passion. In his poem *Euthymiae Raptus, or The Teares of Peace*, originally composed as a verse letter addressed to Henry, Prince of Wales, to accompany Chapman's 1609 edition of the *Iliads* when it was presented to its royal dedicatee, Chapman unravels the paradox that "Griefe in Peace, and Peace in Griefe might dwell," or rather that cheerfulness – *euthymia* – may result from conflict aroused by the passions.[268] At the beginning of the poem, the spirit of Homer appears to guide Chapman "through Earths peace-pretending strife, / To that true Peace" that is the ethical and spiritual destination of Homeric epic. Homer's spirit teaches Chapman that, howsoever much the *Iliad* and *Odyssey* might appear to dramatize the ill effects of "perverse" contention, the poems in fact teach that the attainment of true peace involves and even necessitates strife and affliction.[269] Until he is properly guided by Homer's spirit, Chapman's narrator cannot understand how contentment might be achieved by men perturbed by heroic passion, or how true peace – who then appears, personified in the form of a goddess – could be so "afflicted" by grief. The goddess of Peace resolves Chapman's doubt: "Homer tould me that there are / Passions, in which corruption hath no share," legitimate and ennobling passions that include anger, grief, and "free sufferance for the truth," or zeal.[270]

When the goddess of peace defends her "tears of anger" and justifies her licence to vent a "kind of spleene," she provides a thinly veiled justification of the "predominant perturbation" that motivates Homer's Achilles, whose "teares of unvented anger" are defended by Chapman against the common charge that they are "unworthie and fitter for children or women than such an Heroe as Achilles."[271] Perhaps in an effort to disprove Plato's criticisms of Homer's tearful hero in the *Republic*, Chapman exonerates the weeping Achilles by defending "the fitnesse of teares generally," especially when shed by "the greatest and most renowmed men" such as Aeneas, Alexander the Great, and above all, Christ. Scaliger had, in typical form, mocked Achilles for crying in front of his mother, but Chapman counters the criticism by arguing that the "naturall" tears wept by Achilles are not a sign of his "softnesse or faintnesse" but rather his "hardinesse and courage," for such "teares of manlinesse and magnanimitie" are produced out of the "point and sting of ... unvented anger," an affliction common among men of a "fierie" spirit such as Achilles.[272] The tears of Peace in *Euthymiae Raptus* are similarly the product of righteous indignation: if Homer allows his Achilles to shed heroic tears that do not compromise his masculine prowess, then Chapman's Peace may likewise vent her anger and grief without undermining the tranquillity she personifies.

In the *Euthymiae Raptus,* as well as in his Homeric commentaries, Chapman's defence of passions such as anger and grief challenges the common critical assumption that Chapman interprets the Homeric poems as Stoic allegories about the triumph of right reason over passion. Like many other readers of his era, Chapman could and did make distinctions along the Homeric spectrum of rage, from the most irrational and damaging expressions of anger to the most justifiable and ennobling. But Chapman never praises a single Homeric character for *apatheia*, and in fact often defends the virtuousness of Homeric anger. One of the epigrams accompanying Chapman's 1612 translation of *Petrarchs Seven Penitentiall Psalms* defends Achilles's wrath as "compose[d] ... of industrie" by Homer, while in a gloss explaining the "corselike" appearance of its grieving heroine, Chapman's 1614 *Eugenia* defends her poignant vulnerability to passion with a Homeric allusion. The marginal note reads, "[De]lectati fueri[mus] luctu. [Ho]m. ψ.v.10," referring to a passage at the beginning of Book 23 of the *Iliad* in which Thetis "stirr'd up a delight in griefe" in the heart of Achilles after the death of Patroclus.[273] These and other defences of heroic passion complicate Chapman's apparent assertion that Odysseus is a Stoic sage whose mind remains "unbroken, unalterd with any most insolent and tyrannous infliction."[274] Perhaps Odysseus represents an ideal for Chapman, one unmatched by any of Homer's other heroes and not even fulfilled consistently by Odysseus himself. But Chapman is quite forgiving of the many Homeric heroes who fall short of that ideal, often portraying their vulnerability to passion as a Christian virtue, rather than a Stoic vice.

Gladiators of Letters

In his 1656 *Wit and Fancy in a Maze*, Samuel Holland provides a parodic account of the Poets' War that resembles the wedding of Peleus and Thetis. Cast as Eris, Ben Jonson rudely interrupts the festivities by throwing an "apple of discord" into the crowd, thus precipitating a literary battle every bit as fierce as the Trojan War.[275] In Holland's Lucianic fable, Chapman emerges as one of Jonson's key adversaries, as well as a critic of poetic rivalry more generally. When Jonson engages in a bit of literary *aristeia* after the Homeric fashion, claiming that he is the "first and best" of English poets, Chapman becomes "wondrously exasperated at Bens boldness" and instead lends his support to Spenser, who only belatedly enters the skirmish after finishing his *Faerie Queene*.[276] Holland's satire offers a mock-aetiology of the literary quarrel that engrossed both Jonson and Chapman in the opening years of the seventeenth century, and it gives the "fire of Emulation" that fuels his squabbling banquet of writers a distinctly Homeric origin. Zara and Lamia, the heroes of Holland's mock-romance, meet Jonson, Chapman, and a number of other British bards in an underworld that dramatizes in miniature the history of poetic competition and discord. There, they witness an argument between Odysseus and Thersites in which the latter upbraids the former for his cowardice, accusing him of attaining Achilles's shield by "connivance" rather than by "oraculous Eloquence." Several other Greek and Trojan worthies join the fray, until a brawl breaks out between Homer and Hesiod, the latter poet boasting that he is "in all respects [Homer's] Rivall."[277] An audience composed of later classical writers assembles, splitting down the expected party lines – authors of pastoral and georgic for Hesiod, and authors of epic and tragedy for Homer – until the contention between the two Greek poets gives way to another, larger imbroglio when Statius claims to be equal to Virgil, thus precipitating an epic battle of the books that anticipates and invigorates the rivalries among Chapman, Jonson, and other writers of their generation.

Holland's fable captures many of the concerns about rivalry and discord that animate Chapman's poems and Homeric commentaries. Chapman completed the bulk of his Homeric translations during and shortly after the feud that gripped the English stage between 1599 and 1603, a series of "wit-combats" among rival playwrights that eventually turned into a full-scale "literary civil war" between Jonson and his enemies.[278] In his prologue to *All Fools*, a comedy composed in 1599 but not printed until six years later, Chapman complains that the "bitter spleens" of the day have abandoned the "ancient comic vein" of "merely comical and harmless jests" in favour of the more pungent flavour of "satirism's sauce."[279] Chapman's participation in the Poets' War appears to have shaped his attitudes towards strife and contention in Homeric epic, particularly since the battlefield repartee of Homer's heroes exercises many of the same rhetorical skills – and arouses similar concerns about verbal abuse – as the flyting matches of rival playwrights.

Yet Chapman's periodic repudiation of verbal contestation during the Poets' War is hard to reconcile with the scornful and mocking voice he assumes throughout his Homeric commentaries. Chapman's critics tend to find him combative and "querelous" – a poet driven by "resentment," or a "disgruntled" man whose disdain for his audience manifests itself in "stormy and rancorous abuse."[280] Even as Chapman depicts himself as a reluctant participant in the literary controversies of his age, he often articulates his dislike of verbal aggression in ways that self-consciously implicate him in the contestation he criticizes. This conflicted attitude towards literary rivalry is especially pronounced in Chapman's criticisms of his self-proclaimed arch-rival J.C. Scaliger, the "reviler" of Homer whom Chapman depicts throughout his Homeric commentaries as heir to Zoilus, the ancient critic regarded by the Renaissance as the "father of animadversions against poets" [*animadvertens poetarum parentem*].[281] The vehemence of Scaliger's attacks upon Homer makes him, in Chapman's mind, a tainted reader who soils the object of his criticism by "putting the *putidum mendacium* upon Homer" and "muddily dawb[ing]" his poems.[282] Despite the serious-sounding nature of these accusations,

Chapman may well have been aware that Book 5 of Scaliger's *Poetics*, the book that attacks Homer most vociferously, was composed as a ludic denunciation, addressed to a fellow critic with whom Scaliger was engaged in a quarrel.[283] Scaliger's condemnations of Homer in the *Poetics* are partly designed to flaunt his Latin skills by inventing the most insulting epithets imaginable, and Chapman seems to take up this same game in his commentaries, insulting Scaliger in turn. In a note on a verse in Book 3 of the *Iliad*, Chapman refutes one of Scaliger's many imprecations against the more ridiculous elements of Homeric epic – specifically, his faulting of Homer for representing "lightning in winter before snow or raine." Calling Scaliger a "reviler," a "scold," and a "bawd," Chapman assails the "sencelesse reprehensions" of his fellow scholar with vividly excremental imagery: Scaliger "belcheth" against Homer and then returns to his "vomit," an image that inverts, with parodic grotesqueness, the ancient statue supposedly carved by Galataeon for a temple erected to Homer, which (according to Nashe's account) depicts the poet "vomiting in a baso[n] ... and the rest of the Succeeding Poets after him greedily lapping up what he disgorged."[284]

Chapman's attacks against the "soule-blind Scalliger" and his "impalsied diminution of Homer" may well have been the inspiration for Jonson's satirical portrait of Ovid Senior in *Poetaster*, the poet who rails against anyone who thinks that Homer's "worme-eaten statue must not be spewd against, but with hallowed lips, and groveling admiration."[285] More than a decade after the first performance of *Poetaster*, after the two former collaborators parted ways, Jonson annotated his personal copy of Chapman's 1616 *Works of Homer*. In his margins, Jonson takes a dim view of Chapman's hostile treatment of Scaliger: next to Chapman's derogatory comments about Scaliger's "French wit," Jonson remarks sardonically, "I am sorry, my Chapman, that you have forgotten that Scaliger *père* was Italian, not French" [*Doleo, mi Chapmanne, te non meminisse Scalig: Pat: fuisse Italum, non Gallum*]. On the next page, Jonson responds with similar disgust to Chapman's continued execration against Scaliger, writing "*scurriliter*" and "*profanè et putidè*" in the margins of Chapman's attacks.[286] Jonson's marginal notes portray Chapman, rather than Scaliger, as the truly profane reader of Homer, a reaction that is especially understandable if Jonson's annotations were written after around 1623, the likely date of composition for Chapman's *Invective ... against Ben Johnson*. In this rather nasty piece of verse, Chapman depicts his rival poet as a "*Hercules Furens*," a cruel and biting satirist who "must bee Muzzelde" lest his "petulant will / ... Fliebowe all men with thy great swans Quill."[287] Such a depiction of Jonson is not, of course, particular to Chapman. During the Poets' War, Jonson's verbally combative ways become a frequent subject of satire by fellow dramatists such as Marston and Shakespeare, whose Chrisoganus (in *Histriomastix*) and Ajax (in *Troilus and Cressida*) each mock Jonson's eristic and boastful behaviour, the latter by granting it a Homeric foundation.

At work on his translation of the *Iliad* during the Poets' War, Chapman's conflicts with fellow poets and playwrights help to inject a topical significance into his representation of the aggressive rivalries among Homer's heroes. Deeply sensitive to the envy and hostility of his literary rivals, Chapman constructs the Homeric poet as a figure similarly maligned by the "envious looke" of detractors and yet able to rise above the sorts of rivalries that haunt Chapman's own literary career.[288] In the dedication to his 1598 *Seaven Bookes of the Iliades*, Chapman asks for an Achilles's shield to protect him from the "doting and vitious furie of the two Atrides – Arrogancie and Detraction," a request that reinvents the heroic fortitude of Homer's Achilles in terms of the poet's immunity to envy and criticism.[289] Yet Chapman also portrays himself in his prefaces and commentaries as the undeserving victim of a "rabble of maligners," thus establishing a kinship with Homer that rests upon their mutual status as targets of unmerited or unsound blame.[290] Chapman's self-identification with Homer also rests, paradoxically, upon the singularity of the Greek poet. As the only poet, according to Chapman's reckoning, who lacks peers or predecessors, Homer is his "owne Master onely," a position that enables him to remain detached from the rivalries and contests that define all subsequent poetic identity.[291] Taking pride in a similarly Phoenix-like self-sufficiency, Chapman even declares, in the final line of his elegy for Henry, Prince of Wales, that "Homer, no Patrone founde; Nor Chapman freind," a claim that unites the two poets through their shared singularity.[292]

At the beginning of his career, in his *Shadow of Night*, Chapman reworks Homer's golden chain into a symbol of the poet's ability to rise up above envy and competition and to inoculate himself against the "Ambition" and "cursed avarice" of fellow poets who tug on the chain in order to displace the Olympian poet from his "setled height."[293] For Chapman, this passage from Book 8 of the *Iliad* represents neither divine omnipotence nor sovereign authority but rather the self-sufficiency of the ideal poet able to resist the "Herculean vigor" exerted by the corrupting forces of his culture that work to "constraine / Men from true vertue."[294] The fantasy of a poet untouched by intellectual and institutional pressures – or one unchallenged and unruffled by rivals – courses throughout Chapman's Homeric commentaries. Entranced by the apparition of Homer at the beginning of *Euthymiae Raptus*, Chapman describes how he "remainde / (Like him) an onely soule" such that only the kindred spirit of Homer is able to penetrate the "hidden places of my Solitude."[295] In calling Homer an "onely soule," Chapman may have in mind Poliziano's description of Homer's apotheosis in his *Ambra*, where the poet rises up above the "horrid tempest of unjust Envy" [*iniquae / tempestas foeda Invidiae*] and gazes down in perfect security from his serene perch, "free and unharmed" [*liber et innocuus*] by the "contending winds" below, winds that, in Chapman's more paranoid rendition of the image, become the hostile murmurings of adversaries and detractors.[296] If the Homeric poems provide a guide for some of the rhetorical strategies needed to participate in the wit-combats of the late Elizabethan stage, they also encourage Chapman to construct for himself an ideal model of the poet capable of rising above such petty controversies.

Shakespeare's Ironic Homer

Shaped by the hostile atmosphere of the war of the theatres, the earliest instalments of Chapman's Homer in turn animate Shakespeare's *Troilus and Cressida*, a play saturated with precisely the sort of "abusive quarrel" that Chapman so assiduously analyses in his Homeric commentary.[297] Inasmuch as the play dramatizes a "parodic recreation of the stage-quarrel between Jonson and Marston," *Troilus and Cressida* resituates that quarrel in the context of the Trojan War, a conflict defined not by the "heroic rivalry" between Achilles and Hector but rather by the "scurrilous contention" between anti-heroic figures such as Ajax and Thersites.[298] Although based principally on Chaucer's *Troilus and Criseyde* and on Caxton's *Recuyell of the Historyes of Troye* – two medieval retellings of Trojan legend that debase the ancient originals on which they are modelled – most critics agree that Shakespeare was familiar with Chapman's *Seaven Bookes of the Iliades*, printed in 1598, as well as his *Achilles Shield*, an excerpt from Book 18 of the *Iliad* printed that same year.[299] But most critics of Shakespeare's play also agree that *Troilus and Cressida* diverges radically in its tone and outlook from Chapman's translation as well as from Homer's Greek original, arguing that *Troilus and Cressida* "revamps Homer's lexicon of heroic gestures" and that it "differs greatly from that of George Chapman" inasmuch as while Chapman insists upon the "primacy of sovereign, unpolluted Homer," Shakespeare's version of Trojan legend is always "already irrevocably infected by later 'foul hands.'"[300]

Such readings of *Troilus and Cressida* are predicated on interpretations of Chapman's Homer blind to the translation's sustained attention to the ironic and scoptic dimensions of Homeric epic. Shakespeare is a prime beneficiary of Chapman's ironic interpretation of Homer, even as he directs that interpretation towards different philosophical and literary ends. If *Troilus and Cressida* provides a "sardonic version of the classical past to counter Jonson's antiseptic pseudohistory," as James Bednarz has argued, it also provides a more pessimistic and spiritually bankrupt version of Chapman's ironic Homer, directing that irony towards exposing the absurdity and futility of epic conflict.[301] Critics have, of course, long recognized *Troilus and Cressida* to be a deeply ironic play: Northrop Frye argues that its "ironic emphasis" distinguishes the play from most of Shakespeare's other comedies in that its ironies are "too strong for the drive toward deliverance," while François Laroque discerns irony in the play's tendency to "debun[k] and undermin[e] Homer's legendary story."[302] Yet such observations about Shakespeare's play fail to acknowledge how Chapman's emphasis upon the ironic and scoptic dimensions of the *Iliad* may well have nurtured the dark humour of Shakespeare's play, informing the perspectival shifts and discontinuities that foster its powerful ironies. Although some readers of Shakespeare's play perceive the "complex and ambiguous morality" of Homeric epic to be at the foundation of its ironies, Shakespeare's satirical handling of characters such as Agamemnon has never been traced to Chapman's analysis of the similar strategies employed by the Homeric narrator.[303] It may be true, as Bevington has argued, that Shakespeare treats Agamemnon as a "figure of ridicule" whereas Homer does not. But Chapman, as we have seen, most certainly *does* subject Agamemnon to precisely the kind of "mirthful parody" and "satirical comedy ... of contradiction" that also pervades *Troilus and Cressida*.[304] The "scurril jests" played by Shakespeare's Achilles and Patroclus (I.3.148), Agamemnon's ironic praise of the "noble Ajax" (II.3.147–56; IV.5.3–10), the sceptical deflation of values such as chivalry and fame, the reliance upon mockery and reproach as weapons – all of these characteristics and episodes suggest a profound engagement with Chapman's anatomy of the ironic and scoptic dimensions of Homeric epic.[305]

The practice of revising and parodying Homeric narratives was a popular literary sport during the sixteenth and early seventeenth centuries, a technique partly derived from the burlesque tradition of Greek sophists such as Lucian and Dio Chrysostom and resuscitated in sixteenth-century farces such as the 1537 *Thersites* as well as by the tradition of learned jest practised by writers such as Erasmus, Rabelais, Harington, Nashe, and Harvey.[306] Irreverent treatments of Homer abound in England around the turn of the seventeenth century: works such as Anthony Gibson's 1599 *A Womans Woorth* take perverse pleasure in dethroning the gods and heroes of the *Iliad*, calling Achilles a "brothel hunter," Patroclus a "kitching fellow," and Vulcan and Iris a "drunkard" and a "bawde."[307] Shakespeare, too, "twists, disorders, and occasionally inverts" his Homeric and para-Homeric sources: by pitting rival versions of a given story, scene, or character against each other, *Troilus and Cressida* undermines the legitimacy of any single authority, calling attention to the discontinuities between Homeric epic and the medieval versions of Trojan legend composed by Dares Phrygius, Dictys Cretensis, and Chaucer.[308] Shakespeare also stresses the moral bankruptcy of his characters and the pettiness of the conflicts gripping them. Announcing, "The ravished Helen, Menelaus' queen, / With wanton Paris sleeps; and that's the quarrel," the play's prologue uses the same word ("quarrel") that Hobbes will later adopt as a keyword of his own, bathetic interpretation of the *Iliad* (*Troilus*, Prologue, 9–10). In order to underscore the triviality of its central conflict, *Troilus and Cressida* turns to parodic effect the Renaissance *topos* of the *multum in parvo*, or "the extremity of great and little."[309] When Ulysses complains of Achilles that "[t]hings small as nothing ... / He makes important," his observation is a synecdoche for the play as a whole, which muddles the "extremity of great and little" by refocusing its energies on minor characters such as Thersites and Pandarus, as well as by undercutting the heroic greatness that inheres in virtues such as valour, honour, and truthfulness (II.3.168–9; IV.5.79).

Chapman's translation urges its readers to heed the "voice or manner of utterance" of each character as a "key that discovereth his wisdome or folly," and Shakespeare's play likewise distinguishes its characters according to their habits of speech. The Aristotelian distinctions between the boor (*agroikos*) and the buffoon (*bômolochus*) and between the *alazôn* and the *eiron* are reincarnated, respectively, in the figures of Pandarus and Thersites and Ajax and Ulysses.[310] In a play dominated by the complementary rhetorical figures of hyperbole (or "surplusage") and deflation (or "diminishing"), Thersites, Ajax, and Ulysses are not merely satirical portraits of Shakespeare's contemporaries; to their Elizabethan audiences, they are also "walking, talking figure[s] of speech" who dramatize many of the conventions so carefully noted by Chapman in the margins of his translations.[311] Thersites in particular exhibits both the affective and the rhetorical characteristics embodied by Chapman's term *scoptichè*. Already represented as a "railing detractor" in sixteenth-century rhetorical handbooks such as Leonard Cox's *The Arte or Crafte of Rhethoryke* and in various works by Melanchthon, Shakespeare's Thersites is a "porcupine"

(II.1.24) whose "gall coins slanders like a mint" (I.3.193), a character who raises reproach to a high art form.[312] Not only does Shakespeare amplify Thersites's character far beyond the minor role assigned to him by Homer and Caxton, he also turns Thersites into the play's ethical prism, the fulcrum at which its conflicting perspectives intersect. Thersites is a "knower" (II.3.46) in that whatever self-knowledge the play's other characters possess is "refracted through the deforming glass of Thersites."[313] Whereas Chapman aspires to peel away the ironic layers of Homeric epic to uncover a true vision of human nature that is at once "variant" and harmonious, Shakespeare refigures Homer's pervasive irony in order to demonstrate that truth only exists as "rendered and distorted" by Thersites's derisive and grim commentaries on the action of the play.[314] In a play where "no man is the lord of anything … / … Till he communicate his parts to others" (III.3.116–18), fame is both an obstacle to self-knowledge and the sole, limited means of achieving it, an elusive and "false good" in a competitive arena in which "to have done is to hang / Quite out of fashion, like a rusty mail / In monumental mock'ry" (III.3.152–4).[315] Shakespeare comes closer than any other Renaissance writer save perhaps Hobbes in accentuating the ironies that surround Homer's treatment of *kleos*, refashioning the heroes of the *Iliad* in a manner that works to arouse suspicion of the epic values to which they aspire.[316]

With Thersites the "grotesque satirist" at its centre, providing a "warped kind of choric voice," *Troilus and Cressida* frustrates the ethical and spiritual purpose of ironic and scoptic speech as understood by Chapman.[317] Rather than produce moral clarity or concord, the abusive and scornful language that fills Shakespeare's play is not a means to self-knowledge but rather an obstacle to it, less a "derision medicinable" (III.3.44) than a symptom of the infectious pride and envy that distort each character's view of himself. As the "symbol and faithful interpreter" of a discordant world reduced to "mere oppugnancy" (I.3.111), Thersites thwarts the play's characters as they struggle to "harmonize the conflicting evidence of [a] universe" fraught with paradoxes and contradictions – a universe fuelled by the "sportful combat" (I.3.336) of emulation and by the "noblest hateful love" (IV.1.35) that inheres between enemies who are also kin.[318] *Troilus and Cressida* thus contributes to an ongoing debate rooted in Homeric epic, one initiated by Homer's ancient readers, reinvigorated by Poliziano and Erasmus, and extended by Chapman's translation, over whether insult is a nobler form of combat than physical violence. The play calls into question whether there exists such as a thing as "mere words" (V.3.108) or whether injurious speech may, as Laurie Maguire puts it, "enact power relations as well as reflect them."[319]

Yet the explosive volleys of insult and invective that fill *Troilus and Cressida* also prove a potent form of counter-discourse capable of altering social structures by destabilizing language itself. Shakespeare illustrates this powerfully in Ulysses's famous speech on degree (I.3.75–137), an elaborate reworking of Odysseus's assertion at *Il.* 2.204 that "it is not a good thing to have a multitude of kings" [*ouk agathon polukoiraniê*] and a speech that, like its Homeric antecedent, naturalizes social rank on the grounds that "Degree being vizarded, / Th'unworthiest shows as fairly in the mask" (I.3.83–4). The *Iliad* voices similar concerns about the "vizarding" of social distinctions and its effects: whereas Menelaus (*Il.* 17.252–3) argues for the essential lack of distinction among his soldiers in order to urge them to perform distinguishing acts of heroic excellence, the threat of equivalence prompts other characters to reject war and its accompanying rewards of honour and renown. These are the terms according to which Achilles, in a passage of Book 9 of the *Iliad* here translated by Chapman, justifies his withdrawl from combat:

> Even share [*isê moira*] hath he that keeps his tent and he to field doth go:
> With equall honour cowards [*kakos*] die and men most valiant [*esthlos*],
> The much performer and the man that can of nothing want.[320]

Shakespeare amplifies Achilles's observations about the essential sameness of cowards and heroes, transforming the lines – as do many of Homer's ancient parodists before him – into a vehicle for interrogating the foundations of epic heroism. Both Lucian and the authors of the *Greek Anthology* discredit the epic virtues of fame and heroic excellence in underworld visions that blur the distinction between the best and the worst of men: "in Hades," they imagine, "Thersites is as highly honoured as Minos," or as Achilles.[321] This erosion of distinction haunts every page of *Troilus and Cressida*, a play in which to "lose distinction" in the joys of love is as frightful, according to Troilus, as to join an indistinguishable throng of soldiers in "battle, when they charge on heaps / The enemy flying" (III.2.26–8).

In one camp of the play are Ulysses and Agamemnon, defenders of "degree, priority, and place" who fear for their continued authority in a world where "bold and coward, / The wise and fool, and artist and unread, / The hard and soft, seem all affined and kin" (I.3.86; I.3.23–5). In the other camp are the purveyors of parody, irony, and satire – Thersites, Achilles, Pandarus – whose travesties of the characters around them threaten to erode distinction by highlighting the artificiality or the precariousness of authority founded upon degree or social rank. In the opening two books of the *Iliad*, there is already perilously little difference between Thersites and Achilles. Both figures rail against Agamemnon with strikingly similar language, but the former is consigned to obscurity after one brief, albeit memorable, speech while the latter harnesses his righteous indignation and ends the poem a hero. Whereas Chapman is tentative in his endorsement of the blunt and tart speech that binds together Achilles and Thersites as kindred critics of the world they inhabit, Shakespeare is downright enthusiastic about the partnership, going far beyond his Homeric source in forging an alliance between men who share "factious feasts" and strive to "match" their rivals through the parodic imitation of them (I.3.191; I.3.194).[322] As he works through the *Iliad*, Chapman grasps that Homeric irony is often created when one character unintentionally parodies another – or strives to resemble another character but fails to do so. In Shakespeare's play, it is no longer even possible to distinguish between the parody and its original – as Ulysses complains, all the "abilities, gifts, natures, [and] shapes" of each character are rendered indistinct once swallowed up and spit out by the "mastic jaws" of Thersites, or once distorted into the "stuff" of Achilles's parodic pageants (I.3.179; I.3.73; I.3.184). Like Homer's Menelaus, a few characters in *Troilus and Cressida* cling foolishly to the hope that war might animate what Shakespeare's Agamemnon calls the "broad and powerful fan" of "distinction," which separates those of "mass or matter" from "the light" by "[p]uffing at all" (I.3.27–9). Yet neither the brutality of war nor the violence of abusive language helps to distinguish Shakespeare's heroes and leaders from his villains and cowards. Both sides of the conflict are "aware of the ironies that link them to one another," and as Bevington rightly observes, they also "come increasingly to resemble each other as they compete for the same woman."[323]

The eristic spirit that infuses *Troilus and Cressida* thus places on a level everyone it afflicts. For some readers of the play, this levelling creates a bathos that is distastefully indecorous. As he undertakes to "remove the heap of rubbish under which many excellent thoughts lay wholly buried," John Dryden's 1679 adaptation of *Troilus and Cressida* measures Shakespeare's original against the neoclassical standards of Boileau and Rapin and deems it necessary to excise his predecessor's "co[a]rse" language.[324] Yet despite Dryden's aversion to the "fury of [Shakespeare's] fancy," a fancy that "often transported him beyond the bounds of Judgment … into the violence of a Catachresis," Dryden nonetheless acknowledges the "admirable genius" of the play, finding a peculiar sublimity in the grim and terrible jests that Chapman and Shakespeare esteem so highly in Homeric epic.[325]

Chapter Five

The Razor's Edge: Homer, Milton, and the Problem of Deliberation

Part 1. The Razor's Edge

At the end of *The Doctrine and Discipline of Divorce*, John Milton laments the two kinds of errors that men commit when weighing moral dilemmas such as the legitimacy of divorce. On the one side are those who "abandon" themselves to "serv under the tyranny of usurpt opinions," while on the other are those who "never leave subtilizing and casuisting till wee have straitn'd and par'd that liberal path into a *razors edge* to walk on between a precipice of unnecessary mischief on either side: and starting out at every false alarum, wee do not know which way to set a foot forward with manly confidence and Christian resolution."[1] In that thin sliver of right reason between its two contrary abuses – the tyranny of opinion and the fallacy of casuistical subtlety – the umpire conscience walks a tightrope that is "straitn'd and par'd" all the more by the political and religious factionalism of the early 1640s.

Milton's decision to describe the slender verge between contrary moral errors as a "razor's edge" is a distinctly Homeric metaphor, one that captures both the fearfulness and the exigency of making urgent choices. In Book 10 of the *Iliad*, in the middle of the night before the Great Day of Battle, Nestor wakes Diomedes to communicate to his fellow Achaean the urgency of this decisive moment in the war: "now for all it stands upon a razor's edge [*xurou histatai akmês*], / Either woeful destruction for the Achaeans, or life" (*Il.* 10.173–4). In one of only two uses of the phrase in English prior to 1700, George Chapman's translation of the *Iliad* renders the Greek *xurou histatai akmês* as "the eager razors edge," a possible borrowing from Erasmus's *Adages*, which derives the expression from Homer and from a proverb popularized by Thucydides.[2] Whether via Erasmus, Chapman, both, or neither, Milton's source for the phrase is certainly the *Iliad. Paradise Lost* makes repeated use of similar Homeric images to signal decisive moments: characters tottering on a precipice between contrary moral choices; unresolved battles threatening to tilt one way or another; divine judgments hanging in the balance.[3] All these conventions, as well as the language used to represent them, are vividly and conspicuously Homeric, marking what Milton calls "the moments and turnings of humane occasions."[4] By adopting and transforming Homeric pondering scenes, the Homeric conception of war as *akrita* [unresolved] or as *alloprosallos* [impartial], and the *talanta* or scales of Zeus, Milton imitates Homer in order to "justify" God and to establish a heroic model of Christian liberty that resides in "patience" and in "fortitude" but also in the ability to stride the razor-sharp edges of moral and spiritual choice.

Like so many Miltonic values, the moral tightrope-walking required by decisive moments can be, and is, distorted and abused. In *Paradise Lost*, as well as in *Paradise Regained*, Satan misappropriates Nestor's simile of the razor's edge in order to fashion himself into a hero who embraces "danger on the utmost edge / Of hazard," substituting the sham virtues of risk and recklessness for the prudence and courage required to "set a foot forward with manly confidence" in the manner endorsed by *The Doctrine and Discipline of Divorce*.[5] In the opening book of *Paradise Lost*, Beelzebub, a character who travesties the virtues of deliberation and counsel exemplified by Homer's Nestor, advises Satan how best to revive the waning courage of the rebel angels, inclining them towards "hope in fears and dangers" while they totter on the brink of "the perilous edge / Of battle" (*PL* 1.274–7). Beelzebub uses the metaphor inaptly, for the rebel angels are already *over* the edge: neither danger nor hope can exist for them any longer now that they have been expelled permanently from heaven. But his image of the "perilous edge / Of battle" both anticipates and impersonates the precarious counterpoise of battle achieved during the war in heaven, in which God's temporary suspension of victory is conveyed by means of similarly precipitous – and similarly Homeric – metaphors such as "the rough edge of battle" (6.108) and "the ridges of grim war" (6.236).

In his 1695 *Annotations on Milton's Paradise Lost*, a work largely devoted to identifying the poem's classical allusions, Patrick Hume notes the Homeric derivation of these phrases but remains silent on the possible reasons why Milton might have wished to make use of this cluster of Homeric metaphors for the lines, ridges, edges, and cords of battle. Richard Bentley was befuddled by Milton's "ridges of grim war," proposing to emend it to "bridges," while C.S. Lewis guesses that Milton's "ridges" of war reproduce the "*polemoio gephuras*" [lines of battle] of *Il.* 4.371 but then confesses, "what *they* were, I do not know."[6] In the *Iliad*, as well as in Milton's rereading of it, the "ridges" and "edges" of war dramatize morally and spiritually precipitous moments, the turning points and trials of the individual will as it totters on the brink between alternative choices.

In addition to the battle taunts and the flyting matches typical of Homeric combat – conventions likewise imitated widely and inventively by Milton – the *Iliad*'s battle scenes often depict characters engaging in a solitary process of "pondering" that pushes them onto, and over, moral thresholds. Odysseus "ponders in his mind and in his heart" [*hormaine kata phrena kai kata thumon*] whether to flee or to fight when he finds himself alone on the battlefield, choosing the route of courage over safety, while Menelaus similarly "ponders in his mind and heart" [*hormaine kata phrena kai kata thumon*] whether to risk his life in order to recover the arms of the dead Patroclus or to flee, ultimately opting for the latter (*Il.* 11.411; 17.106). Both during the war in heaven and elsewhere, *Paradise Lost* adapts many of the conventions associated with Homeric pondering scenes in order to dramatize the vexed and imperfect process of deliberation, whether internally (within the individual conscience of characters both human and divine) or collectively (in councils, assemblies, and conversations). In Milton's hands, Homeric scenes of deliberation, of temporarily unresolved conflict, and other "decisive" moments instruct readers how best to employ their own faculties of deliberation while at the same time justifying God as exempt from blame no matter the result of that deliberation.

At its foundation, Milton's poem is about pondering: about the human freedom to make choices; the responsibility of choosing rightly; the influences, both internal and external, that may interfere with rational deliberation; and above all the consequences of human choices when they are pondered, or weighed, by God. Less obvious, perhaps, is Homer's profound and wide-ranging influence upon *Paradise Lost*'s representation of deliberation and judgment, an influence that counterbalances whatever discomfort Milton may have had with "stern Achilles" or "Neptune's ire" and anchors the strong moral and spiritual affinity between the two poets (*PL* 9.14, 9.17). *Paradise Lost* holds deliberative relationships and trials of choice up for scrutiny through the lens of the *Iliad* and *Odyssey*, imitating episodes, images, and conventions that concern various aspects of human and divine decision-making, including the extent to which God assists in or shapes human choices and the advantages and liabilities of collective versus individual deliberation.

Homer's readers have long disagreed about how to interpret the pondering scenes in the *Iliad* and *Odyssey*, about whether the frequent use of verbs such as *mermêrizô* and *hormainô* imply the Homeric poet's conception of a single, autonomous moral faculty akin to free will. In this respect, Milton's interpretation of Homer diverges greatly from that of his contemporary, Thomas Hobbes, whose very different treatment of moral agency and deliberation in his translations of the *Iliad* and *Odyssey* is addressed in the next and final chapter of this book. Working only a decade or two apart, Milton and Hobbes arrive at strikingly different conclusions about the nature and efficacy of the deliberative faculty as represented by stock Homeric phrases such as "he pondered inwardly in his mind and his heart" or "my heart was divided in counsel" – phrases which do not translate easily into seventeenth-century conceptions of faculty psychology or theological conceptions of the will. If Milton and Hobbes disagree about how best to make sense of scenes of deliberation such as *Od.* 9.299, where Odysseus "forms a plan in my great heart" [*bouleusa kata megalêtora thumôn*] to blind Polyphemus, or 20.5, where he "ponders in his evil mind and heart" [*mnêstêrsi kaka phroneôn eni thumô*] how to overthrow the suitors, it is in part because these and other instances of Homeric pondering present deliberation as neither wholly intellectual nor wholly impulsive but rather as a process that occurs simultaneously in the *phrên* (mind) and the *thumos* (heart or chest). Homeric scholars still disagree over the extent to which formulaic phrases such as "*diandicha mermêrizen*" [to be of two minds, to deliberate], "*eipe pros on megalêtora thumon*" [he spoke to his proud heart] or "*hormaine … kata thumon / dichthadi*" [he pondered in his divided heart] make Homeric heroes agents in the fullest sense of that word, particularly since – as Bruno Snell argued a century ago – there is no single word for the "self" in Homeric epic and thus, at least according to Snell's logic, no way to imagine a self in dialogue or deliberation with itself.

Recent work by Homeric scholars has persuasively demonstrated that "Homer's agents live in a world which repeatedly and generously serves them up preponderating reasons for action," an argument that accords with Milton's interpretation of Homeric scenes and motifs of deliberation.[7] Yet even for those scholars who maintain that "Homeric heroes make real decisions," the problem remains that Homeric heroes often make the *wrong* decisions, a problem compounded in Homeric epic, as in *Paradise Lost*, by instances of collective deliberation in assemblies, councils, and conversations. Milton recognizes that *eubolia*, or excellence in council, is a key Homeric virtue, and that the assemblies [*agorai*] and councils [*boulai*] of Homer's poems often act as the "motive forces" behind epic action.[8] While Milton's reworking of some Homeric council scenes reflects his deep distrust of the political and moral efficacy of collective deliberation, he transforms other council scenes so as to suggest sympathies between his own struggles and those of the Homeric poet in imagining a kind of council in which "reason only swaies."[9] As vexing as Homer's Olympian councils may be to Renaissance readers – a concern made patently clear by Tobias Gregory's study of divine action in Renaissance epic – council scenes prove integral to *Paradise Lost*, where they dramatize both the urgency and the fallibility of deliberative processes, giving voice to Milton's damaged republican ideals, articulating his anti-Trinitarian theology, and illustrating the ways in which divine justice is accommodated to the imperfect faculties of human judgment.

Although scholarship addressing Homer's influence on Milton has lagged behind work on the influence of other classical writers such as Virgil and Ovid, scholars have acknowledged for centuries that "Homer [was] Milton's favorite classical poet" and the *Odyssey* his favourite epic poem.[10] In addition to leaving behind a fragment of a poem on *Alfred*, written in imitation of the *Odyssey*, Milton was rumoured during the early eighteenth century to have been asked to translate Homer, a job for which Jonathan Richardson coyly assesses him as "the Best Fitted of any Man on Some Accounts, on Others not at all."[11] Milton's affection for Homer is inseparable from his appreciation of the moral and spiritual sympathies between Homeric epic and the scriptures, an affinity documented with particular fervour in the decade before the publication of *Paradise Lost* by works such as James Duport's 1660 *Homeri Poetarum omnium seculorum facile Principis Gnomologia* and Zachary Bogan's 1658 *Homerus Hebraizôn: sive, comparatio Homeri cum scriptoribus Sacris quoad normam loquendi*. Both texts argue that the kinship between Homer and the Bible rests on the similarly persuasive theodicy mounted by each.[12] Influenced by contemporary treatises on pagan religion by Causabon, Gale, and Stillingfleet, the "Hebraized Homer" of Duport and Bogan presents a poet whose foremost aim is to exonerate God as "the author of civil strife and discord" [*litis ac discordiae civilis autorem*] and to prove that God does not create evil or license mortals to commit it [*Non permisit Deus ut malefaceret mihi*].[13]

Although Duport and Bogan enthusiastically reveal the many correspondences between Homeric epic and the scriptures, the latter often regarded as providing competing models of heroic action by seventeenth-century readers, neither writer makes the sort of bold claims about the correspondences between Hellenic and Hebraic wisdom that characterize earlier Renaissance scholarship. Milton follows suit. He may have assumed the habit of noting stylistic and thematic parallels between Hebrew and Greek poetry at St Paul's school, as Mary Ann Radzinowicz has suggested, or he may have developed it later, under the influence of mid-century scholarly fashions.[14] Yet though Hellenic and Hebraic elements frequently intersect in Milton's poetry –in *Samson Agonistes*, or in his Greek translations of the Psalms – their intersection does not always imply consonance, and at times Milton accentuates the "perilous gulfs" he discerns between pagan and Judaeo-Christian sensibilities.[15] The God of *Paradise Lost* is a synethesis of Homer's Zeus and the "jealous (prerogative-claiming) Jehovah" of the Old Testament, but instead of aiming to collapse these two traditions into one, Milton's synthesis of Hebraic and Hellenic wisdom seeks to test out the limits of their correspondence, at times finding the affinities between classical and scriptural texts compelling, and at times finding them lacking.[16] The result is an engagement with classical epic that "refuses uncomplicated allegiances and values," as Nigel Smith has astutely observed.[17]

Milton's Achillean Choice

Milton's imitations of Homeric epic, much like his imitations of other classical and biblical sources, are "flexible, complex," and resistant to univocal equivalencies.[18] Nowhere is this flexibility more evident than in the choice of Achilles, the moral crux of the *Iliad* which shapes *Paradise Lost*'s appropriation of Homeric scenes of deliberation and also informs Milton's own autobiography. In the *Defensio Secunda*, Milton invokes the dilemma faced by Achilles – the choice between duty and self-preservation – in order to describe the two alternative fates [*duasque sortes*] he faced when obliged to choose whether to "incur the loss of my eyes" or "desert a sovereign duty [*officium*]." Milton compares that choice to "the two-fold destiny, which the son of Thetis reports that his mother brought back concerning himself, when she went to consult the oracle at Delphi," an event described in a passage from Book 9 of the *Iliad* that Milton cites in Greek and Latin.[19] Achilles speaks not of Fate but of *fates*, plural and divided (Gr. *dichthadias kêras*; Lat. *duplicia fata*), a phrase that accentuates the authenticity and the urgency of his choice. Although later in the *Defensio Secunda* Milton cautiously distinguishes himself from the *kleos*-hungry Homeric hero, protesting that he "covet[s] not the arms of Achilles" and that he bears "a real not a painted burden," his invocation of Achilles nonetheless conveys the extent to which Milton discerns in Homer a sympathetic recognition of the vital and agonizing choices demanded by the continual exercise of political and spiritual liberty.[20]

In the *Defensio Secunda*, Milton presents Achilles as having made the *correct* choice in preferring self-sacrificing duty over self-preservation. But *Paradise Lost* throws doubt on Achilles's choice by reworking his posthumous expression of regret in Book 11 of the *Odyssey* – "I would rather serve as the hireling of another, of some portionless man whose livelihood was but small, rather than to be lord over all the dead" – in multiple and contradictory ways in order to dramatize competing conceptions of the relationship between liberty and servitude (*Od.* 11.489–91). Satan's claim that it is "[b]etter to reign in Hell, than serve in Heav'n" (1.263) neatly inverts Achilles's speech. Inasmuch as Satan "aspires to that which Achilles rejects," he lacks the hindsight of Homer's hero even when both characters find themselves in underworlds whose chief torment is the threat of dwindling fame.[21] Yet in a counter-heuristic turn, Milton later permits Abdiel to correct his adversary's erroneous idea of servitude: "This is servitude, / To serve the unwise," Abdiel chastises Satan, dismissively commanding him to "Reign then in hell thy kingdom, let me serve / In heaven," a plea that does not simply reclaim but also improves upon Achilles's original speech by embracing the most noble form of servitude – obedience to God – as both superior to and a precondition of the liberty enjoyed by mortal men on earth (6.178–9; 6.183–4).

Satan repeatedly proves a naive and impure reader of Homer who perverts even the noblest epic sentiments to their worst abuse. Yet by showing how Achilles's lines may be manipulated to demonic as well as heroic ends, Milton also expresses his own ambivalence towards a figure whose ruling passion – a petulant wrath that finally gives way to pity – occupies a broad ethical spectrum in its various incarnations in *Paradise Lost*, from the most malevolent (Satan's wrath, his sense of injured merit, and his pretence of self-sacrifice) to the most sanctified (the Son's virtuous self-sacrifice, his pity, and his Achilles-like re-entry into battle) to a mixture of the two (Adam's foolish self-sacrifice, his Achilles-like rage, and his ultimate, ennobling capitulation to pity).[22] Milton's splintering of Achilles into these discrete and divergent aspects demonstrates what is both attractive and dangerous about the character's heroic temper, parts of which are reconcilable to Milton's ethical and spiritual outlook and parts of which are not.

When characters in *Paradise Lost* are presented with conflicting models of heroism and obliged to choose between them, these decisive moments are sometimes symbolized by Achilles's shield, an *ekphrasis* transformed by Milton into a master-metaphor of deliberation that represents in miniature the exigencies of heroic pondering. The description of Satan's shield at *Paradise Lost* 1.284–91, an object likened to the moon as viewed through Galileo's "optic glass," is one such adaptation of Achilles's shield, likened to the moon for its bright gleam at *Il.* 19.373–4. But Milton embeds in Satan's "ponderous" (1.284) shield a dense and deeply ironic set of Homeric allusions that point to the failure of Satan's deliberative faculties. Cast behind him, over his shoulder, Satan's shield reflects his blindness to the consequences of his choices, a lack of hindsight that distinguishes him from Achilles elsewhere in *Paradise Lost.* Resembling the moon as seen through Galileo's telescope, the shield also represents "Satan's diminished radiance and heavenly estrangement," as Stephen Dobranski argues, for the "spotty globe" of the telescope obscures the moon even as it also amplifies and enhances it.[23] Whereas Homer's two-sided shield is a symbol of moral distinction or *dikê*, Satan's shield is insistently one-dimensional: like the moon as viewed through the lens of a telescope, it provides a single and partial perspective that in turn symbolizes Satan's inability to make judicious discriminations, a spiritual frailty reflected in his boast that "[t]he mind is its own place, and in itself / Can make a heaven of hell, a hell of heaven" (1.254–5). So too does Satan's spear (1.292–4), whose immensity echoes the "wooded peak of lofty mountains" to which Homer compares the club of Polyphemus, the unsociable and barbarous Cyclops who "mingled not with others, but lived apart, his heart set on lawlessness" [*oude met'allous / pôleit, all apaneuthon eôn athemistia êdê*] (*Od.* 9.192, 9.188–9). Linking him to the *athemista* Polyphemus, Satan's spear symbolizes his refusal to observe the *themistas* – the divine laws or decrees guarded by Themis, the Homeric and Hesiodic goddess who presides over assemblies and ensures justice by "straightening crooked judgements" [*skoliôn de dikeôn*].[24]

Achilles's shield is often interpreted during the Renaissance as an emblem of the irreparable distance between God and fallen humankind or between an irretrievably lost golden age and the injustice of the present time. In the *Iliad*, the shield dramatizes this disparity by juxtaposing the violent conflict of battle with a scene of orderly strife [*neikos*], a trial presided over by an assembly of wise elders who ensure the proper dispensation of justice. In the panorama of Old Testament history that Michael affords to Adam at *Paradise Lost* 11.638–711, however, Milton transforms Achilles's shield by emphasizing the imperfections of juridical deliberation as a means of resolving conflict. In Michael's adaptation of the Homeric *ekphrasis*, a scene of "bloody fray" (11.651) is complemented and compounded, rather than remedied, by a scene of "council in the city gates," in which reasoned argumentation in an assembly gives way to "harangues" and to "factious opposition" (11.663–4) until Enoch, "the only righteous in a world perverse," emerges to salvage the deliberative process from a council unable to distinguish between "right and wrong" (11.666). Reworking it into an aetiological emblem of the intrusion of injustice into the postlapsarian world, Milton transforms Achilles's shield into a deeply pessimistic meditation on the failures of collective deliberation and the limitations of the assembly as an instrument of justice. These failures are chastised but not corrected by Enoch's bold reassertion of individual moral reasoning. His heroic defence of "justice, of religion, truth and peace, / And judgment from above" is animated by his conscience rather than by the collective judgments of the community (11.667–8).[25]

Milton's Homeric Theodicy

Milton's reliance upon Homeric metaphors of unresolved conflict is acknowledged by the author of *In Paradisum Amissum Summi Poetae Johannis Miltoni* [On the excellent poet John Milton's *Paradise Lost*], a panegyric probably written by Samuel Barrow that first appeared in the 1674 edition of *Paradise Lost.* Praising Milton for conveying an element of contingency and suspense during the war in heaven, the poem recounts how "Olympus waits, doubtful to which side it must yield, / And fears it may not survive its own conflict" [*Stat dubius cui se parti concedat Olympus, / Et metuit pugnae non superesse suae*].[26] Milton, like Homer, is always "sowing the seeds of future events" in order to keep his audience in a state of expectation. Yet in *Paradise Lost*, God knows exactly which way victory will go, even as He pretends, in a notorious moment of irony, to be somewhat less than "sure / Of our omnipotence" (5.721–2). In depicting Milton's heaven and his God as *dubius* – doubtful, two-sided, impartial – the commendatory poem strives to vindicate one of the most theologically disturbing moments in *Paradise Lost*, when God jokes with the Son that they may "unawares … lose / This our high place, our sanctuary, our hill" (5.731–2). Despite William Empson's objection that God's sardonic humour is "appallingly malignant," the mock-uncertainty voiced by Milton's God does not show Him "doubting his empire," as Empson would have it, but rather shows Him to be *dubius* – impartial, inclined either way, or *alloprosallos*, to use the term that caught Erasmus's attention in his own vindication of Homer's free-will theology.[27]

Although never in doubt of his ultimate victory or his omnipotence, Milton's God preserves the liberty of his creatures by ensuring the counterbalance of an even fight, allowing humankind to "stand / On even ground against his mortal foe, / By me upheld," lines that Dennis Danielson has interpreted as illustrating the "aequilibrium" that is the essence of divine justice in *Paradise Lost*.[28] By allowing Satan to remain on the "perilous edge of battle" until the intervention of the Son – an "edge" that symbolizes the persistently urgent power of choice in shaping the outcome of the war in heaven – Milton's God safeguards both human will and divine impartiality, an equilibrium symbolized by the scales that He grasps by the middle as well as the battle which He lets hang in "even scale" (6.245).

Milton's God inherits these emblems of divine neutrality from Homer's Zeus, and the inheritance sheds light on the ways that *Paradise Lost* emulates Homer's theological project to "justify" the ways of Zeus to men and exonerate him from blame for human error. Milton sees in Homer a poet who shares his concern for "man's freedom and his moral responsibility," and he repeatedly singles out Homer among pagan writers as an especially passionate defender of divine justice.[29] In the *De Doctrina Christiana*, a work that only rarely enlists classical texts to elucidate Christian doctrines, Milton invokes Zeus's opening speech in the *Odyssey* to support his own repudiation of predestinarian theology, which errs in making God the author of sin. Those who "impugn [*accusant*] the justice of God" by blaming Him for human error may, according to Milton, be "justly reproved [*redarguuntur*] in the words of the heathen Homer," who "in the person of Jupiter" claims that mortals "die self-destroyed by their own fault" [*Suis enim ipsorum flagitiis perierunt*] and that we blame the gods and fate on our own errors. Milton translates Zeus's opening speech in the *Odyssey* as follows:

> Papae, ut scilicet Deos, mortales accusant!
> Ex nobis enim dicunt mala esse: illi vero ipsi
> Suismet flagitiis, praeter fatum, Dolores patiuntur.[30]

The same passage, used in 1654 by Henry Hammond to disprove the argument that God is the "author of sin," also appears in Milton's *Doctrine and Discipline of Divorce*, where it serves to prove that "man is the occasion of his owne miseries, in most of those evils which he imputes to Gods inflicting."[31] Later in that same work, Milton may still have Zeus's speech in mind when he identifies Homer as endorsing the doctrine that "mans own freewill self-corrupted is the adequat and sufficient cause of his disobedience," the prefix "self-" (a turn of phrase favoured by both God and Satan in *Paradise Lost*) duplicating the emphatic "*autos*" of Zeus's assertion that mortals bring evils upon themselves "by themselves" [*oi de kai autoi*].[32] Milton's claim that "the justice of God stood upright ev'n among heathen disputers" such as Homer solves the interpretive difficulties posed by other Renaissance commentators on Homer such as Jean de Sponde, who remarks in his annotations to *Il.* 4.66–72 that he "cannot accept the idea that Homer makes his gods the cause of evils" [*Quanquam non possum probare, ut Diis suis malorum causam Homerus tribuat*].[33] Given that the entire argument of *The Doctrine and Discipline of Divorce* rests on the premise that God is not "the author of sin," Zeus's eloquent self-defence helps Milton prove that legal divorce vindicates divine goodness by allowing for the dissolution of ungodly marital unions.[34]

Dedicated both to the elimination of sin and to the upholding of the law, the God of Milton's divorce tracts achieves a "counterpoise" by weighing these two values "like two ingots in the perfect scales of his justice."[35] *Paradise Lost* articulates this perfect counterpoise of divine justice – and tackles the related task of exonerating God from responsibility for sin – through a number of Homeric conventions and motifs. The *Odyssey* opens as Zeus reassigns "blame" or "cause" [*aitioôntai*] for sin or error to the human sphere, and yet Zeus is "morally on the defensive" from the very opening lines of the poem, when he offers a corrective to those mortals who fault the gods for ills they bring upon themselves.[36] When Milton's God first appears at the beginning of Book 3, he launches a similarly pre-emptive strike against a similar set of accusations when he asserts that the rebel angels "themselves decreed / Their own revolt, not I" (3.116–17), a claim reinforced by God's decision to send Raphael on an errand to Eden to "render man *inexcusable*" for his own sin (4, Argument). Like Homer's Zeus, Milton's God understands that he must not simply *be* just but must also *appear* to be just by thwarting unfounded suspicions of tyranny, indifference, or whimsy, a task made more difficult, in both poems, because of the "imperfect comprehension of man."[37]

In *Paradise Lost*, as in *De Doctrina*, Milton interprets the *Odyssey* "as a theodicy, justifying the ways of god to men."[38] Milton is by no means the first Renaissance writer to read Homer's poem in this manner. Sponde's commentary on the *Odyssey* praises Zeus's opening speech as full of Christian truth because it shows how the evils that befall men are "not to be traced to God but to the iniquities and dishonesties in man himself."[39] Both Sponde and Milton invest heavily in Zeus's speech as a mark of Homer's essential compatibility with their own theology. Despite Dennis Burden's claim that *Paradise Lost* reinterprets the *Odyssey* as a poem about "victimization rather than justice" in which the gods distress and perplex the poem's protagonist, Milton grasps the fact that Homer's epic task – much like his own – depends upon illustrating how such victimization is the result of human misperception rather than actual divine enmity.[40]

Milton's choice of the word "justify" in the opening lines of *Paradise Lost* hints at the Homeric and Hesiodic origins of his own theodicy. Both Greek poets "justify" Zeus by emphasizing the disparity between the actual rectitude of divine judgments and the apparent crookedness of those judgments when viewed from a human perspective. As Milton puts it in *The Doctrine and Discipline of Divorce*, God's judgments are "constant and most harmonious" but they often appear "variable and contrarious" to us.[41] Milton's first and most definitive articulation of his poetic project in *Paradise Lost* – to "justify the ways of God to men" (1.26) – stakes its claim with a distinctly Homeric and Hesiodic vocabulary: Hesiod begins the *Works and Days* by asking his readers to "make judgements straight with righteousness" [*dikê d'ithune themistas*] and to "make straight their crooked judgements" [*skoliôn de dikeôn*], phrases that further develop Homer's depiction of Zeus as a god who makes the *themistas* – judgments or decrees – straight with his *dikê*.[42] When Adam, in the final book of *Paradise Lost*, repeats Michael's lesson that God "by small / Accomplish[es] great things, by things deemed weak / Subverting worldly strong, and worldly wise / By simply meek," he echoes the opening lines of the *Works and Days*, where Zeus "easily ... brings the strong man low; easily he humbles the proud and raises the obscure, and easily he straightens the crooked [*de t'ithunei skolion*] and blasts the proud."[43] As a god who ensures justice by straightening [*t'ithunei*] the crooked [*skolion*], the Zeus of Homer and Hesiod bears a close resemblance to the levelling and justifying God of Isa. 40.4–5 and Luke 3.5, parallel verses with which Milton is intimate: "Every valley shall be lifted up, every mountain and hill brought down [*tapeinôthêsetai*]; rugged [*skolia*] places shall be made smooth [*eutheian*] and mountain ranges become a plain."[44] Resonating powerfully in their sentiment and diction with classical Greek analogues, these biblical verses reveal the Christian fulfilment of a conception of divine justice born in many of the ancient Greek writers – Homer, Hesiod, Pindar, Aeschylus, Solon – whom Milton admires most.[45]

Milton's Contrafactual Theodicy

Milton's reliance on Homer in his effort to "justify the ways of God to men" sheds light on some of the theological motives informing *Paradise Lost*'s adaptation of several related Homeric rhetorical conventions – similes, irony, and conditional and contrafactual clauses – that each help to elucidate the workings of divine justice by accommodating divine truth to the human intellect.[46] Although contrafactuals may suggest a deterministic cosmos as well as a contingent one, *Paradise Lost* employs these Homeric conventions in order to depict causation as complex, rooted in a compatibilist theology in which human and divine decision-making are interwoven, by depicting two possible outcomes for the same event or by depicting that event from two divergent perspectives.[47] Contrafactuals are past-tense, contrary to fact statements that usually follow the pattern "And now X might have happened, had not (or 'else') Y intervened," and they appear frequently throughout *Paradise Lost*, where they work to foster narrative suspense and theological contingency as well as to dramatize the mysteriousness of divine grace.[48] The ten examples of this construction in *Paradise Lost* are modelled principally, if not exclusively, on Homeric epic: the *Aeneid* contains only four contrafactuals, while Homer employs more than sixty of them in the *Iliad* alone. Like the many events that the Homeric narrator describes as occurring "*huper moiran*" [against or beyond divine dispensation], contrafactual statements afford the reader a twofold view of the narrative, demonstrating how characters both human and divine enjoy the liberty to have chosen otherwise at crucial moments in the narrative. In *The Doctrine and Discipline and Divorce*, Milton helps to explain his own motives for emulating the Homeric contrafactual when he praises Homer (along with Manilius) as a poet who "with an industrious cheerfulness acquits the *Deity*" of being the author of sin and then paraphrases Zeus's assertion that "mans own freewill self-corrupted is the adequat and sufficient cause of his disobedience *besides Fate*," rendering Homer's *huper moiran* into the ambivalent "besides Fate," a phrase which suggests that the human will is capable of working alongside, next to, or even against fate.[49]

During the war in heaven, Milton's repeated use of contrafactuals makes legible the contingency of the war's outcome upon the intervention – or, at times, the deliberate non-intervention – of various characters. Early on in Book 6, the narrator tells us that the warring angels would have disturbed (though not destroyed) heaven "Had not the eternal king omnipotent / … overruled / And limited their might" (6.227–9), and on the third and final day of the war, "all heav'n /Had gone to wrack" had not God "foreseen / This tumult, and permitted all, advised" in the moment before he declares "[a]ll power … transferred" to the Son (6.669–71; 6:673–4; 6:677–8). Both passages adhere to the "near miss" pattern typical of Homeric epic, in which the *apodosis* (then clause) precedes a negated *protasis* (if clause).

Both passages demonstrate Milton's subtle appropriation of the convention for his own theological purposes.[50] Only rarely is Homer's Zeus the agent of contrafactual interventions, which are usually performed by subaltern gods such as Apollo or Hera. When Zeus does intervene, it is to uphold his impartiality or the fairness of an even fight.[51] *Paradise Lost* dissociates its God even further from the theological determinism at times implied by the contrafactual interventions of Homeric epic: when Milton's God intercedes, He does so to prolong or defer battle rather than to end it, as at *Paradise Lost* 4.993–5, where God hangs out his "golden scales" so as to prevent "the horrid fray" between Satan and the squadron of angels who have come to Gabriel's defence.[52] This contrafactual, like the ones that mark God's intervention during the war in heaven, establishes an equipoise between adversaries, placing them on a level in a manner similar to the conflict between Hector and Ajax, which ends in a tie because both men are "loved by Zeus" and resolve not to fight again "until a god judges [*diakrinê*] between us, and gives victory to one side or the other" (*Il.* 7.280, 7.291–2).

When Satan enters into conflict with adversaries such as Gabriel and Abdiel, judgment is likewise deferred to God, even if both parties are not equally deserving of His affection. At such moments, Milton adapts the Homeric convention of unresolved conflict and deferred victory – the "great strife of equal war" [*neikos homoiiou polemoio*], to use the Homeric formula – to a millenarian outlook that postpones Satan's decisive defeat until the Last Judgment (*Od.* 18.264). During the suspended fight that erupts between Satan and Death in Book 2, the two adversaries assume the stance of well-matched Homeric warriors as they "stand front to front / Hovering a space ... so matched they stood; / For never but once more was either like / To meet so great a foe" (*PL* 2.716–22). This contest must be deferred, but for reasons different from those that tend to suspend Homeric battles: neither party may either prevail or suffer defeat until the Last Judgment, when God will "obstruct the mouth of hell / For ever," sealing up Sin and Death in its "ravenous jaws" (10.636–7). Moreover, contrafactual interventions in *Paradise Lost* assume the form of counsel rather than divine fiat. Unlike Sin, the holder of "the fatal key" (2.725) who interrupts the evenly matched confrontation between Death and Satan and thus threatens to upset the balance of power between them, Milton's God intervenes by "foresee[ing]" and by "advis[ing]" rather than by inhibiting or constraining action. Milton recognizes the convention as capable of providing "an additional means of emphasizing ... the free will which God assigns even to Satan," and thus demonstrating God's ability to ensure both divine justice and human liberty by adjudicating (but not determining) the alternative possibilities identified by the contrafactual phrase.[53] In this respect, Milton's use of Homeric contrafactuals fosters the kind of "free and open encounter" advocated by *Areopagitica* (*YP* 2:561), preserving liberty for divine and human actors alike while simultaneously illustrating the contrary outcomes that might result depending upon what actions a given character takes.

The contrafactual that concludes Book 4 of *Paradise Lost* is partly inspired by Book 23 of the *Iliad*, where the arbitration of Achilles during the funeral games is marked several times by contrafactual formulae.[54] In that episode, Achilles's intervention adjudicates rather than alters the outcome of an *eris* between adversaries; he acts as judge or umpire ("*theiomen amphô*") rather than participant in a potentially volatile contest and ensures its impartial resolution through prudent counsel, not force. A similarly conciliatory impulse motivates the most pivotal contrafactual moment in all of *Paradise Lost*, the Son's intercession during the celestial council of Book 3:

> on man's behalf
> Patron or intercessor none appeared,
> Much less that durst upon his own head draw
> The deadly forfeiture, and ransom set.
> And now without redemption all mankind
> Must have been lost, adjudged to death and hell
> By doom severe, had not the Son of God,
> In whom the fullness dwells of love divine,
> His dearest mediation thus renewed. (3.218–26)

Even the grim definitiveness of divine justice ("*Must* have been lost"; "doom severe") is shown to be conditional by the "mediation" of the Son's voluntary sacrifice. As the theological climax of the poem, the narrator's "had not" – a phrase that closely approximates Homer's "*kai nu … ei mê*" – captures the utter and miraculous contingency of divine grace, powerfully affirming the decisive power of the Son's free choice to intercede.[55] That choice is motivated by the "fullness" of his love for humankind but also by his wish to "end the strife / Of mercy and justice" (3.406–7) that inheres between, and within, Father and Son, an image which implies that Christ's sacrifice, like his intervention during the war in heaven, resolves a potentially insoluble conflict between justice and pity.

Though pivotal, the intercession of the Son is by no means determining: it provides the means for humankind to embrace divine grace but still leaves open the possibility that those who "accept not grace" will be condemned (3.302). By adapting the Homeric contrafactual into a convention that lays bare the motives for divine intercession, Milton reworks it into a vehicle for articulating his theological compatibilism. In Homeric epic, contrafactuals often represent the intervention of the subaltern gods as mediated by human will. At *Il.*17.319–41, for instance, Apollo assists Aeneas in battle by reassuring him that "Zeus desires the victory" of the Trojans over the Greeks, a piece of counsel that while patently untrue nonetheless temporarily alters the balance of war when Aeneas relays Apollo's message to his fellow Trojans, inspiring them to fight more boldly. The contrafactual that introduces the Homeric passage underscores the intended *psychological* effect of a divine intervention that works by enhancing or inhibiting the respective courage of each side: had the Trojans not been inspired by courage through the intervention of Apollo, "the Argives would have won glory beyond the dispensation of Zeus [*huper Dios aisan*] because of their might and their strength" (17.319–22).

In the two contrafactual statements made by Eve and Adam in their respective accounts of their creation, Milton's God intervenes in a similarly non-determining manner, providing moral guidance that Adam and Eve may or may not choose to heed. Eve explains how she might have "fixed / Mine eyes" forever on the reflection of her own image "Had not a voice warned me" (*PL* 4.465–7) to transfer her affection to Adam, a formula repeated at 8.311–12, where Adam states that he would have "new begun / My wandering, had not he who was my guide" appeared to instruct him. In neither case does the offer of divine counsel diminish Adam or Eve's liberty of conscience. The two contrafactuals dramatize the mystery of divine intervention but also its self-imposed limits: neither Adam nor Eve ultimately follows God's advice, thus generating a poignant irony through the proleptic glimpse offered by each contrafactual. The technique is a distinctively Homeric one: according to one scholar's reckoning there are 156 prolepses and 388 analepses, or moments of retrospection, in the *Iliad* alone, and they often create dramatic irony by drawing attention to a character who will act, or has acted, "in ignorance of his condition."[56] Although anticipated by God and by the reader, the fall in *Paradise Lost* is hardly inevitable, a theological point emphasized by the poem's frequent imitation of the *Iliad*'s "reversal passages," moments that "suggest alternatives" to the actual narrative of the poem by "transgressing" that narrative in a "speculative" or hypothetical manner.[57] Whereas the Homeric poet uses this convention in order to distinguish his version of events from the heroic tradition in which (or against which) he works,

Milton adapts contrafactuals and related formulae in order to disentangle divine foreknowledge from theological determinism.

Milton adapts the Homeric contrafactual into a strategy to "justify" God by demonstrating that divine intervention in human affairs does not eclipse liberty of conscience. Unlike the Zeus of Hesiod's *Theogony*, who requires all his *biê*, or force, to defeat the Titans, both Homer's Zeus and Milton's God reserve a power that they choose, repeatedly, *not* to use. Readers of both poets have periodically been troubled by the conditional and unrealized threats issued by Homeric and Miltonic deities, but by displaying an omnipotence that is potential rather than actual, Homer's Zeus and Milton's God engage neither in pretence nor in self-doubt but rather labour to preserve the human liberty upon which divine justice rests. By removing himself from the war in heaven, Milton's God allows each angel to decide for himself whether and how "to advance, or stand, or turn the sway / Of battle" (6.234–5), thus conserving individual spiritual agency and the opportunity for internal deliberation even in the midst of a hectic melée. God's decision to "suspen[d] their doom" for three days before the Son's intervention preserves that agency even more. Nothing in Milton's war in heaven *has* to happen the way it does; its entire outcome is constituted by a set of choices made by God, the Son, Satan, Abdiel, and each and every angel fighting on both sides.

The decision of Milton's God to remain uninvolved during the war in heaven also reflects the problem that (as Homer's Achilles puts it to Asteropaeus) "it is not possible to fight with God the son of Kronos" [*all'ouk esti Dii Kroniôni machesthai*] since combat with Zeus – as with Milton's God – would bring the battle, and the entire poem, to a grinding halt (*Il.* 21.193). Even as Milton's war in heaven imitates the Homeric idiom of "endless strife" [*akrita neikea*] and of "evenly strained conflict" [*isa machê tetato ptolemos*] that likewise marks the protracted fighting of Books 11 through 15 of the *Iliad*, the cords of war are stretched only so taut before the decisive intercession of Achilles and of Milton's Son, figures whose parallel roles reveal the sympathies between Homer's and Milton's conceptions of filial obedience and sacrifice (*Il.* 14.205, 15.413). As the only "solution" (*PL* 6.694) proposed by God to the war in heaven, Milton's Son has the duty of untying (Lat. *solutio*, untying or loosening) the cords of an otherwise "perpetual" battle between adversaries who regard themselves as equally matched in strength, using force only against those who "reason for their law refuse" (6.41).[58]

The voluntary sacrifice of Milton's Son, without which "all mankind / Must have been lost" (3.222–3), is answered by God's willingness to part with "my only Son" and "spare / Thee from my bosom and right hand" (3.278–9), a choice that imitates but also perfects Zeus's choice to sacrifice his mortal son Sarpedon in Book 16 of the *Iliad*.[59] Milton's Homeric source presents Zeus at what may well be his moment of greatest emotional conflict, when his "heart is divided [*dichtha*] in counsel" as he "ponder[s] in my thought" [*phresin hormainonti*] whether to save Sarpedon or to let him die (16.435–8). The decision is agonizing, and when it is made, Zeus "sheds bloody rain drops on the earth" (16.459) in an image that horrifies some of Homer's early Christian and Renaissance readers but gratifies others who find in Zeus's struggle between justice and pity pagan antecedents to Christian passion or *pietas*. Although Hera warns Zeus that if he preserves Sarpedon, he will "arouse dread resentment" among the other gods (16.459), Zeus's decision not to intervene on behalf of his son also prompts immediate accusations of injustice against him, laying bare the divine struggle to balance a pity that threatens to look like partiality against a justice that threatens to look like cruel indifference.

Many of Homer's Renaissance readers try to redeem Zeus's tears over Sarpedon from the criticisms of Plato and other ancient philosophers, who object to the idea that a god could prove so vulnerable to the emotion of grief.[60] Christian readers of the *Iliad* grasp with special intensity the anguish of a father who despite abundant paternal love willingly chooses to part with his son, even as they also struggle with the problem that Zeus's sacrifice may look like weakness, inconsistency, or indifference.[61] Sponde tackles the second of these objections in his commentary on *Od.* 3.236, where Athena observes that the gods cannot prevent the mortals they love from suffering death. Calling the sentiment "bold and too dangerous" [*audax & nimium periculosa*] if interpreted "nakedly" [*nudè*] or literally, Sponde reconciles Athena's claim to Christian doctrine by interpreting it to mean that if a god revokes a decree, he is "no god but a fickle and changeable monster" [*non erit Deus, sed monstrum aliquod mobile & incertum*].[62] Sponde's effort to make sense of the cruel indifference of the gods resurfaces in the mouths of the satanic and the fallen in *Paradise Lost*. Sin even quotes a phrase from the *Iliad* – citing it grossly out of context – when she resolves to join the "gods who live at ease" (2.868), an allusion to *Il.* 6.138, where Glaucus recounts how the "gods who live at ease" [*theoi rheia zôontes*] get angry at Lycurgus and blind him.[63] Glaucus's story in fact shows the Homeric gods to be rather distressed over, and involved in, mortal affairs. Its moral – "I would not wish to fight against the blessed gods" – is one that Sin might do well to heed (*Il.* 6.140).

Scales, Ploughmen, and Moral Threshing

This chapter began by proposing that Homeric metaphors of the "edges" or "ridges" of battle symbolize the central and persistent power of choice in *Paradise Lost*, whether in the war in heaven or in the poem's many scenes of deliberation. Milton likewise imitates Homer by creating a series of intermissions that punctuate the war in heaven: the "grateful truce" (6.407) of night, the numerous battlefield debates and councils, and the other pregnant pauses that make even "expectation [stand] / In horror" (6.306–7). Both poets have been criticized for their representation of these interstitial moments of combat, regarded by some readers as lacking in verisimilitude, disruptive to the narrative, or even mock-heroic. Yet such interludes make up the theological and moral core of the war in heaven, an event that would "surmoun[t] the reach / Of human sense" were it not accommodated, for Adam's benefit, to the "corporal forms" of epic combat (5.571, 5.573).[64]

Milton's decision to allow the war in heaven to hang "long time in even scale" (6.245) uses the intertwined Homeric motifs of counterpoise, hesitation, and uncertain victory to provide a symbolic commentary on the nature of divine justice and the consequences of human and angelic deliberation. Although the balance of Zeus, the even scales of war, and related images of weighing and pondering are imitated habitually and variously by later classical and Renaissance poets, only in Homeric epic do such formulae work together to produce such a resonant emblematic language for describing cosmic justice and conveying the urgency of moral counterpoise in the human sphere both within and outside the arena of war. In one of the *Iliad*'s most famous similes, an evenly matched battle is likened to the motions of a spinner as she "holds the balance [*talanta*] and raises the weight and the wool in either scale, making them equal [*isazous*]."[65] Although the simile may appear to conjure up associations with the Parcae, or Fates, as they spin, card, and cut the threads of human destiny, such a reading is contravened by the precarious counterbalance within the image, which depicts moments of decision that may end, for their participants, on either side of the perilous edge. The spinner's skill in balancing her weight and wool resembles the two-handed justice of Zeus, who grasps his scales "by the middle" [*de messa*], a detail that in Milton's handling transforms Zeus's scales into a metaphor for divine foreknowledge and judgment that does *not* convey God's foreordaining of human actions. When Homer's supreme God "stretches out his balances" [*etitaine talanta*] he does not decide the outcome of a conflict but rather ensures an even fight.[66]

Milton's most direct imitation of Zeus's balance, at *PL* 4.997–1002, reveals his effort to turn the subtle theological sympathies embedded in Homer's image into an explicit demonstration of "God's avoidance of unconditional predestination" that illustrates to its audience their liberty of conscience as well as the "sequel," or consequences, of the choices available to them.[67] Milton's simile is carefully interlaced with two other Homeric conventions, the contrafactual and the epic simile, both of which dramatize the razor-sharp edge of decisive moments whose outcomes are determined by the workings of the umpire conscience. The appearance of God's "golden scales" is occasioned by such a *krisis*: Satan has just concluded a scornful and threatening speech to Gabriel, prompting the squadron of angels surrounding God's messenger angel to turn "fiery red" and to "hem him round / With ported spears" (4.978–80). The gesture leads to one of Milton's most masterful imitations of a Homeric simile:

> With ported spears, as thick as when a field
> Of Ceres ripe for harvest waving bends
> Her bearded grove of ears, which way the wind
> Sways them; the careful ploughman doubting stands
> Lest on the threshing floor his hopeful sheaves
> Prove chaff. (4.980–5)

As an image of the "anxious assessment and uncertain weighing of alternatives," the simile epitomizes both the liberty and the fallibility of "deliberative reason" at work.[68] Illustrating what Danielson has called "the balance model of choice," the scales of Milton's God manifest a divine foreknowledge freed from suspicions of determinism. As Milton's God later explains, he does not "touch with lightest impulse" man's will but rather "to her own inclining left / In even scale" (10.45–7), a position seconded by the seventeenth-century theologian Henry Hammond, who uses the Homeric-biblical metaphor of the divine scales to explain how God foresees the decisions that "hang in the balance of humane indetermination" and how He "also foresee[s] which end of the balance doth at length overpoise."[69]

The simile's theological richness – and the identity of the mysterious ploughman, whose analogical counterpart in the poem's narrative has been much debated by Milton's critics – emerge into view when contrasted with its chief Homeric source at the beginning of Book 2 of the *Iliad*. Agamemnon relates his dream to the Achaean assembly and urges them to flee rather than persist in fighting towards a victory no longer deemed certain.

Nestor then relays Agamemnon's speech to "all those throughout the multitude who had not heard the council," at which point *hoi polloi* in this second, larger assembly [*agorê*] are "stirred like the long waves of the Icarian sea by the East Wind" and run towards their ships with "loud shouting ... / ... so eager were they to return home" (*Il.* 2.142–54). The Homeric simile describes a scene of mass panic, the most ignoble form of cowardice and one that Milton would have interpreted as an illustration of how the tyranny of false opinion makes it difficult to safeguard justice and liberty among the "throng and noises of Vulgar and irrational men."[70] Yet Milton adapts the simile into an emblem of the "better fortitude / Of patience" (9.31–2) on the part of angels who neither flee (like Homer's mob) nor rush headlong into battle, but instead choose "parting" – a temporary deferral of the conflict – as the most judicious option, an example of the best kind of "deliberate valour" (1.560) that Satan attempts to reproduce among the fallen angels but fails to achieve despite his repeated hesitations. For Milton, stubborn resolve must not be confused with true valour; only the latter involves the kind of battlefield pondering that prompts Milton's good angels to defer conflict until a later date.

The courage displayed by the good angels in Milton's simile thus offers a corrective to the shallow and reflexive heroism of Satan's troops, whose "fixèd thought" makes them resemble Homer's Trojans, soldiers whose "minds swerv[e] not" as they advance in battle (*PL* 1.560; *Il.* 13.135). When Achaean and Trojan troops confront each other in battle, Homer compares the cloud of white dust raised by the hooves of the warriors' horses to the effect of the wind separating the grain from the chaff such that the "heaps of chaff grow white" (*Il.* 5.499–504). Overlaid with scriptural implications, this Homeric simile is transformed by Milton into a scene of moral threshing in which the "careful ploughman" comes to symbolize the value of seasonableness and just deliberation over hasty and reckless action. The ploughman also constitutes Milton's most striking departure from his principal Homeric source: there is no ploughman in the simile from the *Iliad*, and thus no figure to preside over the unruly, windswept waves of the rabble and help them thresh out truth from fancy and opinion.[71] Although various identities have been proposed for Milton's ploughman, including Gabriel, God, and even Satan, none of these readings adequately accounts for *whose* deliberative process is represented by the simile. When studied alongside its Homeric analogues, the simile emerges as a vivid dramatization of the concurrent yet discrete operation of each angel's conscience, for Milton transforms Homer's mob, impelled by the contagious passions of rumour and fear, into a unified yet distinct group of individuals, each exercising his "careful" faculties of deliberation and of morally constructive "doubting."

There *are*, however, plenty of ploughmen embedded in other Homeric similes. As a translator of the Psalms, which begins with an image of God blowing away the ungodly "as chaff [*chnous*]," Milton discerns the moral and philological sympathies between Homeric and scriptural threshing and works these latent connections into his own simile.[72] When Homer describes how the wind, or winnowers, "separate [*krinê*] the grain from the chaff" on the "holy threshing-floors," he uses a verb [*krinein*] that means to separate physically but also to judge or to discriminate (*Il.* 5.501). Although shaped by the moral and spiritual threshing of the Psalms, the ploughman of Milton's simile also take their inspiration from the ploughmen on Achilles's shield, who appear alongside judges in the assembly as a symbol of *dikê* or distributive justice, a virtue instantiated in the two-way motion they create as they wheel their teams of oxen, "driving them back and forth" [*zeugea dineuontes elastreon entha kai entha*] (*Il.* 18.543). Next to Homer's ploughmen, on the shield, some reapers hold sickles in their hand as sheaves of wheat fall to the ground and are bound up with straw by another group of men while a "king, staff [*skêptron*] in hand" watches in gladness (18.555). Milton's simile shares a remarkable number of features with this image of distributive justice on the shield: as the fallen sheaves are carefully tended by labourers who separate wheat from chaff, a "king" – in Milton's case, God – watches closely but does not intervene except to lift up the scales whose juridical function is mirrored by the moral "ploughing" of his angels.

The appearance of God's scales at *PL* 4.997–1002 is designed to assist this process of moral threshing – to clarify the angels' choices and perhaps to remind them that the choice of "parting" is the one favoured by God. Unlike Homer's Achaeans, Milton's angels are not motivated by fear, thus explaining why God intervenes so as to thwart not flight but "fight" – to "prevent" the "horrid fray" which "[m]ight have ensued" had the angels chosen to initiate violence against Satan (4.990–1, 4.996). Like the other contrafactuals analysed above, this one stresses the conditional and consular nature of divine intervention: all God does to impede the horrid fray is to hold aloft a pair of scales in order to help clarify a moral decision that still remains the responsibility of each angel, such that the fray "might" not have ensued even without His intercession.

The theological weight of the passage derives from Milton's subtle and complex rereading of the first 130 lines of Book 8 of the *Iliad*, in which Homer interlaces two contrafactual statements with the related metaphors of the golden chain and the scales of Zeus. These images are also tightly interwoven in the final lines of Book 4 of *Paradise Lost*, where they participate collectively in illustrating the mutually supportive relationship between human liberty and divine justice. The theodicy articulated in the final moments of Book 4, moreover, is startlingly similar to that of *Iliad* 8: in both poems, God (or Zeus) counsels but does not confine the human will with his balance, an instrument that in Homer's version strikes "wonder, and pale fear" into the Achaeans rather than constraining their still-plural – and thus still undecided – *kêres*, or fates (*Il.* 8.77, 8.73). Milton's God likewise lifts up his scales in order to provoke fear and awe, and although the angels are assisted by this demonstration of justice, Satan is not, suggesting that even a divine sign as heavy-handed as a pair of scales may, in Milton's cosmos, be vulnerable to misinterpretation.

Milton's interlacement of this trio of Homeric conventions (ploughman simile, contrafactual, and the scales of Zeus) in the final lines of Book 4 of *Paradise Lost* demonstrates his imitation of Homeric epic to be less mediated by later epic than some recent critics have claimed. Nowhere save perhaps in Tasso's *Gerusalemme Liberata* do these interrelated Homeric symbols and narrative strategies form such a coherent ethical and spiritual idiom for describing both divine and human processes of deliberation and adjudication. Milton crowns his imitation of Iliadic metaphors of pondering at the end of Book 4 by reworking Homer's conception of justice as *dikê* – that is, as distribution or division: "all things created first [God] weighed, / The pendulous round earth with balanced air / In counterpoise" (4.999–1001). Enfolding Homer's scales of Zeus into the distinctly Homeric image of a "pendulous" or "pendant" (2.1052) world, Milton's image envisions the golden chain as the result of divine justice, the consequence of Zeus stretching out his golden scales and thus sustaining the "counterpoise" that is the defining feature of justice in the *Iliad* as well as in *Paradise Lost.*

Miltonic *Dusboulia*: Satanic Pondering

With his golden scales, Milton's God "*ponders* all events" (*PL* 4.1001) in the fullest and most Latinate sense of the word. *Paradise Lost* derives from Homeric epic a conception of justice as a truly deliberative act.[73] Yet Satan also ponders: he is a character who deliberates almost obsessively throughout the poem but often "falls into many doubts with himself, and many passions" (*PL* 4, Argument). These repeated hesitations are mirrored and perhaps even parodied in Chaos: where the "high arbiter" of Chance, rather than divine justice, "governs all," atoms "poise" ever so briefly before resuming their incessant motion, thus permitting a "moment" of counterpoise among the striving elements (2.905–10). Yet unlike the umpire conscience, the adjudication of Chaos "by decision more embroils the fray / By which he reigns," its judgments perpetuating strife rather than resolving it (2.908–9). Milton's image of atoms "poising" – as if pausing to arbitrate between alternate courses of action – articulates on a cosmological level the dangers posed by Satanic pondering, by the habit of returning again and again to a razor's edge of contrary choices and, invariably, choosing wrongly. As in Chaos, where the temporary "poise" of atoms is disrupted by only by the impulse to factionalize into "clans," Satan's infernal peers achieve a fleeting "suspense" by "[p]ondering ... with deep thoughts" yet resolving nothing, suggesting that anarchy is not so much a perpetual state of disorder as it is a perpetual state of indecision (2.901, 2.418, 2.421).

Satan's predilection for pondering yokes him, albeit ironically, to Odysseus, the epic hero most adept at skills of deliberation and planning for which he is alternately celebrated and demonized by Renaissance readers of the *Odyssey*. At the beginning of *PL* 4, as the sun, "high in his meridian tower," totters on the perilous edge of noon, Satan engages in "much revolving" before delivering a soliloquy that reveals a mind tottering on the brink between alternatives before it ultimately regresses to its original plan (4.30–1). The image of his "revolving" mind links Satan's deliberative process to the motions of the planetary bodies around him, the diurnal revolutions of day and night that set down a cosmic pattern imitated by the umpire conscience. At high noon, a "timeless moment during which the course of nature is interrupted," Satan is poised on the razor's edge of alternative choices, gripped by an irresolution that is reflected in the momentary ambivalence of a sun that appears, for one brief instant, as if it might dip down on either side of the horizon.[74] Yet here, as at the beginning of Book 9, where "after long debate, irresolute / Of thoughts resolved" (9.87–8) he opts to assume the form of a serpent in order to tempt Eve, Satan's deliberative faculty is shown to be defective: were his will not corrupted by Sin, Satan might instead be deliberating *whether* to tempt Eve, rather than how to do so most effectively. Satan's irresolute "revolving" of this question – the wrong question – shows just how feebly his fallen conscience is able to "judge between the alternatives which persistently confron[t]" it. As Milton points out in *The Reason of Church Government*, "vertue that wavers is not vertue, but vice revolted from itselfe, and after a while returning," a circular pattern mirrored by the revolutions of Satan's thought process.[75]

Satan's predilection for "pondering" perverts the judicious prudence of Odysseus, a character who repeatedly weighs alternatives by "turning over in his mind and heart" [*hôrmaine kata phrêna kai kata thumon*] the decisions that confront him (*Il.* 11.410–11).[76] At times, Odysseus's capacity for pondering seems calculating or even sinister, as when, struck by a footstool thrown at him by Antinous, he does not retaliate but instead remains silent, "pondering evil [*kaka bussodomeuôn*] deep in his heart" (*Od.* 17.465). But whereas Odysseus benefits from the wisdom of Athena in his deliberations, Milton's Satan has the rather dubious assistance of Sin, Athena's demonic alter ego, a creature likewise born out of a cannibalistic union between a figure of counsel and his *mêtis* that symbolizes the grotesque perversion of the deliberative process. Even as Milton "systematically alludes to Odysseus" in his depictions of Satan, Satan ultimately "contravenes the values that Odysseus embodies" even (and especially) at those very moments where he ponders his situation in explicitly Odyssean terms.[77]

In a similar manner, Milton's rebel angels diverge from Odysseus's deliberative habits of mind when they contemplate their course of action during the war in heaven, concluding wrongly that they will suffer shame regardless of whether they flee or fight:

> What should they do? If on they rushed, repulse
> Repeated, and indecent overthrow
> Doubled, would render them yet more despised,
> And to their foes a laughter; for in view
> Stood ranked of seraphim another row
> In posture to displode their second tire
> Of thunder: back defeated to return
> They worse abhorred. (6.600–7)

If Milton's rebel angels fail to see their options in the terms laid out by Odysseus, who deliberates whether to flee or to "hold his ground boldly" when he finds himself alone on the battlefield (*Il.* 11.410–11), it is partly because they are immortal, and thus cannot weigh the shame of a cowardly escape against the glory of a noble death. It is also because the choices open to Homeric heroes in their battlefield deliberations are morally insufficient in the world of *Paradise Lost*, a poem in which to enter battle (or to avoid it) may or may not prove shameful depending upon the side for which one fights. Certain of their righteous cause, the angels who remain on God's side need not deliberate at all: "no thought of flight, /

None of retreat" enters their minds (6.236–7).[78] Rather than cling with Satanic irresolution to the razor's edge between moral alternatives, Milton's good angels exercise their "manly confidence" through their spiritual autonomy: "each on himself relied, / As only in his arm the moment lay / Of victory," a self-reliance that devalues traditional epic virtues of cooperation and unity in battle in favour of a singular and "momentous" conscience (6.238–40).

In Pandaemonium, as in Chaos, the attainment of a fleeting equilibrium between moral alternatives is in and of itself an insufficient guarantor of virtue. Milton's devils also ponder – indeed, they do so more frequently and more perceptibly than do the poem's other characters. Acting as an agent of demonic "deliberation" and "counsel" (2.303–4), Beelzebub triggers a moment of collective pondering when he concludes his final speech in Book 2's infernal council:

> This said, he sat: and expectation held
> His look suspense, awaiting who appeared
> To second, or oppose, or undertake
> The perilous attempt: but all sat mute,
> Pondering the danger with deep thoughts. (2.417–21)

The scene imitates the Achaean reaction to each of Hector's two challenges in the *Iliad*, both of which conclude with the line, "So he spoke, and they all became hushed with silence" (3.95, 7.92). Like Homer's Achaeans, who "were ashamed [*aidesthen*] to refuse [Hector] but feared [*deisan*] to take up the challenge," Milton's rebel angels deliberate silently whether the honour to be gained from Beelzebub's proposed mission outweighs its potential risks.[79] Even as they comprehend the choice that lies before them in distinctly Homeric terms – they are weighing the dangers of honour-seeking against the shame that accompanies the coward's retreat to safety – Milton's devils fail to consider the full weight of those alternatives, committing an error that becomes more visible when we compare their reaction to that of Homer's Menelaus, who responds to the first of Hector's two challenges by affirming his obedience to "the oaths of God" [*Dios horkia*] and by stressing the wisdom of "looking both before and after" [*hama prossô kai opissô / leussei*] (*Il.* 3.107, 3.109–10). The latter phrase, repeated by Achilles at *Il.* 3.343, is interpreted by Sponde as a lesson about the "prudent man," who must "not ignore both the antecedents and the consequences of a course of action" [*principia et causas rerum videre, earumque progressus, et quasi antecessiones non ignorare*].[80] By contrast, neither the imprudent Satan nor the rebel angels in the infernal council display much capacity for the forward- and backward-looking wisdom that together constitute Homeric *mêtis*, nor do they exercise the good judgment exemplified by Menelaus in his reaction to the second of Hector's challenges to the Achaean council. In that scene, Menelaus responds to the hushed silence of his fellow Greeks by reviling them and then volunteering for the mission himself, a gesture of heroic recklessness that might appear to make him a convincing analogue for Satan were it not for the fact that Agamemnon restrains him, counselling Menelaus that he is "mad" [*aphrosunês*] to "fight in rivalry [*eridos … machesthai*] with one better than you" and thus "turning [*parapeisen*] his brother's mind" (*Il.* 7.110–11, 7.120). With advisors that make "the worse appear / The better reason," Satan lacks the good counsel that preserves Menelaus from committing the similarly hubristic folly of fighting against an invincible adversary: there is no one in Pandaemonium able to "counsel rightly" [*aisima pareipôn*; literally, counterweigh evenly] as Agamemnon does for his brother (*PL* 2.113–14). Moreover, Satan has even more *aphrosunê* than Homer's Menelaus: whereas Menelaus foolishly believes he can vanquish Hector, a powerful mortal, Satan believes he can vanquish an omnipotent God.

Milton's reliance upon this episode from the *Iliad* to accentuate Satan's delusional pride develops out of his appreciation that Homer's repeated moralizing on the danger of fighting against God has parallels in both the Old and New Testaments, parallels frequently noted by other seventeenth-century scholars. Duport catalogues several Homeric proverbs about the folly of taking on the gods as adversaries: he compares Aphrodite's observation that "that man endures not for long who fights with the immortals" (*Il.* 5.407) to Acts 23.9 ("*Ne pugnemus cum Deo*"), while Menelaus's assertion that "with Zeus, you may be sure, no mortal man can vie [*erizoi*]" (*Od.* 4.78) corresponds to Isa. 45.9 ("*Vae contendenti cum fictore suo*"), the verse in which the clay is chastised for contending with its potter.[81] Milton's program of classical and scriptural allusions in *Paradise Lost* shares certain methodological sympathies with Duport, who was only two years older than Milton, his contemporary at Cambridge, and from 1639 onwards, Robert Creighton's successor as the Regius Professor of Greek.[82] Yet unlike Duport's *Homeri Gnomologia* and other contemporary scholarship that aims to collate Homeric epic with verses in the Old and New Testaments, the analogical relationships and parallels forged in *Paradise Lost* are complex and unstable. In the infernal council of Book 2 alone, Beelzebub encompasses aspects of Nestor and Odysseus, Belial echoes the voice of the dream sent by Zeus to Agamemnon as well as

Thersites's approval of the dream's message, Moloch incorporates aspects of Achilles, Thersites, and Odysseus, and Satan alternately assumes the roles of Agamemnon, Achilles, Odysseus, and a host of Homeric gods including Eris, Ares, and Zeus.[83]

This dizzying kaleidoscope of shifting correspondences reflects Milton's ambivalence towards certain Homeric characters and values. It also reflects the skill with which Satan and his fallen angels perform a self-conscious impersonation of Homeric heroism. The world of classical epic is a stage on which Satan plays many parts, most of them rather unconvincingly.[84] Within the space of five hundred lines, Milton casts Satan as a reckless and unrestrained Menelaus, a fierce yet obtuse Ajax, an Agamemnon-like leader struggling to maintain authority over his assembly, a flawed Sarpedon who fails to grasp the mutuality of honour, a Diomedes who refuses to acknowledge the value of cooperation, and a deviously "prudent" Odysseus who "prevent[s] all reply" by his council so that he may undertake the journey to Eden alone (2.467–8). By modifying, repeatedly, the epic roles assumed by Satan, Milton reveals his demonic powers of mimicry: if the Son assumes aspects of Achilles, or Sarpedon, then so may his devilish rival, thus allowing Milton to forge *in bono et in malo* versions of various Homeric characters in order to "invit[e] discriminations that are at once literary and moral" on the part of the reader.[85] Satan's impersonation of various Homeric heroes also exposes the errors or defects in his own process of deliberation: when confronted with choices similar to those faced by Homer's heroes, Satan invariably makes the wrong decisions, decisions based on his flawed understanding of heroic virtue.

A closer examination of Book 2's infernal council bears out the pivotal role played by problems of deliberation in Milton's program of Homeric allusions. Only after Agamemnon restrains Menelaus – as Satan, too, should and could have been restrained had the spirit of Homeric *eubolia* thrived more vigorously in his own assembly – does Nestor propose to cast lots [*klêros*] in order to determine which of the Achaeans will face Hector in combat. As the rebel angels rejoice at their "matchless chief" (2.487) after their leader volunteers for his *aristeia*, the scene casts Satan as Ajax, who elicits a similar joy in his fellow Argives when he emerges fully armed for combat "with a smile on his grim face" [*meidoôn blosuroisi prosôpasi*] (*Il.* 7.212). Yet unlike Satan, who manipulates his assembly so that his own "devilish counsel" (2.379) may prevail, Ajax is chosen by lottery. Although this lottery uncannily yields the very result for which the Greek troops have prayed (*Il.* 7.177–80), Homer's contest is decided by chance rather than by demonic calculation, underscoring the fraudulence of Satan's repeated appeals to "hazard" (1.89, 2.473) and "danger" (4.934) in order to authenticate his heroic virtue.

While some of *Paradise Lost*'s adaptations of Homeric "pondering" scenes reflect Milton's perceived affinity between the liberty of conscience enjoyed by Homer's heroes and his own theology of free will, Book 2's infernal council works the convention in a different direction by representing the "pondering" of the rebel angels to be deficient and disingenuous. Not a single member of the assembly chooses to set a foot forward with the "manly confidence" required to stride the razor's edge between the peril of honour and the dishonour of safety. This is, of course, the desired result: Beelzebub's speech is "first devised / By Satan, and in part proposed" (2.379–80), a detail that reveals the proceedings of Satan's assembly to be "mere theatre" orchestrated by a thinly disguised tyrant whose manipulation of his audience resembles the Charles I of Milton's *Eikonoklastes*.[86] Even though the narrator comments, sardonically, that the rebel angels "vote" with "full assent," it is not at all clear whether that vote is the product of "inclination or sad choice" (2.388–91, 2.524).

While many critics have observed that Milton's Pandaemonium allows for little, if any, deliberation, a few readers have detected "genuine debate" in hell, and many more have interpreted the scene as a "classic presentation of the abuses of democratic assembly" in which debate is staged only to be shut down by a ruler whose most salient difference from Milton's God is his intolerance of conflict.[87] While "unity is the keynote" in Book 3's heavenly council, too, the unity of Milton's heaven is produced by different means – it is voluntary, not constrained, rooted in love and reason, not in fear or in "doubtful consultations" (2.486). Regardless of whether one views the infernal assembly as a "genuine exercise in deliberation," a failed attempt at parliamentary procedure, or a tyranny in disguise, *Paradise Lost* represents the institution of the council as an exclusively Satanic and postlapsarian mode of deliberation. Milton's interweaving of Homeric allusions in the council scenes of Book 2 must be interpreted accordingly. Each and every instance of the words "council" and "counsel" (as well as related terms such as "counsell'd" and "counselors") in the poem describes an action taking place in Pandaemonium or on earth after the fall, perhaps reflecting Milton's belief that councils, of which he finds "no trace in Scripture," are not institutions sanctioned by divine "inspiration" and thus are "liable to error."[88] The sole reference to God's "inmost counsels" (1.168) comes from Satan's mouth, and the only time Milton's good angels use the term is to condemn the "counsels vain" of their apostate brethren (7.610), a censure that echoes Psalms 1, 5, and 83, all translated by Milton.[89] After the fall, intuitive reasoning gives way to the highly flawed deliberative mode of counsel: Adam "counsel[s]" Eve to cover up her naked body (9.1099); Eve, in a moment of despair, asks for Adam's "counsel" (10.920) but is not comforted or swayed by it; Enoch disrupts and rebukes the "council" described by Michael when its participants fall to "harangues" and "factious opposition" (11.663–4).

Milton's alarm at the moral and political inefficacy of deliberation in council helps to explain his frequent borrowings of similes drawn from the Achaean assembly in Book 2 of the *Iliad*, an episode that illustrates Homer's keen awareness of the threat posed to assemblies by the tyrannical grip of passion and opinion. Adapting Homer's comparison of the Greek troops fleeing the Achaean agora to "tribes of swarming bees emerg[ing] from some hollow rock, constantly coming on afresh," Milton characterizes the unruly and impulsive behaviour of Satan's infernal peers in the assembly to "bees" who "[t]hick swarmed" as they "expatiate and confer / Their state affairs" (*Il.* 2.87–8; *PL* 1.768, 1.774–5). The simile owes almost everything to Homer, and almost nothing to Virgil: Milton's bees epitomize a superficial or instinctive conformity that masks both hostility and hierarchy. Like Homer's bees, Milton's atoms "[s]warm populous," and his "numberless" hordes of rebel angels "[t]hick swar[m]" as they gather in assembly, metaphors that draw upon Homeric representations of the eristic spirit of the agora in order to give voice to Milton's concern that England has failed to establish a "full and free Councel ... where no single person, but reason only swaies."[90]

Milton's Homeric bees partake of none of the true "commonalty" enjoyed by the "parsimonious emmet," the creature praised in Milton's account of creation as a "[p]attern of just equality" and a blueprint for a republicanism rooted in nature (*PL* 7.484, 487–9). Not all equality in *Paradise Lost* is "just equality," however, and Satan repeatedly corrupts this Miltonic value by conflating it with conformity. Satan's principal vehicle for enforcing this conformity is the council, an institution that in *Paradise Lost*, as in the *Iliad*, threatens to allow the collective fear or moral turpitude of the mob to extirpate individual agency. The events of the 1650s heighten Milton's concern that councils and assemblies allow passion, opinion, and blind partisanship to triumph over right reason.[91] When Milton reworks Homeric council scenes for the opening books of *Paradise Lost*, he places conventional personifications of *dusboulia* in Pandaemonium as well as in Chaos, a nightmarish vision of a council gone awry, governed by "Rumour," "Tumult and Confusion all embroiled, / And Discord with a thousand various mouths" (2.964–6). The "hubbub universal wild" (2.951) of Chaos reflects Milton's genuine fear that the tyrannous sway of "usurpt opinions" throws parliamentary governments into disorder, but it also reflects the spiritually misguided and politically questionable dread of rebellion embodied by Satan, who contrives to represent Pandaemonium as a place where devils united in "mutual league" (1.87) may cooperate and "share" in their adversity like "associates and copartners" rather than rivals (1.265, 1.267).

Satan travesties not only the solitary heroics of Homer's Odysseus but also the collaborative and cooperative values intrinsic to Homeric heroism. In assembly, Satan makes solitary decisions *appear* to be communal, decided by a "vote" after "long debate" (2.390–1). Milton dramatizes this process by infusing irony into a tissue of Homeric allusions in the infernal council of Book 2 of *Paradise Lost*. For all of Satan's virtuoso imitations of Homeric heroism, including his Homeric emphasis upon unity and cooperation ("union, and firm faith, and firm accord"), Milton's council scenes rework Homeric scenes of assembly in order to voice a deep distrust of communal deliberation, a distaste for popular democracy that Milton discerns in the Homeric poems (*PL* 2.36).[92] The problem that majority rule does not always yield the correct decision informs two episodes in the *Odyssey* in which Odysseus's crew act against their leader's better judgment, first opening Aeolus's windbag and then eating the cattle of the sun. In both episodes, Odysseus is unable to sway his crew because they are greater in number. Duport turns Odysseus's observation at *Od.* 10.46, "the evil counsel of my comrades prevailed" [*Boulê de kakê nikêsen etairôn*], into a Latin adage, "*Consilium malum vicit sociorum,*" collating the line with several scriptural parallels, including 1 Kgs. 12.14, where Rehoboam rejects the advice given to him by the elders of his assembly, and 2 Sam. 17.14, where Absalom dismisses the good counsel of Achitophel in favour of the bad advice of another counsellor.[93] Milton highlights the danger posed by majority rule in councils and assemblies by demonstrating the failures of the popular vote as a deliberative tool in Pandaemonium, a lesson reinforced at the end of the poem where we meet Noah, Enoch, and other biblical heroes who appear as Old Testament analogues to Odysseus, figures who rise up in "factious opposition" against majority opinion only to be rejected or ignored.

The hollowness of Satan's repeated appeals to unity and cooperation is reinforced by Milton's revision of several related scenes from the *Iliad* in which heroes choose to enlist the assistance of fellow soldiers or companions to bolster their honour or their military advantage. Despite his jingoistic appeal to the "mutual league" into which he has entered with his "faithful friends" – language that travesties the heroic convention of rousing battlefield speeches made by characters ranging from Achilles to Shakespeare's Henry V – Satan is unwilling to share the hazard or the honour of his "glorious enterprise" (1.87, 1.264, 1.89). Satan's stifling of his "rivals" (2.468) inverts the normal outcome of Homeric pondering scenes, in which warriors such as Deïphobus "debated [*mermêrizen*] whether he should give ground and take as comrade some one of the great-hearted Trojans, or should make trial [*peirêsaito*, literally, test the limits] by himself alone" (*Il.* 13.455–7). In a more familiar version of this kind of dilemma, Diomedes requests the company of Odysseus during the *Doloneia* in Book 10 of the *Iliad*, reasoning that a partner will provide "greater comfort" and "greater confidence" since "When two go together, one discerns before the other the most profitable course; alone, if one discerns anything, his discernment [*noos*] is weaker, and his skill [*mêtis*] the smaller" (*Il.* 10.222–6). Despite his pretentions to be a newfangled Odysseus whose heroic virtue resides in his prudence and his submission to trials of experience, Satan in fact forsakes Odyssean *mêtis* at the very moment that he "prevent[s] all reply, / Prudent," thus disallowing any additional volunteers for the journey to Eden and exemplifying a prudence that only serves to distance him from his Homeric model (2.467–8).[94]

When Homeric warriors such as Diomedes or Deïphobus debate whether to enlist a companion-in-arms, their decision is predicated on the belief that honour is not a quantifiable and finite commodity but rather a substance that increases when it is shared. Satan fails to grasp that the pursuit of honour is not a zero-sum game. His decision to embark alone on his voyage to Eden casts him as an inverted Diomedes and also an inverted Sarpedon, the Trojan warrior and mortal son of Zeus who achieves heroic stature by embracing the spirit of cooperation that is the essential counterpart to Homeric *timê*. In a speech regarded by many Renaissance readers as the pinnacle of Homeric heroism, Sarpedon asks Glaucus "why it is that we two are most held in honour" [*Glauke, ti ê dê nôi tetimêmessa malista*] and asserts that the honour they share obliges both soldiers to "take our stand amongst the foremost Lycians," a sentiment that prompts Sarpedon to invite Glaucus to "go forward" with him into battle "whether we shall give glory to another, or another to us" (*Il.* 12.310, 315, 327–8). For Sarpedon, *kudos* is not a quantifiable prize that must be seized from a competitor; instead, it is a virtue that, like charity or mercy, may be gained, or increased, by sharing it or giving it away. Although *Paradise Lost* is filled with figures of heroic singularity who establish themselves as moral authorities by resisting the centripetal forces of community,

Milton is careful to distinguish the courageous solitude of Abdiel, Enoch, and Noah from the satanic misapprehension that the solitary hero gains a greater share of honour. When Satan tempts Eve, he does so by reversing the logic of Sarpedon's speech to Glaucus, persuading her that the "odds" of honour and power might tilt in her favour should she undertake her pseudo-heroic trial without "copartner" (9.820–1). In his refusal to grant any "collegial role in counsel or in action to others," Satan fails to emulate the Homeric hero whom Milton appears to admire above all others, praising Sarpedon in the *Pro Populo Anglicano Defensio* as a virtuous ruler who wisely recognizes how "the mob is wont to flatter its kings."[95]

Miltonic Fables of Mêtis

The complex tissue of Homeric allusions interwoven into the texture of *Paradise Lost*'s infernal council scenes indicates that while Milton admires Homer's attention to the deliberative process and approves of the moral choices made by some of his characters, he also recognizes how easily individual and collective deliberation can both go awry. Satan's persistent misrepresentation of the political and spiritual values of harmony and unity reflects Milton's concern that conformity is a damaging force in the assembly, a force that extirpates right reason. Satan's perversion of true concord into "horrid sympathy" (10.540) alerts Milton's readers to the dangers of collective decision-making in the assembly as in marriage, institutions in which *homophrosunê*, or like-mindedness, may become overvalued or distorted so as to erode the primacy of the individual conscience.[96]

Nowhere are these dangers better illustrated than in the incestuous liaison between Satan and Sin, a union that travesties the conciliar intimacy enjoyed by God and the Son by misappropriating Homeric models of good counsel. Sin's plea to Satan to desist from fighting against his own son constitutes what Barbara Lewalski has called a "grotesquely comic reprise" of one of the *Iliad*'s conventional type-scenes of familial love, in which a female supplicant (Andromache, Thetis, or Hecuba) implores her husband or son not to enter battle.[97] Knit together in *stasis* by what Colin Burrow has called a "hideously etiolated version of Homeric fellow-feeling," Milton's counter-trinity of Satan, Sin, and Death engage in a form of kinship founded upon the mutual "destruction" of adversaries "so matched" that each is "involved" in the other's "end" (2.807).[98]

As the protagonists in an allegorical fable of *dusboulia*, or bad counsel, Satan and Sin dramatize the dangers inherent in conciliar relationships, in particular the relationship between king and counsellor. The cannibalistic union of Zeus and Mêtis, narrated in full by Hesiod and also alluded to by Homer, is routinely interpreted as a myth of *eubolia* (good counsel) for Renaissance poets and mythographers, a "secret of government" that instructs rulers how best to digest the "wise counsel" [*epiphrona boulên*] offered by their counsellors so as to "preserve their authoritie and Majestie free and entire."[99] According to Francis Bacon, the myth of Zeus and Mêtis illustrates how rulers should "tie themselves to their councils with a bond like that of wedlock" yet cultivate the appearance of an "unconstrained authority and will" so that their strategies and decisions seem "shaped in the womb" rather than hammered out through debate.[100] Milton's Satan does precisely the opposite in Book 2's infernal assembly, using Beelzebub as a mouthpiece to ventriloquize his own "devilish counsel" in a reversal that reveals Satan's cunning pretence of deflecting authority to his counsellors in order to perpetuate the illusion that he is a republican leader rather than an absolute monarch.

Paradise Lost's revisionary interpretation of the myth of Zeus and Mêtis is fuelled by Milton's concern, particularly acute after the end of the Protectorate, that the perpetual establishment of a "full and free Councel" in England has been compromised by the rapacious tyranny of popular opinion in which members of parliaments are guided by "fear or perswasion" rather than by "reason" or "safetie." In *The Readie and Easie Way*, Milton laments how some parliaments have become "so heartless and unwise in their counsels, as not to know how to use it, value it, what to do with it or with themselves," a complaint refracted in his monstrous rewriting of the myth of Zeus and Mêtis.[101] In Milton's version of the myth, Satan and Sin consummate their diabolical union "at the assembly" of the empyreal host in heaven – the very assembly at which God anoints the Son – thus spawning the "[d]eep malice" and "disdain" that begin to fester inside Satan at 5.666. Once swallowed, Sin is reborn, springing out of Satan's head "a goddess armed," much like the "*poluboulos*" [much-in-counsel] Athena as she appears in the *Iliad* and in the *Homeric Hymn to Athena*, which recounts (in Chapman's fanciful translation) her birth out of "Jove-the-great-in-counsaile's very braine."[102] Engendered at an assembly, Sin conveys Milton's deep distrust of such institutions, creating an aetiology of sin that locates its origin not *within* Satan but rather as inherent in the pernicious relationship that develops *between* two participants in the celestial council.[103]

Despite being cast as the protagonist in Milton's version of the fable of Zeus and Mêtis, Satan in fact *lacks mêtis* – good counsel, prudence, or foresight – throughout the poem. This shortcoming, accentuated by his ironic imitation of Odysseus, is also evident in the germination of Satan's plan to overthrow God. When describing how the malicious plot is hatched, Milton's narrator wryly inserts the detail that Satan's design is to "dislodge, and leave Unworshipped" God's throne, as if it has not yet occurred to Satan that he might take God's place (6.669–70). At the very moment that Satan "conceiv[es]" Sin, he wakes Beelzebub in order to issue a sinister rendition of a famous piece of Homeric good counsel: "Sleepst thou companion dear, what sleep can close / Thy eyelids?" (5.673–4), Satan asks, chastising his "next subordinate" (5.671) for failing to live up to the Homeric ideal of the wakeful and vigilant commander. In the opening lines of Book 2 of the *Iliad*, quoted by Milton in an early prolusion, a dream of rather suspect origins counsels Agamemnon: "Do you sleep, son of battle-minded, horse-taming Atreus? A man that is a counsellor [*boulêphoron andra*] must not sleep the whole night through" (*Il.* 2.23–5).[104] These lines attained the status of a proverb for many Renaissance readers, but Milton treats the adage ironically, making Satan, for the second time in the poem, the mouthpiece for a dream that deludes rather than advises.[105] Like Homer's Zeus, Milton's God stays up all night: the "roseate dews" that arrive at the end of Book 5 "disposed / All but the unsleeping eyes of God to rest" (5.646–7). But wakefulness is not in and of itself a guarantor of virtue in *Paradise Lost*, for while it symbolizes divine omniscience, it also provides Satan with the opportunity to "infuse[e] / Bad influence" into the "unwary breast" of his counsellor (6.694–5). Despite the superficial parallels between the nocturnal council scenes of both poems (*Il.* 9.1–181 and *PL* 6.406–97) and between *Il.* 8.485–7 and Milton's description of night approaching on the eve of the war in heaven, sleepless vigilance does not ensure the healthy deliberation or moral insight in *Paradise Lost* that it does in the *Iliad*.

Contrary to Renaissance mythographers, who interpret the myth of Zeus and Mêtis as a parable about how leaders should ponder and digest the counsels received by them, Milton distorts this moral in order to cast doubt on the spiritual and political efficacy of collective deliberation. When Satan, newly arrived in Pandaemonium, tells the rebel angels that "these thoughts / Full counsel must mature," he is endorsing a conventional definition of *mêtis*, or prudent deliberation, that Milton has already questioned and modified in *The Reason of Church Government*, writing that "many things are first crude and hard to digest, which only time and deliberation can supply, and concoct. But in religion wherein is no immaturity, nothing out of season, it goes farre otherwise. The doore of grace turnes upon smooth hinges wide opening to send out, but soon shut[s]."[106]

In matters of faith, decisions made quickly and according to right reason are likelier to be correct than those arrived at through the full gestation of council, a process that may generate irresolution or downright error. When the rebel angels draw "[m]illions of flaming swords" in order "to confirm [Satan's] words," their gesture imitates Achilles, who unsheathes his sword against Agamemnon only to be restrained by Athena (*PL* 1.663–4; *Il.* 1.194–8). In the midst of "pondering [*hormaine*] in his mind and his heart" whether to kill Agamemnon or curb his *thumos*, Achilles is assisted by the goddess of wisdom, born out of the union of Zeus and Mêtis. Milton's rebel angels receive no such guidance, either because they do not ponder sufficiently or, perhaps, because theirs is a dilemma not to be resolved through pondering.

Miltonic *Themistas* and the Politics of Council

The failure of the English Civil War was, for Milton, largely a failure of the institution of the council. Particularly from the mid-1650s onwards, Milton laments the reflexive partisanship that grips human assemblies, recalling how the Rump Parliament laid a strong foundation for the Commonwealth but then fell into a "wors confusion, not of tongues, but of factions, then those at the tower of Babel."[107] Political disorder is not, for Milton, the product of rebellious singularity; rather, it is fostered by the misguided conformity of the throng, a belief that motivates his imitations of Homeric assembly scenes as well as his use of the term "anarch," a word used twice in Book 2 of the *Iliad* to describe the threat posed by leaderless armies.[108] Milton's interpretation of Homeric council scenes, scenes often regarded as the "motive forces" behind epic action in the poems, rests on his perception that councils and assemblies may generate both beneficial and injurious expressions of conflict.[109] By the 1650s, Milton had come to accept that the most dangerous form of conflict in council is produced by the fear-induced conformity of the "rabble" and by the tendency for participants in political and ecclesiastical assemblies to produce "endles matter of dissention."[110] While Milton clearly regards "free and open" debate as necessary for the preservation of political liberty, his political writings of the late 1650s reflect an increasing disgust at the "triviall and vaine" disputes that grip councils and thus "unsettle" the commonwealth by "breed[ing] commotions, changes, novelties and uncertainties."[111] Yet Milton is careful to distinguish between "tedious and unprofitable" disputes in councils and the productive conflict that aims to establish truth in the assembly: as he argues in the *Readie and Easie Way*, "seams in the same cloath, neither hurt the garment, nor misbecome it" so long as the cause for disagreement is just and valid.[112]

Paradise Lost contains several figures who emulate this wisdom by protesting injustice in the agora. But when Enoch and Noah rise up against their respective assemblies by combatting "factious opposition" and preaching "Conversion and repentance," they are (respectively) harassed and ignored, a poignant testimony to the unattainable Miltonic ideal of a council in which "no single person but reason only swaies" (11.665, 11.724). It is impossible to ignore that in *Paradise Lost*, discord enters the world through a council, as well as through the "synod unbenign" formed by the erratic motions of the stars after the fall (10.661). To dramatize the spiritual and political failures of assembly, Milton transforms the epic convention of the council scene so as to downplay the threat posed by "division of opinions" and to substitute for it the greater threat of conformity.[113] Sharon Achinstein has persuasively shown how Milton revises for his own political ideology many of the conventions associated with the infernal council, a genre that mainly served Royalist propaganda during the 1640s.[114] Royalist specimens of the "Parliament of Hell" genre aggrandize the threat posed to political authority by seditious rhetoric and religious zeal. A 1649 post-regicide tract entitled *The Famous Tragedie of King Charles*, for instance, casts Cromwell as Achilles and Hugh Peters, the Independent preacher, as a Thersites who has prepared "a pithy formal speech against the essence and the power of Kings" in order to sway his audience "like Reeds."[115] Works of Royalist propaganda, as well as Royalist editions of the *Iliad* such as the 1648 text printed by Roger Daniel, cast Charles I as Agamemnon and tend to interpret Book 2 of the poem as a defence of the nobility of kingship. Milton inverts this equation in *Eikonoklastes*, turning Charles I into a furious Achilles who rages against tumults and condemns "distempers which his own inordinate doings had inflam'd."[116]

Milton's anti-Royalist interpretation of the council scene in Book 2 of the *Iliad* lays the groundwork for later and more thoroughgoing efforts to recuperate Homer for republican uses. *Paradise Lost*'s renditions of Homeric council scenes switch both the roles and the moral valences of a model reclaimed from Milton's Royalist adversaries, aligning Satan with Agamemnon and with the Odysseus of *Iliad* 2 in order to demonstrate how tyrannical rulers and those who support them co-opt the discourse of unity when faced with the threat of rebellion. Renaissance readers of the *Iliad* are divided about the extent to which the challenges to Agamemnon's authority issued by Achilles, Calchas, and Thersites in the poem's opening books reflect the poet's desire to undermine the claims on which Agamemnon's authority is founded or to illustrate his abuse of that authority. Although a number of Renaissance readers try to make Homer a staunch defender of monarchy – usually by invoking Odysseus's assertion that "it is no good thing to have a multitude of rulers" [*ouk agathon polukoiraniê eis koiranos estô*] – Milton generates a republican interpretation of Homer out of a well-established tradition that regards Agamemnon as "first among equals rather than a single sovereign" and thus regards Achilles as justified and even heroic in his objection to Agamemnon's seizure of a political and juridical authority that does not belong exclusively to him.[117] Such a reading is very much at odds with the palpably Royalist-leaning representation of the scene by Rubens, whose tapestry and oil renditions of *The Wrath of Achilles*, the latter of which appears on the cover of this book, both place Agamemnon firmly on the throne and make Achilles obviously inferior in height, age, and the visible trappings of political authority. Perhaps following Chapman, who imbues Achilles with "an ethical language charged with rebellious energy," Milton establishes an extended analogy between Agamemnon and Satan in order to critique the tyrannical encroachment of power that Achilles decries in the de facto ruler of the Achaeans. Even Odysseus, his leader's staunchest supporter, acknowledges that Agamemnon has been given "the sceptre and judgements" [*skêptron t'êde themistas*] from Zeus in order that he might "take counsel from his people" [*hina sphisi bouleuêsi*] – hardly a knock-down defence of absolute monarchy, even if Odysseus's speech was used that way by some Renaissance writers. In *Paradise Lost*, as well as in his *Pro Populo Anglicano Defensio*, Milton pays close attention to the sceptre mentioned by Odysseus, and he is especially sensitive to the ways in which Agamemnon "mistakenly uses *themis* as a royal prerogative," an intrusion censured by Achilles at *Il.* 1.234–9, who swears an oath by the *skêptron* that, although wielded by Agamemnon as a symbol of royal power, is in fact the communal property of the Achaeans and represents the foundations of that communal authority as rooted in the *themistas*, divine judgments or decrees issued by Zeus and carried out by Themis, the goddess of the assembly who helps to bring the dooms of Zeus to fulfilment.[118]

Achilles expresses his contempt for Agamemnon's unrightful seizure of communal authority by appealing to the *skêptron* as a symbol of "those who guard the laws [*themistas*] that come from Zeus" rather than as a symbol of monarchical authority (*Il.* 1.234–9). In his *Defensio Pro Populo*, Milton cites the final two lines of Achilles's speech not once but twice, appealing to the "judges who at Zeus's hand guard the dooms" [*judices qui leges / ab Jove custodiunt*] as evidence that "it is by God that kings reign" and as proof that Homer, like Solomon, "considers that even lesser officers also, namely judges, are from the same God."[119] Milton is no doubt thinking of Prov. 8.15–16: "Through me kings are sovereign and governors make just laws. Through me princes act like princes, from me all rulers on earth derive their nobility."[120] Both the Old Testament passage and its Homeric analogue inform Milton's rebuttal of Salmasius's defence of Charles I in the *Defensio Pro Populo*, which challenges "Homer's account of kings being descended from Jove."[121] Milton does not disagree with the essential nature of this genealogy – he understands that Homer's kings, like those of Solomon, are made and unmade by God – but rather takes issue with Salmasius's emphasis upon this divine genealogy as evidence that Homer supports absolutist monarchy. Maintaining that Lycurgus "might have learned from Homer ... that even in the heroic times kings were subject to the very same laws" as their subjects, Milton counters Salmasius's reading of the *Iliad* by arguing that "Homer's Achilles, having found that Agamemnon was himself a pestilence unto his people ... did not, though himself a king, hesitate, in an assemblage of the Greeks frequent and full [*in concione frequentissima Graecorum*], to submit a king to his own subjects for judgment," reproving Agamemnon as a "devourer of the people" and warning him that he has "committed outrage for the last time."[122] This Achilles sounds suspiciously like Milton, and this Agamemnon behaves suspiciously like Charles I.

Milton's dispute with Salmasius over Homer's political allegiances corroborates Paul Salzman's claim that unlike romance, which is "virtually without exception, a Royalist genre" during the 1640s and 1650s, epic is "available to writers with a very wide range of political sympathies" and serves those on all sides of the era's ideological divides.[123] Among the epic poets of Greece and Rome, Homer proves an especially unstable mediator of political debates during the English Civil War, since he neither celebrates the establishment of monarchy or empire (as Virgil was often read) nor laments the end of Roman Republicanism (as did Lucan).[124] In an effort to counter contemporary misconstructions of Homer as an Erastian quasi-Royalist who advocates the political expediency, if not the divine authority, of monarchy, Milton makes Homer a zealous defender of the *themistas*, the "dooms" or laws of God that apply to rulers and subjects alike. A number of seventeenth-century English writers, Milton included, invoke Themis as the figure responsible for dispensing divine laws or judgments, a "scribe of God" or the "Justice or Righteousness [which] sits in Counsel with God."[125] They also invoke Themis as a defender of justice against tyranny and a guarantor of political liberty, precisely the way Milton invokes the goddess of the assembly in his sonnet to Cyriack Skinner, written around 1655.[126] If Skinner sits on the "Royal Bench / Of Brittish *Themis*," it is because he upholds the law against claims of royal prerogative, acting as a defender of liberty and justice against tyranny. In *The Tenure of Kings and Magistrates*, Milton's interpretation of the Homeric concept of the *themistas* lends support to his belief that the most "wise and religious" of the Heathen "have don justice upon Tyrants" and have taught "lawless Kings ... [that] Justice is the onely true sovran and supreme Majesty on earth."[127]

This lesson is adapted in *Paradise Lost*, which transforms the council scene of Book 2 of the *Iliad* in order to link Satan's "perversion of liberty's principles" to Agamemnon, a ruler who justifies his authority as expedient and exercises it by fomenting fear.[128] Milton's attunement to Homer's presentation of Agamemnon as a king who has unjustly seized control of a sceptre – the living symbol of Themis, which derives from Zeus and rightfully belongs to the people – explains his multiple imitations of several scenes on Achilles's shield that offer (from Milton's perspective) a sounder conception of the divine origins of political authority as vested in elders who compete to determine "which one among them renders judgement in the straightest manner," each in turn taking the "*skêptron*" in his hand (*Il.* 18.506, 18.508). Agamemnon has abused the power symbolized by that sceptre.[129] As a corrective to this abuse, Achilles's shield eliminates "the juridical authority of earthly kings" in favour of judges appointed to enforce the *themistas*.[130]

For Milton, the contestation over the sceptre in the *Iliad* illustrates the danger posed by earthly kings whose power is borrowed from God, a reading strengthened by Isa. 14.5, where God breaks the sceptre of the wicked ruler. In *Paradise Lost*, the sceptre that rightfully belongs only to God is reclaimed after being misused by the priests who pollute the Temple at Jerusalem and "at last ... seize / The sceptre ... / Then lose it to a stranger," thus barring the "true anointed king Messiah" of his right (12.356–9). Milton's Messiah has his sceptre returned to him. But even when he is most impressively "armed" with the "might" and the "terrors" of God (6.735, 6.737), the Son behaves like an ideal king in his willingness to acknowledge that the sceptre ultimately belongs not to him, but to the Father: "Sceptre and power, thy giving, I assume, / And gladlier shall resign, when in the end / Thou shalt be all in all" (6.730–2).[131]

God the Counsellor: Zeus and Themis

Milton regards Themis not only as an ancient guardian of political liberty but also as a mediator of divine justice who promises to solve some pressing theological questions concerning the nature of divine intercession and divine counsel. For seventeenth-century English writers such as Cudworth and Henry More, the relationship between Zeus and Themis in archaic Greek literature resonates powerfully with several key doctrines of Protestant theology.[132] In her capacity as an intercessor, Themis facilitates prayer and repentance – exactly how she appears at the beginning of Book 11 of *Paradise Lost* – and she also communicates divine law, often tempering or softening it in the process. As the medium through which Zeus fulfils his judgments, Themis is the incarnation of *religio* in its most literal, etymological sense: she creates and protects the ligatures between divine justice and the human articulations of that justice through laws, customs, and ceremonies. For some seventeenth-century English writers, Themis is a figure of accommodation: she moulds Zeus's judgments to "[t]heir fit Composures" and "[w]edds them together," the description provided by Chapman's translation of *The Homeric Hymn to Zeus* (1624).[133] For some writers of the period, this intimate alliance between Zeus and Themis offers a striking analogy for the relationship that inheres between Father and Son as well as for the mediation of divine justice (or natural law) through human laws and customs. In *Paradise Lost*, a poem deeply vexed by the accommodation of divine "ways" to human ones, the figure of Themis helps to articulate some of the dilemmas that arise in Milton's presentation of a God whose divine will works through council as well as through intermediaries such as the Son, Raphael, Michael, and the poem's narrator.

In *Paradise Lost*, the relationship between Zeus and Themis informs Milton's efforts to represent the coexistence of divine providence and human liberty as predicated on a conception of God as both counsellor and counselled. In the *Iliad* and *Odyssey*, according to an oft-repeated phrase, it is the counsel [*boulê*], rather than the will, of Zeus that brings things to their fulfilment [*Dios d'eteleieto boulê*], a formula that preserves Zeus's authority while simultaneously legitimating that authority as the product of rational deliberation rather than fancy or whimsy (*Od.* 11.297). Milton transforms for a Christian context the Homeric conception of a supreme deity who wills through counsel and who is, according to the pseudo-Plutarchan *Life*, "constantly thinking."[134] Such a conception of

God preserves divine and human liberty, confirms Milton's anti-Trinitarianism, and challenges conventional, monotheistic interpretations of Homer that were troubling for political reasons to republican readers resistant to the "one Zeus, one king" interpretation of the *Iliad* espoused by Royalist scholars such as Salmasius.

Readers have frequently noted that the celestial council of Book 3 of *Paradise Lost* resembles the divine assembly at the beginning of the *Odyssey*. Yet the consiliar dynamics of Homer's Pantheon prove both compelling and challenging to Milton's conception of God as both the instrument and the recipient of counsel.[135] Like his classical models working within the epic tradition, Milton risks accusations of anthropomorphism and polytheism by placing multiple deities in dialogue with each other in an assembly. The heavenly councils of *Paradise Lost* might best be understood as an accommodation for mortal minds that cannot grasp God "as he really is, but in such a way as will make him conceivable to us."[136] Milton may also intend for his heavenly council to illustrate Eph. 1.11, a biblical verse central to his theory of divine decision-making that states that Christ "works all things according to the counsel of his will" [*ta panta energountos kata tên boulên tou thelêmatos autou*].[137] Invoked by Hooker and Bacon, the verse is used during the seventeenth century to support the radical Arminianism of thinkers such as John Goodwin as well as to reinforce the more Calvinist-leaning theology of the Westminster Confession of Faith, which asserts that "God from all eternity, did, by the most wise and holy Counsell of own Will, freely, and unchangeably ordaine whatsoever comes to passe."[138] The doctrine that God acts according to the counsel of His will solves several theological problems for its adherents. First, a God who acts "according to the counsell of his own will" rather than "by meer arbitrarious will" is, as Joseph Glanvill argues in 1662, a "Free Agent, because none can compel him to act, none can hinder him from acting."[139] For Milton, too, God's moral freedom to act in accordance with the counsel of His will reinforces divine goodness without undermining divine providence: the God who wills "not by necessity of nature but by counsel," as William Ames observes, is a God who freely chooses good even though he is not constrained to do so.

By depicting God and the Son conversing and even debating with each other in assembly, the celestial councils of *Paradise Lost* dramatize how divine will works through counsel so as to support the kind of "free and open encounter" that guarantees spiritual liberty in heaven as on earth. Milton's celestial assemblies also serve as a "vehicle for revealing God's secret counsel" by disclosing the reasons for divine decrees.[140] Yet the convention of the celestial council poses some risks similar to those posed by Trinitarianism: both may make God appear to have "two wills" or even "two contrary" wills, a doctrine Milton repudiates in *The Doctrine and Discipline of Divorce* and again in *De Doctrina Christiana*, when he invokes Zeus's speech to his Olympian council at the beginning of the *Odyssey*.[141] As a model for God's first speech in Book 3 of *Paradise Lost*, Zeus's opening address allows God to "justify" his ways and also resolve any perceived conflict between divine omnipotence and human liberty.

Following the church fathers, who tend to represent Homer as an honorary monotheist, sixteenth- and seventeenth-century Protestant writers fashion Zeus into an omnipotent and immutable deity who resembles the Hebrew God of the Old Testament.[142] Some early Christian and Renaissance writers struggle to arrive at such an interpretation, however, often resorting to moral or cosmological allegory to explain the existence, not to mention the erratic behaviour, of the subaltern gods. Lactantius accommodates the *Iliad* to his own monotheism by interpreting its account of "gods at war with each other" as a "fiction" designed to caution against polytheism by highlighting how a "multiplicity of gods" will inevitably "want different things, which leads to dispute and contest among them."[143] For most of Homer's Renaissance readers, too, the wrangling and fighting among the Homeric gods is a veil through which the poet's monotheism is easily spied.[144] Even Sponde, who is deeply troubled by the conflicts between Zeus and the subaltern gods, distinguishes in the index to his edition of Homer between *theos* [god] and *theoi* [gods], and he finds compelling evidence of a single, omnipotent God in the epithet "father Zeus" [*Zeus pater*] as well as in the image of a supreme God who sits apart from all the other gods on the peak of Olympus.[145]

Despite the obvious theological attractions of a monotheistic Homer, Milton complicates standard monotheistic interpretations of Zeus because of their risky political implications. Many of the early modern writers who identify Homer as monotheistic do so in order to rest upon that monotheism the analogical principle that one God requires one king.[146] Odysseus's vindication of Agamemnon's authority in Book 2 of the *Iliad* makes this argument an easy one for Tasso, who arranges for the hermit Piero to imitate Odysseus's speech in order to yoke the sovereign rule of a single monarch to Christian piety and obedience, cautioning Goffredo about the danger of "authority balanced out among so many / that no one properly possesses any" [*a quello autorità che, in molti e vari / d'opinioni quasi librata, è pari*].[147] Milton would hardly applaud Piero's argument that the "power and sceptre" should be vested in "one king," for both in *Paradise Lost* and elsewhere, he goes to great pains to refute the Royalist manipulation of "Homer's account of kings being descended from Jove," an interpretation evident in Ogilby's 1660 translation as well as in the 1648 Cambridge edition of the *Iliad* printed by Roger Daniel, the latter probably edited by James Duport.[148] Even so, Michael's account of the establishment of human government in the final book of *Paradise Lost* demonstrates how the pristine correspondence between divine and earthly authority is eroded by Sin such that "paternal rule" of a "fraternal state" is compromised by "one ... / Of proud ambitious heart" who grows discontented with the "fair equality" of this arrangement and tries to "arrogate dominion undeserved / Over his brethren" (12.24–8). The best solution – albeit a highly imperfect one, according to *The Tenure of Kings and Magistrates* – is to add "Counsellors and Parlaments" to limit the authority of rulers and to remedy their "partialitie."[149] Milton interprets the Achaean assembly in Book 2 of the *Iliad* as narrating a similar degeneration from a loosely organized "fraternal state" to the consolidation of power under one ruler who claims a "second sovereignty" from heaven and strengthens that sovereignty by accusing his subjects of rebellion. For Milton, Homer is one of the "wise and religious" heathens who have "don justice upon Tyrants," but he is also a poet who demonstrates that, at certain times, "tyranny must be."[150]

Milton also complicates conventional monotheistic interpretations of Homeric epic by reworking the relationship between Zeus and the subaltern gods in order to bear witness to an anti-Trinitarianism articulated through what he calls a "drama of the personalities in the Godhead" [*personalitatum illud totum drama advocem*].[151] The celestial council of Book 3 of *Paradise Lost* represents an "impassioned, emotionally charged" God who is "imbued with a sense of genuine conflict," yet that conflict is quickly resolved when God expresses "delight" at receiving from the Son counsels identical to his own judgments: "All hast thou spoken as my thoughts are" (3.166, 3.171).[152] As the "Word" (3.170), Milton's Son is an antidote to the figure of Mêtis embodied by Sin, a figure of "undigested" counsel who maintains his autonomy even though the advice he delivers is anticipated by God and consistent with His own will. Rather than incorporate the Son's counsel as his own, Milton's God encourages him to articulate what He, "all-knowing," already knows, "mixing intercession sweet" as Adam likewise does for Eve (10.227–8). This mediation may seem puzzling because it is so unnecessary. Like Homer's Zeus, who chooses to convene divine assemblies when he need only "nod" to bring his will to fulfilment, Milton's God solicits advice and thus encourages the kind of "wrestling" also typical of the God of Isaiah, who invites the penitent to "come, now, let us argue it out" in order to turn their scarlet sins as "white as snow," or the God of the Psalms, who stands in His "great assembly" (as Milton renders the Hebrew *ba-ă-dat*) and "judges and debates."[153] By inviting dialogue and debate, "unfallen" modes of discourse in *Paradise Lost* whose "passing dissonances ... enrich the song," Milton's God lays bare his own deliberative processes to wider scrutiny, so that mortals may emulate divine deliberation, and also so that God's just motives may be rightly understood.[154]

Part 2. Moral Horizons: Milton's Horai

In ancient Greek mythology, the union of Themis and Zeus yields the Horai, sisters who safeguard the timely and mutual interchange of the hours and the seasons. In the *Iliad* and in Hesiod's *Theogony*, the Horai guard the cosmological crossroads of day and night, and of spring and autumn, and they also protect the natural ligatures of human communities bound together by a "collective conscience" forged through marriage or through council.[155] The temporal seams of noon and twilight that embellish *Paradise Lost*'s most decisive moments are deeply and complexly indebted to Homeric and Hesiodic cosmology and in particular to the figures of the Horai, who provide a macrocosmic counterpoint to Milton's representation of the juridical process of the umpire conscience. Noon and twilight mark those junctures of Milton's poem that are, to borrow the Homeric term, *alloprosallos*: events and choices whose outcome is undecided or contingent on forces that are impartial, evenly balanced, or subject to the turn and counter-turn of "revolving" minds.[156] In Homer and Hesiod, the three Horai – Dikê, Eunomia, and Eirene – complement the juridical responsibilities of their parents by presiding over diurnal and seasonal change, thus preserving a cosmic order [Eunomia] that is linked through her sororal bonds to the perpetuation of peace [Eirene] and of distributive justice [Dikê]. The "darkness visible" (1.63) of Pandaemonium suggests the absence of this diurnal alternation: outside the realm of the Horai, Hell does not enjoy the "grateful vicissitude" (6.8) of night and day, a condition related to the oxymoronic self-cancellation associated with Satan throughout the poem.[157] By contrast, both in heaven and in Eden, Milton calls upon the Horai to ensure that day and night revolve "in perpetual round" and "[l]odge and dislodge by turns" (6.6–7).

In *Paradise Lost*, the theological and cosmological significance of the Horai is further strengthened by the sense of spiritual urgency that accompanies their appearance. Milton may have recognized an affinity between the mythography of the Horai and the scriptural emphasis, particularly in the Psalms, upon what is *eukairos* or *horaios*: the seasonable, proper, or ripe time to perform spiritual actions. He may also discern a more particular correspondence between the pagan triplets and Paul's description of salvation as determined at the *horae momentum* [*arti hôras*] – in the moment of an hour, or the blink of an eye. As Thomas Bastard explains in a sermon on the Christian Soldier, paraphrasing 1 Cor. 4.11, human life "is a kind of warring: for we encounter on every side in the moment of an houre, either quick death commeth, or ioyfull victory ... This *horae momentum*, is mans whole life ... in this moment of an houre we are all lost or saved."[158] *Paradise Lost* represents the temporal interstices of twilight and noon as the *horae momentum* of the natural world: fleeting, decisive intervals that, like so many other Homeric "pondering" conventions – balances and scales, edges and ridges, images of hesitation or of suspended conflict – mark the critical junctures at which arbitration occurs (or fails to occur) throughout the poem. Presiding over "moments" of pondering, Milton's Horai demarcate moral horizons, their function deriving from the etymology proposed by Socrates in Plato's *Cratylus*, who attributes their name to their power to "divide [*horizousi*]" the winter from the summer.[159]

Although the "darker veil" of night never fully envelops Milton's heaven, *Paradise Lost* teaches that even the "high mount of God" enjoys the "roseate dews" of "grateful twilight," intermediate states between day and night that exemplify the perfect counterpoise of divine judgment as well as its fallible mediation through the human conscience (5.645–6; cf. 6.12). Imitating Homer, who depicts the rising and setting of the sun occurring on Olympus as well as on earth, Milton is deliberate in his repeated use of the word "twilight," which denotes both dusk and dawn and conveys a powerful sense of the cosmological and moral intermediacy represented by both states. In addition to the pleasing variety of "[l]abour and rest" afforded to Adam and Eve by the alternation of "day and night ... successive" (4.613–14), twilight – those fleeting spells during which night becomes day, and day night – also comes to denote any moral or spiritual state of "twixtness," whether the moment of hesitation before making a decision or the ambiguous appearance of the newly fallen Satan, whose partially obscured brightness is likened to the "twilight" of a "sun new ris'n" – or that same sun about to descend "behind the moon / In dim eclipse" (1.596–7). In heaven, as in Eden, the "grateful vicissitude" (6.9) of day and night requires that both do not occur simultaneously, whereas

Pandaemonium enjoys only the "disastrous twilight" (1.597) of an eclipse, an event that muddles night and day rather than keeping them distinct.[160] As the moment at which day and night seem to coincide, Miltonic twilight makes visible the workings of *dikê*, or distributive justice, and it accommodates that justice to the realm of human experience. Worshipping God as the "Maker Omnipotent" (4.725) of night and day, Adam and Eve display their intuitive understanding of divine creation as an act of *dikê* in which God divides "light from darkness" (7.250), thus creating the "first Evening" and the "first Morn" (7.260). Divine creation separates day and night from each other – in the Septuagint, God "divided" [*diechôrisen*] them – but also creates the potential for interchange and crossing between them. When the angels present at Milton's Creation see "Orient Light / Exhaling first from Darkness" (7.255–6), the joyful harmony of their celestial choir at this first dawn celebrates not divine light per se but rather God's capacity to convert darkness into light, a dynamic process mirrored by the "dark descent" of Milton's narrator into the domain of Chaos and Night and his subsequent re-ascent to the "Sovran vital Lamp" of God at the beginning of Book 3 (3.20–2).

It is a rare epic poem that does not imitate the Homeric convention of introducing and concluding scenes with the rising and setting of the sun. But Milton is not particularly interested in reproducing the vividness of Homer's descriptions – the *rhododactylos* [rosy-fingered] or *krokopeplos* [saffron-robed] dawns that usher in the dawn of poetic similitude itself. Rather, he labours to capture the sacred pleasure of these interstitial moments, as well as the precariousness and moral urgency they mark. The "Twilight gray" that descends upon the middle of Book 4 of *Paradise Lost* attires everything in a "sober liverie," a drabness that evokes Milton's damp and foggy England, the "dim suffusion" (3.26) of his blurry vision, and above all the ethical *grisaille* of his Eden, a place where moral distinctions are fuzzy and evil appears enshrouded in mist. Book 9 announces the decisiveness of its subject by commencing at the arrival of "Twilight upon the earth, short arbiter / Twixt day and night" (9.50–1), a metaphor which reminds us how Adam and Eve each pause, momentarily, upon a morally grey horizon before each chooses to eat, their disobedience unsettling the cosmic justice and harmony once guarded by the Horai. Like the "precarious stasis" of twilight, noon in *Paradise Lost* signals a fleeting and delicate counterbalance between opposites: as the "perfect balancing midpoint between day and night," it marks the moment at which a character strides the razor's edge between moral alternatives.[161] It is noon when Satan "revolv[es]" over whether to destroy Eden and it is once again "noon" (9.739) when Eve, "[p]ausing a while," considers for the last time whether to eat the apple (9.744).[162] The special threat posed by the "noonday demon" of *acedia* explains why Raphael arrives to converse with Adam when the latter has "from the heat of noon retired" (5.231), a time of day associated with spiritual vulnerability and moral indolence as well as with urgent choice.

The divine errand on which Raphael is sent – to remind Adam that he is free and also free to fall – is reticulated in the diurnal motions of a sun that Adam and Eve instinctively recognize, in their morning prayer, as replicating God's "eternal course" in its rising and falling.[163] The prayer fittingly acknowledges the divine origins of the Horai: as the daughters of Themis – the goddess whom Natale Conti identifies as an embodiment of "equity" [*aequitas*] and "law" [*nomos*] – the Horai symbolize the "observance of divine ritual and compliance with civil laws" evident in the visible workings of the cosmos.[164] Given Milton's suspicion of ritual, it may seem odd that he incorporates into *Paradise Lost* such a coherent program of allusions to an archaic trio of goddesses conventionally associated with religious ceremony.[165] But Milton's Horai preside over the uncorrupted "rites" of unfallen nature, ceremonies such as prayer and sex that are "mysterious" and pure only as long as they remain tethered to the natural motions of the cosmos.

Milton adapts a Homeric idiom of twilight in order to accommodate several related theological lessons about the liberty and mutability of the will, and also about the imperfection of human deliberation. The symbolic language of twilight represents the sharp edge between mutually exclusive values or the decisive moment at which one must choose between them, thereby adapting to Milton's Christian ethics Hesiod's account of Day and Night greeting each other as they pass in opposite directions [*ameibomenai*] over the threshold of the House of Night.[166] In *Utrum Dies an Nox praestantior sit* [Whether day is more excellent than night], a prolusion steeped in allusions to Homer, Hesiod, and Plutarch, Milton proposes that day and night are not teammates in a cosmic relay race but rather antagonists in a Manichean struggle between good and evil: "light and darkness have disagreed among themselves with bitterest hatred from the very beginning of things."[167] In the Eden of Book 4, the Horai appear in their capacity as the Seasons, dancing hand in hand with the Graces as they perform the Miltonic values of reciprocity and mutuality as distinct from the "mutual amity" (4.376) sought by Satan with Adam and Eve, a "league ... so strait, so close" that it eliminates any possibility of achieving the kind of *concordia discors* embodied by the Horai or their partners, the

Graces.[168] Inasmuch as it creates both a threshold and a barrier between Day and Night, twilight comes to represent mutuality and reciprocity but also the urgency of choosing between the antagonistic and mutually exclusive forces of good and evil.

Phaiakia and Eden: Paradises Lost

In Milton's Eden, the dance of opposites performed by the Horai reflects the harmonious simultaneity of unfallen nature, the concord of a divinely appointed cosmos that is superior but not invulnerable to the coercive concord imposed by Satan. Like Adam and Eve, whose *homophrosunê* permits them to utter, simultaneously, the same spontaneous prayers without adhering to a scripted rite, Eden enjoys "Blossoms and fruits at once" (4.148) because "spring and autumn" dance "hand in hand" (5.394–5), forging a voluntary and fragile coincidence of opposites mirrored in Milton's ideals of marriage. The concurrence of the seasons in Eden imitates Homer's description of Phaiakia (*Od.* 7.112–32), where the coincidence of spring and fall likewise yields abundance and also reflects the value of *seasonableness* – of a decorum rooted in nature rather than in human custom or law. Though frequently noted in passing, the numerous allusions to Phaiakia embedded in Milton's descriptions of Eden and of the unfallen Adam and Eve have not yet been interpreted as forming a systematic and coherent program of heuristic imitation. Phaiakia provides Milton with more than just the decorative touches of a pagan paradise in which Eve's naked modesty rivals that of Nausicaa, and Adam's "hyacinthine locks" (4.301) surpass the hairdo that Athena twice gives Odysseus to make his tresses "flow in curls like the hyacinth flower" (*Od.* 6.231, 23.158).[169] In addition to serving as a frame for Raphael's accounts of the war in heaven and the Creation, Milton's Eden possesses a number of moral and structural similarities to Homer's lost paradise. Both places nurture strikingly domestic virtues such as hospitality, moderation, modesty, and marital harmony, and both allow for contact and communication between gods and men as they join together at feasts presided over by a divine bard who enjoys privileged access to "what surmounts the reach / Of human sense" (*Od.* 8.43; *PL* 5.571–2).[170]

Seventeenth-century Dutch and Flemish painters such as Jan de Bray (see figure 9) draw on Odysseus and Penelope as a model for the domestic bliss of bourgeois marriage, and Milton does something similar as he imitates those aspects of the *Odyssey* that "celebrat[e] the decorum" of domestic life while at the same time stressing the "difference between gods and mortals" to convey "the danger of trying to cross that boundary."[171] Eden and Phaiakia are both homes to which one cannot return, places where gods and mortals enjoy an intimacy with each other no longer possible. In both poems, the familiarity between divine and mortal creatures – a familiarity cultivated through shared food and conversation, and strengthened by divine messengers and poets – is imperfect and fragile. In *Paradise Lost* the proximity between God and man is irremediably severed by the fall, after which time there is "[n]o more of talk where God or angel guest / With man, as with his friend, familiar used / To sit indulgent, and with him partake / Rural repast" (9.1–4).[172] The opening lines of Book 9 of *Paradise Lost* offer a deeply pessimistic commentary on a speech made by Homer's Alkinous about how in Phaiakia, the gods "have been wont to appear to us in manifest [*enargeis*] form … and they feast among us, sitting even where we sit" (*Od.* 7.201–3).[173] As Milton understands it, both the Homeric poems and the New Testament prize hospitality for its theological value: glossing Hebr. 13.2 in *De Doctrina*, he cautions, "be not forgetful to entertain strangers, for thereby some have entertained angels unawares" (*CW* 17:382–3). Yet by emphasizing the hospitality that Adam and Eve show to their "godlike guest" (5.351) as well as the familiarity with which Adam and Raphael converse "as friend with friend" (5.229), Milton adapts the Odyssean value of hospitality to underscore the decisive and tragic termination of intimacy between gods and men.

Unlike Odysseus, who is given "food and drink such as mortal men eat" by Calypso while she herself enjoys nectar and ambrosia, Milton's Raphael does not find the food served him in Eden "unsavoury … / To spiritual natures," and he eats it "with keen dispatch / Of real hunger" (*Od.* 5.197; *PL* 5.401–2; 5.436–7).[174] Milton's deviation from Homeric epic, in which the immortal gods "do not eat bread nor do they eat ruddy wine, and so are bloodless," conveys the greater intimacy that Adam and Eve enjoy with divine creatures before the fall, as well as their greater physical resemblance to them (*Il.* 5.341–2). The feast that Adam and Eve share with their "godlike guest" (5.351) nourishes the monistic spiritual continuum that Raphael, a divine messenger explicitly modelled on "Maia's son" (5.285), later explains to his host, playing Hermes to Adam's Odysseus. Yet whereas Odysseus departs Calypso's island reverently attuned to the fundamental distinctions between gods and mortals, Adam and Eve have more difficulty grasping the slippery and dynamic continuum between flesh and spirit, which according to Raphael holds the promise that "time may come when men / With angels may participate" (5.493–4). Although Calypso tempts Odysseus with the prospect of immortality, she also

Figure 9. Jan de Bray, *Couple Represented as Ulysses and Penelope* (1668). Oil on canvas. Courtesy Speed Art Museum, Louisville, KY.

declares in no uncertain terms that "mortal women should [not] vie with immortals in form or looks," a precept neglected by Adam, who falters in finding his wife "absolute ... / And in herself complete," as well as by Eve, whose "goddess-like demeanour" proves a temptation as Satan entices her to become a "goddess among gods" (*Od.* 5.213; *PL* 8.547–8, 8.59, 9.547).

Milton is hardly the only Christian reader of the *Odyssey* to discern the theological import of Homer's repeated injunction to respect the difference between gods and mortals.[175] Yet *Paradise Lost* incorporates this Homeric motif into the monistic spectrum that scaffolds its vitalistic cosmos, in which the contingent promise of a potentially greater intimacy between gods and men heightens the sense of alienation between them after the fall. When Eve plucks fruit from the very spot "where / Alcinous reigned" in order to "entertain our angel guest," the allusion poignantly reminds us that the convivial symposium enjoyed between gods and men in Milton's Eden (as in Phaiakia) will come to a definitive end once Eve plucks a different kind of fruit from the garden (5.340–1, 328).[176] And, when Satan first spies Eve, the lush landscape that surrounds her is likened to "those gardens feigned / Or of revived Adonis, or renowned / Alcinous, host of old Laertes' son," the comparisons hint at Eden's transitoriness but also throw into relief the profound difference between the conclusion of the *Odyssey* and that of *Paradise Lost* (9.439–40). Whereas Laertes's son returns to his homeland and is at long last reunited with a father who has given up kingship in favour of tending a simple yet well-ordered garden, Adam and Eve are exiled from their garden home and alienated from their divine father. Odysseus's reunion with his father is the result of a trial in which he "tests [Laertes] with mocking words" [*kertomiois epeessin peirêthênai*]; Adam and Eve, by contrast, are exiled when they fail the trial set for them by God (*Od.* 24.240).

In *Paradise Lost*, the fragile intimacy between gods and mortals is nurtured by "winged messengers" who mediate between heaven and earth by likening spiritual to corporeal forms. This poetic accommodation is temporal as well as spatial: Milton's Raphael follows the Homeric bards in minimizing the disjuncture between divine and human conceptions of temporality. Odysseus commends Demodocus for singing his rhapsodies "*kata kosmon*" [in order, sequentially], praising the blind bard for recounting the matter of Troy "as though you yourself were present, or had heard the tale from another" [*ôs te pou ê autos pareôn ê allou akousas*]. Imitating Demodocus as well as Homer's muses, who are "present and know all things" [*pareste te, iste te panta*], Milton solicits a similar chronological immediacy from his muse: "Instruct me, for thou knowst; thou from the first / Wast present."[177] Raphael exhibits a similar power when he recounts to Adam "what before thy memory was done / From the beginning," a tale at which Adam "still stood fixed to hear" much as the Phaiakians stand "hushed in silence" when Odysseus completes his narrative at the exact halfway mark of the *Odyssey* (*PL* 7.637–8, 8.3; *Od.* 13.1). The poetic authority of both the Homeric bard and his Miltonic counterpart resides in the ability to reverse and transcend temporal limitations, creating a sense of immediacy that transfixes the audience by appearing to stop time.

Milton, Homer, and Future Contingency

Milton recognizes in Homer a poet who likewise grasps the plenitude of divine knowledge in terms of temporal as well as spatial omnipresence. *Paradise Lost* consistently represents God as speaking in the present tense, at times shifting abruptly from past to present or vice versa (as at *PL* 6.26 and 6.669–78) in order to highlight the discrepancy between divine pantemporality and the limited, sequential temporality of human narrative. Milton's use of the present tense to convey the "[i]mmediate" nature of divine knowledge and divine action, "more swift / Than time or motion," also forestalls the Satanic objection that divine foreknowledge compromises spiritual liberty: if God is omnipresent, the distinction between foreknowledge and retrospection exists only as an accommodation to the temporal constraints of the human mind, which "measures all things durable / By present, past, and future" (5.581–2). Howsoever much this limitation might hinder the mortal ability to comprehend God as temporally "all in all," it is a limitation essential to Milton's theology, since without an understanding of temporal sequence (*post hoc*) it is impossible to conceive of causal sequence (*propter hoc*) and thus to admit responsibility for choices and actions. In other words, thinking in temporal terms, for mortals, is a necessary precondition for pondering the consequences of moral decisions: like God's scales, the mortal conception of time makes manifest the "sequel" of causes by showing what may happen *after* – and, more importantly, *because of* – something else.[178]

In *Paradise Lost*, divine omnipresence is accommodated to sequential temporality through the "process of speech" (*PL* 7.177). In his imitations of scenes and episodes from Homer's Phaiakia, Milton is keenly attuned to the theological significance of the temporal distinctions made possible by Homeric Greek, particularly those tenses and modes (including the imperfect, aorist, optative, future less vivid, and middle passive voice) that denote present or past conditionality – what *may* happen or what *might have* happened rather than what will happen or what has happened. Like the contrafactual, a Homeric convention used by Milton to depict the divine and human liberty to choose otherwise, the conditional tenses, modes, and prepositional phrases that pervade certain speeches and episodes of the *Odyssey* resurface in *Paradise Lost* as vehicles for justifying the ways of God to men. Milton shows this process of temporal accommodation to be *imperfect* in both senses of the term; as Martin Evans points out, "[t]he abstract idea of an 'eternal present' is simply not translatable into narrative terms."[179] But Milton also minimizes the difficulty of translating divine omnipresence into the sequential temporal chain of past, present, and future through recourse to conditional and subjunctive clauses (particularly "if" and "until") that grow out of a Homeric grammar of contingency. When Milton's God explains that his foreknowledge has no effect on the outcome of future events, He speaks of that foreknowledge in hypothetical and past conditional terms: "if I foreknew, / Foreknowledge had no influence," phrasing that wreaks havoc upon human distinctions of time and tense (3.117–18). God's "if" reflects his effort to accommodate divine to human temporality: although divine knowledge exists in eternity, mortals imagine a future that is at once contingent and unknown, thus explaining why both God and Raphael explain their most crucial theological precepts ("if they will hear" their umpire conscience, "if not depraved from good") in hypothetical form.[180]

Unlike Milton's paradise, which is "lost" at the poem's title, the destruction of Homer's Phaiakia is postponed indefinitely, suspended by means of a narrative interruption that breaks away from the episode in the midst of the Phaiakians' desperate supplication to Poseidon and whisks the reader back to Odysseus washing up on the shores of Ithaca. The theological implications of this deferral resonate powerfully with *Paradise Lost*'s rejection of determinism, its accompanying emphasis on future contingency, and its powerful representation of the anxieties attendant upon an uncertain future. When Homer's Alkinous first predicts that Poseidon "would smite" one of Phaiakia's ships "some day" and "would fling a great mountain about our city," thereby cutting them off from the sea, he uses the conditional tense in order to highlight the uncertainty of the prediction that "these things the god may bring to pass or may leave unfulfilled [*teleseien / ê k'atelest'eiê*], as may please his heart" (*Od.* 8.564–71). When Homer's narrator abruptly bids the Phaiakians adieu five books later, Poseidon's threat to destroy them by piling a mountain on top of them is unrealized – or rather has not been realized *yet*, an ambiguity that leaves open the question of when, if ever, Poseidon's conditional threat might be fulfilled or whether the prayers and sacrifices of the Phaiakians have been (and may continue to be) effective at averting that threat.[181]

The unrealized prophecy of Poseidon's destruction of Phaiakia leaves its inhabitants in a confused and uncertain state: "they knew not," Homer's narrator comments, "how these things were to be" [*ta d'ouk isan hôs etetukto*] (*Od.* 13.178, 13.170).[182] In his invocation to Book 9 of *Paradise Lost*, when Milton's narrator condemns "Neptune's ire" for having "[p]erplexed the Greek," he does not indict divine wrath per se but only those expressions of wrath that bewilder their victims or remain unexplained by the poet (9.19).[183] Milton may be protesting Poseidon's motiveless malignity against Odysseus, the principal victim of the sea god's anger; a similarly inexplicable Poseidon, his face turned away from the viewer in right foreground, looms in Pellegrino Tibaldi's gory and terrifying rendition of Odysseus's shipwreck (sometimes referred to as *The Revenge of Neptune*) in the Stanza di Ulisse at the Palazzo Poggi in Bologna. But Milton may also be protesting the fact that, because Poseidon's threats do not always come to pass (or do not come to pass in expected ways), the unpredictability of divine wrath puts the *Odyssey*'s human subjects in spiritual peril or perplexity. In the *Odyssey*, the uncertainty generated by the mysterious deferral of divine wrath requires precisely the kind of "patience" identified by Milton's narrator in the invocation to Book 9 of *Paradise Lost* as a truly heroic virtue. If patience is a cornerstone of Miltonic heroism, it is in part because the poet understands waiting, especially waiting for death, as a difficult and perplexing trial, particularly when prophecies and threats are not immediately realized.[184] Inheriting a distinctly Odyssean brand of endurance, Adam and Eve learn to wait for a wrath deferred, spending much of Book 10 in nervous anticipation of a death that is ordained but not yet realized, a "long day's dying" (10.964) that breeds anxiety about an uncertain future.

After the fall, as Adam and Eve await the "future change" (11.193) brought about by the "slow-paced evil" (10.963) of death, they struggle to interpret divine omens such as the "bird of Jove" that "stooped from his airy tower, / Two birds of gayest plume before him drove" (11.185–6). This "mute sig[n] in nature" (11.194) is closely modelled on a portent that appears repeatedly throughout the *Iliad* and *Odyssey*, an omen interpreted in such various and conflicting ways that it comes to epitomize the "baffling and unclear meaning" [*amêchanoi akritomuthoi*] of divine signs and of dreams that "do not at all find fulfillment" [*oude ti panta teleietai*] according to Penelope's exposition of signs and dreams.[185] Penelope's speech on the two gates of sleep exerts a complex influence upon the dreams that bracket Eve's entrance into and her exit from Eden, and it also illustrates to the poet of *Paradise Lost* how dreams, like divine signs, may either perplex and unperplex, creating a "confused field of signs" that pose an "interpretive challenge" for their readers.[186]

Reworked out of a series of Homeric allusions concerning the unintelligibility and contingency of dreams and omens, the divine sign that appears to Adam and Eve in Book 11 of *Paradise Lost* creates an uncertainty about the future that in turn demands that they exercise "[t]rue patience" and "temper joy with fear" as they anticipate an open-ended doom (11.361). Particularly in the final two books of *Paradise Lost*, during which Adam and Eve learn to live in the indefinite future that defines their fallen existence, Milton relies heavily on many of the conditional phrases – in particular "until" and "if" clauses – that Homer frequently uses to convey future contingency.[187] Of the more than 120 "till" clauses in *Paradise Lost*, the vast majority of them are uttered after the fall, in anticipation of a death that *will* come, but at an unknown time and in an unknown form. Adam resolves not to live in fear "*till* we end / In dust"; the Son describes how Adam will live out his "days / Numbered, though sad, *till* death, his doom" arrives; God describes the happiness in which Adam and Eve might have lived "*Till* I provided death"; and Adam counsels Eve that although they have been from "death released" for a certain time, "how long, and what *till* then our life, / Who knows, or more than this, that we are dust, / And thither must return and be no more" (10.1084–5, 11. 39–40, 11.61, 11.198–200). Milton's use of "till" clauses to capture the disquiet of a death foretold but not yet realized reproduces a distinctly Homeric technique for conveying contingency, one used throughout Tiresias's prophecy to Odysseus at *Od.* 11.104–13. Issued as a "riddling task" dependent upon "four consecutive conditions," Tiresias's prophecy is couched in numerous "if" and "until" clauses that create a "deliberate ambiguity" and underscore the contingency of its fulfilment.[188] No matter how Tiresias's prophecy achieves fulfilment, Odysseus will ultimately die, at least outside the confines of the poem. But the prophecy steers Odysseus towards the best death he can hope for – one that comes gently, in old age, much like Michael's description of the ideal death to which Adam should also aspire: "mayst thou live, till like ripe fruit thou drop / Into thy mother's lap, or be with ease / Gathered, not harshly plucked, for death mature" (11.535–7). Yet whereas Odysseus consigns himself to a death that is inevitable albeit uncertain in nature, Adam and Eve confuse the future less vivid implied by "till" with the utter contingency of perhaps, expressing the false hope that "perhaps [we] shalt not die" (9.928) and that "perhaps one hour of life" remains (10.923) until at long last they resign themselves to their "appointed day / Of rendering up" and promising to "patiently attend / My dissolution" (11.550–2).

Through Adam and Eve's confusion over the words "till" and "perhaps," Milton attempts to recreate the perplexity generated by the two different kinds of "until" clauses in ancient Greek, one indicative (and thus definite) and the other conditional (and thus indefinite). Although the two constructions may be differentiated in the past tense, they are indistinguishable in the present tense, a feature of Greek grammar that produces ambiguity and irony at several junctures in the *Odyssey*.[189] Although impossible to reproduce in English, the distinction is crucial to Milton's theology, where it infuses uncertainty into phrases such as "till one greater man / Restore us" (1.4–5), a verse glossed by some readers as an allusion to the opening word of the *Odyssey* (*andra*, or man). Like many of the "till" clauses used by Adam and Eve after the fall, which wishfully turn indicative into subjunctive, the "till" of Milton's invocation does not throw into uncertainty *whether* the Son will indeed restore humankind but rather *when* and *how* he will do so. Tottering on the brink between indicative and subjunctive moods, Milton's "till" clauses also drive home the disparity between divine and creatural knowledge. When God employs a similar construction in Book 3, declaring of Adam and Eve that "free they must remain, / *Till* they enthral themselves" (3.124–5), the statement functions in one mood or the other depending upon the perspective from which it is understood. God's foreknowledge of the fall injects certainty into His "till" even as that same word operates conditionally from the mortal perspective: Adam and Eve are "free to fall" (3.99) even though their fall "had no less proved certain unforeknown" (3.119).[190]

Paradise Lost also uses "till" clauses, a convention adapted from the language of the *Odyssey*, in order to underscore the irremediable gap between pre- and postlapsarian existence. Satan's frequent "tills" during the war in heaven mark crucial turning points in his own moral descent, including his reaction to the apotheosis of the Son (God "till now / Omniscient thought") and his first experience of pain, "[t]ill now not known" (6.429–30, 6.432). For Adam and Eve, "till" marks the horizon between innocence and sin: Eve never experiences "such delight till then" (9.787), and she describes her transformation in terms of an "agony of love till now / Not felt" (9.858–9). When he tastes the apple, Adam likewise declares that they did not "kno[w] till now / True relish," a formula that ironically foreshadows Michael's account of their "original lapse," which did "to servitude reduce / Man till then free" (9.1023–4, 12.83, 12.89–90). When used to voice projections into a conditional future, "if" and "until" clauses emphasize the spiritual liberty given by God to His creatures. Yet in the past tense, these same clauses often signal the perversion or diminution of that liberty, a provisional gift that has been revoked with the entrance of sin into the world. When fallen characters speak in the conditional and hypothetical modes of "if," "until," and "perhaps," they show themselves unaware of the extent to which their liberty has been extirpated by sin, no longer capable of perceiving the limits of contingency in their fallen state. Eve's repetition of the word "perhaps" in her first speech after her fall resists the definitive and irreparable nature of her action: "I perhaps am secret," she muses, since "other care perhaps / May have diverted" God's attention from her such that she might "keep the odds of knowledge" in her power by rendering herself "more equal, and perhaps" even "superior" to Adam (9.811–25). Both her language and her logic are Satanic, mimicking the barrage of "ifs" and "perhaps" in speeches that reflect a false sense of hope in the speaker.[191]

Homeric Hindsight and the Miltonic Ethics of Shame

Paradise Lost imitates the *Odyssey* in representing paradise as a place of moderation, marital harmony, and variety, as well as a place void of the "guilty shame" that accompanies the entrance of sin into the world. Eve's "innocence and virgin modesty" (8.501) before the fall is modelled partly on Homer's Nausicaa, the maiden who proves immune to "dishonest shame" when, emboldened by Athena, she withstands the sight of the naked Odysseus.[192] While the program of Odyssean allusions in Eden reinvents Homeric *homophrosunê* as a Miltonic marital ideal, *Paradise Lost* also reworks other Homeric marriages in order to explore the various threats posed by marriage to individual liberty, as well as the threats posed to marriage by sinful passions such as "anger, hate, / Mistrust, suspicion, discord" and, above all, shame (*PL* 9.1123–4).

The union of Zeus and Hera, directly invoked twice by Milton in his descriptions of Adam and Eve, embodies both the ideals of Edenic marriage and the perils to which it is subject. The earth gives "signs of gratulation" (8.514) when Adam first leads Eve into their nuptial bower, an effect similar to the one produced by the union of Zeus and Hera at *Il.* 14.347–9, when the "bright earth made fresh-sprung grass to grow, and dewy lotus, and crocus, and hyacinth thick and soft."[193] The idea that sex might yield such capillary effects in the macrocosm is congenial to Milton's vitalistic cosmos, in which "various degrees / Of substance" derive from "one first matter" (5.472–4) such that there exists an implicit correspondence between body and spirit and between creatural and cosmic love.[194] But Milton's invocations of Hera and Zeus also hint at the dark cloud of shame that will descend upon Eden after the fall. When Hera seduces Zeus, she does not want to be seen while making love, declaring that if "the gods who are forever should look on us two as we sleep ... that would be a shameful [*nemessêton*] thing" (*Il.* 14.332–3, 14.336). Zeus solves this problem by enfolding his wife in a cloud, a remedy that proves less effective for Adam and Eve, who find that their shame persists even when they are hidden from view.

All three of the Homeric couples to whom Eve and Adam are compared – Hera and Zeus, Nausicaa and Odysseus, and Andromache and Hector – experience shame (*aidôs* or *nemesis*) in the sphere of love. On the surface, Hera's fear of shame, like the modesty that prompts Odysseus to cover up his naked genitals at *Od.* 6.127–9, appears to offer a tidy analogue for the "guilty shame" felt by Adam and Eve after the fall. But Hera does not in fact feel shame: like Hector, the Homeric character whom Milton regards as the noblest embodiment of pagan *aidôs*, she merely *anticipates* shame, and she expresses that anticipation in the same conditional mode as does Hector when he imagines the shame he *would* feel "if like a coward I were to skulk away from the battle" (*Il.* 6.443). In Homeric epic, the power of shame can be *hypothetical* as well as actual: this is why Aristotle argues that shame [*aidôs*] is not a virtue but rather a feeling [*pathei*], since it "can only be virtuous conditionally [*hupotheseôs*] ... in the sense that a good man would be ashamed *if* he were to do so and so; but the virtues are not conditional."[195] This distinction helps to explain why Milton sees no contradiction in ascribing to the unfallen Eve an innocent (because hypothetical) shame that is distinct from the actual *experience* of shame after the fall. Like the contents of her dream, Eve's virgin modesty allows for the anticipation of shameful feelings to "come and go, so unapproved, and leave / No spot or blame behind" (5.118–19). Inasmuch as the actual experience of shame results from the inability to anticipate (and thus to avoid) actions that might arouse shame, *aidôs* often marks a lack of foresight – a failure to ponder adequately the consequences of certain choices or actions. The hypothetical shame anticipated (but not in fact experienced) by Hector reflects the efficacy of his moral faculties: his choices are guided by what Milton calls an "honest shame," an emotion that turns out to be strikingly similar to the *mêtis* or prudent foresight of Odysseus.[196]

Milton's admiration for the *aidôs* that shapes Hector's deliberations is not, however, without its qualifications. Although he praises the shame, "or to call it better, the reverence of our elders," that inspires Hector in battle as "the greatest incitement to vertuous deeds" that existed "of old in Philosophy," Hector's fear of dishonour nonetheless falls short of the most "ingenuous and noble degree of honest shame," which for Milton subsists in "inward reverence" or "esteem."[197] In *The Reason of Church Government*, Milton plots these different aspects of shame along an ethical spectrum, beginning (at the bottom) with "terror" and ending with reverence for God.[198] Although often interpreted as a wholesale rejection of Greek *aidôs* – a term whose flexibility and subtlety Milton seems to grasp in opting for the English "reverence" over "shame" – the anatomy of shame provided by *The Reason of Church Government* preserves many of the moral distinctions – and much of the moral ambivalence – already present in Homeric epic. Both the *Iliad* and *Odyssey* endorse the idea that "shame both harms men greatly and profits them" [*aidôs / gignetai hê t'andras mega sinetai êd'oninêsi*], a principle asserted in its most explicit form by Achilles (*Il.* 24.44–5) and echoed by Agamemnon (at *Il.* 10.237–8) and by Telemachus (*Od.* 17.347) when each warns against the deleterious effects of *aidôs*.[199]

Achilles's observation that *aidôs* both helps and hurts men, a well-known verse cited by Hesiod and Plutarch, helps to associate Homer with precisely the kind of casuistical thinking concerning shame in which Milton also engages.[200] The argument that shame may be harmful or helpful depending upon whether it is felt or merely anticipated is supported in *Paradise Lost*, as in the *Iliad* and *Odyssey*, by a shift in verb tense from present conditional (were I to do X, I would feel shame) to a suppressed conditional (had I not done X, I would not feel ashamed), the latter of which appears throughout Homeric epic.[201] Milton adapts this Homeric formula of regretful hindsight into the episodes of "mutual accusation" in which Adam and Eve engage after the fall. "Hadst thou been firm and fixed in thy dissent," Eve tells Adam, "Neither I had transgressed, nor thou with me," a blame that Adam reassigns to her one book later, telling Eve that "had not thy pride / And wandering vanity" prompted her to disregard Adam's advice, "this mischief had not then befallen" (9.1187, 9.1160–1, 10.874–5, 10.895). Unlike Hector and Odysseus, however, neither Adam nor Eve are "self-condemning" (9.1188) in their retrospection; rather, they pervert typical Homeric expressions of shame and regret in order to rebuke each other, a distinction also evident at 9.1144, where Eve chastises Adam for reproaching her with a Homeric commonplace that circulates widely among Renaissance readers: "What words have passed thy lips, Adam severe."[202] The allusion reflects Milton's appreciation that in the *Iliad*, as in *Paradise Lost*, self-delusion manifests itself through the false or specious assignation of blame to the gods or to women. After the fall, Adam and Eve are briefly recast as Paris and Helen: not only does Eve stir in Adam an ardour that resembles the "sweet desire" [*glukus himeros*] aroused by Helen in Paris at *Il.* 3.446, but she also emerges as his "*neikeos archê,*" the imagined source of his sin.[203] Both the Homeric passages and Milton's imitation of them call into question the anti-feminist impulse to blame female attractiveness or sexual allure for the overpowering effects of male desire, instead treating the male tendency to blame women for their own wayward passions as a corollary to the problem that mortals all too readily "charge" [*aitioôntai*] the gods with their own "blind folly" [*atasthaliêsin*].[204]

Milton understands the moral value of shame as varying according to its imagined cause, whether the disapproval of fellow men, the "severe and modest eye" of the conscience, or the all-seeing eye of God. This spectrum closely resembles the definitions of *aidôs* proposed by recent Homeric scholars such as Douglas Cairns, who has argued that in Homeric epic, shame is connected to *deinos* [terror; awe], to *nemesis* [righteous indignation], and to *opis theôn* [divine vengeance or pious reverence], the last of these concepts, a dread or awe inspired by the gods, constituting the most righteous and the most powerful form of shame.[205] For Milton, too, the "pious and just honouring of our selves" that he terms 'esteem' – a shame measured not by the "offence and reproach of others" but rather by dispassionate "reflection" upon one's own actions – is ethically superior to the inhibitory emotion exhibited by Hector, a shame fuelled by "feare of infamy."[206] Not all of Homer's heroes are susceptible to the same kind of shame. Achilles approaches the Miltonic ideal of esteem when he claims that "in one honor are held both the coward and the brave" [*en de iê timê êmen kakos êde kai esthlos*], a bold repudiation of Hector's honour-seeking *aidôs* in favour of an inward reverence that, like Raphael's definition of esteem, is "grounded on just and right / Well managed" (*Il.* 9.319; *PL* 8.572–3). In both poems, the noblest expressions of *aidôs* result from a process of pondering in which competing systems of moral value – divine and human, internal and collective – are weighed and found to be incommensurate. When Achilles points out that both the coward and the brave soldier may end up with "the same allotment" [*isê moira*], he is acknowledging that the Homeric gods do not judge human actions according to the same scales that humans themselves use: to him, Zeus may not value courage or honour any more than Milton's God values Adam's valour or Eve's sweet attractive grace.[207]

The Shrine of Themis: Hope and Prayer in Milton's Fallen Eden

This chapter has already explored how Milton adapts the Homeric and Hesiodic motif of day and night passing over a threshold in opposite directions, turning the image into a complex metaphor throughout the middle books of *Paradise Lost* for various forms of "horizontal" interchange: the process of deliberation, the pleasures of variety and of conversation, and the cultivation of reciprocal values such as hospitality, charity, and mutual sympathy. After the fall, the crossing of day and night also comes to symbolize the perilous moral horizons of the fallen world, a world in which alternatives are inevitable, perplexing, and as sharp as a razor's edge. Appropriately, the "Spartan Twins" (10.674), or the Dioscuri, herald the flux and antipathy of a world out of joint, divided into hemispheres and seasons, beset by extremes of cold and heat (10.675–91). Their chiastic structure mirroring the voluntary sacrifice of the Son, the Dioscuri's exchange of places conveys the urgency of choosing between mutually exclusive alternatives.[208] After the fall, the world is a place in which alternatives distress rather than delight and in which vicissitude is disagreeable rather than delectable. Milton transforms several Homeric conventions to convey the disharmony of fallen existence or the incongruity between divine and mortal knowledge. *Paradise Lost*'s epic similes, more deeply indebted to Homer than to any subsequent epic poet, dramatize the disparity between divine and mortal points of view, identifying "our vision as fallen" or reflecting the "incertitude" of the fallen condition.[209] Other techniques borrowed from Homeric epic that are put to similar use are ironic apostrophes, the use of multiple names or different idioms (divine and mortal), the not-naming of gods and heroes, and the repetition of identical lines by different speakers.[210]

Paradise Lost adapts Homeric techniques of repetition in order to convey a range of theological and hermeneutic problems concerning the perils of mediation. In Homeric epic, different speakers often use the same words unaware that other speakers have already spoken them, a technique that in *Paradise Lost* serves to highlight the potential for misinterpretation as concepts are "translated" from heaven to earth in a cosmic game of telephone that has profound spiritual consequences after the fall, when "to God [there] is no access / Without mediator" (12.239–40).[211] Milton marshals these scenes of repetition to present a complex account of the mediatory power of prayer. When, at *PL* 10.1099–1104, the narrator repeats Adam's prayer (10.1087–92), he assists in the mediation of that prayer, interceding along with the Son and the Holy Spirit on behalf of

Adam and Eve. As prevenient grace descends to remove the "stony from their hearts," Adam and Eve breathe "sighs" that the "spirit of prayer / Inspired, and winged for heaven with speedier flight / Than loudest oratory," an image that adapts Homer's *epea pteroenta* [winged words] to testify to the greater immediacy and efficacy of Christian prayer over pagan supplication (11.6–8). Yet that immediacy is quickly undercut. The prayer uttered by Adam and Eve is separated from God by the "intermission" between Books 10 and 11, and although we are reassured that their prayer flies up to heaven, "nor missed the way, by envious winds / Blown vagabond or frustrate" (11.15–16), the narrator's comparison between Adam and Eve and the image of "Deucalion and chaste Pyrrha … / … before the shrine / Of Themis" (11.9, 12–14) calls into question the extent to which prayers may bend divine will.

In classical mythology, Themis and the Horai are goddesses of prayer and supplication who possess intercessory powers.[212] According to Thomas Heywood, who links the Horai etymologically to *oratum*, the Latin word for prayer, Themis and her daughters "have the power to admit of our devotions, and give them accesse unto the gods," a role also accorded them by the *Iliad* and by Ovid's *Fasti*, where the Horai appear as heaven's gatekeepers.[213] Although Adam and Eve's prayer at the beginning of Book 11 of *Paradise Lost* is chiefly indebted to the "second" creation story in Book 1 of Ovid's *Metamorphoses*, where Deucalion and Pyrrha restore humankind by creating a new race after the flood, Milton's interest in the "shrine of Themis" also derives from her mythographic status as a goddess who reconciles human effort and divine grace and is thus supportive of Milton's compatibilist theology. In sixteenth- and seventeenth-century mythographies, the intercession of Themis and the Horai is commonly explained not in terms of irresistible grace but rather in terms of the mutual contribution of human effort and divine pity. According to Heywood, Themis and her daughters have the power to "ripen all mens actions by their care," while Conti observes that Themis and the Horai watch over mortals to "see how industrious we are" [*inspectarent diligentioribusque*], since "God always takes pity on men for the work that they do" [*Nam humanam industriam nunquam deserit divina clementia*].[214] Both explanations reveal the circumscribed nature of Themis's intervention in the human sphere: unlike their sisters the Moirai, the Horai do not "fate" or "doom" but merely "ripen" human actions, using natural means to realize and sustain natural ends.[215] All actions performed by the Horai can and may be neglected, negated, or otherwise undone by the vicious impulses of human nature.

In the final books of *Paradise Lost*, Milton imitates several Homeric passages concerning the Horai in order to raise questions about the efficacy of human prayer. In the *Iliad*, although the Horai assist in acts of supplication by opening and closing the doors of Olympus for the entreaties of mortals beneath, the gates of Olympus open and shut *automatai* [by themselves], as do those of Milton's heaven, "self-open[ing] wide / On golden hinges turning" in a manner that hints at the unconstrained nature of divine strength as well as the mysteriousness of divine grace (*Il.* 5.749, cf. 8.393; *PL* 5.254–5).[216] Although God's "heavenly doors" (11.17) – or rather the "living doors" (7.566) of his ears – do open for Adam and Eve's prayer, Adam can hardly be certain of the efficacy of his supplication. Three times in the space of five hundred lines, Adam expresses doubt that prayer will make God "relent and turn / From his displeasure" (10.1093–4), his lack of confidence punctuated each time by an "if":

If prayers
Could alter high decrees, I to that place
Would speed before thee, and be louder heard. (10.952–4)
... if we pray him, will his ear
Be open, and his heart to pity incline. (10.1060–1)
... if by prayer
Incessant I could hope to change the will
Of him who all things can. (11.307–9)

Although Adam is correct that his supplications will not change God's "absolute decree" (11.311) – he still must leave Eden and suffer death – he underestimates the power of the Son to "mitigate" that decree by interpreting his prayer so as to "bend" God's ear (11.41, 11.30). Adam's ongoing deliberation about whether and to what extent his prayer might bend God's will internalizes the pivotal question raised by one the most famous passages in the *Iliad*, the fable of Atê and the Litae that Phoenix recounts to Achilles in order to persuade him to put aside his wrath and make amends with Agamemnon. Phoenix placates Achilles by arguing that "even the very gods can bend [*streptoi*]": when men employ "incense and reverent vows and libations and the savor of sacrifice," according to Phoenix, they can "turn [the gods] from wrath with supplication [*lissomenoi*]" even when they transgress or err [*huperbêê kai hamartê*] (*Il.* 9.497, 499–501). Phoenix's emphasis upon the conciliatory effect of the sweet odours produced by the sacrifices of the remorseful helps to explain the uncharacteristically Laudian accoutrements of Milton's Son when he appears as a "priest" who combines "sighs / And prayers" in a "golden censer, mixed / With incense" in order to produce a concoction of "pleasing savour" to God (*PL* 11.23–6). The imagery is overtly scriptural: Rev. 5.8 describes the prayers of the saints as "golden bowls full of incense" rising up to heaven. Yet Milton's ambivalence towards the efficacy of prayer is invigorated by his Homeric source more than its scriptural parallel. Phoenix explains to Achilles:

> For Prayers [Litai] there are as well, the daughters of great Zeus, halting and wrinkled and of eyes askance, and they are ever mindful to follow in the steps of Atê. But Atê is strong and fleet of foot, so she far outruns them all, and goes before them over the whole earth making men to fall, and Prayers follow after, seeking to heal the hurt. (*Il.* 9.502–7)

The Homeric parable leaves it unclear if the crippled deities of forgiveness will ever catch up to swift-footed Atê, a problem foregrounded by Alciati's emblem of the parable, "Remedia in arduo, mala in prono esse" [Remedies ascend a steep and difficult path; woes descend in a downward direction], which focuses on the stooped postures and the canes of the slow-paced prayers (see figure 10). This problem is likewise refracted in the delay between Phoenix's speech and the scene of supplication and forgiveness that concludes the *Iliad* fifteen books later. As Milton adapts this typically Homeric narrative technique of delay, the delay couches divine pity in mystery: prayers work, as Phoenix, suggests, but they do so in inscrutable ways and at unpredictable times. When Adam exclaims that "justice divine / Mends not her slowest pace for prayers or cries," his metaphor inverts Homer's fable: prayers may rise swiftly to heaven, but divine justice – as manifested by the punishment of death – moves slowly (10.858–9).[217]

The various correspondences established between Achilles and Adam in the final books of *Paradise Lost* are grounded in Milton's recognition that the power of prayer to transform wrath into pity is an uncertain and gradual process, one that depends upon Adam's ability to set aside his "blame" when Eve, here cast as Priam, appears before him as a "suppliant" (10.958, 10.917).[218] As Colin Burrow has argued, the "commiseration" (10.940) produced by their reconciliation is modelled upon the "Homeric fellow-feeling" that knits together Achilles and Priam.[219] Priam supplicates Achilles by imploring him to "Remember thy father ... whose years are like mine," words that knit a chiastic knot of sympathy between the two men: Priam remembers Hector and weeps, while "Achilles [weeps] for his own

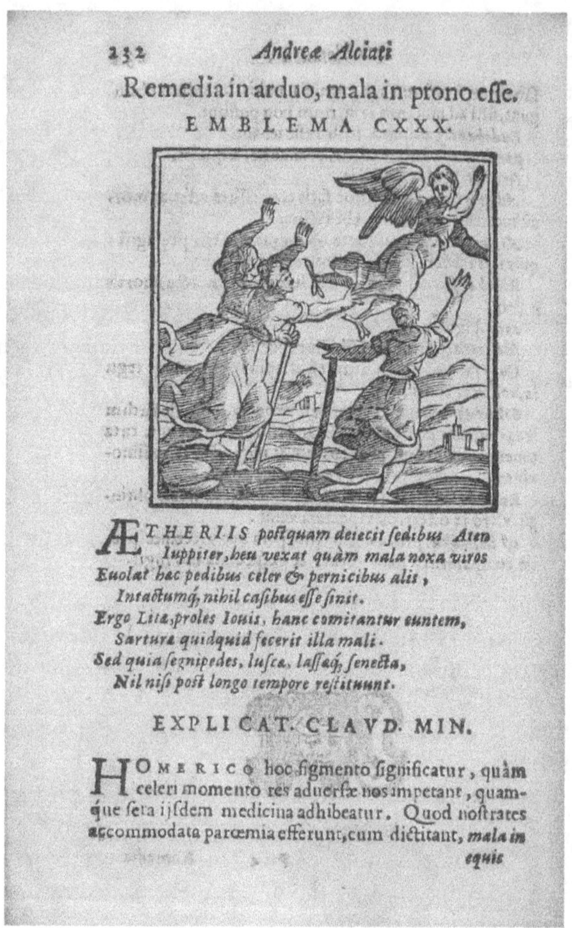

232 *Andreæ Alciati*

Remedia in arduo, mala in prono esse.

EMBLEMA CXXX.

ÆTHERIIS postquam deiecit sedibus Aten
Iuppiter, heu vexat quàm mala noxa viros
Euolat hæc pedibus celer & pernicibus alis,
Intactumq́, nihil casibus esse sinit.
Ergo Litæ, proles Iouis, hanc comitantur euntem,
Sartura quidquid fecerit illa mali.
Sed quia segnipedes, lusca, lassaq́, senecta,
Nil nisi post longo tempore restituunt.

EXPLICAT. CLAVD. MIN.

HOMERICO hoc figmento significatur, quàm celeri momento res aduersæ nos impetant, quamq́ue sera iisdem medicina adhibeatur. Quod nostrates accommodata parœmia efferunt, cum dictitant, *mala in equis*

Figure 10. Andrea Alciati, *Emblemata* (Padua: Pietro Paolo Tozzi, 1618), p. 232: Emblem 130: "*Remedia in arduo, mala in prono esse.*" Courtesy Rubenstein Rare Book and Manuscript Library, Duke University.

father" (*Il.* 24.486–7, 24.509–11). One of Adam's most anguished moments in the final books of *Paradise Lost* is precipitated by a similar emotional reciprocity between son and father, although in Adam's case, the father whose grief he feels as his own is God. Witnessing the destruction brought about by the flood, he grieves "as when a father mourns / His children, all in view destroyed at once" (11.760–1), a sorrow that the childless Adam has yet to feel except in sympathy with a God who "[g]rieved at his heart, when looking down he saw / The whole earth filled with violence" and depravity before the flood (11.887–8). Lamenting his own foreknowledge of the flood, Adam feels an agony that helps him commiserate with God.

The bond of sympathy between Achilles and Priam is knit by Iris, the swift-footed messenger who visits Priam before the final scene of the *Iliad*, advising him to pacify Achilles with gifts and reassuring him that "I am a messenger to you from Zeus, who, far away though he is, cares for you greatly and pities you" (24.173–4). In Homer and Hesiod, Iris has three principal attributes: she is quick; she is accurate, often speaking "winged words"; and she is a peacemaker who resolves disputes and assists in relaying prayers up to Olympus.[220] In her two appearances in *Paradise Lost*, Iris arrives at moments that promise a joy or harmony that is not to be. She first appears, as "Iris all hues" (4.698), in the catalogue of flowers adorning Adam and Eve's nuptial bower, her irenic influence mirrored in the "hymenean" (4.711) song that celebrates their union. She next appears as the "triple-coloured bow" sent by God to Noah as a symbol of His new covenant after the end of the flood, a bright portent of peace and regeneration that is dimmed all too soon by the rise of Nimrod at the beginning of Book 12. As an "Internuntia Deorum," Iris is often identified by Renaissance scholars and mythographers as a pagan counterpart to the rainbow of Gen. 9.8–14, a "Token of the Covenant between God and Man" that brings a message of "Peace and Reconciliation with the New World" or guarantees "a certain correspondence and concatenation of earthly with celestial things."[221] In "On the Morning of Christ's Nativity," Milton follows mythographic convention when he imagines how "Truth, and Justice then / Will down return to men, / Orbed in a rainbow."[222] Yet in *Paradise Lost*, the rainbow is not a "pacific sign" of reconciliation (11.860) but rather an emblem of the mixed lot of human experience, her stippled streaks of colour symbolizing the mottled condition of fallen existence. Although Adam initially construes the rainbow as the "brow of God appeased" (11.880), Michael corrects this misinterpretation and explains that

> when he brings
> Over the earth a cloud, [God] will therein set
> His triple-coloured bow, whereon to look
> And call to mind his covenant: day and night,
> Seed-time and harvest, heat and hoary frost
> Shall hold their course, till fire purge all things new. (11.895–900)

Michael's explanation is not very comforting: the harsh extremes of fallen nature will persist in discordant alternation until the Apocalypse, a pattern reticulated in the appearance of Noah, the "only son of light / In a dark age" (11.808–9), as well as in the rainbow itself, produced out of an interaction between sun and clouds. The moral significance of the rainbow is evident in Michael's advice "to temper joy with fear / And pious sorrow" (11.361–2), a lesson already instilled in Adam through the experience of prayer, which allows for "new hope to spring / Out of despair, joy, but with fear yet linked" (11.138–9).

The hope felt by Milton's Adam after the fall – a hope that springs from despair – is a far cry from the virtue praised by Paul at 1 Cor. 13.13. At several points in the final books of *Paradise Lost*, Milton adapts elements from the final book of the *Iliad* in order to inject pessimism into the Old Testament narratives related by Michael, narratives that validate hope theologically, through the promise of the fulfilment of the old law by the new. In addition to invoking a distinctly Homeric rainbow to signal the mixed lot of fallen existence, Milton likewise transforms another episode from Book 24 of the *Iliad* – Achilles's speech about Zeus's two jars – to justify the existence of evil and to correct the misapprehension that God creates evil in the fallen world. Milton allows God to answer this charge one final time in a speech that imitates one of the most vexing passages of Homeric epic and renders that speech theologically compatible with *Paradise Lost*'s own theodicy. In the *Iliad*, Achilles explains to Priam, "two urns are set on Zeus's floor of gifts that he gives, the one of ills, the other of blessings." To some mortals, Zeus gives a "mixed lot" such that they "meet now with evil, now with good," while to others he gives only from the baneful urn, subjecting them to madness, dishonour, and sorrow (24.527–32). Since antiquity, Homer's readers had struggled with the theological implications of the speech: in the *Republic* (380c), Plato objects to it for attributing evil to the gods, but Proclus later solves this problem by interpreting the two urns as "the unified source of mutable things," a defence echoed by many of Homer's Renaissance readers. In his paraphrase on the Psalms, Henry Hammond quotes Achilles's speech as a testimony to "God's gifts and dispensations," proposing it as a pagan analogue to Ps. 11.6, which depicts the wicked receiving an evil portion from a cup as God rains down fire and brimstone upon them.[223] Guillaume Paquelin comes even closer to Milton's own treatment of the passage when he interprets Zeus's two jars as exemplifying a monistic theory of matter: man is created good "but is changed into evil" on account of sin.[224] Explaining what has become of the "two fair gifts" with which he first endowed Adam and Eve, Milton's God adapts Zeus's two jars into a defence of a monistic cosmos in which humans enjoy a free will that exonerates God from the creation of evil.

Although God gives Adam and Eve "happiness / And immortality" at their creation, the former is "fondly lost" with the fall: since the latter "served but to eternize woe" after the fall, becoming a curse rather than a gift, God "provided death" (11.57–61), thus explaining how good is transformed into evil ("of incorrupt / Corrupted") while also vindicating God as the agent of that transformation.

God's explanation of how his two gifts to Adam and Eve are "tainted" by the "sin, that first / Distempered all things" (11.52 11.55–6) resolves some the theological problems provoked by Achilles's speech and also evokes another ancient urn of Zeus, this one also laden with gifts. Right after the allusion to Iris, Milton's narrator calls the innocent Eve "more lovely than Pandora, whom the gods / Endowed with all their gifts" (4.714–15), an ominous prolepsis of the fall that also sets into motion an investigation into the uses and perils of hope that dominates the final books of *Paradise Lost*.[225] When Hesiod's Pandora opens her box, she unleashes countless evils and miseries on the world, leaving only *Elpis* – Hope or Anticipation – in its "unbreakable home under the lid of the storage jar, according to the plans [*boulêsi*] of Zeus" (*WD*, 96–9). Zeus's preservation of hope is an antidote to the "countless ... miseries" that Pandora unleashes on the world, an act of divine beneficence that spares humankind the agony of anticipating future pain, instead allowing sickness and evil to "come to mortals in silence" (*WD*, 100–3). Yet Hesiod, like Homer, is ambivalent about hope, which is "good if it inspires men to work ... and bad if it lulls an idle man into illusory expectations for the future."[226]

The final books of *Paradise Lost* share this ambivalence, inheriting from its Homeric and Hesiodic sources a similar hesitancy about the hope that is ubiquitous in Pandaemonium yet conspicuously absent from Michael's catalogue of virtues in Book 12 ("add faith," he tells Adam, "Add virtue, patience, temperance, add love" [12.581–2]). Milton's rebel angels, by contrast, fall victim to a "[f]allacious hope" (2.568) evident in their abuse of subjunctive and conditional phrases and modals – if, until, perhaps, may, might. The misguided optimism reflected in Satan's conditional language either lulls the rebel angels into spiritual complacency or fosters an overconfidence that, as Satan puts it, makes them believe that they "may with more successful hope resolve" a second battle against God (1.120).[227] Belial, another purveyor of false hope, proposes that "[o]ur supreme foe in time may much remit / His anger," musing that the rebel angels cannot know for sure "what hope the never-ending flight / Of future days may bring, what chance, what change / Worth waiting" (2.210–11, 2.221–3). Yet both of these expressions of hope display a blindness to the workings of divine providence, a blindness confirmed by the simile of the pilot who drops his "fixèd anchor" only to discover that he has landed on a whale rather than an island (1.200–6). Often interpreted as an emblem of "false presumptuous hope" (2.522), the simile demonstrates how the "reinforcement" that the rebel angels "may gain from hope" (1.190) only compounds the illusions and fallacies to which they are vulnerable.[228]

Milton's denunciation of the fallacy of hope culminates in Satan's soliloquy at the beginning of Book 4, a speech that illustrates how erroneous beliefs and ambitions may grow out of the hope that springs from despair. Bidding "farewell" to "fear" and "remorse," Satan anticipates that he will hold "[d]ivided empire" with God, hoping that "more than half perhaps will [I] raign" (4.108–9, 4.111–12). The speech casts a dark cloud on the "new hope" that will later "spring / Out of despair" for Adam and Eve after they issue their remorseful prayer (11.138–9). Although this hope does not reflect the same degree of delusion that accompanies satanic hope in *Paradise Lost*, it must nonetheless be tempered and limited in order to serve its proper spiritual function.[229] Even the hope awakened by their prayer is limited in the good it can accomplish: the foresight afforded by Michael's final vision of the Last Judgment is circumscribed by his admonition to "hope no higher," a warning echoing the one issued by the narrator after he compares Eve to Pandora in Book 4: "Sleep on, / Blest pair; and O yet happiest if ye seek / No happier state, and know to know no more" (4.773–5). While Promethean foresight is essential for effective deliberation before the fall – for the anticipation and prevention of future ills – all that remains after the fall is an Epimethean hindsight that proves a source of misery for Adam, who like Prometheus's brother does learn to be wise, "but too late."[230] As a mark of the deficiency of fallen human judgment, Adam's regretful hindsight is the limited knowledge of one who has opened Pandora's *pithos* and is left with the very imperfect antidote of hope.[231] At the end of *Paradise Lost*, Adam and Eve are "looking back" (12.641) even as they advance towards a world that is "all before them" (12.641, 12.646), replicating Michael's pregnant pause as he suspends his narrative "[b]etwixt the world destroy'd and world restor'd" (12.3). In this momentary counterbalance between foresight and hindsight, between the prescience demanded by deliberation and the retrospective knowledge that comes with regret, Adam and Eve are poised on a razor's edge between the two forms of moral knowledge that Milton's poem inherits from Homeric epic and makes its own.

Chapter Six

Hobbes's Homer and the Idols of the Agora

The previous chapter argues that *Paradise Lost* adapts and transforms certain elements of Homer's *Iliad* and *Odyssey* in order to accommodate them to Milton's theological and political beliefs. Milton reinvents Homer as a poet who prizes rational deliberation and labours to vindicate God from charges of injustice and partiality. Hobbes, meanwhile, reinvents Homer according to the core principles of his own moral and political philosophy. Hobbes's translation of Books 9 through 12 of the *Odyssey* appeared in 1673; his complete translation of the *Odyssey* was printed in 1675, and his translation of the *Iliad* followed one year later. Eric Nelson has aptly called Hobbes's Homer a "*Leviathan* by other means," and his recent edition of the translations argues that the work may have provided a refuge for Hobbes after he was barred from publishing political and theological works in the mid-1660s.[1]

Despite the fact that Hobbes undertook the task of translating Homer only in his extreme old age, there is plenty of evidence to suggest that he had long been an admirer of the poet. His library catalogue, composed during the 1620s while he was serving as tutor to William Cavendish, includes a hand-signed edition of Chapman's translation of the *Hymns* and *Batrachomyomachia*; it is quite possible that Homer's two early English translators knew each other personally, since they moved in similar circles and shared a close friend in Ben Jonson during the 1620s. John Aubrey reports that although Hobbes owned "very few books" and hardly ever kept more than "half a dozen about him in his chamber, Homer and Virgil were commonly on his table" (HH 1:xvii–xix). In his original works, though they are on the whole remarkably devoid of classical allusions, Homer is the ancient author most frequently quoted by Hobbes, winning out over Euripides's *Medea*, which he had translated into Latin in 1602 at the tender age of fourteen.[2] One of Hobbes's few stated motives for translating Homer is that he "felt that his Greek and Latin were gradually slipping away from him" during his years spent on the European continent; upon his return, he resolved to "appl[y] himself with diligence to the historians and the poets," a resolution that culminates in his translation of Homer, begun in his eighty-first year and finished at age ninety-one, when he finally completed his translation of the *Cyclometria*.[3]

Hobbes's attraction to Homer is at once ideological and stylistic. Jerry Ball has remarked that it is especially fitting that Hobbes, who "regarded motion as the one great inarguable fact," produced a translation of Homer "that read[s] with something approaching Homer's celebrated rapidity," and other critics have observed that his translations replicate the low diction, the brevity, and the clarity that he favoured in his own writing, thus illustrating Quentin Skinner's observation that Hobbes often practises his preferred rhetorical precepts in his texts.[4] In his *Answer to Davenant*, Hobbes had observed that Greek and Latin "have put off flesh and blood, and are become immutable, which none of the modern tongues are like to be." This immutability, with its accompanying lack of ambiguity, attracts Hobbes to Homer in particular; the preface to his 1675 translation of the *Odyssey* praises the Greek poet for excelling Virgil in "clearness of Images (or Descriptions)" (*HH* 1:xcvii).[5]

Few of Hobbes's modern critics, however, have seriously contemplated the significance of his Homeric translations to the rest of his career.[6] Partly by virtue of his own observations in works such as *The Elements of Law*, Hobbes is understood by the majority of his modern readers as turning away from humanistic endeavours in the 1630s, rejecting "dogmatical" knowledge in favour of "mathematical" knowledge on the grounds that only the latter is "free from controversies and dispute."[7] Hobbes's stated reasons for undertaking a translation of the *Iliad* and *Odyssey* are coyly unhelpful in making sense of his true motives. In his prose autobiography, Hobbes dismisses his translations as works of his dotage done to pass the time "once his adversaries were silenced," a claim that neglects the fact that Hobbes was still under attack from some of those adversaries as well as the fact that a "Hobbesian" translation of Homer may well have constituted an effective if subtle counteroffensive against those adversaries. While Homer's treatment of "justice and policy" may well be fraught with the kind of "contradiction" that Hobbes professes to avoid in his moral and political philosophy, Homeric epic nonetheless provides a platform for many of his most controversial and hard-fought principles. Nelson's edition provides abundant evidence that Hobbes intended to turn

Homer into a "seventeenth-century Erastian monarchist," an interpretation strengthened by Hobbes's remark in his *Philosophical Rudiments* that ancient writers "preferred the monarchical state before all others, ascribing the rule of the gods to one Jupiter."[8] At numerous places in both poems, Hobbes excises passages that undermine sovereign authority and elaborates upon those that cement it.[9] Moreover, many of Hobbes's chief concerns in earlier works such as *Leviathan* and *Elements of Law* are reticulated in the alterations he makes to the text of the *Iliad* and *Odyssey*: Hobbes accentuates Homer's intermittently dim view of factionalism and dissent, particularly in scenes of council; he inflates Homer's distrust of rhetoric and of the "divine pretensions of poets"; he redefines key terms such as *timê* [honour] and *zêlos* [emulation or rivalry] according to the definitions laid down in his own writings; and he casts doubt on certain Homeric religious beliefs and practices as superstitions that befit the Kingdom of Faeries envisioned in the closing pages of *Leviathan* (*HH* 1:36).

Hobbes's translations thus provide a corrective to Milton's interpretation of Homer – an interpretation that strives to make the Greek poet a spokesman for political and theological liberty. In *Leviathan*, Hobbes had complained that the reading of "Greek, and Latin Authors" nurtures in certain contemporaries a love of "tumults, and of licentious controlling the actions of their Soveraigns," a role in which Homer is enlisted by many republican readers during the 1640s and 1650s.[10] Although he never says so explicitly, Hobbes certainly conceives of his translations as an antidote to readers "deceived, by the specious name of Libertie" as they read works of classical literature and philosophy.[11] The Homer who emerges in the pages of Hobbes's translations is a poet who strives to explain the causes of discord and to identify possible solutions to it, not to license it. Moreover, the origins of and resolutions to strife underscored by Hobbes's translations of Homer are strikingly similar to the views he espouses in works such as *Elements of Law*, which depicts human life as a "race" whose prize is "no other garland, but being foremost," or *Leviathan*, which depicts it as a "perpetuall and restless desire of Power after Power, that ceaseth only in death."[12] Particularly in its opening two books, the *Iliad* dramatizes many of the conflicts analysed by these works and offers a similar resolutions to them. Although Achilles and Agamemnon may be seen as fundamentally equal – both justifiably lay claim to the epithet "*aristos Achaiôn*" [best of the Achaeans] – their persistent competition over honour and power, as well as their diffidence or mistrust of each other, necessitates the recognition of a "coercive power" able to reduce a "plurality of voices" in the Achaean council "unto one Will," as Odysseus famously argues during the council scene of Book 2.[13] The Achaean willingness to "conferre all their power and strength upon one Man" in the form of Agamemnon ensures both victory and peace through unity, a lesson that Hobbes extracts from Homer's account of the Trojan War as early as 1628, when he observes in the margins of his translation of Thucydides that the "name of Hellenes [was] not given to all the Grecians in the time that Homer wrote his poems" and that the "Trojan Warre was the first Enterprise when the Grecians combined their forces."[14] Such a reading makes the *Iliad* ground zero for the kind of harmony Hobbes sought to impose after the restitution of the English monarchy.

Hobbes's Discreet Epic

Hobbes's reading of the *Iliad* and *Odyssey* as parables about how the "irregular jostling" between men demands a "common Power to keep them all in awe" lest they live in a state of "warre ... of every man, against every man" challenges more conventional Royalist interpretations of scholars such as John Ogilby, whose 1660 translation of the *Iliad* welcomes the restoration of Charles II by presenting the Homeric poet as "a most constant Assertor of the Divine Right of Princes and Monarchicall Government."[15] Although Hobbes may have applauded certain facets of Ogilby's interpretation, such as his claim that Homer's representation of Agamemnon teaches "Good Subjects" to be "meek and peaceable like sheep" instead of "tearing and ravenous wolves," he clearly targets Ogilby's translation in his preface to his own work, where he explains that he omitted "Annotations" by demurring that "I had no hope to do it better than it is already done by Mr. Ogilby."[16] The remark is aptly interpreted by Nelson as a piece of irony, not only because Ogilby was somewhat less than a stellar scholar but also because his translation interprets the *Iliad* as a wholesale endorsement of the Stuart ideals of divine right kingship, a poem that enthusiastically applauds the restoration of Charles II (*HH* 1:xcix). Given Hobbes's "remorseless barrage of scornful comment" against his adversaries in earlier works, the absence of annotations in his translations of Homer may also reveal his reluctance to continue engaging in the kind of "copious ... jearing" for which Henry More faults Hobbes in a 1662 work.[17] The absence of a commentary may also reveal Hobbes's reluctance to lay bare the resemblances between his own moral and political philosophy and that of Homer. At the end of *Leviathan*, Hobbes explains that he has "neglected the Ornament of quoting ancient Poets, Orators, and Philosophers" because "it is many times with a fraudulent Designe that men stick their corrupt Doctrine with the Cloves of other mens wit," an accusation directed primarily at the erudition of contemporaries who bring "Greek and Latine Sentences unchewed ... up again" to defend the republican cause through what Hobbes contemptuously calls an "argument of Indigestion."[18] Disinclined to expose his sympathies with Homer in the heavy-handed manner of Ogilby, Hobbes is equally reluctant to spell out too explicitly the key principles of Homer's moral and political philosophy, a technique that confirms his observation in *De Cive*, where Hobbes commends the prudence of ancient writers "who rather chose to have the science of justice wrapped in fables, than openly exposed to disputations."[19] The influence of Bacon's *Wisdom of the Ancients* is evident here, as in Chapman's earlier translation, but without any whiff of the involuted mystery that Chapman delights to find in Homer.

By refusing to establish Homer as the forerunner of his own philosophical program, Hobbes sidesteps the sorts of disputes that had come to define his career for the previous three decades. Abraham Cowley suggests as much when, in an epigram printed in 1680, he praises Hobbes for rejecting the "cursed Strife" of political and philosophical disagreements in favour of translating Homer:

Tom's grown Another Man, and now himself betakes
To poetry, and Sonnets makes
Of Gods, and Goddesses, and such like things:
He's now the Eccho of what HOMER sings.[20]

Despite Cowley's mock-praise for Hobbes's abandonment of the combative arena of philosophical dispute ("Opposing Truths") in favour of the irenic world of rhyme, these two fields form the complementary opposites of Hobbes's temperament, defined by Cowley as a jumble of "contradictions" between "Old Age, & Youth, Aetnean Cold & Heat." Hobbes's Homer is no olive branch; in fact, it constitutes a final assault against his adversaries, albeit a discreet one. Such discretion is, according to Hobbes, the key virtue of Homeric epic: in the preface to his translation of Homer, he asserts that the qualities required by "Heroick" poetry are comprehended by "one word, Discretion" (*HH* 1:67). As Nelson has pointed out, Hobbes's desire to "inject discretion into the greatest of the ancient epics" is puzzling, if only because quite a few of Homer's Renaissance readers faulted his poems for being less than discreet (*HH* 1:xxxvii). While it is possible that Hobbes "truly believes in Homer's towering discretion," it is more probable that "it is not the actual Homer, but rather *Hobbes's*

Homer" who is being celebrated for its discretion in his prefatory essay (*HH* 1:xli).

Sixteenth- and seventeenth-century writers are all too eager to align Homer with a broad and conflicting spectrum of political positions ranging from republicanism to monarchy to the kind of proto-Hobbesian Erastianism espoused by Ulysses in Shakespeare's *Troilus and Cressida*.[21] Hobbes is more tentative than many of his contemporaries about making Homer a vehicle for "public policy" in this manner. Even so, a number of passages in Hobbes's translations of the *Iliad* and *Odyssey* are rendered into maxims that echo the key principles of his own moral and political philosophy. Hobbes transforms a line spoken by Odysseus to reflect the view that "men's desires inherently conflict," changing Odysseus's observation that "different men take joy in different works" [*allos gar t'alloisin anêr epiterpetai ergois*] to "Many things are there wherein one delights, / Which to another man unpleasant be" (*HH* 2:189; *Od.* 14.228). At *Od.* 22.331–2, Hobbes alters a maxim spoken by Odysseus – "doing good is much more profitable than doing bad" [*kakoergiês euergesiê meg'ameinôn*] – so as better to conform with his own, rather different views of profit or self-interest (*HH* 2:293, translating *Od.* 22.374).

These are, admittedly, subtle changes, and the creation of rhymed *sententiae* in English and Latin editions of Homeric epic is common enough during the period.[22] But the above adages confirm the value that Hobbes places throughout his translation on discretion and disinterestedness. Hobbes goes further than even Milton in celebrating Zeus's neutrality: according to his preface, "Homer indeed maketh some Gods for the *Greeks*, and some for the *Trojans*; but always makes *Jupiter* impartial. And never prefers the judgment of a Man before that of *Jupiter*" (*HH* 1:xcvii). To confirm the impartiality of Homer's supreme deity, Hobbes removes several lines at *Il.* 8.225, which describe how Zeus is moved by the sight of Agamemnon weeping; at the beginning of Book 6, he adds several lines to confirm that, despite the events of the previous book, "The Gods to neither side assistance yield, / But on his own hand each mans fortune lies" (*HH* 1:124, 1:92). Whereas Milton is attracted to Homer's representation of gods swayed by passion and pity, Hobbes most certainly is not, taking several opportunities to help Homer's deities rise up above the passion and self-interest that so often motivate their actions in the *Iliad* and *Odyssey*. At *Od.* 20.260, for instance, Hobbes eliminates three lines (20.284–6 in the Greek) that depict Athena encouraging the suitors to persist in insulting Odysseus in order to enrage him (*HH* 2:271). For Hobbes, such behaviour is a far cry from the wisdom that Athena is supposed to embody. In addition to presenting the Homeric pantheon as dispassionate, Hobbes also presents Homer as dispassionate, a poet capable of tempering his "Elevation of Fancie" with a "discretion" that demands both self-restraint and impartiality (*HH* 1:xciv).

One of the most striking alterations made by Hobbes to the text of the *Odyssey* is his rearrangement of the last four lines of the poem so that its final line reads, "And thus it was agreed that War should cease" (*HH* 2:319). This is a much more concrete and definitive conclusion than the Greek, which ends not with the "truce" [*horkia*] but rather with a somewhat haunting and mysterious image of "Pallas Athene, daughter of Zeus, who bears the aegis, in the likeness of Mentor both in form and in voice" [*Pallas Athênaiê, kourê dios aigiochoio, / Mentori eidomenê êmen demas êde kai audên*] (*Od.* 24.547–8). Hobbes's rearrangement of the *Odyssey*'s final lines confirms one of the central aims of his own political philosophy: the establishment of a covenant that ensures peace and harmony. The line thus comes to affirm his own hope for a "pacified post-Civil war English society" achieved through an Act of Oblivion that resembles the truce established by Homer's Athena.[23] The translation subtly confirms Hobbes's belief in the physical principle that peace is the cessation of motion, a harmonious stillness "imposed upon the conflicts and collisions of constantly moving, desiring individuals."[24] While the "endless striving" depicted in *Leviathan* hinders rather than celebrates heroic achievement, since there is no "terminal achievement" or climax, Hobbes's translation finds a way to stop the "cycle of order and disorder, of government formation and sedition" that characterizes his view of politics.[25]

The Best of the Philosophers: Hobbes's Heroic Philosophy

Hobbes's translations of Homer may usefully be understood as the culmination of his career as a "heroic political philosopher" whose principal task is to narrate an aetiology of strife and provide possible resolutions to it.[26] In his *Answer to Davenant*, Hobbes distinguishes between "ancient Ethnick Poets" and contemporary divines, arguing that while both groups regard themselves as priests who claim for themselves divine inspiration in order to gain "dominion," the latter "raise *Discord*" instead of truth and foster "*Reformation*, *Tumult*; and *Controversie* instead of *Religion*."[27] Whereas the theologians and philosophers of his own era endanger sovereign authority through their claims of inspiration, classical poets such as Homer instead secure that authority. Various moments in Hobbes's translations of Homer confirm his belief that the principal task of the heroic poet is to use any means necessary to mitigate strife – in particular the strife caused by conflicts between disparate passions and interests – and thus to guarantee concord and peace. As such, Hobbes recognizes Homer's Achaeans as capable of transcending the political and moral discord that he himself laboured to neutralize during and after the English Civil War in works such as *Leviathan*, whose "epic scale" reflects what Sheldon Wolin has termed the "epical aim" of Hobbes's philosophical career.[28] Recent critics including Wolin, Charles Cantalupo, and David Johnston have argued that Hobbes modelled his writings upon a heroic or epic tradition of political philosophy, a tradition that originates with Plato's counteroffensive against Homer in his *Republic*. According to Wolin, the structure of *Leviathan* reveals "strong traces of and resemblances to epic poetry," an interpretation taken even further by Cantalupo, who argues that the "epic descent" in Book 4 of *Leviathan* presents a "satirical vision of disorder" in keeping with the mock-epic poems of Homer's comic imitators.[29] In his *Answer to Davenant*, Hobbes argues that when the "Precepts of true Philosophy" fail to communicate their truths, authors may legitimately turn to heroic poetry, a move that Hobbes himself had already made in his political and moral writings by assuming the role of an "agonal figure," one who approaches "intellectual disputation as a form of physical combat."[30]

Hobbes's most thoroughgoing attempt to produce a translation of Homer that reflects and validates his own philosophical doctrines is evident in his treatment of political authority. According to Nelson, "Hobbes saw a great deal of danger in the English reception" of Homer, and he crafted his translation to reflect the conviction that "no discreet epic should ever provoke sedition by speaking ill of monarchs" (*HH* 1:xxi, 1:lxii). At *Il.* I.218, for instance, he omits the phrase *dêmoboros basileus* [kings, devourers of the people], an epithet that had provided "fodder for republican pamphleteers" and for critics of monarchical arrogance since the time of Erasmus and Rabelais (*HH* 1:10). In *Behemoth*, one of the last political works he wrote before translating Homer, Hobbes had observed that like the ancient Saxons, the "Grecian army in the Trojan war" was not united into a commonwealth but was instead a "league of diverse petty" lords and states who possessed no "other obligation" to each other apart from "that which proceeded from their own fear and weakness," an interpretation of the *Iliad* that legitimates Hobbes's own political philosophy even as it also makes sense of the urgency of Odysseus's call to political unity in Book 2 of that poem.[31]

As the disunity of the Achaean troops in the opening books of the *Iliad* gives way to a harmony that clinches their ultimate victory over the

Trojans, Hobbes rewrites Homer's account of how Agamemnon comes to be acknowledged as "best of the Achaeans" so as to reflect his theory that a civil society is created out of a "concourse of wills" that agrees to recognize one supreme authority.[32] This interpretation is reinforced by Hobbes's alterations to *Il.* 1.80–5, where Calchas refers only to Agamemnon, and not to Achilles (as he does in the Greek text), as the "best of the Achaeans" [*aristos Achaiôn*] (*HH* 1:6). The *eris* between Agamemnon and Achilles is a conflict that revolves around the rightful owner of the "prize" [*geras*] of Briseïs as well as around the question of which man may rightfully claim the title of *aristos*, thus illustrating Hobbes's observation that men, apt to overvalue themselves and to undervalue others, continually dispute titles of honour, "from whence continually arise amongst them, Emulation, Quarrells, Factions, and at last Warre" (*Il.* 1.118).[33] In the *Iliad*, this dire conclusion is averted by Odysseus, who calls upon his fellow kings in the Achaean council to grant Agamemnon supreme authority, an argument that closely mirrors Hobbes's call in *Leviathan* for the English people to "conferre all their power and strength upon one Man ... that may reduce all their Wills, by plurality of voices, unto one Will."[34] In Homer's Troy, as well as Hobbes's England, this process is imperfectly achieved, thanks to the existence of councils or parliaments that undermine the king's authority and provoke disunity through rhetoric. Perhaps in response to the threat posed by the Achaean council – a council that bears a close resemblance to seventeenth-century English parliaments throughout his translation – Hobbes is forceful in his attempt to depict Agamemnon as sole and supreme authority: at *Il.* 2.532, he adds a line that identifies Agamemnon as "chief Commander," and at *Il.* 9.58–9, he cuts a half-line in which Diomedes refers to the plural "kings of the Argives" [*Argeiôn basilêas*], a phrase that undercuts his claim that Agamemnon is "most kingly" [*basileutatos*] (*HH* 1:36, 1:133; *Il.* 9.69). Similar motives drive Hobbes's omission of *Il.* 2.74 (2.86 in the Greek text), where he eliminates the narrator's reference to "sceptered kings" [*skêptouchoi basilêes*], and his omission of 1.316 (1.331 in the Greek), where two of Agamemnon's messengers visit Achilles in his tent only to be "seized with dread and respecting the king" [*tô men tarbêsante kai aidomenô basilêa*] at the sight of him, a reaction that casts serious doubt on Agamemnon's supremacy over his rival (*HH* 1:23, 1:14).

Hobbes makes a number of other alterations to speeches in the *Iliad* that concern the nature and origin of Agamemnon's authority – an authority more vigorously contested in the original Greek and also more ambiguous in its foundation and scope. In Book 9 of the *Iliad*, Hobbes translates Nestor's statement to Agamemnon that he is "the greatest king" [*basileutatos*] as "you are our General" so as to obscure the fact that Agamemnon is "one king among many" (*Il.* 9.69; *HH* 1:134). Softening an especially harsh speech that Diomedes makes to Agamemnon in the same book of the *Iliad*, Hobbes embellishes several lines so as to underscore the contractual (but still absolute) nature of Agamemnon's authority. In the Greek text, Diomedes tells Agamemnon that "with the sceptre [Zeus] has granted you to be honoured [*tetimêsthai*] above all, but valour [*alkên*] he gave you not, in which is the greatest might" (*Il.* 9.38–9). Hobbes alters the speech – one that closely resembles Odysseus's more forceful defence of Agamemnon at *Il.* 2.205–6 – in order to stress that Agamemnon's lack of valour does not compromise his authority: "*Jove* giv'n you has the Right to be obey'd, / And grac'd you with the title of our King," Hobbes's Diomedes tells his king, sidestepping the issue of Agamemnon's possible shortcomings as a ruler (*HH* 1:133).

From Hobbes's perspective, Agamemnon's faults and vices – his lack of valour or his susceptibility to passions such as anger – are irrelevant to his capacity to rule, or his authority to do so. Because he holds passions to be compulsive, and therefore blameless, Hobbes would not have understood Agamemnon's vulnerability to wrath as a threat to his authority because, as he explains in chapter 15 of *Human Nature*, men are fundamentally equal and the "little odds ... of strength or knowledge between men" means that "he that is weaker in strength or in wit; or in both, may utterly destroy the power of the stronger."[35] For similar reasons, Hobbes omits Achilles's harshest accusations against Agamemnon at *Il.* 1.323–5, where the former complains that the latter's murderous wrath has prompted him to confiscate Achilles's rightful prize. The speech is one of several passages where Hobbes either exorcises Agamemnon's anger or labours to turn it into a political virtue; the latter motive is evident at *Il.* 2.173–5, where Odysseus warns his fellow Achaeans to take care that Agamemnon "in his anger [*cholôsamenos*] ... not harm" them, since "Proud is the heart of kings, nurtured by Zeus; for their honour is from Zeus" [*thumos de megas esti diotrepheôn Basilêôn, / timê d'ek dios esti*] (2.195–6). In Hobbes's version, Odysseus asserts that "Deep rooted is the Anger of a King, / To whom high *Jove* committed has the Law, / And Justice left to his distributing," an argument that vests Agamemnon's authority in his wrath rather than depicting his passions as a threat to that authority (*HH* 1:26). Yet Hobbes also excises a few especially indecorous descriptions of kingly passion, including an extended comparison between the pain of Agamemnon's war wound and the pain of childbirth at *Il.* 11.243 (11.269–72 in the Greek) and a line in Book 8 of the *Iliad* describing how Zeus is moved by the sight of Agamemnon weeping (*HH* 1:124).

Hobbes also departs from Homer's Greek text to drive home "his central conviction that all property is from the sovereign," a principle to which he makes the text of the *Iliad* adhere as he rewrites the conflict between Agamemnon and Achilles over Briseïs. At *Il.* 1.281–5, where Nestor counsels Agamemnon, "mighty as you are," to return Briseïs to Achilles, Hobbes's translation makes it clear that Agamemnon is perfectly within his rights to claim the girl as his own, and he adds a half-line to Nestor's advice, "Atrides take not from him, *though you can*," in order to counteract Nestor's claim that Achilles's fellow Achaeans, and not Agamemnon, awarded her as a prize in the first place (*HH* 1:12, my italics). Nestor points out in the same breath that although Achilles "be strong, and on a Goddess got, / Atrides is before you in command," a much stronger assertion of Agamemnon's supremacy than one finds in the Greek, where Nestor simply states that Agamemnon has more power because he rules over more men (*HH* 1:12). Other changes in the opening books of the *Iliad* are designed to inflate Achilles's threat to Agamemnon's authority: at *Il.* 1.273, for instance, Agamemnon accuses Achilles of wishing to "give the Law to all as he thinks fit," even though the Greek contains no mention of Achilles's usurping any juridical authority (*HH* 1:12; *Il.* 1.289). By presenting Achilles as a rebel who refuses to obey or to be commanded, Hobbes's translation turns him into a personification of *pleonexia*, or encroaching, a central concept in *Leviathan*, which defines it as the "desire of more than [one's] share."[36] Even the title that Hobbes bestows on the opening book of the *Iliad* – the "discontent and secession of Achilles" – suggests Achilles's violation of laws of nature that Hobbes would recognize from his own writings: the law against contumely, which provokes men to fight; the law against pride, which prevents men from acknowledging all others as their equals according to nature; and the law against arrogance, which hinders men from entering into "conditions of Peace" by prompting them to wish "to reserve to himself any Right, which he is not content should be reserved to every one of the rest."[37]

A distinctly Hobbesian language of covenant and contract permeates his translation of the *Iliad*, where it often serves to illustrate the difference between the state of nature and a civil society. In a speech that neatly sums up Hobbes's understanding of the foundation of conflict in a state of nature, Achilles tells Hector, "Talk not of Oaths and Covenants to me, / That nothing worth 'twixt Lions are and Men, / And Wolves with Lambs on nothing can agree" (*HH* 1:354). Yet Hobbes ensures that the human world of the *Iliad* places great value on oaths and covenants as instruments of concord and consent. At *Iliad* 3.39–43, Hector assails his brother Paris for being "mad after women," a "deceiver," and an "object of scorn to other men"; Hobbes adds another insult to the mix, "one that durst not his own word maintain," an accusation which reflects the importance of keeping covenants in Hobbes's own political theory (*HH* 1:45). At *Il.* 3.107, after Hector issues his challenge to the Achaean army, Hobbes inserts a line into a speech by Menelaus: "'Tis good for both that makes a Contract bind" (1:47). Whereas Homer simply has Menelaus request that Priam be called upon to "swear an oath [*horkia*]" upon the challenge, Hobbes heightens the power of this "contract" to bind enemies in peace, thus permitting the "rest from woeful war" described at 3.110–12 as "best for both sides" [*arista met'amphoteroisi*]. Hobbes thus turns the scene into what his political writings call a "union," the voluntary subjection of individual will to the sovereign that takes the form of a "contract ... not to resist the will of that [sovereign]" in order to preserve peace (1:47).[38] Hobbes sometimes renders Homer's Greek *horkia* [oath] as "contract," a translation that reflects his belief that political order is "dependent upon linguistic order" such that rational discourse may guide men to a covenant with each other.[39] As a "nominalist and an empiricist" Hobbes insists upon the "need for language to have material conceptual correlatives," and his Homeric translations provide evidence that words should be binding: "Where are your promises," Nestor chides his fellow Achaeans at *Il.* 2.306–7, "and whither gone / Our oaths and vows [*sunthesiai te kai horkia*]?" (*HH* 1:30).[40] In order to add additional weight to verbal agreements reached in councils and assemblies, Hobbes prefers the term "consent," a word that according to *Human Nature* denotes a "concourse of wills" towards "some one and the same action."[41] At *Il.* 1.26 and again at 1.362, the Achaean princes "all gave their consent / Except King Agamemnon" to the request that he return Chryseis; at *Il.* 2.10–11, Hobbes depicts how the gods "consented have for Juno's sake," their agreement much firmer than in the Greek, where Homer's Olympians are "no longer divided [*amphis*] in counsel" (*HH* 1:4, 1:15, 1:21; *Il.* 2.13).

Hobbes recognizes, however, that the consent of a council carries only limited authority in the world of Homeric epic, which he understands as ruled by a single sovereign. When Nestor gives Agamemnon advice, Hobbes is careful to render his speech so as to reflect the belief that "assemblies may offer counsel, but cannot bind sovereigns" (*HH* 1:134). At *Il.* 9.69, Hobbes's Nestor tells Agamemnon, "Hear their advice, and do what you think fit," a rather radical departure from the Greek, which has Nestor tell his leader that "when many are gathered together, you will follow whoever devises the wisest counsel" [*pollôn d'agromenôn tô peiseai hos ken aristên / Boulên bouleusê*] (*HH* 1:134; *Il.* 9.74–5). His words shaped by theories of political authority laid out in works such as *Leviathan*, Hobbes's Nestor is well aware that Agamemnon is under no obligation to heed the advice of his counsel: "do then as I advise. / For I conversed have with men as good, / That yet my counsel never did despise," Hobbes's Nestor tells his leader at *Il.* 1.246–8, his phrasing suggestive of the fact that Agamemnon may choose to ignore that advice (*HH* 1:11). When a sovereign consults with his counsellors, according to chapter 25 of *Leviathan*, all ultimate decisions should still rest with the sovereign: "because many eyes see the same thing in divers lines, and are apt to look asquint towards their private benefit; they that desire not to misse their marke, though they look about with two eyes, yet they never ayme but with one."[42] Sponde construes the argument between Achilles and Agamemnon as a conflict between private and public interest, and Hobbes elaborates on this interpretation in both poems. Accordingly, at *Od.* 3.331–2, Mentor tells Telemachus that "Not with Authority, / But my advise they'll follow for respect," a distinction illustrating how Mentor's good counsel may be followed by those who deem him wise, even if he lacks the sovereign authority to issue commands (*HH* 2:38).

Hobbes's translation thus accentuates the difference between *command* and *counsel*: whereas the former must be obeyed, the latter may be disregarded, a distinction crucial to Hobbes's political philosophy as well as to his philosophy of language. According to *Leviathan*, counsel is inferior to command as a rhetorical mode because it relies upon "Exhortation, and Dehortation" and often resorts to "Similitudes, Metaphors," and "other tools of Oratory, to persuade [its] Hearers," thus making it an especially effective way for "corrupt Counsellors" to sway a "multitude" in the direction of their own self-interest.[43] The distinction between counsel and command emerges even more clearly in Hobbes's rendering of *Il.* 14.103, a passage rewritten so as to stress the superior authority of command: "Yet not *command* but *counsel* 'twas I gave" (*HH* 1:222). In scenes where one character counsels another, Hobbes's translation often conveys a diminished sense of the political weight of counsel: at *Il.* 14.59–60, for instance, Nestor advises Agamemnon, "let's consult what course to take were best, / If counsel can do any thing at all," whereas the Greek text has him doubt the efficacy of *noos*, or prudent planning (*HH* 1:221; *Il.* 14.62). An even more pessimistic assessment of the political utility of counsel emerges in Hobbes's translation of *Il.* 16.623–5, where Patroclus, in the heat of battle, chastises Meriones for fighting with words rather than weapons. In the Greek, Patroclus is arguing a point of decorum: "*epeôn d'eni boulê*" – the place for words is in council, and not on the battlefield, "[s]o we must not multiply words, but we must fight" (*Il.* 16.630–1). Yet Hobbes's translation has Patroclus observe that "[i]n council words may somewhat signify" and on the battlefield not at all, thus casting doubt upon the value of verbal conflict even in the assembly (*HH* 1:268).

Homeric *Basileus* and Hobbesian Sovereign

Many of the Hobbesian principles that Hobbes teases out of Homer's poems are genuinely present in the texts of the *Iliad* and *Odyssey* – so much so, in certain cases, that the correspondences suggest Homer's potent influence on Hobbes's moral philosophy, his faculty psychology, and his attitudes towards rhetoric. But Hobbes faces greater obstacles when he strives to use Homer as a vehicle to articulate his own conception of sovereignty. Although many of Homer's Renaissance readers interpret the poet as a defender of monarchy, the vast majority of these readings root that defence in the argument that royal power is, as Jean Bodin puts it, "natural, that is, instituted by God."[44] Yet a few, including Etienne de la Boëtie, interpret Homer's defence of royal authority rather differently. In his *De la Servitude Volontaire ou Contr'un*, La Boëtie quotes Odysseus's famous defence of single rule ("*D'avoir plusiers seigneurs aucun bien je n'y voy: / Qu'un sans plus soit le maistre, et qu'un seul soit le Roy*") and then explains that these lines do not in fact constitute an endorsement of divine right monarchy but rather are designed "to appease the revolt of the army" [*appaiser la revolte de l'armée*].[45] Although La Boëtie's ultimate goal is to distance Homer from Odysseus's defence of monarchy, whereas Hobbes wishes to align them, both interpretations rest on the premise that Odysseus's justification of single rule – "we cannot all be Kings," as Hobbes translates one key phrase in the speech – is a direct response to political turmoil (*HH* 1:27).[46] Both La Boëtie and Hobbes interpret Odysseus's speech as embodying a conception of monarchy as a human rather than a divine institution, a politically useful artifice that may at times pretend to a divinely ordained legitimacy that it does not in fact possess. In various alterations to and expurgations of the Greek text of the *Iliad*, Hobbes aligns Homer with this conception of kingship and simultaneously illustrates the dangers of setting up a "Ghostly Authority against the Civill," as he puts it in *Leviathan*.[47] At *Il.* 1.278–81, Nestor cautions Achilles not to "strive with a king, might against might" [*erizemenai Basilêi / antibiên*] because it is "no common honour that is the portion of a sceptred king to whom Zeus gives glory" [*epei ou poth'homoiês*

emmore timês / skêptouchos basileus, hô te Zeus kudos edôken]. But in Hobbes's version, Nestor provides a subtly different account of the divine origin of Agamemnon's authority, explaining that "the man / Whom *Jove* hath crown'd is made of *Jove* a limb," an image whose instrumentality accords with Hobbes's theory of sovereignty as the "artificiall chains" of a contract that binds together a civil society (*HH* 1:12).

In order to make Homer the mouthpiece for his own conception of sovereignty, Hobbes must craft a distinction in his translation between natural and positive (or civil) law that does not exist – or at least does not exist with any real clarity – in the language or culture of the Homeric poet. Hobbes's theory of sovereignty rests on the premise that the "Artificiall Chains, called *Civill Lawes*" are able to restrain the laws of nature through the "terrour of some Power."[48] In his translations of Homer, as in other works, Hobbes uses the term "justice" to indicate the "dictates of man-made law" as distinct from the laws of nature; according to his definition, justice is "conventional," and it presupposes a "civil society."[49] In his translations of the *Iliad* and *Odyssey*, Hobbes implicitly argues that the Cyclopes lack the justice that distinguishes a civil society from the state of nature: they possess "no Courts of Councel, nor of Right," and when Hobbes translates Alkinous's question to Odysseus at *Od.* 8.547–8: "What kind of People, *civil*, or without Law, / Civil [*dikaioi*] or kinde to Strangers, godly or no," he renders *dikaioi* [just] as "civil," repeating the word (as the Greek does not) in order to emphasize how the barbarous groups encountered by Odysseus, such as the Cyclopes, do not constitute civil societies (*HH* 2:114, 2:111). Although the two men were adversaries, Hobbes may have been thinking of Alexander Ross's *Mystagogus Poeticus*, which interprets Polyphemus as symbolizing a "Commonwealth without a king," consisting of "nothing but Cyclopian cruelty and oppression, great men feeding on the flesh of the poor; then is nothing, but intestine Wars and broils."[50] But Hobbes's translation of *dikaioi* [just] as "civil" also suggests that strife and war result from a failure to adhere to the "artificiall chains" of civil law. This interpretation is evident in Hobbes's rendering of Nestor's oft-quoted condemnation of civil war, verses beloved by earlier Renaissance humanists such as Erasmus. Whereas the Greek text has Nestor assert that only a "clanless, lawless, hearthless [*aphrêtôr athemistos anestios*] man ... loves the horror of war among his own people," Hobbes rearranges the diction so as to highlight the claim that only those who lack the "benefit of law" could desire civil strife: "For none but such as have no Law, no Kin, / Nor House, in *civil* discord can delight" (*Il.* 9.63–4; *HH* 1:134, my italics). Elsewhere, Hobbes accentuates the distinction between natural and positive law so as to illustrate that Homer's Achaeans and Trojans understand the concept of a civil society in which "the law of nature is eternal" and yet the "opportunities for obeying it outwardly" vary according to circumstance.[51] His translation intercedes at several junctures to drive home a strict distinction between natural and positive law. At *Il.* 4.465, Hobbes describes Priam's bastard son as a "lawful Son where Nature is the Law," a line inserted to highlight the discrepancy between natural and positive law (*HH* 1:68). At *Il.* 11.131, where the two sons of the Trojan Antimachus plead with Agamemnon for their life only to be told that their father "gave advice to murther *Menelaus* ... / ... When of the *Greeks* Ambassador he was," Hobbes interjects the phrase, "Contrary to the Laws of honesty," thus introducing into the passage one of his own laws of nature from *Leviathan* 1.15, namely, that "all men that mediate Peace, be allowed safe Conduct" (*HH* 1:168).

In spite of the fact that the two translations form the bookends of a career that spans more than a half-century, Hobbes's interpretation of Homer is heavily mediated by Thucydides, whose *History of the Peloponnesian War* he translated in 1628. Although Hobbes's translation of Thucydides was composed with the "wars of religion looming," while his translation of Homer was composed after the restoration of Charles II and accordingly imagines what a "pacified post-Civil war English society" might look like, the two projects are united by Hobbes's conviction that they offer valuable insight into the origin and containment of civil strife.[52] In his preface to the *History of the Peloponnesian War*, Hobbes observes that Homer and Thucydides are comparable stylists; both, moreover, are hostile to sedition, have a distaste for *hoi polloi*, and write with a "frank realism" that dramatizes the effects of human passion on a polity.[53] At different times in Hobbes's career, Homer and Thucydides each provide an antidote to the period's excessive reliance on Aristotle, whose "Civill Philosophy" teaches its seventeenth-century readers "to call all manner of Common-Wealths but the Popular ... *Tyranny*" according to *Leviathan*.[54] Looking back on his early work, Hobbes writes in his *Vita* that Thucydides taught him about the absurdity of popular government: "He says Democracy's a Foolish Thing / Than a Republick Wiser is one King."[55] There is abundant evidence to suggest that Hobbes approaches Homer from a similar perspective. As if to confirm his claim that "the praise of Ancient Authors, proceeds not from the reverence of the Dead, but from the competition, and mutuall envy of the Living," Hobbes looks to both writers as defenders of monarchy, and as writers able to stop the ears of his contemporaries tempted by the "siren song of classical republicanism."[56]

Hobbes is certainly not the only Renaissance writer to note the ideological and stylistic sympathies between Homer and Thucydides. Martin Crusius regarded both works as a "palaestra" of "civil prudence," and in his commentary on Book 1 of the *Iliad*, Crusius cross-references Nestor's account of the war between the Lapiths and the Centaurs at *Il.* 1.247–84 with a passage from Hemocratis's oration in Book 4 of Thucydides's *History*, a speech that condemns the "transgression of civil war" ["*Stasis … hamartias*"].[57] According to Grafton, Crusius's lectures on Thucydides "carefully analyzed the political rhetoric of all parties in the Peloponnesian War," and Hobbes employs a similar method in his translations of both writers, accentuating their rational and disenchanted account of the rhetorical, psychological, and political origins of civil strife.[58] Moreover, Hobbes borrows from both Homer and Thucydides in order to enumerate the three chief sources of discord – competition, diffidence, and glory – as well as the three chief motives for human behaviour: fear, honour, and profit or self-interest.[59]

One of the most powerful sympathies between the two writers for Hobbes is their shared recognition that "war … is a most violent master, and conformeth most men's passions to the present occasion," as Hobbes translates the line from Book 3 of Thucydides's *History*.[60] Thucydides depicts the extremity of civil war as a period of heightened ambition and rivalry, passions that demand a "particular climate and the willingness to unleash them."[61] Although neither the *Iliad* nor the *Odyssey* depicts a civil war, strictly speaking, Hobbes appreciates that the dissent and internecine strife in the Achaean camp, on Olympus, among Ithaca's suitors, and among the members of Odysseus's crew encapsulate Thucydidean lessons about human nature in a state of war, a state that puts fear of death and a desire for glory into conflict with each other such that "interest and sociability" cannot coexist.[62] Thucydides's *History* begins with an account of Agamemnon's unification of the Greek forces at Troy, a unity fostered "not so much upon favour, as by feare" that erodes as soon as "seditions" and "innovations" arise among the Greeks after their victorious return from Troy.[63]

Hobbes interprets Homer through this lens, focusing upon many of the Greek historian's key concerns, including the threat posed by councils or assemblies, the effects of fear (both beneficial and detrimental), the social dynamics of ambition and rivalry, and the abuses of rhetoric that make it necessary to distinguish between "legitimate and illegitimate appeals to the passions."[64] In the prefatory essay to his translation of Thucydides, Hobbes explains the importance of differentiating between "truth and elocution," a formula he later refines in *Elements of Law* into a distinction between "reason and persuasion," the latter of which appeals to the passions while the former does not.[65] For Hobbes, both Homer and Thucydides illustrate how civil strife throws language into disarray and how moral and political disorder may result from the fact that men "differ in their use of evaluative terms."[66] Thucydides explains that in times of sedition, the "received value of names imposed for signification of things, was changed into arbitrary. For inconsiderate boldness, was counted true-hearted manliness: provident deliberation, a handsome fear: modesty, the cloak of cowardice."[67] This destabilization of language during periods of conflict prompts Hobbes to regard rhetoric as a "dangerous weapon" during war: in *Behemoth*, he even transforms a very Homeric deity of strife into "Impudence," a "'goddess of rhetoric' in Parliament" who presides over and nurtures verbally eristic behaviour.[68] Used principally to "argue about what is good and evil," language is a chief "source [of] contention" for Hobbes, and in certain works he makes little if any distinction between verbal conflict and physical combat: in *Elements of Law*, for instance, he argues that when the "wills of two divers men produce such actions as are reciprocally resistances to each other, this is called CONTENTION," and when that resistance is "upon the persons of one another" it is called battle – a difference of degree but not ultimately of kind.[69]

Idols of the Agora

The threat posed by verbal warfare is exacerbated for Hobbes by the fact that "universal selfishness and ambition devalues rhetoric" such that no politician is disinterested enough to use rhetoric for "deliberative purposes."[70] The title page of Hobbes's translation of Thucydides hints at this intersection between rhetorical and political strife in its depiction of the two chief adversaries of the war: Archidamas, king of the Lacedaemonians, and Pericles, the Athenian statesman and orator. Underneath the first figure, in a vignette on the bottom left-hand side of the engraving, are represented "*hoi aristoi*" [the few, the aristocracy], while under Pericles, on the bottom right, are *hoi polloi*, the multitude whose spirits are roused, for better and for worse, by their leader's inspiring speeches. The title page emblematizes two key political conflicts of Thucydides's *History*, the clash between aristocratic and popular forms of government and the one between two very different styles of political leadership, the latter of which (as Hobbes understands it, and as Thucydides does to a lesser extent) relies on the power of persuasion to coalesce and inspire the multitude.

Hobbes's translation accentuates Thucydides's cautionary treatment of rhetoric, particularly the use, or rather the abuse, of rhetoric in assemblies and councils. In *Philosophical Rudiments*, Hobbes provides a testimonial to the lesson that "the tongue of man is a trumpet of war and sedition" with the figure of Pericles, of whom it is "reported … that he sometimes by his elegant speeches thundered and lightened, and confounded whole Greece itself."[71] Particularly during the English Civil War and its aftermath, many English readers look to Thucydides and Homer to mediate their concerns about the advantages and liabilities of debate in parliaments and assemblies. In *Oceana*, James Harrington extracts from his reading of Thucydides the lesson that excessive debate is dangerous to the stability of a state: whereas the government of ancient Athens consisted of a senate and an "assembly of the people resolving and too often debating – which was the ruin of it," the Lacedaemonians were governed by a "congregation of the people resolving only, and never debating – which was the long life of it."[72] Hobbes goes further still in interpreting both Thucydides and Homer as cautioning against the danger of rhetoric in council. Although he praises Thucydides as a writer whose "perspicuity and efficacy … setteth his Reader in the Assemblies of the People, and in the Senates, at their debating; in the streets, at their Seditions; and in the Field at their Battles," such vivid recreations of conciliar strife are not without risk.[73] After Cleon delivers an oration in which he warns his audience "not [to] be carried away with combats of eloquence and wit" while in the assembly, Hobbes echoes the sentiment in a rather sardonic marginal note that reads, "The nature of the multitude in council, lively set forth."[74]

Distrustful of orators whose rhetorical skill is fuelled by their self-interested pursuit of glory or their desire to provoke sedition, Hobbes is equally alarmed by the prospect of audiences too easily swayed by eloquent invective.[75] His scorn for the susceptibility of the multitude to the oratorical skills displayed in the agora also informs Hobbes's translations of the *Iliad* and *Odyssey*, where he repeatedly injects highly topical language into Homer's representation of council scenes in order to highlight the political perils of the institution. The council scenes that fill Homeric epic – thirty-seven of them, according to one scholar's reckoning – demonstrate a high tolerance for dissent and verbal abuse as participants showcase their rhetorical virtuosity through aggressive displays of insult.[76] Such verbal and political belligerence in the Homeric *bouleutêrion* attracts a range of Renaissance readers for various reasons: for some, council scenes serve as a platform to demonstrate different rhetorical styles; for others, they illustrate Homer's commitment to *parrhêsia* or to the legitimate expression of dissenting viewpoints even during periods of heightened political conflict. By contrast, Hobbes systematically alters Homeric council scenes so as to minimize the threat of dissent, to stress the limited authority of council, and to downplay the value of rhetorical skill, particularly the skills of exhortation and rebuke that garner the admiration of contemporary readers as diverse as Sturm, Crusius, Chapman, and Milton.[77]

In *Leviathan*, Hobbes quips that "to accuse, requires lesse Eloquence … than to excuse."[78] The Homeric translations bear out a similarly dim view of speakers who display an excessive gusto for verbally eristic behaviour in the assembly. The chorus of dissenting opinions in the Homeric council, a convention so masterfully imitated by Milton in the celestial and infernal councils of *Paradise Lost*, proves a challenge to Hobbes's view that governments are weakened by the "long and set orations" given in "great assemblies," in which speakers aim to "incline and sway the assembly to their own ends."[79] Whereas Hobbes holds democracy to be nothing more than "an aristocracy of orators" in which disputes between "opposite factions" eventually "dissolve into civil war," the single and undivided voice of a sovereign, who is "one by nature," ensures that there is always a "certain set time for deliberation," that the ruler "always [be] in a present capacity to execute his authority," and that the "finall Resolution" of all deliberations rests "in one man."[80] Particularly in the opening two books of the *Iliad*, Hobbes stifles the plurality of voices in the Achaean assembly, mitigating both the authority and the eloquence of those voices in order to lend credence to his assertion that "many eyes see more than one; yet [this] is not to be understood of many Counsellors."[81] Early on in Book 1, Hobbes omits a line in which the assembly shouts at Agamemnon, "respect [*aideisthai*] the priest, accept the shining ransom," a demand that would hardly please the translator given his professed distaste for rhetorical combat and his profoundly anticlerical views (*HH* 1:4; *Il.* 1.23). In Book 2, as Agamemnon concludes his speech proposing that the Achaean army return to their ships, Hobbes inserts a half-line in which the audience cries "Ha la la," an exclamation designed to "express contempt for the multitude" more explicitly than does the Greek text, which stops at comparing the reaction that courses through the assembly to waves and ears of grain stirred by the wind – precisely the simile transformed by Milton, as argued by the previous chapter of this book, into a pivotal moment of effective angelic ratiocination (*Il.* 2.146–9; *HH* 1:25). Whereas Homer's similes convey how fear precipitates velocity – the army rushes so quickly to their ships that they raise dust under their feet – Hobbes's diction instead suggests the ease with which Agamemnon persuades his audience to agree to his imprudent, cowardly plan: "with applauses high / [They] [c]onsented all," Hobbes writes, like waves "rolled ... by some great Wind at Sea" or like fields of grain that "encline" and "bo[w] their heads ... / When their consent they to the King exprest" (1:25). The inarticulateness of that consent, in combination with verbs ("encline," "bow") that convey an irrational capitulation to the winds of rhetoric, allow the passage to speak to Hobbes's suspicion that deliberation is a failed mode of discourse because most men are rhetorically "unskillful" or otherwise "incapable" of political reasoning.[82]

In order to underscore the problem that councils aggravate discord and even provoke civil war, Hobbes frequently translates the Greek *agorê* [assembly or place of assembly] as "parliament," a word that indicates the degree to which his distaste for English republicanism shapes his attitudes towards the political dynamics of the Homeric poems. At *Il.* 8.444, Hector calls his army to "Parliament," and at *Od.* 2.26, an Ithacan elder points out to Telemachus that "We ne'r convoked were to Parliament" since Odysseus's departure for Troy twenty years earlier (*HH* 1:130, 2:19). Such anachronisms are common enough in seventeenth-century translations of classical texts, but they are not always so pointed. Hobbes's use of the term is, as Nelson has argued, designed to "highlight the failure of public deliberation and debate," as are other phrases drawn from a contemporary political idiom, such as "common-councel" (2:19). At *Il.* 11.120, a vote settled in a "Common-Councel" suggests a political body whose judgments are implicitly corrupt (1:167), while the "legalistic, Parliamentarian language" used by Poseidon at *Il.* 15.156–71 underscores the illegitimacy of his complaint that Zeus, his brother, aims to "usurp upon my liberty":

> Let *Jove* then with his share contented be,
> And not encroach on me. For well 'tis known
> I hold not any thing of him in Fee,
> But live as he should do, upon my own.[83]

Whereas Homer's Poseidon justifies his claim according to the concept of *moira*, or portion – each god has been "apportioned his own domain" over which to rule – Hobbes's Poseidon argues that earth and Olympus do "Common lye" such that what appears in the Greek text to be a jurisdictional conflict among three distinct kingships is transformed into the discordant jostling among three leaders of a republic in which all things are, very problematically, held in common (*HH* 1:238). In other words, Hobbes's Poseidon mistakenly thinks of himself as one member of a triumvirate, whereas Zeus and Hobbes both recognize Olympus to be governed by one supreme ruler.

In *Philosophical Rudiments*, Hobbes appears to have Homer's Olympians foremost in his mind when he argues that the ancients "preferred the monarchical state before all others, ascribing the rule of the gods to one Jupiter."[84] This is a striking departure from the interpretations of sixteenth-century mythographers such as Vincenzo Cartari, who identifies the twelve principal Olympian gods as "counsellors of the celestial senate" [*conseilleurs du senat celeste*], explaining that "whenever there was some affair of importance, Jupiter would assemble the council to deliberate it" [*quand il y avoit quelque affaire d'importance, Iupiter faisoit assembler le conseil pour en deliberer*].[85] In *Leviathan*, Hobbes attributes the failure of council to the "factions" that arise in a commonwealth when "equal orators do combat with contrary opinions and speeches."[86] Since councils "cannot move but by the plurality of consenting opinions ... retarded by the part dissenting," it is best for a sovereign to have "no Second at all" and rely wholly on his own judgment, a model that Hobbes attempts to extract from Homeric epic as well as from other ancient sources.[87] In the preface to his *Philosophical Rudiments*, Hobbes even engages in a rare flight of allegorical fancy (albeit a Baconian flight) when he proposes to interpret the union of Ixion and Juno as a fable about councils. Invited to a banquet by Jupiter, Ixion falls in love with Juno, but when he embraces her, she metamorphoses into a cloud, a transformation which symbolizes how "private men being called to councils of state ... prostitute justice" to their "own judgments and apprehensions" and yet ultimately embrace a "false and empty shadow."[88] Such is the wisdom that Hobbes's Athena imparts to Telemachus at *Od.* 2.267–8 when she advises him "no more with th' Woo'rs in Council sit, / Expect from Fools to have no more redress," a translation that presents the political threat posed by his mother's suitors in terms of the foolish clamour of discordant voices in the assembly (*HH* 2:25).[89] According to Hobbes's allegory, the union of Ixion and Juno yields the Centaurs, a "fierce, fighting, and unquiet generation" whose hybridity symbolizes the inherently contradictory, agonistic nature of dissonant voices jarring in council. As Hobbes observes of the Rump Parliament in *Behemoth*, "contrary commands cannot consist in one and the same voice," a principle literalized by the centaur's grotesque fusion of man and horse.[90]

Interpretations of Homeric council scenes have been moulded since antiquity by concerns about the deleterious effects of dissent. Maximus of Tyre cites Agamemnon's complaint that "among the uproar of many, how may a man either hear or speak?" [*andrôn d'en pollô homadô pôs ken tis akousai / ê eipoi*] in order to illustrate the problem that it is difficult to "hear the voice of law and authority in a noisy and tumultuous democracy."[91] Hobbes addresses a similar concern when, at *Il.* 18.489, he renders *eris* [strife] and *kudoimos* [confusion] as "Disorder" and "Debate," thus implying that the war-torn city represented on Achilles's shield has descended into conflict because of its excessive tolerance for debate in the assembly (*HH* 1:306). And when Telemachus convenes the people of Ithaca to demand solidarity against the suitors but they fail to do so because of their rhetorical skills, Hobbes, "alone among translators, refers to the failed gathering as a 'Parliament'" (*HH* 1:lx–lxi).

In his translation of the scene featuring Thersites, Hobbes plays up the physical and moral deformities of the "railing knave" whose "peevish humour" threatens to undermine Agamemnon's authority (*HH* 1:28). Hobbes sharpens his attack and also intensifies Odysseus's counter-attack: in the Greek, Odysseus threatens to strip Thersites and inflict "shameful [*aidô*] blows" upon him that will send him "wailing" back to the ships, but in Hobbes's version, Odysseus tells Thersites that he will "strip you naked to the skin, / And send you soundly beaten to the Ships / With many stripes and ugly to be seen," a punishment that operates through physical violence as much if not more than through shame (*Il.* 2.261–4; *HH* 1:28). Moreover, although Hobbes's translation makes clear that Thersites is hardly an eloquent speaker – he is "[o]ne that to little purpose could say much, / And what he thought would make men laugh, would say" – the reaction of the Achaean assembly conveys their dangerous vulnerability to his virulent invective, no doubt confirming Hobbes's suspicion that certain orators in the assembly speak for "the applause of their motley orations" rather than for the best interest of the commonwealth (1:27).[92] The rabble "cannot chuse but laugh," according to Hobbes's rendering, turning their laughter into an uncontrollable impulse that can only be stifled by Athena, who intervenes in the likeness of a herald and commands the audience to"keep silence" [*siôpan*] so that they might "hear [Odysseus's] words and learn his counsel" [*muthon akouseian kai epiphrassaiato boulên*] (HH 1:28; *Il.* 2.280–2). By turning Pallas Athena into a "Crier," one of his preferred terms for the messengers that populate Homeric epic, Hobbes makes the crowd appear even more vulgar and disorderly than they appear in the original text (1:28). Incited by Thersites, they behave "like many brands, that enflame one another (especially when they blow one another with Orations) to the setting of the Common-wealth on fire," a complaint voiced in *Leviathan* that re-emerges in the texture of Hobbes's Homeric translations.[93]

If orators, as Hobbes asserts in *Leviathan*, are the "Favourites of Soveraigne Assemblies, though they have great power to hurt, [and] have little to save," then the damage done by Thersites is remedied to some degree by Odysseus, whose legendary eloquence complicates Hobbes's attempt to denigrate rhetorical skill in his translations.[94] In addition to expurgating many of the epithets that characterize Odysseus's rhetorical prowess – Odysseus *polumêtis*; Odysseus *pantoios* – Hobbes provides some moral undergirding to Odysseus's displays of eloquence by emphasizing the wisdom of his judgment or counsel, faculties closely linked to what Hobbes calls discretion. When Odysseus delivers his defence of monarchy (*Il.* 2.200–6 in the Greek text), Hobbes calls the oration a "deed" rather than a speech, since his words produce the desired effect of restoring order to the Achaean army. The palpably advantageous impact of the speech is evident in the alterations made by Hobbes to the simile that follows Odysseus's speech. In the Greek text (2.209–10), the Achaean troops hurry noisily to the agora "as when a wave of the loud-resounding sea thunders on the long beach, and the depths roar," an image that suggests the deafening tumult of a multitude. But Hobbes transforms the image so that it conveys the silence which follows the breaking of a wave: "Then to th'Assembly back again they pass'd, / With noise like that the Sea makes when it breaks / Against the Shore, and quiet were at last" (*HH* 1:27).[95] In Hobbes's handling, Odysseus's rhetorical skill resides in his ability to stifle a boisterous mob, persuading them to heed his better judgment.

Hobbes is guided by similar motives in his alterations to *Il.* 3.213–16, the famous comparison between Odysseus's voice and the falling of snowflakes:

> But when his voice was raised to the height,
> And like a Snow upon a Winters day
> His gentle words fell from him, no man might
> With him compare; so much his words did weigh. (*HH* 1:50)

The snowflakes in Hobbes's translation convey not delicacy or subtlety but substance: if Odysseus's words "weigh" it is not because they are delivered with particular fluency but rather because he is "among the people most esteem'd," a man whose good counsel wins him "most reverence" (1:50). Accordingly, Hobbes removes from the passage the narrator's multiple allusions to "*polumêtis*" and "*pantoios*" Odysseus, a man who "knows all manner of tricks and cunning devices" [*pantoious te dolous kai mêdea pukna*] and who is adept at "weav[ing] the web of words and devices" [*de muthous kai mêdea pasin huphainon*] (*Il.* 3.200, 3.202, 3.212). He also adds the detail that Odysseus's voice is "gentle": whereas the Greek text describes how Odysseus's "great voice emerges from his chest" [*dê opa te megalên ek stêtheos*], Hobbes softens his voice so as to reinvent Odysseus as the poem's master of discretion, a speaker who observes decorum in the assembly and exercises restraint even when tempers flare (*Il.* 3.221; *HH* 1:50).

Whereas Elpenor, the *Odyssey*'s chief exemplar of poor judgment, does not possess "very much discretion" when he tumbles from the roof on Circe's isle, Odysseus is praised for being discreet again and again in Hobbes's translation, which uses the term to translate the Greek *pinutos* [prudent], *pepnumena* [wise], and *kata moiran* [fittingly] (*HH* 2:141).[96] The qualities of prudence, good judgment, and decorum that Hobbes identifies as discretion are often manifested through speech acts: to speak discreetly, according to Hobbes, is to restrain the impulse to engage in the witty insults and severe rebukes so often classified by Homer's ancient and early modern readers as instances of eloquence. At *Il.* 9.249–50, Hobbes embroiders upon Phoenix's advice to Achilles so that it explicitly proscribes verbal contention: where Homer's Phoenix counsels Achilles to "desist from strife, contriver of mischief" [*lêgemenai d'eridos kakomêchanou*], Hobbes's character tells him to "[d]ecline all contestation of the tongue, / And let your conversation gentle be" (*Il.* 9.257; *HH* 1:139). Such a change accords with Hobbes's various criticisms of verbal abuse or *katachrêsis*: in *Leviathan*, he censures speakers who use words "metaphorically; that is, in other sense than that they are ordained for" in order to "grieve one another," and both *De Cive* and *Elements of Law* attack the rhetorician as a "commotrix" who seeks to arouse passions or to secure victory rather than to reveal the truth.[97]

Nelson rightly argues that Hobbes consistently "suppresses the Homeric *topos* that excellence for men is to be found in public debate and rhetorical skill," and he also labours to circumscribe Homer's valorization of Odysseus's talent for improvisation, lies, and storytelling by distinguishing between eloquence and discretion, only the latter of which reflects good judgment (*HH* 1:240).[98] Often, Hobbes accomplishes this by injecting a note of sarcasm into passages that praise eloquence: in the opening books of Hobbes's *Odyssey*, Antinous sounds more sardonic than he does in the Greek when he commends the "high strain / Of Language, and undaunted Oratory" exhibited by Telemachus, whom he appears to mock by calling him a "bold and brave Orator" (*HH* 2:16, 2:26).[99] When Penelope rebukes Antinous in turn, Hobbes presents her as scorning him for his rhetorical skill – "In *Ithaca* the Glory you have got / Of Wit and Eloquence" – rather than for the absence of it, as is suggested by the Greek (*HH* 2:221).[100] Like Plato before him, who rewrites portions of the *Iliad* "in plain narrative" in order to get rid of the "seductive appeal of personal speech," Hobbes aims to make Homer's characters less susceptible to the charms of rhetoric.[101] In Book 4 of the *Odyssey*, for instance, he omits a line in which Pisistratus tells Menelaus that he "delights in your voice as if some god were speaking" [*tou nôi theou hôs terpometh'audê*] (*HH* 2:46). Four books later, when Odysseus explains how the gods compensate men who lack physical beauty with the gift of superior rhetorical skill, Hobbes replaces eloquence with discretion, removes a reference to the divine origin of human gifts, and even injects a note of scorn into Homer's description of how other men gaze upon the skilled *rhetor* as a god. In Hobbes's version, the man given "Language steddy and discreet, / ... honour'd is i'th' Publike Place, / And men gaze on him going in the street," a rather derisive and backhanded compliment that reflects the translator's more widespread contempt for the Homeric bards whom (as discussed at further length below) Hobbes turns into minstrels and fiddlers, artisans who occupy no special status and exert no special power over their audience (*HH* 2:100).[102]

When Aeneas chastises Achilles for wrangling in a passage of the *Iliad* discussed at length in previous chapters of this book, Hobbes translates:

> What need we like two women in the street,
> When they cannot agree, to rail and scoff?
> Who say they true or false, are *undiscreet*. (*HH* 1:326; my italics)

In Hobbes's rendering, one finds none of the admiration for heroic raillery evident in Chapman's translations of Iliadic flyting scenes, or in Milton's imitations of them. Discretion is not ultimately defined for Hobbes by the truth or falsehood of a given statement but rather by the judgment necessary to determine when it may or may not be prudent to speak harshly – or at all. Such a reading is corroborated by Hobbes's alterations to *Il.* 9.31–2, where Diomedes tells Agamemnon that "so far as 'tis fit / In such a publick place I must you chide" (1:132). In the Greek text, Diomedes claims that "it is my right [*themis*]" to "contend" [*machêsomai*] with Agamemnon in the agora, but Hobbes tones down Diomedes's rebuke and makes him acknowledge the "limits" of what is "appropriate to say about kings" in the assembly (1:133). Although Hobbes usually uses the term "discretion" to denote prudence or good judgment, he also employs it to mean forthrightness or honesty. As Nelson has pointed out, this meaning is particularly apparent in Hobbes's handling of Phoenix's speech to Achilles in Book 9 of the *Iliad*, in which he explains that Achilles that was sent to Agamemnon "a mere child" [*nêpion*] who had "no knowledge yet of evil war, nor of assemblies in which men become preeminent" [*ou pô eidoth'homoiiou polemoio, / oud'agoreôn, hina t'andres ariprepees telethousi*] until taught by Phoenix to become "a speaker of words and a doer of deeds" [*muthôn te rhêtêr emenai prêktêra te ergôn*] (*Il.* 9.440–3). Hobbes fundamentally alters the nature of Achilles's rhetorical instruction: instead of learning how to become "preeminent" in the assembly and thus to cultivate the agonistic behaviour that makes Hobbes so uncomfortable elsewhere in his translation, Achilles learns how to speak his mind:

When you to Agamemnon first were sent,
You were a Child and understood not War,
Unable to say clearly what you meant,
Which the first principles of Honour are. (*HH* 1:144)

This passage is one of several in which the moral virtue of speaking one's mind trumps eloquence as Hobbes "replace[s] Homer's perfect orator with his own discreet hero" (1:lviii). When Odysseus brings word to Achilles in Hades of the accomplishments of his son, Hobbes has him report that "In Councel always he / First spake his minde, and never spake but well," a rendering that de-emphasizes the competitive verbal *aristeia* conveyed in the Greek: "he always spoke first, and never erred in his words" [*aiei prôtos ebaze kai ouch'hêmartane muthôn*] (*HH* 2:155; *Od.* 11.511).[103]

Hobbes's Impulsive Hero

Particularly in the *Odyssey*, a text in which spoken words and inner thoughts are often depicted as conflicting with each other, Hobbes often uses the formulae "he speaks his mind" or "he begins to speak his mind" in order to mark speech that is discreet, forthright, or transparently reflective of an undivided or resolute mind.[104] When Euryalus tells Laodamas to speak to Odysseus in order "his mind to see," the phrasing suggests speaking is – or at least ought to be – a means of making visible the workings of the inner mind (2:99). Hobbes's reliance on these formulae reflect his interest in Homer's representation of what Jeffrey Barnouw has termed "discursion," the deliberative practises signified by Homeric verbs such as *hormainô* and *mermêrizô* that depict deliberation as a "conflict of warring impulses within the self."[105] Hobbes's translations of Homer are shaped in various ways by his understanding of the relationship between physics and moral philosophy – between physical motion and what, in *De Corpore Politico*, he calls "the motions of the mind, namely appetite, aversion, love."[106] In particular, Hobbes's renderings of Homeric pondering scenes demonstrate his efforts at reconciling Homeric faculty psychology with his own conception of deliberation as a "series of alternating desires" or motions that he terms endeavours, or *conatus*.[107] In *Leviathan*, Hobbes explains that when *conatus* inclines "toward something which causes it, [it] is called APPETITE or DESIRE" and when it is "fromward something, it is generally called AVERSION," terms that correspond to the Greek words *hormê* and *aphormê*, the contrary "impulses or action tendencies" that are understood to move or urge the mind in different directions.[108] For Hobbes, deliberation involves a process of contrary oscillations between appetite and aversion that produce a "constant stream of internal bodily motions" or desires ending in an act of will, defined as the "last desire before an action."[109] According to this model, "deliberation is nothing but the succession of appetites and aversions" or rather "a summation of infinitesimal impulses" such that every human decision is "externally caused" by contrary impulses or *hormê* that serve Hobbes as an explanation of "how purpose works in the mind as the principle underlying the organization of thought."[110]

The Renaissance is heir to two rival interpretations of Homeric faculty psychology, one dominated by Plato and the other by the ancient Stoics.[111] Ancient and early modern debates over Homer's conception of will and appetite often revolve around the meaning of pondering scenes such as *Od.* 20.15–20, in which Odysseus admonishes his "barking" heart. Both Plato and Chrysippus understand the scene as dramatizing a "mental conflict" within Odysseus, but they disagree as to the origin and nature of that conflict.[112] Whereas Plato holds that Homeric deliberation engages a "hierarchically organized system of distinct, sometimes conflicting faculties" in which the *thumos* at times requires restraint by the higher faculties, the Stoics interpret Homeric pondering scenes as illustrating how "every inner tendency and intention has its intellectual as well as its impelling aspect" such that "deliberation is not a contest between impulse and reason but between competing impulses or intentions."[113] As Barnouw has argued, Hobbes is much more indebted to the Stoic model, which posits "actual (not metaphorical) motions within the mind" and also affirms the "unity and plasticity of the mind" in conceiving of deliberation as a "contest" of conflicting desires or urges rather than as an *agôn* between reason and passion.[114]

In a number of places where Homer uses the verb *hormainô* [to ponder], the term seized upon by Milton in his effort to "translate" Homeric scenes of deliberation into illustrations of the umpire conscience, Hobbes refines the meaning of this word so as to privilege his own, more mechanistic interpretation of the process of deliberation. At *Od.* 4.120, where Menelaus "ponder[s] in his mind and in his heart" [*hôrmaine kata phrena kai kata thumon*] whether he should question Telemachus or give him leave to speak, Hobbes eliminates the formulaic "in his mind and in his heart" and instead supplies "Consider'd whether best it were or no," thus eradicating any sense of conflict between mind and *thumos* (*Od.* 4.116, *HH* 2:45). In other Homeric scenes of "doubting," as Hobbes terms that aspect of deliberation in which "we ... ask, as it were, reasons of our consultation," he likewise eliminates any hint of struggle between competing faculties.[115] At *Il.* 14.20–1, Nestor weighs two choices with what the Homeric narrator calls a "divided thumos" [*thumon / dichthadi*], but Hobbes grants him only "two thoughts distracted" as he ponders his alternatives (*HH* 1:220). At *Od.* 2.156, when the observers of an omen "pondered in their hearts" [*hôrmênan d'ana thumon*] the significance of two eagles fighting each other in the sky, Hobbes simply presents them as "seek[ing] ... what this should mean," without any reference to the *thumos* as an actor in that search (*HH* 2:22). Hobbes makes an especially odd choice in translating a passage that describes how Odysseus "ponders standing on the threshold" [*hôrmain'histamenô*] of Alkinous's palace (*Od.* 7.83). In Hobbes's version, as Odysseus prepares to enter, "long he laid the Law / Unto himself before he would adventure," his rendering replaces the involuntary impulses of *hormai* with a rational assessment of "the Law" and thus presents deliberation not as an internal struggle between impulses in competition with each other but rather as a process of "reflective intellectual consideration."[116] Similarly, in Book 18 of the *Odyssey*, Hobbes presents Odysseus "casting in his mind" for the best plan of attack against the suitors rather than "pondering in his mind" [*hôrmaine phresin*], as Homer has it (*HH* 2:247; *Od.* 18.345).

At first glance, Hobbes's handling of these passages appears inconsistent: certain passages highlight the workings of Odysseus's "mind" while others suppress the appearance of ratiocination in favour of words and phrases that uphold Hobbes's understanding of *hormai* as a stream of contrary physical impulses. The motives behind these competing methods of translation emerge more clearly when studied alongside Hobbes's remarks on deliberation in works such as *Thomas White's De Mundo Examined*, which compares the "oscillation" between impulses to the operation of a "balance … now one pan is depressed, now the opposite one, as fresh weights are thrown in from one side or the other; likewise deliberation is a *conatus*."[117] For Hobbes, human decisions are "voluntary" only inasmuch as no obstacle impedes them; liberty, which Hobbes defines as "consist[ing] in motion," is nothing more than a lack of physical restraint.[118] By truncating Homer's conventional pondering formulae, thus speeding up the process of deliberation, and by removing the influence of the heart or *thumos* from those deliberations, Hobbes distils Homeric moments of "doubting" into a brief forward or fromward motion (appetite or aversion) in which choice – so prized as a moral faculty by Milton in his own imitation of similar scenes – is reduced to "the last act of the judgment in a conflict between fear and hope."[119]

Hobbes's Phobic Epic

According to Leo Strauss, Hobbesian man understands his choices in terms of "a conflict between vanity and fear," and Hobbes construes the choices made by Homer's heroes in similar terms, interpreting both poems according to the principle that competition over riches, honour, or power goads men into "Contention, Enmity, and War" while "Desire of Ease" and "Fear of Death" inclines them to obedience and harmony.[120] The dilemma posed by these contrary impulses perfectly describes Achilles's predicament, for he must choose between a short but honourable life and a long but ignoble one, stating plainly that there is no "price" sufficient the "life of any man though poor to buy. / Horses and kine, and sheep, and household stuff, / May be recover'd, but man's life cannot" (*HH* 1:143). Hobbes's interpretation of the *Iliad*, predicated upon the conflict between the instinct of self-preservation and the competitive impulse to seek honour, creates a world in which "good and evil" are connected by a "chain … so necessarily linked together, that the one cannot be taken without the other."[121] All choices carry risks, and all human interactions put into motion a long "chayn of consequences" in which "are linked together both pleasing and unpleasing events," even if no human being understands causation sufficiently to see the end of that chain.[122] Hobbes dramatizes this interlacement of contrary impulses, and of divergent consequences, in a line added by him at *Il.* 3.326. As the Greek army emerges, impressively armed for battle "(The people stupid sat 'twixt hope and fear)," their suspension between opposing passions is informed by Hobbes's claim that aversion combined with hope produces courage, while aversion combined with "opinion of Hurt" produces fear and cowardice.[123]

Throughout his translations of Homer, Hobbes amplifies the passion of fear, altering the Greek text in various ways so as to explore both its origins and effects. When Terror, Fear, and Strife – Deimos, Phobos, and Eris – make their appearance on the battlefield in Book 4 of the *Iliad*, Hobbes reduces their number to two, "Fright" and "(Mars his sister) Strife" – a pair that corresponds to his idea that the life of man in a state of nature consists of a "perpetuall and restless desire of Power after Power, that ceaseth only in death" or because of the fear of it.[124] Often, Hobbes intensifies the experience of fear by translating the passion of shame into terror or fright: at *Il.* 17.512, Hobbes's Athena rouses Menelaus's courage in battle by telling him, "Do not fear," whereas in the Greek text she threatens shame [*oneidos*] should Menelaus flee (*Il.* 17.556). At *Il.* 24.435, Homer's Hermes admits that he has "fear and respect" [*deidoika kai aideomai*] for Achilles, but Hobbes distils this compound emotion into "great fear" and omits any mention of reverence or *aidôs* (*HH* 1:396). In both cases, Hobbes seeks to clarify Homer's submerged contrast between two very different kinds of fear, the fear of the coward (loss of life) and the fear of the man with *arête* (loss of honour): the former is conducive to peace and the latter to war. Lessons about the consequences of acting upon these contrary impulses are embedded throughout the battle scenes of the *Iliad*, where Hobbes does his best to accentuate the difference between them: in a speech contrasting the brave man and the coward, for instance, Idomeneus tells Meriones that "fear and courage are discerned best" in combat, which the valiant man "quietly abides without afright" (*Il.* 13.257, 13.267). But whereas Hobbes conceives of fear as a singular and pre-eminent passion stimulated by man's natural impulse towards self-preservation, Homeric epic represents war as a dilemma between equal but opposite fears – the fear of death and the fear of dishonour. In Book 15 of the *Iliad*, Ajax encourages the Argive troops by telling them that "slain are alwaies more of those that fly / Than those that of base flight ashamed are," an observation that both confirms and complicates Hobbes's political and moral philosophy, founded as it is on the conflict between fear of death (those that fly) and the desire for honour, power, or glory (those ashamed of base flight).[125] Recognizing that Homer's soldiers need not be encouraged to choose the honour of bravery over the shame of safety – the choice warriors make over again and again in the *Iliad* – Hobbes adds a line and a half at the end of Ajax's speech: "This said, though of it no great need there was / Amongst the Greeks, they presently obey'd" (*HH* 1:247). His modification highlights the utility of fear in instilling obedience and unity among an army already predisposed to evaluate decisions in terms of a choice between honour and safety.

Hobbes gleans from Homer as well as from Thucydides the "equation between lack of fear and civil disobedience," and his translations of the *Iliad* and *Odyssey* illustrate the uses of fear and superstition as tools for cementing political authority.[126] Translating a line that describes Priam as "revered" [*aidoios*] and "worthy of awe" [*deinos*], Hobbes grants the description "more ideological heft" by turning him into a ruler to whom "all men owe more reverence and fear" (*HH* 1:49). Hobbes's recognition that Homer's rulers are canny manipulators of their subjects' fears and apprehensions helps to explain why he excises four lines (*Il.* 13.107–10) in which Poseidon rouses the Achaeans by claiming that Agamemnon has been "slack in war," a passage that proves challenging to Hobbes's view that sovereigns are supposed to instil fear rather than feel it (*HH* 1:200).

In *Leviathan*, Hobbes argues that the heathens deified all sorts of objects and forces of nature, superstitions cultivated by their rulers so that the "common people ... were the lesse apt to mutiny against their Governors."[127] In that work, obedience to the laws of nature requires the "terrour of some Power" for their enforcement, but Hobbes complicates this principle in his translation of the *Iliad* by demonstrating the ways in which fear and superstition cement political authority and shape human action for better and for worse.[128] At *Il.* 2.33, Hobbes displays a rare show of contempt for Agamemnon, "Vain man presuming from a Dream *Jove's* will," a translation that overlays on the Greek text the idea that Agamemnon's folly derives from his false assumption that it is possible to receive God's will through a dream (*HH* 1:22). Hobbes repeatedly debunks the idea that deities communicate with mortals through dreams and omens: when three black serpents appear in the sky in Book 11 of the *Iliad*, the Homeric narrator calls them "a portent for mortal men" [*teras meropôn anthrôpôn*] but Hobbes describes them as "shown by Jove for men to wonder at," thus injecting an air of arbitrariness and uncertainty into the meaning of the divine sign (*Il.* 11.28; *HH* 1:165). In Book 15 of the *Iliad*, where the Greek text describes how the "Trojans heard the sound of Zeus' thunder," Hobbes presents them as "by their hopes interpreting *Jove's* mind," a translation that accentuates the degree to which divine signs are accommodated to mortal hopes and fears and are thus subject to misinterpretation (*Il.* 15.379–80; *HH* 1:242). If *Leviathan* is, as it is sometimes read, a kind of heroic poem stripped of its divine machinery, then Hobbes's translation of the *Iliad* supplies an originary model for the genre, a poem that casts doubt on the trustworthiness of divine signs and mocks the absurd behaviour of gods whose inconsistencies and ironies point not to their mysteriousness or superior wisdom (as is the case for Chapman) but rather their probable non-existence.

Hobbes's Disenchanted Epic

Even as Hobbes scorns the superstitious outlook of Homer's heroes, he appreciates the *Iliad*'s frequent demonstrations of the political and moral value of fear, a passion central to the worship of God as a "confession of his power" according to Hobbes as well as to the maintenance of sovereign authority.[129] In a chapter of *Leviathan* devoted to demonology, Hobbes argues that the "Governours of the Heathen Common-Wealths" manipulated the fear of demons in order to regulate the fear of the people, a task for which "the Poets, as Principall Priests of the Heathen Religion, were specially employed, or reverenced."[130] Hobbes's translation of Homer implicates the poet-priest in precisely such a process so as to "debunk the *Homerus Sophos* tradition of Platonism and Priestcraft" upheld by Cambridge Platonists such as Ralph Cudworth and Henry More as well as by other seventeenth-century English scholars interested in ancient theology, such as Michael Drayton and John Selden.[131] Homer's various prophets and poets – figures related, in Hobbes's view, by virtue of their kindred roles as purveyors of fear and wonder for the benefit of sovereign authority – acquire the most disdainful and bathetic of epithets throughout his translation. Tiresias is dubbed a "Wizard" at *Od.* 11.462, a title intended to poke fun at the intricacy and obscurity of his prophecies. Hobbes turns the bard Thamyris into a "Thracian Fidler" at *Il.* 2.546, and at *Od.* 8.99, Hobbes's Demodocus plays neither a "harpe" nor a "cithara" (as Chapman and Sponde have it) but rather a lowly "Fiddle" (*HH* 1:36, 2:98). Both passages reflect Hobbes's anxieties about the "divine pretensions of poets" and shed light on Pope's claim that Hobbes's translation seems to have "been writ on purpose to ridicule the poet" rather than to honour him, a point that helps us distinguish between Chapman's interest in Homeric bathos and irony and that of his successor, since Chapman's ironic interpretations labour at every turn to apotheosize both Homer and himself as divinely inspired poets.[132] Struggling to free Homer from the "ghostly Commonwealth" into which he is enlisted by More, Cudworth, and their fellow seekers of the *prisca theologia*, Hobbes strips Homer's bards and prophets of their heroic stature, thus confirming his argument in the *Answer to Davenant* that the heathen poets were regarded as "Divines" and "Prophets" and that they "[e]xercised amongst the People a kinde of spiritual Authority" akin to the "unskilful Conjurers" or fraudulent preachers of his own day.[133] This disenchanted view of poetic invention, which is part of Hobbes's larger strategy to "assault Platonism and the doctrine of essences," manifests itself most clearly in his translation of Book 11 of the *Odyssey*, where Anticlea, Odysseus's mother, speaks of her fellow shades as "Substances Incorporeal" and Achilles then scorns the title of "Supreme Head" of "all things Incorporeal" (*HH* 2:147, 2:155). These phrases, added by Hobbes in order to make a "sarcastic dig" at the "priestcrafty" speech of his theological adversaries, reveal Hobbes's translation to be an "extended meditation on the danger of false beliefs" in which the foolish and the unlucky blame their lot on the devil (Hobbes's preferred translation of *daimôn*) while the prudent maintain a healthy scepticism that enables them to resist the "false belief / Of things they know not, but uncertain are," as Hobbes's Odysseus puts it to Eumaeus in a passage much altered by the translator.[134] Hobbes's *Odyssey* is a foundational text of scepticism for other Renaissance readers, too, but the scepticism that Hobbes injects into the poem is aimed at debunking superstition rather than at strengthening the kind of knowledge that is gained only through faith.

Such moves accord with Hobbes's anticlerical sentiments, his belief in the materiality of the soul, and his distaste for the improbabilities and marvels of romance, the "impenetrable Armors, Inchanted Castles, invulnerable bodies, Iron Men, flying Horses" mocked by his *Answer to Davenant* as "not onely ... exceed[ing] the *work*, but also the *possibility* of nature."[135] Although Hobbes does not "assen[t] to those that condemn either Homer or Virgil" on such charges of excessive fancy, his translations do present the Homeric poet as taking special delight in duping gullible readers, and he may well have agreed with Tommaso Campanella that Homer was a "mountebank" who sang in public squares "in order to attract the gawking populace – as our charlatans do and the Blindman from Forlì."[136] In a note on *Od.* 10.85 that appears only in the 1673 edition of his translation, Hobbes comments upon the narrator's description of Laestrygonia "seated just 'twixt day and night" that "*Homer* knew well there could not be a Town, at one end whereof was Day, at the other Night at the same time; but had a minde to tell the Learned how much the Unlearned can believe" (*HH* 2:129). Hobbes may have been inspired in his remark by Strabo's observation, here paraphrased by Edward Stillingfleet in his *Origines Sacrae*, that Homer's outlandish fables are designed "partly to delight the people, and partly to awe them ... such things do hugely please the natural humours of weak people."[137] Despite his contempt for the excessive credulity exhibited by various characters in both epics, Hobbes shares the poet's appreciation that "men can be moved by imaginary rewards and punishments" even more powerfully than by actual, corporeal causes and effects.[138] Even as he illustrates the extent to which false beliefs may generate a fear that in turn guarantees obedience and peace, the Homeric narrator strikes Hobbes as a thoroughly disenchanted thinker capable of explaining the rational and material causes and effects of human actions. Twice in his translation of the *Iliad*, Hobbes transforms an allusion to *tuchê*, usually translated as fortune, luck, providence, or fate, into "the chance of war," a phrase that strips conflict of its supernatural dimensions and denies opportunities for heroic excellence to its mortal participants.[139] Unlike Erasmus and Milton, who each inject into the Homeric concept of war as *alloprosallos* an underlying sense of divine justice or balance even when it is not apparent, Hobbes interprets Homeric war as evidence of cosmic randomness, proof that conflict may devolve, in a godless universe, into a free-for-all guided not by moral rules but simply by physical ones.

The idea that the outcome of war depends upon something akin to chance does appear in the Greek text of the *Iliad*, but Hobbes amplifies this idea, transforming the Homeric concept of war as "common to all" in order to stress the fundamental equality of adversaries, the "little odds … of strength or knowledge between men" that exists in a state of nature such that "he that is weaker in strength or in wit; or in both, may utterly destroy the power of the stronger."[140] As Hobbes's translation makes clear at several places, such equality both fosters strife and makes its outcome uncertain. At *Il.* 11.75–6, Hobbes's rendering of Eris as she descends into the midst of battle highlights her delight in parity during combat: both armies advance "In number equal; and gave great delight / To Eris, who (and no god else) was by" (*HH* 1:166). In two separate scenes in later books of the *Iliad*, Hobbes similarly accentuates the degree to which what the Homeric poet calls *homonoia* – sameness or equality – promotes conflict: speaking of Agamemnon, Achilles complains at 16.52 that his heart grieves because "my equal should oppress me by meer might," a statement which no doubt confirms Hobbes's own suspicion that recognition of Agamemnon's sovereignty is a crucial antidote to the fundamentally "equal" [*homoion*] status of Homer's Achaeans (1:253). Later in the same book, Hobbes turns a simile describing a lion and boar who meet at a fountain to drink into a parable about how discord arises through equality: only in Hobbes's translation do the two creatures share "equal thirst," an equivalence that explains the violence that follows: "drink they both would fain, / But fight who shall drink first, slain is the boar" (1:273).

Hobbes's emphasis on the chance of war and on the essential equality of antagonists devalues the *aretê* or heroic excellence that, according to a number of Homer's more recent interpreters, is tested and challenged by an agonal culture that affords little security to the victors of wars and contests, who are continually "threatened by the envy and ambition" of their co-competitors.[141] One of the principal casualties of Hobbes's anti-heroic and materialistic interpretation of Homeric epic is the sublimity or height so highly prized by other seventeenth- and eighteenth-century readers. As Nelson observes, Hobbes's "great target seems to have been the Homeric sublime," and it is useful to distinguish the various causes and symptoms, both ethical and stylistic, of that assault to understand what makes Hobbes's interpretations of Homer so profoundly different from those of his contemporaries and direct successors (*HH* 1:lxxiv).

Hobbes's representation of the emotion of fear perhaps reveals the most striking distinction between his understanding of the Homeric sublime and that of contemporary scholars such as René Le Bossu, John Dennis, and Alexander Pope. Hobbes was almost certainly influenced by Boileau, whose French translation of Longinus's *On the Sublime* was first printed in 1674. Moreover, he shares with many of his contemporaries an interest, derived partly from Longinus, in the effects of fear on the readers of Homeric epic. Yet Hobbes understands the effects of that fear rather differently, conceiving of it as an ethical and political force rather than an aesthetic or spiritual one, a force that helps to manage and curb strife rather than to intensify the perverse pleasure fostered by it.[142] Whereas Dennis speaks of the pleasure produced by the "Enthusiastick Terrour" aroused by Homeric epic, a terror that "proceeds from our reflecting that we are out of Danger at the very time that we see it before us," Hobbes understands this same fear, when stimulated in Homer's readers, as a vital means of *involving* the audience in the poem's aetiology of discord in order to instruct them how to avoid or manage strife.[143] Pope may be echoing Hobbes when he argues that Homer's "chief Moral ... was to dispose the ill Effects of Discord" by demonstrating how the Trojans profit, at least temporarily, from "[d]isagreement" among the Greeks, but it is hard to imagine that Hobbes would have agreed with Pope's praise for the "wonderful sublimity" of Homer's Eris as she descends into the battlefield at the beginning of Book 11 of the *Iliad*, a passage that, in Pope's hands, follows Longinus in identifying strife as a key source of the sublime.[144]

In Hobbes's translations, strife is more often bathetic than sublime: the *eris* between Zeus and Hera at *Il.* 1.494 turns into a "quarrel," a word that evokes Lucianic parodies of epic combat as well as the anti-heroic world of

Shakespeare's *Troilus and Cressida*. Hobbes has Agamemnon describe the poem's chief conflict as a "quarrel with *Achilles* for a maid" – not exactly the stuff epic is made of, according to most early modern reckonings (*HH* 1:19, 1:31).[145] Closer to Pope's *Rape of the Lock* than to his translation of Homer, Hobbes's *Iliad* trivializes the causes of discord by turning verbal disputes into catfights – in one, Aphrodite calls Helen a "Hussie" – and by employing language deemed "homely" and "vulgar" by later readers including Cowper and Coleridge (*HH* 1:55).[146] Hobbes's "unstudied and unpretending language" may well be "less remote from the original" than the "smooth and glittering lines of Pope," as Molesworth argues in the advertisement to volume 10 of Hobbes's *Works*.[147] But Hobbes's reliance on rhetorical devices such as *asteismus* and *tapinosis*, the latter defined by Peacham as "when the dignitie or majestie of a high matter is much defaced by the basenesse of a word," does not reflect Hobbes's effort to recreate Homer faithfully in English as much as his desire to debase the image of Homer as a prophet or theologian, the very Homer venerated by the "school divines" whom he counted among his adversaries.[148] While the tone of "ironic condescension" that dominates Hobbes's Homer may not have been intended "to ridicule the poet," as Pope claimed of his predecessor's translations, Hobbes's tendency to heighten "unHomerically low" instances of humour in both poems reflects his appreciation of the deftness with which Homer's heroes wield scorn and ridicule against their adversaries, a technique also employed by Hobbes in many of his original works of political and moral philosophy.[149]

At the very beginning of his career, Hobbes wrote a mock-epic poem entitled *De Mirabilibus Pecci*. Composed in the late 1620s – its dedicatee, the Earl of Devonshire, died in 1628 – the work was twice printed during Hobbes's lifetime, in an undated edition probably printed in the late 1620s and again in 1666; it was translated into English in 1678 as *The Wonders of the Peak in Darby-Shire, Commonly called the Devil's Arse of Peak*.[150] According to Skinner, who describes the poem as modelled after the "Homeric idea of a memorable journey," *De Mirabilibus Pecci* was quite popular during the seventeenth century; both Locke and Newton owned copies of it.[151] One of two accounts of a journey through the Peak District near Chatsworth – the other was written by Richard Andrewes – Hobbes's poem is interpreted rather seriously by the few modern readers who have paid any heed to it, examined for its classical allusions or read in light of the author's supposed "phobia of heights and darkness."[152] But much like Andrewes's companion piece, which A.P. Martinich describes as "uncivil and uncouth" in its repeated analogies between geological phenomena and human anatomy, Hobbes's poem is clearly satirical and, in certain places, patently vulgar, a work akin to La Mothe Le Vayer's *Explication de L'Antre des Nymphes* and similar parodic allegories written by the erudite libertines with whom Hobbes associated during the late 1630s and 1640s.[153]

The *De Mirabilibus Pecci* provides a devastating parody of the marvellous, that aspect of epic romance so disdained by Hobbes. The poem also mocks the aesthetic experience that, a half-century later, would commonly come to be described as the sublime. It begins by describing the rugged countryside in the Peak district near Chatsworth; Hobbes recounts how his entourage "Towards a steep Hill's high top, doe climbing go; / And after many a tug and weary strain" reach the summit, where they feel "wonder" at the sweeping vista.[154] Both the origins of the mountain's name – the Devil's Arse – and the comical dimensions of the poem become clearer as the narrator describes how the peak emerges into view:

> Swelling into two parts, which turgent are
> As when we bend our bodies to the ground,
> The buttocks amply sticking out are found.[155]

This physiognomic allegory develops further as Hobbes and his companions enter a cave, inside of which they "with wonder and amaze admire / The tall prodigious Rocky Hemisphere" as they are guided through it by a "she-Native of the place."[156] Struggling to find an "apt simily" to describe this "hiatus" in the earth through which pours a strong "fount" of water, Hobbes resorts to the pseudo-learned glossing also typical of libertine allegory and observes that the "mouth of the hole be of a cunnoid form or like the privities of a woman."[157] Terrified by the sight of this "vast abyss," the climbers toss stones and other large objects into its watery depths only to discover that the giant hole "swallow'd all," a mystery that prompts further investigation as they seek out the source of the stream coursing through the watery chasm: "As we go, / We searching strive by ev'ry sign to know / From what hid cause, so great a strife should Spring."[158] The answer, found in a pool of water that rises from underground and passes through a narrow vent, is hardly the stuff of epic, and the poem ends as the men refresh themselves in a pool and enjoy a meal of roasted lamb, wine, and tobacco.

When Hobbes turns a half-century later to his translations of Homer, he adheres to this fundamental definition of epic as an aetiology of strife. Despite the long and varied career that divides the two works, there are some striking similarities between *De Mirabilibus Pecci* and Hobbes's translations of the *Iliad* and *Odyssey*. Both evince a profound distrust of wonder and sublimity, and both imagine the epic quest (whether earnestly or mockingly) as a search for the root causes of discord. In this respect, Hobbes has more in common with sixteenth- and seventeenth-century readers of Homer than with the new generation of classical scholars who emerge at the beginning of the eighteenth century. For these younger scholars, "Homer's poetry reveal[s] in its warp and its woof the perplexities of a mind still frightened by natural forces," a naive primitivism consonant with Hobbes's emphasis on the experience of fear in his translations, but not with his repeated puncturing of the poems' "primeval" sense of wonder and sublimity.[159] Like many earlier Renaissance readers, Hobbes treats the *Iliad* and *Odyssey* as poems that seek to rationalize and delimit conflict, an approach at odds with proto-Romantic interpretations that stress the unfathomable grandeur of Eris or the mysteriousness of her effects. For Hobbes, Eris is not a force to be celebrated, or to be marvelled at, but rather to be controlled and put in her place.

Epilogue: The Homeric Contest from Vico to Arendt

In the hands of Alexander Pope, Richard Bentley, Thomas Blackwell, Giambattista Vico, Friedrich Wolf, and other eighteenth-century scholars, Homer assumes his place in the opening chapter of a new set of narratives that recount a progression from barbarism to civility, from lawlessness to order, from superstition to religion, and from war to peace.[1] In Homeric epic, as Vico argues in his *New Science*, "we may discover the natural law of the Greeks when they were still a barbarous people," composing poems whose "clumsy and indecorous language reflect[s] the awkwardness under which the Greeks laboured to express themselves while their language was still taking shape and was extremely poor."[2] The primitive behaviours and naive beliefs that Vico locates in Homeric epic go hand in hand with the constant "warfare" that makes archaic Greek culture "so fierce that human laws no longer have a place among them," a condition remedied only by the intervention of "divine providence," which leads "fierce and violent men" away from their "lawless condition" into a civility roused in turn by a "confused idea of divinity."[3] Hobbes likewise reads Homeric epic as a clue to the maze – a way out of the seemingly insoluble conflicts that afflict not just primitive man but also seventeenth-century England and Europe. Yet Hobbes understands Homer's antidote to conflict as inhering in his assertion of the superiority of monarchy and in his admonitory treatment of rhetorical prowess and its capacity to sway human passion and opinion. Observing that "Hobbes failed to see the providential origin of human institutions" in Homeric epic, Vico distinguishes his own, rather Whiggish, way of reading of Homeric epic from that of his English predecessor by arguing that religion and positive law, rather than the institution of monarchy, are the solutions provided by later Greek culture for the ceaseless strife of the Homeric world. Whereas Hobbes, according to

Vico's appraisal, interprets Homeric epic as demonstrating that the "generall inclination" of human nature is towards the "perpetuall and restless desire of Power after Power," Vico employs Homeric epic in order to narrate the eventual triumph of civility over barbarism and of harmony over discord.[4]

Both Hobbes and Vico interpret Homeric epic according to the principle that "war, like motion, continues until some means can be found to stop it," yet those means are human and artificial for Hobbes, whereas for Vico they are natural and divine.[5] Hobbes's interpretation of Homeric epic is, as we have seen, animated by his belief in a physical world that consists only of bodies and motions, a doctrine that makes conflict inevitable and even necessary for the perpetuation of physical processes and human interactions.[6] By contrast to the "endless striving" that Hobbes discerns in Homeric epic, Vico reads the Homeric emphasis on the ubiquity of conflict as a sign of the poet's primitivism, a problem to be overcome by the forces of law [*nomos*] and civility that emerge and prevail only in more advanced civilizations.[7] Although both Hobbes and Vico strip the Homeric poet of the "esoteric wisdom" with which he had been credited by earlier Renaissance readers, Hobbes understands Homer's representation of conflict as banal and familiar, whereas Vico interprets the eristic forces that animate Homeric epic as primitive, sublime, and utterly alien to his own culture, so much so that the "gruesome atrocity of Homeric battles and deaths is the source of all the astonishing power of the *Iliad*."[8]

Vico's relegation of Homeric violence and conflict to an archaic, unrecoverable past shapes an interpretation of the *Iliad* and *Odyssey* – and of human history more generally – that dominates for the better part of two centuries. Yet with the emergence of late nineteenth-century German writers such as Friedrich Nietzsche (1844–1900) and Jakob Burckhardt (1818–97), whose classical scholarship reasserts Homeric *agôn* as intellectually and politically productive, the spirit of noble conflict and competition that animates early Greek civilization – the two centuries after Homer that Burckhardt terms the "agonal age" – re-emerges as a valuable and beneficial force. In their respective *The Greeks and Greek Civilization* (first delivered as a series of lectures in 1872) and *Homer's Contest* (also drafted in 1872), Burckhardt and Nietzsche recuperate the Homeric ideal of *aristeia*, the urge "always to be the first and outdo all the others," as a form of "noble victory without enmity" expressed in "[m]any different aspects of life," from the conversations and songs of symposiasts, to the institutions of "philosophy and legal procedure," to athletic competition.[9] Burckhardt and Nietzsche both regard the Homeric lust for conflict not as a mark of the culture's primitive barbarity but rather as a fertile soil out of which grow all the finest political, cultural, and artistic accomplishments of the Greeks, evidence of a "good" Eris that must nonetheless be cultivated in order to be put to good use – in Nietzsche's case, to preserve the unity and strength of the new German nation, created one year before the composition of *Homer's Contest*. In that work, Nietzsche argues that contest, or *Wettkämpfe*, in the early Greek world makes strife meaningful by yoking artistic and athletic competitions to the grand conflicts of the Olympian gods, by nurturing "natural gifts" among agonists, and above all by making a heroic virtue out of the eristic impulses that Hesiod, in Nietzsche's view a poet who predated Homer, regarded as a curse.[10] Whereas early modern readers of Homer often bristle at the "tiger-like pleasure in destruction" evident in the Homeric cosmos, Nietzsche celebrates the early Greek capacity to heighten the heroic dimensions of struggle by stylizing it, whether through the retelling of myths featuring "exemplary agonists" such as Herakles, or in the habitual retelling of "fighting scenes of the *Iliad*."[11] And, whereas early modern readers of the *Iliad* and *Odyssey* labour to redeem the unabashedly agonistic spirit of the Homeric poems by assimilating it to more civilized, virtue-building, or spiritually enlightened modes of conflict, Nietzsche narrates the devolution of Homeric *agôn* by Plato and later by Pauline Christianity, philosophical outlooks that devalue struggle, respectively, by stripping glory of its worth and by relegating *eris* to a purely internal and individual struggle.

In works ranging from *The Greek State* (1871–2) and *Philosophy in the Tragic Age of the Greeks* (1873) to *The Genealogy of Morals* (1887), Nietzsche narrates the evolution of Greek thought and culture from Hesiod (inventor of the "bad" Eris) to Homer (inventor of the "good" Eris) and beyond. This genealogy forms the basis of his political and moral philosophy, which repeatedly prioritizes Homeric ideals of contest over those of Hesiod by aligning the Homeric world view with the doctrines of Heraclitus, the pre-Socratic philosopher who affirms that all things in the cosmos are united, and ennobled, by perpetual conflict. This idea would later be elaborated by Heidegger, who argues that *eris* and *polemos* give rise to "position and order and rank" such that "a world comes into being."[12] It would also be developed by Burckhardt, who echoes and also helps to shape Nietzsche's account of the civilizing force of *eris*. The cultivation of institutionalized forms of conflict features prominently in Burckhardt's own narrative of the transition between medieval and Renaissance culture as the pivotal moment when primitive eristic impulses – those evident, say, in the warrior culture of the *Nibelungenleid* – organize themselves into the public, political culture of Quattrocento Italy, a culture animated by debate, by artistic rivalries that produce works of unprecedented excellence, and above all by an "egotism" that Burckhardt regards as culturally and intellectually generative even as it breeds violence and factionalism.

A century and a half later, looking back through the lens of two world wars and countless revolutions and civil wars, this narrative might sound naive at best and morally treacherous at worst, particularly as corrupted versions of Nietzsche's and Burckhardt's theories of the civilizing power of *eris* resurface in the unabashedly selfish heroes of Ayn Rand or in the self-justifying logic of *The Third Man*'s Harry Lime (1949), Graham Greene's black marketeer who reasons that the peaceful democracy of the Swiss yields only a "cuckoo clock," while in Italy, the "warfare, terror, murder, and bloodshed" of the Borgias produces countless Leonardos and Michelangelos. Yet even under the shadow of the Second World War, interpretations of the eristic forces in the Homeric world reflect a kaleidoscopic set of reactions to the horrors of war. At one end of the spectrum is Simone Weil (1909–43), the French philosopher and Marxist-turned-Christian mystic whose *The Iliad or the Poem of Force*, first published in the *Cahiers du Sud* in winter 1940–1, offers an uncompromisingly stark condemnation of Iliadic violence in readings that "isolate and intensify scenes of horror" in the poem order to demonstrate their dreadful kinship with the violent upheavals of contemporary Europe.[13] Treating Homer as an ancient counterpart to Goya, whose Disasters of War she viewed at an exhibition in Geneva on the eve of the Second World War, Weil's interpretation of the *Iliad* disallows readers from revelling in the work's militaristic celebration of heroic excellence, and it allows us no glimmer of hope that the poem's tenderest moments, those set off the battlefield, foreshadow any of the "Christian" values of forgiveness, humility, or cooperation so enthusiastically detected by early modern readers.[14] Instead, Weil gives us a poem without heroes, arguing that "force" is the *Iliad*'s sole protagonist and its sole victor: "The author of the *Iliad* ... neither lionizes victors nor denigrates losers; Homer well knows that force is the only winner."[15] Force, for Weil, is the power that turns human agents of the *Iliad* into "purely passive inert matter" or the "blind forces of sheer impetus." Force is at once universal, levelling, and fundamentally amoral, operating according to a principle of counterbalance enacted through the "seesaw movement" so dimly foreseen by Hector, whose god of war "slays him who would slay" [*te ktaneonta katekta*].[16] Weil's depiction of Homeric conflict as neutral and totalizing may speak more powerfully to the Anschluss than it does to the *Iliad*'s actual representation of war. But as Weil herself admits, the *Iliad* is not a "historical document" but rather the "purest and loveliest of mirrors" for our own complex understanding of war and violence.

Weil's observation helps to explain why Rachel Bespaloff (1895–1949), another twentieth-century European scholar whose life was ravaged by war, extracts from the *Iliad* a very different set of lessons for those living under the threat of Nazism. A Bulgarian emigré to France, and later a war refugee to the United States who taught at Mount Holyoke College until her suicide, Bespaloff's *De l'Iliade* (1943) agrees with Weil that "[w]ar devours differences and disparities, shows no respect for the unique" and yet manages, unlike Weil, to detect a certain "beauty" in the poem's representation of violence, a beauty that resides in the poet's ability to turn "warlike emulation" into the "fountainhead of creative effort."[17] Both Weil and Bespaloff treat force in the *Iliad* as ruthlessly mathematical – "geometrical," to use Weil's preferred term – in its capacity to reduce people to things, to soulless bodies or instruments of state power. Yet Bespaloff holds out the possibility that the "plurality of antagonistic energies that hold each other in check" throughout the *Iliad* might offer a route to harmony, or at least to a temporary serenity, rather than to mutual destruction.[18] Homer might have had a "virile love of war" according to Bespaloff, but he also had a "virile horror of it."[19]

For Nietzsche, Homeric epic provided a compelling answer to the question, "What is a life of struggle and victory for?"[20] We should not be surprised, therefore, that sixteenth- and seventeenth-century writers interpret Homer as a means of establishing the underlying purpose and validity of intellectual disputes, wars, and other forms of conflict and rivalry. For these generations of readers, the *Iliad* and *Odyssey* provide various and contradictory answers to Nietzsche's question, showing them that conflict is alternately ennobling and brutal, necessary and trivial, a means of preserving the political order or a threat to justice or stability. Successive generations of readers have supplied their own answers to Nietzsche's question, some valorizing conflict in Homeric epic as productive of ethical or political good and others condemning it as frivolous or destructive. Attentiveness to this rich interpretive tradition enlarges our own understanding of the poems, making them appear lithe and flexible as they pass through the hands of readers with concerns at times distant, and at other times not so distant, from our own.[21]

One of the peculiar delights of literary reception work is to stumble across interpretations of a familiar text that are radically alien to our own critical methods or sensibilities. This book provides abundant examples of such readings. But to study the reception of Homer is also to experience the rarer pleasure of discovering how certain texts – call them classics, if you will – are unusually receptive to being vested with divergent and contrary interpretations. Hannah Arendt attributes this malleability in Homer to his "[a]gonal spirit," a reading that reveals the enduring influence of the interpretive traditions addressed in this book. For Arendt, Homer's agonal spirit is ancestor both to Socratic scepticism and to the democratic spirit of public debate: "this Homeric way of showing that all things [have] two sides," she writes, illustrates how "all things with two sides make their real appearance only in struggle."[22] If literary reception work underscores the difficulty – or even the folly – of recovering "authentic" or "pristine" texts untainted by later hands and minds, it also serves to remind us why we continue to read the *Iliad* and *Odyssey* in the first place: because such poems, as Arendt observes, "appear in as many perspectives as there are people to discuss [them]." Although we may no longer aspire to "discover" a "true Homer," as Vico did, we can relish the capaciousness of poems that have yielded, over the centuries, such diverse interpretations.

Notes

Introduction: Homer and the Question of Strife

1 Plato, *Rep.* 8.3 [545d].
2 Hugo, *Vera Historia Romana*, 110–11, 138, 146–7. For a discussion of the work in the context of Renaissance allegory, see D.C. Allen, *Mysteriously Meant*, 100–2.
3 Hugo, *Vera Historia*, 149, 141.
4 Hugo, *Vera Historia*, 150, 120.
5 Lipsius, *Politica*, 532–3. Lipsius quotes the lines in Latin as "depravant publica iura, / Iustitiamque fugant, divum nil verba verentes" and "Caussa horum poenas misit Deus, et quoque mittet."
6 Petrarch, *Letters of Old Age* 1:149–50. Letter IV.5.
7 Budé, *De Transitu*, ed. Garanderie, 114, 118. On Budé's *De Transitu* and the relationship between his Hellenism and his Lutheranism, see Saladin, *La Bataille du Grec*, 397–400. Compare Conti, *Mythologiae*, 1:267–8, excoriating the "wicked offspring of Luther" and their schisms. On Homeric epic as a locus for conflicts over sovereignty during the French religious wars, see Bizer, *Homer and the Politics of Authority*, 5; and Christine Deloince-Louette, "Les lieux homériques de Jean de Sponde: une lecture éthique de l'*Iliade* à l'usage du Prince," in *Homère*, ed. Capodieci and Ford, 383–98.
8 Mexio, *The treasvrie of auncient and moderne times*, 579.
9 Hobbes, *Behemoth*, *EW* 6:213.
10 Sarpi, *Trent*, 2. On the sixteenth-century tendency to interpret ancient texts as reflecting contemporary civic ideals, see Godman, *From Poliziano to Machiavelli*, 134–79.
11 *Homeri quae extant omnia*, ed. Sponde, 2:267, 1:152, vol. numbers refer to *Iliad* (1) and *Odyssey* (2). All subsequent citations of Sponde's Homer will be from this edition.

12 Lipsius, *Politica*, 666–7, citing *Il.* 9.63.
13 Dorat, *Mythologicum*, 10.
14 See Pertusi, *Leonzio Pilato*. There are a number of important new contributions to Homeric scholarship in the early Italian Renaissance, including recent editions of Poliziano's Homeric translations and orations by Paola Megna and Luigi Silvano.
15 Moul, *Jonson*, 4.
16 Burkert argued (*Greek Religion*, 248) that the "multiplicity" of Homeric polytheism "always implies opposition" yet for early modern readers, it may imply conflict but not necessarily outright opposition.
17 Greek editions of Homer during the first half of the sixteenth century north of the Alps include editions of *Iliad* 1 (Strasbourg, 1516); *Iliad* 1 and 2 (Louvain, 1518, and Paris, 1523); *Odyssey* 1 and 2 (Basel, 1520); *Odyssey* 1–4 (Wittenberg, 1520); complete *Iliad* (Louvain, 1523), and complete *Odyssey* (Strasbourg, 1525). Latin translations include editions of the Valla-D'Arezzo *Iliad* (Paris, 1511; Leipzig, 1512, et al.), editions of the Maffei translation of the *Odyssey* (Rome, 1510; Lyon, 1541); Andreas Divus's translation of both poems (Paris, 1538; Lyon, 1538; Basel, 1539); Eobanus Hessus's translation of the *Iliad* (Basel, 1540). For a more comprehensive list of sixteenth-century editions and translations of Homer, see Irigoin, "La Tradition homérique," and Young, *The Printed Homer*.
18 Wilson-Okamura, *Virgil*, 48. On the collecting of "pithy sayings" out of ancient texts, see also Bolgar, "From Humanism to the Humanities," 11.
19 Kallendorf, *The Other Virgil*, 14; on the role of Homeric epic in the history of scepticism, see Zerba, *Doubt and Skepticism*, 5–8, 10–17.
20 Castiglione, *Book of the Courtier*, 336.
21 On Dolce, see Terpening, *Lodovico Dolce*, 30 and Steadman, "Achilles and Renaissance Epic," 141. Steadman argues that Achilles was an especially problematic figure during the sixteenth century because of his flagrant breach of chivalric ideals.
22 On Virgil as a poet of praise, see Kallendorf, *The Other Virgil*, 31, and Wilson-Okamura, *Virgil*, 59.
23 For similar justifications, see Wilson-Okamura, *Virgil*, 3, and Martindale, *Redeeming the Text*, chapters 2 and 3.
24 On this point, see Rutherford, "From the *Iliad* to the *Odyssey*," in *Oxford Readings*, ed. Cairns, 142; Havelock, *The Greek Concept of Justice*, 89; West, "Homer's *Iliad*," 4. Homeric scholars including Long ("Morals and Values") and Hogan ("Eris in Homer") have argued that *Od.* recuperates and redeems the eristic forces of *Il.* in order to put them to more beneficial use or to demonstrate how *eris* may nurture cooperative values and even thrive within

a harmonious community so long as its expression is governed by propriety and good sense.

25 Cartari, *Les Images*, 5.
26 Hogan, "Eris in Homer," 25.
27 Hogan, "Eris in Homer," 45. On the distinction between *eris* and *polemos*, see also Nagler, "Towards a semantics of ancient conflict," 83–5. For a different argument concerning the role played by *eris* within a community, see Louden, *The Iliad*, 161, who argues that *Il.* 1–17 are framed by an "eris myth" but that the latter books "restore eris to its correct application, outside the community."
28 See Peele, *Arraignment of Paris* (1584), *The Rare Triumphs of Love and Fortune* (1582), and *Locrine* (ca 1591), where Atê serves as prologue; Discord serves as Prologue in *Caesar and Pompey or Caesar's Revenge* (Trinity College, Oxford, 1592–6). Thanks to Alan Dessen for bringing these references to my attention.
29 BL 653 G8/G9/G10, *Eustathius … in Homeri Iliadis*, annotated by Isaac Casaubon, 377; Aristotle, *Politics* 1303b.
30 Firestone Library, Princeton, NJ, PA4018.A31 M52 1541q, *Poiêseis Homêrou amphô*, annotated by Martin Crusius, 88; back endpapers.
31 Pope, *Rape of the Lock*, 1.
32 Hesiod, *Works and Days*, ls. 13–15, 23–5, hereafter abbreviated as *WD*. Unless otherwise noted, the poems of Hesiod are cited from *Hesiod, the Homeric Hymns, and the Lesser Homerica*. On Hesiod's conception of *eris* in the *WD*, see Clay, *Hesiod's Cosmos*, 7–9, and Michael C. Nagler, "Discourse and conflict in Hesiod: Eris and the Erides," *Ramus* 21 (1992): 79–96.
33 Heraclitus, *Homeric Problems*, section 29.5, 54–5. The work was first printed at Venice in 1505. On Homer and Hesiod as contemporaries and rivals, see M.L. West, "The Contest of Homer and Hesiod," 433–50; Graziosi, *Inventing Homer*, 169–99; A. Ford, *The Origins of Criticism*, 277. Several of Homer's Renaissance translators, including Jean de Sponde and George Chapman, also translated Hesiod's *WD*.
34 Friedrich Nietzsche, "Homer's Contest," 55.
35 Nietzsche, "Homer's Contest," 55.
36 Nietzsche, "Homer's Contest," 54; Whigham, *Ambition and Privilege*, 78.
37 Whigham, *Ambition and Privilege*, 80.
38 Huizinga, *Homo Ludens*, 71; Nietzsche, "Homer's Contest," 62, argues that "nothing separates the Greek world more from ours" more than the "ethical ideals … of Eris and of Envy," or *zêlos*.
39 Burckhardt, *The Greeks*, 207; *The Civilization of the Renaissance in Italy*, 87, 93.

40 See, for example, Andrea Alciati's *Concordia* (*Emblemata*, 48), which depicts Ulysses and Diomedes along with the motto, "Unum nihil, duos plurimum posse" [One can do nothing; two can do much], a line derived from *Il.* 10.224.
41 Wilson, *Ransom*, 109.
42 Le Bossu, *Treatise of the Epick Poem*, 49; contrast Machiavelli, *Discourses*, 34, arguing that "discord can actually strengthen a state."
43 Lord, *Heroic Mockery*, 17.
44 Mueller, "Knowledge and Delusion," 108.
45 Hobbes, *Leviathan*, 86–7: as Hobbes puts it, no man "can thereupon claim to himself any benefit, to which another may not pretend, as well as he."
46 Burkert, *Greek Religion*, 105; Gouldner, *Enter Plato*, 13.
47 Rutherford, *Homer*, 42; *Problèmes de la Guerre*, ed. Vernant, editor's introduction, 10.
48 *Oxford Readings*, ed. Cairns, editor's introduction, 21.
49 Cairns, *Aidôs*, 140. Compare Lateiner, "The *Iliad*: an unpredictable classic," in *The Cambridge Companion to Homer*, ed. Fowler, 22.
50 Martin, *Language of Heroes*, 66–7; Rutherford, *Homer*, 42; Cairns, *Aidôs*, 50–1; see also Dodds, *The Greeks and the Irrational*, 17–18, 28, 47–50.
51 On this "ideological contradiction," in which "aristocratic individualism" is both "vital to the community" in Homeric epic and also a "danger to be controlled by the community," see Seaford, *Reciprocity and Ritual*, 5–6; Heraclitus, *The Art and Thought of Heraclitus*, introduction, 13–14. For other interpretations of Homeric epic that emphasize how playful contests may "defuse" more serious conflicts or cultivate *philophrosunê*, see Beck, *Homeric Conversation*, 282; W. Harris, *Restraining Rage*, 76, 149.
52 Seznec, *Survival of the Pagan Gods*, 17.
53 Proclus, *Commentaire sur la République*, 1:162 (XV.142.30–143.1); Heraclitus, *Homeric Problems*, section 40.14, 73–5.
54 The pseudo-Plutarchan *Life*, printed alongside two other *Lives* of Homer attributed to Dio and Herodotus, was widely available in Latin translation: in Sebastian Castellio's edition of Homer (*Homeri Opera graeco-latina*, Basel: Nicolaus Brylingerus, 1561), Henri Estienne's *Poetae Graeci heroici carminis* (Geneva: Fugger, 1566), and Wilhelm Xylander's edition of Plutarch's *Moralia* (Basel: Oporinus, 1566, rpt. 1570, 1572, and 1574). On the popularity of the pseudo-Plutarchan *Life*, see P. Ford, *De Troie à Ithaque*, and Sowerby, "Early Humanist Failure with Homer (II)," 171. The D-Scholia were edited by Lascaris in 1517; by contrast, the Venetus A scholia, although familiar to a few fifteenth-century scholars such as Martino Filetico, was largely unknown. Eustathius's commentaries, discussed below, were in print from 1542 to 1550 but accessible only to scholars with excellent Greek. On the Renaissance familiarity with the Homeric scholiasts, see Pontani, "Homeric Readings," 392–5.

55 [Plutarch], *Essay on the Life and Poetry of Homer*, 164–5. The pseudo-Plutarchan *Life* quotes a fragment by Empedocles (DK B17.7–8; fragment 25 in *The Poem of Empedocles. A Text and Translation*, 217). A similar argument appears in Heraclitus, *Homeric Problems*, 69.1–16, 110–11. On the applications of the allegory of Ares and Aphrodite to Renaissance philosophy and literature, see Wind, *Pagan Mysteries*, 86–9, and D. Cheney, *Spenser's Image of Nature*, 236, which argues that Spenser's invocation of Mars and Venus provides an ethic derived from the "linking [of] these two antithetical elements as the basis of the dialectic working throughout the poem."

56 Aristotle, *Nic. Ethics* VIII.1.6, 454–5 [1155b]; compare *Eudemian Ethics* 1235a.

57 Diogenes Laertius, *Lives* VIII.57, and Stobaeus, *Eclogae* 1.10.11b, both cited from *The Poem of Empedocles*, Testimonia A1, 147; A33b, 165–6.

58 Heraclitus, *Homeric Problems*, 25.3, 48–9; [Proclus], *Lucubratio*, 42r. Compare Eustathius, *Comm. ad Hom. Iliadem*, 3:224–5 (985.1–41, on *Il.* 14.272–81); *Johannes Tzetzae Liber Historicus*, Chiliad V.24 ("De Pomo Contentionis"), 93, ls. 772–6, which offers an allegorical reading of Eris's intrusion into the wedding as the "generation of the world" [*mundi generatione*].

59 La Primaudaye, *French Academie*, 654–6.

60 Poliziano, *Oratio*, ed. Megna, 23–4; Pansa, *De Osculo Ethnicae* 1.12 (1601), 44–5. On mythographic interpretations of Homeric epic during the sixteenth century, see Seznec, *Survival of the Pagan Gods;* Allen, *Mysteriously Meant*; on Pansa, see Schmitt, "Perennial Philosophy," 529.

61 Both the Homeric *Scholia* and Heraclitus's *Homeric Problems* offer similar theodicies, arguing that while the Trojan War might appear futile from a mortal perspective, Homer's gods nonetheless preserve cosmic harmony and justice: "Wars and battles seem terrible to us," the Venetus B Scholia to *Il.* 4.4–8 reads, "but not to the gods, for the deities accomplish all things in thinking about the harmony of all else" (*Scholia* [Venetus B] to *Il.* 4.4, cited in Buffière, *Les Mythes d'Homère*, 298). On the publication history of the Homeric Scholia and of Heraclitus's *Homeric Problems*, see P. Ford, *De Troie à Ithaque*, 6–7. On the allegorical exegesis of this episode and on Platonic interpretations of Homer's theomachy during the sixteenth century, see Hutton, *Themes of Peace*, 201–2.

62 Poliziano, *Oratio*, in *Opera Omnia*, 1:487.

63 Reynolds, *A Treatise of the Passions,* 119.

64 *L'Odyssée d'Homere*, trans. Salomon Certon, sig. a3r.

65 Philostratus, *La Suite de Philostrate*, fol. 7b.

66 [Ovid], *Ovide Moralisé* 4:148 (XI.1265, XI.1284); 4:152 (XI.1418–29); Lemaire de Belges, *Les Illustrations de Gaule*, 1:275, imitating Pseudo-Clement, *Recognitions*, 10:41; on Lemaire's interpretation, see also Kem, *Jean Lemaire de*

Belges, 20, and Moss, *Poetry and Fable*, 17–21. A similar interpretation appears in Heraclitus, *Homeric Problems*, 22.8, 42–3, which attributes to Homer the doctrines of Thales and of Anaxagoras, who "joined earth with water ... so that the wet, combined with the dry, blended with its opposite to produce a harmonious system" [*antipalou phuseôs eis mian homonian anakpathê*]. Sallust, *Concerning the Gods*, similarly maintains that the apple thrown by Eris represents the universe, "which, as it is made of opposites, is rightly said to be thrown by strife" (Sallust, IV.10, cited in Wind, *Pagan Mysteries*, 270).

67 The latter reading may derive partly from the relationship between the wedding of Peleus and Thetis and the *Charites*, or Graces, who are conceived as Eurymone makes her way home from the wedding. The Graces are interpreted by classical and early modern allegorists as symbols of the principle that harmony is born out of concordant discords; on this reading, see Wind, *Pagan Mysteries*, 82–6.

68 Conti, *Mythologiae*, 1:139.

69 Lambinus, *Pridie Quam Homeri Iliadis,* 18: "Empedocles ex quattuor elementis oriri omnia, & in ea interire putavit, adiunctis tamen duobus aliis principiis amicitia, & lite ... Homerus hanc quattuor elementorum discordem concordiam, per furtivum Martis & Veneris concubitum non obscure describit ... Iam Apollo a Neptuno assidue & implacabiliter dissidens quid aliud declarat, quam calidum, & siccum, frigid, & humido contrarium?"

70 Reynolds, *Mythomystes*, in *Critical Essays*, ed. Spingarn, 1:171; *Ovids Metamorphosis Englished,* trans. Sandys, "The Minde of this Frontispeece," ls. 2–3. On Achilles's shield as a master metaphor for the concept of unity in multeity, see Heninger, *Touches of Sweet Harmony*, 174.

71 Benserade, *La Mort d'Achille*, 15.

72 Leroy, *De La Vicissitude*, 210, 32: "banquets, rises, convoitises, plaintes, lamentations, fascheries, choleres, haynes, differens, discords, combats, guerres, et batailles."

73 Leroy, *De La Vicissitude*, 32. On the tradition of interpreting Homeric epic as endorsing the "opposition of contraries as a principle derived from nature," see Austin, "The One and the Many," 229.

74 Quattrehomme, *Discours*, 9: "Nostre Homere dit donc sagement que celuy qui blasme la contention, blasme la Nature, chaque chose si gra[n]de & petite qu'elle soit aya[n]t deux genies qui co[n]tinuelleme[n]t l'entourrent co[n]trarians ensemble."

75 Heraclitus, *On the Universe* LVI, in Hippocrates, *Works*, 4:489; the same passage is cited by Plutarch in his *Isis and Osiris* 369B (*Moralia* 5:109) and his *On Tranquility of Mind* 473F (*Moralia* 6:219).

76 Heraclitus, *Cosmic Fragments*, 51. Heraclitus explains how cosmic forces are "at variance" but also "agree" with each other such that "there is a connection

working in both directions, as in the bow and the lyre [*toxou kai lurês*]." Early modern comparisons between Homer and Heraclitus persist in spite of the fact that Heraclitus was a staunch critic of Homer who assails Achilles for being "wrong when he said, 'Would that Conflict [*Eris*] might vanish from among gods and men!' For there would be no attunement [*harmonia*] without high and low notes, nor any animals without male and female, both of which are opposites." See *The Art and Thought of Heraclitus*, Fragment LXXXI, 66–7, preserved in Aristotle, *Eudemian Ethics* VII.1 [1235a25] and in the A *Scholia* to *Il.* 18.107.

77 Stillingfleet, *Origines Sacrae*, 475–6.

78 Lorris and De Meun, *Roman de la Rose*, 16.786–7; Chaucer, *Knights Tale*, ls. 2136–52, describes the "faire cheyne of love" that binds the elements and ensures the stability of the world. For other treatments of the interpretation of the golden chain in medieval and Renaissance literature, see Edelstein, "The Golden Chain of Homer"; Wolff, *Die goldene Kette;* Lévêque, *Aurea Catena Homeri*; Arthur Lovejoy, *The Great Chain of Being: a study of the history of an idea.*

79 Hutton, *Themes of Peace*, 177–8. On the popularity of allegories concerning the chaining of Discord by Harmony (or Harmony reconciled to Discord) during the 1550s and 1560s in France, see Hutton, 106–17. For Landino's interpretation of the golden chain, see his *Disputationes Camaldulenses*, 177–8; on interpretations by Ficino and Bruno, see Catana, *The Concept of Contraction*, 82–3, and Brisson, *How Philosophers Saved Myths*, 114–17.

80 Le Caron, *Dialogues*, 286; compare Fraunce, *Amintas dale*, in *Yuychurch,* 15, which explains that the golden chain ensures the "cohoerent concatenation and depending of things united so in order, as none but only the almighty Jupiter can dissolve the same."

81 La Boëtie, *De la Servitude Volontaire*, 66–7. On Lucian's use of the metaphor, see Anderson, *Lucian*, 33.

82 Knevet, *Stratiotikon,* 126–7, ls. 402, 408–9, 412, 416–17.

83 Bruni, *De Studio Litterarum*, 247.

84 *Homeri Ilias*, ed. Giphanius, 3; *Homeri Quae Extant Omnia*, ed. Sponde, dedicatory epistle to Henri III, sig. A2v. On this passage, and on Sponde's reading of Homeric epic for contemporary political lessons, see Bizer, "Men are from Mars," 167.

85 Scaliger, *Poetices*, ed Deitz and Vogt-Spira, 4:418.

86 Lipsius, *Politica,* 538–9, citing *Il.* 3.179.

87 Le Caron, *Dialogues*, 287: "l'amitié et la dissention [qui] sont les commencements des choses, qui a esté l'opinion d'Empedocle." Compare Wilson, *Ransom*, 113.

88 See Philostratus, *La Suite de Philostrate*, 56a, which argues that the two sides of the shield are symbols of peace and war, the more desirable condition represented by the city that illustrates "the peace [created] by Justice and the policing by which cities should be regulated" [*la paix de Justice & police dont les villes doibvent estre reglees*]. Compare Eustathius, *Comm. ad Hom. Iliadem*, 4:90–2 (1158.1–10 on *Il.* 18.498; 1158.39–62 on *Il.* 18.508–9), arguing that the peaceful city represents the virtue of *homonoia* and reflects the high estimation of justice among the ancient Greeks.

89 Lambinus, *Pridie Quam Homeri Iliadis*, 17.

90 S. Morgan, *Armilogia*, 110.

91 *L'Iliade d'Homere*, trans. Souhait, 617.

92 I. Johnston, *Ironies of War*, 88–9; on the shield as a cosmological allegory, see also Hardie, "Imago Mundi," 11–31. This interpretation was, however, disputed by Homer's early Christian readers, particularly by Origen, *Contra Celsum* VI.42, who attacks the idea that war and strife, as represented by Homer, are part of a larger cosmic design. On the shield as a union of contraries, see Conche, *Essais sur Homère*, 158, 160; on Achilles's shield as a symbol of the union of contraries, see also Taplin, "The Shield of Achilles within the *Iliad*," in *Oxford Readings*, ed. Cairns, 342–64.

93 Jonson, *Haddington Masque* (1608), in *Works*, 7:258. *Ovids Metamorphosis Englished*, trans. Sandys, 602.

94 See I. Johnston, *Ironies of War*, 27, who emphasizes the "ironic tension" in the *Iliad*'s representation of the "dual nature of warfare," which both "exalts men and impartially destroys them."

95 On Heraclitus's cosmology, see Nietzsche, *Philosophy During the Tragic Age of the Greeks*, Later Preface (1879), in *Works*, 2:101.

96 Aristotle, *Nic. Ethics* VIII.1.6, 454–5 [1155b]. For Heraclitus's comments on the epithet *xunos Enualios*, see *The Art and Thought of Heraclitus*, 62–3 [Fragment LXXXII], 66–7 [Fragment LXXV], and editor's commentary, 205–7; these fragments are preserved by Origen, *Contra Celsum* VI.28, and by Aristotle, *Nic. Ethics*.

97 Heraclitus, *Homeric Problems*, 31.5, 56–7, argues that the term *alloprosallos* conveys how the "fortune of battle often passes now to one side and now to the other" [*machais amphibolias allote pros allous metaphoitôsês*], thus depicting war as an ongoing process of "opposition and reversals [*tropai*]" that preserves the counterbalance of the natural world. On this epithet as conveying a "cosmology of inversion," see Vacca, "The Theology of Disorder," 8; Nietzsche, *Philosophy During the Tragic Age*, in *Works*, 2:101.

98 L. Morgan, *Patterns of Redemption*, 205–7; Hadot, *The Veil of Isis*, 205.

99 Quint, *Epic and Empire*, 8.

100 Collins, *Master of the Game*, 58. Conte, *The Rhetoric of Imitation*, 183–4, and Kallendorf, *The Other Virgil*, 74–6, both make similar arguments about *The Aeneid*, arguing that Virgil opens up the "epic norm" to "multiple points of view," thus making the epic tradition rich in "contradictory registers."

101 Nagy, *Homeric Questions*, 1, discusses the ancient tradition of works by Aristotle and Porphyry, among others, that address Homeric Questions [*Zêtêmata*], a term used by Plato to denote philosophical puzzles or problems.

102 Griffin, *Homer on Life and Death*, 199. On the comic and satirical elements in Homeric epic, see Halliwell, *Greek laughter*; Nagy, *The Best of the Achaeans*; Giangrande, *The Use of Spoudaiogeloion*; Lateiner, *Sardonic Smile*, and the discussions in chapters 2 and 4 of this book.

103 On Casaubon's detection of the *Batrachomyomachia* (printed in Henri Estienne's 1566 *Poetae Graeci*) as a counterfeit, see Grafton, *Defenders of the Text*, 147–8.

104 The passage, located at Quintilian, *Inst. Orat.* X.1.46 and XII.10.64, is cited frequently during the period: see Tortelli, *Orthographia* (1493), sig. n3r; Valla, *De Voluptate*, 244–5; Poliziano, *Ambra*, ls. 489–91, in *Silvae*, 100–1: "Whether [Homer] wishes to spin his verse with a slender thread or holds to a middle style or rises more forcefully with full strength" [*sive libet tenui versum deducere filo, / seu medium confine tenet, seu robore toto / fortior assurgit*]. Compare Poliziano's paraphrase in his preface to *Homerou Odysseias Bibloi A & B*, sig. C3r: "Hunc nemo in magnis rebus sublimitate, in parvis proprietate superav[er]it."

105 Aulo Giano Parrasio, *In Q. Horatii Flacii autem poeticam commentaria* (1531), preface, 2r–2v, as cited in *The History of Literary Criticism in the Italian Renaissance*, ed. Weinberg, 1:371: "vi sua comediarum, tragoediarum, dithyramborum, omniumque poematum argumenta suis operibus inservit."

106 Cinthio, *Discorsi*, 225; Vossius, *De Artis Poeticae*, 67; Vossius goes on to point out that some regard the *Margites*, and not the *Odyssey*, as the prime example of Homer's comic genius.

107 On these and other works of tragicomedy based on the *Odyssey*, see E. Hall, *The Return of Ulysses*, 39.

108 Simmaco de Jacobiti, *Batracomiomachia* 62, ls. 601, 607–8: "ingegno in basse cosi / pilgiar principia alti e gloriosi."

109 Peradotto, *Man in the Middle Voice*, 53.

110 Heywood, *Gynaikeion*, 13. The view that Homer was a beggar persists through the eighteenth century: see, for instance, the discussion of "poor Homer" singing his rhapsodies for "small earnings" in Richard Bentley, *Remarks Upon a Late Discourse of Free-Thinking*, in *A Letter to F.H.D.D. by Phileleutherus Lipsiensis*, 8th ed. (Cambridge, 1745), 25–6.

111 J.S., *Innovation of Penelope and Ulysses*, 157, 139–40, 150.
112 Gratius, *Dialogue between Mercury and a Potlicker*, in *Scheming Papists and Lutheran Fools*, ed. Rummel, 52–3.
113 Nuttall, "Action at a Distance," in *Shakespeare and the Classics*, ed. Martindale and Taylor, 216–17.
114 Thalmann, *Swineherd*, 134.
115 Visa-Ondarçuhu, *L'Image de l'Athlète*, 40, 63; on rhetorical performance as one of the "primary agonistic arenas" for Homer's heroes, see also J. Heath, *Talking Greeks*, 120.
116 Thalmann, *Swineherd*, 111, 120.
117 Lord, *Heroic Mockery*, 17. On the culture of play (or serious play) in Renaissance culture, see Huizinga, *Homo Ludens*; Colie, *Paradoxia Epidemica*; Bakhtin, *Rabelais and his World*; Marcus, *The Politics of Mirth*; Whigham, *Ambition and Privilege;* Daston and Park, *Wonders and the Order of Nature, 1150–1750.*
118 Leroy, *De la Vicissitude*, 207: "si grande diversité de natures, multitude de disciplines, varieté d'actions, d'exercises, et oeuvres."
119 Valens, *De Laudibus Homeri Oratio*, 29: "Homerus omnis scientiae ac sapientiae Oceanus est."
120 Rubenstein, "The Notes to Poliziano's *Iliad*," 213. On Poliziano's conception of Homer as source or "ocean," see also Maier, "Une Page Inédite de Politien," 9–10; Poliziano, *Ambra*, ls. 12–13; ln. 481, in *Silvae*, 70–1, 98–9. Compare Salel, *L'Apologie d'Homère*, in *Oeuvres*, 89, who identifies Homer as the fount of all things.
121 Heywood, *The Golden Age*, n.p.; Jehasse, *La Renaissance de la Critique*, 136, points out that for early modern philologists such as Henri Estienne, all "filiations" of meaning begin with Homer, making him a linguistic as well as a philosophical and rhetorical point of origin.
122 *Les XXIIII Livres de l'Iliade*, trans. Salel, sig. A3r: "Il n'est passage en la Philosophie, / Tant soit divers, qui ne se fortifie, / Par quelque dict, ou sentence notable, / De ce poete." Compare Deimier, *L'Academie de L'Art Poetique*, 232, on the "mouth" [*bouche*] of Homer as a source from which all poetry flows, as well as "the diverse regimes of old philosophers" [*les regimes diverses / Des Philosophes vieux*].
123 *Les XXIIII Livres de l'Iliade,* trans. Salel, sigs. A2v–A3v. Salel's translation of *Il.* 1 and 2 first appeared in 1542, without this epistle. *Iliad* 1 to 10 were printed in Paris in 1545, with 11 and 12 in 1554 and the whole *Iliad* (along with Jacques Peletier's translation of *Od.* 1 and 2) in 1580. Although Renaissance scholars also quibble about Virgil's philosophical loyalties, he is often held to be either a Platonist or an Epicurean (or a combination of the two). On this point, see Wilson-Okamura, *Virgil*, 80.

124 Porphyry, *Homeric Questions*, trans. Schlunk, 2–3; Seneca, Epistle 88.5, in *Epistulae Morales* 2:351–3. On this passage and its relevance to the reception of Homer, see N.J. Richardson, "Homer and his Ancient Critics," in *Homer's Iliad: a Commentary*, ed. Kirk, 6:37, and Murrin, *Allegorical Readers*, 9.

125 Quattrehomme, *Discours*, 185–6: "Homère semble un Palais à plusieurs éstages, où tout un monde peut loger."

126 Collop, "Of Homer," ls. 3–6, in *The Poems of John Collop*, 108.

127 Rabelais, *Quart Livre*, 49, in *Oeuvres*, 712; Poliziano, *Oratio*, in *Opera Omnia*, 1:479.

128 Du Bartas, *Divine Weekes and Works*, 431; Poliziano, *Ambra*, ls. 516–17, in *Silvae*, 100–3: "doctaq[ue] multiiugae post hunc divortia sectae / Hinc haustum"; Garasse, "Invective contre Homere et Virgile," in his *Nouveau Jugement*, 143: "sur tous d'Homere pour authorizer ses contentions Philosophiques, par les meilleures sente[n]ces qu'il tiroit d'eux."

129 Maximus of Tyre, Oration 26, in *Orations*, 216.

130 [Plutarch], *Life of Homer*, 165–7; compare Heraclitus, *Homeric Problems*, sections 24 and 69, 46–7, 110–11.

131 Petit, *Homeri Nepenthes*, sig. A2r: "Ante omnia locus hic Poetarum & literarum parentis ponendus in medio; cum sit fundamentum, vel certe occasio totius disputationis."

132 Finkelberg, "Homer as a Foundation Text," 92; Halbertal, *People of the Book*, 32–3.

133 Compare Wilson-Okamura, *Virgil*, 7: "Idiotic or insightful does not matter: if an idea about Virgil had currency during the Renaissance, then we want to know about it."

134 Filippo Sassetti, *Sopra Dante* (BNF VII, 1028), 4v, cited in Weinberg, *History of Literary Criticism* 1:531; the paraphrase of Cinthio's *Discorsi* appears at Weinberg, 2:968.

135 Antonio Minturno, *Arte Poetica*, 32–3, cited in Weinberg, *History of Literary Criticism* 2:971: "che una volta è vero, convien che sia sempre, & in ogni etâ."

136 Niccolo degli Oddi, *Dialogo … contra gli Academici della Crusca* (1587), 63, cited in Weinberg, 2:1033: "non è se non vitio voler seuguitare Homero in quelle cose, che come à suoi tempi convenivano, hora sono disconvenevoli; oltre che … l'età di Homero, & I costume de'suoi tempi, e le singolari virtù che si ritrovano in esso, fecero tolerabili quelle cose in lui." On the quarrel between ancients and moderns in the Renaissance, see Baron, "The Querelle," 3–22; Jones, *Ancients and Moderns*; J.B. Bury, *The Idea of Progress; an inquiry into its origin and growth*, 2nd ed. (New York: Macmillan, 1932); Grafton, *Commerce with the Classics*.

137 Grafton, *Defenders of the Text*, 26–7; compare Steadman, "Achilles and Renaissance Epic," 140–1.
138 Bolgar, *The Classical Heritage*, 349; Peletier, *Au Roy Tres Chrestien*, in *Oeuvres Poétiques*, 7.
139 Martindale, "Introduction: Thinking Through Reception," 12, in *Classics and the Uses of Reception*, ed. Martindale and Thomas, 1–13.
140 Goldhill, *Who Needs Greek?*, 297.
141 Tim Whitmarsh, "True Histories: Lucian, Bakhtin, and the Pragmatics of Reception," 104, in *Classics and the Uses of Reception*, ed. Martindale and Thomas, 104–16.
142 M. West, "Homer's *Iliad* and the Genesis of Mock-Heroic," 3.
143 Sowerby, "Early Humanist Failure with Homer (I)," 44.
144 Lamberton, *Homer the Theologian*, 81–2.
145 Budé, *De Transitu*, ed. Lebel, 231. Budé addresses the correspondence between Homeric epic and the scriptures throughout *De Transitu* and other works. In his *De Studio litterarum recte et commode instituendo*, 20, 24, Budé argues that Homer adorned his poems with elements borrowed from the ancient Hebrews and that the ancientest poets borrowed "the seeds of their theology ... from the sanctuary of sacred philosophy."
146 Sponde, *Homeri quae extant omnia*, Prolegomena, 1:11; Jehasse, *La Renaissance de la Critique*, 539n59, remarks on the fact that thirty citations of Homer in Lipsius's *Politica*, around twenty percent of the total number, are also cited by Clement of Alexandria.
147 Budé, *De Transitu*, ed. Lebel, 176.
148 *L'Odissea d'Homero tradotta in volgare fiorentino da M. Girolamo Baccelli*, n.p.: "Le ferite, I furti, le vergogne, e le altre cose humane, che Homero attribuisce a gli Dii, sono alti misteri di quella Teologia."
149 Guggisberg, *Sebastian Castellio*, 158.
150 Scapula, *Lexicon Graecolatinum* (London, 1619), column 516, sig. Y4v.
151 Hammond, *A Paraphrase and annotations upon all the books of the New Testament*, 29.
152 Hammond, *Paraphrase*, 487.
153 Hammond, *Paraphrase*, 576, 538; Hammond also calls Paul's language "Agonistical" at Phil. 3.12 (644).
154 Ross, *Mystagogus Poeticus*, 2–3.
155 Fotherby, *Atheomastix*, 53.
156 Duport, *Homeri ... Gnomologia*, 101.
157 Duport, *Homeri ... Gnomologia*, 290–1.
158 Wilson-Okamura, *Virgil*, 1.
159 Poliziano, *Ambra*, ls. 12–13, in *Silvae*, 70–1: "de gurgite vivo / combibit arcanos vatum omnis turba furores."

160 Compare Hepp, *Homère en France au XVIIe Siècle*, 96, which argues that the study of Homer "is almost always undertaken through screens" [*se fait Presque toujours à travers des écrans*]. In her discussion of the ancient authors cited by Sponde's commentary on Homer, Deloince-Louette (*Sponde, Commentateur d'Homère*, 88–91) provides useful insight into the variety of classical and early Christian texts through which early modern interpretations of Homer were mediated.

161 Hutten, *Letters of Obscure Men*, 481–2.

162 Montaigne, "Of Physiognomy," in *Complete Essays*, 808.

163 *Homeri Poetae Clarissimi Odyssea, Andrea Divo ... interprete*, Ad Lectorum, *Odyssea*, fol. 2r: "qui Poetam hunc graecum legent, eundem etiam habeant latinum ita excusum, ut uno intuitu omnia in utroque videre posit." On the popularity of Greek-Latin editions of Homer, see P. Ford, *De Troie à Ithaque*, 145.

164 Sowerby, "Early Humanist Failure with Homer (I)," 37, and "Early Humanist Failure with Homer (II)," 167.

165 See Gregory, *From Many Gods to One*; Warner, *The Augustinian Epic*; Wilson-Okamura, *Virgil*, 133; Van der Laan, "'What virtue and wisdom can do'"; Demetriou, "'Essentially Circe'." Zatti, *l'Ombra del Tasso*, 94n55, argues that a preference for Homer over Virgil during the period is "heterodox" but nonetheless embraced by Trissino, among others.

166 Collop, "On Scaliger," ls. 6, 8, in *The Poems*, 109.

167 Vida, *De Arte Poetica* 1:10–11, ls. 126–8.

168 See, for instance, Andrea Menichini's 1572 *Delle lodi della poesia d'Omero, et di Virgilio*, Paolo Beni's 1607 *Della comparazione d'Omero, Virgilio, e T. Tasso*, and "Homeri loca magis insignia quae Virgilius imitatus est," a concordance of the two poets printed in *Opera Pub. Virgilii Maronis*, ed. Paolo Manuzio and Georg Fabricius (Antwerp: Plantijn, 1572). None of these works compare Homer entirely unfavorably to Virgil, nor do later seventeenth-century treatises by Rapin (*Comparaison des poëmes d'Homère et de Virgile*, 1664) or Le Bossu (*Traité du poëme epique*, 1675).

169 Giulio Del Bene, *Due Discorsi* (1574), cited in *Trattati di Poetica e Retorica del Cinquecento*, ed. Weinberg, 3:189: "Omero, che fu il primo poeta, non ebbe alcuno maestro che gli insegnasse ma fu perfettissimo poeta."

170 A. Ford, *Homer*, 95.

171 Poliziano, *Ambra*, ls. 461–6, in *Silvae*, 98–9. Not all Renaissance writers thought that Homer had no models or predecessors: for the dissenting view, see Peletier, *Art Poétique* (1555), in *Traités*, 257.

172 Donatus, *Life of Virgil*, trans. David Wilson Okamura (www.virgil.org), 46.

173 Aesop, Fable 534, in *Fables*, 129.

174 Greene, *The Light in Troy*, 40.
175 Longinus, *On the Sublime*, 210–13. On "eristic" imitation, see Pigman, "Versions of Imitation in the Renaissance," 4n9.
176 Longinus, *On the Sublime*, 212–13, citing Hesiod, *WD*, ln. 24.
177 Paquelin, *Apologeme pour le grand Homere*, sig. A3r, calls Homer "le Platon des Poetes, [et] que Platon est appellé l'Homere des Philosophes." Compare Dalechamp, *Artis Poeticae et versificatoriae encomium*, rpt. in Binns, *Latin Treatises*, 160–1, who calls Plato "Homerus philosophorum." On Paquelin's interpretation of Homer, see Mino Gabriele, "Le premier commentaire sur Homère en langue française: *l'Apologeme* de Guillaume Paquelin, 1577," in *Homère*, ed. Capodieci and Ford, 93–104.
178 Proclus, *Lucubratio*, fol. 82r: "Platoni in omnibus suis scriptis Homerum aemulari tum in divinis tum in humanis rebus."
179 On the sympathies between Homeric epic and Platonic philosophy, see Deneen, *The Odyssey of Political Theory*, 82, 13.
180 Heywood, *The Hierarchie of the Blessed Angells*, 109.
181 Ong, *Interfaces of the Word*, 222–4; A. Ford, *Homer*, 93.
182 *Robert Dover and the Cotswold Games*, ed. Whitfield, 21; William Denny, "An Encomiastick to his worthy Freind Mr. Robert Dover, on his Famous Annual Assemblies at Cotswold," in *Annalia Dubrensia*, ed. Grosart, 15; also see Semenza, *Sport, Politics, and Literature*, 127; Graziosi, *Inventing Homer*, 180, 198–9.
183 A. Ford, *Homer*, 96.
184 R. Martin, *The Language of Heroes*, 238, 94. On the textual history of the *Certamen*, which survives in a second-century CE manuscript but probably derives from the fourth-century BCE *Mouseion* of Alcidamas, see Nietzsche, "Die Florentinischer Tractat"; N.J. Richardson, "The contest of Homer and Hesiod and Alcidamas' *Mouseion*"; Martin West, "The Contest of Homer and Hesiod," 433–50. On poetic contests in early Greece, see Kahane, *Diachronic Dialogues*; Griffith, "Contest and contradiction in early Greek poetry"; Graziosi, "Competition in Wisdom." The title page of Daniel Pareus's 1627 *Mellificium Atticum*, which depicts Hesiod and Homer flanked by Apollo and his lyre, may be a reference to the *Certamen*; retellings of the contest are common throughout the Renaissance.
185 Graziosi, "Competition in Wisdom," 59, 71; Graziosi, *Inventing Homer*, 109, 169–70.
186 M.L. West, "The Contest of Homer and Hesiod," 443: "The judgment of Panedes comes down to a choice between peace and war." On this point, compare A. Ford, *Origins of Criticism*, 276–7.

1. Homer, Erasmus, and the Problem of Strife

1 More, *Letter to the University of Oxford* (29 March 1518), in *Complete Works of Thomas More*, 15:133. The most immediate cause for the debate was the provision made by Bishop Fox for the first permanent establishment of a Greek lecturer at the foundation of Corpus Christi College in 1516. On the relationship of the quarrel to the Reuchlin affair and the debate over trilingual pedagogy in the early sixteenth century, see Saladin, *La Bataille du Grec*, 173–8, and Sandys, *Classical Scholarship*, 2:230. Epigraph: Aeschylus, *Seven Against Thebes*, ln. 1057: "eris perainei muthon hustatê theôn."

2 Desiderius Erasmus, Adage II.v.98: *Esernius Cum Pacidiano*, cited from *CWE* 33:286–8 and from *Opera Omnia* (ASD) II.3:474. Unless otherwise noted, all subsequent citations from Erasmus are cited (in English) from *CWE* and (in Latin) from the ASD or LB. I have made occasional alternations to the English translations provided by the *CWE*.

3 On Erasmus's interest in establishing a decorum of conduct for scholarly debates, see Rummel, "Argumentis, Non Contumeliis," 305–15.

4 Budé, *De Transitu*, 114; Pontani, "Homeric Readings," 407. On Budé's *De Transitu* and the relationship between his Hellenism and his Lutheranism, see Saladin, *La Bataille du Grec*, 397–400.

5 Ep. 131, in Erasmus, *Epistolae*, ed. Allen, 1:305–6. On this letter, and on the possibility that Erasmus undertook (or planned to undertake) a translation of *Od.*, see Allen 1:305n, and Thomson, "Erasmus and Paris," 120–3. On Erasmus's Latin translations of Homer in the *Adages*, also see Cytowska, "Erasme de Rotterdam, Traducteur d'Homère," 341–53.

6 In *Érasme: une abeille laborieuse*, 105, Margolin counts 666 allusions to Homer in the 1517 edition of the *Adages*, making Homer second only to Cicero in frequency of citations. In selecting passages for the work, Erasmus used the 1488 Florentine *editio princeps* of Homer by Nerlius, the same edition owned by Budé; according to Ep. 1437, Erasmus felt that the Aldine edition was corrupt ("Aldina sunt depravatissima"). On Erasmus's translations of Homer in the *Adages*, see also Cytowska, "Homer bei Erasmus."

7 Rummel, "The Use of Greek," 65, 63, points out that the compound nature of the Greek language lends itself especially well to "witty, sarcastic, or hyperbolic" phrasing.

8 Erasmus, *Institutio Principis Christiani*, *CWE* 27:251; compare Erasmus's letter to Duke Ernest of Bavaria [(Louvain), 4 Nov. 1517], which served as the dedicatory letter to his edition of Quintus Curtius Rufus's *History of*

Alexander the Great, printed at Strasbourg in June 1518 (Ep. 704, *CWE* 5:184–5).

9 Spitz, *The Religious Renaissance,* 210–11; Rummel, "The Use of Greek," 60.

10 The abridgment was printed as *Proverbia quaedam Homerica D. Erasmi Roterodami labore exquisitissimo e Graeco in linguam Latinam versa, ingenii ac eruditionis plenissima* (Antwerp: Martin de Keyser, 1529); it contains a brief preface followed by a list of the Homeric adages in Latin. Rummel, "The Reception of Erasmus' *Adages*," 21.

11 Firestone Library, Princeton UL, 2681.1488q, *Hê tou Homêrou poiêsis hapasa* (Florence: Nerlius, 1488), annotated by Guillaume Budé, 2:113a; BNP Res. YB 151, *Homêrou Ilias* (Louvain: Bartholomaeo Gravio, 1535), inscribed "Christophorus Comes a Manderscheit" on inside front cover, sigs. I2r, Mr, O2v.

12 Vat. Stamp. Pal. IV.801, *Homêrou Odysseiae A ke E Angeli Politiani in Homerum Praefatio* (Basel, 1520), annotated by Achilles Pirminius Gasser, signed "A.P.G.L.Vuittenberg 1523" on the title page; cross-references to Erasmus's *Adages* appear on pages 1 and 20 of the text, which is bound with *Iliados D Homêrou Rhapsodias Hupodesis*, transcribed by Achilles Gasser and dated "anno 1523 Nuremberge," fols. 20v–21r.

13 *Seculorum Longe Principis Homeri Ilias*, trans. Hessus, 151, glossing *Il.* 6.236; see Erasmus, Adage I.ii.1. P. Ford, *De Troie à Ithaque*, 73, notes that in his *Homeri Iliados libri duo* (1523), Melchior Wolmar also includes cross-references to Erasmus's *Adages.*

14 Epo, *Omnium Scriptorum Principis Homeri Sententiae*, sigs. B3v, F2v. In her "Homer for the Court of François I," 744, Rothstein notes a similar tendency in Salel's French translation of Homer, in which marginal notes identify speakers and mark out *sententiae* with "the usual inverted quotation marks."

15 Lambinus, *Pridie quam Homeri Iliadis librum A. explicare inciperet*; BNP mss. Fonds Francais 19.035, fols. 60–176 (Séguier, *Receuil des Mythologies apophtegmes et sentences d'Homere, extraict des commentaries d'Eustathe*). On these and other collections of proverbs based on Homeric epic, see Hepp, "Homère en France au XVIe Siécle," 425; P. Ford, *De Troie à Ithaque*, 299.

16 Hartung, *Chilias Homericorum Locorum*, poem by Oporinus to Hartung, n.p. (back endpapers).

17 On the exemplary copia of Homeric epic, see *Lingua* (*CWE* 29:283), where Erasmus argues that "only Homer seems to have escaped causing surfeit through the marvelous variety of his stories, although perhaps not everywhere, since Virgil pruned back many passages." The ancient scholiasts frequently praise Homer as *philopoikilos*, or a lover of variety; on *poikilia* or variety in the scholia, see N.J. Richardson, "Literary Criticism in the exegetical Scholia," 266–7.

18 In the same letter, Budé explains how several several other nuggets of Homeric wisdom help him to patch up his disagreement with Erasmus, citing two lines from *Il.* (21.150–1) in order to explain why he has been dissuaded from further strife. See Ep. 583, *CWE* 4:362 [Allen 2:570].

19 In his annotation on 1 Cor. 14.11, a verse in which Paul states that "I will be a foreigner to the speaker [*lalounti barbaros*] and the speaker a foreigner to me [*lalôn ... barbaros*]," Erasmus glosses the verse by mentioning Homer's use of the term *barbarophônôn*, a probable reference to *Il.* 2.867 (ASD VI.8:270).

20 Marsuppini, *Praefatio in Homeri Libros*, 56–7, ls. 130–2, 56–7, paraphrasing Quintilian, *Inst. Orat.*, II.17.8; compare Seneca, *Ep.* 40.2 and Gellius, *Noctes Atticae*, VI.14.7. On Homeric epic as demonstrating the three styles of oratory, see G. Kennedy, "The Ancient Dispute over Rhetoric in Homer," 23–27, and the excellent discussion by Wilson-Okamura, *Virgil*, 73–4.

21 Bruni's treatment of the three speeches in *Il.* 9 is indebted to Quintilian, *Inst. Orat..* II.17.8, and to Gellius VI.14.7. His *Homeric Orations* were widely available in manuscript during the fifteenth century; they were printed in *Homeri Opera et Graeco Traducta* (Venice, 1516), an edition that also contains Guarino of Verona's Latin translation of pseudo-Plutarch's *Life of Homer*. They were also printed in a freestanding edition as *Tres Orationes in triplici dicendi genere* (Nuremberg: Brassicanus, 1523). For a modern edition, see *Die Orationes Homeri des Leonardo Bruni Aretino*, ed. Thiemann. On Bruni's orations, see Sowerby, "Early Humanist Failure with Homer (I)," and P. Ford, *De Troie à Ithaque*, 26, 31. On praise and blame in fifteenth-century Italy, see Kallendorf, *In Praise of Aeneas*, 78.

22 Monfasani, *Byzantine Scholars*, 178; compare chapter 2 of Kendrick, *Ancient Epics, Renaissance Translations*, which argues that Bruni's interest in Homer was predicated on the belief that ancient Greece and fifteenth-century Florence shared a commitment to rhetorical excellence and to democratic debate.

23 Valla's translations of Homer were widely available in printed editions, including the *Ilias ... in Latinum* (Brescia, 1474; rpt. 1497), the *Homeri poetae clarissimi Ilias* (Venice, 1502), and a 1512 edition of the *Iliad* printed at Leipzig. Poliziano's autograph translation of *Il.* 2 and 3 [MS Vat. Lat. 3298] and his autograph translation of *Il.* 4 and 5 [MS Vat. Lat. 3617] are discussed (and the notes transcribed) by Rubenstein, "The Notes to Poliziano's *Iliad*." Poliziano's preface to Homer was also printed in *Homêrou Odysseias [bibloi] 1. kai 2* (Basel: Andreas Cratander, 1520).

24 On Valla as the "most argumentative of the humanists," see Seigel, *Rhetoric and Philosophy*, 141; for a contemporary view of the disputatious Valla, see Pontano, *De Semone*, 27.

25 Erasmus, Ep. 272 (*CWE* 2:250), the dedicatory epistle to Henry VIII of England [Cambridge, July 1513] that accompanied his translation of

Plutarch's essay [now Cambridge UL MS Add. 6858]. The translation was eventually printed in *Plutarchi Opuscula* (Basel: Froben, August 1514).

26 Rom. 15.4; 2 Tim. 4.2. On Erasmus's use of the verse from Timothy, see his Letter to Dorp, *CWE* 71:12. His paraphrase of the verse appears at *CWE* 44:51. In his *Annotations* on Rom. 16.18 ("dia tês chrêstologias kai eulogias") Erasmus proposes changing the Vulgate "per dulce sermones et benedictiones" [through soft words and benedictions] to "per blandiloquentiam et assentationem" [through smooth speaking and flattery] in order better to convey Paul's hatred of the vice of flattery (*CWE* 56:430).

27 Petrarch uses the phrase in his *Invective Against a Doctor*, in *Invectives*, 368–9, citing *Il.* 4.350.

28 Adage III.viii.6, *CWE* 35:285 [ASD II.6:486], citing *Od.* 1.64 and Gellius, *Noctes Atticae* I.xv.3–4; Poliziano, marginal note to *Il.* 4.405 (fol. 13v), cited by Rubenstein, "The Notes to Poliziano's *Iliad*," 227.

29 Gellius, *Noctes Atticae* I.xv.3, 72.

30 Gellius, *Noctes Atticae* I.xv.4, 74.

31 Capito, *The Letters of Wolfgang Capito*, 1:97.

32 Mackie, *Talking Trojan*, 10; Beck, *Homeric Conversation*, 242. See also Martin, *The Language of Heroes*, and J. Heath, *The Talking Greeks*.

33 2 Cor. 12:20–1; compare 2 Tim. 4.2; Rom. 13:13; Gal. 5.20. For additional "Homeric" adages that condemn harsh speech, see *In clamosos* [Adage III. viii.91; *CWE* 35:315], *Aeacidinae minae* [Adage IV.x.91, *CWE* 36:537], and *Contemnentis inimicum* [Adage III.viii.54; *CWE* 35:302].

34 Erasmus's perception of the rhetorical and ethical continuities between Homeric epic and the New Testament is not as far-fetched as it might appear. Recent scholarship by Dennis MacDonald and others has argued persuasively that the apocryphal Acts of Andrew constitute a "Christianizing of Homer" whose protagonist is an "evangelizing Odysseus" (see MacDonald, *Christianizing Homer*, 5–6).

35 Compare Erasmus's *Paraphrase* on Acts 4.31–2 (*CWE* 50:37): "just as saffron and some other things are more productive through injury, so it rises up and forces its way out against a world that is bearing down upon it."

36 Compare Erasmus's *Paraphrase* on Titus 1.13: "reprove them severely that they may be healthy in faith."

37 Erasmus, Adage I.vi.96, *CWE* 32:64 [ASD II.2:120]; for a similar use of this Homeric proverb, see *Lingua*, *CWE* 29:270.

38 See Acts 4.13, where Peter speaks frankly [*parrêsian*]; Acts 9.28, where Paul is praised by Barnabas for "speaking boldly" [*parrêsiazomenos*]; similar commendations of frank speech appear at Acts 13.46, 14.3, and 19.8. Erasmus renders the word variously in his Latin translation of Acts: "Petri in dicendo

libertatem" (4.13), "cum fiducia loquens" (9.28), "sumpta fiducia" (13.46), "fortiter agentes," "libere loquebatur" (19.8); see ASD VI.2:244, VI.2:300, VI.2:348, VI.2:350, VI.2:402.

39 Joseph Scaliger, Jean Vassan, and Nicolas Vassan, *Scaligerana* (Amsterdam, 1740), 20, as cited by Grafton, *Defenders of the Text*, 36.

40 BNP Res. YB-151. *Homeri Ilias. Ulyssea, Batrachomyomachia, Hymni XXXII* (1535), annotated by Christopher Comes, sig. D2v; Rom. 13.1.

41 Hugo, *Vera Historia*, 118: "Paulem Thersiten, hoc est, Tharsiten, à Patria Tharsi appellatum, ob hoc grande crimen deformem depingit, & Regibus, hoc est, Christianis, regali oleo Christi delibutis, semper adversantem, eidumque Achilli Christo, & Ulyssi Petro inimicissimum."

42 Compare *Aperte simpliciterque loqui* [Speaking literally and simply], Adage III.ix.71, *CWE* 35:345 [ASD II.6:540], citing *Od.* 4.348–9, also spoken by Menelaus.

43 Erasmus, *Libanii Sophistae sub persone Menelai* (Louvain, 1519), preface (also printed as Ep. 177, in Allen 1:390–3).

44 For Erasmus's citation of the speech in the *Querela Pacis*, see *CWE* 27:319 [ASD IV.2:96], citing *Il.* 13.636–9.

45 Compare Adage III.x.52: *Iactantiae comes invidia* [Envy is the companion of boasting], derived from *Od.* 18.142: "Let him keep in silence whatever gifts he may have of the gods" (*CWE* 35:375) and Adage IV.iv.65: *Admoto capite* [With head brought near], a phrase from Plutarch, *Moralia* 71c, which derives from a verse used several times in *Od.* (at 1.157, 4.70, and 17.592) (*CWE* 36:105–6).

46 One of Erasmus's adages misconstrues Agamemnon's use of the epithet "watermelon" to describe Menelaus ("*ô pepon, ô Menelae*"), interpreting it as a compliment rather than (in its usual sense) as a "proverbial insult applied to weak, effeminate men" who are "soft and inedible." See Adage IV.i.81, *CWE* 35:490–91 [ASD II.7: 87], citing *Il.* 6.55.

47 Rummel, "Argumentis non Contumeliis"; Clement, *Exhortation to the Greeks*, 211.

48 Erasmus's practice of adapting Homeric phrases to contemporary contexts is also inspired by Cicero, who makes frequent and biting use of lines from Homer in his adversarial writings. The adage *Qui prior laesit* [The first to wound] is a Homeric phrase (*Il.* 24.369) "usurped" [*usurpat*] by Cicero (*Ad Atticus* 2.ix.3) to serve philosophical rather than military altercations (see Adage V.i.39, *CWE* 36:564 [ASD II.8:286]). Glossing the adage *Hinc illae lachrymae* [Hence those tears], Erasmus once again mentions how Cicero uses the Homeric phrase "I fear the Trojans" to sardonic effect (Adage I.iii.68, *CWE* 31:293, citing Cicero, *Ad Atticus* 2.v.1).

49 These criticisms are echoed by Mosellanus, *De Ratione Disputandi* (Augsburg, 1519), a work that holds up Erasmus as a "model polemicist" and criticizes antagonists who "tur[n] their pens into weapons" or try to overwhelm their opponents with "contentious clamour" [*rixoso clamore*]. On Mosellanus's work, see Rummel, "Argumentis, Non Contumeliis," 306–8.

50 In his *Novum Instrumentum*, Erasmus translates this verse as "amarulentia, & tumor, & ira, & vociferatio" (LB VI:850B).

51 On the clamour of Homer's Trojans and the silence of his Achaeans, see Mackie, *Talking Trojan*, 15–17.

52 Erasmus's *Lingua* criticizes those "barbarians according to Homer" who "rush into the fight with a great shouting" [*apud Homerum Barbari magno clamore ruunt ad praelia*] (*CWE* 29:305 [ASD IV.1:278]).

53 Erasmus's frequent use of the image of Stentor no doubt influenced the author of the satire *Theologists in Council* (ca 1521), which features a character named Stentor, presumably based on Jacob Hoogstraten, Reuchlin's principal enemy and a man known for his "sermons and loud declamations." On Hoogstraten's text, see *Scheming Papists and Lutheran Fools*, ed. Rummel, 64.

54 Poliziano, note to *Il.* 4.1–4, cited by Rubenstein, "The Notes to Poliziano's *Iliad*," 213. Poliziano closely follows pseudo-Plutarch's *Life of Homer*, chap. 72, 136–7, which devotes considerable attention to the "various kinds of styles," or *plasmata*, employed by Homer's speakers, including "the grand style, the plain style, and the intermediate style" [*to mên adron, to de ischnon, to de meson legetai*]. The pseudo-Plutarchan *Life* was printed in Nerlio's 1488 *editio princeps* of Homer's *Iliad* and *Odyssey* as well as in 1504 and 1517 Aldine editions of Homer.

55 [Plutarch], *Life of Homer*, 252–3, 262–5.

56 [Plutarch], *Life of Homer*, 256–7.

57 Poliziano, *Ambra*, ls. 311–12, in *Silvae*, 88. Budé was also extremely familiar with the pseudo-Plutarchan *Life*: the work was printed in his copy of Homer and heavily annotated by him. Grafton "How Guillaume Budé Read his Homer," 162–3, notes Budé's interest in the work.

58 Christ, too, is *omnia omnibus*. In his *Ratio*, Erasmus describes Christ as playing "the role of a kind of Proteus in the variety of his life and doctrine," a figure who "conducted himself differently toward different persons, so much so in fact that on occasion his words appear at first sight to be contradictory" (*Ratio*, H 214:31–3, 211:28). Later in the *Ratio*, Erasmus defends such polymorphousness on the grounds that the "variety of Christ renders a fuller harmony. He indeed became all to all, but in such a way that in nothing was he dissimilar to himself" (*Ratio* 286:6–11).

59 See Gal. 4:20: "I wish I were present with you now and could change my tone [*allaxai tên phônên mou*]."
60 Acts 14.12; Col. 4.6.
61 In his *Annotations* (ASD VI.6:214), Erasmus uses the phrases "libertatem" and "in dicendo audaciam" to describe Peter's bold speech. In his translation of the *New Testament*, Erasmus uses "lenitas" for softness in one edition and "levitas" (smoothness, fluency) in another (*CWE* 50:189n26).
62 Budé, *De Transitu*, ed. Garanderie, 160: "ab Homerica philosophia mutuari quippiam nostra non gravabitur orthodoxia." Erasmus presents Paul as a figure willing "change myself into everything" [*In omnia me mutarem*] in order to "better accommodate my speech to the varieties of your moods and to the present matter" [*orationem melius ad varietates animorum & ad rem praesentem accommodarem*] (*CWE* 42:118 [LB VII:959B]).
63 Erasmus, *Paraphrase on Acts* 18.18 (*CWE* 50:114 [LB VII:740C]). For similar arguments, compare his Argument to the *Paraphrases on Romans* (*CWE* 42:8) and his paraphrase on Rom. 12.16 (*CWE* 42:72).
64 Paraphrasing Acts 23.5–8, where Paul pits the Sadducees and the Pharisees against each other, Erasmus observes that "it is permissible to avoid danger by cunning when no advantage appears to be forthcoming" (*CWE* 50:133).
65 On the influence of Plato and Pythagoras on Erasmus's attitude towards friendship, see Eden, *Friends Hold All Things in Common*, 4–5, 25–33; Charlier, *Érasme et l'Amitié*, 31–42; E. Bury, "L'Amitié savante," 729–47. On *homonoia*, which Aristotle (*Nic. Ethics* IX.6.2) defines as "civic concord" [*politichê philia*], see Hutton, *Themes of Peace*, 26–7.
66 On Erasmus's attitudes towards war, contention, and polemic, see Adams, *The Better Part of Valor*, 26–111, and *Guerre et Paix*, ed. Margolin, editor's introduction, 9–11. On Erasmus's use of adages in his controversial writings, see Asia Rowe, "The Erasmian Adage in the Controversy with Luther," *ERSY* 30 (2010): 41–55, and Ari Wesseling, "Intertextual Play: Erasmus' use of Adages in *The Colloquies*," *ERSY* 28 (2008): 1–27.
67 For Erasmus's Latin translation of the passage, see Adage I.vii.13 (ASD II.1:136–7).
68 Hutten, *Expostulation*, and Erasmus, *Spongia*, both in *The Polemics of Erasmus*, 109, 149.
69 Compare Budé, *De Philologia*, 72–4, which blames the *obloquentia* of his intellectual adversaries on the "golden apple of discord" [*malum auream discordiae*] tossed into the scholarly community, an event brought about by the "faction of word-haters" [*misologica factio*] opposed to the humanists.
70 On Jean Briart Atensis and Erasmus's identification of him with Homer's Atê, see Margaret Mann Phillips's introduction to the *Antibarbarorum Liber* (*CWE*

23:12–14). Erasmus also refers to Atê in a July 1519 letter to Edward Lee (Ep. 998, in Allen 4:9–10), and in the colloquy *Ichthyophagia*, where the butcher alludes to the "pestilential Strife" [*pestilens Ate*] who has brought about "a calamitous war between the two most powerful kings in the world," Charles V and Francis I (*CWE* 40:687). In the anonymous 1519 pamphlet entitled *A Dialogue between the Two Tongued and the Trilinguals* [*Dialogus saneque festivus Bilinguium ac Trilinguium*], Jean Briart is likewise identified with Atê; this pamphlet has occasionally been attributed to Erasmus but was more likely written by someone familiar with Erasmus's identification of Briart as Atê in writings dated prior to 1519. On this work, see Nesen, *Les Funerailles de la Muse*, and *La Conférence Macaronique*, ed. Saladin, 5–7, 33–5.

71 In a letter to Martinus Gertophius, written 13 August 1520 (*Letters* 1:95), Wolfgang Capito uses the same Homeric allusion to describe how Erasmus's adversary Edward Lee "has very much disturbed the peace of scholarship. Eris, when she was passed over, threw a golden apple among the assembled gods and caused a quarrel. Edward Lee was able to destroy the tranquility of scholars with his shitty little book."

72 Compare Montaigne's discussion of the "inane causes" of the Trojan War in his *Apology for Raymond Sebond* (*Complete Essays*, 348). Citing Horace ("All because Paris loved another's wife, / Greeks and barbarians clashed in baneful strife"), Montaigne writes, "All Asia was ruined and consumed in wars for Paris' lechery. The envy of one single man, a spite, a pleasure, a domestic jealousy, causes which should not move two fishwives to scratch one another – that is the soul and motive of this great turmoil."

73 Plato, *Symposium* 178e. *Philotiméomai* means to love or seek after honour, to strive eagerly, or to be ambitious, emulous, or jealous; the term has both positive and negative connotations in classical Greek.

74 Ep. 704, Erasmus to Duke Ernest of Bavaria [(Louvain) 4 Nov. 1517], *CWE* 5:185 [Allen 3:130]; on Erasmus's condemnation of Achilles and Alexander the Great and on his general dislike of ancient epic and chivalric romance, see Adams, *The Better Part of Valor*, 170, 223–30.

75 In *Scarabeus aquilam quaerit* (Adage III.vii.1), Erasmus similarly criticizes the *thumos* – the spirited or irascible aspect of man – that is praised by both Plato and Homer. On Erasmus's negative attitude towards the pagan valorization of *gloria* and war, see Tracy, *The Politics of Erasmus*, 35–9.

76 See Adage I.iii.1: *Aut Regem Aut fatuum oportere* (*CWE* 31:227–8 [ASD II.1:304]). Erasmus may be echoing Tertullian: "what ridiculous things I find [in pagan literature] that for Trojans and Greeks the gods fought amongst themselves like pairs of gladiators" (*Apologeticus Adversus Gentes*, 29).

77 Budé, *De Philologia*, ed. Lebel, 68.

78 Heraclitus, *Homeric Problems*, 29.6–7, 55.
79 Compare Erasmus's *Letter to Dorp*: "the reciprocal exchange of injuries is not seldom the source of some dangerous conflagration" (Ep. 337, in *CWE* 3:114).
80 Erasmus, *Annotations on 1 Tim. 6.4* (LB VII:1054B). On Erasmus's understanding of *mataiologia*, see Rummel, *The Humanist-Scholastic Debate*, 28, discussing Erasmus's Annotations on 2 Tim. 1.6. Paraphrasing 1 Tim. 6.4, Erasmus writes that "quarrelsome debates" [*verbis digladians*] escalate when, in the "growing heat of the quarrel no one wants to yield to another" [*dum gliscente rixarum calore, nullus alii vult concedere*], finally giving rise to "abusive language when the affair ends in a mad rage" [*convitia, quoties res exit in rabiem*] (*CWE* 44:35 [LB VII 1054B]). Frivolous squabbling is also a major preoccupation of the *Adages* and of Erasmus's controversial writings; see, for example, *A Lasso rixa quaeritur* [Weariness loves a wrangle] and *Parni scaphula* [Parnus' skiff], which concerns how "for some affair of no moment [men] raise endless quarrels and complaints" (Adage I.vi.46, *CWE* 32:34–5 and Adage II.v.17, *CWE* 33:249).
81 Titus 1.10; compare 1 Tim. 6.4; Titus 3.9; Erasmus, *Annotations on 1 Timothy* 6.4 (LB VI:943F–944C) and his *Paraphrase* on Titus 3.9 (LB VII:1074B), which translates Paul's condemnation of foolish controversies and quarrels as "stultas & indoctas quaestiones" and "contentiosas dissertationes."
82 Race, *Pindar*, 23.
83 *Agôn* means an assembly or gathering; by extension, it may describe a struggle, trial, or danger, martial, athletic, legal, or otherwise. *Neikos* means wrangle, quarrel, or strife; it can denote a battle, a dispute before a judge, or verbal railing or abuse. *Machê* means battle, fight, strife, wrangling, or contest; it may denote legal and verbal disputes as well as physical combat. On the relationship between *philia* and *Eris* and on Homeric attitudes towards strife, see Nagy, *Best of the Achaeans*, 130–42; Clay, *The Wrath of Athena*, 176–84; Loraux, *The Divided City*, 90–2, 111–14; Vernant, "Weaving Friendship," 75–87.
84 On ritualized contest as a safety valve that stifles more serious hostilities, see Beck, *Homeric Conversation*, 232. On Erasmus's distaste for ancient Greek athleticism, see his 1526 translation of Galen, *Exhortatio ad Bonas Artes, praesertim medicinae*, a "tirade against professional athletes" that cites various ancient authorities on the deleterious effects of strenuous physical exercise (*CWE* 29:221, 235 [ASD I.1:652]).
85 See, for example, 2 Tim. 2.5: "if anyone competes as an athlete [*athlêtis*], he is not crowned unless he competes according to the rules [*nomimôs athlêsê*]."
86 Waswo, *Language and Meaning*, 218.
87 Some key verses include 1 Cor. 9:24–5, in which Paul compares Christian believers to runners in a race but then distinguishes the two kinds of striving:

the runner competes "to obtain a corruptible crown [*phtharton stephanon*]; but we an incorruptible [*aphtharton*]." Compare 2 Tim. 2.5; 2 Tim. 4.7–8; and Hebr. 12.1–2. On athletic metaphors, see also Erasmus's paraphrase of Acts 7.55 and 20.24 (*CWE* 50:55, 123). On Paul's use of the term *agôn* and his transformation of the ancient Greek spirit of competition and self-assertion, see Pfitzner, *Paul and the Agon Motif*, 3–7, 76–90, and Zerbe, "Paul's Ethic of Nonretaliation," 178–9.

88 Erasmus appears to have been particularly influenced by Plutarch's critique of the Homeric ethos of rivalry and competition in the *Table-Talk*, where Homer is chided for representing banquets in which the participants are unable to put aside their enmity and achieve "fellowship and communion." See *Table-Talk* 643F, in Plutarch, *Moralia* 8:189.

89 On Erasmus's polemic with Lefèvre, see Charlier, *Érasme et l'Amitié*, 233–43.

90 On verbal abuse and railing in Homeric epic, see Nagy, *The Best of the Achaeans*, 245–63; Adkins, "Threatening, Abusing, and Feeling Angry," 7–21.

91 *Hê tou Homêrou poiêsis hapasa*, annotated by Budé, vol. 1, 167a, annotating *Il.* 20.245–50; Erasmus, Ep. 990, *CWE* 6:406. Erasmus's complaint may also be indebted to Plato's proscription against disputation or verbal abuse [*amphisbêtôn*] at *Laws* 934e–935a, which states that it is "unseemly [*ou prepon*] ... in a well-regulated state" to see men "cursing one another and foully abusing each other in the manner of fish-wives."

92 Adage I.i.41: *Sus cum Minerva certamen suscepit*, *CWE* 31:91 [ASD II.1:156].

93 Plato, *Theaetetus* 167e; *Protagoras* 337a–b; Plato also distinguishes between dialectic and wrangling [*erizein*] at *Rep.* 5.4 [454a] and 6.12 [498c–d].

94 Gagarin, "The Ambiguity of Eris," 174, 180, points out that for Hesiod, the "good" Eris is "not unequivocally good," since the use of the verb *zêloô* "raises a suspicion that this spirit of rivalry may have other, less desirable consequences" such that Hesiod aimed "not to resolve but [rather] to affirm" the tension between the two Erides.

95 Compare Erasmus, *Paraphrases on Acts* 2.44, which describes how the "love of Christ implanted in their [the apostles'] hearts joined together such disparate people with so much oneness of heart" (*CWE* 50:25 [LB VII:674E]).

96 Adage I.ii.22 (*CWE* 31: 168 [ASD II.1: 240]), derived from *Od.* 17.218 and cited by Plato, *Lysis* 214a, and by Aristotle, *Nic. Ethics* VIII.1.2 [1155a34].

97 Compare adage I.ix.95, *Aequalitas haud parit bellum*, which "extol[s] equality, which is according to Pythagoras both parent and nurse of friendship, while inequality is the mother of discord and war" [*cum aequalitatem anteferemus, quam Pythagoras dixit amicitiae tum parentem tum altricem, contra inaequalitatem discordiarum bellorumque matrem*] (*CWE* 32:230 [ASD II.2:406]).

98 Compare Adages I.viii.71 and I.viii.72, *Vespa cicadae obstrepens* [Wasp buzzing against cricket] and *Pica cum luscinia certat, epopa cum cygnis* [Jay strives with nightingale, hoopoe with swan], which both argue that strife in the animal world is the result of dissimilarity.

99 On Adages I.ii.21 through I.ii.25, see *CWE* 31:167–70; Plato, *Lysis* 214a, 215d. On Erasmus's attitude towards the principle of *similia similibus* (like to like) and his contrary belief in "the basic dualism of things," see Hoffmann, *Rhetoric and Theology*, 107–14. Compare Adages II.iv.83 (*Prius duo echini amicitiam ineant* [Sooner would two urchins make friends]), II.ii.3 (*Lusciniae nugis insidentes* [Nightingales Perching on Trifles]), and IV.vi.4 (*Musarum aves* [Birds of the Muses]), each illustrating how some animals cannot maintain harmonious relations even within their own species.

100 On the concept of *máchimos*, which derives from the Greek *máchê*, or battle, see Plutarch, *Moralia* 8:43. Compare adage I.ii.25, *Inimicus et invidus vicinorum oculus*, added in 1533, where Erasmus once again fails to acknowledge any virtue in "honest emulation" [*honestam ... aemulationem*], as the cautionary title of the adage suggests: "Unfriendly and envious is the neighbour's eye."

101 Adage III.viii.31: *Aequa concertatio*, *CWE* 35:293 [ASD II.6:494]; on these Homeric phrases for equal contest, see *The Iliad: A Commentary*, ed. Kirk, 4:93.

102 For additional adages addressing the problem of equally matched contestants, see *Cadmea victoria* [Cadmean Victory], *Testa collisa testae* [One pot smashed against another], and *Victoria non incruenta* [Not a bloodless victory], the last of which is derived from a line plucked out of a particularly bloody battle scene in the *Iliad*; Adages II.viii.34 [*CWE* 33:61–2]; III.vii.29 [*CWE* 35:233], and III.ix.2, [*CWE* 35:319], the last derived from *Il.* 17.363.

103 Compare Erasmus, *Parabolae* (*CWE* 23:155), citing Plutarch, *Moralia* 486c–d: "Those who set out on different roads cannot give each other any help; but those who follow different ways of life escape rivalry and are more prone to help each other."

104 Erasmus does cite Odysseus's challenge (*Od.* 8.205–6) in *Omni certaminis genere* [In any sort of contention]; see Adage III.x.13, *CWE* 35:362.

105 See, for example, Erasmus's annotations on Rom. 14.2 (*CWE* 56:367 [LB VI:639C]).

106 See Erasmus, *Spongia*, 245. Erasmus often translates the Greek *zêlos* as *aemulus*: striving, rivalrous, or emulous, usually in a negative sense. On Erasmus's understanding of the term *zêlos*, see Adage III.iii.6 (*CWE* 34:283–4; ASD II.4:193–4): *Azêlos ploutos*, in which he explains that *azêlos*

signifies "unenvied" or "admired by no one." Erasmus's scholarship on The New Testament reveals both positive and negative uses of the term: positive at 2 Cor. 11.2, the "godly jealousy" [*theou zêlô*] of Paul for his audience, and negative at Acts 5.17, where the Sadducees are "filled with jealousy" [*eplêsthêsan zêlou*] against the Apostles, and at Acts 13.45, where the Jews are filled with "*zêlou*" when contradicting Paul.

107 Compare Erasmus's comments on Gal. 4.17 and 4.18 (*CWE* 42:65, 118, 155n4).

108 On the "confused continuum" of the concept of *zêlos* in Hesiod, see Gagarin, "The Ambiguity of Eris," 175, 180; compare Pucci, *Hesiod and the Language of Poetry*, 132. See Erasmus's annotations on Rom. 10.2, where he proposes translating Paul's "hoti zêlon theoû" [that *zêlos* for God] as "quod studium" [that strong devotion] rather than the Vulgate's "quod aemulationem" [that emulation], since while *aemulatione* can mean imitation or jealous rivalry, neither the positive nor the negative sense are adequate for the verse, whereas *studium* conveys a virtue that may, if excessive, become a vice (*CWE* 56:276–7).

109 Erasmus translates 1 Cor. 14.1 as "Sectamini charitatem, aemulamini spiritualia" and 1 Cor. 13.4 as "charitas non invidet" (LB VI:728A, VI:726A); in the *Paraphrases*, Erasmus instead has "charitas non aemulatur" (LB VII:901B). Compare his *Annotations* on 1 Cor. 12.31 ("Aemulamini autem charismata") (ASD VI.8:266, VI.8:248).

110 While the Vulgate translates *paroxusmos* [disagreement] as *dissensio*, a Latin term rarely used in a positive sense, Erasmus's 1516 New Testament translates the Greek as "acris …disceptatio," a phrase that underscores the harsh tone used by the Apostles but at the same time downplays any harm (such as schism) resulting from their disagreement (ASD VI.2:370; see also *CWE* 50:272n73).

111 On the relationship between concord and consensus in Erasmus's thought, see McConica, "Erasmus and the Grammar of Consent," 77–99.

112 Ep. 1011, Budé to Erasmus, *CWE* 7:68 [Allen 4:62]. For examples of Erasmus's attitude towards scholarly competition, see *Sphaeram inter sese reddere* [To throw the ball from one to another], Adage III.i.99 (*CWE* 34:222–3 [ASD II.5:100]), an adage based closely on Plutarch, *Moralia* 80b (1:426–7), cited by Erasmus in his *Parabolae* (*CWE* 23:179).

113 On the "intellectual communalism" of Erasmus's *Adages*, see Eden, *Friends Hold All Things in Common*, 162; 25–33. On Erasmus's theory of friendship and its ancient sources, also see Seth Lobis, "Erasmus and the Natural History of Friendship," *ERSY* 30 (2010), 23–39. Erasmus appears aware of an alternative tradition in which the exchange of weapons between Diomedes and Glaucus reveals the generosity of the latter, a reading that

hinges upon the interpretation of the word "*exeleto*" at *Il.* 6.234 as raised (or exalted) rather than removed. On this passage, see William M. Calder, "Gold for Bronze: *Iliad* 6.232–36," in *Studies Presented to Sterling Dow on His Eightieth Birthday* (Durham, NC: Duke University Press, 1984), 31–5.

114 Alciati, *In Dona Hostium* [The Gifts of Enemies], in *Emblemata*, 181, relates the exchange of weapons between Hector and Ajax at *Il.* 7.300–5. On gift-exchanges in Erasmus's intellectual community, see Charlier, *Érasme et l'Amitié*, 525, 61–3. Erasmus's reading of Diomedes's and Glaucus's exchange of weapons is diametrically opposed to that of Maximus of Tyre, who argues that "both sides of the bargain are equally satisfactory to both parties, since the equality of goodwill in the giving cancels out the disparity of the materials" (Oration 40, in *Philosophical Orations*, 314).

115 Adage IV.i.37: *Alybantis hospitis munera* (*CWE* 35:463 [ASD II.7:64]), paraphrasing *Od.* 24.304–6 and Eustathius, *Comm. ad Hom. Odysseam* 1961.60; compare Adage I.iv.5: *Cyclopis donum* (*CWE* 31:323 [ASD II.1:412–13]), in which "the gift of the Cyclops" – his promise to eat Odysseus last – is proverbial for "any useless gift" [*munus inutile*]. Similar morals are extracted from Homeric sources by the adages *Verbo tenus amicus* [A friend in words alone], derived from *Od.* 18.282–3, and by *Nihil recusandum, quod donatur* [Never refuse a gift], which comes from a line spoken by the greedy suitor Antinous at *Od.* 18.287 (*Adages* III.x.53 and III.x.54, *CWE* 35:375–6).

116 In his *Annotations* on the New Testament, Erasmus invokes the adage in order to draw attention to an even more unequal exchange: when the Roman soldiers at John 19.34 decide not to break the legs of the crucified Christ because he is already dead, Erasmus likens the scene to "Diomedis et Glauci permutatione" (ASD VI.6:162).

117 Compare Poliziano, Letter to Pico della Mirandola (I.vi, ln. 2), in Poliziano, *Letters* 1:24–5; compare II.x, Poliziano to Girolamo Donà, in *Letters* 1:117.

118 Ep. 531 (*CWE* 4:228 [Allen 2:463]); Clement, *Exhortation to the Greeks*, 245, citing *Il.* 6.236.

119 "In quibus neque labor neque senium neque morbus est vllus, nec usquam in agris asphodelus, malua, squilla, lupinumue, aut faba, aut aliud hoc genus nugarum conspicitur. Sed passim oculis simulque naribus adblandiuntur moly, panace, nepenthes, amaracus, ambrosia, lotus, rosa, viola, Hiacynthus, Adonidis hortuli" (*CWE* 27:89 [ASD IV.3:78]). Hesiod mentions the "great advantage" of "asphodel and mallow" at *WD*, ls. 41–2.

120 *CWE* 27:94 [ASD IV.3:88]. The phrase *rheia zôontes* appears at *Od.* 4.805 and at 5.122; Folly's epithet instead means "taking away [or carrying away] ease."

121 *CWE* 27:89, 76 [ASD IV.3:76, 88, and 89n]; for Homer's use of phrases resembling *en philotêti michtheis*, see *Il.* 3.445, 6.25, 14.295; *Od.* 8.271.

122 *CWE* 27:142 [ASD IV.3:178], echoing Horace, Epistle I.2, ln. 5, "*stultorum et regum populorum*" (*Epistles*, 13).
123 On Homer's use of the word *nêpios*, see J. Heath, *The Talking Greeks*, 95; Edmonds, *Homeric Nêpios*, 60–97.
124 Gordon, *Humanist Play and Belief*, 189.
125 *Il.* 11.336, 16.662, 14.389, 17.389–99; on imagery of cords and tugging see *The Iliad: A Commentary*, ed. Kirk, 3:263.
126 See *Il.* 13.358–9, where Homer describes how Zeus and Poseidon "knotted [*epallaxantes*] the ends of the cords of mighty Strife and equal war [*eridos kraterês kai homoiou ptolemoio*], and drew them taut [*tanussan*] over both armies" or the tug or war played between Ajax and Odysseus during the funeral games, in which the two men "strive for victory" [*phoinikoessai*] through the "violent tugging of bold hands" [*thraseiaôn apo cheirôn*] (*Il.* 23.717, 23.714).
127 The phrase "homoiiou ptolemoio" is used at *Il.* 13.358 and elsewhere; on the meaning of the phrase, see *The Iliad: A Commentary*, ed. Kirk, 4:93.
128 Compare Adage III.6.84: *Utroque nutans sententia* [Wavering both ways in his opinion], developed from *Il.* 13.281 into the original phrase, "dischôloi gnômai," a mind turning this way and that, and thus, a phrase "applicable to a man of slippery faith and uncertain allegiances" (*CWE* 35:167).
129 On the phrase "xunos enualios" as a maxim during antiquity, see *The Iliad: A Commentary*, ed. Kirk, 5:182, which cites Aristotle, *Rhetoric* II.21.11 and Archilochus, Fragment 10 as examples.
130 Heraclitus, *Homeric Problems*, 31.5, 57, proposes that Ares is called "alloprosallon" because "wars bring retribution as they swing back and forth" [*nemesêtai gar ai polemôn ep'amphotera rhopai*] and because "the fortune of battle passes now to one side and now to the other" [*machais amphibolias allote pros allous metaphoitôsês*].
131 [Plutarch], *Life of Homer*, 310–11.
132 For other verses concerned with the impartiality of God in the New Testament, compare Rom. 2.11 and Col. 3.25.
133 Erasmus, *Pangyricus*: "et notum est illud de Andromacha Homericum *dachruoen gelasasa*, id est lachrymabile ridens, ita lachrymas suas habet & gaudium" (ASD IV.1:90). In addition to *Il.* 6.484, Erasmus also mentions *Od.* 16.215 and 19.471 as examples of the mixing of joy (or laughter) and sorrow. The AB-T scholiast praises Homer's depiction of Andromache at *Il.* 6.484 as "powerfully expressed and impossible to analyze" [*dunatôs rhêthen anermêneuton*] because of its conflicting emotions; on this gloss, see Richardson, "Literary Criticism in the Exegetical Scholia," 275.
134 Compare Erasmus, *Carmen* 23, an early poem (ca 1489) that "entertains the opposing notions of joy and sadness. Happiness can turn into bitterness;

pleasure never comes unmixed." *Carmen* 23, ls. 37–40 and 87–8, cited by Gordon, *Humanist Play and Belief*, 43.

135 Scaliger, *Poetices* (1561), 227.

136 [Plutarch], *Life of Homer*, 304–5. His ancient scholiasts argue that Homer is skilled at providing relief to tense or suspenseful moments. On this point, see Richardson, "Literary Criticism," and Nünlist, *The Ancient Critic at Work*, 150–1.

2. The Remedy of Contraries: Melanchthon, Rabelais, and Epic Parody

1 Nietzsche, "Homer and Classical Philology," 154–5.

2 Nietzsche, "Homer and Classical Philology," 155. Such debates persist among Homeric scholars. On the question of whether it is better to privilege one Homeric text (or variant of a text) over another, see M. L. West, *Studies in the Text and Transmission of the Iliad*, 159.

3 Wolf, *Prolegomena to Homer*, 156–7.

4 Dio Chrysostom, Discourse 53, in *Discourses*, 360–1. On Stoic interpretations of Homer, see A.A. Long, "Stoic Readings of Homer," in *Oxford Readings in ancient literary criticism*, ed. Laird, 212–33.

5 Timon (ca 320–230 BCE) wrote a Homer-parody in mock-heroic style that includes a descent to the underworld modelled on *Od.* 11 in which the author, guided by Xenophanes, interrogates the shades of philosophers belonging to different schools. On Timon, see A.A. Long, "Post-Aristotelian Philosophy," in *The Cambridge History of Classical Literature*, ed. P.E. Easterling and B.M.W. Knox, 1, part 3, 144. Written in mock-Homeric hexameters, *silloi* were often written as attacks against various philosophical schools: on the genre, see Jaeger, *The Theology of the Early Greek Philosophers*, 39–41 and Rose, *Parody*, 17.

6 On Conradi and on the teaching of Greek in early sixteenth-century Wittenberg, see Grossmann, *Humanism in Wittenberg*, 47–8, 96–7. On Greek learning in early sixteenth-century Germany, see also Spitz, *Religious Renaissance*, 131–3, 164–6, 243–9.

7 [Homer], *Batrachomyomachia*, ln. 32, in *Homeric Hymns, Homeric Apocrypha, Lives of Homer*, ed. M.L. West, 266–7.

8 On Camerarius's Homeric commentaries, see below. The edition of Homer produced by Camerarius and Micyllus was published as *Opus Utrumque Homeri Iliados et Odysseae* (Basel: Hervagius, 1541); the text of the poems is a reprint of the 1535 Hervagius edition.

9 Crusius, *In Batrachomyomachiam Homeri, Martini Crusii Praefatio*, pp. 42–64 of Langius, *Ad Poesin Barbaro-Graecam*, 54. On page 60, Crusius's preface is identified as having been delivered at Tübingen, "in

aula vetere" [in the old court], on 3 April 1581. On page 23, Langius dates Demetrius Zeno's translation of the poem into *koinê* Greek to 1529; Zeno's translation is accompanied by Crusius's preface and a Latin translation of the poem also attributed to him.

10 Crusius, *In Batrachomyomachiam Homeri*, 55–6. In the first of these passages, Crusius cites *Il.* 22.262 in Latin: "Non bene conveniunt homines pacto, atque leones."

11 Crusius, *In Batrachomyomachiam Homeri*, 59.

12 Crusius, *In Batrachomyomachiam Homeri*, 60.

13 Crusius, *Commentationes in I Lib. Iliad. Homeri* (n.p.: Gotthardi Voegelini, [1612]), Prolegomena, sig. **2v: "Ex Homero, Epigrammatum, Comoediarum, Tragoediarum, & Satyrarum origo est."

14 On these and other works of Reformation satire, see Rummel's introduction to her *Scheming Papists*.

15 On the influence of Lucianic dialogue on Reformation satire, see Rummel, *Scheming Papists*, 25; Dandrey, *L'Eloge Paradoxale*; Marsh, *Lucian and the Latins*. On early sixteenth-century humanist attitudes towards sophistry, see Rummel, *The Humanist-Scholastic Debate*, 19–25, and her "'Et cum Theologo bella poeta gerit'," 713–26.

16 Erasmus, Adage III.viii.23 (*CWE* 35:291 [ASD II.6:491]).

17 *In Homeri Batrachomyomachiam scholia Philippi Melanchthonis*, in *HOMÊROU BATRACHOMYOMACHIA= Homeri Ranarum & Murium Pugna*, preface, sig. A2r.

18 Melanchthon, "On the Usefulness of Fables," English text quoted from *Orations on Philosophy and Education*, 56; Latin from *Opera Omnia* 11:118–19.

19 *Aesopi Phrygis Fabellae Graece et Latine* (Basel: Froben, 1518), includes the *Batrachomyomachia* and several other mock-epic poems; see also the editions produced at Basel (1530 and 1541), Venice (1542), Paris (1549), Lyon (1551 and 1570), and Wittenberg (1564).

20 Rhein, "Melanchthon and Greek Literature," 150. On Melanchthon's scholarship on Homer, see also Bleicher, *Homer in der Deutschen Literatur*, 72–86; on the activities of Homeric scholars in Melanchthon's Wittenberg circle, see P. Ford, *De Troie à Ithaque*, 20–2, 34–5. On Melanchthon's lectures on Homer, which he gave regularly from 1518 until 1543, see Hartfelder, *Philipp Melanchthon*, 283–95.

21 Melchior Lotther published an edition of the first four books of *Od.* (*Odyssea Homeri*, Wittenberg, 1520); Lonitzer published a two-volume Greek edition of *Il.*, *Od.*, *Batrachomyomachia*, and *Hymns* (*Homêrou Ilias* and *Odysseia*, Strasbourg: Wolf Köpfel, 1525); Opsopoeus's translations of

Il. 1, 2, and 9 were first printed as *Homericae Iliados Libri duo* (Nuremberg: Friedrich Peypus, 1527; books 2 and 9 only) and were reprinted (along with the translations of Nicolao Valla) in *Homeri Iliados libri aliquot* (Hagenau: Johann Setzer, 1531); Camerarius produced commentaries on *Il.* 1 and 2, the *Commentarius Explicationis primi libri Iliados Homeri* (Strasbourg: Kraft Mueller, 1538) and the *Commentarii Explicationum Secundi Libri Homericae Iliados* (Strasbourg: Kraft Mueller, 1540); Hessus produced a Latin translation of the *Iliad* (*Poetarum Omnium Seculorum Longe Principis Homeri Ilias*, Basel: Robert Winter, 1540); Capito collaborated on a 1542 Strasbourg edition of the *Iliad* dedicated to Melanchthon; Simon Lemnius published a Latin verse translation of *Od.*, *Odysseae Homeri libri XXIII* (Basel: Oporinus, 1549). On Luther's Greek studies at Wittenberg, see Spitz, *Religious Renaissance*, 243–9.

22 Achilles Gasser's annotated edition of Camerarius's *Commentarius Explicationis primi libri Iliados Homeri* (1538), dated May 1538, is preserved at Vat. Stamp. Pal IV.801 and bound with Camerarius's *Commentarii Explicationum Secundi libri Homericae Iliados* (1540), also signed by Gasser and dated 1540. On Gasser's notes to Melanchthon's 1521 lectures on the *Canones Apostolici*, see Rhein, "Melanchthon and Greek Literature," 152. On Silberborner, whose translation of *Il.* 2.182–206 was printed on fol. 8r of a collection of poems and translations from the Greek by Melanchthon and his students that was published in 1528, see Rhein, 155–6.

23 Melanchthon, "On Correcting the Studies of Youth," in *A Melanchthon Reader*, 48.

24 Titus, 3.9, 1.15. At the end of his 1518 oration *De corrigendis adolescentiae studiis*, Melanchthon writes, "we have Homer in our hands, and we have Paul's Epistle to Titus" [*Homerum habemus in manibus, habemus et Pauli epistolam ad Titum*] (*Melanchthons Werke*, 3:41). On Melanchthon's 1518 lectures, see *Melanchthon on Christian Doctrine*, xxv, and Schofield, *Philip Melanchthon and the English Reformation*, 10.

25 Melanchthon, *Preface to Homer*, in *Orations*, 40, 43 [Latin: *Opera Omnia* 11:400, 403].

26 Vat. Stamp. Pal. IV.801, Manuscript transcription of excerpts from the *Iliad* by Achilles Pirminius Gasser, dated 1523, fol. 20v; Erasmus, *Homo bulla*, Adage II.iii.48 (*CWE* 33:157).

27 Vat. Stamp. Pal. IV.801, fol. 21r. Additional marginal cross-references to Erasmus's *Adages* can be found on fols. 21v–22r.

28 Vat Stamp. Pal. IV.801, Achilles Gasser's copy of *HOMÊROU ODYSSEIAS BIBLOI A to E, Angeli Politiani in Homerum Praefatio* (Basel, 1520), fols. C2v, C3r. In the margins of two consecutive pages of the *Oratio*, Gasser jots

down the terms "apophthegmata" and "gnomę"; later, in the margins of his text of *Od.*, he marks several lines containing pithy snippets of proverbial wisdom.

29 See Melanchthon, *Loci Communes*, 47, 94; compare 53, where Melanchthon praises Achilles because he "checked himself, sheathed the sword." Melanchthon, *Preface to Homer*, in *Orations*, 51 [Latin: *Opera Omnia* 11:410] praises Homer for making his heroes intermittently vulnerable to their passions rather than cultivating a "stupid and imaginary Stoic *apatheia*" [*stultam … et imaginariam Stoicorum apatheian*]. Cambridge University Library Adv. d.13.4: *Homerou Ilias* (Aldus, 1504), annotated by Philipp Melanchthon, 403. Next to Achilles's complaint about the futility of strife at the beginning of book 18, Melanchthon writes "IRA" [anger] in capital letters. For further discussion of Melanchthon's annotations on the *Iliad*, see P. Ford, *De Troie à Ithaque*, 63–4.

30 Melanchthon, *Preface to Homer*, in *Orations*, 38 [Latin: *Opera Omnia* 11:398].

31 Cambridge UL Adv. D.13.4, Melanchthon's annotated copy of *Il.*, 469 (annotating *Il.* 21.464–6); 444–5 (annotating *Il.* 20.246–7, 254–5).

32 Melanchthon, *Preface to Homer*, in *Orations*, 44 [*Opera Omnia* 11:404].

33 Melanchthon, *Preface to Homer*, in *Orations*, 45–6 [*Opera Omnia* 11:405–6]. On Melanchthon's "bias" for *Od.*, see Pontani, "Homeric Readings," 387n40.

34 Melanchthon, *In Praise of Eloquence*, in *Orations on Philosophy and Education*, 68; Latin text quoted from *Encomium Eloquentiae* (1523), in *Melanchthons Werke* 3:52. P. Ford, *De Troie à Ithaque*, 64, points out that Melanchthon interprets the shield as embodying an "irenic attitude" [*attitude irénique*], by contrast to Heraclitus the Homeric allegorist, who regards the shield as representing "two contrary forces" [*deux forces contraires*].

35 On Homer's poverty, see Dio Chrysostom, *Discourse* 53, in *Discourses*, 364. The Greek text of pseudo-Herodotus's *Life of Homer*, entitled *Herodotou Halikarnassos Exegesis Perites Toi Homêrô genesis ê biotos*, begins on sig. Pr of Melanchthon's *Grammatica Graeca* (Hagenau: Johan Secerium, 1531), and the Latin translation, entitled the *Vita Homeri ex Herodotus*, begins on sig. R2v.

36 Melanchthon, *Preface to Homer*, in *Opera Omnia* 11:412–13.

37 1 Cor. 3.18.

38 Bakhtin, *Dialogic Imagination*, 55–6.

39 Bakhtin, *Problems of Dostoevsky's Poetics*, 126; Rose, *Parody*, 146, 161.

40 Rose, *Parody*, 65; compare Donaldson, *The World Upside Down*, 7–8, and Schwartz, "Irony," in Zegura, ed. *The Rabelais Encyclopedia*, 130–2.

41 Rose, *Parody*, 47.

42 On the "dialectic of opposites," see Masters, *Rabelaisian Dialectic*, 3; on the "bipolar structure" of Rabelais's work, see Chesney, *The Countervoyage of Rabelais and Ariosto*, 209. Duval has called *Pantagruel* both an "epic New Testament" and an "anti-epic" work, while Chesney argues that Rabelais uses the "hybrid mock-epic genre" of the "countervoyage," a genre characterized by "antithesis." See Duval, *The Design of Rabelais' Pantagruel*, 92; Chesney, *Countervoyage*, 209–10, 6, 11. Compare Demerson, *Humanisme et Facétie*, 24, who calls Rabelais's work a "burlesque" epic but an epic nonetheless; Tetel, "The Function and Meaning of the Mock Epic Framework in Rabelais," 158, describes this combination as "an interplay between the sublime and the vulgar, the serious and the ludicrous." On Rabelais as a Homer parodist, see also Coleman, "Language in the *Tiers Livre*," 45; on the Homeric origins of sceptical suspension of belief, see Zerba, *Doubt and Skepticism*, 94.

43 François Rabelais, *TL* 35, in *Oeuvres Complètes*, 498. English translations (with some minor modifications) are cited from the translation of J.M. Cohen, with the French text cited parenthetically in the text from the Demerson edition.

44 Defaux, "Une Rencontre Homerique," 110. Pontani, "Homeric Readings," 390, admits that Homer has an "ubiquitous presence" in Rabelais.

45 Duval, *The Design of Rabelais' Pantagruel*, 11; Tetel, *Etude sur le Comique de Rabelais*, 35 ("une parodie de l'épopée"); Demerson, *Humanisme et Facétie*, 33.

46 Compare E. Hall, *The Return of Ulysses*, 147, who argues that Odysseus is an antecedent of the "shabby philosopher" such as Diogenes, Aesop, and Socrates.

47 Cook, *The Odyssey in Athens*, 10. Cave, "Panurge and Odysseus," 52, argues that Rabelais produces a "parody" of Homeric epic but not one "coterminous with satirical demolition."

48 See Augustine, *On Christian Teaching*, 104–7, on how Christian orators need not follow the rules of classical rhetoric and how the "grandiloquence" of classical orators is not compatible with the humble grandeur of Christian piety.

49 La Fresnaye, *L'Art Poétique*, 135.

50 Martial, *Ep*. XIV:183, in *Epigrams* 3:298–9.

51 For Socrates's comments on the *Margites*, see *Second Alcibiades* 147b, in *Homeric Hymns*, ed. M.L. West, 247. *La Batrachomyomachie d'Homere*, trans. Royhier, Dedicatory Epistle to M. Hugues le Marlet, sig. A2v.

52 *La Batrachomyomachie*, trans. Royhier, sig. A2v.

53 In his *Politia Literaria*, Angelus Decembrius calls the *Batrachomyomachia* a "jocosum opus, et poetae iunioris" that was written before Homer's epic

works and not afterwards, in parody of them, as is now commonly assumed; on Decembrius, see Fabbri, "Carlo Marsuppini e la Sua Versione Latina Della 'Batrachomyomachia'," 560.

54 On Poliziano's conception of Homer as a master of all three rhetorical styles, see pp. 35, 74 of this book. The idea is an ancient commonplace: see Aristotle, *Poetics* 1448b34–1449a6; Quintilian, *Inst. Orat.* 4:29, 4:487 (X.1.46; XII.10.64); Gellius, *Noctes Atticae*, 2:61 (VI.14.7) On the idea of Homer as "*philpoikilos*" [a lover of variety] in the Greek scholia, see N.J. Richardson, "Literary Criticism in the Exegetical Scholia," in *Oxford Readings in ancient literary criticism*, ed. Laird, 266.

55 On antilogic or eristic, see Kerferd, *The Sophistic Movement*, 29–31, 62–6. On 63, Kerferd defines antilogic as "opposing one *logos* to another *logos*, or in discovering or drawing attention to the presence of such an opposition in an argument or in a thing or state of affairs."

56 Plato, *Phaedrus* 261b–c, where Socrates comments that both Nestor and Odysseus wrote treatises on the art of rhetoric, and Phaedrus responds that he "must be disguising Gorgias under the name of Nestor and Thrasymachus ... under that of Odysseus," thus identifying Homer's most skilful speakers with two contemporary sophists. On this passage, see Sprague, *The Older Sophists*, 64. Plutarch, *Lives of the Ten Orators* 832e (*Moralia* 10:347), mentions that Antiphon, a sophist, was nicknamed Nestor because of his eloquence and quick wit. Compare Nehamas, "Eristic, Antilogic, Dialectic," 3–6; E. Hall, *The Return of Ulysses*, 37, on how Odysseus's reputation for rhetorical skill lends itself to Sophocles's depiction of him as "the master sophist-demagogue" in plays such as *Ajax* and *Philoctetes*.

57 Dio Chrysostom, *Discourse* 11, in *Discourses*, 514–15; on Homer as the mentor of Socrates, see Discourse 55, 382–3.

58 N.J. Richardson, "Homer and his Ancient Critics," in *A Commentary on the Iliad*, ed. Kirk, 6:26, 6:29.

59 On the Sophistic emendation of Homeric texts, see Philostratus, *Heroikos*, xlix; on the Sophistic use of the paradoxical encomium, also see K. Morgan, *Myth and Philosophy*, 118–28, and Pease, "Things Without Honor."

60 Verdenius, "Gorgias' Doctrine of Deception," 127.

61 Defaux, *Pantagruel et les Sophistes*, 172, 206; on Rabelais's reliance on sophistic techniques, see also Jeanneret, "Quand la Fable se met à Table," 164–5.

62 C. Robinson, *Lucian and his Influence*, 42–3. On Lucian's relationship to Homer, also see Briand, "Lucien et Homère."

63 On the Aristarchan principle of clarifying Homer with Homer, see Reynolds and Wilson, *D'Homère à Érasme*, 10, and Porphyry, *Homeric Questions*, trans. Schlunk, 47.

64 C. Robinson, *Lucian and his Influence*, 43.
65 Lucian, *True History*, in *Dialogues*, 1:323. On Lucian's satirical techniques, see Branham, *Unruly Eloquence*, 116–18, 136–8, and C. Robinson, *Lucian and his Influence*, 43.
66 Rabelais, *Gargantua*, Prologue, 40: "Croiez-vous en vostre foy qu'oncques Homère, escrivent l'*Iliade* et *Odyssée*, pensast ès allegories lesquelles de luy ont calfreté? Plutarche, Heraclides Ponticq, Eustatie, Phornute, et ce que d'iceulx Politian a disrobé?"
67 Rabelais, headnote to *TL* 3, in *Gargantua and Pantagruel*, trans. Screech, 422.
68 Masters, *Rabelaisian Dialectic*, 25; compare Chesney, *Countervoyage*, 70, on Rabelais's imitation of Lucian's "pulverization of the Great Chain of Being," and Gauna, *The Rabelaisian Mythologies*, 138.
69 Greene, *Rabelais*, 66.
70 Eichel-Lojkine, *Excentricité et Humanisme*, 222–4, argues that Rabelais often uses Homer in order to undermine Plato. Panurge's Homeric chain of debts may be a nod to one of the possible etymologies for the Greek *homêros*, "from homou, together, and eirein, to connect, because a guarantor binds a creditor and debtor together" according to Giambattista Vico, "Discovery of the True Homer," in his *New Science*, 375.
71 Eustathius, *In Homeri Iliadis et Odysseae Libros Parekbolai* (Basel: Froben, 1560), annotated by Isaac Casaubon, 572, annotating *Il.* 8.1–25: "Hanc fabulam peri tan dios seiras, soluta oratio elegantissime expressit Lucianus in dialogo Martis et Mercurii" [This is the fable about the god's chain, a speech elegantly expressed by Lucian in his dialogue on Mars and Mercury].
72 Lucian, *Zeus Catechized* and *Zeus Rants*, both in *Dialogues*, 2:65, 2:110–13.
73 On insult or *bômolochia* in Homer, see Nagy, *The Best of the Achaeans*, 245–59, and Lateiner, "The *Iliad*: an unpredictable classic," in *The Cambridge Companion to Homer*, ed. Fowler, 15–23.
74 Lateiner, "The *Iliad*: an unpredictable classic," 15. On the "reciprocal exchange" of blame speech in Homeric epic, see Martin, *The Language of Heroes*, 18–21.
75 Szabari, "Rabelais *Parrhesiastes*," 94, 88; compare Bakhtin, *Rabelais and His World*, 168.
76 On the "therapeutic" nature of insult in Rabelais, see Greene, "Rabelais and the Language of Malediction," 105–9; on the "cleansing and homeopathic process" of insult and vituperation in Rabelais, see also Defaux, "Rabelais and the Monsters of Antiphysis," 1027.
77 On the adage "war is the father of all things" [*polemos pantôn men patêr esti*], see Heraclitus, *Cosmic Fragments*, 53; the passage is quoted or paraphrased by Lucian, *Icaromenippus* (*Dialogues* 2:281), by Plutarch, *Isis*

and Osiris 370d (*Moralia* 5:116–17), and by Erasmus, *Bellum omnium pater* [*O polemos apantôn patêr*], Adage III.v.36 (*CWE* 35:87 [ASD II.5:315]).

78 See Erasmus, Adage IV.i.1 (*Dulce bellum inexpertis*), which argues that *bellum* (war) is so called "by antiphrasis because it has nothing good or *bellum* … about it; war is *bellum* in the same way that Furies are the Eumenides, 'the kindly ones'" [*quorum alii bellum kat'antiphrasin dictum volunt, quod nihil habeat neque bonum neque bellum, nec alia ratione bellum esse bellum quam Furiae sunt Eumenides*] (*CWE* 35:405 [ASD II.7:16]).

79 Collins, *Master of the Game*, 153–4, argues that Heraclitus's criticism of Homer is based on the belief that his poetry does not "sufficiently distinguish between the surface differences of appearance and their underlying unity." In a fragment preserved in Porphyry's *Quaestiones Homericae*, a work printed by Aldus (Venice, 1521), by Rihelius (Strasbourg, 1539), and by Camerarius and Micyllus in their edition of Homer (Basel, 1541), Heraclitus justifies the depiction of the gods gazing down from the tranquillity of Olympus at the beginning of *Il.* 4 by observing that "wars and battles seem dreadful to us, but to God not even these are dreadful; for God accomplishes all things with a view to a harmony of the universe." See Heraclitus, *Cosmic Fragments*, 62b.

80 Marsh, *Lucian and the Latins*, 72–3.

81 In Lucian's version of the scene (*Dialogues* 4:99), equally steeped in Homeric allusions, Menippus relates how, upon his arrival in Hades, he could not tell the difference between "Thersites [and] the handsome Nireus, or the mendicant Irus [and] the king of the Phaeacians, or the cook Pyrrhias [and] Agamemnon" – that is, between the ugliest and the most attractive, and the most ignoble and noble, of Homer's characters. The observation lends itself to a proverb; see, for instance, Thomas Lodge, *Defence of Poetry*: "You compare Homer to Methecus, cookes to Poetes" (in *Elizabethan Critical Essays*, ed. Smith, 1: 77).

82 Branham, *Unruly Eloquence*, 140.

83 Duval, *The Design of Rabelais's Pantagruel*, 103–4.

84 Peradotto, *Man in the Middle Voice*, 53; see also Giangrande, *The Use of Spoudaiogeloion*, 43. Henri Estienne, *Traicté de la Conformité du Langage François avec le Grec*, 124, notes Homer's tendency towards hyperbole and exaggeration.

85 Dufresny, *Parallele Burlesque*, 3:194–5, 3:205, 3:209.

86 Rapin, *Comparaison des poemes d'Homère et de Virgile*, 85.

87 Le Bossu, *Treatise of the Epick Poem*, 120–1, citing Horace, *Ars Poetica*, ls. 137–9.

88 Erasmus, Adage I.ix.14 (*CWE* 32:188 [ASD II.2:336]), citing Horace, *Ars Poetica*, ls. 137–9; on Rabelais's use of this adage, see Duval, "History, Epic, and the Design of Rabelais' *Tiers Livre*," 128–32. At *TL* 22:449, Rabelais cites

another passage from Horace (*Satires* II.5, ln. 59) by way of Erasmus, *Adage* III.3.35.

89 Horace satirizes such poets by asking, "What will this boaster produce in keeping with such mouthing? / Mountains will labour, to birth will come a laughter-rousing mouse" [*Quid dignum tanto feret hic promissor hiatu? / parturient montes, nascetur ridiculus mus*].

90 Horace, *Ars Poetica*, ls. 136–41, in *Satires, Epistles, and Ars Poetica*, 462–3. On Horace's deliberate misrepresentation of lines from Homer "for humorous effect" and his "debasement of epic language into the clichés of Maeonian song," see Ahern, "Horace's Rewriting of Homer in *Carmen* I.6," 301–14.

91 Erasmus, *Elephantum ex musca facis* [You are making an elephant out of a fly], Adage I.ix.69 (*CWE* 32:219), derived from *Il.* 17.570–3, where Menelaus is compared to a fly.

92 On Virgilian and Homeric forms of copiousness or fecundity, see Wilson-Okamura, *Virgil*, 99, 119–31.

93 On Erasmus, see Defaux, *Pantagruel et les Sophistes*, 49.

94 Rabelais may be associating the story with Erasmus, Adage V.i.1 (*CWE* 36:543), "*Tu in legione, ego in culina*" [You in the camp, I in the kitchen].

95 Plato, *Rep.* 3.13 [404c]; on Plato's attitudes towards cooking, see *Gorgias* 462f–463c (*Plato* 5:313).

96 Decembrius, *De Politia Literaria*, 50.

97 On the debate between La Motte and Dacier over Homer representing his kings cooking meat, see Foerster, *Homer in English Criticism*, 14. On the objections of Claude Fleury, who protests in his 1728 *Remarques sur Homère* that Homer represents "kings and army generals making their own food" [*Rois et des generaux d'armée fassent eux mesmes leur cuisine*], see Hepp, *Deux Amis d'Homère*, 146.

98 On the names of the frogs and mice in the *Batrachomyomachia*, see *Homeric Hymns*, ed. M.L. West, 233.

99 Coleman, *Rabelais*, 8.

100 Screech, *Laughter at the Foot of the Cross*, 289.

101 See Clarke, "The Humor of Homer," 251: "Odysseus is almost always hungry, and his quest consists mainly of eating – and not being eaten."

102 See Cave, "Panurge and Odysseus," 48–9; Defaux, *Rabelais Agonistes*, 258–9, and "Une Rencontre Homerique," 116.

103 *Od.* 14.124–6; on the significance of this passage and on the motif of hunger in *Od.*, see Cave, "Panurge and Odysseus," 48–9; Segal, *Singers, Heroes, and Gods*, 179; on Cratinus, see E. Hall, *Return of Ulysses*, 39.

104 Erasmus, *Venter auribus caret* (Adage II.viii.84, *CWE* 34:83); see also *Ventres* (Adage II.viii.78, *CWE* 34:80); *Glôssogastores* (Adage IV.v.99; *CWE* 36:207); and *Necessitas magistra* (Adage IV.vii.55, *CWE* 36:314). Compare *Molestus*

interpellator venter, which Erasmus derives from *Od.* 7.216–18, explaining that "the stomach is a shameless intruder which never allows anyone to forget it" (Adage III.x.9, *CWE* 35:360–1). Several of these adages duplicate maxims contained in *De Ventre* [On the Stomach] in Stobaeus, *Gnomologia Graecolatina* (Basel: Oporinus, 1557), 303.

105 Erasmus, Adage II.viii.78 (*CWE* 34:80 [ASD II.4:198]); IV.vii.55 (*CWE* 36:314 [ASD II.8:98]), citing Persius, *Prologus*, ls. 10–11; IV.v.99 (*CWE* 36:207). Compare Adage IV.ii.48 (*CWE* 35:528 [ASD II.7:120]): *Multa docet fames* [Hunger teaches many things], which quotes Persius on "that dispenser of genius, the belly, who often has a rare skill in getting at words that are not his own" [*Magister artis ingenique largitor / Venter, negates artifex sequi voces*].

106 Erasmus, Adage IV.v.99 [*Glossogastores*], ASD II.7:292.

107 See *Od.* 17.286–7: "a ravenous belly [*gastera*] no man may hide, an accursed plague that brings many evils on men."

108 [Plutarch], *Life of Homer*, 240–1, argues that Epicurus was misled by Homer's description of Alkinous's feast at *Od.* 9.5–11 and out of this misreading developed his doctrine that "pleasure [*hêdonên*] is the goal of the fortunate life [*eudaimonia*]"; Heraclitus, *Homeric Problems*, 129–31, similarly argues that Epicurus stole his doctrines from Homer's Phaiakians.

109 On the proverbial status of Homer's observation that wine is "arbiter of peace, concord, and friendship" [*pacis, concordie, amicie arbiter*] and also "the father of sweet sleep" [*dulcissimi somni pater*], see Valla, *De Voluptate*, 118–19.

110 Clay, "Goat Island: *Od.* 9.116–141," 264.

111 On the tyrannous appetite of Homer's Polyphemus, see R. Hunter, "Homer and Greek Literature," in *The Cambridge Companion to Homer*, ed. Fowler, 245: "the only authority which [Homer's] Cyclops recognizes is his own appetite, *thymos*," a quality Euripides turns into a "'blasphemous cult' of his own belly."

112 Lateiner, *Sardonic Smile*, 171, argues that in the cave of Polyphemus, "every body and every thing is magnified and parvified, from stature to voices to the toxicity of wine."

113 On this point, see Segal, *Singers, Heroes, and Gods*, 157–8, who argues that in *Od.*, the "beggar, belly and all, has … a connection with the resourcefulness, inventiveness, and flexibility of the bard." On hunger as a dominant theme in *Od.*, see also Graver, "Dog-Helen and Homeric Insult."

114 A. Berry, "Les Mithologies Pantagruelicques," 475, calls chapters 29–35 and 37–47 of *QL* an "Odyssée du Ventre" [Odyssey of the stomach] that ends only when Panurge beshits himself and is reborn. On the "Histoire de Gorgias" episode at the end of *Pantagruel*, see Gaignebet, "Histoire des Gorgias."

115 Victor Hugo, *William Shakespeare*, in *Oeuvres Complètes* (Paris, 1937), 41:39–40, cited in A. Berry, "Les Mithologies Pantagruelicques," 475.
116 On Erasmus's use of the phrase, from *Il.* 1.231, see *Scarabeus aquilam quaerit*, Adage III.vii.1 (*CWE* 35:184 [ASD II.6:400]) and *Institutio Principis Christiani*, *CWE* 27:315 [ASD IV.1:160].
117 Rabelais attributes the phrase at *Il.* 18.104 to Hesiod, even though he correctly attributes the phrase in a letter to Guillaume Budé, 4 March 1521: "to tou Homêrou etôsion achthos" [Homer's useless burden on the earth]. See Budé, *Correspondance* 1:284. It is possible that Rabelais wished to link the phrase to *Theogony*, ln. 26, where Hesiod launches an attack against the tyranny of appetite and distinguishes his poetry from that of "mere bellies" [*gasteres oion*] who sing for money and thus without regard for truth.
118 Gumpert, "Homer," in *The Rabelais Encyclopaedia*, ed. Zegura, 118.
119 On Rabelais's punning on the word *farci* in chapter 59 of *QL*, see Screech, *Laughter at the Foot of the Cross*, 291.
120 Erasmus, Adage IV.x.70 (*CWE* 36:525); on Rabelais's debt to this adage, see Screech, *Rabelais*, 373.
121 Thalmann, *Swineherd*, 103, argues that Margites derives his name from *margos* [ravenous], the same word used to describe the belly of the beggar Irus at *Od.* 18.2; Nagy, *Best of the Achaeans*, 231, 259 points out that Homer's Irus (or Iros) is a blame poet and is also *margos*, or gluttonous and that the contents of the *Margites* resemble blame-poetry.
122 The 1573 *Homeri et Hesiodi Certamen ... Matronis et Aliorum parodiae, ex Homeri versibus parva immutatione lepidè detortis consultae*, printed by Henri Estienne at Geneva, includes Homer parodies by Matro, Hegemon, and Hipponax, reprinted in Estienne's 1575 *Parodiae Morales*. After the 1514 Aldine edition of Athenaeus, a second edition of the Greek text was printed in Basel in 1535, and a Latin translation by Natale Conti was printed in Venice in 1556.
123 Athenaeus, *Deipnosophists*, 1:37–81 (I.8e–14e); Plutarch, *Convivial Questions* 736e–737c, in *Moralia* 9:221–3 (736e–737c); on symposiastic recitations of Homer-parodies, see also Collins, *Master of the Game*, 184–5, and Rose, *Parody*, 14.
124 Hipponax, as cited by Athenaeus, *Deipnosophists*, 7:243 (XV.698c), also cited in *Matro of Pitane*, 16.
125 On Archestratus and the Egyptian *Iliad*, see *Matro of Pitane*, 9–10; Archestratus, *The Life of Luxury*, 15; Athenaeus, *Deipnosophists*, 3:251 (VII.278d); at 3:279, Athenaeus calls Archestratus a "Daedalus of tasty dishes."
126 *Matro of Pitane*, 56–7; see page 20 for the Homeric sources of these passages. The fragments of Matro are also preserved by Athenaeus, *Deipnosophists*, 2:117–27 (IV.134d–137c).

127 Folengo, *Baldus* 1:ix–x, 1:1–2 (I.15–16), 1:4 (I.36–9). On the influence of Folengo on Rabelais, see A. Russell, "Epic Agon," 119–48, and Scalamandre, *Rabelais e Folengo*.

128 Bakhtin, *Problems of Dostoevsky's Poetics*, 127; on Scaliger's Virgil parodies, see Rose, *Parody*, 9.

129 Aristotle, *Poetics*, 38–41 (1448b30, 1448b33–1449a2).

130 Plato, *Second Alcibiades* 147a, cited in *Homeric Hymns*, ed. M.L. West, 246–7. Compare Erasmus, *Margites*, Adage II.iii.71 (*CWE* 33:174), a poem by Homer and consequently a name used by Lucian to denote a stupid man, derived from *mê* (not) and *ergon* (work) because he was no good at anything.

131 On this fragment from the *Margites* [P. Oxy.2309] see *Homeric Hymns*, ed. M.L. West, 250–1, and West's discussion on 225–6. On the *Cercopes*, see *Homeric Hymns*, ed. M.L. West, 228.

132 Pulci, *Morgante* XVIII.118, 365. On the influence of Homer on Pulci, see Everson, *The Italian Renaissance Epic*, 242–3.

133 Pulci, *Morgante* XIX.147–8, 411.

134 Erasmus, *Emori risu*, Adage IV.i.86 (*CWE* 35:493 [ASD II.7:89]). Estienne, *Traicté de la Conformité du Langage*, 120, also notes that Homer is the origin of the French expression "it makes me die with laughter" [*il me fait mourir de rire*].

135 Textor, *Officina* (1526), 373–4; Textor also mentions the story on 209. The riddle is also told in the *Lives* of pseudo-Herodotus and pseudo-Plutarch, both reprinted in *Homeric Hymns*, ed. M.L. West, 399, 409–11. For additional sixteenth-century discussions of Homer's death by riddle, see Melanchthon, *Grammatica Graeca*, sig. Tr; Berni, *Dialogo contra I Poeti*, 208; Quattrehomme, *Discours*, 308–9.

136 BNP Fonds Français 12.407. *Extraict d'Homere. Et du Commentaire Grec. Par monsieur Marcassus*, fol. 108v, fol. 132v; Pulci, *Morgante* XXVII.139–40, XXVII.701.

137 Joubert, *Traité du Ris*, 88–9.

138 Joubert, *Traité du Ris*, 88–9; on the influence of Homer on Joubert's theories of laughter, see Daniel Ménager, *La Renaissance et le Rire*, 58.

139 Joubert, *Traité du Ris*, 44. In his *De Risu*, 351, Politianus calls this phenomenon "antiperistasis" or "contrarii coactio."

140 Joubert, *Traité du Ris*, 44, 42.

141 Joubert, *Traité du Ris*, 42; on dying of laughter, see also 61–2. On the question of whether laughter is produced by two contrary passions, see also Vallesio, *Controversiarum Medicarum*, 236.

142 Joubert, *Traité du Ris*, 105.

143 Ricchieri, *Lectionum Antiquarum* 3.12 (1566), col. 86a: "Homerus quoque de caloris copia risum profluere, inibi videtur indicare, ubi *gelôta asbestos*, id est inextinguibilem dicit risum." Compare Girardus, *Meditationes in Librum Primum Iliados Homeri*, 102, on *Il.* 1.599: "Risum vocat inextinguibilem, qui fusus copiosus est, & velut incendium restingui non potest ... Fortasse huc respexit Homerus, quod qui naturae sunt calidioris, in risum sint propensiores. Vulcanus tantu[m] excitavit risum, ut nullus Deorum se a vehementer ridendo continere potuerit."

144 Persona, *Noctes Solitariae,* Colloquy 59, 374.

145 Paquelin, *Apologeme*, 40–1, 45.

146 Joubert, *Traité du Ris*, 127.

147 [Plutarch], *Life of Homer*, 292–3. On debates over the Homeric diet in Athenaeus, see *Deipnosophists*, 1:43–7, and M. Heath, "Do Heroes Eat Fish?"

148 Valet, *Oratio in Scholis medicorum ... Quâ Medicinae antiquitas ex antiquissimo Poetarum Homero obiter & allegorica describitur* (Paris: Johannes de Bordeaux, 1570).

149 On Rabelais's medical training, see chapters 7 and 8 of Jean Plattard, *The Life of François Rabelais* (London: Frank Cass, 1930; rpt. 1968).

150 *Peri Phusôn* [On Breaths] I.33–4, in Hippocrates, *Works* 2:228–9; compare *Aphorisms* II.22 (2:112–13), *Regimen*, I.6 (2:238–9), and *Regimen* I.16 (2:254–5). On the relationship between the cosmology of Heraclitus and the doctrines of Hippocrates and the Sophists, see Rankin, *Sophists, Socratics, and Cynics*, 55.

151 Heraclitus, *On the Universe*, in Hippocrates, *Works* 4:455. For Hippocrates's reliance on Heraclitus's concept of *palintonos harmoniê*, see *Regimen* I.6 (*Works* 2:237–9). On the relationship between the allopathic medical theories of Hippocrates and the Presocratic cosmologies of Heraclitus and Empedocles, see Arikha, *Passions and Tempers*, 8, 91–2, and G. Kennedy, "Sophists and Physicians of the Greek Enlightenment," in *Cambridge History of Classical Literature* 1, part 3, ed. Easterling and Knox, 60–5. On Heraclitus's concept of the unity of opposites and his criticisms of Homer, see Collins, *Master of the Game*, 153–5.

152 Heraclitus, *Cosmic Fragments*, 203 (as cited in Hippolytus, *Refutatio* IX.9.1); compare Heraclitus, *On the Universe*, as cited in Hippocrates, *Works* 4:489: "[t]he attunement of the world is of opposite tensions [*palintonos*], as is that of the harp or bow." This second passage is also cited twice by Plutarch, *On Tranquility of Mind* 474a; *Isis and Osiris* 370d.

153 The term *palintonos* appears five times in Homeric epic, always in connection with a *toxon*, or bow: see *Il.* 8.266, 10.459, 15.443; *Od.* 21.11 and 21.59. On the Homeric and Heraclitean concepts of *palintonos*, see

Heraclitus, *Cosmic Fragments*, 213–16, and *The Presocratic Philosophers*, ed. Kirk, Raven, and Schofield, 192. Heraclitus, *On the Universe*, as cited in Hippocrates, *Works* 4:485; the passage is linked to Homer by Eustathius, who quotes it in his commentary on *Il.* 18.197. For an example of a sixteenth-century interpretation of the god Apollo as a symbol of Heraclitean cosmology, see Thenaud, *La Lignée de Saturne*, 77r–v, citing *Od.* 3.276–85. On Apollo's associations with the bow and the lyre, see also Burkert, *Greek Religion*, 145–6. Although Heraclitus's fragments were not printed until Estienne's 1573 *Poesis Philosophica*, his doctrines were familiar to sixteenth-century readers through the many fragments preserved in Plato, Aristotle, Plutarch, Clement of Alexandria, Cicero, and Diogenes Laertius, the last of whose *Lives of the Philosophers* was first printed at Basel in 1533. On the reception of Heraclitus in sixteenth-century France, see Joukovsky, *Le Feu et le Fleuve*, 7–12.

154 On the influence of Heraclitus on ancient Stoicism, see Hahm, *The Origins of Stoic Cosmology*, xiv, 6, 107, 154; Whitman, *Allegory*, 33–4.

155 Defaux, *Pantagruel et les Sophistes*, 209.

156 Defaux, *Pantagruel et les Sophistes*, 43–4; Bridoye is paraphrasing Aristotle, *Categories*; Defaux, 44, provides Peter Ramus's French paraphrase of the passage from his 1555 *Dialéctique*: "Et les opposez sont de leur nature entre soy esgallement notoires ... et neantmoins, l'un mis devant l'autre est plus clairement apperceu."

157 Defaux, *Pantagruel et les Sophistes*, 43.

158 Defaux, "Rabelais and the Monsters of Antiphysis," 1032, 1035; Schwartz, *Irony and Ideology in Rabelais*, 167.

159 Huizinga, *Homo Ludens*, 116.

160 On Rabelais's contempt for sophistry, see Seiver, "Cicero's *De Oratore* and Rabelais," 655–71. Defaux, *Pantagruel et les Sophistes*, xix, calls Rabelais a master of "*pro et contra*" disputation whose work is characterized by dialectic and antithesis.

161 Defaux, *Rabelais Agonistes*, 172.

162 [Plutarch], *Life of Homer*, 264–5.

163 According to De Romilly, *Magic and Rhetoric in Ancient Greece*, 83, Hippodromus also claimed that Homer was the father of the sophists.

164 A. Ford, "Sophistic," 48; on antithesis and antilogy as sophistic argumentative techniques, see De Romilly, *Magic and Rhetoric*, 9, 27, and Griffith, "Contest and Competition." On "*hysteron proteron*" as a Homeric rhetorical device, see Nünlist, *The Ancient Critic at Work*, 326–34.

165 *Hesychii Dictionarum* (1521), sig. h3v, column 231, defines *eirôneia* as a "word moving from opposite to opposite" ("*logos ek tô enantis enantion*");

Nashe, "To the Gentleman Students," prefatory epistle to Robert Greene, *Menaphon*, in Nashe, *Works*, ed. McKerrow, 3:314.

166 Rabelais, headnote to *TL* 49, in *Gargantua and Pantagruel*, trans. Screech, 598.

167 Bernardete, *The Bow and the Lyre*, 86–7, argues that Homer's Moly is a symbolic lesson in *physis*, or nature, reminiscent of the doctrines of Heraclitus.

168 On the relationship between scepticism and sophistry, see Kerferd, *The Sophistic Movement*, 62–3, 34. Kerferd, *Sophistic Moment*, 34, argues that scepticism "originated from within the sophistic movement" even though Plato eventually came to enforce a strict distinction between the truth-seeking aims of Socratic dialectic and the antilogic of his sophistic adversaries.

169 Lucian, *Dionysius*, in *Dialogues*, 1:57.

170 On this point, see W. Stephens, *Giants in Those Days*, 322, who argues that Rabelais's Alcofribas is even more like Homer than he realizes and that "[h]is words are indeed a Silenus, since they contain a wisdom that must be sought beneath the surface of his naively eclectic and venal attempts to garner authority."

171 Alcofribas's comment is derived from Horace, *Epistle* I.XIX, ls. 2, 6, in Horace, *Satires, Epistles, and Ars Poetica*, 380–1. On the influence of this passage on Rabelais's conception of Homer, see Defaux, *Rabelais Agonistes*, 371.

172 Demerson, *Humanisme et Facétie*, 19; L. Morgan, *Patterns of Redemption*, 23, 36.

173 Erasmus, *Enchiridion* (*CWE* 66:67–8). On the concept of *huponoia* and its relevance to techniques of interpreting Homeric epic, see N.J. Richardson, "Homeric Professors in the Age of the Sophists," in *Oxford Readings in ancient literary criticism*, ed. Laird, 63–6.

174 Erasmus, *Sileni Alcibiades*, Adage III.3.1 (*CWE* 34:262 [ASD 2.5:160]): "fronte vilis ac ridicula videatur, tamen interius ac proprius contemplanti sit admirabilis."

175 Poliziano, *Oratio*, ed. Megna, 53, ln. 4.

176 An idea that Rabelais could certainly have gotten from Lucian: see Branham, *Unruly Eloquence*, 22–5, on Tiresias's advice to Menippus to move through life "laughing [*gelon*] a great deal and taking nothing seriously [*meden espoudakôs*]," an ironic detachment that counterbalances *alazoneia*, or boastfulness.

177 Aristotle, *Nic. Ethics*, IV.7.1–17, 240–5 [1127a13–32].

178 Gumpert, "Homer," in *The Rabelais Encyclopedia*, ed. Zegura, 119.

179 Diogenes Laertius, *Lives* IX.67, 2:481.

180 Diogenes Laertius, *Lives* IX.71, 2:483–5. Sextus Empiricus makes similar claims at *Adversos Mathematicos* VII.126–9, citing *Od.* 19.136–7 as evidence of

Homer's sceptical tendencies; on Sextus, see Pérez, "Allégorie et Doxographie Sceptique," 245.

181 Diogenes Laertius, *Lives* IX.71, 2:483–5.

182 Montaigne, *On the Uncertainty of Our Judgment*, in *Complete Essays*, 205.

183 Montaigne, *Apology for Raymond Sebond*, in *Complete Essays*, 371, 377.

184 Montaigne, *Apology*, in *Complete Essays*, 442–3. On Montaigne's knowledge of Homer, see P. Ford, "Montaigne's Homer: poet or myth?" *Montaigne Studies* 17, nos. 1–2 (2005): 7–16.

185 Melanchthon, *Encomium Eloquentiae*, in *Melanchthons Werke* 3:51: "... Graecorum grammaticorum vulgus, qui ad physiologian totum Homeri Carmen referunt mireque sibi placent, cum nova metamorphosi belli nugatores ex Iove aethera, ex Iunone aerem faciunt, quae ne per febrim quidem unquam somniaturus erat Homerus." On the influence of this passage on Rabelais, see P. Ford, *De Troie à Ithaque*, 400–5.

186 [Plutarch], *Life of Homer*, 311.

187 Schwartz, *Irony and Ideology in Rabelais*, 50.

188 Frame, *François Rabelais. A Study*, 32. Compare Grafton, "Renaissance Readers of Homer's Ancient Readers," in *Homer's Ancient Readers*, ed. Lamberton, 157, on how sixteenth-century humanists "both ridiculed and practiced the various forms of allegory when reading Homer."

189 Schwartz, *Irony and Ideology in Rabelais*, 88.

190 Gumpert, "Homer," in *The Rabelais Encyclopedia*, ed. Zegura, 118.

191 Cavaillé calls the treatise "an ironic allegory of eleven lines of Homer" in which, "by contrast to the neoplatonic tradition, which uses the sensible world to figure intelligible realities and which raises up sensual desire to a love of ideas, allegory is used here to ground itself in the dense thicket of the sensible world." See La Mothe Le Vayer, *L'Antre des Nymphes*, 16, 14.

192 La Mothe Le Vayer, *L'Antre*, 69, 71.

193 La Mothe Le Vayer, *L'Antre*, 66.

194 La Mothe Le Vayer, *De la Philosophie Sceptique*, in *Dialogues*, 20.

195 La Mothe Le Vayer, *L'Antre*, 69: "Socrate disait en riant que Platon lui en avait bien fait dire dans ses dialogues à quoi il n'avait jamais pensé, qu'Homère aurait bien plus de sujet de se moquer de tant de sens differents que l'on donne."

196 I. Casaubon, *Notae ad Diogenes Laertii*, 270 on *Lives* IX.12.

197 Cicero, *De Oratore* III.34.137, in *Cicero* 4:108–9; compare Hesychius of Miletus (in *Suda* o251), cited in *Homeric Hymns*, ed. M.L. West, 429–31, on how Homer "did not write the *Iliad* all at once or in sequence" but rather "wrote each rhapsody and performed it as he went round from town to town to make a living ... and subsequently the poem was put together by various people, above all Peisistratus."

198 Borges, "Some Versions of Homer," 1135; compare Lianeri, "The Homeric Moment? Translation, Historicity, and the Meaning of the Classics," chapter 12 (pages 141–52) of *Classics and the Uses of Reception*, ed. Martindale and Thomas, 142.

199 Montaigne, *Apology*, in *Complete Essays*, 455.

200 P. Ford, *De Troie à Ithaque*, 203.

201 Rabelais, *Gargantua and Pantagruel*, trans. Screech, xxxv.

202 Budé, De *Philologia*, 256–7; McNeil, *Guillaume Budé*, 78, points out that Budé and Rabelais are among the first French writers to use the term *philologue*.

203 Jeanneret, "Signs Gone Wild," 65.

204 Cave, *Cornucopian Text*, 327; "Panurge and Odysseus," 52; on Rabelais's "agelastes" readers, see *QL*, Dedicatory Epistle to the Cardinal of Chatillon (1552), 564–5, and the discussions by Szabari, "Rabelais Parrhesiastes," 91–3, and Emily Butterworth, "Calumny," in *The Rabelais Encyclopedia*, ed. Zegura, 26–7.

205 Quintilian, *Inst. Orat.* IX.ii.35, defines *parôde* as a song sung in imitation "but employed as an abuse of language to designate imitation"; on the meaning of *para-*, see Rose, *Parody*, 47.

206 Rose, *Parody*, 15, 19.

207 On Tiraqueau's and Cardano's attitude towards the *sortes* and their possible influence on Rabelais, see Rabelais, headnote to *TL* 10, in *Gargantua and Pantagruel*, trans. Screech, 445.

208 Cicero, *De Divinatione* II.xli, 467–9; Agrippa, *De Incertitudine*, trans. as *The Vanity of arts and sciences*, 23.

209 On the "pastiche and transposition" of Homeric elements in chapter 9 of *P*, see Cave, "Panurge and Odysseus," 51.

210 [Homer], *Histoire Facetieuse des Rats contre les Grenouilles*, trans. Sara, 14.

211 Clement, *Protreptique* I 9.1–9.2, 63–4; on this passage see Dawson, *Allegorical Readers*, 199.

212 Clement, *Stromates* 7, 16.96.1–3, pp. 290–3.

213 Cave, "Panurge and Odysseus," 51.

214 Zeitlin, "Visions and Revisions of Homer," 241.

215 On these works, see Lesky, *Greek Literature*, 815–16.

216 On the Homeric centos, see *Centons Homeriques* [Homerocentra], ed. Rey, 65–70.

217 Irenaeus of Lyons, *Against the Heresies*, 47; Tertullian, *Prescriptions Against Heretics*, 262.

218 Jerome, Letter 6 (to Pantinus), trans. Erasmus, *CWE* 61:211.

219 Erasmus, Adage II.iv.58 (*CWE* 33:221 [ASD II.3:370]); *Ciceronianus*, *CWE* 28:438 [ASD I.2:701].

220 Erasmus, *Ciceronianus*, *CWE* 27:438 [ASD I.2:703].
221 Le Loyer, *Edom ou les Colonies iduméans en l'Asie et en l'Europe*, 224 ; on Le Loyer's interpretation, see Hepp, *Homère en France au XVIIième Siècle*, 112–13.
222 [Plutarch], *Life of Homer*, 228–9.
223 *Parodiae Morales*, ed. Estienne, 2–3, 33. Estienne's treatment of problems of inconsistency in Homeric epic differs from that of later scholars such as François D'Aubignac, whose 1715 *Conjectures académiques*, published posthumously, launched the "disintegrationist" theory that the *Iliad* was a collection of poems composed by various rhapsodes. On D'Aubignac's argument that the inconsistencies, contradictions, and mixture of styles in Homeric epic indicated more than one author, see Murrin, *Allegorical Epic*, 175–7.
224 *Homêri Poemata Duo*, ed. Estienne, sig. ¶3r: "Ex quibus alii quidem iam ante nostrum aetatem ad proverbalem accommodare usum fuerunt, alii autem (praeter paucos quosdam) non minus accommodari posse visi sunt."
225 On the relations between the cento and parody, and on the connections between both genres and the carnivalesque, see Bakhtin, *Dialogic Imagination*, 70.
226 Lucian, *Charon*, in *Dialogues* 2:441–3; Prustus, *Theotokion Homêrikon* (Paris: Morellus, 1610).
227 *Homêrou kai Hesiodou Agôn*, ed. Henri Estienne (1573), preface; 75, 96.
228 Lipsius, *Politica*, ed. Waszink, preface, 234–7.
229 Homer, *Od.* 19.564–7 and editor's note a.
230 BNP Fonds Français 12.407. *Extraict d'Homere*, fols. 141v–142r.
231 Erasmus, *Homo bulla*, Adage II.iii.48 (*CWE* 33:157 [ASD II.3:258]).
232 Canter, *Novarum lectionem*, 260–1.
233 *Homeri Ilias*, ed. Giphanius, 15.
234 J. Morrison, *Homeric Misdirection*, 104.
235 Erasmus, *Enchiridion* (*CWE* 66:68). On the Sibyl as a feminine version of Erasmus's *Silenus*, see F. Weinberg, "Written on the Leaves," 729.
236 *Pantagrueline Prognostications of 1533*, To the Kindly Reader, in Rabelais, *Gargantua and Pantagruel*, trans. Screech, 174.
237 Erasmus, Adage III.iii.35 (*CWE* 34:293 [ASD II.5:207]), citing Horace, *Satires* II.5, ln. 59.
238 Irenaeus, *Against the Heresies*, 47.
239 Montaigne, *Apology*, in *Complete Essays*, 442–3.
240 Poliziano, *Oratio*, in *Opera Omnia* 1:478, echoing Virgil, *Aen.* 6.98–100; Dorat, *Sibyllarum … duodecim oracula*, sig. B2r, and *Mythologicon*, 7r, 13r, both cited in P. Ford, "Classical Myth and its Interpretation in

sixteenth-century France," 340–1. Sebastian Castellio makes similar but less boldly phrased claims in his 1546 Latin edition of the *Oracula Sibyllina*.

241 "Sibylline" was synonymous with textually obscure in the sixteenth century, thanks to maxims such as "Praeter Sibyllam Leget Nemo" [Legible to no one but the Sibyl]. See Erasmus, Adage IV.ii.41 (*CWE* 35:524–5). On the obscurity of the Sibylline Oracles, see Cicero, *De Divinatione* II.liv, 495–7, on oracles that were "embellished with an acrostic" so that the initial letters of each line spell out the subject of the prophecy; at II.lvi, Cicero complains of oracles "so intricate and obscure that interpreter needs an interpreter ... and some so equivocal that they require a dialectician to construe them."

242 Cicero, *De Divinatione* II.lvi, 501; Plutarch, *The Oracles at Delphi* 398F, in *Moralia* 5:282–3.

243 Cave, *The Cornucopian Text*, xiii–xv.

244 Cave, "Panurge and Odysseus," 59; Mornay, *Christian Religion*, 462.

245 Beni, *Comparatione*, 149: "I am not surprised to read that according to many, Homer was reputed to be verbose and noted for garrulity" [*io non prendo maraviglia di leggere che Homero da molti sia stato riputato verbose e notato de garrulità*]. Compare Dufresny, *Parallèle Burlesque*, 183, who calls Homer and Rabelais "digressers and babblers" [*digressioneurs and babillards*].

246 *Il.* 20.248–51; Diogenes Laertius IX.73, in *Lives* 2:487.

247 *Hê tou Homerou poiêsis hapasa*, annotated by Budé, 1:167a, glossing *Il.* 20.245–7.

248 Ong, *Orality and Literacy*, 41.

249 Melanchthon, *Grammatica Graeca*, sig. O4v.

250 Rapin, *Comparaison*, 105–6, 119, 132. On Renaissance notions of Homeric and Virgilian style, see Wilson-Okamura, *Virgil*, 129–31.

251 Scaliger, *Poetices Libri Septem*, ed. Deitz, 4:48.

252 Peletier, *Oeuvres Poétiques*, 157; *Oeuvres*, ed. Laumonier, 156–7.

253 Peletier, *Art Poétique* (1555), in *Traités*, 228.

254 Ronsard, *Franciade*, in *Oeuvres*, 16:5; the passage is discussed by P. Ford, *De Troie à Ithaque*, 294.

255 On winged words as birds or arrows, see Martin, *Language of Heroes*, 35 and Combellack, "Words that Die," 22. On the meaning of the epithet, see Vivante, "On Homer's Winged Words," 8; Calhoun, "The Art of Formula in Homer," 215–17; Combellack, 25, proposes that its meaning approaches the adage, "scripta manent, verba volant," while Vivante, 3–5, and Martin, 30–1, both propose that it conveys the irrevocability or the permanence of words that cannot be retracted, a reading often grounded in the line spoken by Aeneas to Achilles at *Il.* 20.250: "Whatever word you speak, you will also hear."

256 Erasmus, Adage III.1.18 (*CWE* 34:189 [ASD II.5:52]); compare Girardus, *Meditationes*, 44; Horace, *Epistle* I.XVIII, ln. 71, in *Satires, Epistles, and Ars Poetica*, 374–5. Glossing the Homeric epithet, Combellack, "Words that Die," 24, cites the bT *Scholia* to *Il.* 16.101, which observes, "words disappear, being winged."

257 Erasmus, Adage II.i.94 (*CWE* 33:72 [ASD II.3:118]), citing *Od.* 8.408–9. Compare Erasmus, Adage III.viii.22 [*Malorum oblivio*], which cites *Il.* 4.363: "And may the gods blow all these things away and bring them to naught" [*Ta de panta theoi metamônia theien*] (*CWE* 35:291).

258 Martin, *Language of Heroes*, 18–19; Montiglio, *Silence in the Land of Logos*, 61.

259 T. Greene, "Rabelais and the Language of Malediction," 113.

260 Aristotle, *Rhetoric* 1411b11–12a, 406–7; Plutarch, *Moralia* 398a, 5:298–9; compare Cicero, *De Oratore* I.35.161, 110–11, where Cotta describes the language of his interlocutor Crassus as "swiftly winged" [*evolavit*] and full of "rushing energy" [*vim ... incitationem aspexerim*].

261 On Homeric *energeia* and *enargeia*, see Erasmus, *De Duplici Copia* (*CWE* 24:580 [ASD I.6:202]); the passage is also discussed by Cave, *Cornucopian Text*, 20, 29–30. On discussions of *enargeia* and *energeia* in Homer by his ancient scholiasts, see N.J. Richardson, "Literary Criticism in the Exegetical Scholia," 278, and Schlunk, *The Homeric Scholia and the Aeneid*, 41.

262 On Gorgias's and Democritus's understanding of the mechanics of language, see A. Ford, *Origins of Criticism*, 165–6, 174–5. For a sixteenth-century articulation of this idea, see Tyard, *The Universe*, 69, on how "air serves human understanding greatly and especially to incorporate its conceptions into words by the voice, which happens when air is knocked, pushed, and moved by the tongue and by other instruments that Nature has provided for this marvelous effect" [*l'air serve de beaucoup à l'humain entendement & singulierement à incorporer invisiblement ses conceptions en parolles par la voix, qui se fait quand l'air est frappé, poussé, & esmeu de la langue, & autres instrumens que Nature ordonne pour cest effect merveilleux*].

263 Gorgias, *Helen*, and Democritus (DK 68B21), both cited in A. Ford, *Origins of Criticism*, 176, 169–70; the Democritus passage is cited by Poliziano, *Oratio*, ed. Megna, 14. On Stoic views of Homeric language and on the view that allegory and etymology might repair the breach of "human language from its natural foundation," see Whitman, *Allegory*, 37.

264 Whitman, *Allegory*, 37; A. Berry, "Les Mithologies Pantagruelicques," 477; on the "mort spirituelle" of language, compare Defaux, "A Propos de paroles gelées et dégelées," 158,

265 See Le Caron, *Dialogues*, 288–9, discussing Plato, *Cratylus* 391d–e, and arguing that Socrates relies on Homer to "understand the nature and truth

of names" [*apprendre la cause et verité des noms*]. On the influence of the *Cratylus* on sixteenth-century commentaries on Homer, see P. Ford, *De Troie à Ithaque*, 217–19.

266 Cave, *Cornucopian Text*, 147; on Rabelais's Moses as "logotherapist, see A. Berry, "Les Mithologies Pantagruelicques," 476–7.

267 Whitman, *Allegory*, 33–4.

268 See chapters 119, 134, 143, and 144 of pseudo-Plutarch, *Life of Homer*; on the Stoic influences upon Heraclitus's *Homeric Problems*, see Russell and Konstan's introduction, xx–xxi.

269 Democritus, *DK* B18 and the discussion by A. Ford, *Origins of Criticism*, 136, 168.

270 Melanchthon, *Preface to Homer*, as cited in Cave, *Cornucopian Text*, 177.

271 Hahm, *The Origins of Stoic Cosmology*, 167–8.

272 On the meaning of Ruach, see Screech, *Rabelais*, 789. On the transformation of Homer's Aeolus by Virgil and Lucretius, see Hardie, *Cosmos and Imperium*, 90–1. Conti, *Mythologiae* 2:742, offers a conventional interpretation of Aeolus as an allegory about anger, since it is a "very useful skill to be able to turn one's anger on and off at will, just as Aeolus checks and releases the winds whenever he wants."

273 Cave, *Cornucopian Text*, 213.

274 Cave, *Cornucopian Text*, 213; Cook, *Odyssey in Athens*, 88; V. Allen, *On Farting*, 61.

275 Terry, *Mock Heroic*, 17.

276 *Homeric Hymn to Hermes*, ln. 296, in *Homeric Hymns*, ed. M.L. West, 136–7.

277 Gellius, *Noctes Atticae* III.xvii.16, 1:299; also see Rose, *Parody*, 17.

278 Frame's translation of *bûcheron* as "butcher" and Screech's as "baker" are disputable, hence my interpolation.

279 Erasmus, *Subventanea parit*, Adage III.vii.21 (*CWE* 35:229 [ASD II.6:436–7]).

280 Jonson, *Poetaster* I.ii.84, in *Works* 4:211.

281 Gager's translation is preserved in manuscript (BL Add. MS. 22,583, fols. 1–8); on his *Ulysses Redux*, see Binns, *Intellectual Culture*, 129.

282 Gager, "Ad Criticum," *Ulysses Redux*, cited in Binns, *Intellectual Culture*, 129.

283 Nashe, *Lenten Stuffe*, in *Works* 3:176. Compare the epilogue to Nash, *Quaternio*, 276, which calls Homer the "most auncient and *learnedst* of Poets" and places him first in a similar catalogue of paradoxical encomiasts, since he "writ of the Combate betweene the Frog and the Mouse."

284 Nash, *Quaternio*, Epilogue, 276.

285 See, for example, Nashe's epilogue to *Summers Last Will and Testament*, in *Works* 3:293; Coryate, *Coryats Crudities*, sigs. b2v, e1r.

286 Coryate, *Crudities*, sigs. i2r–v.

3. Spenser, Homer, and the Mythography of Strife

1 Edmund Spenser, *The Faerie Queene*, ed. Roche, 2.x.1, 2, 2.x.3, 1. All subsequent references to *The Faerie Queene* are cited parenthetically from this edition.

2 I.O. [John Ogle], *The lamentation of Troy for the death of Hector*, sig. B2r, ln. 145, calls Spenser the "only Homer living"; on Spenser's inheritance of "Homers soule," see Fitz-Geffrey, *Sir Francis Drake*, sig. B5r.

3 The 1561 statutes of the Merchant Taylors' School, modelled on those of St Paul's School, stipulate that Homer is to be taught in the upper forms, with the assistance of commentaries and dictionaries. While no particular text is dictated in the earlier statutes, a 1611 statute alludes to the preparation of an anthology for Greek study that includes *Il.* 1 through 4; see Baldwin, *William Shakespere's small Latine and lesse Greeke*, 1:417–19, 2:660. On Spenser's Greek studies at Merchant Taylors' School and Cambridge, see Judson, *The Life of Edmund Spenser*, 14, 27, 106–7; on Greek studies at Pembroke Hall, Cambridge, in the Elizabethan period, see Tilley, "Greek Studies at Cambridge in Early Sixteenth-Century England II," 443.

4 On Henry Hutchinson's book inventory, see, *Private Libraries*, ed. Fehrenbach and Leedham-Green, 4:133–9. On Spenser's "perfect" Greek, see Bryskett, *A Discourse of Civill Life*, 21. On Tunstal's gifts to Cambridge University Library, including manuscripts of Eustathius's commentary on Homer [Kk.6.29] and Johannes Tzetzes's *Chiliades* [Ee.6.35], see Oates, *Cambridge University Library*, 1:64–6. The 1558 Junius edition of Eustathius's commentary on Homer, entitled the *Copiae Cornu*, has a dedication by Lawrence Humphrey, president of Magdalen College, Oxford, who was in exile during Mary's reign in Basel, Frankfurt, and Geneva.

5 On Harvey's edition of the *Iliad*, which includes Books 6, 8, and 10 through 24, see V. Stern, *Gabriel Harvey*, 221. Given their availability as well as the religious outlook of their translators, likelier candidates for Greek-Latin editions of Homer consulted by Spenser include those by Henri Estienne, Adrian Turnebus, Sponde, and Giphanius. According to P. Ford, *De Troie à Ithaque*, 115–16, both William Cecil and George Buchanan owned copies of Turnebus's edition, now both held at Cambridge University Library.

6 Elyot, *The Boke named the Governour*, 2:360, citing Eustathius, *Comm. ad Hom. Iliadem* 10.7–10 on *Il.* 1.1; Sir John Harington, *A Preface, or rather a Briefe Apologie of Poetrie* (1591), cited from *Elizabethan Critical Essays*, ed. G.G. Smith, 2:198.

7 See Heninger, *Touches of Sweet Harmony*, 287–397, 160–3; Durling, *The Figure of the Poet in Renaissance Epic*, 123–4; Quint, *Origin and Originality*,

133–66; Quitslund, *Spenser's Supreme Fiction,* 162–3. Durling, 123, argues that analogies between a poem (or a work of art) and the cosmos often hinge on the idea of cosmic and poetic harmony as the product of a "reconciliation of opposites."

8 On the crossroads or crisis as a feature of allegorical interpretations of Achilles and Hercules, see Whitman, *Allegory*, 23; on the Renaissance iconography of the choice of Hercules and similar myths, see Bull, *The Mirror of the Gods,* 97–8.

9 For a comprehensive treatment of the sources and analogues for Spenser's golden chain, see Wolff, *Die Goldene Kette*, and Hutton, "Spenser's Adamantine Chains." Other sources and analogues for the golden chain not discussed at further length in the text of this chapter include Macrobius, *Commentary on the Dream of Scipio*; Prudentius's *Psychomachia*; Chaucer, *Troilus and Criseyde* III, ln. 1744, *Boece* II.8, *Knight's Tale* V, ls. 2987–9; Lorris and De Meun, *Roman de la Rose* XVI.786–7; numerous poems by Ronsard, including *Ode de la Paix*, *Hymne des Astres*, *Hymne d'Eternité*, *Exhortation de la Paix*, *La Paix, au Roy*; Antoine de Baïf, *Hymne de la Paix*; and Amadys Jamyn, *Hymne des Estoiles.*

10 Quattrehomme, *Discours*, 57.

11 Chapman, *Shadow of Night*, ls. 159–62, in *Poems*, ed. Bartlett, 23.

12 MacCaffrey, "Place and Patronage in Elizabethan Politics," 108; John Naunton, *Fragmenta Regalia*, 16, as cited in Whigham, *Ambition and Privilege,* 49. It is instructive to compare the social and political tensions of the Elizabethan court as represented by Spenser to the arguments of Seaford, *Reciprocity and Ritual,* 5–6, who discusses the "ideological contradiction" of the *Iliad* as the problem that "aristocratic individualism is on the one hand vital to the community and on the other hand a danger to be controlled by the community."

13 Compare Phineas Fletcher, *The Purple Island, or The Isle of Man* VIII.38, in *The Poetical Works* 2:113, which describes the "climbing minde" of Philotimus, one of Mammon's "children of the world," who perceives the world around him as a series of "rising ladders," but when he "gain'd the top, with spite accurst / Down would he fling the steps by which he clamb'red first," thus preventing anyone from imitating his ascent.

14 La Primaudaye, *The French Academie*, chapter 23, 236, chapter 1, 18.

15 Xenophon, *Cyropaedia* 8.3, trans. Holland, 186; compare *Cyropaedia* 2.4, 38, where Cyrus commands "games of price and triall of masteries" among his soldiers because "men be more willing to practise all those feats, about which ariseth an emulation and contentious desire of victory." On the role of tournament and mock combat in Elizabethan culture and Spenserian

epic, see McCoy, *The Rites of Knighthood*, 24, which argues that "mock combat" functions at times as a "socially sanctioned and carefully regulated release of aggressive energies" that may preserve concord instead of threatening it.

16 John Davies, "To the same truelie-noble Earle, and his most honorable other halfe Sir James Haies, Knight," in his *Wittes Pilgrimage*, sig. A3r.

17 Conti, *Mythologiae* 1:119. This passage is discussed in Nohrnberg, *The Analogy of The Faerie Queene*, 51, 307, and in Spenser, *Works. A Variorum Edition* 2:261 (hereafter cited as *Variorum Spenser*).

18 On the relationship between *philotimia* and envy, see Aristotle, *Rhetoric* II.x.3 [1387b]; on the difference between *zêlos* and *phthonos* (envy), see *Rhetoric* II.xi.1 [1388b] and Plutarch, *On Brotherly Love* [*Peri Philadelphous*], 486b–488a, in *Moralia* 7:292–301. On the relationship between *philotimia* and envy in ancient Greece, see Walcot, *Envy and the Greeks*, 16–18.

19 On *philotimia*, see Aristotle, *Nic. Ethics* II.7.8 [1107b], IV.3.17–18 [1123b–24b], IV.4.1–6 [1125b]; Thomas Aquinas, *Summa Theologica* II.i.q.60. art. 5, cited from Nohrnberg, *Analogy*, 46–7, 51.

20 See, for example, the description of Lucifera at *FQ* 1.iv.11–17, where she first proclaims herself equal to Zeus and is then described as striving "to match ... / Great Junoes golden chaire."

21 On the adamantine spindle of necessity, see Plato, *Rep.* 10.14 [616c].

22 Calvin, *Institutes of the Christian Religion*, 1:214, citing *Il.* 19.86.

23 [Plutarch], *Life of Homer*, 190–1.

24 Du Bartas, *The Divine Weekes and Workes*, 132. In *City of God* 5.8, Augustine follows Cicero in noting that *Od.* 18.136–7 is also invoked by the Stoics to testify to the inextricability of fate, since for them Jupiter is the "supreme god" from whom "hangs the whole chain of fates" (*City of God*, 90).

25 Quitslund, *Spenser's Supreme Fiction*, 144–5.

26 Perkins, *A Golden Chaine*, 199: "A Frame of the Doctrine of Predestination." Other contemporary theological works whose titles refer to the golden chain include Radford Mavericke, *Saint Peters Chaine: consisting of eight golden Linckes* (London, 1596); Hermann Rennechero, *Aurea Salutis Catena* (Marburg, 1597); John Andrewes, *Andrewes Golden Chaine, to link the penitent sinner unto Almighty God* (London, 1645); Johann Gerhard, *A Golden Chaine of Divine Aphorismes*, trans. Ralph Winterton (Cambridge, 1632); and William Nisbet, *A Golden Chaine of Time Leading unto Christ* (Edinburgh, 1650).

27 Boethius, *Consolation*, 4.6, 362–3, ls. 86–7; 5.2, 390–1, ls. 1–5.

28 Fraunce, *Yuychurch*, 15.

29 Bacon, *Advancement*, 79. Compare Reynolds, *Mythomystes*, in *Critical Essays*, ed. Spingarn, 1:174, who interprets the golden chain in light of Saint

Paul's instruction to remain humble and "not sawcily to leap, but by the golden linckes of that golden chaine of *Homer*, that reaches from the foote of *Jupiters* throne to the Earthe."

30 Puttenham, *The Arte of English Poesie*, in *Elizabethan Critical Essays*, ed. G.G. Smith, 2:147. On the Gallic Hercules and the use of the golden chain as a metaphor for eloquence, see Alciati, *Emblemata* (Lyon, 1550), 194, "Eloquentia fortitudine praestantior"; Valeriano, "Lingua," in *Hieroglyphica* XXXII, 39; and discussions in Nohrnberg, *Analogy*, 696, and P. Cheney, *Spenser's Famous Flight*, 142–3.

31 Wind, *Pagan Mysteries*, 119. On the use of these rhetorical devices in *FQ* 6, see *Variorum Spenser*, 6:189.

32 Quitslund, *Spenser's Supreme Fiction*, 142–6; McCabe, *Pillars of Eternity*, 158–61.

33 See Hesiod, *Theogony*, ls. 211–25.

34 Linche, *The Fountaine of Ancient Fiction*, sig. R1v; on Spenser's attitude to sleep, compare Quitslund, *Spenser's Supreme Fiction*, 175.

35 Clement, *Stromates*, 2:66–9.

36 Upton, in *Variorum Spenser*, 1:268: "Our knights do not part without mutual presents, and this is agreeable to Homer: Diomed and Glaucus, Ajax and Hector, part not without gifts, though engaged in different interests."

37 For Erasmus's adage, see pages 97–8 of this book; for Alciati's emblem "In dona hostium" [The Gifts of Enemies], which is explained by way of Homer's account (*Il.* 7.299) of the exchange of weapons between Ajax and Hector, see *Emblemata*, 181. On reciprocity and gift-giving in *Il.*, see Blundell, *Helping Friends*, 28, 87.

38 *Problèmes de la Guerre*, ed. Vernant, editor's introduction, 12. In addition to the wedding of Peleus and Thetis, Vernant also cites the example of the marriage of Cadmus and Harmony, to which Eriphylus ("lover of strife") brings a necklace that sparks discord.

39 Nohrnberg, *Analogy*, 342. Giamatti, *The Earthly Paradise and the Renaissance Epic*, 233–4, also expresses confusion at Mammon's silver stool, asking why a stool, and "Why a *silver* stool?"

40 *Ovid, Metamorphoses*, trans. Golding, 29, ls. 217–18.

41 On the motif of the deaf Odysseus in English Renaissance literature, see Harry Vredeveld, "Deaf as Ulysses to the Siren's Song: the Story of a Forgotten Topos," *RQ* 54, no. 3 (2004): 846–82.

42 Jaeger, *Paideia*, 1:20.

43 Plato, *Rep.* 10.16 [620c–d]. On Plato's reading of Odysseus, see Deneen, *The Odyssey of Political Theory*, 82, 108–11.

44 Harington, *A Preface, or rather a Briefe Apologie of Poetrie*, in *Elizabethan Critical Essays*, ed. G.G. Smith, 2:215.

45 On the iconographic relationship between temperance and Nemesis in emblems by Valeriano, Alciati, and Geoffrey Whitney, see D. Greene, "The Identity of the Emblematic Nemesis."

46 Weil, *The Iliad or the Poem of Force*, 54, argues that nemesis in Homeric epic operates according to a "geometrically stringent chastisement" that "spontaneously punishes" its victims out of a sometimes uncontrollable sense of indignation.

47 Charles Lemmi, cited in *Variorum Spenser* 2:200; Phoenix's discussion of the Erinnys, Atê, and the Litae appears at *Il.* 9.454–571.

48 Clement, *Exhortation to the Greeks*, 245.

49 W.L., "When stout Achilles heard of Helens rape," ls. 3–4 and 13–16, *Commendatory Verses*, in *Faerie Queene*, ed. Roche, 21–2. The episode is related by Apollodorus, *Library* 3.xiii.8, and alluded to by Achilles at *Il.* 9.410–15, where he describes his choice between immortal fame and a long life.

50 The four lines in question, whose authenticity have been long debated, read, "Ille ego qui quondam gracili modulatus avena / carmen et egressus silvis vicina coegi / ut quamvis avido parerent arva colono, / gratum opus agricolis, ac nunc horrentia Martis." For an English translation of the passage, see Aelius Donatus, *Life of Virgil*, 42, trans. David Wilson-Okamura (http://virgil.org/vitae/).

51 According to Whitman, *Allegory*, 23, allegorical interpretations of Achilles, like those of Hercules, focus on the "critical turning point" at which he finds himself at a crossroads or crisis.

52 See, for instance, Michael West, "Spenser and the Renaissance Ideal of Christian Heroism," and his "Spenser's Art of War," 655, arguing that Spenser demonstrates "considerable moral ambivalence about the activity of warfare."

53 On *phulattein* (to save for later; to keep in store) as a Homeric technique, see Nünlist, *The Ancient Critic at Work*, 49, discussing the bT scholiast on *Il.* 20.376.

54 Homer, *Il.* 5.739–40. In a similar vein, Quitslund, *Spenser's Supreme Fiction*, 172, notes that Spenser uses "the imagery of elemental strife" in order to "dramatize [Britomart's] emotions." For a similar reading of the temple of Concord and of Spenser's poetics of *concordia discors*, see Berger, *Revisionary Play*, 19–36; Bono, *Literary Transvaluation*, 167–90, interprets Shakespeare's treatment of the myth of Venus and Mars in *Anthony and Cleopatra* in terms of the relationship between sexual conflict and complementarity.

55 See Porphyry, *On the Homeric Cave of the Nymphs*, trans. Taylor, 158; Bieman, *Plato Baptized: Toward the Interpretation of Spenser's Mimetic Fictions*, 106–7, notes Spenser's debt to Porphyry's interpretation of the cave as a "coincidentia oppositorum."

56 Quitslund, *Spenser's Supreme Fiction*, 157.

57 Aristotle, *Nic. Ethics* VIII.1.6, 455 [1155a]: "Heracleitus says, 'Opposition unites [*antixoun sumpheron*],' and 'The fairest harmony springs from difference,' and ''Tis strife [*erin*] that makes the world go on.' Others maintain the opposite view, notably Empedocles, who declares that 'Like seeks after like [*to gar homoion tou homoiou ephiesthai*].'" Compare *Eudemian Ethics*, 1235a.

58 Both pseudo-Plutarch and Heraclitus, *Homeric Problems*, interpret Homer's Phaiakia as an Epicurean society. Pico della Mirandola, *Examen Vanitatis doctrinae gentium & Veritatis disciplinae Christianae*, in *Opera Omnia* (1573), 2:939, argues that "many believe that Epicurus drew from Homer his idea that the greatest good lies in pleasure" [*multi existiment Epicurum ex Homero traxisse summum bonum esse in voluptate*].

59 Quitslund, *Spenser's Supreme Fiction*, 156; Heraclitus, *Homeric Problems* 69.8–9, 110–11 argues that Homer confirms Empedocles's doctrine by "calling strife Ares and love Aphrodite. He therefore represents these old adversaries as giving up their former contention [*philoneikias*] and coming together in concord [*homonoian*]."

60 On "heuristic imitation," see T. Greene, *The Light in Troy*, 40–1; on Spenser's heuristic imitation of Virgil, also see Watkins, *The Specter of Dido*, 11.

61 On the accusation that Epicurus stole his philosophy of pleasure from Homer's Phaiakians, see Heraclitus, *Homeric Problems*, 79.2, 128–9; Athenaeus, *Deipnosophists* XII.7 (513a–b), which comments on *Od.* 9.5–11 as a defence of *hêdone*; and the A scholia to *Od.* 9.28, cited in Pépin, *Mythe et Allégorie*, 135. See also note 58, above. Paraphrasing Eustathius, Marcassus calls the Phaiakians "lax and unused to war, because they were brought up in soft pleasures" [*lasches et Inhabiles a la guerre, pour ce qu'ilz estoient nourris dans les molles voluptez*]. See BNF MS fonds français 12.407 (Marcassus, *Extraict de l'Odyssee d'Homere*, fol. 48v), commenting on *Od.* 6.9–10 and paraphrasing Eustathius, *Comm. ad Hom. Odysseam*, 1:235 [1549.18–22]).

62 On the maxim "He who blames contention blames nature," see Leroy, *De La Vicissitude*, 32, and my discussion on page 26 of this book.

63 Ripa, *Iconologia*, "Congiuntione delle cose humane con le divine," 72–3.

64 *Ten books of Homers Iliades*, translated out of the French by A[rthur] H[all], 135; Lucian, *Dialogue of the Gods*, in *Dialogues* 7:241.

65 In Lucian's *Charon, or the Inspectors* (*Dialogues* 2:405), Hermes recounts the story of Otus and Ephialtes to Charon, first proposing that they try something similar so as to overthrow Zeus but then pointing out that Homer "has made it possible for us to scale heaven in a jiffy with a pair of verses." The story of Otus and Ephialtes is also told by Ovid, *Metam.* 1.151–4 (ls. 171–81 in Golding's translation), and Virgil, *Georg.* 1.281–2.

66 Eustathius, *Comm. ad Hom. Iliadem,* 2:183–4, 694.60–695.30 (on *Il.* 8.10–19); Proclus, *Commentaire sur le Timée* 2:171–4; Joachim Camerarius, *Quaestiones Promiscuae*, 123–4.
67 Plato, *Theaetetus* 153d.
68 Plato, *Theaetetus* 153c.
69 Jonson, *Hymenaei*, ls. 317, 320–6, in *Works*, 7:221.
70 Knevet, *Stratiotikon*, ls. 401, 419, 458–60, 490, in *The Shorter Poems of Ralph Knevet*, 126, 129.
71 See, for instance, Ronsard's 1550 *Ode de la Paix au Roi*, ls. 43–50, where God divides the world into the four elements and "links them with adamantine nails" [*Les lia de clous d'aimant*], forcing them to love each other with a "peaceful constraint" [*paisible contrainte*]; compare *Hymne du Ciel*, ln. 115, and *Hymne des Astres*, ls. 83–4, both of which also depict the universe as bound together by an adamantine (or loving) chain [*un lien aimantin*]. Ronsard, *Œuvres Complètes*, 3:6, 7:149, 7:153.
72 Hutton, "Spenser's 'Adamantine Chains,'" 573–4; on Ronsard's use of similar images, see "Spenser's 'Adamantine Chains,'" 579, and his *Themes of Peace in Renaissance Poetry*, 106–7, 209–10.
73 For a similar account, see Fraunce, *Yuychurch*, sig. A2v, which describes Demogorgon's reduction of the confused mass of elements and "seedes of things disagreeing" into order. For Plato's account of the elements, see *Timaeus* 32b–34b. Compare Ebreo, *Dialoghi D'Amore* 2:110, which decribes how the first creature to emerge out of chaos is "Litigio" – strife, or "the division of things" [*la divisione de le cose*], and explains that this division "is called Litigio because it consists in contrariety" [*Chiama questa divisione 'litigio' perché consiste in contrarietà*].
74 Quitslund, *Spenser's Supreme Fiction*, 156, also notes that *FQ* 2's motif of elemental strife finds parallels on psychological and physiological levels, since each manifestation of a character's passionate excess or humoral disorder corresponds to an element, such as Pyrochles's wrath with fire.
75 La Primaudaye, *The French Academie*, 704.
76 Du Bartas, *The Second Weeke*, in *The Divine Weekes and Workes*, 319. Compare Jonson, *Masque of Queenes*, in *Works* 7:287, marginal note o, where Atê is represented as the chief link in an enchained procession of vices; Jonson's note explains that the "chayning of these vices" should be staged and understood "as if one lincke produc'd another, and the Dame were borne out of them all."
77 Malatesta, *Della Poesia Romanzesca,* 247, 243: "credo ancora che per la catena che hanno insieme tutte le cose humane d'attacarsi l'una con l'altra, è quasi impossibile à segregare una di loro talmente dall'altre, che stia come divisa &

ritirata da tutte, ne habbia interesse ò miscuglio con qualche sua vicina, ò contigua attione diversa da lei."

78 Lombardelli, *Discorso Intorno,* 68–70: "tutte le parti di questa sua poesia così ben habbia saputo annodare, e legare ... il prometter di cantar' il glorioso raquisto, e poi tanto sospenderlo, attraversarlo, interomperlo, e condurlo quasi in disperazione ... e con tal ... intrecciatura, e rispondenza dell'una con l'altra parte; che non mai vi rimangon dubbi, che importino, ò perturbata la memoria, ch[e] non rattacchi subito l'una cosa con l'altra: finche al fine tutti gli ostacoli cedono."

79 Nohrnberg, *Analogy*, 36; on the importance of "multiple unity" or "e pluribus unum" as a cosmological and narrative concept for Spenser, see also Heninger, *Touches of Sweet Harmony*, 147.

80 Thanks to the near-homonymic Greek words for poet [*aêdôn*] and nightingale [*aêdonis*], Homer's myth of Thamyris is often conflated with the story of Aêdôn, the daughter of Pandareüs who appears in Penelope's complaint (*Od.* 19.518–28) as well as with the nightingales who appear in Hesiod and Virgil (*Georg*. 4.514). In many post-classical allusions, the nightingale provides a mythical aetiology of poetic rivalry or competitiveness; see Du Bartas, *Divine Weekes and Workes*, 176 and Robert Burton, *The Anatomy of Melancholy* 1:262–3, who explains how Virgil's plaintive bird evolved out of Homeric *Philotimia*, comparing men who would rather die than suffer "defamation of honour" to the nightingale who "dies for shame, if another bird sing better, he languisheth and pineth away in the anguish of his spirit." On Homeric and post-Homeric myths of envy and rivalry, see Walcot, *Envy and the Greeks*, 4–6.

81 While Spenser's competitive mermaids are also indebted to the various fables by Homer, Hesiod, and Ovid mentioned above, they may also be partly inspired by the fable of Glaucus and Scylla as told by Ovid, *Metamorphoses*, Books 13 and 14, and subsequently moralized by Textor, *Officina* 5.61, 669, under the heading *Zelotypia* (Envy or Emulation).

82 *FQ* 2.vii.12, 7, 2.vii.21, 5–6. On Mammon's relationship to Strife, see Heninger, *Touches of Sweet Harmony*, 170–5; Hughes, *Virgil and Spenser*, 378; Nohrnberg, *Analogy*, 336. Spenser's sources for Atê and for Eris's intrusion into the wedding of Peleus and Thetis may include Hyginus, *Fabulae*, 92; Virgil, *Aen.* 6.280; Statius, *Thebaid* 7.50; and Chaucer, *Knight's Tale*, ln. 2005.

83 On Tasso's Armida, see Giamatti, *Earthly Paradise*, 196–7.

84 Quitslund, *Spenser's Supreme Fiction*, 170.

85 Mulcaster, *Positions*, 84. Jacob wrestles with the angel at Gen. 32.34; Satan's wrestling match with Christ is described at *Luke* 4.9–4.13 and Matt. 4.1. Rachel wrestles with Leah at Gen. 30.8 (*Geneva Bible*, sig. d1v). On wrestling

as a theological motif in Book 2 of *FQ*, see Nohrnberg, *Analogy*, 300. On the scriptural language of wrestling and its deviation from pagan concepts of agôn, see Pfitzner, *Paul and the Agon Motif*, 16–44 and 76–139.

86 Bacon, *Advancement*, 25.

87 Fraunce, *Yuychurch*, 47v. On Circe as a symbol of the elements or the seasons, see Gesner, *Moralis Interpretatio Errorum Ulyssis Homerici*, Error XI, 14r; *Ovids Metamorphoses Englished*, trans. Sandys, *On the Fourteenth Booke*, 480, explains that Circe is the daughter of Sol and Persis (daughter to Oceanus), and "Circe is so called of mixing, because the mixture of the elements is necessary in generation which cannot be performed but by the motion of the Sun." Bruno, *Heroic Frenzies*, 75, argues that Circe represents the "generative matter of all things," and that she transforms all things by means of a "secret harmony."

88 For a similar reading see Giamatti, *Earthly Paradise*, 280.

89 Spenser's character is identified by the spelling "Ate," while Homer's is distinguished by the accented spelling "Atê."

90 Colonne, *The Life and Death of Hector*, trans. Lydgate, 63–4, 81; according to Clarke, *Homer's Readers*, 48–9, Lydgate emphasizes the danger of Discord as a catalyst for the fall of Troy; Spenser may have Lydgate's version in mind as he creates the narrative structure of the 1596 *FQ*.

91 Compare Tonkin, *Spenser's Courteous Pastoral*, 32, which argues that *FQ* 4 focuses on "discord between individuals" while *FQ* 6 focuses on "discord in society"; McCoy, *Rites of Knighthood*, 138, argues that "discord and disruption prevail in the narrative" of *FQ* 4 and intensifies in *FQ* 5; C. Smith, *Spenser's Theory of Friendship*, 490–500, cited in *Variorum Spenser* 4:310, argues that the tension between concord and discord takes on a social dimension in *FQ* 4 and a cosmic one in the *Cantos of Mutability*.

92 On Ariosto's use of this metaphor, see *Orlando Furioso*, XVIII.12 and XXVI.77, trans. Harington, 138, 206.

93 Fletcher, *Purple Island* VII, 59–60, in *Works*, 2:99.

94 C. Estienne, *Dictionarium Historicum, Geographicum, Poeticum*, "Ate," 81, col. 3; Peele, *Arraignment*, ln. 20, in *Works* 1:6; on Homer's concept of Atê as a "temporary clouding" of mind, see Dodds, *The Greeks and the Irrational*, 5; compare Doyle, *Atê Its Use and Meaning*, 3–16.

95 While the common source are the descriptions in *Il.* 4 and 19, Spenser's Ate is also modelled on Virgil's Fama (*Aen.* 4.174–95), Ovid's House of Fame (*Metam.* 12.42–69), Statius's Temple of Mars (*Thebaid* 7. 40–62); Chaucer, *Knight's Tale*, ls. 1112–92, 1977–80.

96 Quitslund, *Spenser's Supreme Fiction*, 271.

97 Boccaccio, *Genealogia deorum gentilium* 1.3, 32–4; Giraldi, *De Deis Gentium*, 44b–45a; the latter description is based on Pausanias and Aristides as well as Homer and Virgil. Compare *FQ* 4.i.26–7, which describes Ate as having "squinted eyes," a "loathly mouth," and a generally "monstrous shape."

98 Roche, *Kindly Flame*, 17. For a different interpretation of the concept of friendship as likeness during the English Renaissance, see Shannon, "The Early Modern Politics of Likeness: Sovereign Reader-Subjects and Listening Kings," chapter 1 of her *Sovereign Amity*, 17–53. On the idea of a "copula sacra" or sacred embrace, see Capella, *Marriage of Philology and Mercury*, 99.

99 On this passage from *Od.* and its afterlife in classical and Renaissance theories of friendship, see chapter 1 of this book. Cicero, *De Amicitia* VII.24, mentions Empedocles as one who "sang in inspired strain ... that in nature and the entire universe whatever things are at rest and whatever are in motion are united by friendship and scattered by discord [*contrahere amicitiam, dissipare discordiam*]."

100 Plato, *Symposium* 186b; compare Plato, *Lysis*, 214a, 215c–d and Aristotle, *Nic. Ethics* VIII.1.2, 451 [1155a–b]. Compare Plutarch, "On Having Many Friends," in *Moralia*, 95a–b, which cites Empedocles's idea that "friendship draws together and holds together" striving forces, and the discussion of this passage in *The Poem of Empedocles*, 67, 120. On Spenser's understanding of friendship as based on equality and similarity, an idea found in Plato, Aristotle, Cicero, and Erasmus, see Charles G. Smith, *Spenser's Theory of Friendship* (Baltimore: Johns Hopkins University Press, 1935), 32–6.

101 Roche, *Kindly Flame*, 30.

102 In his depiction of Priamond's death at 4.iii.12–13, Spenser almost certainly has Achilles and Patroclus in mind, as well as Castor and Pollux; *Variorum Spenser* 4:184 detects an echo of Homer's description of Patroclus's death at *Il.* 16.856–7, though Priamond's soul does not, of course, flee to Hades. On Spenser's attitude towards communalism in friendship, see *Variorum Spenser* 4:332.

103 Guazzo, *Civile Conversation*, 34r, 36r. Shannon, *Sovereign Amity*, 47, observes that flattery poses an epistemological dilemma in that "mere simulation can look alot like the similitude friendship celebrates."

104 Jonson, *A Marriage at Tilt*, ls. 217–18, in *Works*, 7:395.

105 Whigham, *Ambition and Privilege*, 78–80; McCoy, *The Rites of Knighthood*, 7, 22.

106 Mulcaster, *Positions*, 247.

107 While the suffix (*bellum*=war) is self-explanatory, the prefix is not. Spenser may be adapting the Greek prefix *kam-*, which like *kata-* can mean either toward or against. A more probable reading is that Cambell shares a prefix with Cambina, whose name suggests change, transformation, or combination; together, the pair thus symbolizes either the transformation of war into peace, or their synthesis.

108 Alciati, *Emblemata* (1550), 48.

109 Prustus, *Homeri Epitheta*, "Bellum," 30. For other uses of "the strife of equal war" [*neikos homoiion polemoio*] and related phrases in Homer, see *Il.* 4.444, 9.440, 13.358, 13.635, 15.670, 18.242, 21.294; *Od.* 24.543.

110 BL 653 G8/G9/G10, *Eustathius... In Homeri et Odysseae Libros Parekbolai* (Basel: Froben, 1560), 3 vols., with marginal notes by Isaac Casaubon, 1:377, notes to Eustathius's commentary on *Il.* 4.47–50, where Casaubon cross-references the passage by writing "Vide *Iliad* u pag. 529, ln.29." Casaubon cross-references the phrase with a similar passage at *Il.* 13.358–9, where Zeus and Poseidon, intervening on opposing battle lines of the Trojan war, are described as "knotting the ends of the cords of mighty strife and equal war" [*eridos kraterês kai homoiiou ptolemoio*], pulling the two armies together in a tight knot. On this passage and the Homeric "bond of conflict," see Loraux, *The Divided City*, 113–14.

111 *Od.* 24.543; Ausonius, *Periochae Homeri Iliades et Odyssiae*, in *Oeuvres* 2:286, paraphrases this passage, describing how Zeus orders Athena to descend to Ithaca and conciliate the conflict by "effacing the past."

112 Maurice Evans, *Spenser's Anatomy of Heroism*, 186.

113 *The Faerie Queene*, ed. Roche, 1171, editor's note to *FQ* 4.iii.43; Milton, *Comus*, ls. 675–87, in John Milton, *Complete Poems and Major Prose*, ed. Hughes, 106.

114 Clement, *Exhortation to the Greeks*, 6–7, citing *Od.* 4.221.

115 Tasso, *Gerusalemme Liberata* X.65–7; on the two waters of Ardenne, see Ariosto, *Orlando Furioso* I.78. For sixteenth-century allegories of the Lotus, see Erasmus, "Lotum gustavit," Adage II.vii.62 (*CWE* 34:30), and Alciati, "In Oblivionem Patriae" [Forgetfulness of one's country], in *Emblemata* (1550), 125.

116 Lipsius, *Two Bookes of Constancie* 1.6, trans. Stradling and ed. Kirk, 83; for a later attack on the Stoic allegoresis of Helen's Nepenthe, see La Sena, *Homeri Nepenthes*, Part 4, 205, 212–13, 241. *Mnêstôr* means mindful of, while *mnêstis* means remembrance, and *mnêstêr* means wooer or suitor, as well as calling to mind. Spenser's Eumnestes (literally, happy remembrance) conveys the pleasures of memory (particularly as contained in literary or historical narrative). Nohrnberg, *Analogy*, 347–8, and Michael West,

"Spenser and the Renaissance Ideal," 1020, both note the correspondences between Homer's Nestor and Spenser's Eumnestes, and Nohrnberg also points out that the equation of tranquillity and forgetfulness is a problematic concept throughout *FQ* 2. My reading of Cambina is also indebted to Detienne, *The Masters of Truth in Archaic Greece*, 48, and Loraux, *The Divided City*, 155–8.

117 *Homeri Quae Extant Omnia*, ed. Sponde, 1:175 on *Il.* 10.10.

118 O[gle], *The Lamentation of Troy*, A4r; *Hecubaes Mishaps*, in *Fennes Frutes*. On the Homeric dimensions of Elizabethan complaint literature, see Heald, *Tears for Dido*.

119 La Sena, *Homeri Nepenthes*, 213, 240, 248.

120 Persona, *Noctes Solitariae*, Colloquy 12, 84–6.

121 Chapman, *Ovids Banquet of Sence*, stanza 10, in *Poems*, ed. Bartlett, 55; Sir John Davies, "Of Tobacco," ls. 3–4, in *Poems*, 144.

122 Eustathius, *Comm. ad Hom. Odysseam*, 1:160 [1493.58–63], on *Od.* 4.220–3.

123 La Sena, *Homeri Nepenthes*, Part 3, 146–7. For the argument that Renaissance interpretations of *Od.* tend to "consider the problems of the aftermath," including the aftermath of war, see Van Der Laan, "'What Virtue and Wisdom Can Do,'" 5.

124 Compare Petit, *Homeri Nepenthes*, B3r, E6v, which distinguishes between true "laetitia" and "inania gaudia," the former produced by Nepenthe and the latter by alcohol; see also La Sena, *Homeri Nepenthes*, 128.

125 Compare Quitslund, *Spenser's Supreme Fiction*, 156, commenting on Hate and Love bound by Concord: "the fact that the younger is always victorious in debate does not deprive the elder of legitimacy ... Hate is evident in the natural strife among the elements, while the most basic form of love appears in their tempering throughout the sublunary creation."

126 Several critics identify the temple of Venus in Boccaccio, *Teseida* VII.51–66, as a source for Spenser's temple; see also *Variorum Spenser* 4:226 on the episode illustrating the Empedoclean doctrine of *philia* and *eris* or the philosophical doctrine that "universal concord is established by particular disagreements and opposite principles." Alanis Insulis, *Complaint of Nature*, Metre V, ls. 1–2; Boethius, *Consolation of Philosophy*, 2.8, 226–7, ls. 1–4, 15–21.

127 *The Poem of Empedocles*, Fragment 25, 214–17, ls. 1, 7–8, 19. Much of Spenser's knowledge of Empedoclean cosmology is probably derived from other classical sources, many of which are reproduced in Inwood's edition of the *Fragments* under the headings "Fragments in Context" and "Testimonia." These sources include Diogenes Laertius, *Lives of the Philosophers* VIII, 51–77; Lucretius, *DRN* 1.714–33; Plutarch, *De Tranquilitate Animi* 474b–c,

and *Isis and Osiris* 370e; Aristotle, *Eudemian Ethics* VII.1 [1235a10–12], *Metaphysics* I.iv [985a21–b3].

128 *The Poem of Empedocles*, Fragment 61, 242–3, ls. 5–9.

129 Paraphrasing Boccaccio, *Genealogia deorum gentilium* 5.35, 198, E.K. writes, "Bocace saith, that they be painted naked ... the one having her backe towarde us, and her face fromwarde, as proceeding from us: the other two toward us, noting double thanke to be due to us for the benefit, we have done" (*Aprill*, *SC*, gloss to ln. 109, in *Shorter Poems*, ed. McCabe, 69). On Spenser's reliance upon the twinned impulses of "forward" and "fromward" (or "froward") movement, see Nelson, *The Poetry of Edmund Spenser*, 180–98, and Quitslund, *Spenser's Supreme Fiction*, 156, both arguing that Spenser's notion of Temperance is based on affective "conflicts between innate 'forward' and 'froward' tendencies."

130 Roche, *Kindly Flame*, 163; Nohrnberg, *Analogy*, 630.

131 On Spenser's possible sources for the myth of the two Helens, which include Book 6, chapter 23 of Conti's *Mythologiae* and Charles Estienne's entry on Proteus in his *Dictionarium*, see Roche, *Kindly Flame*, 152–63.

132 *Hermeias Alexandrinus, In Platonis Phaedrum Scholia* 98–101, ed. Couvreur, 77–8, glossing Plato, *Phaedrus* 243a; see the discussion in Nohrnberg, *Analogy*, 117. Compare Proclus, *Lucubratio* 21, 87r, which explains that Homer's blindness makes him blind to physical beauty but able to see with the mental eyes of contemplation [*mentis oculo contemplatus*], while Helen, by contrast, "represents the whole sensual world and the beauty it generates, over which our spirits are in perpetual conflict" [*omnem sensilis mundi & generationis pulchritudinem significare, circa quam animaru[m] pugna perpetuò committitur*].

133 Boccaccio, *Genealogia deorum gentilium* 4.47, 153; see also 3.22, 114, following Lactantius in glossing the girdle as a guarantor of marital fidelity ("*Hoc cingulum, dicit Lactantius ... Venerem non ferre nisi ad honestas nuptias*"). On Spenser's reliance on Boccaccio in this episode, see *Variorum Spenser* 4:193.

134 Aristotle, *Nic. Ethics* VII.6.3 [1149b17]

135 *The Iliad of Homer*, trans. Pope, *Observations on the Fourteenth Book*, 688, note to ln. 218.

136 Plato, *Theaetetus* 43–5 [152e]; Socrates is referring to *Il.* 14.201, 14.302, and concludes from these passages that "all things are the offspring of flow and motion"; Montaigne, *Apology for Raymond Sebond*, in *Complete Essays* 2.12, 455. For similar readings, see Stobaeus, *Eclogae* 1.10.11b, and Empedocles, Fragment 25, ls. 7–8, both cited in *The Poem of Empedocles*, *Testimonia* A33b, 165–6, and *Fragments*, 215–16.

137 Landino explains that the highest link in Homer's golden chain is the *Essentia Dei*, and the lowest is *hulê*, or matter, "the mother of all forms." See Landino, *Disputationes*, 177–9, cited in Quitslund, *Spenser's Supreme Fiction*, 113; compare Browne, *Garden of Cyrus*, in *Major Works*, 386, on Proteus as "the Symbole of the first matter."

138 On Proteus as unformed or "shapeless matter," see Heraclitus, *Homeric Problems*, 65.1, 104–5; Eustathius, *Comm. ad Hom. Odysseam*, 1:174 [1503.9–11, 1503.20–1]. This interpretation is also present in the Homeric scholia: see *Scholia Graeca in Homeri Odysseam* 1 209, on *Od.* 4.384; compare Conti, *Mythologiae*, 2:726. For critical discussions of Proteus's cave, see Nohrnberg, *Analogy*, 581–4; Bieman, *Plato Baptized*, 106–7; and Giamatti, "Proteus Unbound," 437–75. On the figure of Proteus in the Renaissance, see Pesic, "Shapes of Proteus in Renaissance Art," and Burns, "A Proverb of Versatile Mutability."

139 Evans, *Spenser's Anatomy of Heroism*, 183.

140 Della Porta, *Natural Magick* 1.4, 6; 1.6, 7–8.

141 On the relationship between the fate of Marinell and that of Achilles, see Roche, *Kindly Flame*, 188–9; Michael West, "Spenser and the Renaissance Ideal," 1025.

142 For the epithet "silver-footed Thetis," see *Il.* 1.538 and 18.369. Capella, *De Nuptiis Philologiae et Mercurii*, in *Martianus Capella* 2, 5; Insulis, *Complaint of Nature*, Prose III, ls. 76–79.

143 [Plutarch], *Life of Homer*, section 93, 159, which cites *Il.* 14.246 ("Oceanus who gave birth to all things") and compares the passage to Thales; compare Eustathius, *Comm. ad Hom. Iliadem* 3:214–15 [978.8–61] on *Il.* 14, 202–4 on why Homer calls Oceanus the father of all things because water is the foundation of all the other elements and because humidity is the principal cause of generation. For a sympathetic reading of the allegorical meanings that accrue to Oceanus in Virgil and Spenser, see Quint, *Origin and Originality*, 33–7, 149–66.

144 L. Morgan, *Patterns of Redemption*, 32–3. On Virgil's debt to Hellenistic allegories of Homer, see also Morgan, 92–5, and Hardie, *Cosmos and Imperium*, 36–7, 51–2. On the associations between Homer and Ocean, see also Brink, "Ennius and the Hellenistic Worship of Homer," 553–6. Virgil's treatment of the transformation of Proteus and of the songs of Clymene (*Georg.* 4.345–7) and Iopas (*Aen.* 1.742ff) each offer elemental interpretaions of Homeric epic.

145 Mornay, *Christian Religion*, 9, 132; Lambinus, *Pridie quam Homeri Iliadis Librum A. Explicare*, 18, which holds that the union of Ares and Aphrodite, as well as the conflicts between Pallas and Ares and Apollo and Poseidon, represent the Empedoclean principle of love and strife as well as the

agreement and hostility among the four elements [“*duobus aliis principiis amicitia, & lite: per quae elementorum qualitates partim co[n]cordeis, partim inter se contrarias significat*”]. The association of Homer with the doctrine of Thales [“*omnium rerum initium aquae*”] also appears in Poliziano, *Oratio*, ed. Megna, 20. Classical sources linking Homer and Thales include Heraclitus, *Homeric Problems*, 22.1–22.7, 40–3; Stobaeus, *Eclogae* I.10.2; and Plutarch, *Isis and Osiris*, 364d.

146 On the wedding of Peleus and Thetis, see Conti, *Mythologiae*, 2:560. Conti goes on to explain that Discord was absent from the wedding because units of matter, once created, cannot survive unless “they get along with each other.”

147 Lemaire, *Illustrations de Gaule*, 1:275; see also Kem, *Trojan Legend*, 20. *Ovide Moralisé*, 4.11, 152, ls. 1418–29, also explains the elemental and humoural allegories conveyed by Peleus and Thetis.

148 Cymochles’s name presumably derives from *kyma-* (wave), and *-kleis* (a bar or bolt) or *-kleiô* (to shut, close, or bar), thus accurately describing Phaedria’s enervating effect on him. The suffix of Cymodoce’s name derives either from *dochê* (receptacle, reception) or *dokê* (vision, fancy), the former suggestive of her overprotective behaviour towards her son and the latter perhaps suggestive of her fearful reactions to Proteus’s prophecy. In Book 3, she is referred to as Cymoent (from *kyma-* and either *entasis*, tension or limitation, or *entanyuô*, to limit, strain, or stretch tight), no doubt signifying her desire to protect Marinell by limiting his exposure to the fluctuations of fortune and love. These etymologies confirm Quitslund’s remark (*Spenser’s Supreme Fiction*, 154) that Spenser’s sea is “an ally of fortune and a symbol of it.” For a similar reading of the aquatic imagery in *FQ* 2, see Quint, *Epic and Empire*, 249.

149 D. Cheney, *Spenser’s Image of Nature*, 235; at 224, he argues that the comparison between Paris and Calidore “reminds the reader that during his stay on Mount Ida Paris not only courted and won Oenone, but was involved also in the choice which occasioned the Trojan War.”

150 Stewart, “Spenser and the Judgment of Paris,” 182

151 D. Cheney, *Spenser’s Image of Nature*, 231, 226.

152 Clay, *The Wrath of Athena*, 176.

153 Statius, *Thebaid* 6.358; 6.360–1: “*orsa deum ... / ... tunc aperit, quis fulmen agat, quis sidera ducat / spiritus, unde animi fluviis, quae pabula ventis.*”

154 Spenser confuses Mount Pelion, where the wedding took place, with Hæmus Hill; *Variorum Spenser* 6:299 notes that the error is probably due

to Spenser's misreading of Ovid, *Metam.* 11.229, which begins the story of Peleus and Thetis with the phrase "Et sint Haemoniae."
155 Speroni, *Dialogo della Discordia*, in *Dialoghi*, 72a–b, 71a.
156 Nohrnberg, *Analogy*, 80, 749–51; Lucian's *Parliament of the Gods* casts Momus as the protagonist of an account of an Olympian assembly that attempts to purge divine society of its aliens and subversives.
157 Fraunce, *Yuychurch*, B2v; compare P. Fletcher, *The Purple Island* VII.51, in *Works*, 97, whose Eris is a shrewish lover of contention whose weapons are "bitter words" and who insists upon having the "last word" or else she will "never leave to scold."
158 Peele, *Arraignment*, in *Works* 1:5; Baron, *Apologie for Paris*, 5. The source for both works, as well as for Spenser, may be Apuleius, whose retelling of the story of the "rusticall Judge and shepheard appointed by the counsell of great Jupiter, [who] sold his judgement for a little pleasure" is moralized by the lament that "many of our judges now a daies sell their judgements for money." See Apuleius, *The Golden Asse* 10.46, 257.
159 Du Bartas, *Divine Weekes and Workes*, Week 1, Day 1, 19.
160 Augustine, *Citie of God* 3.25, 143; 19.13, 770.
161 Leslie, *Spenser's "Fierce Warres and Faithfull Loves,"* 35.
162 Heninger, *Touches of Sweet Harmony*, 149, 176.
163 Wilson, *Ransom, Revenge, and Heroic Identity*, 113.
164 Heraclitus, *Fragment* LXXXII (Origen, *Contra Celsum* 6.28), in *Life and Thought of Heraclitus*, 62–3; editor's commentary, 205–7. Heraclitus, *Homeric Problems*, 49.2–49.3, 86–7 provides one of several interpretations of the shield that argues that it its border, depicting the "great might of Oceanus" [*mega sthenos Okeanoio*, *Il.* 18.607), parent of all the gods, represents the universal, complementary cosmic and political forces at work on both sides of the shield.
165 Heraclitus, *Fragment* LXXV (Aristotle, *Nic. Ethics* VIII.1.6 [1155b]), cited from *Life and Thought of Heraclitus*, 66–7, and commentary, 205–7.
166 Spenser may also have been familiar with the doctrines of the Presocratic Heraclitus through Origen, *Contra Celsum* 6.42, which attacks Celsus for endorsing Heraclitus's doctrine that a "divine war" governs the universe and that "everything comes into being through strife and necessity" (trans. Chadwick, 357). This passage is based on Heraclitus, *Fragment* LXXXII, in *Life and Thought of Heraclitus*, 66. On the sixteenth-century interest in Heraclitus, see Joukovsky, *Le Feu et le Fleuve*, and chapter 2 of this book.
167 Quitslund, *Spenser's Supreme Fiction*, 270.

168 Spenser's recognition of the reparative function of Themis and her daughters the Litae is reinforced by the allusion to Pyrrha and Deucalion in the Proem to *FQ* 5: in Ovid's account (*Metam.* 1.371–494) it is Themis – the goddess of law and custom – who assists the pair by giving them the riddle that, once solved, enables them to salvage humanity from its near-destruction after the flood.

169 Spenser's representation of the Litae is probably also indebted to Hesiod, *Theogony*, 145, ls. 901–2, and to Conti, *Mythologiae* 4.16, 130, which both identify the Horai (Eunomia, Dikê, and Eirênê), and not the Litae, as the daughters of Jove and Thetis. Spenser also may have known Alciati, *Emblemata* 130: "Remedies ascend a steep and difficult path; woes descend in a downward direction" [*Remedia in arduo, mala in prono esse*], fig. 10 of this book, which depicts Atê tumbling down from heaven while the crippled Litae toil up a rocky hill. On the iconography of this episode, see *Variorum Spenser* 5:241, and Aptekar, *Icons of Justice*, 16–21.

170 Taplin, "The Shield of Achilles within the *Iliad*," in *Oxford Readings*, ed. Cairns, 357, 361.

171 Alciati, *Emblemata* (1550), 35, based on *Od.* 11.541–5; on Paridell's perception of injustice and partiality amongst the gods, see Roche, *Kindly Flame*, 62–3.

4. Chapman's Ironic Homer

1 Randolph, *The Muses looking-glasse*, 50–1. The epigraph is cited from Tasso, *Discourses on the Heroic Poem*, 163.

2 Randolph, *Muses*, 54, 50, 54. The exchange as a whole is probably indebted to Lucian's *The Fisherman, or The Dead Come to Life*, which contains an exchange between Plato and *Parrhêsiadês* [Blunt Speaker] in which the latter explains, "Homer, in whom I had my greatest hope, is useless to me. I suppose I must take refuge with Euripides" (*Dialogues*, 3:7).

3 Aristotle, *Nic. Ethics* IV.7.15, 244–5 [1127a].

4 Randolph, *Muses*, 50.

5 Unless otherwise noted, all quotations from Chapman's translation of the *Iliad* and *Odyssey* are cited from *Chapman's Homer: the Iliad* and *Chapman's Homer: the Odyssey*, ed. Nicoll. On the use of *skôptein* and related terms by Homer's ancient scholiasts, see Nünlist, *The Ancient Critic at Work*, 214. Chapman's conception of the term *scopticè* is very close to that of Johannes Scapula, *Lexicon*, col. 1490, who defines *skôptikos* as "qui scommatis dicterisq[ue]; falsis incessere solet. Exponitur etiam, cavillis valens, mordax, dicax." According to Schoell, *Etudes sur l'Humanisme*, 147–50, Chapman relied heavily upon Scapula's lexicon.

6 For critical treatments of Homeric irony, see Lateiner, *Sardonic Smile*; A. Dekker, *Ironie in De Odyssee*; Peradotto, *Man in the Middle Voice*; C. Segal, "*Kleos* and its Ironies in the *Odyssey*"; Seeskin, "The Comedy of Gods in the *Iliad*"; Pucci. *The Song of the Sirens*, 22–5; DeJong, *Narrators and Focalizers*, 81–7; *The Iliad: A Commentary*, ed. Kirk, 1:284 (on *Il.* 3.152), 2:333 (on *Il.* 8.452–3), and 4:316 (on *Il.* 16.7–19). On the ancient and Byzantine tradition of ironic interpretations of Homer, see Stanford, *Ambiguity*, 64, 103.

7 MacLure, *George Chapman*, 189; Lord, *Homeric Renaissance.* Lord's *Heroic Mockery* does intermittently address the comic dimensions of Homeric epic but nowhere acknowledges Chapman's recognition of them; Gutsell, in *Irony in the Fallen World*, 16, 85, is unusual in noticing Chapman's interest in Homeric irony.

8 J. Stephens, *Essays and Characters*, 29.

9 Hoskyns, *Directions for Speech and Style*, 125; Joseph Hall, *Virgidemiarum* 3 (London, 1598), Prologue, 43.

10 Compare Shaftesbury, *Characteristics* 1:71–2, also cited in N. Knox, *The Word Irony*, 44: "[i]f Men are forbid to speak their minds seriously on certain subjects, they will do it ironically. If they are forbid to speak at all upon such Subjects, or if they find it really dangerous to do so; they will then redouble their Disguise, involve themselves in Mysteriousness, and talk so as hardly to be understood."

11 N. Knox, *The Word Irony*, 147; Peacham, *Garden of Eloquence*, 38–9, defines *Mycterismus* as a "privie kind of mocke ... yet not so privie but that it may well be perceived," explaining that even this more rudimentary and obvious form of irony should not be directed towards "simple and ignorant persons, which do want the capacitie & subtlety of wit to perceive it."

12 Chapman, *Ovids Banquet of Sence*, title page, in *Poems*, 428. On the epigraph and its relationship to Chapman's irony, see Waddington, "Chapman and Persius," 158–62.

13 Dane, *The Critical Mythology of Irony*, 11.

14 Homer, *Ten Bookes of Homers Iliades*, trans. Hall, Preface, sig. A2v, 25.

15 Fraunce, *The Arcadian Rhetorike*, ed. Seaton, 10.

16 *Iliad*, trans. Chapman, 342, marginal note to 16.677–82 [=745–50]; Fraunce, *Arcadian Rhetorike*, 68–9. Fraunce also praises Thersites's speech as an example of *paronomasia*, or wordplay; at page 13, he cites Achilles's speech to Thetis in *Il.* 1 as an example of paralepsis or *Praeterito*, a subset of irony.

17 On the use of these and other terms by Eustathius and Hermogenes, see Lindberg, *Studies in Hermogenes and Eustathios*, 165, 168–9, 258–60.

18 *Iliad*, trans. Chapman, "Preface to the Reader," 17, ln. 160.

19 D. Knox, *Ironia*, 153. Knox identifies the Latin translation of the pseudo-Plutarchan *Life*, printed in Sebastian Castellio's 1567 Latin translation of

Homer, as an important source for the transmission of terms and concepts related to irony.

20 Compare Chapman, *Shadow of Night*, in *Poems*, 19, Dedicatory Epistle to Mathew Roydon.

21 *Iliad*, trans. Chapman, 470, marginal note to 23.582–83 [= 674–5].

22 Aristotle, *Nic. Ethics*, IV.7.15 [1127a].

23 *Iliad*, trans. Chapman, 23.584, 23.589 [= 670; 677], 23.471.

24 [Plutarch], *Life of Homer*, 135.

25 *Iliad*, trans. Chapman, 70–1, commentary to 2.355 [= 408].

26 *Iliad*, trans. Chapman, 71–2, commentary to 2.355 [=408].

27 *Iliad*, trans. Chapman, 3.234–6 [= 213–15], 80. It was a commonplace during the sixteenth century that the *Iliad* represented the three chief styles of oratory: Nestor the Grand style, Odysseus the middle style, and Menelaus the low style.

28 *Iliad*, trans. Chapman, 3.242–3 [= 221–2], 80. Philostratus, *Heroikos*, 112–13, describes Odysseus as "skilled in public speaking" and as a "dissembler" [*eirôna*]; Demetrius, *On Style*, 427 and 499, notes the forceful [*deinotês*] quality of Odysseus's speech.

29 *Iliad*, trans. Chapman, 89, commentary to 3.234 [= 213], responding to Sponde's commentary on *Il.* 3.213–16 (*Homeri Quae Extant Omnia*, 1:55). Liddell and Scott translate *epitrochadên* as "trippingly, fluently, glibly"; Chapman's definition reveals his recognition that the word is related to *epitrechô*, to run over, to graze the surface, to treat lightly.

30 *Iliad*, trans. Chapman, 89, commentary to 3.324; Liddell and Scott define *ligus* as both "clear, whistling" and as "shrilly."

31 *Iliad*, trans. Chapman, 42, introductory commentary to book 1. Compare Poliziano, *Ambra*, ls. 517–19, in *Silvae*, ed. Fantazzi, 102–3, on Homer's depiction of the triumph of harmony over strife in the "infant world" as "natural causes conspir[e] together in an aggressive alliance, [making] discordant accords, and engendering seeds of things [*infantes cunabula saecli, / seu conspirantes pugnaci foedere causas / discordemque fidem et genitalia semina rerum*].

32 On the Homeric cosmos as defined by "the opposition of contraries," see Austin, "The One and the Many in the Homeric Cosmos," 229; [Plutarch], *Life of Homer*, 164–7. On Chapman's understanding of the "contrarieties" of character, see Gutsell, *Irony in the Fallen World*, 16; discussing Chapman, *Tragedie of Biron* 5.3.189–94.

33 Compare Porphyry, *Homeric Questions*, ed. MacPhail, 83, who observes that Homer depicts Paris (at *Il.* 3.441) as "simultaneously ... bold and cowardly in war ... to show what sort of man he was."

34 *Iliad*, trans. Chapman, 90, commentary to 3.235 [=215].

35 *Iliad*, trans. Chapman, 90, commentary to 3.325.

36 Ben Jonson, *Discoveries*, in *Works*, 8:625. Earlier in the *Discoveries* (574), Jonson bears out this observation by contrasting Homer's Thersites, who "speak[s] without judgement, or measure," with Odysseus, a "long-thinking man" who thinks "before hee speaks." The sentiment derives from Quintilian, *Inst. Orat.* II.i.30, and Seneca, *Epistolae* 114.1.
37 *Iliad*, trans. Chapman, 89, commentary to 3.235.
38 *Iliad*, trans. Chapman, 71, commentary to 2.355.
39 *Iliad*, trans. Chapman, 71, commentary to 2.355.
40 *Iliad*, trans. Chapman, 71, commentary to 2.355.
41 See Erasmus, *De Copia*, *CWE* 24:485.
42 For example, see *Iliad*, trans. Chapman, 2.356–8 [= 408–9], 56–7 and commentary, 71–2, where Menelaus comes unbidden [*automatos*] to dinner with Agamemnon, a scene that according to Chapman is narrated "*Scopticè*, or by way of irrision." Sponde's translation of *Il.* 2.408 (*Homeri Quae Extant Omnia*, 1:38) acknowledges that some readers understand the poet to praise Menelaus here, while others understand the passage as condemnatory.
43 *Iliad*, trans. Chapman, 90, commentary to 3.235; Helen refers to the "warlike Spartan King" [*arêiphilos Menelaos*] at 3.252 [= 232] and the epithet is used again by the herald Idaeus in the Greek text at *Il.* 3.253, though Chapman does not translate it.
44 *Iliad*, trans. Chapman, 90, commentary to 3.235. The reading is borrowed in part from Sponde (*Homeri Quae Extant Omnia*, 1:75), who similarly concludes that to award Menelaus the epithet may appear "ridiculum" depending on how it is interpreted.
45 Porphyry, *Homeric Questions*, ed. MacPhail, 116–17, commenting on *Il.* 6.265.
46 *Iliad*, trans. Chapman, 13.542–3 [= 602–3], 267.
47 Chapman frequently marks the "insultations" exchanged between soldiers in battle. At *Il.* 11.319–35, 225, he notes how Diomed "insults on Hector" and Paris "insults on Diomed"; at *Il.* 14.375–88, 291–2, his marginal notes read "Polydamas his insultation" and "Ajax insults in requitall of Polydamas," and a marginal note at 344 (*Il.* 16.762) reads "Hector's insultation over Patroclus."
48 *Iliad*, trans. Chapman, 13.570–4 [= 636–9], 268.
49 *Iliad*, trans. Chapman, 277, commentary to 13.556. On the convention of the "flyting exchange" in the *Iliad*, see Martin, *Language of Heroes*, 127; Lateiner, "The *Iliad*: an unpredictable classic," chapter 2 of *The Cambridge Companion to Homer*, ed, Fowler, 15–23; Parks, *Verbal Dueling in Heroic Narrative*, 42–5; Fenik, *Typical Battles Scenes in the Iliad*, 219–28.
50 *Iliad*, trans. Chapman, 13.562 [= 626], 268.
51 *Iliad*, trans. Chapman, 277, commentary to 13.556. Chapman is principally responding to a note in Sponde's translation (*Homeri Quae Extant Omnia*, 1:255), which asserts that Helen was raped before she married Menelaus.

52 *Iliad*, trans. Chapman, 278, commentary to 13.556.
53 *Iliad*, trans. Chapman, 278, commentary to 13.556.
54 Booth, *Rhetoric of Irony*, 25.
55 *Iliad*, trans. Chapman, 278–9, commentary to 13.556.
56 Chapman, *Ovids Banquet of Sence*, "To the Trulie Learned ... Mathew Royden," in *Poems*, 49.
57 Chapman, *The Shadow of Night*, "To my Deare and Most Worthy Friend Master Mathew Royden," and *Ovids Banquet*, "To ... Mathew Royden," both in *Poems*, 19, 49.
58 *Iliad*, trans. Chapman, "Preface to the Reader," 15.
59 *Odyssey*, trans. Chapman, 211, marginal note to 12.101.
60 Chapman, *Ovids Banquet*, "To ... Matthew Royden," in *Poems*, 49.
61 Chapman, *Ovids Banquet*, "To ... Matthew Royden," in *Poems*, 50; *Iliad*, trans. Chapman, "Preface to the Reader," 18.
62 *The Iliad of Homer*, trans. Pope, 166, *Observations on the Third Book*, note to ln. 278.
63 *Iliad*, trans. Pope, "Speeches or Orations," in *Poetical Index*, 1169–70.
64 *Iliad*, trans. Chapman, 17.488–9 [= 569–70], 363.
65 *Iliad*, trans. Chapman, 370, commentary to 17.489; compare *Homeri Quae Extant Omnia*, ed. Sponde, 1:329 on *Il*. 18.570.
66 *Iliad*, trans. Chapman, 370, commentary to 17.489.
67 *Iliad*, trans. Chapman, 9, "To the Reader," ls. 109–10 and marginal note. Ironically enough, Chapman's translations are full of small misprints and errors, as Loane, "Misprints," points out.
68 *Iliad*, trans. Chapman, 17.71–3 [= 93–5] and marginal note, 350. Chapman may read Menelaus's speech as a comic version of the battlefield deliberations made by Achilles, Hector, Agenor, and Odysseus at other places in the *Iliad*, for instance at 11.360–1 [=407–10], 226, where Odysseus debates whether he should risk death in battle or "flie the ods in feare" and suffer the "high dishonour" faced by "pale cowards."
69 Elsewhere in *Il*. 17, Chapman notes the poet's "direct scoffe" and "notable Ironie" against Menelaus: see *Iliad*, trans. Chapman, 365–6, 370–1, notes to 17.581 and 17.611 and commentary to 17.489 and to 17.588.
70 *Iliad*, trans. Chapman, "Preface to the Reader," 16–17.
71 *Iliad*, trans. Chapman, 42, introductory commentary to Book 1.
72 Chapman uses the term "abuse" several times to describe the misinterpretations of his predecessors: see his discussion of the "strange abuse" of the term *arizêlos* (commentary to *Il.* 2.275, 70) and his attack against those who "abuse the name of Criticks" in his commentary to *Il.* 13.556, 277.
73 *Iliad*, trans. Chapman, marginal notes to 1.521 (p. 39); 2.193 and 2.215 (52); 3.417 (85); 3.458 (87); 4.430 and 4.439 (104); 5.403 (120). Homer's

ancient scholiasts were likewise attentive to sounds and rhythms, and to the representation of various noises; on this point, see N.J. Richardson, "Literary Criticism in the Exegetical Scholia," in *Oxford Readings in ancient literary criticism*, ed. Laird, 205–7.

74 *Iliad*, trans. Chapman, 3.162–3 [= 153–5], 78.

75 *Iliad*, trans. Chapman, 89, commentary to 3.162.

76 *Iliad*, trans. Chapman, 89, commentary to 3.162.

77 *Odyssey*, trans. Chapman, 12.135–7 [= 85–7] and marginal note, 212.

78 *Iliad*, trans. Chapman, 468, marginal note to 23.489–96 [=576–85] and to 504–5 [=587–8].

79 *Iliad*, trans. Chapman, 23.505–8 [= 587–90], 468.

80 *Iliad*, trans. Chapman, 23.515–18, 469.

81 *Iliad*, trans. Chapman, 17.587, 589–91 [= 674–8], 365 and commentary, 371.

82 On the Homeric simile as a means of "ironical inversion," see Buxton, "Similes and other Likenesses," chapter 9 of *The Cambridge Companion to Homer*, ed. Fowler, 149.

83 *Iliad*, trans. Chapman, 12.433–4 [= 433–5] and marginal note, 251.

84 *Iliad*, trans. Chapman, 251, marginal note to 12.426–31, paraphrasing *Homeri Quae Extant Omnia*, ed. Sponde, 1:238 on 12.432–3: "Admiranda & penè inimitabilis comparatio."

85 Nashe, preface to Robert Greene, *Menaphon* (1589), in Nashe, *Works*, ed. McKerrow, 3:314.

86 Demetrius, *On Style* 2.84, 401–2.

87 Longinus, *On the Sublime* 1.7, 189.

88 Longinus, *On the Sublime*, 189.

89 Quintilian, *Inst. Orat*. VIII.vi.54 (3:332–3).

90 Ramus, *Scholae in Liberales Artes*, 296–9, defines irony as a change of meaning "from opposite to opposite" [*ex oppositis ad opposita*] while Prideaux, *Sacred Eloquence,* 12, follows Cicero in defining irony as the "turning upside down of a thing, or contrary to the right form."

91 *Odyssey*, trans. Chapman, 5, "To Robert Earl of Somerset," ls. 85–9.

92 Shankman, *Pope's Iliad,* 103–4. Chapman mentions Longinus by name in his dedicatory epistle to the Earl of Somerset (*Odyssey*, 5, ln. 87). Shankman claims that "no other Elizabethan or Jacobean critic, apart from Chapman, appears ever to have mentioned Longinus," a claim I have not been able to disprove. Shankman suggests that Chapman could have read Longinus in Robortello's 1554 edition, although the passage of the *Peri Hupsous* cited by Chapman in his epistle to Somerset also appears in the general introductory remarks of Eustathius's commentary on *Od.*, a more likely source for Chapman, since he cites this text elsewhere in his commentary.

93 Aristotle, *Poetics*, 41 [1448b33–7].

94 Poliziano, *Ambra*, ls. 560–1, in *Silvae*, 103–4.
95 *Odyssey*, trans. Chapman, "To the Earle of Somerset," 5, ls.100–2; *Iliad*, trans. Chapman, "To the High Borne Prince of Men," 6.
96 Poliziano, *Ambra*, ls. 479, 519–20, in *Silvae*, 98–9, 102–3.
97 *Odyssey*, trans. Chapman, 8.489–91 [= 359–62] and marginal note, 141.
98 Plato, *Symposium*, 197e, in *Plato III*, 160–1.
99 Plato, *Phaedrus*, 267a, in *Plato I*, 538–9.
100 On the concept of the *spoudaiogeloion*, a term also used by Cynic and Stoic philosophers to describe their habit of "speaking the truth under a jest," see Grant, *The Ancient Rhetorical Theories of the Laughable*, 20. At *Gorgias* 481b–c (*Plato* III, 378–9), Socrates is asked whether he is serious [*spoudazei*] or joking [*paizei*], a question to which he never provides an entirely satisfactory response. See also Aristotle, *Rhetoric* 466 [III.18.7], which praises Gorgias as skilful in creating the dignified irony that consists in opposing or "confound[ing] [*enantiôn*] his opponents' earnest [*spoudên*] with jest [*gelôti*] and their jest with earnest [*gelôta spoudê*]."
101 Verdenius, "Gorgias' Doctrine of Deception," 122–3.
102 Plato, *Phaedrus*, 261b–c; on the relationship between Homer and the sophists, see also Plato, *Protagoras*, 316d; A. Ford, *Origins of Criticism*, 161–87; Griffith, "Contest and Contradiction," 187; Verdenius, "Doctrine of Deception," 118–27; K. Morgan, *Myth and Philosophy*, 111, 170–1.
103 Plato, *Symposium*, 216e, describes how Socrates, like the Silenus, must be "caught ... in a serious moment and opened" so as to reveal the "divine and golden" [*theia kai chrusa*] wisdom inside.
104 *Odyssey*, trans. Chapman, "To the Earle of Somerset," 4–5, ls. 71–4.
105 Plato, *Sophist*, 234c–d. See Erasmus, *Enchiridion* (LB 5:29b), which explains that the Silenus conceals "pure divinity within, under a sordid and ridiculous cover" [*sub tectorio sordido ac pene ridiculo, merum Numen claudunt*]. Pico's similar use of the image is quoted by Erasmus in the *Adages* (ASD 2.5, 159–61n): "if you look at the outside you see a beast; if you look within, you will recognize the divine" [*Ita extrinsecus si aspexeris, feram videas, si introspexeris, numen agnoscas*].
106 *Iliad*, trans. Chapman, 21, "Of Homer," ls. 97–8. On Scaliger's condemnation of Homer as "ridiculous," see *Poetices* 5.3 (1561), 227, condemning Homer's description of Eris: "It is ridiculous. It is fatuous. It is Homeric" [*Ridiculu[m] est. Fatuum est. Homericum est*].
107 *Iliad*, trans. Chapman, 20, "Of Homer," ln. 65. Chapman uses the word "ridiculous" throughout his commentaries on the *Iliad*: see 42, 71 (commentary to 2.355), 268 (marginal note to 12.566), 277 (commentary to

12.566), 346 (commentary to 16.111), 369–70 (commentary to 17.480–9), 404 (commentary to,19.191, and 468 (marginal note to 23.489).

108 *Odyssey*, trans. Chapman, "To the Earle of Somerset," 5, ls. 79–80.

109 Ibid., ls. 74–80. Compare Puttenham, *The Arte of English Poesie*, ed. Willcock and Walker, 150, who praises Homer's "trifling worke of *Batrachomyomachia*" as evidence that the "loftie style may be decently used in a meane and base subject & contrariwise," since although frogs and mice are "but litle and ridiculous beasts, yet to treat of warre is an high subject, and ... asketh martiall grandiloquence."

110 Chapman, *Hero and Leander*, "Dedication to Lady Walsingham," ls. 11–12, in *Poems*, 132.

111 Chapman, *The Crowne of all Homers Workes*, in *Chapman's Homeric Hymns and Other Homerica*, ed. Scully, 54, "To the Earle of Somerset. The Occasion of this Impos'd Crowne," ls. 5–6. On Chapman's attitude towards the *Batrachomyomachia*, see MacLure, *George Chapman*, 204.

112 Chapman, *A Free and Offenceles Justification*, in *Poems*, 327.

113 Chapman, *The Shadow of Night*, "To ... Mathew Roydon," in *Poems*, 19; Chapman also refers to his poems as trifles in the dedication to *Hero and Leander* (*Poems*, 132).

114 For an extended version of this argument, see chapter 5 of my *Humanism, Machinery, and Renaissance Literature*.

115 *Iliad*, trans. Chapman, "To the Most Honored ... Earle of Essexe," dedication to *Seaven Bookes of the Iliades*, 505, ls. 105–7.

116 Chapman, *Ovids Banquet*, "To ... Mathew Royden," in *Poems*, 49. Ancient treatises on rhetoric by Aristotle, Longinus, Demetrius, Cicero, Quintilian, and the pseudo-Plutarchan *Life* all acknowledge Homer as the unsurpassed master of vivid description. On Homer's ability to make the inanimate seem animate, see Aristotle, *Rhetoric*, 407 [III.xi.3]. For other discussions of vividness in Homeric epic, see Longinus, *On the Sublime*, 249–53; Demetrius, *On Style*, 4.209–19, 471–9; Cicero, *Tusculan Disputations* V.39.114–16; [Plutarch], *Life of Homer*, 133. On ancient conceptions of vividness in Homer, see Zeitlin, "Visions and Revisions of Homer," 218–25.

117 Quintilian, *Inst. Orat.* VIII.3.82 [3:387]; at IX.3.50, Quintilian points out that when such brevity obscures rather than clarifies, it is called "brachyology." On Chapman's debts to Quintilian's conception of *enargeia*, see Huntington, *Ambition, Rank, and Poetry*, 91.

118 See Chapman, *Ovids Banquet*, stanza 117, in *Poems*, 82. On Chapman's understanding of *enargeia* as reconcilable to irony, see Gless, "Chapman's Ironic Ovid," 22. On the debate over whether to read *Ovids Banquet* as

ironic, see also Kermode, "The Banquet of Sense," 68–99; Waddington, "Chapman and Persius"; and Dundas, *Pencils Rhetorique*, 130.

119 Chapman, *Ovids Banquet*, "To ... Mathew Royden," ls. 29–30, in *Poems*, 49.

120 Chapman, *Ovids Banquet*, "To ... Mathew Royden," ls. 30–4, in *Poems*, 49; on possible sources for Chapman's discussion of poetic obscurity, see Quintilian, *Inst. Orat.* VIII.3.56–7 [3:241–3], and Demetrius, *On Style*, 5.254, 493: "even obscurity [*asapheia*] is often a sort of forcefulness [*deinotês*], since what is implied is more forceful, while what is openly stated is despised."

121 For Erasmus's discussions of Homeric *enargeia*, see *De Copia*, *CWE* 24:577, 580. In Homeric epic, *enargês* means not simply vivid but also the fleeting, often blinding visibility of sacred things normally invisible to mortal sight; see, for example, *Od.* 3.420. On the concept of *enargês* in Homeric epic, see Loraux, *Tiresias*, 213; Pucci, *Song of the Sirens*, 21–2.

122 [Plutarch], *Life of Homer*, 97. Snare, *Mystification*, 136, notes the relevance of this definition for Chapman, citing it from Xylander's edition of Plutarch: "an oration varying in some creative way from common usage by some sort of invention either for the sake of utility or adornment" [*schema est oratio a communi consuetudine varians fictione aliqua, idque ornatus aut utilitatis gratia*].

123 Ahl and Roisman, *The Odyssey Re-Formed*, 15.

124 [Plutarch], *Life of Homer*, treats *emphasis* and *schêma* successively in chapters 26 and 27; the text (95) defines *emphasis* as a trope "which by things implied adds tension to what is actually said" [*esti kai hê emphasis, hêper di'huponoias epitasin tou legomenou paristêsin*]. Quintilian, *Inst. Orat.* IX.2.65 [3:414–15] writes that *schêma* is a useful trope when "we want something other than what we actually say to be understood ... something which lurks there for the reader to discover." For discussions of this passage in the context of Homeric epic, see Ahl and Roisman, *Odyssey Reformed*, 16 and Stanford, *Ambiguity in Greek Literature*, 18.

125 Nünlist, *The Ancient Critic at Work*, 157–9, 173, 167.

126 See, for instance, Chapman, *Ovids Banquet*, stanza 3, in *Poems*, 54, which describes a statue of Niobe that is not visible when "neerly viewed" but may be seen from "a farre of[f]." On irony and optical illusion in Chapman's poetry, see Dundas, *Pencils Rhetorique*, 123–30; Gutsell, *Irony*, 98.

127 Compare Gless, "Chapman's Ironic Ovid," 41, on how "only an ironic reading of *Ovids Banquet* can make sense of all the poem's richly various details."

128 Booth, *Rhetoric of Irony*, 128.

129 For example: *XV Bookes of Ovids Metamorphoses*, trans. Golding, "Preface to the Reader," ls. 167–8: "For to the pure and Godly mynd are all

things pure and cleene, / And unto such as are corrupt the best corrupted beene."

130 *Achilles' Shield*, in *Iliad*, trans. Chapman, "To the Understander," 548.

131 Plato, *Symposium*, 216d–e, in *Plato III*, 222–3.

132 Chapman, *Free and Offenceles Justification*, ls. 1–5, 13–14, in *Poems*, 327.

133 Chapman, *Free and Offenceles Justification*, ls. 26–8, in *Poems*, 327. The quotation is attributed in the margin to "Plat. in Alcib. 2."

134 Chapman, *Free and Offenceles Justification*, ls. 29–32, in *Poems*, 327.

135 [Plato], *Second Alcibiades*, 147a.

136 Chapman, *Free and Offenceles Justification*, in *Poems*, 329–30.

137 Chapman, *Free and Offenceles Justification*, in *Poems*, 330. On Chapman's adaptation of Erasmus's adage about a young man who was supposed to have made tremendous leaps while at Rhodes, see Schoell, *Etudes*, 44.

138 Chapman, "To M. Harriots," dedicatory epistle to *Achilles' Shield*, ls. 91–3, in *Poems*, 383.

139 *Odyssey*, trans. Chapman, Verse epilogue, 421, ls. 11–14.

140 Compare Vida, *De Arte Poetica* 2:44–5, ls. 40–4, on how the Homeric poet intimates through "covert references and recondite circumlocutions" but nonetheless permits "the likeness of things [to] shin[e] through quite clearly ... as through a light-suffused cloud." The example provided by Vida (2, ls. 46–50) is the not-naming of Odysseus in the opening lines of *Od.*, a passage often cited as an example of Homeric irony.

141 *Iliad*, trans. Chapman, 295, commentary to 14.343 [= 334–6].

142 *Iliad*, trans. Chapman, 295, commentary to 14.343.

143 For another example of Chapman's scorn for gratuitous obscurity, see Chapman, *Dialogus*, ls. 89–96, 94, in *Poems*, 334, also paraphrasing Lucretius, *DRN* 1.641–2: "*omnia enim stolidi magis admirantur amantque / inversis quae sub verbis latitantia cernunt.*"

144 D. Knox, *Ironia*, 73.

145 Sixteenth-century readers often recognize that claims of obviousness (as reflected in phrases such as "sanè vero" [of course] and "quasi vero" [as if; indeed] are intended ironically. On this point, see Erasmus, *De Copia*, *CWE* 24:485. Girardus, *Meditationes in librum primum Iliados*, 49, points out Homer's use of this technique, glossing an adverb that means "sanè" [of course] as an example of "irony and biting irrision" [*ironia & mordax irrisio*].

146 *Iliad*, trans. Chapman, "To the Reader," 9–10, ls. 106, 143–4, 139.

147 Liceti, *Hieroglyphica*, 359.

148 Chapman's concern to reconstruct Homer's intent may reflect the influence of Sponde (*Homeri Quae Extant Omnia*, 2:132 on *Od.* 10.21), who protests,

"it is not possible to deform them [Homer's fables] any way one likes" [*sed quia eas quo uolueris detorquere, non liceat*].

149 *Odyssey*, trans. Chapman, "So wrought divine Ulysses" (epilogue), 421, ls. 16–17, 22, 27.

150 *Odyssey*, trans. Chapman, epilogue, 421, ls. 27–30.

151 Ovid, *Metamorphoses*, trans. Golding, "Preface to the Reader," ln. 218.

152 Chapman, "To M. Harriots," ls. 82; 89–90, in *Poems*, 382–3.

153 *Odyssey*, trans. Chapman, 7, "To the Earl of Somerset," ls. 190–3; compare *Euthymiae Raptus*, ln. 48, in *Poems*, 174, where Chapman describes how he emulates Homer's solar presence by putting on "[a]s confident a countnance, as the Sunne" in order to beam his rays on the readers below.

154 *Iliad*, trans. Chapman, 17, "Preface to the Reader," ls. 127–30, 155. Compare Chapman's verse epistle "To the Reader," (*Iliad*, 9–10, ls. 117–27), attacking the "word-for-word traductions" of Homer's other translators and justifying his own use of "needfull periphrases" to "make cleare the Author."

155 *Iliad*, trans. Chapman, "To the Reader," 17, ls. 133–5.

156 *Iliad*, trans. Chapman, "To the Reader," 17, ls. 135–7; compare 369, the commentary to *Il.* 17.335, where he answers the "objector that would have no more words than Homer used in his translator" and explains that he uses more words than Homer because it is "necessarie to expresse such a sence as I understand in Homer," unlike Valla, who "with his briefenesse utterly maimes" a simile that Chapman professes to translate correctly.

157 *Odyssey*, trans. Chapman, 18.188–9 [=130–1], 316.

158 *Homeri Extant Quae Omnia*, ed. Sponde, 2:266, on *Od.* 18.130, citing Sophocles, Fragment 13.

159 Chapman, *Homeric Hymns and Lesser Homerica*, 53, *Crowne*, "To ... the Earle of Somerset," ln. 131, *Eugenia*, Vigilia Prima, ls. 258–9; 261, in *Poems*, 277–8; also see *Poems*, 457, note to ln. 261, which identifies the phrase as from Strabo. Chapman's direct source is most likely Sponde, whose source in turn is Sophocles, Fr. 13 and its close parallel at *Ajax*, ls. 125–6, where Odysseus comments on the mad Ajax, "I see we are, all of us, nothing / But images and an empty shadow [*zômen ê kouphên skian*]" (quoted from *Sophocles* I, 44–5). Another source for Chapman (and for Sponde) may be Erasmus's adage *Homo bulla* [Man is a bubble], which traces the phrase to Pindar.

160 Compare Gutsell, *Irony*, preface, iv, which argues that the principal irony dramatized by Chapman's dramatic works is an "irony of self-deception and of consequential self-defeat."

161 Rutherford, *Homer*, 45; Golden, "*To Gêloion* in the *Iliad*," 57; compare Seeskin, "The Comedy of Gods in the *Iliad*," 301, 304; Griffin, *Homer on Life and Death*, 178–83. Michael West, "Homer's *Iliad* and the Genesis of the Mock-Heroic," 14–16, argues that the "detachment" of the Homeric

gods "affords a sort of double perspective" on the human action of the poems; compare Griffin, 178–81, and S. Richardson, *The Homeric Narrator*, 122–3.

162 Peacham, *Garden of Eloquence*, 36, 24–5; compare Aristotle, *Art of Rhetoric* II.24, 184–5.

163 Chapman, *Euthymiae Raptus*, ls. 48–9, in *Poems*, 174.

164 Rutherford, *Homer*, 46. On the comic dimensions of the Homeric gods, compare Griffin, *Homer on Life and Death*, 199; K. Reinhardt, *Das Parisurteil*, 25, on the "*erhabener Unernst*" [sublime frivolity] of the gods of the *Iliad*; Clarke, "The Humor of Homer," 246–52.

165 *Odyssey*, trans. Chapman, 4.662–3 [=493–4], 75. He elaborates greatly upon the Greek text here.

166 *Odyssey*, trans. Chapman, 4.470–4 [=347–50], 71.

167 Peradotto, *Man in the Middle Voice*, 35–8, provides a lengthy analysis of the structural similarities between Menelaus's account of Proteus in *Od.* 4 and Odysseus's later interaction with Tiresias in *Od.* 11.

168 Harvard, Widener Library f HEW 6.11.3, Chapman's presentation copy to Henry Reynolds, author's inscription, also cited in MacLure, *Chapman*, 204. Chapman's inscription is echoed by Reynolds's later claim that Homer "hid the misteries of his doctrine ... within the foults and involvements of fables" and "Hieroglyphicks" (*Mythomystes*, in *Critical Essays*, ed. Spingarn, 1:156).

169 *Odyssey*, trans. Chapman, 15.216–19; 228 [=169–71, 174–6], 264.

170 *Odyssey*, trans. Chapman, 19.767–8 [=560–1], 345.

171 *Odyssey*, trans. Chapman, 1.47 [=29], 13.

172 *Odyssey*, trans. Chapman, 13, marginal note to 1.47–50.

173 *Odyssey*, trans. Chapman, 1.50–4 [=32–4], 13.

174 On the irony of Homer's heroic epithets, see M. Clarke, "Manhood and Heroism," in *The Cambridge Companion to Homer*, ed. Fowler, 81, which argues that the epithet *amumôn*, or blameless, is "so far from moral approbation" that it clearly does not imply "univocal praise" on the part of the poet. Ironic readings of the epithet are not universally accepted, however; the Loeb edition explains the epithet as follows: "Used to the formulaic style as we are not, Homer's audience was more able than we to separate the generic description from the particular event," for instance at *Od.* 16.4, "The loud-barking dogs fawned and did not bark" (note to 1.29, 14–15).

175 *Odyssey*, trans. Chapman, 13, marginal note to 1.47; compare 14, marginal note to 1.90, where Chapman glosses Pallas's allusion to "Atlas' wise mind," proposing that *oloophrôn*, defined in the previous note as "mente perniciosus," can also mean "qui universa mente agitat." For Cleanthes's

interpretation of the passage, which he takes to denote Atlas's providential concern for the whole universe, see *Stoicorum Veterum Fragmenta* 1:549.

176 *Odyssey*, trans. Chapman, 4, "To the Earle of Somerset," ln. 64. Mueller, "Knowledge and Delusion in the *Iliad*," in *Essays on the Iliad*, ed. Wright, 108, argues that Odyssean heroism is a "form of knowledge."

177 Hesiod, *Georgicks*, trans. Chapman, 3, ln. 88 and note 22.

178 Hesiod, *Georgicks*, trans. Chapman, 3, note 22, summarizing Bacon, *De Sapientia Veterum* 26: Prometheus; or the State of Man.

179 Bacon, *De Sapientia Veterum* 26, in *Works*, ed. Spedding 6.1, 752–3.

180 Bacon, *De Sapientia Veterum*, Preface, in *Works* 6.1, 695.

181 *Iliad*, trans. Chapman, 277, commentary to 13.556 [= 619]; *Odyssey*, trans. Chapman, 421, verse epilogue, ls. 21–2.

182 Bacon, *De Sapientia Veterum*, in *Works* 6.1, 749.

183 Chapman, "Dedicatory Epistle to Robert, Earl of Somerset," ls. 51–2, in *Poems*, 406; Poliziano, *Ambra*, ls. 27–30, in *Silvae*, 72–3, represents Homer as a poet who "disdains empty honours and, far-removed from the crowd, despises the rewards of hollow fame; having reached the summit, he laughs at the multitude panting to scale the steep heights" [*honores / fastidit vanos et ineptae praemia famae / despicit, exemptus vulgo ac iam monte potitus, / ridet anhelantem dura ad fastigia turbam*].

184 *Iliad*, trans. Chapman, 42, introductory commentary to Book 1.

185 *Iliad*, trans. Chapman, 7, "To the Reader," ls. 1–5; Poliziano, *Manto*, ln. 373, in *Silvae*, 28–9.

186 Poliziano, *Oratio*, in *Opera Omnia* 1:478; on the late antique understanding of allegory as an initiation into sacred mysteries, see Brisson, *How Philosophers Saved Myths*, 57–61. On Chapman's allegories of Homer, see Tania Demetriou, "George Chapman's *Odysses*: translation and allegory," in *Homère*, ed. Capodieci and Ford, 281–99.

187 Waddington, *The Mind's Empire*, 183, calls the poem an "initiation rite."

188 *Iliad*, trans. Chapman, 6, "To the High Borne Prince of Men," ls. 136–7.

189 See, for example, Dove, *A Confutation of Atheisme*, 38; Prideaux, *Sacred Eloquence*, 12. Dove cites Gen. 3.22 and Ps. 50 as examples of irony.

190 Lavezola, *Osservationi ... Sopra il Orlando Furioso*, 30, also cited in D. Knox, *Ironia*, 170.

191 *Odyssey*, trans. Chapman, 20.523–7 [=345–9], 359; *Iliad* 5.426–7 [=441–2], 121.

192 Levine, "Homeric Laughter," 97–8, 102. On the laughter of the gods, see also Friedländer, "Lachende Götter," 219, who argues of Zeus that "*sein Lächeln aber ist der genuss dieser erneuten Majestät.*"

193 *Iliad*, trans. Chapman, 5.401–3, 5.412, 5.414–15 [=418–25], 120–1.

194 *Iliad*, trans. Chapman, 21.379–82 [=408–11], and marginal note, 433.

195 *Iliad*, trans. Chapman, 8.34–5 [=38–40], 167.

196 *Iliad*, trans. Chapman, 8.393–6, 8.398, 8.403 [=413–24], 177–8.

197 [Plutarch], *Life of Homer*, 137. Often etymologized by sixteenth-century lexicographers as deriving from *sarkazô* or *sarkizô* [to rip or tear the flesh], sarcasm is often noted by Eustathius, who associates it with *barus*, the Hermogenean form that denotes bitter or scornful speech. Like the pseudo-Plutarchan *Life*, Eustathius associates *sarkasmos* with the distinctively Homeric gesture of the Sardanian (or Sardonian) smile, a metaphor of obscure origins at times rendered as "Sardinian" by those who trace its roots to a plant from Sardinia whose leaves are so bitter that they elicit a grimace when eaten. For a discussion of pseudo-Plutarch's definition of sarcasm as a species of irony, see D. Knox, *Ironia*, 177.

198 Eustathius, *Comm. ad Hom. Odysseam* 3:707, on 20.302; Chapman (*Od.* 20.477–8) translates Homer's description of Odysseus's gesture as "a laughter raising most Sardinian, / With scorne and wrath mixt" (p. 357) while his translation of *Il.* 15.99 has Hera laughing "meerely from her lips" (300). For Renaissance discussions of the Sardonian smile, see Schott, trans. *Paroimiai Hellenikai,* 12.63, 527–8, "Sardonicus Risus, id est simulatus," with reference to *Od.* 20.302.

199 Erasmus, "Risus Sardonicus," Adage III.v.1 (ASD II.5, 289–97); Joubert, *Traité du Ris*, 88–9; Goclenius, *Physiologia De Risu & Lacrymis*, 26; Nicander, *De Voluptate et Dolore, De Risu et Fletu,* 346–7; on Sardonian laughter in the Renaissance, see Ménager, *La Renaissance et du Rire*, 58.

200 *Iliad*, trans. Chapman, 15.97–101 [=100–3], 300. Compare Lateiner, *Sardonic Smile*, 12, 184n14, which argues that Odysseus "smiles inwardly" and that these "involuted" smiles "heighte[n] [the] ironies" of the poem. On laughter in *Od.*, see also D. Levine, "*Odyssey* 18: Iros as Paradigm for the Suitors," 200–4, and his "Homeric Laughter and the Unsmiling Suitors," 97–104.

201 *Iliad*, trans. Chapman, 15.112, and marginal note, 300. Pope, *Iliad*, 732, *Observations on the Fifteenth Book*, note to ln. 114 calls the speech "a masterpiece in that sort, which seems to say one thing, and persuades another."

202 *Iliad*, trans. Chapman, 15.169, 15.173–4 [=180–3] and marginal note, 15.181, 15.186 [=196, 198], 302–3.

203 Sherry, *Treatise*, 26b, defines *Mycterismus* (from Gr. *muktêrizô*, to turn up the nose, ridicule, sneer at) as a subset of ironic speech accompanied by "counterfayted laughter"; compare Peacham, *Garden of Eloquence*, 38–9. The word is used by Homer's ancient scholiasts.

204 *Od.* 18.100; on the laughter of the suitors as a sign of their "presumed eminence," see D. Levine, "Homeric Laughter," 97–8, and his "*Odyssey* 18," 200–4.

205 Fraunce, *Arcadian Rhetorike*, 68–9, 10.

206 *Iliad*, trans. Chapman, 16.682–3 [=744] and marginal note, 342.

207 *Iliad*, trans. Chapman, 16.786, 791 [=853–4] and marginal note, 345.

208 *Iliad*, trans. Chapman, 10.388 [=456–7], 211.

209 *Iliad*, trans. Chapman, 15.329–32 [=361–6], 307.

210 *Iliad*, trans. Chapman, 307, marginal note to 15.329–30.

211 *Iliad*, trans. Chapman, 13.112–15 [=118–22], 255–6.

212 On the fifteenth-century tendency to interpret Homeric epic as a rhetorical manual that teaches readers to speak "safely, tactfully, and effectively in every imaginable situation," see Ahl and Roisman, *Odyssey Re-Formed*, 13–14.

213 Puttenham, *Arte of English Poesie*, 209–10.

214 *Iliad*, trans. Chapman, 225, marginal notes to 11.320 and 11.337; Suter, "Paris and Dionysos: Iambos in the *Iliad*," 8. In the *Homeric Hymn to Demeter*, rediscovered in 1777 and thus unfamiliar to Chapman, the character of Iambe scolds and mocks the grieving goddess with "*paraskôptous*" (ln. 203) – the ritual abuse, obscenity, or *aischrologia* common to Eleusinian cults. On this passage, see Clay, *The Politics of Olympus*, 234.

215 Sowerby, "Chapman's Discovery of Homer I," 43.

216 Chapman's interpretation of scoptic speech appears highly indebted to Sponde, who frequently defends the epic decorum of scoffing and reviling speech. Commenting on a speech made by Agamemnon at *Il.* 8.228–44 (*Homeri Quae Extant Omnia*, 1:137–8), Sponde praises the way in which the Greek general reprimands his fearful troops rather than comforting them, since "acerbic and injurious words" [*acerbis & contumeliosus uerbis*] work better than "blandishment and soft speech" [*blanda eos oratione demulceat*].

217 *Iliad*, trans. Chapman, 294, commentary to 14.81.

218 Eustathius, *Comm. ad Hom. Iliadem* on 2.223; 9.11; 10.114; 13.735; 16.21–31; for a discussion of the concept of *barus* in Eustathius and Hermogenes, see Lindberg, *Studies in Hermogenes and Eustathios*, 215–16, and Nünlist, *Ancient Critic at Work*, 214. Sixteenth-century treatises on rhetoric call this bittersweet mixture of praise and blame *Charientismus*, often classifying it as a species of irony, used "when thinges that be hardely spoken, be mollifyed with pleasante wordes" (Sherry, *Treatise*, 25b–26b).

219 *Iliad*, trans. Chapman, 182, marginal note to 9.32–5 [=32–5]. Diomedes is silent in response to Agamemnon's rebuke at *Il.* 4.401; in the Greek, he does not mention his former silence but only points out that he has been reviled by his fellow Achaeans for being "lacking in valor."

220 Montiglio, *Silence in the Land of Logos*, 16, 26.

221 On Odysseus's exemplary silence, see Montiglio, *Silence*, 266, 263; see *Od.* 9.316, 17.465, 20.184.

222 See *Od.* 20.13–21; Plato repeatedly praises Odysseus's capacity for silence: see *Rep.* 3.4 [390d] and *Phaedo* 94d, both discussed by Montiglio, *Silence*, 287–8.

223 On Diomedes's silence to Agamemnon in *Il.* 4, see Martin, *The Language of Heroes*, 143. On silence as hostile or threatening, see also Montiglio, *Silence*, 55–63. For ancient discussions of Homeric silence, see Longinus, *On the Sublime*, 185; [Plutarch], *Life of Homer*, 106–7: both praise the sublimity of Ajax's silence towards Odysseus at *Od.* 11.543–67.

224 *Iliad*, trans. Chapman, 6.340–8 [=326–31] and marginal note, 146.

225 Eustathius, *Comm. ad Hom. Iliadem* 1:378 on *Il.* 3.39–45.

226 *Odyssey*, trans. Chapman, 22.360–1 [=287–8] and marginal note, 383. Compare Girardus, *Meditationes in librum primum Iliados,* 94, glossing "kertomiosi" as "mordacibus, amarulentis, & contumeliosis."

227 *Odyssey*, trans. Chapman, 22.363–5 [=288–9], 383.

228 *Odyssey*, trans. Chapman, "To the Earle of Somerset," 4, ls. 64, 66–7.

229 *Odyssey*, trans. Chapman, 166, marginal note to 9.673–7.

230 *Odyssey*, trans. Chapman, 14, marginal note to 1.97.

231 Eustathius, *Comm. ad Hom. Odysseam* remarks in his introductory essay to his commentary that the poem is "more pungent" or "sharper" [*drimutêros*] than the *Iliad*; see also Eustathius on *Il.* 2.340–53 and Demetrius, *On Style*, 429. On pungency and jest in Homeric epic, also see Segal, *Singers, Heroes and Gods*, 12, and Lindberg, *Studies in Hermogenes and Eustathios*, 183–4, 215–16, 257–60.

232 Demetrius, *On Style*, 3.129–30, 426–7, quoting *Od.* 9.369–70. At 5.262, 488–9, Demetrius once again cites *Od.* 9.369, "No-man will I eat last" [*Outin egô pumaton edomai*] as an example of Homer's skill at mixing playfulness and terror; at 497, Demetrius observes that mixing in an element of "playfulness" produces *deinos* – that is, vigour or terror.

233 Ide, "Exemplary Heroism in Chapman's *Odysses*," 128.

234 *Homeri Quae Extant Omnia*, ed. Sponde, 1:7 on *Il.* 1.85.

235 [Homer], *Poiêseis Homêrou amphô, ete Ilias kai e Odysseia*, ed. Micyllus and Camerarius, with annotations by Crusius, 159 (on *Il.* 9.107–8) and 237 (on *Il.* 13.725–30). Crusius also includes speeches "cum parrhêsia" in his list of oratorical styles provided in the unpaginated endpapers. 1 Cor. 12.8: "One man, through the Spirit, has the gift of wise speech [*logos sophias*], while another, by the power of the same Spirit, can put the deepest knowledge [*logos gnôseôs*] into words."

236 Melanchthon, *Elementorum Rhetorices*, 296; Crusius, *Quaestiones*, 308, 311.

237 *Iliad*, trans. Chapman, 1.66 [=72], 25, 16.791 [=859], 345.
238 Eustathius, *Comm. ad Hom. Iliadem*, on 13.374–84; compare 14.479–505 and 21.184–99 and the discussion in Lindberg, *Studies*, 180. On Eustathius's usage of these rhetorical terms, see Lindberg, *Studies*, 168–9, 183–4, 215–16, and 244–5.
239 *Iliad*, trans. Chapman, 141, commentary to 6.148–222.
240 Vida, *De Arte Poetica* 2:62–3, ls. 307–10: "cum Glauco medio aequore belli / Tydides ferus occurrit, vix credere possunt, / Tot traxisse moras longas sermonibus usos / Inter sese ambos, dum fervent omnia caede."
241 *Iliad*, trans. Chapman, 141–2, commentary to 6.148–222.
242 *Iliad*, trans. Chapman, 20.230–1 [=252–3], 413.
243 *Iliad*, trans. Chapman, 2.293, 2.302–3 [=337–40], 55.
244 *Iliad*, trans. Chapman, 346, commentary to 16.89.
245 *Iliad*, trans. Chapman, 346, commentary to 16.89.
246 *Iliad*, trans. Pope, *Observations on the Thirteenth Book*, 641–2, note to ln. 471.
247 Thersites and Irus have both been identified with Archilochus and with the authors of *silloi*, or versified invectives; on the Homeric foundations of iambic blame poetry and invective, see Nagy, *Achaeans*, 231, 253–9. A number of recent critics have argued that Irus is a precursor of the iambic tradition: see Nagy, *Achaeans*, 253–7, 231, 245; Thalmann, *The Swineherd and the Bow*, 100, 83.
248 Gager, *Ulysses Redux*; on the performance and reception of this play, see Binns, *Intellectual Culture in Elizabethan and Jacobean England*, 129. Gager's translation of the *Batrachomyomachia* is preserved in the British Library as BL MS Add. 22,583, fols. 1–8.
249 On Chapman's debts to Homer's Irus in these comedies, see Weidner, "The Dramatic Uses of Homeric Idealism," 121; the characters in question are Irus (*Blind Beggar*), Dowsecer (*A Humorous Day's Mirth*), and Clarence (*Giles Goosecap*).
250 On Chapman's revisions to his Homeric translations, see Tania Demetriou, "'Strange Appearance': the reception of Homer in Renaissance England." University of Cambridge PhD thesis, 2008.
251 Aristotle, *Nic. Ethics*, III.7.7–9 [1115b]. On Aristotle's understanding of *thrasutes*, see Loraux, *Tiresias*, 243. Lucian, *The Fly*, which Chapman mentions in his commentary to *Il.* 17.489, also discusses the difference between *tharsos* and *thrasos*. On this issue, see Thalmann, "Thersites," 16.
252 *Od.* 18.415; compare *Od.* 20.323 and the discussion of these phrases by J. Heath, *The Talking Greeks*, 122, and Walsh, *Fighting Words*, 141–62. On attitudes towards verbal combat in the Renaissance, see Whigham, *Ambition and Privilege*, 137–84; Martines, *Strong Words*, and Ong, *Fighting for Life*.

253 *Seaven Bookes*, 1.155 [=149–51], in *Iliad*, trans. Chapman, 513; Briggs, "Chapman's *Seaven Bookes of the Iliades*," 69, 71–2.
254 *Seaven Bookes*, 1.301, and *Il.* 1.211–12, both in *Iliad*, trans. Chapman, 517, 29. Chapman's revision of this passage has also been noted by Smalley, "The Ethical Bias of Chapman's Homer," 179.
255 *Seaven Bookes*, 1.215, 1.217–18, in *Iliad*, trans. Chapman, 515.
256 *Seaven Bookes*, 1.199–200, 1.202, in *Iliad*, trans. Chapman, 514.
257 *Iliad*, trans. Chapman, 1.192, 1.194 [=189–92], 29.
258 Fraunce, *Arcadian Rhetorike*, 107–8.
259 *Iliad*, trans. Chapman, 70, commentary to 2.275.
260 *Iliad*, trans. Chapman, 2.275–6, 2.290, 54–5 and commentary to 2.275, 70. The Loeb edition [=2.318] has *aizêlon*, a word that Zenodotus emended to *arizêlon* or *aridêlon*. Line 319, "for the son of crooked-counselling Kronos turned him [i.e., the dragon] to stone," was rejected by Aristarchus.
261 *Iliad*, trans. Chapman, 18.184–5 [=220–1], 377, and commentary to 18.184, 389–90.
262 *Iliad*, trans. Chapman, 18.25, 373; 4.463, 105; 12.343–4, 248; 5.858–9, 134; 11.9–10, 216.
263 Demetrius, *On Style*, 1.49, 378–9, notes that Homer conveys grandeur by means of ugly and harsh sounds; at 2.105, 412–13, he praises Homer's use of cacophony.
264 *Iliad*, trans. Chapman, 324, marginal note to 16.80; 216, marginal note to 11.9–10.
265 *Iliad*, trans. Chapman, 215–16, argument to 11, 11.2, 11.11–14.
266 Hesiod, *Georgicks*, trans. Chapman, ls. 22, 46 and note 17, in *The georgicks of Hesiod*, 2–3.
267 *Iliad*, trans. Chapman, 18.485 [=535], 386.
268 Chapman, *Euthymiae Raptus*, ln. 199, in *Poems*, 177.
269 Chapman, *Euthymiae Raptus*, ls. 97–8, in *Poems*, 175.
270 Chapman, *Euthymiae Raptus*, ls. 181, 184–5; 190, in *Poems*, 177.
271 *Iliad*, trans. Chapman, 44, commentary to 1.359.
272 Scaliger, *Poetices* (1561), 216; *Iliad*, trans. Chapman, 44–5, commentary to 1.359. Plato's complaint about Achilles's tears, at *Rep.* 3.2 [387d–388b], was refuted by various ancient commentators, including Porphyry, *Homeric Questions*, ed. MacPhail, 231, on *Iliad* 18.22.
273 Chapman, *Eugenia*, ln. 854 and marginal note, in *Poems*, 291; *Iliad*, trans. Chapman, 23.10–11, 454, a misreading of the passage, which in fact describes the Myrmidons resolving to eat once they have their fill of "dire lamenting."
274 *Odyssey*, trans. Chapman, "To the Earle of Somerset," 4, ls. 64, 66–7.
275 Holland, *Wit and Fancy in a Maze*, 101.
276 Holland, *Wit and Fancy in a Maze*, 100–1.
277 Holland, *Wit and Fancy in a Maze*, 100.

278 Bednarz, *Poets' War*, 1, 3. On Marston's satire of Jonson, see Bednarz, 23.
279 Chapman, *All Fools*, Prologue, ls. 16–19, in *Plays: Comedies*, 1:101.
280 On Chapman's "resentment," see MacLure, *Chapman*, 21, and Huntington, *Rank*, 5, 65; on the "rancorous" and "disgruntled" Chapman, see Acheson, *Shakespeare and the Rival Poet*, 71, and Snare, *Mystification*, 22.
281 Giraldi, *Historiae Poetarum* (1545), Dialogue 1, 70.
282 *Iliad*, trans. Chapman, 88, commentary to 3.121.
283 Shephard, "Scaliger on Homer and Virgil," 316.
284 Nashe, *Lenten Stuffe*, in *Works*, ed. McKerrow, 3:155.
285 *Iliad*, trans. Chapman, 545, Dedication to Earle Marshall, *Achilles' Shield*, ls. 100, 103; Jonson, *Poetaster*, I.2.81–7, in *Works*, 4:211.
286 On the annotations in Jonson's copy of the 1616 edition of Chapman's *Whole Works of Homer*, held by the Fitzwilliam Museum, see Simpson, "Ben Jonson on Chapman," *T.L.S.* 3 March 1932, 155. Jonson's signature does not appear in the Fitzwilliam volume. Jonson did own Chapman's 1598 *Iliads* and the 1598 *Achilles' Shield*; on these volumes and on the ascription to Jonson of the 1616 volume, see David McPherson, "Ben Jonson's library and marginalia: an annotated catalogue," *SP* 71, no. 5 (1974): 1–106, 52.
287 Chapman, "An Invective Wrighten ... Against Mr. Ben: Johnson," ls. 124, 27, 10–11, 60 in *Poems*, 374–6.
288 *Iliad*, trans. Chapman, epilogue, 498.
289 *Iliad*, trans. Chapman, 505, *Seaven Bookes*, Dedication to the Earl of Essex, ls. 89–90.
290 *Iliad*, trans. Chapman, 17, "Preface to the Reader," ls. 157–8, 161.
291 Chapman, Epilogue to the *Hymns* of Homer, ln. 41, in *Poems*, 417.
292 Chapman, "To the Immortall Memorie, of the Incomparable Heroe, *Henrye* Prince of Wales," from *The Whole Workes of Homer* (1616), in *Poems*, 389. On Chapman's memorial engraving to Henry, Prince of Wales, and his relationship to his patron, see John A. Buchtel, "Book Dedications and the death of a patron: the memorial engraving in Chapman's Homer," *Book History* 7 (2004): 1–29.
293 Chapman, *Shadow of Night*, ls. 159–62, in *Poems*, 23.
294 Chapman, *The Shadow of Night*, ls. 164–5, in *Poems*, 23. On the significance of the figure of Hercules for Chapman, see Buchtel, "Book Dedications," 11–13.
295 Chapman, *Euthymiae Raptus*, ls. 65–6, 103, in *Poems*, 174–5.
296 Poliziano, *Ambra*, ls. 458–63, in *Silvae*, 98–9.
297 Bednarz, *Poets' War*, 47.
298 Bednarz, *Poets' War*, 257.

299 On the sources of Shakespeare's play, see Bednarz, *Poets' War*, 260, 386. Caxton's *Recuyell of the Historyes of Troye* is a translation of Raoul Lefevre's *Receuil des Histoires de Troye*, in turn a translation of Guido Delle Colonne's *Historia Trojana*. Caxton's text was printed in 1502, 1503, 1553, and 1596.

300 R.J. Kaufmann, "Ceremonies for Chaos: the Status of *Troilus and Cressida*," *ELH* 32, no. 2 (1965): 139–59, 149; J. Harris, "'The Enterprise is Sick,'" 24. See also Shakespeare, *Troilus and Cressida*, ed. Bevington, introduction, 21, which argues that Shakespeare was sufficiently familiar with Chapman's translation "to have savoured its tragic grandeur and its insistence on the war's great significance to the gods and to the human race" but that he departs from Chapman in his focus on "the absurd" dimensions of the conflict.

301 Bednarz, *Poets' War*, 260.

302 Frye, *The Myth of Deliverance*, 61; François Laroque, "Perspective in *Troilus and Cressida*," in John M. Mucciolo, ed., *Shakespeare's Universe: Renaissance Ideas and Conventions. Essays in honour of W.R. Elton* (Brookfield, VT: Scolar Press, 1996), 239.

303 I. Johnston, *The Ironies of War*, 6; compare Rabkin, *Meaning and Shakespeare*, 104.

304 Shakespeare, *Troilus and Cressida*, ed. Bevington, introduction, 22–3.

305 On scoptic speech in *Troilus and Cressida*, see Patricia Thomson, "Rant and Cant in *Troilus and Cressida*," *Essays and Studies* 22 (1969): 33–56; Elton, *Inns of Court Revels*, 77–82; Laurie E. Maguire, "Performing Anger: The Anatomy of Abuse(s) in *Troilus and Cressida*," *Renaissance Drama* n.s. 31 (2002): 153–83; David Hillman, "The Gastric Epic: *Troilus and Cressida*," *SQ* 48, no. 3 (1997): 295–313; Kenneth Gross, *Shakespeare's Noise* (Chicago: University of Chicago Press, 2001), 57.

306 Elton, *Inns of Court Revels*, 8, 167; on the Homeric foundations of "learned folly" and serious play, see also Giangrande, *The Use of Spoudaiogeloion*, and Elton, 39, which argues that Ulysses's degree speech effects a "mock-epic inversion suited to the world-upside-down occasion of a revel."

307 Gibbon, trans. Pontaymeri, *A Womans Woorth*, sig. C4v (16v). On late sixteenth- and early seventeenth-century irreverence towards Homer, see Elton, *Inns of Court Revels*, 8–9.

308 James, *Shakespeare's Troy*, 89; compare J. Harris, "Enterprise," 23, who argues that Shakespeare deliberately highlight[s] the multiple and mutually contradictory currencies he encountered in his source materials."

309 Elton, *Inns of Court Revels*, 33.

310 Elton, *Inns of Court Revels*, 26. On Aristotle's distinction between the boor and the buffoon, see *Nic. Ethics* IV.8.3–11 [1128a–b]. On Shakespeare's Ulysses as a Socratic *eiron*, see Robert Grudin, "The Soul of State: Ulyssean Irony in *Troilus and Cressida*," *Anglia* 93, nos. 1–2 (1975): 55–69, 56–7, which remarks upon the "consistent irony which clarifies [Ulysses's] double position as moralist and deceiver" and also describes his opening speech in I.3 as full of "ambiguities" and "shaded with irony." On the irony of Ulysses's degree speech, also see Norbrook, "Rhetoric, Ideology, and the Elizabethan World Picture," 154–6, and Elton, "Shakespeare's Ulysses and the Problem of Value," 97–9.

311 Shakespeare, *Troilus and Cressida*, 80; the rhetorical terms are from Puttenham, *Arte of English Poesie*. On Ajax's braggart status and on evidence that he is a portrait of Jonson, see Elton, "Shakespeare's Portrait of Ajax," 746–7, and Kimbrough, *Shakespeare's Troilus and Cressida*, 39.

312 On the sixteenth-century presentation of Thersites as a "railing detractor," see Kimbrough, *Shakespeare's Troilus and Cressida*, 38.

313 Lombardo, "Fragments and Scraps," 205; on conflicting perspectives in the play, see also John J. Enck, "The Peace of the Poetomachia," *PMLA* 77, no. 4 (1962): 386–96, and Arnold Stein, "*Troilus and Cressida*: the Disjunctive Imagination," *ELH* 36, no. 1 (1969): 145–67.

314 Laroque, "Perspective," 226.

315 On fame as a "false good" in *Troilus and Cressida*, see Grudin, "The Soul of State," 63–4.

316 Pucci, *Song of the Sirens*, 168, 66.

317 On Thersites as a "grotesque satirist" see Laroque, "Perspective," 226; on Thersites as a warped chorus, see Shakespeare, *Troilus and Cressida*, 66.

318 Lombardo, "Fragments and Scraps," 205; for a similar reading, see Una Ellis-Fermor, "'Discord in the Spheres': the Universe of *Troilus and Cressida,*" 56–76 of her *The Frontiers of Drama*, 2nd ed. (London: Methuen, 1964), 64. On discord in *Troilus and Cressida*, see also M. T. Jones-Davies, "Discord in Shakespeare's *Troilus and Cressida*; or, The Conflict between 'Angry Mars and Venus Queen of Love,'" *SQ* 25, no. 1 (1974): 33–41. Richard Fly, 'Suited in Like Conditions as Our Argument': Imitative Form in Shakespeare's *Troilus and Cressida*," *SEL* 15, no. 2 (1975): 273–92, 277–82, argues that the "'disjunctive and nonsequential' shape of the play" jolts the audience out of its "complacent expectation of conventional design" and adds to the sense of disorientation. On emulation in *Troilus and Cressida*, see Joel Fineman, "Fratricide and Cuckoldry: Shakespeare's Doubles," in, *Representing Shakespeare: New Psychoanalytic Essays*, ed. Murray M. Schwartz and Coppelia Kahn (Baltimore: Johns Hopkins University Press, 1980): 70–109,

94; René Girard, "The Politics of Desire in *Troilus and Cressida*," in *Shakespeare and the Question of Theory*, ed. Patricia Parker and Geoffrey Hartman (New York: Methuen, 1985), 188–209.

319 Maguire, "Performing Anger," 177. Compare Burton, *Anatomy of Melancholy*, 1:337–41: "The Gods had their Momus, Homer his Zoilus, Achilles his Thersites ... the bitter jest ... pierceth deeper then any losse, danger, bodily paine, or injury whatsoever."

320 *Iliad*, trans. Chapman, 9.307–9 [= 318–20], 189. The 1598 translation of these lines (*Seaven Bookes*, 84) is identical save a few variant spellings.

321 *The Greek Anthology* 2: 387 (Book 7, Epigram 727); compare Lucian, *Charon* (*Dialogues* 2:441), in which the title character creates parodic pastiches out of lines from Homer which assert that death will level out the distinctions between Agamemnon and Irus and between Achilles and Thersites. On inversion and misrule in *Troilus and Cressida* see Elton, *Inns of Court Revels*, 49.

322 On the relationship between Achilles and Thersites in the *Iliad*, see Thalmann, "Thersites," 19, which argues that Thersites's reproach is a "parody of Achilles' earlier reproaches of Agamemnon" and, "since parody implies an irreducible element of similarity … Thersites is Achilles' comic double."

323 Shakespeare, *Troilus and Cressida*, 21.

324 Dryden, *Troilus and Cressida, or, Truth found too late*, preface, sig. b2v.

325 Dryden, *Troilus and Cressida*, preface, sig. b2v. On Dryden's reinterpretation of *Troilus and Cressida*, see Hopkins, "'The English Homer': Shakespeare, Longinus, and English 'neo-classicism'," chapter 15 (261–76) of *Shakespeare and the Classics*, ed. Martindale and Taylor, 269.

5. The Razor's Edge: Homer, Milton, and the Problem of Deliberation

1 Milton, *Doctrine and Discipline of Divorce*, in *Complete Prose* 2:343, hereafter cited as *YP*. All citations from *PL* are from *Paradise Lost*, ed. Fowler.

2 *Iliad*, trans. Chapman, 204 (10.150); Erasmus, Adage I.i.18 (*CWE* 31:66). The other usage appears at Shakespeare, *Love's Labors Lost* V.2.257, where Boyet calls the "tongues of mocking wenches … as keen / As is the Razors edge, invisible." In his *Psyche, or Loves Mysterie in XX Canto's*, 140, Beaumont uses the phrase "the edge of Rasors" to describe a sharp stare. In his opening speech in *Henry IV, Part 1* 1.1.18, the king speaks of the "edge of war." But no English writer except Chapman and Milton uses the phrase in its Homeric sense – to describe the precipice between two contrary choices or outcomes. On Milton's knowledge of Erasmus's *Adages*, see G. Butler, "Milton's Pandora: Eve, Sin, and the Mythographic Tradition," *MS* 44 (2005): 153–78.

3 Compare Milton, *Paradise Regained* 2.455, in *Complete Works* 2(2): 440 (hereafter cited as *CW*) where Christ cautions Satan that a desire for riches may "slacken virtue, and abate her edge."

4 Milton, *Reason of Church Government*, hereafter abbreviated *RCG*, in *YP* 1:751.

5 Milton, *Paradise Regained* 1.94–5, in *CW* 2(2): 408.

6 Hume, *Annotations on Paradise Lost*, 6.108; *Milton's Paradise Lost. A New Edition by Richard Bentley*, 190 on *PL* 6.236; Lewis, *Preface to Paradise Lost*, 135.

7 See Snell, *The Discovery of the Mind*, 1–23; Gaskin, "Do Homeric Heroes Make Real Decisions?" 15; Zerba, *Doubt and Skepticism*, 32–6.

8 Schofield, "Eubolia in the *Iliad*," 220–4; Barnouw, *Odysseus, Hero of Practical Intelligence*, 7–8. On Homeric pondering scenes and other conventions governing deliberation both within and outside of assembly, see also Edwards, "Convention and Individuality in *Iliad* I." This chapter uses the terms *council* and *assembly* somewhat interchangeably, although Milton did distinguish in later writings between councils (permanent) and parliaments (transitory and successive).

9 Milton, *Readie and Easie Way*, *YP* 7:427. On Milton's transformation of Homeric council scenes, see Quint, "Ulysses and the Devils," 23–4.

10 Martindale, *John Milton and the Transformation of Ancient Epic*, 53; Tillyard, *The English Epic*, 438. Revard, *Pindar*, 119, describes Milton's admiration for the "Greek sisterhood ... that sustained Homer and Hesiod and Pindar."

11 On Milton's Alfred poem, see *CW* 18:266; for Richardson's comment, see his *Explanatory Notes and Remarks on Milton's Paradise Lost* (London, 1734), lxxxv–lxxxvi, rpt. in *CW* 18:387. Richardson also asserts that Milton could "almost repeat [Homer] without book" and that, had Milton been represented in "the Parnassus," one of Raphael's frescoes in the Vatican, "Homer and he ought to have been Embracing each other, he knew him perfectly" (xiv, cxlix).

12 On these and other Hebraizing interpretations of Homeric epic, see Allen, *Mysteriously Meant*, 67–75, 100–3; and chapter 3 of Shoulson, *Fictions of Conversion*. On seventeenth-century attitudes towards the scriptures as epic or heroic, see Ryken, "*Paradise Lost* and Its Biblical Epic Models," in *Milton and Scriptural Tradition*, ed. Sims and Ryken, 53. On Milton's use of Homeric quotations to support his Arminian theology, see Van Der Laan, "Milton's Odyssean Ethics."

13 Bogan, *Quae Spectant ad Deum*, in his *Homerus Hebraizon*, 396, 399; according to Bogan, these doctrines are endorsed by passages including *Od.* 3.132, 20.44, 20.273, and 22.39.

14 Radzinowicz, *Psalms*, 8, argues that the marginalia in Milton's books suggests that "Hebrew and Greek poetry were introduced to him as subjects of comparison" at school.

15 Hale, *Milton's Languages*, 43–6, 70, argues that Milton's Greek translation of Ps. 114 uses the "energetic verbs and amplitude of epithetizing" typical of the *Iliad*, qualities that prompt Hale to argue that his translations of the Psalms fuse "Hellenic with Hebraic" and "operat[e] where Homer and David intersect in heroic." On Milton's translations of the Psalms and his familiarity with the Septuagint, see also Radzinowicz, *Psalms*.

16 Hale, *Milton's Languages*, 198. In *Areopagitica* (*YP* 2:508–9), Milton appeals to the model of Saint Paul, who "thought it no defilement to insert into Holy Scripture the sentences of three Greek poets," and he concurs with Church fathers such as Jerome, Chrysostom, and Basil, who regarded it as "an injury … to be depriv'd of *Hellenick* learning." On Milton's synthesis of "incompatible materials," see also Turner, *One Flesh*, ix, and Van Der Laan, "Milton's Odyssean Ethics," 49–50.

17 N. Smith, "*Paradise Lost* from Civil War to Restoration," chapter 14 (251–67) of *The Cambridge Companion to Writing of the English Revolution*, ed. Keeble, 263.

18 Kallendorf argues that as *PL* unfolds, Satan first appears to be the "new" Aeneas but then turns out to be the new Turnus, while Adam takes up the role of Aeneas and Eve is alternately cast as his Dido, his Lavinia, and his Venus. See his "Virgil, Milton, and the Modern Reader," chapter 6 (67–79) of *Classics and the Uses of Reception*, ed. Martindale and Thomas, 72–4. On the "flexible" and "complex" aspects of Milton's comprehension of generic form, see Lewalski, *Paradise Lost*, 23.

19 Milton, *Defensio Secunda*, *YP* 4(1):589, citing *Il.* 9.411–16. For Milton's Latin translation, see *CW* 8:68.

20 Milton, *Defensio Secunda*, *CW* 8:85. That choice, as Quint, "Ulysses and the Devils," 26–7, points out, is a choice between "public heroism and the heroism of private conscience."

21 Porter, *Reading the Classics*, 90–1.

22 On Satan as a "parody" or perversion of Achilles, see Harding, *The Club of Hercules*, 46–7; Rumrich, *Matter of Glory*, 28; Lewalski, *Paradise Lost*, 60–2; Steadman, *Milton and the Paradoxes of Renaissance Heroism*, 46. On Christ as an Achilles-figure, see Quint, *Epic and Empire*, 48; Lewalski, 126–8. On Adam as an Achilles figure, see Mueller, "*Paradise Lost* and the *Iliad*," 301–2; and Revard, "Milton, Homer, and the Anger of Adam."

23 On the symbolism of Satan's shield and his incorrect handling of it, see Dobranski, "Pondering Satan's Shield in *Paradise Lost*."

24 Hesiod, *WD*, ln. 264; compare ls. 8–9 and *Il.* 16.387 for similar formulae. On Achilles's shield (*Il.* 18.506–8), the judges of the assembly compete for "two talents of gold" [*duô chrusoio talanta*] to be given to the judge who utters "the straightest judgement" [*dikên ithuntata*].
25 Martindale, *John Milton and the Transformation of Ancient Epic*, 56–7, notes several allusions to Achilles's shield in Michael's vision of fallen man at *PL* 11.638–71.
26 Barrow, *In Paradisum Amissum Summi Poetae Johannis Miltoni*, ls. 27–8, in Milton, *Paradise Lost*, ed. Fowler, 51. On Homer's cultivation of expectation and suspense, see N.J. Richardson, "Literary Criticism in the Exegetical Scholia," in *Oxford Readings in ancient literary criticism*, ed. Laird, 180–3.
27 Empson, *Milton's God*, 96–7. If Milton's God is "dubius," it is perhaps intended as an antidote to the lack of doubt manifested by Satan and his rebel angels as they stand "scoffing, heightened in their thoughts beyond / All doubt of victory" (*PL* 6.629–30).
28 *PL* 3.178–9; Danielson, *Milton's Good God*, 142. Compare Martz, *Milton: Poet of Exile*, 99, arguing that "the whole poem depends upon this promise."
29 Lord, "Homer, *Paradise Lost*, and the Renaissance," in *The Milton Encyclopedia*, ed. Hunter, 4:25.
30 Milton, *De Doctrina Christiana*, *CW* 14:174–5, hereafter abbreviated as *DDC*, citing *Od.* 1.7 and 1.32–4: "It is astonishing how ready mortals are to blame the gods. It is from us, they say, that evils come, but they by themselves, through their own blind folly, have sorrows beyond that which is ordained by fate." The Homeric passage was a favorite of the church fathers: see, for instance, Alexander of Aphrodisias, *The Banquet of the Ten Virgins*, in *Ante-Nicene Fathers* 6:340.
31 Hammond, *Of Fundamentals in a notion referring to practise*, 177, 184–5; Milton, *Doctrine and Discipline*, *YP* 2:234. Sixteenth- and seventeenth-century readers of Homer's *Odyssey* often draw similar theological conclusions from the passage; see, for instance, the marginal notes in BL C.66.b2, sig. aa2r, Lemnius's 1549 *Odyssey*, in which the annotator has written "Deus non est causa malorum" (God is not the cause of evil) and "Quis mali sui faber" (Every man makes his own evil) next to Zeus's speech.
32 Milton, *Doctrine and Discipline*, *YP* 2:234, 2:294.
33 Milton, *Doctrine and Discipline*, *YP* 2:294; *Homeri Quae Extant Omnia*, ed. Sponde, 1:64 on *Il.* 4.66–72; the passage depicts Zeus, at Hera's prodding, ordering Athena to coerce the Trojans to forswear their oath; compare Sponde's comments on *Od.* 18.347, where Athena does not permit the suitors to "abstain from bitter outrage."
34 Milton, *Doctrine and Discipline*, *YP* 2:294.

35 Milton, *Tetrachordon*, *CW* 4:161.
36 Griffin, *Homer on Life and Death*, 192.
37 Milton, *DDC*, *CW* 14:31–3.
38 Lord, "Homer, *Paradise Lost*, and the Renaissance," in *A Milton Encyclopedia*, ed. Hunter, 4:25.
39 *Homeri Quae Extant Omnia*, ed. Sponde, 2:4 on *Od.* 1.32–5: "malorum quae hominibus contingunt, causam non esse in Deum, sed in ipsas hominum nequitias & improbitates referendam." On Sponde's reading of Zeus's speech in the *Odyssey*, see Lord, "Homer, *Paradise Lost*, and the Renaissance," 25.
40 Burden, *The Logical Epic*, 12. This reading confirms and complicates Stanley Fish's argument that *Paradise Lost* teaches readers to "distrust [their] own abilities and perceptions" (Fish, *Surprised by Sin*, 22).
41 Milton, *Doctrine and Discipline*, *YP* 2:321.
42 Hesiod, *WD*, ls. 9, 264. In Homeric epic, the terms *dikê* and *themis* are quite close; both are associated with the *agora*: see *Od.* 4.691, 11.569–70, 12.439–40, 14.83–8, and the discussion by Cook, *Odyssey in Athens*, 97–100. On the ancient Greek understanding of Themis and her connection to *dikê*, see also Rudhardt, *Themis et les Hôrai*, 32.
43 Milton, *PL* 12.566–9; Hesiod, *WD*, ls. 5–8.
44 See also Prov. 2.15, a lament for those whose "paths are crooked" [*triboi skoliai*].
45 The resonance is especially striking given that *dikê* and *dikaiôn* are the preferred Septuagint translations for "justice" and "just" (or "righteous").
46 On God's willingness to "accommodate himself to our capacities" see Milton, *DDC*, *CW* 14:31–3.
47 On the relationship between similes and irony in Homeric epic, see chapter 4 of this book. For similar arguments concerning Milton's use of the word "or," which produces a "poetics of incertitude" by denoting the possible distinction or choice between values or objects that "have not just differing, but fundamentally opposite valences," see Herman, "*Paradise Lost*, the Miltonic 'Or,' and the Poetics of Incertitude," 183, 188.
48 Louden, "Milton and the Appropriation of an Epic Technique," 326; see also his *The Odyssey. Structure, Narration, and Meaning*, 123–7, and his "Pivotal Counterfactuals in Homeric Epic," 181–98. Additional discussions of Homeric contrafactuals appear in Mabel Lang, "Unreal Conditions in Homeric Narrative," *Greek, Roman and Byzantine Studies* 30, no. 1 (1989): 5–26; De Jong, *Narrators and Focalizers*, 70–2; and Morrison, *Homeric Misdirection*, 32.
49 Milton, *Doctrine and Discipline of Divorce*, *YP* 2:294.
50 Louden, "Milton and the Appropriation of an Epic Technique," 326; compare B. Berry, *Process of Speech*, 212, and Nünlist, *The Ancient Critic at Work*,

142–8, on how Homer's ancient scholiasts analysed contrafactuals in terms of the agony they create in the reader.

51 When Athena scolds Ares for interfering in battle, she tells him "it would be best to leave the Trojans and Achaeans to fight, so that father Zeus may grant glory to whichever side he wishes" (*Il.* 5.32–4).

52 On the non-intervention of Milton's God, see Fallon, "To Act or Not," 448, which argues that God's liberty includes the freedom not to act: "God … can do only right, but he is free to act or not."

53 Louden, "Milton and the Appropriation of an Epic Technique," 339. On divine intervention in Homeric epic as reconcilable with human liberty, see Nünlist, *The Ancient Critic at Work*, 269–70.

54 Ajax and Idomeneus would have created "strife" [*eris*] "if Achilles himself had not stood up and spoken" (*Il.* 23.491); Achilles acts once again as "*theiomen amphô*" (umpire; literally, "standing between two sides") during the boxing match between Ajax and Odysseus, who would have continued to wrestle "if Achilles himself had not stood up and held them back," awarding victory to both men (*Il.* 23.486, 23.734). On the significance of the *histôr* or umpire during the funeral games of *Il.* 23, see Nagy, *Pindar's Homer*, chapter 9.

55 Louden, "Milton and the Appropriation of an Epic Technique," 328. On Christ as "our Mediator" and "*theanthropôs*" [god-man], see Milton, *DDC*, *CW* 15:278–9, and the discussion by Hugh MacCallum, *Milton and the Sons of God. The Divine Image in Milton's Epic Poetry* (Toronto: University of Toronto Press, 1986), 32, 58.

56 On the frequency of prolepses and analepses in the *Iliad*, see E. Balensiefen, *Die Zeitgeitaltung in Homers Ilias* (PhD dissertation, University of Tubingen, 1955), 19, and De Jong, *Narrators and Focalizers*, 86. On scholiastic interpretations of Homeric prolepses and analepses, see Nünlist, *The Ancient Critic at Work*, 37–8, 47.

57 Morrison, "Alternatives to the Epic Tradition," 66, 62, 68–9.

58 Since strength is the only "measure" according to which the rebel angels are willing to assess the outcome of the war in heaven, "of other excellence / Not emulous, nor care who them excels" (*PL* 6.821–2), the Son chooses to employ physical force only to accommodate the moral infirmity of his enemies.

59 Louden, "Milton and the Appropriation of an Epic Technique," 336.

60 In his *Commentary on Plato's Republic* 144 (124.27–8), Proclus proposes that the tears of the gods represent their providence towards mortals, who are born and die. Paquelin, *Apologeme*, 89, refutes Plato by arguing

that no father, even a divine one, "should have such an adamantine heart" [*auroit tant le Coeur adamantin*] that he does not weep over the death of a son.

61 Clement, *Exhortation*, 183, cites *Od.* 2.47 ("*patêr d'hôs êpios*," as tender as a father) in order to describe the gentle chastisement of the Christian God, who "speaks not as a teacher to disciples, nor as a master to servants, nor as God to man, but as a 'tender father' admonishing his sons." Compare Clement, *Stromates* 14, 116.1, p. 215.

62 *Homeri Quae Extant Omnia*, ed. Sponde, 2:34 on *Od.* 3.236.

63 Sin's Homeric allusion is a good example of what Julia M. Walker calls an "antitext"; see her "The Poetics of Antitext and the Politics of Milton's Allusions," *SEL* 37 (1997): 151–71.

64 On the "military metaphor" of the war in heaven as a "vehicle for accommodation," see William McQueen, "*Paradise Lost* V, VI: The War in Heaven," *SP* 71, no. 1 (1974): 89–104, 99. For additional discussions of whether Milton's war in heaven should be read literally or allegorically, see Lee A. Jacobus, *Sudden Apprehension. Aspects of Knowledge in Paradise Lost* (Paris and The Hague: Mouton, 1976), 93, which argues that the war in heaven is not a "concession to Adam's understanding" because Adam has no experience of war; Murrin, *Allegorical Epic*, 162–71; J.B. Broadbent, *Some Graver Subject. An Essay on Paradise Lost* (London: Chatto & Windus, 1960), 230, argues for an allegorical reading, stating that the Son's weapons are "not military, but the immaterial fire of the *Logos*."

65 *Il.* 12.433–5: Chapman translates the verb "*isazous*" as "just paise stand" and praises the simile as "beyond comparison and admiration" (*Iliad*, trans. Chapman, 251). *The Iliad: A Commentary*, ed. Kirk, 3:362, notes the similarity between this simile and that of Zeus's scales: "As an image, scales express balance, as here, or the moment of decision, when the balance inclines in one direction, as at [*Il.*] 8.69, 22.209."

66 On the image of Zeus stretching out his scales at *Il.* 8.69–72 (repeated at 22.209–13), see Kirk, *The Iliad: a Commentary*, 2:303. Although routinely mistranslated as "raising aloft" his scales, Homer's Zeus in fact "stretches" [*etitaine*] them out, a verb that corresponds to his juridical role as a "counselor" who straightens crooked judgements.

67 Treip, "Reason is Also Choice," 169. Compare Frank Harper Moore, "Astraea, the Scorpion, and the Heavenly Scales," *ELH* 38, no. 3 (1971): 350–57, 351: "the scales are to be regarded …as weighing the consequences of the two courses of action open to Satan at one particular crisis of his career."

68 Treip, "Reason Is Also Choice," 167–8; also see Martz, *Poet of Exile*, 90, on the "careful plowman" whose "doubting" implies a "state of uncertainty and ... of fear." In *DDC* (*CW* 16:218–19), Milton discusses the wheat and chaff imagery at Matt. 3.12 and 13.24–5.

69 Hammond, *A Pacifick Discourse of Gods Grace and Decrees*, 585; on this Miltonic passage, see Danielson, *Milton's Good God*, 141. On Dan. 5.27 ("you have been weighed in the balance and found wanting") as another key source for Milton's image, see Broadbent, *Some Graver Subject*, 201.

70 Milton, *Tenure of Kings and Magistrates*, *YP* 3:192. For a similar interpretation of Milton's transformation of the Achaean Council, see Lewalski, *Paradise Lost*, 86, which argues that Satan's address to his assembly is intended to prevent the disunity evident in the Homeric council and that Satan, like Agamemnon, meets with opposition, "as Belial and Mammon play Thersites' role in urging abandonment of the war."

71 On ploughman and threshing metaphors as images of epistemological or moral distinction, see Sansone, "How Milton Reads," 335, who points out that "[w]innowing and threshing are common biblical metaphors for judgement, appearing especially in the books of the prophets" and provides numerous examples of these metaphors and their influence on Milton's *Lycidas*.

72 See Milton's translation of Ps. 1.11–14: "Not so the wicked, but as chaff which fann'd / The wind drives, so the wicked shall not stand / In judgment, or abide their trial then, / Nor sinners in th'assembly of just men." Compare Isa. 17.13: nations will fly away "driven like chaff on the hills before the wind."

73 In an early poem entitled *Naturam non pati senium* [That Nature Submits not to Decay], Milton cleaves even more closely to Homer with an image of God holding "weights inerrant, *pondering* in perfect balance the scales of the fates [*certoque peregit / Pondere fatorum lances*]. See *Naturam non pati senium*, ls. 34–5, *CW* 1(1): 262.

74 Albert R. Cirillo, "Noon-Midnight and the Temporal Structure of *Paradise Lost*," *ELH* 29, no. 4 (1962): 372–95, 380.

75 Corns, *Regaining Paradise Lost*, 83; Milton, *RCG*, *YP* 1:795. On Satan's irresolution, see also Treip, "Reason is also Choice," 162, which discusses the threat posed to free will by "indeterminatione" as represented by Cesare Ripa's emblem *Libero Arbitrio*. Compare Quint, "Ulysses and the Devils," 30, 37–8, which argues that the devils in Hell continually invent "false alternatives" for themselves, a tendency symbolized in the Odyssean motif of Scylla and Charybdis, the figures of "bad alternatives" and impossible choice.

76 This process of deliberation is the defining feature of Odysseus's heroic temper in the *Odyssey*, where he repeatedly "ponders in his mind and his heart" [*hôrmaine kata phrena kai kata thumon*] before he "makes trial for himself" [*autos peirêsomai*] the better course of action. For this formula, see also *Od.* 6.118, 6.126, 18.345. On Satan as a perverted Odysseus, see Quint, "Ulysses and the Devils."

77 Lord, "Homer, *Paradise Lost*, and the Renaissance," 22–3.

78 Contrast the rebel angels at *PL* 6.840 as they flee, discarding their helms, a formulaic image of flight based on *Il.* 12.22 and similar passages.

79 *Il.* 3.95, where Hector proposes the single combat between Menelaus and Hector, and *Il.* 7.92–3 where Hector challenges Ajax to single combat.

80 *Homeri Quae Extant Omnia*, ed. Sponde, 1:18 on *Il.* 3.343.

81 Duport, *Homeri … Gnomologia*, 25, 164–5; Duport identifies and translates the Homeric passages as *Il.* 5.402 and *Od.* 4.78 ("Utique cum Jove mortalium haud quisqua[m] contenderit").

82 On Duport's career, see Fletcher, *Intellectual Development of John Milton*, 2:276–9.

83 For the Homeric analogues to Belial and Moloch, see James Baumlin, "Epic and Allegory in *Paradise Lost*, book II," *College Literature* 14, no. 2 (1987): 167–77, 169–70; M. Hammond, "*Concilia Deorum*"; Quint, "Ulysses and the Devils," 24–30.

84 Readers in search of Homeric analogues to the infernal council in Book 2 of *PL* often identify Satan with Ajax, the warrior selected to do single combat with Hector; Satan shares Ajax's audacity and his towering physical presence. *PL* 2's infernal council closely follows the Achaean council scene of *Il.* 7, as well as the contest between Ajax and Ulysses in the so-called *Judicium Armorum* of Ovid's *Metamorphoses*. On the scene's debts to Ovid and on Satan's resemblance to Ovid's Ulysses, who outtalks his rival in a "prearranged debate," see DuRocher, *Milton and Ovid*, 139–40.

85 Lewalski, *Paradise Lost*, 23. On the resemblance of Satan to Achilles, see Lewalski, 3, who argues that Satan is an "Achillean hero motivated by a sense of injured merit." On Achilles and Satan, also see Steadman, *Milton and the Paradoxes of Renaissance Heroism*, 46; Harding, *The Club of Hercules*, 46–7; on the resemblance of the Son to Achilles, see Lewalski, 61.

86 Milton, *Eikonoklastes*, *YP* 3:409 depicts Charles as a king who "summon[s] Parliaments" so that "greatest matters may be there debated and resolv'd" only to "dash all thir resolutions" with his "one single voice."

87 On "genuine debate" in Milton's hell, see Herman, *Destabilizing Milton*, 93; David Daiches, *Milton* (New York: Hutchinson's University Library, 1957), 166.

88 Milton, *DDC*, *CW* 16:310–11: "*Conciliorum vestigium in scriptura nullum reperio.*"

89 See Ps. 5.10–11 ("let them fall / By their own counsels quelled"); Ps. 1.1–2 (blessed is he who "hath not walked astray / In counsel of the wicked"), and Ps. 83.5 (on the sinners who have "taken counsel with one consent" against God).

90 Milton, *Readie and Easie Way*, *YP* 7:427. Compare William Moeck, "Bees in my Bonnet: Milton's Epic Simile and Intertextuality," *MQ* 32, no. 4 (1998): 122–35, who argues (124–5) that the bee simile at *PL* 1.768–76 derives from Virgil, *Aen.* 1.598–609, verses indebted to *Il.* 2.111–17 but lacking the shepherd of Homer's version.

91 Yet Milton's early writings also display an interest in the infernal council convention for the purposes of exposing the dangers of popular opnion. *In Quintum Novembris*, ls. 173–7 (*CW* 1(1):250) depicts the council of plotters presided over by *Fama* – an amalgam of Virgil's goddess of Rumor and Homer's Eris who is accompanied by a "rabble rout."

92 On Milton's dislike of popular votes, see *Readie and Easie Way*, *CW* 6:114, arguing that councils should act upon "what [is] well motiond and advis'd" rather than following a vote decided by "numbring or computing on which side were most voices in Parlament."

93 Duport, *Homeri ... Gnomologia*, 201; on Odysseus's inability to resist the majority opinion of his crew, see Ruzé, *Déliberation*, 84.

94 Lewalski, *Paradise Lost*, 304n5, points out that Satan's actions resemble those of Dolon at *Il.* 10.202: Dolon goes alone on his mission so as not to share glory but is defeated by Diomedes and Odysseus. For another interpretation of Milton's *Doloneia*, see Quint, "Ulysses and the Devils."

95 Lewalski, *Paradise Lost*, 57–8; Milton, *Defensio Pro Populo*, *YP* 4(1):358.

96 On Milton's concept of marriage in Eden, see Luxon, *Single Imperfection*, and McColley, *Milton's Eve*, 22, 49.

97 *PL* 2.681–726; on these scenes, see *Il.* 6.391–493, 18.70–137, and 22.79–93. On Milton's "grotesquely comic" imitation of the *Iliad*, see Lewalski, *Paradise Lost*, 60.

98 Burrow, *Epic Romance*, 278.

99 Hesiod, *Theogony*, ls. 896–900, relates how Zeus, told that Mêtis will give birth to a daughter wiser than him in counsel, swallows Mêtis so that she might "advise [Zeus] about good and evil" [*hôs dê oi phrassaito thea agathon te kakon te*] from the inside of his abdomen, thus allowing Zeus to give birth to Athena – wisdom – from his own head. On the myth as a secret of state see Bacon, *Wisdom* 30, in *Works*, 6.1, 761.

100 Bacon, *Wisdom*, in *Works*, 6.1, 761–2.
101 Milton, *Readie and Easie Way*, *CW* 6:123, 6:114.
102 See *Il.* 5.738–41. The second *Homeric Hymn to Athena* (ls. 8–12) describes Athena's birth out of Zeus's head, fully armed; see Chapman, "To Pallas," ln. 8, in *Odyssey*, 597.
103 *Pandaemonium* derives from a Greek compound meaning "assembly of all the demons." On this point, see King, *Milton and Religious Controversy*, 68.
104 Milton, *Mane citus lectum fuge*, *CW* 12:288–91.
105 See, for example, Duport, *Gnomologia*, 9: "non oportet per totam noctem dormire consiliarum virum" (paraphrasing *Il.* 2.3). The Homeric adage was often compared to Ps. 121.4, "The guardian of Israel / never slumbers, never sleeps."
106 Milton, *PL* 1.659–60, *RCG*, *YP* 1:797.
107 Milton, *Readie and Easie Way*, *YP* 7:423.
108 See *Il.* 2.703, 2.726. *Anarchê* is one of a number of Homeric privatives used in *PL*: see Hume, *Annotations*, 92 (on *PL* 2.988), and the discussion of "negative prefixation" in Corns, *Milton's Language*, 84–6.
109 Schofield, "Eubolia in the *Iliad*," 224.
110 Milton, *Eikonoklastes*, *YP* 3:348; *Considerations Touching the Likeliest Means to Remove Hirelings*, *CW* 6:84.
111 Milton, *Readie and Easie Way*, *CW* 6:127; *Of Prelaticall Episcopacy*, *CW* 3(1):99; *Apology*, *CW* 3(1): 357.
112 Milton, *Of True Religion*, *CW* 6:176–77; *Apology*, *CW* 3(1):357. Compare *Areopagitica* (*YP* 2:555) on the "many schisms and many dissections made in the quarry and in the timber, ere the house of God can be built."
113 M. Hammond, "Concilia Deorum," 11. On Milton's debts to and his transformation of the *Concilia Deorum*, see also Achinstein, "Milton and the Fit Reader. *Paradise Lost* and the Parliament of Hell," chapter 5 (177–223) of her *Milton and the Revolutionary Reader*; M. Christopher Pecheux, "The Council Scenes in *Paradise Lost*," chapter 4 of *Milton and Scriptural Tradition*, ed. Sims and Ryken, 82–103; Olin H. Moore, "The Infernal Council," *MP* 16, no. 4 (1918): 1–25; Gertrude C. Drake, "Satan's Councils in *The Christiad*, *Paradise Lost*, and *Paradise Regained*," in *Acta Conventus Turonensis* (1980), ed. Jean-Claude Margolin, 2:979–89; Lewalski, *Paradise Lost*, 115.
114 Achinstein, *Revolutionary Reader*, 203; at 179–88 she argues that Royalist works such as *The Devil in his Dumps* (1647) and *The Devil and the Parliament* (1648) represent their titular anti-heroes as republican dissenters, "source[s] of schism" who infuse "contentious spirits" into their audiences

in order to "stir up Faction, and Rebellion." Compare Lawrence Venuti, "The Destruction of Troy: translation and royalist cultural politics in the Interregnum,"*JMRS* 23, no. 2 (1993): 197–219. On the use of the Satanic council in civil war-era pamphlets, see also Diana Benet, "Hell, Satan, and the New Politician," in *Literary Milton: Text, Pretext, Context*, ed. Benet and Lieb, 91–113.

115 *Famous Tragedie*, 1–2, cited in Achinstein, *Revolutionary Reader*, 192.

116 Milton, *Eikonoklastes*, *YP* 3:387, 3:356. On the 1648 Cambridge edition of the *Iliad*, possibly edited by James Duport and designed to "bolster royalist sentiments," see Machacek, "Royalist Homer," 331–2.

117 *Il.* 2.204–6: "No good thing is a multitude of kings; let there be one lord, one king, to whom the son of crooked-counseling Cronos has given the scepter and judgements [*skêptron t'êde themistas*], so that he may take counsel for his people." For pro-monarchical interpretations of Homer, see Lipsius, *Sixe Bookes of Politickes or Civil Doctrine* 2.2, trans. Jones, 18, and Ovid, *Metam.*, trans. Sandys, 63–4. On republican interpretations of Agamemnon, see Burrow, *Epic Romance*, 218.

118 Hammer, *The Iliad as Politics*, 130. For Homer's conception of the *themistas*, see *Od.* 2.68–9. On the role of Themis in governing "debate" in the assembly, see also Hammer, *The Iliad as Politics*, 119, discussing *Il.* 15.87–93 and 20.4. Ruzé, *Déliberation*, 29, identifies Themis as the goddess "who dissolves and convenes the assemblies of men" (my translation).

119 Milton, *Defensio Pro Populo*, *YP* 4 (1): 358 [*CW* 7:110–11]. Milton's republican interpretation of the *Iliad* has an ancient legacy in writers such as Theophrastus, who paraphrases *Il.* 2.204 in his *Characters*, 143, arguing that "those who covet power and profit … remember only one line from Homer, 'More than one leader is bad'." For a similar argument about Milton's anti-monarchical interpretation of the *Aen.*, see Kallendorf, *The Other Virgil*, 162.

120 In the Septuagint, the passage reads, "Di'emou basileis basileuousi, kai oi dunastai graphousi dikaiosunên. Di'emou megistanes megalunontai, kai turannoi di'emou kratousi gês."

121 Milton, *Defensio Pro Populo*, *YP* 4 (1): 437.

122 Milton, *Defensio Pro Populo*, *YP* 4 (1): 441, citing *Il.* 1.231–2: "Populi vorator rex, quoniam hominibus nihili imperas. / Alioqui enim Atrida, nunc postremum injuriam faceres."

123 Paul Salzman, "Royalist Epic and Romance," chapter 12 (pp. 215–230) of *The Cambridge Companion to Writing of the English Revolution*, ed. Keeble, 216. On the appropriation of epic for the Royalist cause, see also Herman, *Destabilizing Milton*, 39.

124 During the 1640s and 1650s, plenty of Royalists tried to claim Homer as one of their own; see N. Smith, *Literature and Revolution*, 53.

125 Hall, *Virgidemiarum*, Book 2, Sat. 3, ln. 3, p. 30; Cudworth, *The True Intellectual System*, 544; compare Jackson, *A Treatise containing the originall of unbeliefe*, 174.

126 In Part 2, canto 1 of Rous's *Thule, or Vertues Historie*, an allegorized *Themistos* defeats a tyrant. Michael Maier's *Themis Aurea*, translated into English in 1656, urges commonwealths to worship Themis, the "Goddesse of Justice," because it is "by [Themis] [that] kings held their Dominions." See Maier, *Themis Aurea*, 1–3; on Rous's work, also see the discussion in Burrow, *Epic Romance*, 167. Milton, Sonnet XXI ("To Cyriack Skinner"), ls. 1–2, in *CW* 1:67.

127 Milton, *Tenure of Kings and Magistrates*, *YP* 3:237. On this passage, see Fixler, *Milton and the Kingdoms of God*, 157.

128 N. Smith, "*Paradise Lost* from Civil War to Restoration," in *The Cambridge Companion to Writing of the English Revolution*, ed. Keeble, 255.

129 As Nestor boldly points out at *Il.* 9.98–100, telling Agamemnon that "Zeus has put into your hands the scepter and the *themistas*, so that you may take counsel [*bouleuêstha*] for your people. Therefore you must above all others both speak and listen."

130 On Achilles's shield, see Nagy, *Pindar's Homer*, chapter 9; compare Hesiod, *Theog.* ln. 30, where Zeus gives the *skêptron* to the poet rather than to a king.

131 See *PL* 3.339–41 for God's rendition of this same speech; on the passage's significance for Milton's attitudes towards kingship, see Loewenstein, *Representing Revolution*, 231.

132 Homer's association with this myth may have been strengthened during the Renaissance by the claim that Homer's mother was named Themista or (as Vives claims in his commentary on Augustine) that "Themis was a Delphic Sibyl" and that "Homer inserted many of her verses into his Rhapsodie," an argument that grants Homer a remarkably unmediated access to natural and divine laws (Vives, in Augustine, *Citie of God*, 18.23, p. 704).

133 *Homeric Hymn to Zeus*, trans. Chapman, ls. 7–8, in *Chapman's Homeric Hymns and other Homerica*, 146. Cudworth, *True Intellectual System*, 542–4, asserts that Themis was "another name of God" among the Pagans, the "Supreme God" of a religion that despite an appearance of polytheism practises "Polyonomy." For contemporary interpretations of Themis as God or Eternal Law, see also Stephanus Pighius, *Themis Dea, Seu de Lege Divina* (Antwerp: Plantijn, 1568), 38–40, 63.

134 [Plutarch], *Life of Homer*, 185: "aei dianoeitai"; compare Porphyry, *Homeric Questions*, ed. MacPhail, 85 on *Il.* 4.443, glossing the terms "*ekôn*" (willing) and "*akôn*" (unwilling).
135 Lewalski, *Paradise Lost*, 115.
136 Milton, *DDC*, *YP* 6:133.
137 For Milton's treatment of this verse ("*qui agit omnia ex consilio voluntatis suae*"), see *DDC*, in *CW* 14:62–3.
138 Bacon, "Of Counsel," in *Essayes*, 63, argues that "God himselfe is not without [counsel]: But hath made it one of the great Names, of his blessed Sonne, *The Counsellour*"; Hooker, *Laws* 1.2.5, 111: "he worketh all things *kata tên boulên tou thelêmatos autou*, not only according to his own will, but 'the counsel of his own will'. And whatsoever is done with counsel or wise resolution hath of necessity some reason why it should be done"; *The humble advice of the Assembly of Divines, now by authority of Parliament sitting at Westminster, concerning a confession of faith* (London, 1647), 3.1, p. 8.
139 Glanvill, *Lux Orientalis*, 72; Ames, *Marrow of Theology* I.vii.34, 97. On Milton's use of the terms "arbitrarious" and arbitrary, see Leonard, *Naming*, 7.
140 Milton, *Paradise Lost*, ed. Fowler, 171.
141 Milton, *Doctrine and Discipline*, *YP* 2:440; On Milton's use of the celestial council convention, see M. Hammond, "*Concilia Deorum* from Homer through Milton"; Samuel, "Dialogue in Heaven"; and Labriola, "'God Speaks.'"
142 Clement, *Stromates* 6, 151.5, p. 365 cites Agamemnon's description of Zeus at *Il.* 3.277 ("You sun, who see all things and hear all things") as evidence of Homer's monotheism; Justin Martyr, *Hortatory Address to the Greeks*, 280, argues that Homer's use of the singular *theos* to describe Zeus indicates "by the pronoun the real and true God." Homeric scholars including Charles Segal have argued that *Od.* is more monotheistic in its outlook than *Il.*: see his *Singers, Heroes, and Gods*, 204, on how the poem tries to "bring the polycentric, polytheistic world order under the unified morality of Zeus."
143 Lactantius, *Divine Institutes*, 63.
144 Mornay, *Christian Religion*, 40–1, argues that "*Homere* … cannot make a notabler difference betweene the true GOD and al the rest of the Gods whome men worshipped in this time" and that "whensoever there is any greater deede talked of, [Homer] speaketh alwaies but of one God in the singular number." D.C. Allen, *Mysteriously Meant*, 30–2, 44–5, discusses similar arguments for Homer's monotheism in the seventeenth century, including Mutio Pansa's 1601 *De osculo ethnicae* and La Mothe Le Vayer's

1642 *De la Virtu des payens*. Compare Bergmann, *De Theologia Homeri*, sigs. a3v, Br, B2v on the singularity, immortality, immutability, and consistency of Homer's Zeus.

145 *Homeri Quae Extant Omnia*, ed. Sponde, 1:97, commenting on *Il.* 5.761–2; on Sponde's attitude towards the double theology of Homeric epic, see Deloince-Louette, *Sponde*, 186.

146 On Milton's rejection of this analogy, see Ng, *Literature and the Politics of Family*, 66.

147 Tasso, *Gerusalemme*, 1.30; Peter (Piero) continues his imitation of Odysseus's speech in the next stanza: "when rule is not united in one man / whose verdicts deal reward and punishment, / who delegates responsibilities, / you have a fickle and wandering government: / Oh, make one body of members in accord, / one head, to give direction and restraint: / the power and scepter, then, to one man bring – / and let him be acknowledged as a king."

148 Milton, *Defensio Pro Populo*, *YP* 4(1): 437. On Milton's account of Nimrod in the final book of *PL* as an attack against this "patriarchalist myth" that "condemn[s] the origin of kings," see Ng, *Literature and the Politics of Family*, 145–6. On the Royalist leanings of the 1648 Cambridge edition, see Kallendorf, *The Other Virgil*, 141, and Machacek, "Royalist Homer," 331–2.

149 Milton, *Tenure of Kings and Magistrates*, *YP* 3:199–200. On Milton's understanding of the commonwealth as the most ancient form of government and the rise of monarchy as a "result of the degradation ... set into motion by the Fall," see Michael Bryson, "'His Tyranny Who Reigns': the Biblical Roots of Divine Kingship and Milton's Rejection of 'Heav'n's King'," *MS* 43 (2004): 111–44, 116.

150 Milton, *Tenure of Kings and Magistrates*, *YP* 3:237.

151 Milton, *DDC*, *CW* 14:196–7.

152 Lieb, *The Sinews of Ulysses*, 86.

153 Isa. 1.18; Ps. 82.1–2, trans. Milton, *CW* 1:141. The Septuagint translation of Ps. 82 has "sunagôgê" for assembly and "diakrinei" for judges. For similar readings of Milton's translation of Ps. 82, see Lieb, *Sinews of Ulysses*, 92–3, and Pecheux, "Council Scenes," 83–6. For additional examples in the Old Testament, see Ps. 89.7 ("God is greatly to be feared in the assembly of the saints, and to be had in reverence of all them that are about him") and Job 1.6, where Satan takes his place in the assembly to debate with God.

154 On dialogue as "unfallen" discourse in *PL*, see McColley, *Milton's Eve*, 169.

155 In some accounts, Zeus and Themis are also the parents of the *Charites*, or Graces, who are represented as dancing hand in hand (along with Harmonia, Hebe, and Aphrodite) in the *Homeric Hymn to Pythian Apollo*, ls. 194–6, and at *PL* 4.267. They are also linked by Hesiod, *Theogony*, ls. 901–11,

where they are identified, respectively, as the successive offspring of Zeus and Themis (the Horai) and Zeus and Eurynome (the *Charites* or Graces). On Themis and the Horai, see Rudhardt, *Themis*, 90–5; for Themis as the binding force of the "collective conscience," see Harrison, *Themis*, 485.

156 Compare Cirillo, "Noon-Midnight," 373: "virtually every event of thematic importance in *Paradise Lost* occurs at either midnight or noon, polarities that are at once disparate and concordant."

157 See, for instance, *PL* 4.286, where Satan "[s]aw undelighted all delight" the prospect of Eden.

158 Bastard, *Third Sermon* (The Christian Soldier), in *Twelve Sermons*, 37, paraphrasing 1 Cor. 4.11. The Vulgate translation of Isa. 40.15 reads "*momentum staterae*" [moment of a balance].

159 Plato, *Cratylus*, 410c.

160 The fall, appropriately, is signalled by a "real eclipse" at *PL* 10.413. On "partition" and "parturition" in Milton's cosmos, see Budick, *The Dividing Muse*, 42–4, and McColley, "'All in All,'" 27–31.

161 On the "precarious stasis" of twilight, see *Paradise Lost*, ed. Fowler, 471 (on 9.50–1): "Twilight, like prelapsarian life, briefly balances light and dark"; on noon as "the perfect balancing midpoint," see Cirillo, "Noon-Midnight," 375. Hume, *Annotations*, 245, describes twilight as the "quick nimble Umpire between Day and Night, by turns fore-running both, and uncertain, to which most enclining."

162 On the Miltonic imagery of noon and its relationship to moral choice, see Treip, "Reason is also choice," 166–8. While Eve is shown "pausing a while" before she eats the apple, Satan "paused not" before he eats in her dream (*PL* 5.64). When Adam asks for an account of the war in heaven, Raphael's "short pause" (5.562) suggests a similar moment of deliberation before he answers.

163 At *PL* 5.173–4, Adam and Eve's prayer implores the Sun to reflect the glory of God in its "eternal course, both when thou climbst, / And when high noon hast gained, and when thou fallst."

164 Conti, *Mythologiae*, 1:341–2; Latin cited from *Mythologiae* (1637), 226.

165 For a more conventional treatment of Themis and the Horai, see Chapman, *Hero and Leander*, 3.125–51, in *Poems*, ed. Bartlett, 137.

166 Hesiod, *Theogony*, ls. 748–53: "While the one is about to go down into the house, the other comes out at the door. And the house never holds them both within; but always one is without ... while the other stays at home."

167 Milton, *Sixth Prolusion*, *CW* 12:133.

168 On the graces as a symbol of *concordia discors*, see Wind, *Pagan Mysteries*, 28–30, 38–40.

169 Milton may also regard Penelope as a model for Eve's modesty: in *DDC* (*CW* 17:220–1) he cites *Od.* 1.333 ("She ... beaneath the portal of her stately mansion stood") as an example of modesty or "womanly decorum" in Penelope. On Milton's allusion to Odysseus's hyacinthine locks, see Bruce Boehrer, "Milton, Homer, and Hyacinthus: Classical Iconography and Literary Allusion in *Paradise Lost* 4.300–303," *IJCT* 13, no. 2 (2006): 197–216.

170 Raphael is not, strictly speaking, a poet, but his role as mediator parallels that of the Miltonic narrator; both enjoy relative freedom in passing from heaven to earth and back, and both assist in accommodating divine truths to a human audience. Milton may also have in mind Quintus Smyrnaeus, *The Trojan Epic*, 4.134–7, 67, where the Seasons and Themis serve food at the wedding of Peleus and Thetis.

171 Thalmann, *The Odyssey: an epic of return*, 10–11, 49.

172 A. Ford, *Poetry of the Past*, 125, observes that Homer's Phaiakia presents a nostalgic glimpse back at a time when "gods and men had banquets together and were seated together"; Clay, *The Wrath of Athena*, 168, similarly reads the feast at the wedding of Peleus and Thetis as an indication that the "heroic era is coming to a close" and that "[t]he distance separating gods and mortals seems to be increasing." Compare Luxon, *Single Imperfection*, 151.

173 Aryanpur, *Paradise Lost*, 162, notes similarities between the opening of *PL* 9 and Alkinous's speech at *Od.* 7.198–296 (especially in Chapman's translation). Martindale, *Milton*, 85, notes that Milton treats Homer's Phaiakia as a pagan version of his own lost paradise.

174 Griffin, *Homer on Life and Death*, 59n17. Edwards, *Discourse*, 580, compares Calypso's entertainment of Hermes in *Od.* to Gen. 18.5, where Abraham entertains the angels with a morsel of bread, an analogue that Milton may have in mind. See also the discussion by Persona, *Noctes Solitariae*, 126, on the Judaeo-Christian significance of *Il.* 5.341.

175 See, for instance, Clement, *Exhortation to the Greeks*, 240–1, which cites *Il.* 5.128, a line spoken by Athena to Diomedes, "Thus shalt thou well discern who is God and who is but mortal," as a gloss on Ps. 19.8. A number of seventeenth-century scholars cite the same line as evidence of Homer's piety.

176 On Milton's reliance upon the related comic genres of the Platonic symposium and the "entertainment" or feasting of a noted guest, see Lewalski, *Paradise Lost*, 205–9.

177 Homer, *Od.* 8.489, 491; *Il.* 2.485; Milton, *PL* 1.19–20. Milton's invocation is conventionally seen as an imitation of *Il.* 2.484, where the narrator invokes the muses who "are divine and present and know all things." Compare Milton, "Vacation Exercise," ls. 45–52, *CW* 1(1): 20.

178 It is worth noting that one of the dangers of fancy in *PL* is its disruption of temporal order as grasped by the reason, producing "wild work" by "misjoining shapes" but also by "[i]ll matching words and deeds long past and late" (5.110–13).
179 Martin Evans, *Paradise Lost Books IX–X*, 178. But Danielson, *Milton's Good God*, 161, argues that Milton does not fully embrace the Boethian belief that "God dwells in an eternal present that transcends our categories of time and tense." On the extra-temporal nature of divinity in *PL*, see also 10.90–1, where the Son descends straight to earth and the narrator comments that "the speed of gods / Time counts not."
180 *PL* 3.195, 5.471; On this point, see Danielson, *Milton's Good God*, 257n67.
181 This technique is comparable to the Homeric contrafactual in its ability to effect ironic retardation or foreshadowing, through which "we are told that an event *nearly* happened but did not" (Rutherford, *Homer*, 35).
182 The phrase is repeated at *Od.* 23.152 to describe another false assumption: the rumour that Penelope, unable to wait for Odysseus "even until he should come" home, has married one of the suitors.
183 On the terms perplex and perplexity in *PL*, see Achinstein, *Revolutionary Reader*, 213. For a slightly different reading of the invocation to *PL* 9, see Burden, *The Logical Epic*, 11, which describes the invocation as a "characteristic exercise in close discrimination" that turns upon anger but points out that Milton does not go as far as Horace's critique of Achilles's wrath at *Ars Poetica*, ln. 121. Cook, *The Odyssey in Athens*, 21–3, 35, argues that "the cause" of Poseidon's anger is never mentioned by the Homeric narrator and that the entire invocation of the poem inverts the usual archaic epic convention of "ascrib[ing] the miseries suffered ... to divine will." On divine wrath in *PL*, see also Richard DuRocher, "'Tears such as Angels Weep': Passion and Allusion in *Paradise Lost*," *MS* 49 (2009): 124–45.
184 This attitude may also be an index of the extent to which Milton's youthful "millenarian instinct" is diluted later in life "by a sense of the almost infinite postponement of the millennium." See Corns, *Regaining Paradise Lost*, 27; compare Lewalski, "Milton and the Millenium," 15 (citing *YP* 6:618), on how Milton "imagined that the millennium might be close at hand" when the Reformation was going well, "and when it was in difficulties he deduced, in what is probably a late addition in *DDC*, that Christ 'will be slow to come'." For Milton's discussion of scriptural examples of patience at 1 Kgs. 19.4, Job 3.2, and Jonah 4.3, see his *DDC* (*CW* 17:68–9); on death as an "intellectual test" of patience, see Radzinowicz, *Psalms*, 174–5.
185 See *Il.* 24.315 and *Od.* 19.555–62.
186 Achinstein, *Revolutionary Reader*, 213.

187 On Milton's use of subjunctive and conditional clauses and modals, see Emma, *Milton's Grammar*, 105–6.

188 Peradotto, *Man in the Middle Voice*, 69. On the influence of Tiresias's prophecy on the image of the two-handed engine in *Lycidas*, see David Sansone, "How Milton Reads: Scripture, the Classics, and That Two-Handed Engine," *MP* 103, no. 3 (2006): 332–57.

189 See *Od.* 2.97–8, where Penelope tells the suitors that she wishes to postpone marriage to one of them "until" she completes Laertes's shroud, a statement that implies certainty to the suitors (she *will* finish his shroud and then *will* marry one of them) but also implies conditionality: she may or may not complete the shroud (an unlikely event, since she deviously unravels it every night) and if and only if she completes it will she marry one of the suitors. Seymour Chatman, "Milton's Participial Style," *PMLA* 83, no. 5 (1968): 1386–99, 1387, argues that the ambiguity of certain participial phrases is used to similar effect in *PL*. On the "until" clauses in this Homeric passage, see Peradotto, *Man in the Middle Voice*, 72.

190 A similar grammatical ambiguity inflects Michael's promise that "day and night, / Seed-time and harvest, heat and hoary frost / Shall hold their course, *till* fire purge all things new," a prophecy voiced in a Tiresian grammar of contingency whose fulfillment is dependent upon the same kind of conditional necessity that circumscribes divine creation (*PL* 11.898–900).

191 See, for instance, *PL* 1.166–8.

192 *PL* 4.313; *Od.* 6.137. On the parallels between Eve and Nausicaa, see Lord, "Homer, *Paradise Lost*, and the Renaissance," 23; Aryanpur, *Paradise Lost*, 153–60.

193 On the "regenerative connotations" of Milton's allusion to Zeus and Hera, see McColley, *Milton's Eve*, 63, who also argues (69–70) that Milton repeatedly distinguishes between the "regenerative" and the "degenerative" implications of the pagan myths to which he alludes.

194 Compare *PL* 4.499–501: when Adam gazes upon Eve, he is compared to Jupiter when he "on Juno smiles, when he impregns the clouds / That shed May flowers," a consummation interpreted by the Homeric allegorists as symbolizing the synthesis of ether and air. Also compare 9.1037–41, where Adam, after the fall, leads Eve to a "shadie bank / Thick overhead" and filled with "hyacinth, earths freshest softest lap." On this Homeric analogue and its elemental implications, see Revard, "Vergil's *Georgics* and *Paradise Lost*," 266–7.

195 Aristotle, *Nic. Ethics* IV.9.7 [1128b]. On Homeric conceptions of shame, see Cairns, *Aidôs*; Dodds, *The Greeks and the Irrational*, chapter 2; Lloyd-Jones, *The Justice of Zeus*, 24–7.

196 Milton, *RCG*, *YP* 1:841; on Milton's interpretation of Hector's "honest shame," see Martindale, *Milton*, 58; Joshua Scodel, "*Paradise Lost* and Classical Ideals of Pleasurable Restraint," *CL* 48, no. 3 (1996): 189–236, 215–23.

197 Milton, *RCG*, *YP* 1:840–1.

198 Milton, *RCG*, *YP* 1:841.

199 At *Il.* 10.237–8, Agamemnon cautions Diomedes against choosing "as your comrade one who is worse, yielding to respect [*aidoi*] and looking to birth" rather than to the success of his expedition. At *Od.* 17.347, Telemachus offers the disguised Odysseus some bread, observing, "shame [*aidôs*] is no good friend to a man in need."

200 See Hesiod, *WD*, ls. 317–18, on how shame "greatly harms men and also benefits them," and Plutarch, *De Vitioso Pudore*, in *Moralia* 529D, citing *Il.* 24.44 and observing that *aidôs* is only helpful "when reason removes the overplus and leaves us with the right amount."

201 At *Il.* 5.201, Pandarus expresses regret – "But I did not listen, not I – surely it would have been far better" – in a verse repeated by Hector in a pivotal moment of battlefield pondering before his final confrontation with Achilles (*Il.* 22.103–24) and again repeated by Odysseus (*Od.* 9.228) when he expresses regret for having ignored the pleas of his crew to leave Polyphemus's island.

202 For uses of this expression in Homeric epic, see *Il.* 14.83; *Od.* 23.183. Chapter 1 of this book offers a discussion of this Homeric formula and its afterlife in the writings of Erasmus and his contemporaries.

203 *Il.* 22.116. *Il.* 3.446 is repeated at 14.329, where it describes Zeus's lust for Hera. On this Homeric analogue, see Gilbert, "Milton's Defense of Bawdry," 66.

204 *Od.* 1.32–4; Milton, *Paradise Lost*, ed. Fowler, 530, argues that when Raphael cautions Adam to "[a]ccuse not nature," he is attempting to steer Milton's hero away from the "misogynistic sexism" exhibited by Homer's Trojans and Greeks when they falsely identify Helen as the cause of the war.

205 Cairns, *Aidôs*, 87–8, 136. See, for instance, *Od.* 17.188–9, where Eumaeus feels "reverence and fear" [*aideomai kai deidia*] for his master, whose "rebukes are dreadful" [*opissô / neikeiê*], or *Il.* 18.394, where Hephaestus calls Thetis a "dread and reverend goddess" [*deinê te kai aidoiê theos*].

206 Milton, *RCG*, *YP* 1: 841–2; on Hector as exhibiting this sort of shame, see *Il.* 22.105, 22.122–4; Aristotle, *Nic. Ethics* IV.9.1–3 [1128b] on shame as fear of disrepute.

207 Scodel, *Excess and the Mean*, 223, discussing Miltonic images of pondering, points out that Milton's language is indebted to Seneca, *Moral Epistles* 89.14,

which equates wisdom and virtue with the capacity to esteem [*aestimare*] and to weigh [*perpendere*] one's moral worth correctly.

208 Hume, *Annotations*, 280, glossing *PL* 10.674, comments of the Dioscuri that "in the very minute of their Rising and Setting, one of 'em is above the Horizon, while the other is below." On the inadequacy of alternatives in *PL*, compare Quint, "Ulysses and the Devils," 37, which argues that Scylla and Charybdis, invoked at 2.660 and 2.1020, represent Moloch and Belial, serving as twin symbols of "bad alternatives that, because they are bad, are no alternatives at all."

209 Christopher Grose, *Milton's Epic Process. Paradise Lost and Its Miltonic Background* (New Haven, CT: Yale University Press, 1973), 146; Herman, "The Poetics of Incertitude," 183. On Milton's Homeric similes, see also Christopher Ricks, *Milton's Grand Style* (Oxford: Clarendon Press, 1963), 127; Martindale, *Milton*, 121; Fish, *Surprised by Sin*, 22–8.

210 Martindale, *Milton*, 76, shows how Milton imitates the Homeric convention of apostrophizing a character as "fool" [*nêpios*] to demonstrate that he is "acting in ignorance of the reality of the situation," as when Abdiel calls Satan a fool, imitating *Il.* 2.873 and 20.466. On Milton's tendency to assign different names in hell and heaven, see Achinstein, *Revolutionary Reader*, 222.

211 De Jong, *Narrators and Focalizers*, 187–8. See Hume, *Annotations*, 114, on how repetition is "affected after the Homeric manner" in passages including *PL* 3.190–1 and 3.401–10.

212 See Hume, *Annotations*, 290, on Themis as the goddess "supposed to prompt Men those Petitions that were fit to be ask'd of the Gods."

213 Heywood, *Gynaikeion*, 108–9; At *Il.* 5.749–50 and 8.393–95, the gates of Olympus are described as "of themselves [*automatai*] groaning on their hinges, which the Hours had in their keeping."

214 Heywood, *Gynaikeion*, 108–9; Conti, *Mythologiae*, 2:904–5 (Latin, 540).

215 This is why Conti (*Mythologiae*, 1:342; Latin, 226) describes the Horai as "promot[ing] the cultivation of the fields" [*cultum agris inducunt*].

216 See Conti, *Mythologiae*, 1:341, on the Horae as figures who preside over the gates of heaven and "calm the heavens when they feel like it."

217 See Milton, *DDC*, *YP* 6:618, on how "Christ will be slow to come" [*Adventus Christi erit tardus*].

218 Revard, "Milton, Homer, and the Anger of Adam," 32, notes that Eve appears in the "posture of a Homeric suppliant," on her knees and with disordered hair. On delay as a Homeric narrative technique, see Nünlist, *The Ancient Critic at Work*, 49.

219 Burrow, *Epic Romance*, 6.

220 Hesiod, *Theogony*, ls. 782–3, and *Il.* 23.1989.
221 Edwards, *Discourse*, 222–3; Quattrehomme, *Comparaison*, 57–8, compares Homer's Iris to the rainbow of Genesis as well as to the golden chain. The analogies between Noah's flood and its pagan counterpart (the story of Deucalion and Pyrrha) were often noted during the period: Conti, *Mythologiae*, 2:769, argues that the pagan myth "takes its origin from the sacred writings." On Greek and Roman analogues to the story of the flood, see also D.C. Allen, *The Legend of Noah*, 83, 176.
222 Milton, *On the Morning of Christ's Nativity*, ls. 141–3, *CW* 1(1): 7. According to Quint, "Expectation and Prematurity in Milton's Nativity Ode," *MP* 97, no. 2 (1999): 195–219, Milton marked the passage in his copy of *Iphigenia in Tauris* concerning the oracle at Delphi which Earth (Gaia) reserves for her daughter Themis.
223 Hammond, *A Paraphrase and annotations upon the books of the Psalms,* 36.
224 Paquelin, *Apologeme*, sigs. O3r, O4r, 109–11.
225 For a similar reading, see McColley, *Milton's Eve*, 69.
226 Zeitlin, *Playing the Other*, 64.
227 On Milton's use of conditional modals, see Emma, *Milton's Grammar*, 105–6.
228 For readings of this simile, see Bryan Adams Hampton, "Milton's Parable of Misreading: Navigating the Contextual Waters of the 'night-founder'd skiff' in *Paradise Lost* 1.192–209," *MS* 43 (2004): 86–110.
229 Compare *PL* 10.1042–3, where Adam consoles Eve by advising her to forgo the "willful barrenness, / That cuts us off from hope." Even as it produces children – a source of hope – childbirth is painful for Eve, again suggesting how hope and pain are yoked together after the fall. At *DDC* (*CW* 17:202–3) Milton classifies hope (*spes*) as both a virtue and an affection; in the latter category, it is grouped with anger, joy, sorrow, and fear.
230 On Epimetheus as a "tardily-wise" figure of limited hindsight, see Erasmus, Adage I.i.31 (*CWE* 31:78–80): "Trouble experienced makes a fool wise" [*Malo accepte stultus sapit*].
231 On Milton's interpretation of the fable of Epimetheus and Pandora, see G. Butler, "Milton's Pandora."

6. Hobbes's Homer and the Idols of the Agora

1 Hobbes, *Translations of Homer*, 2 vols., ed. Nelson, back cover. Subsequent citations of Hobbes's translation are from this edition (unless otherwise noted) and quoted parenthetically, abbreviated *HH*.
2 Hillyer, "Hobbes's Explicated Fables," 281; Martinich, *Hobbes: A Biography*, 7, 27.

3 Hobbes, *Prose Life*, in *The Elements of Law*, ed. Gaskin, 246.
4 Ball, "The Despised Version," 15; Davis, "Thomas Hobbes's Translations of Homer," 244–7; Skinner, *Reason and Rhetoric*, 4.
5 On Hobbes's admiration of perspicuity in Thucydides and other ancient writers, see also Reik, *The Golden Lands of Thomas Hobbes*, 46.
6 Three exceptions are Skinner, *Reason and Rhetoric*, D. Johnston, *The Rhetoric of Leviathan*, 3–4; and Davis, "Thomas Hobbes's Translations of Homer," 232–3.
7 Hobbes, *Dedication to William, Earl of Newcastle*, in *Elements of Law*, 19.
8 Hobbes, *Philosophical Rudiments*, in *English Works* 2:129, hereafter abbreviated *EW*.
9 For a similar argument, see Hobbes, *Translations of Homer*, *HH* 1:xli.
10 Hobbes, *Leviathan*, ed. Tuck, 150.
11 Hobbes, *Leviathan*, 149.
12 Hobbes, *Human Nature*, in *Elements of Law*, 54, and *Leviathan*, 70.
13 *Il.* 1.91, 2.82, et al.; Hobbes, *Leviathan*, 120.
14 Hobbes, *Leviathan*, 120; Thucydides, *Eight books of the Peloponnesian Warre*, trans. Hobbes, sig. B2r.
15 Hobbes, *Leviathan*, 221; 88; *Homer his Iliads*, trans. Ogilby, "Dedication to King Charles II," n.p.
16 Hobbes, "To the Reader: Concerning the Vertues of an Heroique Poem," in *Translations of Homer*, ed. Nelson, 1:xcix; *Homer his Iliads*, trans. Ogilby, 41, note n.
17 Skinner, *Reason and Rhetoric*, 394, 425, citing Henry More, *Immortality of the Soul*.
18 Hobbes, *Leviathan*, 490.
19 Hobbes, *De Cive*, 272, cited from *Man and Citizen*, ed. Gert, 96–7; compare *Philosophical Rudiments*, *EW* 2, Preface, xii.
20 Cowley, "To Mr. Hobbes," in his *The True Effigies of the Monster of Malmesbury*, sig. B2v.
21 Shakespeare's Ulysses is frequently classified as proto-Hobbesian by virtue of his defence of political hierarchy and obedience, a defence that rests upon political expediency rather than divine right. For "Hobbesian" readings of *Troilus and Cressida*, see Elton, "Shakespeare's Ulysses." Vico spells out this interpretation of Homeric epic more explicitly in his *New Science*, 254–5, which argues that several passages in the *Iliad* have been misinterpreted as evidence that Homer was familiar with monarchy: "In both passages, Homer says that 'only one man is king'. But both refer to wartime, when there can only be one commander-in-chief, as Tacitus observed."
22 See, for instance, the 1648 Cambridge edition of the *Iliad*, which turns nine verses in the opening three books of the poem into "*sententiae* that assert the

legitimacy, even supremacy, of monarchical government" (Kallendorf, *The Other Virgil*, 141).

23 Springborg, "Hobbes and Historiography," 64.

24 Goldsmith, *Hobbes's Science of Politics*, 193.

25 Wolin, *Hobbes and the Epic Tradition*, 28; L. Johnson, *Thucydides, Hobbes*, 70.

26 D. Johnston, *The Rhetoric of Leviathan*, 90.

27 Hobbes, *Answer to Davenant*, in *Critical Essays*, ed. Spingarn, 2:59; for Nelson's discussion of this passage, see *HH* 1:l–lii.

28 Cantalupo, *A Literary Leviathan*, 234; Wolin, *Hobbes and the Epic Tradition*, 4.

29 Wolin, *Hobbes and the Epic Tradition*, 16; Cantalupo, *A Literary Leviathan*, 235–6.

30 Hobbes, *Answer*, in *Critical Essays*, ed. Spingarn, 2:60; D. Johnston, *The Rhetoric of Leviathan*, 19; Wolin, *Hobbes and the Epic Tradition*, 16–17.

31 Hobbes, *Behemoth, EW* 6:259.

32 Hobbes, *Human Nature*, in *Elements of Law*, 72.

33 Hobbes, *Leviathan*, 126; *Il.* 1.85–92 in Grk. text.

34 Hobbes, *Leviathan*, 120.

35 Hobbes, *Human Nature*, in *Elements of Law*, 78.

36 Hobbes, *Leviathan*, 108.

37 Hobbes, *Leviathan*, 107.

38 Hobbes, *Philosophical Rudiments*, *EW* 2:68.

39 D. Johnston, *Rhetoric of Leviathan*, 58.

40 Elizabeth J. Cook, "Thomas Hobbes and the 'Far-Fetched'," *JWCI* 44 (1981): 222–32, 226; Anat Biletzki, *Talking Wolves: Thomas Hobbes on the Language of Politics and the Politics of Language* (Dordrecht, Boston, & London: Kluwer Academic Publishers, 1997), 75.

41 Hobbes, *Human Nature*, in *Elements of Law*, 72.

42 Hobbes, *Leviathan*, 182. For Sponde's reading, see *Homeri Quae Extant Omnia*, ed. Sponde, 1:9.

43 Hobbes, *Leviathan*, 177–8.

44 Bodin, *Method for the Easy Comprehension of History*, trans. Reynolds, 282.

45 Boëtie, *De la Servitude Volontaire ou Contr'un*, 33.

46 Compare Justin Martyr, *Hortatory Address to the Greeks*, 280, who argues that Odysseus's statement, "let there be one ruler," reflects the wars that arise when there are a multitude of rulers, "the fights and factions," whereas "monarchy is free from contention."

47 Hobbes, *Leviathan*, 226.

48 Hobbes, *Leviathan*, 147, 117. That Hobbes cuts much of the exchange between Hera and Themis at *Il.* 15.93–5 may indicate his apprehensions about

Themis, conventionally interpreted as a personification of natural law or a goddess who presides over the connections between natural and positive law.

49 L. Johnson, *Thucydides, Hobbes*, 73; also see Hobbes, *De Cive*, XII.1.This definition of justice is also evident in Hobbes's translation of *Od.* 22.332 (ln. 374 in the Greek), "Justice better thrives than Knavery" (*HH* 2:293).

50 Ross, *Mystagogus Poeticus*, 87.

51 L. Johnson, *Thucydides, Hobbes*, 76.

52 Springborg, "Hobbes and Historiography," 64.

53 Thorpe, *The Aesthetic Theory of Thomas Hobbes*, 21.

54 Hobbes *Leviathan*, 470.

55 Hobbes, *Verse Life*, in *Elements of Law*, 256.

56 Hobbes, *Leviathan*, 490.

57 Grafton, "Martin Crusius Reads his Homer," 85; Crusius, *Commentationes in I Lib. Iliad Homeri*, 129. The comparison between the two stories is already commonplace in antiquity: both the fall of Troy and the battle between the Lapiths and the Centaurs are depicted on the metopes of the Parthenon, features described by Pausanias and thus familiar to early modern scholars.

58 Grafton, "Martin Crusius Reads His Homer," 85.

59 George Klosko and Daryl Rice, "Thucydides and Hobbes's State of Nature," *History of Political Thought* 6, no. 3 (1985): 405–9, 405; see also L. Johnson, *Thucydides, Hobbes*, 41 on Thucydides's argument that the root causes of civil war are the passions of greed and ambition, and springing from these, rivalrousness.

60 Thucydides, *Eight books of the Peloponnesian Warre*, trans. Hobbes, *EW* 8:348.

61 L. Johnson, *Thucydides, Hobbes*, 41; on Thucydides's conception of *phusis anankaia*, "compelling or compulsive nature," to describe the activating principle of aggression in human nature and in the cosmos, see Rankin, *Sophists, Socratics, and Cynics*, 120.

62 L. Johnson, *Thucydides, Hobbes*, 28.

63 Thucydides, *Eight books of the Peloponnesian Warre*, trans. Hobbes, 6, 8.

64 Zappen, "Aristotelian and Ramist Rhetoric in Thomas Hobbes's *Leviathan*," 67.

65 Zappen, "Aristotelian and Ramist Rhetoric," 67, 81.

66 D. Johnston, *Rhetoric of Leviathan*, 39.

67 Thucydides, *Eight books of the Peloponnesian Warre*, trans. Hobbes, *EW* 8:348.

68 L. Johnson, *Thucydides, Hobbes*, 16.

69 L. Johnson, *Thucydides, Hobbes*, 16; Hobbes, *Human Nature*, in *Elements of Law*, 72.

70 L. Johnson, *Thucydides, Hobbes*, 22.
71 Hobbes, *Philosophical Rudiments*, *EW* 2:67.
72 Harrington, *The Commonwealth of Oceana*, 29.
73 Thucydides, *Peloponnesian Warre*, trans. Hobbes, "To the Readers," sig. A3v.
74 Thucydides, *Peloponnesian Warre*, trans. Hobbes, *EW* 8:301–2.
75 On this point, see L. Johnson, *Thucydides, Hobbes*, 159.
76 For a comprehensive list of council scenes in Homeric epic, see Ruzé, *Délibération*.
77 For two different arguments concerning Hobbes's attitudes towards verbal abuse, see Skinner, *Reason and Rhetoric*, 198–211, 393–425, and Whelan, "Language and Its Abuses," 59–75.
78 Hobbes, *Leviathan*, 132.
79 Hobbes, *De Corpore Politico*, in *Elements of Law*, 120.
80 Hobbes, *De Corpore Politico*, 140; *Philosophical Rudiments*, *EW* 2:101; *Leviathan*, 182. Hobbes's interpretation of Homer may be mediated by Aristotle's *Politics*, which argues that though Agamemnon "heard patiently reviling speeches and taunts in publicke assemblies" he also had, outside of assembly, the "free and entire power of putting to death." See *Aristotles Politiques, or Discourses of Government* 3.10 (London: Adam Islip, 1598).
81 Hobbes, *Leviathan*, 182.
82 Hobbes, *Leviathan*, 137.
83 *HH* 1:237.Compare the exchange between Telemachus and Antinous at *Od.* 2.64 and following, where Telemachus urges Antinous to "restrain" the "liberty" of his sons (*HH* 2:20). Nelson notes that Hobbes inserts the term "liberty" twice into the conversation between the two men, both times to stress the importance of restraining it (*HH* 2:20).
84 Hobbes, *Philosophical Rudiments*, *EW* 2:129.
85 Cartari, *Les Images des Dieux des Anciens*, 5.
86 Hobbes, *Leviathan*, 138.
87 Hobbes, *Leviathan*, 182; on this point, see also Goldsmith, *Hobbes's Science of Politics*, 205.
88 Hobbes, *Philosophical Rudiments*, *EW* 2:xiii.
89 The Greek text does not mention a "council" of suitors; Athena merely tells Telemachus at *Od.* 2.281–2 to "put from your mind the suitors' plans and intentions – fools, for they are in no way either prudent or just."
90 Hobbes, *Behemoth*, *EW* 6:359.
91 Maximus of Tyre, Oration 11, in *Philosophical Orations*, 104, citing *Il.* 19.81–2.
92 Hobbes, *Leviathan*, 181.
93 Hobbes, *Leviathan*, 181.
94 Hobbes, *Leviathan*, 132.

95 For similar reasons, at *Il.* 18.453, Hobbes translates the "agora" on Achilles's shield, where the trial takes place, as a "Market place" (*HH* 1:305).

96 See Hobbes's translations of *Od.* 4.212 [=4.211] "discreet" [*pinutous*]; 6.178 [=6.187], "a good man and discreet" [*oute kakô out'aphroni*, literally, not a bad man nor without understanding]; 7.63 [=7.74], "wise woman and discreet" [*hêsi t'eu phroneêsi*, literally, not lacking in good sense]; 7.214 [=7.227], "He speaks discreetly" [*kata moiran eeipen*]; 17.533 [=17.580], "he is discreet" [*mutheitai kata moiran*, literally, he speaks according to order); 18.190 [=18.220], "discretion" [*phrenes … enaisimoi*, literally, right mind); 19.323–4 [19.352], "prudent and discreet" [*pepnumena*].

97 Hobbes, *Leviathan* 25–6; Skinner, *Reason and Rhetoric*, 269, 265.

98 Nelson argues that in Hobbes's translation of Homer, "discretion displaces rhetoric" (*HH* 1:lx).

99 Compare Hobbes's reliance on "satirical" rhetorical techniques and on irony in *Leviathan*, as discussed by Skinner, *Reason and* Rhetoric, 13, 393–422, and Louis Roux, *Thomas Hobbes: Penseur entre deux mondes* (Saint-Etienne: Publications de l'Université de Saint-Etienne, 1981), 103–13.

100 Compare Hobbes's translation of *Od.* 20.247 (20.274 in Greek), "Else we should quickly spoil his eloquence," where, as Nelson notes, eloquence translates *ligun … agorêtên* ("clear orator") and is "being used derisively" (*HH* 2:271).

101 Jasper Griffin, "The Speeches," in *The Cambridge Companion to Homer*, ed. Fowler, 157, discussing Plato, *Rep.* 3.5 [392c] and 3.6–3.9 [393c–398b].

102 The Greek text, by contrast, has Odysseus describe the eloquent man as he whom "some god sets a crown of beauty upon his words, and men look upon him with delight … and as he goes through the city men gaze upon him as a god" (*Od.* 8.169–74). Hobbes's distrust of the marvellous is also apparent at *Od.* 8.436, where he cuts a line (8.459 in the Greek) that depicts Nausicaa marveling [*thaumazen*] at Odysseus's beauty (*HH* 2:107).

103 Hobbes may have in mind Achilles's statement at *Il.* 9.306–8: "Those men I hate / Whose Tongues and Hearts I find to disagree, / As much as I abominate Hell gate" (*HH* 1:141).

104 See *Od.* 1.184, where Telemachus begins "to speak his mind" (*HH* 2:10 and note 17).

105 Barnouw, *Odysseus, Hero of Practical Intelligence*, 307, 316.

106 Hobbes, *De Corpore Politico*, in *Elements of Law*, 199.

107 Hobbes, *Leviathan*, 97; on Hobbes's understanding of *conatus*, see Barnouw, *Odysseus*, 12.

108 Hobbes, *Leviathan*, 38; Graver, *Stoicism and Emotion*, 26; see also Barnouw, *Odysseus*, 117, and Hobbes, *Thomas White's De Mundo Examined*, 407–8,

446–8. Seber, *Index Vocabulorum In Homeri Non Tantum Iliade atque Odyssea*, *2v, translates *hormê* as *conatus*.

109 Martinich, *A Hobbes Dictionary*, "Deliberation," 97. Compare Hobbes, *Thomas White's De Mundo Examined*, 447–8, which summarizes his theory of "appetite" and "avoidance" or "*conatus* towards an object" and "*conatus* in the opposite direction." The "oscillation" between these impulses "is called deliberation," a process he compares to how "[i]n a balance, now one pan is depressed, now the opposite one, as fresh weights are thrown in from one side or the other; likewise deliberation is a *conatus*."

110 J.W.N. Watkins, *Hobbes's System of Ideas*, 43; Barnouw, *Odysseus*, 12, 117.

111 These positions are nicely summarized in Giovanni Battista Gelli's 1549 *Circe*, a series of ten dialogues between Odysseus and various animals; in one, a lion argues that human beings are singularly vulnerable to the passions, calling "rage by the name of courage, lasciviousness by the name of love, envy by the name of emulation, and cowardice by the name of caution" (99) whereas animals possess virtues such as fortitude (102), true courage (103), and so on. But Odysseus dismisses the lion's argument by protesting that his adversary "knows no operations but those which proceed from the body ... so it is no wonder if he calls those things actions of fortitude which are only natural inclinations, without any election or reason to them" (108).

112 Graver, *Stoicism and Emotion*, 72; see Plato, *Rep.* 4.11 [435c], and *Phaedrus* 246a–256d. According to Graver, 74, Galen challenges Chrysippus's reading of the Homeric passage, arguing that at times, neither reason nor *thumos* is "strong enough to pull the other in its direction right away, but there is opposition and conflict between them until in time one defeats the other."

113 Barnouw, *Odysseus*, 121–3; for Plato's interpretation, see *Phaedo* 94c10–d4, *Rep.* 3.4 [390d], and *Rep.* 4.13 [437c].

114 Barnouw, *Odysseus*, 118, 3.

115 Hobbes, *Art of Rhetoric*, *EW* 6:527.

116 *HH* 2:88; Barnouw, *Odysseus*, 296.

117 Hobbes, *Thomas White's De Mundo Examined*, 447–8.

118 L. Johnson, *Thucydides, Hobbes*, 82; Hobbes, *Thomas White's De Mundo Examined*, 446; on Hobbes's understanding of liberty and necessity, see also Mintz, *The Hunting of Leviathan*, 110–14.

119 Mintz, *Hunting of Leviathan*, 113; compare V. Kahn, *Wayward Passions*, 151.

120 Goldsmith, *Hobbes's Science of Politics*, 72; see also Strauss, *Political Philosophy of Hobbes*, 15–21; Hobbes, *Leviathan*, 70.

121 Hobbes, *Elements of Law*, 45.

122 Hobbes, *Leviathan*, 253.

123 Hobbes, *Leviathan*, 41; at *Il.* 3.342, the Greek text only notes the "amazement" [*thambos*] of the people.
124 *Il.* 4.440–1; *HH* 1:67; *Leviathan*, 70. For Hobbes's translation of Homeric personifications of terror and fear, see also *Il.* 11.42, where he renders Homer's "Deimos" and "Phobos" (11.37) as "Terror and Affright." Compare Hobbes's odd account of his birth in his *Verse Life* (in *Elements of Law*, 254): his mother, hearing news of the approach of the Spanish Armada, "[d]id bring forth Twins at once, both Me, and Fear."
125 At *Il.* 5.478–82, Hobbes's Agamemnon tells his troops, "be bold, and fight like men, / Of one another's censure stand in fear. Of them that do so, fewer perish than / Of those that fly and never think upon / The loss of fame." In the Greek text (5.531), Agamemnon contrasts men that have shame [*aidomenôn andrôn*] with those that flee.
126 Gabriella Slomp, "Hobbes, Thucydides, and the Three Greatest Things," *History of Political Thought* 2, no. 4 (1990): 565–86, 570.
127 Hobbes, *Leviathan*, 83.
128 Hobbes, *Leviathan*, 117.
129 Hobbes, *Leviathan*, 251.
130 Hobbes, *Leviathan*, 441.
131 Springborg, "Hobbes and Historiography," 63; see also P. Davis, "Thomas Hobbes's Translations of Homer," 234–6, 240–3; and *HH* 1:xlii–xlv. On Hobbes's disagreements with More and Cudworth, see Mintz, *The Hunting of Leviathan*, 80.
132 *HH* 1:36; *Od.* 8.99, and the comment in *Homeri Quae Extant Omnia*, ed. Sponde, 2:100; Pope, as cited in Joseph Spence, *Observations, Anecdotes, and Characters of Books and Men*, 2 vols., ed. James Marshall Osborn (Oxford: Clarendon Press, 1966), 1:193.
133 Hobbes, *Answer to Davenant*, in *Critical Essays*, ed. Spingarn, 2:58; on this passage and its relationship to Hobbes's translations of Homer, see *HH* 1:l–li and P. Davis, "Thomas Hobbes's Translations of Homer," 243.
134 *HH* 2:147, 2:193; P. Davis, "Thomas Hobbes's Translations of Homer," 235; Springborg, "Hobbes and Historiography," 63. At *Od.* 11.55 and again at 11.572, Hobbes translates *daimôn* as "Devil" (2:143, 2:157).
135 Hobbes, *Answer*, in *Critical Essays*, ed. Spingarn, 2:61. On Hobbes's dislike of romance, see V. Kahn, *Wayward Passions*, 142–51.
136 Tomasso Campanella, *Poetica* (ca 1596), cited by Weinberg, *History of Literary Criticism*, 2:791.
137 Stillingfleet, *Origines Sacrae*, 61.
138 D. Johnston, *Rhetoric of Leviathan*, 149.

139 Hobbes's Athena speaks of the "chance of War" at *Il.* 8.386 (1:128), translating "*hos ke tuchê keinos*" (8.430). At *Il.* 16.614, Meriones tells Aeneas, "Yourself are subject to the chance of Warre," a line added by Hobbes (1:268). It may be for similar reasons that Hobbes cuts two lines spoken by Penelope (*Od.* 19.592–3) in which she observes that the immortal gods give each thing at its proper time (*HH* 2:264).
140 Hobbes, *Human Nature*, in *Elements of Law*, 78.
141 Gouldner, *Enter Plato*, 59.
142 Thorpe, *The Aesthetic Theory of Thomas Hobbes*, 118.
143 Thorpe, *The Aesthetic Theory of Thomas Hobbes*, 248, 250, citing John Dennis, *Grounds of Criticism*, 86; see also John Dennis, *The Grounds of Criticism in Poetry* (1704), in *Critical Works*, 1:356–7. On late seventeenth-century attitudes towards terror and the sublime in Homeric epic, see Swedenberg, Jr, *The Theory of the Epic in England* and Wood, *The Word "Sublime."*
144 Shankman, *Pope's Iliad*, 9, citing Pope, *Obs. on Homer's Iliad* 3.53 (Twickenham 7:191); Homer, *Iliad*, trans. Pope, 544, note to 11.5; for Longinus's comments on the same passage, see his *Peri Hupsous* (1651), xiv.
145 Hobbes translates Homer's *erethêsin* (*Il.* 1.519) as "quarrel"; Skinner, *Reason and Rhetoric*, 232 notes that Hobbes admired Lucianic dialogue.
146 "Hussie" is Hobbes's translation of *schetliê* (hard woman) at *Il.* 3.414. Cowper commented that Hobbes's Homer makes him "laugh immoderately" and that the translation is "ridiculous" while Coleridge called Hobbes's Homer "homely" and "vulgar" but true to the original. For these and other criticisms of Hobbes's low diction in his Homeric translations, see Ball, "The Despised Version: Hobbes' Translation of Homer," 16, citing Cowper, *Letters and Prose Writings*, ed. King and Ryskamp, 4:369, and S.T. Coleridge, "Arrogance or Presumption," in *Collected Works: The Friend*, ed. Barbara Rooke, 1:31n. In the advertisement to his edition of Hobbes's translations of Homer, Molesworth comments that the "unstudied and unpretending language" of Hobbes's translation of Homer is "less remote from the original" than the "smooth and glittering lines of Pope" (*EW* 10:2).
147 Ball, "The Despised Version," 2, citing Hobbes, *EW* 10, advertisement.
148 P. Davis, "Thomas Hobbes's Translations of Homer," 244–6; on Hobbes's attitude towards mock-epic, see also Cantalupo, *Literary Leviathan*, 235–8.
149 On Hobbes's "ironic condescension" and his use of satire, see Skinner, *Reason and Rhetoric*, 210–11, 199–201; on the "unhomerically low" diction of his translations, see P. Davis, "Thomas Hobbes's Translations of Homer," 244. On Hobbes's "scoffing humour" and its contemporary detractors, see also Mintz, *Hunting of Leviathan*, 136.

150 On the dating of Hobbes's poem, see Martinich, "Francis Andrewes's Account of Thomas Hobbes' Trip to the Peak," 436–40 and my forthcoming "The *Arse Poetica* of Thomas Hobbes."
151 Skinner, *Reason and Rhetoric*, 240–1.
152 Skinner, *Reason and Rhetoric*, 240–1; on Hobbes's fear of heights and its relevance to the poem, see Mintz, *The Hunting of Leviathan*, 15.
153 On the associations between Hobbes and La Mothe Le Vayer, see Skinner, "Thomas Hobbes and his disciples in France and England," *Comparative Studies in Society and History* 8 (1966): 153–67, and his *Reason and Rhetoric*, 429; Paganini, "Hobbes among ancient and modern skeptics," 11.
154 Hobbes, *De Mirabilibus Pecci*, 16.
155 Hobbes, *De Mirabilibus Pecci*, 30.
156 Hobbes, *De Mirabilibus Pecci*, 32–4.
157 Hobbes, *De Mirabilibus Pecci*, 42.
158 Hobbes, *De Mirabilibus Pecci*, 62.
159 Vico, *New Science*, Introduction, xxi; Wood, *The Word "Sublime,"* 152.

Epilogue: The Homeric Contest from Vico to Arendt

1 And, one might add, from Homer to Virgil. Pope, Bentley, and Vico all relied heavily on Scaliger's *Poetices Libri Septem* (1561), which aimed at every turn to prove the superiority of Virgil to Homer. In his *New Science*, Vico's lists of Homer's primitive forms of expression are indebted to Scaliger's critique of Homer in his *Poetics* (Vico, *New Science*, Introduction, xxiv).
2 Vico, *New Science*, 6, 371.
3 Vico, *New Science*, 87.
4 Vico, *New Science*, 87; Hobbes, *Leviathan*, 70. In spite of Vico's criticisms of Hobbes, many of his interpretations of Homer and early Greek culture are in fact indebted to the earlier writer; see, for example, *New Science*, 125, where Vico relies on a Hobbesian conception of *conatus*.
5 Goldsmith, *Hobbes' Science of Politics*, 105.
6 Compare Harrington, *Oceana*, 123: "in motion consisteth life." On Hobbes's views of motion, see Martinich, *A Hobbes Dictionary*, "Motion," 212–13.
7 Wolin, *Hobbes and the Epic Tradition*, 28.
8 Vico, *New Science*, 358, 371.
9 Burckhardt, *The Greeks and Greek Civilization*, 164, 166.
10 Nietzsche, "Homer's Contest," in *Works*, 2:58. On Nietzsche's writings on Homer, see James I. Porter, "Neitzsche, Homer, and the Classical Tradition," in *Nietzsche and Antiquity: his reaction and response to the classical tradition*, ed. Paul Bishop (Rochester: Camden House, 2004), 7–26, and chapters 1

and 2 of Christa Acampora, *Contesting Nietzsche* (Chicago: University of Chicago Press, 2013).

11 Nietzsche, "Homer's Contest," in *Works*, 2:51–2.

12 Heidegger, *An Introduction to Metaphysics*, 62; compare 131 and his *Parmenides*, 17–18.

13 Simone Weil and Rachel Bespaloff, *War and the Iliad*, introduction, xv.

14 Weil, *The Iliad or the Poem of Force*, introduction, 7.

15 Weil, *Poem of Force*, 9.

16 Weil, *Poem of Force*, 53–4; 61, citing *Il.* 18.309.

17 Bespaloff, *On the Iliad*, in *War and the Iliad*, pp. 46–7.

18 Bespaloff, *On the Iliad*, 94.

19 Bespaloff, *On the Iliad*, 71.

20 Nietzsche, *Homer's Contest*, 53–4.

21 Recent studies such as Kate McLoughin's *Authoring war: the literary representation of war from the Iliad to Iraq* (Cambridge University Press, 2011) and James Tatum's *The Mourner's Song: War and Remembrance from The Iliad to Vietnam* (University of Chicago Press, 2003) testify to the ongoing inclination to narrate the history of recent war through the lens of Homeric epic. In a slightly different vein, works such as Jonathan Shay's *Achilles in Vietnam: Combat Trauma and the Undoing of Character* (New York: Athenaeum, 1994) and his *Odysseus in America: combat trauma and the trials of homecoming* (New York: Scribners, 2002) invoke Homeric themes and turn them into meditations on contemporary problems such as PTSD and the social challenges faced by soldiers returning home.

22 Hannah Arendt, *The Promise of Politics*, ed. Jerome Kohn (NY: Schocken Books, 2005), 166–7.

Works Cited

Manuscripts and Adversaria

Biblioteca Apostolica Vaticana

MS Vat. Lat. 3298. Angelo Poliziano's autograph translation of *Iliad* II and III.

MS Vat. Lat. 3617. Angelo Poliziano's autograph translation of *Iliad* IV and V.

Vat. Stamp. Pal. IV.801. *Homêrou Odysseiae A ke E Angeli Politiani in Homerum Praefatio*. Basel, 1520. Signed (1523) and annotated by Achilles Pirminius Gasser, bound with *Iliados D Homêrou Rhapsodias Hupodesis*, Joachim Camerarius's *Commentarius Explicationis primi libri Iliados Homeri* (1538), and *Commentarii Explicationum Secundi libri Homericae Iliados* (1540), also signed and annotated by Gasser.

Biblioteca Marciana, Venice

MS Lat. XII.232, no. XIV, fols. 5b–14b. Johannes Reuchlin's Latin translation of the *Batrachomyomachia*, ca 1510, with marginal notes by Reuchlin.

Bibliothèque Nationale de France, Paris

MS. Fonds Francais 19.035, fols. 60–176. Antoine Séguier, *Receuil des Mythologies apophtegmes et sentences d'Homère, extraict des commentaries d'Eustathe*.

MS. Fonds Français 12.407. Pierre de Marcassus. *Extraict de L'Odisée d'Homère. Et du Commentaire Grec.* 154 fols.

MS. Fonds Coislin 182–3. Pierre de Marcassus, "Extraict des choses les plus remarcables, qui se trouvent dans les poètes grecz et dans leurs scholiastes, et premièrement dans Homère et dans Eustathius." 438 fols.

Res. YB 151. *Homeri Ilias. Ulyssea, Batrachomyomachia, Hymni XXXII.* Louvain: Bartholomaeo Gravio, 1535. Inscribed "Christophorus Comes a Manderscheit" on inside front cover, with annotations.

British Library

Add. MS. 22, 583, fols. 1–8. William Gager's translation of the *Batrachomyomachia.*

653 G8/G9/G10. *Eustathius … in Homeri Iliadis et Odysseae Libros Parekbolai.* Basel: Froben, 1560. Annotated by Isaac Casaubon.

C.66.b2. *Odysseæ Homeri libri XXIIII, nuper a Simone Lemnio … Heroico Latino carmine facti and a mendis quibusdam priorum translationum repurgati. Accessit et Batrachomyomachia Homeri.* Basel: Oporinus, 1549. With marginal annotations.

Cambridge University Library

Adv. d.13.4. *Homerou Ilias.* Venice, Aldus, 1504. Annotated by Philipp Melanchthon.

Adv. a.3.3. *Poetae Graeci Principes Heroici Carminis*, ed. Henri Estienne. Geneva: Fugger, 1566. Annotated by Isaac Casaubon.

Firestone Library, Princeton University

PA4018.A31 M52 1541q. *Poiêseis Homêrou amphô, ête Ilias kai ê Odysseia.* Basel, J. Hervagius, 1541. Annotated by Martin Crusius.

2681.1488q. *Hê tou Homêrou poiêsis hapasa.* Florence: Nerlius, 1488. Annotated by Guillaume Budé.

Widener Library, Harvard University

f HEW 6.11.3. George Chapman's presentation copy of his *The crowne of all Homers worckes. Batrachomyomachia, or, the battaile of frogs and mise: his hymn's and epigrams* (London: John Bill, 1624), given to Henry Reynolds, and inscribed by the author.

Editions and Translations of Homer

Homerou Odysseias Bibloi A & B. [*Homeri Ulysseae lib. I & II*]. Basel: Andreas Cratander, 1520.

Homeri Omnium Poetarum Principis Ilias, Andrea Divo interprete. Venice: Jacopo Borgofranco, 1537.

Homeri Poetae Clarissimi Odyssea, Andrea Divo Iustinopolitano interprete, ad verbum translata. Venice: Jacopo Borgofranco, 1537.

La Batrachomyomachie d'Homere, ou est Racontée et Descrite La Bataille des Grenouilles, & Souris, Traduire nouvellement de Grec en vers Francois par G[uillaume] Royhier. Lyon: Jean Temporal, 1544.

Poetarum omnium seculorum longe Principis Homeri Ilias: hoc est de rebus ad Troiamgestis descriptio iam recens Latino carmine reddita Helio Eobano Hesso interprete. Paris: Carolus Guillard, 1545.

Homeri Opera graeco-latina, quae quidem nunc extant, omnia. Hoc est: Ilias, Odyssea, Batrachomyomachia, et Hymni. Edited and translated by Sebastian Castellio. Basel: Nicholas Brylingerus, 1561.

Homerou Batrachomyomachia. Homeri Ranarum & murium pugna. In Homeri Batrachomyomachiam scholia P. Melanchthonis, a studioso quodam, ex ore ipsius olim excerpta. Paris: Thomas Richard, 1562.

Homêrou Ilias, ê mallon hapanta ta sôzomena. Homeri Ilias, Seu Potius omnia eius quae extant opera. Studio & cura Ob[ertus] Giphanii. Strasbourg: Theodosius Rihelius, 1572.

Homêrou kai Hêsiodou agôn = Homeri et Hesiodi Certamen … Matronis et Aliorum parodiae, ex Homeri versibus parva immutatione lepidè detortis consultae … cum duplici interpretatione Latina. [Geneva]: Henri Estienne, 1573.

Les XXIIII Livres de l'Iliade d'Homère … traduicts du grec en vers François. Les XI premiers par M. Hughes Salel … et les XIII derniers par Amadis Jamyn. Paris: Lucas Breyer, 1580.

Ten books of Homers Iliades, translated out of the French by A[rthur] H[all]. London: Ralph Newberie, 1581.

L'Odissea d'Homero tradotta in volgare Fiorentino da M. Girolamo Baccelli. Florence: Sermatelli, 1582.

Homeri quae extant omnia Ilias, Odyssea, Batrachomyomachia, Hymni, Poematia … cum latina versione. Edited and translated by Jean de Sponde. Basel: Eusebius Episcopius, 1583.

Homeri Poemata Duo, Ilias et Odyssea, sive Ulyssea. Alia item carmina eiusdem … Adiecti sunt etiam Homerici centones qui Graecè Homêrokentra: item, Proverbialivm Versuum libellvs. Edited by Henri Estienne. Geneva: Henri Estienne, 1588.

L'Odyssée d'Homere. Au Roy. De la Version de Salomon Certon. Paris: Abel l'Angelier, 1604.

Histoire Facetieuse des Rats contre les Grenouilles.Imitation d'Homere. Seconde edition. Paris: Jean Sara, 1616.
L'Iliade d'Homere … avec la suite d'icelle, Ensemble le Ravissement d'Helene. Translated by Sieur du Souhait. Paris: Nicolas Buon, 1617.
The crowne of all Homers worckes. Batrachomyomachia or the battaile of frogs and mise. His hymn's - and – epigrams. Translated by George Chapman. London: John Bill, [1624].
Homer his Iliads translated, adorn'd with sculpture, and illustrated with annotations by John Ogilby. London: Thomas Roycroft, 1660.
In Batrachomyomachiam Homeri, Martini Crusii Praefatio. In Ioh[annes] Mich[ael] Langius. *Ad Poesin Barbaro-Graecam, succincta Introductio. Accedit Batrachomyomachia Homeri, a Demetrio Zeno Zacynthio in versos Barbaro-Graecos conversa cum Interpretatione Latina & annotationibus B. Martini Crusii*. Altdorf: Jodoci Guilielmi Kohles, 1707.
Odyssey. 2 vols. 2nd ed. Translated by A.T. Murray. Cambridge, MA: Harvard University Press, 1995.
The Iliad of Homer. Translated by Alexander Pope. Edited by Steven Shankman. London: Penguin, 1996.
Chapman's Homer: The Iliad. Translated by George Chapman. Edited by Allardyce Nicoll. Princeton: Princeton University Press, 1998.
Iliad. 2 vols. 2nd ed. Translated by A.T. Murray. Cambridge, MA: Harvard University Press, 1999.
Chapman's Homer: Volume 2. The Odyssey. Translated by George Chapman. Edited by Allardyce Nicoll. Princeton: Princeton University Press, 2000.
Homeric Hymns, Homeric Apocrypha, Lives of Homer. Edited and translated by Martin L. West. Cambridge, MA: Harvard University Press, 2003.
Chapman's Homeric Hymns and other Homerica. Edited by Alardyce Nicoll. Princeton: Princeton University Press, 2008.
Translations of Homer. 2 vols. Translated by Thomas Hobbes. Edited by Eric Nelson. Oxford: Clarendon Press, 2008.

Primary Works

Aeschylus. 2 vols. Translated by Herbert Weir Smyth. London: Heinemann, 1922–6.
Aesop. *Fables*. Edited and translated by Emile Chambry. Paris: Belles Lettres, 1960.
Agrippa, Heinrich Cornelius. *The Vanity of arts and sciences*. London, 1676.
Alciati, Andrea. *Emblemata* (Lyon, 1550). Edited and translated by Betty I. Knott. Aldershot: Scolar Press, 1996.
Ames, William. *The Marrow of Theology*. Translated by John D. Eusden. Boston: Pilgrim Press, 1968.

Apuleius, Lucius. *The Golden Asse*. Translated by William Adlington and edited by E.B. Osborn. New York: Rarity Press, 1931.
Archestratus. *The Life of Luxury*. Edited and translated by John Wilkins and Shaun Hill. Totnes, UK: Prospect, 1994.
Ariosto, Ludovico. *Orlando Furioso: in English Heroical Verse.* Translated by John Harington. London, 1591.
Aristotle. *Aristotles Politiques, or Discourses of Government*. Translated from the French of Louis Le Roy by I.D. London, 1598.
– *Eudemian Ethics*. In *The Athenian constitution: The Eudemian ethics. On virtues and vice*. Translated by H. Rackham. Cambridge, MA: Harvard University Press, 1952.
– *Nicomachean Ethics*. Translated by H. Rackham. Cambridge, MA: Harvard University Press, 1982.
– *Poetics*. In *Aristotle, Longinus, Demetrius*. Edited and translated by Stephen Halliwell. Cambridge, MA: Harvard University Press, 1995.
– *Rhetoric. The Art of Rhetoric. Aristotle XXII*. Translated by John Henry Freese. Cambridge, MA: Harvard University Press, 1982.
Athenaeus. *The Deipnosophists*. 7 vols. Translated by Charles Burton Gulick. Cambridge, MA: Harvard University Press, 1951.
Augustine. *Of the Citie of God: With the Learned Comments of Io. Lo. Vives*. London: George Eld, 1610.
– *On Christian Teaching*. Translated by R.P. H. Green. London: Penguin, 1997.
Ausonius. *Periochae Homeri Iliades et Odyssiae*. In *Oeuvres en vers et en prose*. 2 vols. Translated by Max Jasinski. Paris: Garnier [n.d].
Bacon, Francis. *The Advancement of Learning*. Edited by Michael Kiernan. *The Oxford Francis Bacon*, volume 4. Oxford: Clarendon Press, 2000.
– *De Sapientia Veterum. The Wisdom of the Ancients*. In volume 6:1 of *The Works of Francis Bacon*. 14 vols. Edited by James Spedding, Robert Leslie Ellis, and Douglas Denon Heath. London, 1857–74; rpt. Cambridge University Press, 2011.
– *The Essayes, or Counsells, Civill and Morall*. Edited by Michael Kiernan. *The Oxford Francis Bacon*, volume 15. 2nd ed. Oxford: Clarendon Press, 2000.
Baron, Robert. An *apologie for Paris for rejecting of Juno and Pallas and presenting of Ate's golden ball to Venus*. London, 1649.
Bastard, Thomas. *Twelve Sermons*. London, 1615.
Beaumont, Joseph. *Psyche, or Loves Mysterie in XX Canto's*. London, 1648.
Beni, Paolo. *Comparatione di Torquato Tasso con Homero e Vergilio*. Padua, 1612.
Benserade, Isaac. *La Mort d'Achille et la Dispute de ses Armes*. Paris, 1636.
Bergmann, Nicolaus. *De Theologia Homeri Dissertatio Philologica*. Leipzig, 1679.

Berni, Francesco. *Dialogo contra I Poeti*. In *Renaissance Humanism at the Court of Clement VII: Francesco Berni's Dialogue against Poets in context*. Edited and translated by Anne Reynolds. New York and London: Garland, 1997.

Bespaloff, Rachel. *On the Iliad*. See Weil and Bespaloff.

[*Bible*]. *The New English Bible with Apocrypha. Oxford Study Edition*. Edited by Samuel Sandmel. New York: Oxford University Press, 1976.

[Bible, NT, Greek] *Interlinear Greek-English New Testament. King James Version*. Edited by George Ricker Berry. Grand Rapids, MI: Baker Books, 2002.

[Bible, OT, Greek] *The Septuagint with Apocrypha: Greek and English*. Edited and translated by Sir Lancelot C.L. Brenton. London, 1851, rpt. Peabody, MA: Hendrickson Publishers, 2001.

Boccaccio, Giovanni. *Genealogia deorum gentilium*. Venice, 1472.

Bodin, Jean. *Method for the Easy Comprehension of History*. Translated by Beatrice Reynolds. New York: Norton, 1969.

Boethius. *The Consolation of Philosophy*. Translated by H.F. Stewart, E.K. Rand, and S.J. Tester. Cambridge, MA: Harvard University Press, 1973.

Boëtie, Etienne de la. *De la Servitude Volontaire ou Contr'un*. Edited by Malcolm Smith. Geneva: Droz, 1987.

Bogan, Zachary. *Homerus Hebraizon: sive, Comparatio Homeri cum Scriptoribus Sacris quod normam loquendi*. Oxford, 1658.

Borges, José Luis. "Some Versions of Homer." Translated by Suzanne J. Levine. In *PMLA* 107, no. 5 (1992): 1134–8.

Browne, Thomas. *The Major Works*. Edited by C.A. Patrides. London: Penguin, 1977.

Bruni, Leonardo. *De Studio Litterarum* (1424). Translated as *On the Study of Literature*, in *The Humanism of Leonardo Bruni: Selected Texts*. Edited and translated by Gordon Griffiths, James Hankins, and David Thompson. Binghamton, NY: MRTS, 1987.

– *Die Orationes Homeri des Leonardo Bruni Aretino: Kritische Edition*. Edited by Peter Thiermann. Leiden: Brill, 1993.

Bruno, Giordano. *The Heroic Frenzies*. Translated by Paul Eugene Memmo, Jr. Chapel Hill: University of North Carolina Press, 1965.

Bryskett, Lodowick. *A Discourse of Civill Life*. London, 1606.

Budé, Guillaume. *De Philologia*. Edited and translated by Marie-Madeleine de la Garanderie. Paris: Belles Lettres, 2001.

– *De Studio litterarum recte et commode instituendo*. Paris, 1532.

– *De Transitu Hellenismi ad Christianismum*. Edited and translated by Marie-Madeleine de la Garanderie. Paris: Belles Lettres, 1993.

– *De Transitu Hellenismi ad Christianismum*. Edited and translated by Maurice Lebel. Sherbrooke: Editions Paulines, 1973.

Burckhardt, Jakob. *The Civilization of the Renaissance in Italy: an essay*. Translated by S.G.C. Middlemore. London: Phaidon, 1950.
– *The Greeks and Greek Civilization*. Translated by Sheila Stern. New York: St Martin's Press, 1998.
Burton, Robert. *The Anatomy of Melancholy*. 6 vols. Edited by Thomas C. Faulkner, Nicolas K. Kiessling, and Rhonda L. Blair. Oxford: Clarendon Press, 1989–2002.
Butler, Samuel. *The Authoress of the Odyssey*. Chicago: University of Chicago Press, 1967.
Calvin, John. *Institutes of the Christian Religion*. 2 vols. Edited by John McNeill and translated by Ford Lewis Battles. Philadelphia: Westminster Press, 1960.
Camerarius, Joachim. *Questiones Promiscuae*. In Janus Gruter, *Lampas, Sive Fax Artium Liberalium, Hoc Est, Thesaurus Criticus*. Frankfurt, 1604.
Canter, Guillaume. *Novarum lectionem libri septem*. Basel, 1566.
Capito, Wolfgang. *The Letters of Wolfgang Capito*. Volume 1 (1507–23). Edited and translated by Erika Rummel. Toronto: University of Toronto Press, 2005.
Cartari, Vincenzo. *Les Images des Dieux des Anciens*. Lyon: Estienne Michel, 1581.
Casaubon, Isaac. *Notae ad Diogenes Laertii libros de vitis dictis et decretis principum philosophorum*. Morges, 1583.
Castellio, Sebastian. *Oracula Sibyllina*. Basel, 1546.
Castiglione, Baldassar. *The Book of the Courtier*. Translated by Thomas Hoby and edited by Virginia Cox. London: J.M. Dent, 1994.
Chapman, George. *Chapman's Homer: the Iliad*. Edited by Allardyce Nicoll. Princeton, NJ: Princeton University Press, 1998.
– *Chapman's Homer: Volume 2. The Odyssey*. Edited by Allardyce Nicoll. Princeton, NJ: Princeton University Press, 2000.
– *The Comedies*. 2 vols. Thomas Marc Parrott. New York: Russell & Russell, 1961.
– *The Poems of George Chapman*. Edited by Phyllis Bartlett. New York: Modern Language Association, 1941.
– *The Tragedies*. 2 vols. Thomas Marc Parrott. New York: Russell & Russell, 1961.
Chaucer, Geoffrey. *The Riverside Chaucer*. Edited by Larry D. Benson. Boston: Houghton Mifflin, 1987.
Cicero. *De Natura Deorum*. Translated by H. Rackham. Cambridge, MA: Harvard University Press, 1979.
– *De Oratore*. 2 vols. Translated by H. Rackham. Cambridge, MA: Harvard University Press, 1942.
– *De Senectute. De Amicitia. De Divinatione*. Translated by William Armistead Falconer. Cambridge, MA: Harvard University Press, 1979.
– *Letters to Atticus*. 4 vols. Translated by D. Shackelton Bailey. Cambridge, MA: Harvard University Press, 1999.

– *Tusculan Disputations*. Translated by J.E. King. Cambridge, MA: Harvard University Press, 1971.

Cinthio, Giraldi. *Discorsi intorno al comporre dei romanzi*. Venice, 1554.

Clement of Alexandria. *Exhortation to the Greeks*. Edited and translated by G.B. Butterworth. Cambridge, MA: Harvard University Press, 1982.

– *Les Stromates* II. Edited and translated by Claude Montdésert. Paris: Editions du Cerf, 1954.

– *Les Stromates* VII. Edited and translated by Alain Le Boulleuc. Paris: Editions du Cerf, 1997.

– *Protreptique*. Edited and translated by Claude Montdésert. Paris: Editions du Cerf, 1949.

Collop, John. *The Poems of John Collop*. Edited by Conrad Hilberry. Madison: University of Wisconsin Press, 1962.

Conti, Natale. *Mythologiae*. 2 vols. Edited and translated by John Mulryan and Stephen Brown. Tempe, AZ: ACMRS, 2006.

– *Mythologiae Sive Explicationis Fabularum Libri Decem*. Padua, 1637.

Coryate, Thomas. *Coryats Crudities* (1611). Reprinted with an introduction by William M. Schutte. London: Scolar Press, 1978.

Cowley, Abraham. *The True Effigies of the Monster of Malmesbury, or, Thomas Hobbes in his proper Colours*. London, 1680.

Crusius, Martin. *Commentationes in I Lib. Iliad. Homeri, Grammaticae, Rhetoricae, Poeticae, Historicae, Philosophicae*. [Heidelberg], 1612.

– *Quaestiones*. See Melanchthon, *Elementorum Rhetorices*.

Cudworth, Ralph. *The True Intellectual System of the Universe*. London, 1678.

Dalechamp, Caleb. *Artis Poeticae et versificatoriae encomium*. In his *Exercitationes duae* (1624). Reprinted in *Latin Treatises on Poetry from Renaissance England*. Edited by J.W. Binns. Signal Mountain, TN: Summertown, 1999.

Davies, John. *Wittes Pilgrimage*. London, 1605.

Davies, John, Sir. *Poems*. Edited by Robert Krueger. Oxford: Clarendon Press, 1975.

Decembrius, Angelus. *De Politia Literaria Libri Septem*. Basel, 1562.

Deimier, Pierre. *L'Academie de L'Art Poetique*. Paris, 1610.

Demetrius. *On Style*. In *Aristotle, Longinus, Demetrius*. Edited and translated by Doreen C. Innes. Cambridge, MA: Harvard University Press, 1995.

Dennis, John. *The Grounds of Criticism in Poetry* (1704). In volume 1 of *The Critical Works of John Dennis*. 2 vols. Edited by Edward Niles Hooker. Baltimore: Johns Hopkins University Press, 1939.

Dio Chrysostom. 5 vols. Translated by J.W. Cohoon. London: Heinemann, 1932.

Diogenes Laertius. *Lives of the Philosophers*. 2 vols. Translated by R.D. Hicks. Cambridge, MA: Harvard University Press, 1972.

Donatus. *Life of Virgil*. Edited and translated by David Wilson-Okamura (www.virgil.org).

Dorat, Jean. *Mythologicum*. Edited and translated by Philip Ford. Geneva: Droz, 2000.

Dove, John. *A Confutation of Atheisme*. London, 1605.

Dryden, John. *Troilus and Cressida, or, Truth found too late … to which is prefix'd, a preface containing the grounds of criticism in tragedy*. London, 1679.

Du Bartas, Guillaume Salluste. *Divine Weekes and Works* (1605). Translated by Joshua Sylvester and edited by Francis C. Haber. Delmar, NY: Scholars' Facsimiles and Reprints, 1977.

Dufresny, Charles Rivière. *Parallele Burlesque, ou Dissertation, ou Discours qu'on nommera comme on voudra, sur Homere et Rabelais*. In volume 3 of *Oeuvres de Maitre Francois Rabelais avec des Remarques Historiques et Critiques de Mr. Le Duchat*, 3 vols. Amsterdam, 1741.

Duport, James. *Homeri Poetarum omnium seculorum facile Principis Gnomologia.* Cambridge, 1660.

Ebreo, Leone. *Dialoghi D'Amore*. Edited by Santino Caramella. Bari: Laterza, 1929.

Edwards, John. *A discourse concerning the authority, stile, and perfection of the books of the Old and New-Testament*. London, 1693.

Elyot, Thomas, Sir. *The Boke named the Governour*. London, 1537.

Empedocles. *The Poem of Empedocles. A Text and Translation*. Edited and translated by Brad Inwood. Toronto: University of Toronto Press, 1992.

Epo, Boetius. *Omnium Scriptorum Principis Homeri Sententiae*. Louvain, 1555.

Erasmus, Desiderius. *Collected Works of Erasmus*. Toronto: University of Toronto Press, 1974–.

– *Libanii Sophistae sub persona Menelai, pro cōcione Troianorum, Helenam & res repetentis, ni reddant, armis iniuriam ulturum se denunciantis*. In *Libanii Sophistae Graeci Declamationculae Aliquot…* Louvain, 1519.

– *Opera Omnia Desiderii Erasmi Roterodami.* Amsterdam, 1969–.

– *Opera Omnia*. 10 vols. Edited by J. Leclerc. Leiden, 1703–6.

– *Opus Epistolarum Des. Erasmi Roterodami*. 12 vols. Edited by P.S. Allen, H.M. Allen, and H.W. Garrod. Oxford: Clarendon Press, 1906–58.

– *Proverbia quaedam Homerica D. Erasmi Roterodami labore exquisitissimo e Graeco in linguam Latinam versa, ingenii ac eruditionis plenissima*. Antwerp, 1529.

– *Ratio*. In *Desiderius Erasmus. Ausgewählte Werke*. Edited by Hajo Holborn and Annemarie Holborn. 2nd ed. Munich, 1964.

– *Spongia*. In *The Polemics of Erasmus and Ulrich von Hutten*. Edited and translated by Rudolph J. Klawiter. London and Notre Dame, IN: University of Notre Dame Press, 1977.

Estienne, Charles. *Dictionarium Historicum, Geographicum, Poeticum*. Paris, 1596; rpt. New York & London: Garland, 1976.

Estienne, Henri, ed. *Parodiae Morales … in poetarum vet. sententias celebriores, totide[m] versibus Gr. ab eo redditas*. [Geneva]: Estienne, 1575.

– *Traicté de la Conformité du Langage François avec le Grec*. Geneva, 1565.

Eustathius, *Commentarii ad Homeri Iliadem et Odysseam*. 4 vols. Edited by Gottfried Stallbaum. Hildesheim: Georg Olms, 1960.

Fenne, Thomas. *Hecubaes Mishaps*, in *Fennes Frutes ...* London, 1590.

Fitz-Geffrey, Charles. *Sir Francis Drake, His Honourable lifes commendation, and his tragicall deathes lamentation*. Oxford, 1596.

Fletcher, Phineas. *The Purple Island*. In volume 2 of The *Poetical Works of Giles Fletcher and Phineas Fletcher*. 2 vols. Edited by Frederick S. Boas. Cambridge: Cambridge University Press, 1908–9.

Folengo, Teofilo. *Baldo*. 2 vols. Translated by Ann E. Mullaney. Cambridge, MA: Harvard University Press/I Tatti Renaissance Library, 2007–9.

Fotherby, Martin. *Atheomastix: clearing foure truthes, against atheists and infidels ...* London, 1622.

Fraunce, Abraham. *The Arcadian Rhetorike* (1588). Edited by Ethel Seaton. Oxford: Basil Blackwell, 1950.

– *The third part of the Countesse of Pembrokes Yuychurch Entituled, Amintas dale ...* London, 1592.

Fresnaye, Vauquelin de la. *L'Art Poétique* (1605). Edited by Georges Pellissier. Paris: Garnier, 1885.

Gager, William. *Ulysses Redux: tragoedia nova*. Oxford, 1592.

Garasse, François. *Invective contre Homere et Virgile*. In his *Nouveau Jugement de ce qui a esté dict et escrit pour and contre le livre de la doctrine curieuse des beaux esprits de ce temps*. Paris, 1625.

Gelli, Giovanni Battista. *Circe*. Edited by Robert Adams and translated by Thomas Brown. Ithaca, NY: Cornell University Press, 1963.

Gellius, Aulus. *Noctes Atticae*. 3 vols. Translated by John C Rolfe. Cambridge, MA: Harvard University Press, 1946.

Gesner, Conrad, ed. *Moralis Interpretatio Errorum Ulyssis Homerici. Commentatio Porphyrii de Nympharum antro in XIII. libro Odysseae Homericae ...* Zurich, [1542].

Gibbon, Anthony, trans. Alexandre de Pontaymeri, *A Womans Woorth, defended against all the men in the world. Prooving them to be more perfect, excellent, and absolute in all virtuous actions, then any man of what qualities soever*. London, 1599.

Giraldi, Lillio. *De Deis Gentium Varia & Multiplex Historia*. Basel, 1548.

– *Historiae Poetarum tam Graecorum quam Latinorum Dialogi*. Basel, 1545.

Girardus, Nicolaus. *Meditationes in Librum Primum Iliados Homeri*. Paris, 1566.

Glanvill, Joseph. *Lux Orientalis, or, An enquiry into the opinion of the Eastern sages concerning the praeexistence of souls: being a key to unlock the grand mysteries of providence*. London, 1662.

Goclenius, Rudolph. *Physiologia De Risu & Lacrymis*. In *Hermolai Barbari Patritii Veneti, Scientiae Naturalis Compendium*. Marburg, 1597.
Gratius, Ortuinus. *Dialogue between Mercury and a Potlicker*. Translated in Rummel, ed., *Scheming Papists and Lutheran Fools*.
Greek Anthology, The. 5 vols. Translated by W.R. Paton. London: William Heinemann, 1927–39.
Greene, Robert. *Menaphon: Camillas alarum to slumbering Euphues, in his melancholie cell at Silexedra*. London, 1589.
Grosart, Alexander, ed. *Annalia Dubrensia or Celebration of Captain Robert Dover's Cotswold Games*. London, 1877.
Guazzo, Stefano. *The Civile Conversation ... translated by George Pettie*. London, 1581.
Hall, Joseph. *Virgidemiarum: sixe bookes. First three bookes, of tooth-lesse satyrs*. London, 1597.
Hammond, Henry. *Charis kai eirênê, or, A pacifick discourse of Gods grace and decrees*. London, 1660.
– *Of Fundamentals in a notion referring to practise*. London, 1654.
– *A Paraphrase and annotations upon all the books of the New Testament*. London, 1659.
– *A Paraphrase and annotations upon the books of the Psalms, briefly explaining the difficulties thereof*. London, 1659.
Harrington, James. *The Commonwealth of Oceana*. Edited by J.G.A. Pocock. Cambridge: Cambridge University Press, 1992.
Hartung, Johannes. *Chilias Homericorum Locorum ...* Basel, 1568.
Heidegger, Martin. *An Introduction to Metaphysics*. Translated by Ralph Manheim. New Haven, CT: Yale University Press, 1959.
– *Parmenides*. Translated by André Schuwer and Richard Rojcewicz. Bloomington: Indiana University Press, 1992.
Heraclitus [pre-Socratic philosopher]. *The Art and Thought of Heraclitus: An Edition of the Fragments*. Edited and translated by Charles H. Kahn. 2nd ed. Cambridge: Cambridge University Press, 1999.
– *Cosmic Fragments*. Edited and translated by G.S. Kirk. Cambridge: Cambridge University Press, 1954.
Heraclitus [the allegorist]. *Allegoriae in Homeri fabulas de diis*. Translated by Conrad Gesner. Basel, 1544.
– *Allégories d'Homère*. Edited and translated by Félix Buffière. Paris: Belles Lettres, 1962.
– *Homeric Problems*. Edited and translated by Donald A. Russell and David Konstan. Leiden, Brill, 2005.
Hermeias Alexandrinus. *In Platonis Phaedrum Scholia*. Edited by Paul Couvreur. Paris: E. Bouillon, 1901.

Hesiod. *Hesiod, the Homeric Hymns, and Homerica*. Translated by H.G. Evelyn-White. Cambridge, MA: Harvard University Press, 1936.

Hesiod. *The georgicks of Hesiod*. Translated by George Chapman. London, 1618.

[Hesychius] *Lexikon. Dictionarium locupletiss[ima] ea fide ac diligentia excusum*. Edited by Marcus Musurus. Venice, 1521.

Heywood, Thomas. *The Golden Age*. London, 1611.

– *Gynaikeion*. London, 1624.

– *The Hierarchie of the Blessed Angells*. London, 1635.

Hippocrates. *Works*. 8 vols. Translated by W.H.S. Jones. 2nd ed. Cambridge, MA: Harvard University Press, 1998.

Hobbes, Thomas, *The Elements of Law Natural and Politic, Part I. Human Nature, Part II. De Corpore Politico*. Edited by J.C.A. Gaskin. Oxford: Oxford University Press, 1994.

– *De Mirabilibus Pecci. Being The Wonders of the Peak in Darby-Shire, Commonly Called The Devil's Arse of Peak*. London, 1678.

– *The English Works of Thomas Hobbes of Malmesbury*. 11 vols. Edited by Sir *William Molesworth*. London: Bohn, 1839–45.

– *Leviathan*. Edited by Richard Tuck. Cambridge: Cambridge University Press, 1996.

– *Thomas White's De Mundo Examined*. Translated by Harold Whitmore Jones, based on the Latin text by Jean Jacquot. London: Bradford University Press, 1976.

Holland, Samuel. *Wit and Fancy in a Maze. Or the Incomparable Champion of Love and Beautie. A Mock-Romance*. London, 1656.

[Homeric scholia]. *Scholia Graeca in Homeri Iliadem (scholia vetera)*. Edited by Hartmut Erbse. Berlin: De Gryter, 1969.

[Homeric scholia]. *Scholia Graeca in Homeri Odysseam*. 2nd ed. Edited by Wilhelm Dindorf. Amsterdam, 1962.

[Homerocentra]. *Centons Homeriques*. Edited by Andre-Louis Rey. Sources Chrétiennes 437. Paris: Editions du Cerf, 1998.

Hooker, Richard. *Of the Laws of Ecclesiastical Polity*. Edited by A.S. McGrade and Brian Vickers. New York: St Martin's Press, 1975.

Horace. *Epistles*. Translated by David Ferry. New York: Farrar, Strauss, and Giroux, 2001.

– *Satires, Epistles, and Ars Poetica*. Translated by H. Rushton Fairclough. Cambridge, MA: Harvard University Press, 1929.

Hoskyns, John. *Directions for Speech and Style* (ca 1599–1603). In Louise Brown Osborn, *The Life, Letters, and Writings of John Hoskyns 1566–1638*. 2nd ed. New York: Archon Books, 1973.

Hugo, Jacobus [Jacques Hugues]. *Vera Historia Romana seu Origo Latii vel Italiae ac Romanae Urbis.* Rome, 1655.

Hume, Patrick. *Annotations on Paradise Lost.* In *The poetical works of Mr. John Milton*. London, 1695.

Hutten, Ulrich von. *Expostulation*. See Erasmus, *Spongia*.

– *Letters of Obscure Men*. Edited by Marie Stokes. New Haven, CT: Yale University Press, 1925.

Insulis, Alanis [Alain de Lille]. *The Complaint of Nature*. Translated by Douglas M. Moffat. Yale Studies in English 36. New York: Henry Holt, 1908.

Irenaeus of Lyons, Saint. *Against the Heresies*. Vol. 1. Translated by Dominic J. Unger. New York: Paulist Press, 1992.

Jackson, Thomas. *A Treatise containing the originall of unbeliefe, misbeliefe, or mispersuasions*. London, 1625.

Jonson, Benjamin. *Works*. 11 vols. Edited by C.H. Herford and Percy Simpson. Oxford, Clarendon Press, 1925–63.

Joubert, Laurent. *Traité du Ris*. Translated as *Treatise on Laughter* by Gregory David Du Rocher. Tuscaloosa: University of Alabama Press, 1980.

Justin Martyr. *Hortatory Address to the Greeks*. Translated by Rev. M. Dods. Ante-Nicene Fathers I. Grand Rapids, MI: Eerdmans, 1950.

Knevet, Ralph. *Stratiotikon: or, a Discourse of Military Discipline*. London, 1628.

Lactantius. *Divine Institutes*. Translated by Anthony Bowen and Peter Garney. Liverpool: Liverpool University Press, 2003.

Lambinus, Dionysius. *Pridie Quam Homeri Iliadis Librum A. Explicare Inciperet*. Paris, 1562.

La Mothe Le Vayer, François de. *De la Philosophie Sceptique*. In *Dialogues faits à l'imitation des Anciens* (1606). Edited by André Pessel. Paris: Fayard, 1988.

– *L'Antre des Nymphes*. Edited by Jean-Pierre Cavaillé. Toulouse: Anacharsis, 2004.

Landino, Cristoforo. *Disputationes Camaldulenses*. Edited by Peter Lohe. Florence: Sansoni, 1980.

La Seine [La Sena], Petro. *Homeri Nepenthes Seu De Abolendo Luctu Liber*. Lyon, 1624.

Lavezola, Alberto. *Osservationi … Sopra il Orlando Furioso.* Venice, 1584.

Le Bossu, René. *Traité du poëme epique*. Paris, 1675.

– *Treatise of the Epick Poem Containing Many Curious Reflexions*. Translated by W.J. London, 1695; rpt. Gainesville, FL: Scholars' Facsimiles and Reprints, 1970.

Le Caron, Louis. *Dialogues*. Edited by Joan A. Buhlmann and Donald Gilman. Geneva: Droz, 1986.

Le Loyer, Pierre. *Edom ou les Colonies iduméans en l'Asie et en l'Europe; colonies d'Hercule Phénicien et de Tyr*. Paris, 1620.

Lemaire de Belges, Jean. *Les Illustrations de Gaule et singularitez de Troye.* In *Oeuvres.* 4 vols. Edited by J. Stecher. Geneva: Slatkine, 1969.

Leroy, Louis. *De La Vicissitude ou Variete des Choses en l'Univers* (1577). Edited by Philippe Desan. Paris: Fayard, 1988.

Liceti, Fortunio. *Hieroglyphica, sive Antiqua Schemata Gemmarum Anularium.* Padua, 1653.

Linche, Richard, trans. *The Fountaine of Ancient Fiction, Wherein is lively depictured the Images and Statues of the gods of the Ancients ...* London, 1599.

Lipsius, Justus. *Politica: six books of politics or political instruction.* Edited and translated by Jan Waszink. Assen, Netherlands: Royal Van Gorcum, 2004.

– *Sixe Bookes of Politickes or Civil Doctrine.* Translated by William Jones. London, 1594

– *Two Bookes of Constancie.* Translated by Sir John Stradling (1594) and edited by Rudolf Kirk. New Brunswick, NJ: Rutgers University Press, 1939.

Lombardelli, Orazio. *Discorso Intorno a i contrasti che si fanno sopra la Gerusalemme Liberata.* Basel, 1586.

Longinus. *On the Sublime.* In *Aristotle. Longinus. Demetrius.* Translated by W.H. Fyfe. Cambridge, MA: Harvard University Press, 1995.

– *Peri Hupsous, Or ... the Height of Eloquence.* Translated by John Hall. London, 1651.

Lorris, Guillaume de, and Jean de Meun. *Le Roman de la Rose.* Edited by André Mary. Paris: Gallimard, 1984.

Lucian. *Dialogues.* 8 vols. Translated by A.M. Harmon. London: William Heinemann, 1913–67.

Lucretius. *De Rerum Natura.* Translated by W.H.D. Rouse. 2nd ed. Cambridge, MA: Harvard University Press, 1982.

Lydgate, John, trans. Guido delle Colonne. *The Life and Death of Hector ...* London, 1614.

Machiavelli, Niccolò. *Discourses.* Edited by Bernard Crick and translated by Leslie J. Walker, SJ. London: Penguin, 1983.

Maier, Michael. *Themis Aurea: the laws of the fraternity of the Rosie Crosse.* London, 1656.

Malatesta, Gioseppe. *Della Poesia Romanzesca, Overo Delle Difese Del Furioso, Ragionamento Secondo ... Delle Difese Del Furioso Ragionamento Terzo.* Rome, 1596.

Marsuppini, Carolus Aretinus. *Caroli Aretini Poetae Clarissimi Praefatio in Homeri Libros Ad Nicolaum PP.* In *Carlo Marsuppini, Traduttore d'Omero.* Edited by Alessandra Rocco. Padua: Il Poligrafo, 2000.

Martial. *Epigrams.* 3 vols. Translated by D.R. Shackleton Bailey. Cambridge, MA: Harvard University Press, 1993.

Martianus Capella. *The Marriage of Philology and Mercury (De Nuptiis Philologiae et Mercurii)*. Volume 2 of *Martianus Capella and the Seven Liberal Arts*. 2 vols. Translated by William Harris Stahl with E.L. Burge. New York: Columbia University Press, 1977.

Matro of Pitane. *Matro of Pitane and the Tradition of Epic Parody in the Fourth Century BCE. Text, Translation, and Commentary*. Edited and translated by S. Douglas Olson and Alexander Sens. Atlanta: American Philological Association Scholars Press, 1999.

Maximus of Tyre. *Philosophical Orations*. Translated by M.B. Trapp. Oxford: Clarendon Press, 1997.

Melanchthon, Philipp. *Elementorum Rhetorices Libri Duo*. Basel, 1564.

– *Grammatica Graeca*. Hagenau, 1531.

– *Loci Communes* 1555. In *Melanchthon on Christian Doctrine*. Edited and translated by Clyde L. Manschreck. New York: Oxford University Press, 1965.

– "On Correcting the Studies of Youth." In *A Melanchthon Reader*. Translated by Ralph Keen. New York and Frankfurt: Peter Lang, 1988.

– *Orations on Philosophy and Education*. Edited by Sachiko Kusukawa and translated by Christine F. Salazar. Cambridge: Cambridge University Press, 1999.

– *Philippi Melanthonis Opera Quae Supersunt Omnia*. 28 vols. Edited by Karl Gottlieb Bretschneider. Halle: C.A. Schwetschke and sons, 1834–60.

Milton, John. *Complete Poems and Major Prose*. Edited by Merritt Y. Hughes. Indianapolis, IN: Hackett, 2003.

– *Complete Prose Works*. 8 vols. Edited by Don M. Wolfe. New Haven, CT: Yale University Press, 1953–82.

– *Paradise Lost*. Edited by Alistair Fowler. Harlow: Longman, 1971.

– *The Works*. 21 vols. Edited by Frank Allen Patterson. New York: Columbia University Press, 1931–8.

Mexio, Pedro, and Francesco Sansovino. *The treasvrie of avncient and moderne times* ... Translated by Thomas Milles. London, 1613.

Mirandola, Pico della. *Examan Vanitatis doctrinae gentium & Veritatis disciplinae Christianae*. In *Opera Omnia*. 2 vols. Basel, 1573.

Montaigne, Michel de. *The Complete Essays*. Translated by Donald Frame. Palo Alto, CA: Stanford University Press, 1976.

More, Thomas. *Complete Works of Thomas More*. 15 vols. New Haven, CT: Yale University Press, 1963–97.

Morgan, Sylvanus. *Armilogia Sive Ars Chromocritica ... Mythologized to the Heroical Theam of Homer on the Shield of Achilles*. London, 1666.

Mornay, Philippe de. *A woorke concerning the trewnesse of the Christian Religion*. Translated by Philip Sidney and Arthur Golding. London, 1592.

Mosellanus, Petrus. *De Ratione Disputandi, praesertim in re Theologica … Oratio*. Augsburg, 1519.

Mulcaster, Richard. *Positions concerning the training up of children*. Edited by William Barker. Toronto: University of Toronto Press, 1994.

Nash, Thomas (d. 1648). *Quaternio or A fourefold way to a happie life set forth in a dialogue betweene a countryman and a citizen, a divine and a lawyer.* London, 1633.

Nashe, Thomas (d. 1601). *The Works of Thomas Nashe*. 5 vols. Edited by Ronald McKerrow. Oxford: Basil Blackwell, 1966.

Nicander, Jossius. *De Voluptate et Dolore, De Risu et Fletu, Somno et Vigilia, deque Fame & Siti*. Frankfurt, 1603.

Nietzsche, Friedrich. "Die Florentinischer Tractat über Homer und Hesiod," *Rhetorica* (Rheinisches museum für philologie) 25 (1870): 528–40 and 28 (1873): 211–49.

– *Homer and Classical Philology*. In *On the Future of our Educational Institutions*. Trans. J.M. Kennedy. New York: Macmillan, 1924.

– "Homer's Contest," *Preface to an unwritten book* (1872). Translated by Maximilian A. Mügge. In vol. 2 of Nietzsche, *Complete Works*, 18 vols. Edited by Oscar Levy. Edinburgh: T.N. Foulis, 1909–13.

– *Philosophy During the Tragic Age of the Greeks*, Later Preface (1879). In vol. 2 of *Complete Works*, ed. Levy.

[Ogle, John]. *The lamentation of Troy, for the death of Hector*. London, 1594.

Origen. *Contra Celsum*. Translated by Henry Chadwick. Cambridge: Cambridge University Press, 1965.

Ovid. *Metamorphoses*. 2 vols. Translated by Frank Justus Miller. Cambridge, MA: Harvard University Press, 1916.

– *Ovids Metamorphosis Englished, mythologiz'd, and represented in figures*. Translated by George Sandys. Oxford, 1632.

– *Shakspeare's Ovid: being Arthur Golding's translation of the Metamorphoses*. Edited by W.H.D. Rouse. London: Centaur Press, 1961.

[Ovid]. *Ovide Moralisé*. 5 vols. Edited by C. De Boer. Amsterdam: J. Müller, 1915–38.

Pansa, Mutio. *De Osculo Ethnicae et Christianae Philosophiae*. Chieti, 1601.

Paquelin, Guillaume. *Apologeme pour le grand Homere, Contre la Reprehension du divin Platon*. Lyon, 1577.

Peacham, Henry. *Garden of Eloquence. A Facsimile Reproduction, with an introduction by William G. Crane.* Gainesville, FL: Scholars' Facsimiles and Reprints, 1954.

Peele, George. *Arraignment of Paris*. In *The Works of George Peele*. 2 vols. Edited by A.H. Bullen. London: John Nimmo, 1888.

Peletier, Jacques. *Art Poétique* (1555). In *Traités de Poétique et de Rhétorique de la Renaissance*. Edited by Francis Goyet. Paris: Livres de Poche, 1990.

– *Oeuvres Poétiques*. Edited by Léon Séché and Paul Laumonier. 2nd ed. Geneva: Slatkine, 1970.

Perkins, William. *A Golden Chaine, or the Description of Theologie, Containing the Order of the Causes of Salvation and Damnation, According to Gods Word*. Cambridge, 1591.

Persona, Jo[annes] Baptista. *Noctes Solitariae, sive de lis Quae Scientifice scripta sunt ab Homero in Odyssea*. Venice, 1613.

Petit, Pierre. *Homeri Nepenthes, Sive De Helenae Medicamento luctum ... dissertatio*. Utrecht, 1687.

Petrarch, Francesco. *Invectives*. Edited and translated by David Marsh. Cambridge, MA: Harvard University Press/I Tatti Renaissance Library, 2003.

– *Letters of Old Age. Rerum Senilium Libri I–XVIII*. 2 vols. Edited and translated by Aldo S. Bernardo, Saul Levin, and Reta A. Bernardo. Baltimore: Johns Hopkins University Press, 1992.

Philostratus, Flavius [the Elder]. *Heroikos*. Edited and translated by Jennifer K. Berenson Maclean and Ellen Bradshaw Aitken. Atlanta: Society of Biblical Literature, 2001.

– *La Suite de Philostrate par Blaise de Vigénère*. Paris, 1602.

Pindar. Translated by William H. Race. Cambridge, MA: Harvard University Press, 1997.

Plato. *Cratylus*. *Plato IV*. Translated by Harold North Fowler. Cambridge, MA: Harvard University Press, 1996.

– *Laws*. 2 vols. *Plato X and XI*. Translated by J.B. Bury. Cambridge, MA: Harvard University Press, 1952.

– *Lysis. Symposium. Gorgias. Plato III*. Translated by W.R.M. Lamb. Cambridge, MA: Harvard University Press, 1983.

– *Phaedrus. Plato I*. Translated by Harold North Fowler. Cambridge, MA: Harvard University Press, 1990.

– *Protagoras. Plato II*. Translated by W.R.M. Lamb. Cambridge, MA: Harvard University Press, 1977.

– *Republic. Plato V and VI*. 2 vols. Translated by Paul Shorey. Cambridge, MA: Harvard University Press, 1937.

– *Theaetetus*; *Sophist. Plato VII*. Translated by Harold North Fowler. Cambridge, MA: Harvard University Press, 1977.

[Plato]. *Second Alcibiades*. In *Homeric hymns; Homeric apocrypha; Lives of Homer*. Translated by Martin L. West. Cambridge, MA: Harvard University Press, 2003.

Plutarch. *Moralia*. 16 vols. Translated by Frank Cole Babbitt. Cambridge, MA: Harvard University Press, 1969.

[Plutarch]. *Essay on the Life and Poetry of Homer*. Edited and translated by J.J. Keaney and Robert Lamberton. Atlanta: Scholars' Press, 1996.

Politianus, Antonius. *De Risu*. Printed with Jossius Nicander, *De Voluptate et Dolore, De Risu et Fletu* ... Frankfurt, 1603.
Poliziano, Angelo. *Silvae*. Edited and translated by Charles Fantazzi. Cambridge, MA: Harvard University Press/I Tatti Renaissance Library, 2004.
– *Appunti per un corso sull'Odissea. Editio Princeps dal Par. Gr. 3069*. Edited by Luigi Silvano. Alessandria: Edizioni dell'Orso, 2010.
– *Letters*. Volume 1. Edited and translated by Shane Butler. Cambridge, MA: Harvard University Press/I Tatti Renaissance Library, 2006.
– *Opera Omnia*. 3 vols. Basel, 1553; rpt. Turin: Bottega d'Erasmo, 1970–1.
– *Oratio in Expositione Homeri*. Edited by Paola Megna. Rome: Edizioni di storia e letteratura, 2007.
Pontano, Giovanni. *De Sermone Libri Sex*. Edited by S. Lupi and A. Risicato. Lucca: Thesauri Mundi, 1954.
Pope, Alexander. *Rape of the Lock*. 4th ed. London, 1715.
Porphyry. *Homeric Questions*. Translated by Robin R. Schlunk. New York and Frankfurt: Peter Lang, 1993.
– *Homeric Questions on the Iliad: text, translation, commentary*. Edited and translated by John A. MacPhail, Jr. New York: De Gruyter, 2011.
– *On the Cave of the Nymphs*. Translated by Thomas Taylor. Grand Rapids, MI: Phanes Press, 1991.
Porta, Giambattista della. *Natural Magick ... in Twenty Books*. London, 1658.
Prideaux, John. *Sacred Eloquence: Or, the Art of Rhetorick, As it is layd down in Scripture*. London, 1659.
Primaudaye, Pierre de la. *The French Academie*. Translated by T.B.C. London, 1618.
Proclus. *Commentaire sur la Republique*. 3 vols. Edited and translated by A.J. Festugière. Paris: J. Vrin, 1970.
– *Commentaire sur le Timée*. 5 vols. Edited and translated by A.J. Festugière. Paris: J. Vrin, 1966–.
– *Lucubratio Procli Lycii Diadochi De dictis adversus Homerum & Poeticen in Republica Platonis*. In Gesner, Conrad. *Moralis Interpretatio Errorum Ulyssis Homerici.* Zurich, 1542.
Prustus, Nicolas. *Homeri Epitheta omnia ex Iliade et Odyssea*. Lyon, 1594.
– *Theotokion Homêrikon ad B. Virginem Laurentanam*. Paris, 1610.
Pulci, Luigi. *Morgante*. Translated by Joseph Tusiani. Bloomington: Indiana University Press, 1998.
Puttenham, George. *The Arte of English Poesie*. Edited by Gladys Doidge Willcock and Alice Walker. Cambridge: Cambridge University Press, 1936.
Quattrehomme, Louis. *Discours en Forme de Comparaison sur les Vies de Moyse & d'Homere*. Paris, 1604.
Quintilian. *Institutio Oratoria*. 4 vols. Translated by H.E. Butler. Cambridge, MA: Harvard University Press, 1993.

Quintus Smyrnaeus. *The Trojan Epic*. Edited and translated by Alan James. Baltimore: Johns Hopkins University Press, 2004.
Rabelais, François. *Gargantua and Pantagruel*. Translated by J.M. Cohen. London: Penguin, 1955.
– *Gargantua and Pantagruel*. Translated by M.A. Screech. London: Penguin, 2006.
– *Oeuvres Complètes*. Edited by Guy Demerson. Paris: Seuil, 1973.
Ramus, Peter. *Scholae in Liberales Artes* (1569), rpt. Hildesheim and New York: G. Olms, 1970.
Randolph, Thomas. *The Muses looking-glasse*. London, 1643.
Rapin, René. *Comparaison des poëmes d'Homère et de Virgile*. 3rd ed. (1664), rpt. Hildesheim and New York: Georg Olms Verlag, 1973.
Reynolds, Edward. *Mythomystes*. In *Critical Essays of the Seventeenth Century*. 3 vols. Edited by J.E. Spingarn. Bloomington: University of Indiana Press, 1957.
– *A Treatise of the Passions and Faculties of the Soule of Man*. London, 1640.
Ricchieri [Rhodiginus] Ludovico. *Lectionum Antiquarum Libri Triginta*. Basel, 1566.
Ripa, Cesare. *Iconologia*. Padua, 1618.
Ronsard, Pierre de. *Oeuvres Complètes*. 20 vols. Edited by Paul Laumonier. Paris: Hachette, 1914–75.
Ross, Alexander. *Mystagogus Poeticus or The Muses Interpreter*. London, 1648; rpt. Garland, 1976.
Rous, Francis. *Thule, or Vertues Historie*. London, 1598.
[S., J.] *Innovation of Penelope and Ulysses*, in *Wit Restor'd*. London, 1658.
Salel, Hugues. *L'Apologie d'Homère*. In *Oeuvres Poétiques*. Edited by Louis-Alexandre Bergounioux. 2nd ed. Geneva: Slatkine, 1969.
Sarpi, Paolo. *The Historie of the Councel of Trent*. Translated by Nathaniel Brent. London, 1620.
Scaliger, Julius Caesar. *Poetices Libri Septem*. 5 vols. Edited by Luc Deitz und Gregor Vogt-Spira. Stuttgart-Bad Cannstatt: Frommann-Holzboog, 1994.
– *Poetices Libri Septem*. Lyon, 1561.
Scapula, Johannes. *Lexicon Graecolatinum nouum*. Basel, 1615.
– *Lexicon Graeco-Latinum Novum*. London, 1637.
Schott, Andrea, trans. *Paroimiai Hellenikai. Adagia, sive Proverbia Graecorum ex Zenobio Seu Zenodoto Diogeniano & Suidae Collectaneis*. Antwerp, 1612.
Seber, Wolfgang. *Index Vocabulorum In Homeri Non Tantum Iliade atque Odyssea* ... Frankfurt, 1604.
Seneca. *Ad Lucilium epistulae morales*. 3 vols. Translated by Richard M. Gunmere. Cambridge, MA: Harvard University Press, 1961–2.
Shakespeare, William. *The Riverside Shakespeare*. 2nd ed. Edited by G. Blakemore Evans. Boston: Houghton Mifflin, 1997.
– *Troilus and Cressida*. 3rd ed. Edited by David Bevington. Walton-on-Thames, Surrey: Thomas Nelson & sons, 1998.

Sherry, Richard. *A Treatise of schemes and tropes …* London, 1550.
Simmaco de Jacobiti, Aurelio. *Batracomiomachia. Volgarizzamento del 1456.* Edited by Marcello Marinucci. Padua: Esedra, 2001.
Smith, G. Gregory. *Elizabethan Critical Essays.* 2 vols. Oxford: Clarendon Press, 1904.
Sophocles. *Ajax.* In *Sophocles* I. Translated by Hugh Lloyd-Jones. Cambridge, MA: Harvard University Press, 1994.
– *Philoctetes.* Translated by Robert Torrance and edited by Oscar Mandel. Lincoln: University of Nebraska Press, 1981.
Spenser, Edmund. *The Faerie Queene.* Edited by Thomas P. Roche, Jr. New York: Penguin, 1978.
– *Shorter Poems.* Edited by Richard McCabe. London and New York: Penguin, 1999.
– *The Works of Edmund Spenser. A Variorum Edition.* 11 vols. Edited by Edwin Greenlaw, Charles Grosvenor Osgood, and Frederick Morgan Padelford. Baltimore: Johns Hopkins University Press, 1932–57.
Speroni, Sperone. *Dialogo della Discordia*, in *Dialoghi.* 2nd ed. Venice, 1552.
Spingarn, J.E. *Critical Essays of the Seventeenth Century.* 3 vols. Oxford: Clarendon Press, 1908.
Statius. *Thebaid.* Translated by J.H. Mozley. Cambridge, MA: Harvard University Press, 1967.
Stephens, John. *Essays and Characters. Ironicall and Invective.* 2nd ed. London, 1615.
Stillingfleet, Edward. *Origines Sacrae, Or a Rational Account of the Grounds of Christian Faith …* London, 1662.
Stobaeus. *Gnomologia Graecolatinum.* Edited by Michael Neander. Basel, 1564.
Stoicorum Veterum Fragmenta. 4 vols. Edited by H.V. Arnim. Leipzig: 1903–24; rpt. Stuttgart, 1964.
Tasso, Torquato. *Discourses on the Heroic Poem.* Translated by Mariella Cavalchini and Irene Samuel. Oxford: Clarendon Press, 1973.
– *Gerusalemme Liberata.* Edited by Lanfranco Caretti. Milan: Mondadori, 1899.
– *Jerusalem Delivered.* Translated by Anthony Esolen. Baltimore: Johns Hopkins University Press, 2000.
Tertullian. *Apologeticus Adversus Gentes* and *Praescriptiones adversus Haereticos.* Ante-Nicene Fathers. Vol. 3. Edited by Rev. Alexander Roberts and James Donaldson. 2nd ed. Grand Rapids, MI: W.B. Eerdmanns, 1971–85.
Textor, Johannes Ravisius. *Officina, Sive Theatrum Historicarum et Poeticum.* Basel, 1526.
Theophrastus. *Characters.* Edited and translated by Jeffrey Rusten. Cambridge, MA: Harvard University Press, 1993.

Thucydides, *Eight books of the Peloponnesian Warre*. Translated by Thomas Hobbes. London, 1629.

Tortelli, Giovanni. *Orthographia*. Venice, 1493.

Tyard, Pontus de. *The Universe of Pontus de Tyard. A Critical Edition of l'Univers*. Edited and translated by John C. Lapp. Ithaca, NY: Cornell University Press, 1950.

[Tzetzes]. *Johannes Tzetzae Liber Historicus*. Printed with *Lycophronis Chalcidiensis Alexandra, Sive Cassandra*. Translated by Paul Lacisii Veronensis. Basel, 1546.

Valens [Valentis], Petrus. *De Laudibus Homeri Oratio, habita in regio Cameracensi auditorio*. Paris, 1621.

Valeriano, Pierio. *Hieroglyphica, sive de sacris Aegyptiorum*. Basel, 1547.

Valet, Antoine. *Oratio in Scholis medicorum … Quâ Medicinae antiquitas ex antiquissimo Poetarum Homero obiter & allegorica describitur*. Paris, 1570.

Valla, Lorenzo. *De Voluptate. On Pleasure*. Translated by A. Kent Hieatt and Maristella Lorch. New York: Abaris Books, 1977.

Vallesio, Francesco. *Controversiarum Medicarum et Philosophicarum*. 3rd ed. Frankfurt, 1590.

Vico, Giambattista. *New Science*. Translated by David Marsh. London: Penguin, 1999.

Vida, Marco Girolamo. *De Arte Poetica*. Edited and translated by Ralph G. Williams. New York: Columbia University Press, 1976.

Virgil. *Eclogues. Georgics. Aeneid*. 2 vols. Translated by H. Rushton Fairclough. Cambridge, MA: Harvard University Press, 1934–5.

Vossius, Gerhard. *De Artis Poeticae Natura, ac constitutione liber*. Amsterdam, 1647.

– *Poeticarum Institutionum, libri tres*. Amsterdam, 1647.

Weil, Simone. *The Iliad or the Poem of Force. A Critical Edition*. Edited and translated by James P. Holoka. New York and Frankfurt: Peter Lang, 2003.

– and Rachel Bespaloff. *War and the Iliad*. Translated by Mary McCarthy. New York: New York Review Books, 2005.

Whitfield, Christopher, ed. *Robert Dover and the Cotswold Games: Annalia Dubrensia*. London: Sotheran, 1962.

Xenophon. *Cyropaedia. The Institution and Life of Cyrus*. Translated by Philemon Holland. London, 1632.

Secondary Texts

Acheson, Arthur. *Shakespeare and the Rival Poet*. London and New York: John Lane, 1903.

Achinstein, Sharon. *Milton and the Revolutionary Reader*. Princeton, NJ: Princeton University Press, 1994.

Adams, Robert P. *The Better Part of Valor: More, Erasmus, Colet, and Vives on Humanism, War, and Peace, 1496–1535*. Seattle: University of Washington Press, 1962.

Adkins, A.W.H. "Threatening, Abusing, and Feeling Angry in the Homeric Poems." *JHS* 89 (1969): 7–21.

Ahl, Frederick, and Hanna Roisman. *The Odyssey Re-Formed*. Ithaca, NY: Cornell University Press, 1996.

Ahern, Charles F., Jr. "Horace's Rewriting of Homer in *Carmen* I.6." *CP* 86, no. 4 (1991): 301–14.

Allen, Don Cameron. *The Legend of Noah: Renaissance Rationalism in Art, Science, and Letters*. Urbana: University of Illinois Press, 1963.

– *Mysteriously Meant: The Rediscovery of Pagan Symbolism and Allegorical Interpretation in the Renaissance*. Baltimore: Johns Hopkins University Press, 1970.

Allen, Valerie. *On Farting: Language and Laughter in the Middle Ages*. New York and Basingstoke, UK: Palgrave Macmillan, 2007.

Anderson, Graham. *Lucian: Theme and Variation in the Second Sophistic*. Leiden: Brill, 1976.

Aptekar, Jane. *Icons of Justice: Iconography and Thematic Imagery in Book V of The Faerie Queene*. New York: Columbia University Press, 1969.

Arikha, Noga. *Passions and Tempers: A History of the Humours*. New York: Harper Collins, 2007.

Aryanpur, Manoocher. "*Paradise Lost* and *The Odyssey*." *TSLL* 9, no. 2 (1967): 151–66.

Austin, Norman. "The One and the Many in the Homeric Cosmos." *Arion* n.s. 1, no. 2 (1973): 219–74.

Bakhtin, Mikhail. *The Dialogic Imagination: Four Essays*. Translated by Caryl Emerson and Michael Holquist. Austin: University of Texas Press, 1981.

– *Problems of Dostoevsky's Poetics*. Edited and translated by Caryl Emerson. Minneapolis: University of Minnesota Press, 1984.

– *Rabelais and His World*. Translated by Hélène Iswolsky. Bloomington: University of Indiana Press, 1984

Baldwin, T.W. *William Shakespere's small Latine and lesse Greeke*. 2 vols. Urbana: University of Illinois Press, 1944.

Ball, Jerry L. "The Despised Version: Hobbes' Translation of Homer." *Restoration: Studies in English Literary Culture, 1660–1700* 20, no. 1 (1996): 1–17.

Barnouw, Jeffrey. *Odysseus, Hero of Practical Intelligence: Deliberation and Signs in Homer's Odyssey.* Lanham, Boulder, and New York: University Press of America, 2004.

Baron, Hans. "The Querelle of the Ancients and the Moderns as a Problem for Renaissance Scholarship." *JHI* 20, no. 1 (1959): 3–22.

Beck, Deborah. *Homeric Conversation*. Cambridge, MA: Harvard University Press, 2005.

Bednarz, James. *Shakespeare and the Poets' War*. New York: Columbia University Press, 2001.

Benet, Diana. "Hell, Satan, and the New Politician." In *Literary Milton: Text, Pretext, Context*, edited by Benet and Michael Lieb, 97–113. Pittsburgh: Duquesne University Press, 1994.

Berger, Harry, Jr. *Revisionary Play: Studies in the Spenserian Dynamics*. Berkeley: University of California Press, 1988.

Bernardete, Seth. *The Bow and the Lyre: A Platonic Reading of the "Odyssey."* Lanham, Boulder, and New York: Rowan & Littlefield, 1997.

Berry, Alice. "'Les Mithologies Pantagruelicques': Introduction to a Study of Rabelais' *Quart Livre*." *PMLA* 92, no. 3 (1977): 471–80.

Berry, Boyd M. *Process of Speech: Puritan Religious Writing and "Paradise Lost."* Baltimore: Johns Hopkins University Press, 1976.

Bieman, Elizabeth. *Plato Baptized: Towards the Interpretation of Spenser's Mimetic Fictions*. Toronto: University of Toronto Press, 1988.

Binns, J.W. *Intellectual Culture in Elizabethan and Jacobean England. The Latin Writings of the Age*. Leeds: Francis Cairns, 1990.

Bizer, Marc. *Homer and the Politics of Authority in Renaissance France*. Oxford: Oxford University Press, 2011.

– "Men Are from Mars: Jean de Sponde's Homeric Heroes and Vision of Just French Leaders." In *Masculinities in Sixteenth-Century France*, edited by Philip Ford and Paul White, 167–79. Cambridge: Cambridge French Colloquia, 2006.

Bleicher, Thomas. *Homer in der Deutschen Literatur (1450–1750): Zur Rezeption der Antike und zur Poetologie der Neuzeit*. Stuttgart: J.B. Metzlersche, 1972.

Blundell, Mary Whitlock. *Helping Friends and Harming Enemies: A Study in Sophocles and Greek Ethics.* Cambridge: Cambridge University Press, 1989.

Bolgar, R.R. *The Classical Heritage and Its Beneficiaries*. Cambridge: Cambridge University Press, 1954.

– "From Humanism to the Humanities." *Twentieth-Century Studies* 9 (1973): 8–21.

Bono, Barbara. *Literary Transvaluation: From Virgilian Epic to Shakespearean Tragicomedy*. Berkeley and Los Angeles: University of California Press, 1984.

Booth, Wayne C. *A Rhetoric of Irony*. Chicago: University of Chicago Press, 1974.

Branham, R. Bracht. *Unruly Eloquence: Lucian and the Comedy of Traditions.* Cambridge, MA: Harvard University Press, 1989.

Briand, Michel. "Lucien et Homère le sophiste ou les ambiguïtés d'une 'mimesis' ironique." In *Révolutions Homériques*, edited by Glenn Most, Larry F. Norman, and Sophie Rabau, 27–46. Pisa: Edizioni della Normale, 2009.

Briggs, John Channing. "Chapman's *Seaven Bookes of the Iliades*: Mirror for Essex." *SEL* 21, no. 1 (1981): 59–73.

Brink, C.O. "Ennius and the Hellenistic Worship of Homer." *AJP* 93, no. 4 (1972): 547–67.

Brisson, Luc. *How Philosophers Saved Myths: Allegorical Interpretation and Classical Mythology*. Translated by Catherine Tihanyi. Chicago: University of Chicago Press, 2004.

Broadbent, J.B. *Some Graver Subject. An Essay on Paradise Lost*. London: Chatto & Windus, 1960.

Buchtel, John A. "Book Dedications and the Death of a Patron: The Memorial Engraving in Chapman's Homer." *Book History* 7 (2004): 1–29.

Budick, Sanford. *The Dividing Muse: Images of Sacred Disjunction in Milton's Poetry*. New Haven, CT: Yale University Press, 1985.

Buffière, Félix. *Les Mythes d'Homère et la Pensée Grecque*. Paris: Belles Lettres, 1956.

Bull, Malcolm. *The Mirror of the Gods.* Oxford: Oxford University Press, 2005.

Burden, Dennis. *The Logical Epic: A Study of the Argument of "Paradise Lost."* Cambridge, MA: Harvard University Press, 1967.

Burkert, Walter. *Greek Religion: Archaic and Classical.* Translated by John Rattan. Oxford: Basil Blackwell, 1985.

Burns, William E. "A Proverb of Versatile Mutability: Proteus and Natural Knowledge in Early Modern Britain." *SCJ* 32, no. 4 (2001): 969–80.

Burrow, Colin. *Epic Romance. Homer to Milton*. Oxford: Clarendon Press, 1993.

Bury, Emmanuel. "L'Amitié savante, ferment de la République des Lettres." *XVIIe Siècle* 51, no. 4 (1999): 729–47.

Bury, J.B. *The Idea of Progress: An Inquiry into Its Origin and Growth.* New York: Macmillan, 1936.

Butler, George F. "Milton's Pandora: Eve, Sin, and the Mythographic Tradition." *MS* 44 (2005): 153–78.

Cairns, Douglas L. *Aidôs: The Psychology and Ethics of Honour and Shame in Ancient Greek Literature*. Oxford: Clarendon Press, 1993.

– ed. *Oxford Readings in Homer's "Iliad."* Oxford: Oxford University Press, 2001.

Calhoun, George M. "The Art of Formula in Homer – EPEA PTEROENTA." *CP* 30, no. 3 (1935): 215–27.

Cantalupo, Charles. *A Literary Leviathan: Thomas Hobbes's Masterpiece of Language*. Lewisburg, PA: Bucknell University Press, 1991.

Capodieci, Luisa, and Philip Ford, eds. *Homère à la Renaissance: mythe et transfigurations*. Paris: Somogy, 2011.

Catana, Leo. *The Concept of Contraction in Giordano Bruno's Philosophy*. Aldershot, UK: Ashgate, 2005.

Cave, Terence. "Panurge and Odysseus." In *Myth and Legend in French Literature. Essays in Honour of A.J. Steele*, edited by Keith Murphy, David Bellos, and Peter Sharratt, 47–59. London: Modern Humanities Research Association, 1982.

Charlier, Yvonne. *Érasme et l'Amitié d'Après sa Correspondance*. Paris: Belles Lettres, 1977.

Cheney, Donald. *Spenser's Image of Nature: Wild Man and Shepherd in The Faerie Queene*. New Haven, CT: Yale University Press, 1966.

Cheney, Patrick. *Spenser's Famous Flight: A Renaissance Idea of a Literary Career*. Toronto: University of Toronto Press, 1993.

Chesney, Elizabeth A. *The Countervoyage of Rabelais and Ariosto: A Comparative Reading of Two Renaissance Mock Epics.* Durham, NC: Duke University Press, 1982.

Cirillo, Albert R. "Noon-Midnight and the Temporal Structure of *Paradise Lost*," *ELH* 29, no. 4 (1962): 372–95.

Clarke, Howard W. *Homer's Readers: a historical introduction to the Iliad and Odyssey*. Newark: University of Delaware Press, 1981.

– "The Humor of Homer." *CJ* 64, no. 6 (1969): 246–52.

Clay, Jenny Strauss. "Goat Island: *Od*. 9.116–141." *CQ* 30, no. 2 (1980): 261–4.

– *Hesiod's Cosmos.* Cambridge: Cambridge University Press, 2003.

– *The Politics of Olympus: Form and Meaning in the Major Homeric Hymns*. Princeton, NJ: Princeton University Press, 1989.

– *The Wrath of Athena: Gods and Men in the Odyssey*. Princeton, NJ: Princeton University Press, 1983

Coleman, Dorothy Gabe. "Language in the *Tiers Livre*." In *Rabelais in Glasgow*, edited by James A. Coleman and Christine M. Scollen-Jimack, 39–53. Glasgow: University of Glasgow Press, 1984.

– *Rabelais: A Critical Study in Prose Fiction*. Cambridge: Cambridge University Press, 1971.

Colie, Rosalie. *Paradoxia Epidemica: The Renaissance Tradition of Paradox*. Princeton, NJ: Princeton University Press, 1966.

Collins, Derek. *Master of the Game: Competition and Performance in Greek Poetry*. Cambridge, MA: Harvard University Press, 2004.

Combellack, Frederick M. "Words that Die." *CJ* 46 (1950): 21–6.

Conche, Marcel. *Essais sur Homère*. 2nd ed. Paris: Quadrige, 2002.
Conte, Gian Biagio. *The Rhetoric of Imitation*. Edited and translated by Charles Segal. Ithaca, NY: Cornell University Press, 1986.
Cook, Erwin F. *The* Odyssey *in Athens: Myths of Cultural Origins*. Ithaca, NY: Cornell University Press, 1995.
Corns, Thomas. *Milton's Language*. Oxford: Basil Blackwell, 1950.
– *Regaining "Paradise Lost."* London and New York: Longman, 1994.
Cytowska, Maria. "Erasme de Rotterdam, Traducteur d'Homère." *Eos* 63 (1975): 341–53.
– "Homer bei Erasmus." *Philologus* 118 (1974): 145–57.
Daiches, David. *Milton*. New York: Hutchinson University Library, 1957.
Dandrey, Patrick. *L'Eloge Paradoxale de Gorgias a Molière*. Paris: Presses Universitaires de France, 1997.
Dane, Joseph. *The Critical Mythology of Irony*. Athens: University of Georgia Press, 1991.
Danielson, Dennis. *Milton's Good God: A Study in Literary Theodicy*. Cambridge: Cambridge University Press, 1982.
Daston, Lorraine, and Katherine Park. *Wonders and the Order of Nature, 1150–1750*. New York: Zone Books, 1998.
Davis, Paul. "Thomas Hobbes's Translations of Homer: Epic and Anticlericalism in Late Seventeenth-Century England." *Seventeenth Century* 12, no. 2 (1997): 231–55.
Dawson, David. *Allegorical Readers and Cultural Revision in Ancient Alexandria*. Berkeley: University of California Press, 1992.
Defaux, Gérard. "A Propos de paroles gelées et dégelées (*Quart Livre* 55–56): 'plus hault sens' ou 'lectures plurielles?'." In *Rabelais's Incomparable Book: Essays on His Art*, edited by Raymond C. La Charité, 155–77. Lexington, KY: French Forum, 1986.
– *Pantagruel et les Sophistes*. The Hague: Martinus Nijhoff, 1973.
– *Rabelais Agonistes: Du Rieur au Prophète*. Geneva: Droz, 1997.
– "Rabelais and the Monsters of Antiphysis." *MLN* 110, no. 5 (1995): 1017–42.
– "Une Rencontre Homérique: Panurge Noble, Peregrin, et Curieux." *French Forum* 6, no. 2 (1981): 109–22.
De Jong, Irene J.F. *Narrators and Focalizers: The Presentation of the Story in the Iliad.* Amsterdam: B.R. Grüner, 1989.
Dekker, Annie Femmina. *Ironie in De Odyssee*. Leiden: Brill, 1965.
Deloince-Louette, Christine. *Sponde, Commentateur d'Homère*. Paris: Honoré Champion, 2001.
Demerson, Guy. *Humanisme et Facétie: Quinze études sur Rabelais*. Orléans: Paradigme, 1994.

Demetriou, Tania. "'Essentially Circe': Spenser, Homer, and the Homeric Tradition." *Translation and Literature* 15, no. 2 (2006): 151–76.
Deneen, Patrick. *The Odyssey of Political Theory: The Politics of Departure and Return*. Lanham, Boulder, and New York: Rowman & Littlefield, 2000.
Detienne, Marcel. *The Masters of Truth in Archaic Greece*. Translated by Janet Lloyd. New York: Zone Books, 1996.
Dobranski, Stephen B. "Pondering Satan's Shield in *Paradise Lost*." *ELR* 35, no. 3 (2005): 490–506.
Dodds, E.R. *The Greeks and the Irrational*. Boston: Beacon Press, 1951.
Donaldson, Ian. *The World Upside Down: Comedy from Jonson to Fielding*. Oxford: Clarendon Press, 1970.
Doyle, Richard E., SJ. *Atê, Its Use and Meaning: A Study in the Greek Poetic Tradition from Homer to Euripides*. New York: Fordham University Press, 1984.
Dundas, Judith. *Pencils Rhetorique: Renaissance Poets and the Art of Painting*. Newark: University of Delaware Press, 1993.
Durling, Robert. *The Figure of the Poet in Renaissance Epic*. Cambridge, MA: Harvard University Press, 1965.
DuRocher, Richard J. *Milton and Ovid*. Ithaca NY: Cornell University Press, 1985.
Duval, Edwin. *The Design of Rabelais' Pantagruel*. New Haven, CT: Yale University Press, 1991.
– "History, Epic, and the Design of Rabelais' *Tiers Livre*." In *François Rabelais: Critical Assessments*, edited by Jean-Claude Carron, 121–32. Baltimore: Johns Hopkins University Press, 1995.
Edelstein, Ludwig. "The Golden Chain of Homer." In *Studies in Intellectual History*, 48–66. Baltimore: Johns Hopkins University Press, 1953.
Eden, Kathy. *Friends Hold All Things in Common: Tradition, Intellectual Property, and the Adages of Erasmus*. New Haven, CT: Yale University Press, 2001.
Edmunds, Susan T. *Homeric Nêpios*. New York, 1990.
Edwards, Mark W. "Convention and Individuality in *Iliad* I." *Harvard Studies in Classical Philology* 84 (1980): 1–28.
Eichel-Lojkine, Patricia. *Excentricité et Humanisme: Parodie, dérision et détournement des codes à la Renaissance*. Geneva: Droz, 2002.
Elton, W.R. "Shakespeare's Portrait of Ajax in *Troilus and Cressida*." *PMLA* 63, no. 2 (1948): 744–8.
– *Shakespeare's Troilus and Cressida and the Inns of Court Revels*. Aldershot, UK: Ashgate, 2000.
– "Shakespeare's Ulysses and the Problem of Value," *ShS* 2 (1966): 95–111.

Emma, Ronald. *Milton's Grammar*. Paris and The Hague: Mouton, 1964.

Empson, William. *Milton's God*. 2nd ed. London: Chatto & Windus, 1965.

Evans, Maurice. *Spenser's Anatomy of Heroism: A Commentary on The Faerie Queene*. Cambridge: Cambridge University Press, 1970.

Everson, Jane E .*The Italian Renaissance Epic in the Age of Humanism: The Matter of Italy and the World of Rome*. Oxford: Oxford University Press, 2001.

Fabbri, Renata. "Carlo Marsuppini e la Sua Versione Latina Della 'Batrachomyomachia' Pseudo-Omerica." In *Saggi di Linguistica e di Letteratura in Memoria di Paolo Zolli*, edited by Giampolo Borghello, Manlio Cortelazzo, and Giorgio Padoan, 555–65. Padua: Antenore, 1991.

Fallon, Stephen. "'To Act or Not': Milton's conception of divine freedom." *JHI* 49, no. 3 (1988): 425–49.

Fehrenbach, R.J., and E.S. Leedham-Green, eds. *Private Libraries in Renaissance England: A Collection and Catalogue of Tudor and Early Stuart Book-Lists*. 7 vols. Binghamton, NY: MRTS, 1992–.

Fenik, Bernard. *Typical Battles Scenes in the Iliad: Studies in the Narrative Techniques of Homeric Battle Description*. Wiesbaden: Franz Steiner Verlag, 1968.

Finkelberg, Margalit. "Homer as a Foundation Text. In *Homer, the Bible, and Beyond: Literary and Religious Canons in the Ancient World*, edited by Finkelberg and Guy G. Strousma, 75–96. Leiden: Brill, 2003.

Fish, Stanley. *Surprised by Sin: The Reader in Paradise Lost*. Berkeley and Los Angeles: University of California Press, 1971.

Fixler, Michael. *Milton and the Kingdoms of God*. Evanston, IL: Northwestern University Press, 1964.

Fletcher, Harris Francis. *The Intellectual Development of John Milton*. 2 vols. Urbana: University of Illinois Press, 1956.

Foerster, Donald M. *Homer in English Criticism: The Historical Approach in the Eighteenth Century*. 2nd ed. New York: Archon Books, 1969.

Ford, Andrew. *Homer. The Origins of Criticism: Literary Culture and Poetic Theory in Classical Greece*. Princeton, NJ: Princeton University Press, 2002.

– *The Poetry of the Past*. Ithaca, NY: Cornell University Press, 1992.

– "Sophistic." In *Symposium: Platonic Insults. Common Knowledge* 2, no. 2 (1993): 33–47.

Ford, Philip. "Classical Myth and Its Interpretation in Sixteenth-Century France." In *The Classical Heritage in France*, edited by Gerald Sandy, 331–49. Leiden: Brill, 2002.

– *De Troie à Ithaque: réception des épopées homériques à la Renaissance*. Geneva: Droz, 2007.

– "Montaigne's Homer: poet or myth?" *Montaigne Studies* 17, nos. 1–2 (2005): 7–16.

Fowler, Robert ed. *The Cambridge Companion to Homer*. Cambridge: Cambridge University Press, 2004.

Frame, Donald. *François Rabelais: A Study*. New York and London: Harcourt Brace, 1977.

Friedländer, Walter. "Lachende Götter." *Antike* 10 (1934): 209–26.

Frye, Northrop. *The Myth of Deliverance. Reflections on Shakespeare's Problem Comedies*. 2nd ed. Toronto: University of Toronto Press, 1993.

Gagarin, Michael. "The Ambiguity of Eris in the *Works and Days*." In *Cabinet of the Muses*, edited by Mark Griffith and Donald J. Mastronarde, 173–83. Atlanta: Scholars Press, 1990.

Gaignebet, Claude. "Histoire des Gorgias: Les Mondes Intérieures Renversés de Rabelais." In *L'Image du Monde Renversé et ses Représentations Littéraires et Para-Littéraires de la fin du XVIe siècle au milieu du XVIIe*, edited by Jean Lafond and Augustin Redondo, 49–54. Paris: J. Vrin, 1979.

Gaskin, Richard. "Do Homeric Heroes Make Real Decisions?" *CQ* 40, no. 1 (1990): 1–15.

Gauna, Max. *The Rabelaisian Mythologies*. Madison, NJ: Farleigh Dickinson University Press, 1996.

Giamatti, A. Bartlett. *The Earthly Paradise and the Renaissance Epic*. Princeton, NJ: Princeton University Press, 1966.

– "Proteus Unbound: Some Versions of the Sea-God in the Renaissance." In *The Disciplines of Criticism*, edited by Peter Demetz, Thomas Greene, and Lowry Nelson, Jr, 437–75. New Haven, CT: Yale University Press, 1968.

Giangrande, Lawrence. *The Use of Spoudaiogeloion in Greek and Roman Literature*. The Hague and Paris: Mouton, 1972.

Gilbert, Allan H. "Milton's Defense of Bawdry." In *SAMLA Studies in Milton: Essays on John Milton and His Works*, edited by J. Max Patrick, 173–83. Gainesville: University of Florida Press, 1953.

Gilmore, Myron P. "Les Limites de la Tolérance dans l'oeuvre polémique d'Erasme." In *Colloquia Erasmiana Turonensia*, 2 vols., ed. Jean-Claude Margolin, 2:713–36. Toronto: University of Toronto Press, 1972.

Girard, René. "The Politics of Desire in *Troilus and Cressida*." In *Shakespeare and the Question of Theory*, edited by Patricia Parker and Geoffrey Hartman, 188–209. New York: Methuen, 1985.

Gless, Darryl J. "Chapman's Ironic Ovid," *ELR* 9, no. 1 (1979): 21–41.

Godman, Peter. *From Poliziano to Machiavelli: Florentine Humanism in the High Renaissance*. Princeton, NJ: Princeton University Press, 1998.

Golden, Leon. "*To Gêloion* in the *Iliad*." *Harvard Studies in Classical Philology* 93 (1990): 47–57.

Goldhill, Simon. *Who Needs Greek? Contests in the Cultural History of Hellenism*. Cambridge: Cambridge University Press, 2002.

Goldsmith, M.M. *Hobbes's Science of Politics*. New York and London: Columbia University Press, 1966.

Gordon, Walter. *Humanist Play and Belief: The Seriocomic Art of Desiderius Erasmus*. Toronto: University of Toronto Press, 1990.

Gouldner, Alvin W. *Enter Plato. Classical Greece and the Origins of Social Theory*. New York and London: Basic Books, 1965.

Grafton, Anthony. *Defenders of the Text: The Traditions of Scholarship in an Age of Science*. Cambridge, MA: Harvard University Press, 1991.

– "How Guillaume Budé Read his Homer." In *Commerce with the Classics: Ancient Books and Renaissance Readers*, 135–83. Ann Arbor: University of Michigan Press, 1997.

– "Martin Crusius Reads His Homer." *Princeton Library Chronicle* 64, no. 1 (2002): 63–86.

– "Renaissance Readers and Ancient Texts: Comments on Some Commentaries." *RQ* 38, no. 4 (1985): 615–49.

Grant, Mary A. *The Ancient Rhetorical Theories of the Laughable: The Greek Rhetoricians and Cicero*. Madison: University of Wisconsin Press, 1924.

Graver, Margaret. "Dog-Helen and Homeric Insult." *CA* 14, no. 1 (1995): 41–61.

– *Stoicism and Emotion*. Chicago: University of Chicago Press, 2007.

Graziosi, Barbara. "Competition in Wisdom." In *Homer, Tragedy and Beyond: Essays in Honour of P.E. Easterling*, edited by F. Budelmann and P. Michelakis, 57–74. London: Society for the Promotion of Hellenic Studies, 2001.

– *Inventing Homer: The Early Reception of Epic*. Cambridge: Cambridge University Press, 2002.

Gregory, Tobias. *From Many Gods to One: Divine Action in Renaissance Epic*. Chicago: University of Chicago Press, 2006.

Greene, David M. "The Identity of the Emblematic Nemesis." *Studies in the Renaissance* 10 (1963): 25–43.

Greene, Thomas. *The Light in Troy: Imitation and Discovery in Renaissance Poetry*. New Haven, CT: Yale University Press, 1982.

– "Rabelais and the Language of Malediction." In *François Rabelais: Critical Assessments*, edited by Jean-Claude Carron, 105–20. Baltimore: Johns Hopkins University Press, 1995.

– *Rabelais: A Study in Comic Courage*. Engelwood Cliffs, NJ: Prentice Hall, 1970.

Griffin, Jasper. *Homer on Life and Death*. Oxford: Clarendon Press, 1980.

Griffith, Mark. "Contest and Contradiction in Early Greek Poetry." In *Cabinet of the Muses: Essays on Classical and Comparative Literature in Honour of Thomas G. Rosenmeyer*, edited by Griffith and Donald J. Mastronarde, 185–207. Atlanta: Scholars Press, 1990.

Gross, Kenneth. *Shakespeare's Noise*. Chicago: University of Chicago Press, 2001.

Grossmann, Maria. *Humanism in Wittenberg 1485–1517*. Nieuwkoop: B. de Graaf, 1975.

Grudin, Robert. "The Soul of State: Ulyssean Irony in *Troilus and Cressida*." *Anglia* 93, nos. 1–2 (1975): 55–69.

Guggisberg, Hans R. *Sebastian Castellio, 1515–1563: Humanist and Defender of Religious Toleration in a Confessional Age*. Edited and translated by Bruce Gordon. Aldershot, UK: Ashgate, 2002.

Gutsell, James. *Irony in the Fallen World of George Chapman: A Study of Irony in Chapman's Poems, Comedies, and Tragedies*. PhD dissertation. University of Connecticut, Storrs. 1968.

Hadot, Pierre. *The Veil of Isis: An Essay on the History of the Idea of Nature*. Translated by Michael Chase. Cambridge, MA: Harvard University Press, 2006.

Hahm, David. *The Origins of Stoic Cosmology*. Columbus: Ohio State University Press, 1977.

Halbertal, Moshe. *People of the Book: Canon, Meaning, and Authority*. Cambridge, MA: Harvard University Press, 1997.

Hale, John. *Milton's Languages: The Impact of Multilingualism on Style*. Cambridge: Cambridge University Press, 1997.

Hall, Edith. *The Return of Ulysses: A Cultural History of Homer's Odyssey*. Baltimore: Johns Hopkins University Press, 2008.

Halliwell, Stephen. *Greek Laughter*. Cambridge: Cambridge University Press, 2008.

Hammer, Dean. *The Iliad as Politics: The Performance of Political Thought*. Norman: University of Oklahoma Press, 2002.

Hammond, Mason. "*Concilia Deorum* from Homer through Milton." *SP* 30, no. 1 (1933): 1–16.

Hardie, Philip. "Imago Mundi: Cosmological and Ideological Aspects of the Shield of Achilles." *JHS* 105 (1985): 11–31.

– *Rumour and Renown: Representations of Fama in Western Literature*. Cambridge: Cambridge University Press, 2012.

– *Virgil's Aeneid: Cosmos and Imperium*. Oxford: Oxford University Press, 1986.

Harding, Davis. *The Club of Hercules: Studies in the Classical Background of "Paradise Lost."* Urbana: University of Illinois Press, 1962.

Harris, Jonathan Gil. "'The Enterprise is Sick': Pathologies of Value and Transnationality in *Troilus and Cressida*." *Renaissance Drama* n.s. 29 (1998): 3–37.

Harris, William V. *Restraining Rage: The Ideology of Anger Control in Classical Antiquity*. Cambridge, MA: Harvard University Press, 2001.

Harrison, Jane Ellen. *Themis: A Study of the Social Origins of Greek Religion*. 2nd ed. Cambridge: Cambridge University Press, 1927.

Hartfelder, Karl. *Philipp Melanchthon als Praeceptor Germaniae*. Nieukoop: B. de Graaf, 1964.

Havelock, Eric A. *The Greek Concept of Justice: From Its Shadow in Homer to Its Substance in Plato*. Cambridge, MA: Harvard University Press, 1978.

Heald, A.H. *Tears for Dido: A Renaissance Poetics of Feeling*. PhD dissertation. Princeton University, 2009.

Heath, John. *The Talking Greeks. Speech, Animals, and the Other in Homer, Aeschylus, and Plato*. Cambridge: Cambridge University Press, 2005.

Heath, Malcolm. "Do Heroes Eat Fish? Athenaeus on the Homeric Lifestyle." In *Athenaeus and His World: Reading Greek Culture in the Roman Empire*, edited by David Braund and John Wilkins, 342–59. Exeter, UK: University of Exeter Press, 2000.

Heninger, S.K. *Touches of Sweet Harmony: Pythagorean Cosmology and Renaissance Poetics*. San Marino, CA: Huntington Library, 1974.

Hepp, Noémi. *Deux Amis d'Homère au XVIIe siècle. Textes inédits de Paul Pellisson et de Claude Fleury*. Paris, 1970.

–"Homère en France au XVIe Siécle." *Atti della Accademia della Scienza di Torino II: Classe di Scienze Morali, Storiche, e Filologiche* 96 (1961–2): 389–508.

– *Homère en France au XVIIe Siècle*. Paris: Klincksieck, 1968.

Herman, Peter. *Destabilizing Milton: Paradise Lost and the Poetics of Incertitude*. New York: Palgrave Macmillan, 2005.

– "*Paradise Lost*, the Miltonic 'Or,' and the Poetics of Incertitude." *SEL* 43, no. 1 (2003): 181–211.

Hillman, David. "The Gastric Epic: *Troilus and Cressida*." *SQ* 48, no. 3 (1997): 295–313.

Hillyer, Richard. "Hobbes's Explicated Fables and the Legacy of the Ancients." *Philosophy and Literature* 28, no. 2 (2004): 269–83.

Hogan, James C. "Eris in Homer." *Grazer Beiträge* 10 (1983): 21–58.

Hopkins, David. "'The English Homer': Shakespeare, Longinus, and English 'neo-classicism'." In *Shakespeare and the Classics*, edited by Charles Martindale and A.B. Taylor, 261–76. Cambridge: Cambridge University Press, 2004.

Hughes, Merritt Y. *Virgil and Spenser. University of California Publications in English*, 2, no. 3 (1929): 263–418.

Huizinga, Johan. *Homo Ludens: A Study of the Play Element in Culture*. 2nd ed. Boston: Beacon, 1955.

Huntington, John. *Ambition, Rank, and Poetry in 1590s England*. Urbana and Chicago: University of Illinois Press, 2001.

Hutton, James. *Themes of Peace in Renaissance Poetry*. Ithaca, NY: Cornell University Press, 1984.

– "Spenser's Adamantine Chains': A Cosmological Metaphor." In *The Classical Tradition: Literary and Historical Studies in Honour of Harry Caplan*, edited by Luitpold Wallach, 572–94. Ithaca, NY: Cornell University Press, 1966.

Ide, Richard S. "Exemplary Heroism in Chapman's Odysses." *SEL* 22 (1982): 121–36.

Irigoin, Jean. "La Tradition homérique et les éditions d'Homère en France." In *La tradition des textes grecs: pour une critique historique*, 613–26. Paris: Belles Lettres, 2003.

Jaeger, Werner. *Paideia: The Ideals of Greek Culture*. 3 vols. Translated by Gilbert Highet. Oxford: Basil Blackwell, 1954.

– *The Theology of the Early Greek Philosophers: The Gifford Lectures 1936*. Oxford: Clarendon Press, 1947.

James, Heather. *Shakespeare's Troy: Drama, Politics, and the Translation of Empire*. Cambridge: Cambridge University Press, 1997.

Jeanneret, Michel. "Quand la Fable se met à Table: Nourriture et structure narrative dans le *Quart Livre*." *Poétique* 54 (1983): 163–80.

– "Signs Gone Wild: The Dismantling of Allegory." In *François Rabelais: Critical Assessments*, edited by Jean-Claude Carron, 57–70. Baltimore: Johns Hopkins University Press, 1995.

Jehasse, Jean. *La Renaissance de la Critique: L'essor de l'Humanisme Erudit de 1560 à 1614*. Saint-Etienne, France: Université de Saint-Etienne, 1976.

Johnson, Laurie M. *Thucydides, Hobbes, and the Interpretation of Realism*. Dekalb: Northern Illinois University Press, 1993.

Johnston, David. *The Rhetoric of Leviathan: Thomas Hobbes and the Politics of Cultural Transformation*. Princeton, NJ: Princeton University Press, 1986.

Johnston, Ian C. *The Ironies of War: An Introduction to Homer's "Iliad."* Lanham, New York, and London: University Press of America, 1988.

Jones, Richard Foster. *Ancients and Moderns: A Study of the Rise of the Scientific Movement in Seventeenth-Century England*. St Louis, MO: Washington University Press, 1936.

Joukovsky, Françoise. *Le Feu et le Fleuve: Héraclite et la Renaissance Française*. Geneva: Droz, 1991.

Judson, A.C. *The Life of Edmund Spenser*. In volume 11 of *The Works of Edmund Spenser: A Variorum Edition*. 11 vols. Edited by Edwin Greenlaw,

Charles Grosvenor Osgood, and Frederick Morgan Padelford. Baltimore: Johns Hopkins University Press, 1932–57.
Kahane, Ahuvia. *Diachronic Dialogues: Authority and Continuity in Homer and the Homeric Tradition*. Lanham, MD: Lexington Books, 2005.
Kahn, Victoria. *Wayward Contracts: The Crisis of Political Obligation in England, 1640–1674*. Princeton, NJ: Princeton University Press, 2004.
Kallendorf, Craig. *In Praise of Aeneas: Virgil and Epideictic Rhetoric in the Early Italian Renaissance*. Hanover and London: University Press of New England, 1989.
– *The Other Virgil: "Pessimistic" Readings of the Aeneid in Early Modern Culture*. Oxford: Oxford University Press, 2007.
Kaufmann, R.J. "Ceremonies for Chaos: the Status of *Troilus and Cressida*." *ELH* 32, no. 2 (1965): 139–59.
Keeble, N.H., ed. *Cambridge Companion to Writing of the English Revolution*. Cambridge: Cambridge University Press, 2001.
Kem, Judy. *Jean Lemaire de Belges's "Les Illustrations de Gaule et singularitez de Troye."* New York and Berlin: Peter Lang, 1994.
Kendrick, Robert. *Ancient Epics, Renaissance Translations*. PhD dissertation, University of Chicago, 2005.
Kennedy, George A. "The Ancient Dispute over Rhetoric in Homer." *AJP* 78 (1957): 23–35.
– "Sophists and Physicians of the Greek Enlightenment." In *Cambridge History of Classical Literature*. Volume 1, part 3. Edited by P.E. Easterling and B.M.W. Knox. Cambridge: Cambridge University Press, 1989.
Kerferd, G.B. *The Sophistic Movement*. Cambridge: Cambridge University Press, 1981.
Kermode, Frank. "The Banquet of Sense." In *The Bulletin of the John Rylands Library* 44 (1961): 68–99.
Kilgour, Maggie. *Milton and the Metamorphosis of Ovid*. Oxford: Oxford University Press, 2012.
Kimbrough, Robert. *Shakespeare's Troilus and Cressida and Its Setting*. Cambridge, MA: Harvard University Press, 1964.
King, John. *Milton and Religious Controversy: Satire and Polemic in "Paradise Lost."* Cambridge: Cambridge University Press, 2000.
Kirk, G.S., ed. *The Iliad: A Commentary*. 6 vols. Cambridge: Cambridge University Press, 1985–93.
Kirk, G.S., J.E. Raven, and M. Schofield, eds. *The Presocratic Philosophers*. 2nd ed. Cambridge: Cambridge University Press, 1983.
Knox, Dilwyn. *Ironia. Medieval and Renaissance Ideas on Irony: Columbia Studies in the Classical Tradition* 16. Leiden and New York: Brill, 1989.

Knox, Norman. *The Word Irony and its Context, 1500–1750*. Durham, NC: Duke University Press, 1961.

Labriola, Albert C. "'God Speaks': Milton's Dialogue in Heaven and the Tradition of Divine Deliberation." *Cithara* 25 (1986): 5–30.

Laird, Andrew, ed. *Oxford Readings in Ancient Literary Criticism.* Oxford: Oxford University Press, 2006.

Lamberton, Robert. *Homer the Theologian: Neoplatonist Allegorical Reading and the Growth of the Epic Tradition*. Berkeley: University of California Press, 1986.

Lamberton, Robert, and John J. Keaney, eds. *Homer's Ancient Readers: The Hermeneutics of Greek Epic's Earliest Exegetes*. Princeton, NJ: Princeton University Press, 1992.

Laroque, François. "Perspective in Troilus and Cressida." In *Shakespeare's Universe: Renaissance Ideas and Conventions. Essays in Honour of W.R. Elton*, edited by John M. Mucciolo, 224–42. Brookfield, VT: Scolar Press, 1996.

Lateiner, Donald. *Sardonic Smile: Nonverbal Behaviour in Homeric Epic*. Ann Arbor: University of Michigan Press, 1995.

Laureys, Marc, and Roswitha Simons, eds. *The Art of Arguing in the World of Renaissance Humanism*. Leuven: Leuven University Press, 2013.

Leonard, John. *Naming in Paradise: Milton and the Language of Adam and Eve*. Oxford: Clarendon Press, 1990.

Lesky, Albin. *A History of Greek Literature*. Translated by James Willis and Cornelis de Heer. 2nd ed. New York: Thomas Crowell, 1966.

Leslie, Michael. *Spenser's "Fierce Warres and Faithfull Loves": Martial and Chivalric Symbolism in "The Faerie Queene."* Woodbridge, UK: D.S. Brewer, 1983.

Lévêque, Pierre. *Aurea Catena Homeri: une étude sur l'allégorie grècque*. Paris: Belles Lettres, 1959.

Levine, Daniel B. "Homeric Laughter and the Unsmiling Suitors." *CJ* 78, no. 2 (1983): 97–104.

– "*Odyssey* 18: Iros as Paradigm for the Suitors." *CJ* 77, no. 3 (1982): 200–4.

Lewalski, Barbara. "Milton and the Millenium." In *Milton and the Ends of Time*, edited by Juliet Cummins, 13–28. Cambridge: Cambridge University Press, 2003.

– *Paradise Lost and the Rhetoric of Literary Forms*. Princeton, NJ: Princeton University Press, 1985.

Lewis, C.S. *Preface to Paradise Lost*. London and New York: Oxford University Press, 1942.

Lieb, Michael. *The Sinews of Ulysses: Form and Convention in Milton's Works*. Pittsburgh: Duquesne University Press, 1989.

[Liddell and Scott]. *An Intermediate Greek-English Lexicon, Founded upon the Seventh Edition of Liddell and Scott's Greek-English Lexicon*. Oxford: Clarendon Press, 1994.

Lindberg, Gertrud. *Studies in Hermogenes and Eustathios: The Theory of Ideas and Its Application in the Commentaries of Eustathios on the Epics of Homer*. Lund: J. Lindell, 1977.

Lloyd-Jones, Hugh. *The Justice of Zeus*. Berkeley: University of California Press, 1971.

Loane, George. "Misprints in Chapman's Homer." *NQ* 173 (1937): 398–402, 453–5, and *NQ* 174 (1938): 367.

Lobis, Seth. "Erasmus and the Natural History of Friendship." *ERSY* 30 (2010): 23–39.

Loewenstein, David. *Representing Revolution in Milton and His Contemporaries*. Cambridge: Cambridge University Press, 2001.

Lombardo, Agostino. "Fragments and Scraps: Shakespeare's *Troilus and Cressida*." In *The European Tragedy of Troilus*, edited by Piero Boitani, 199–217. Oxford: Clarendon Press, 1989.

Long, A.A. "Morals and Values in Homer." *JHS* 90 (1970): 121–39.

– "Post-Aristotelian Philosophy." In *The Cambridge History of Classical Literature*, volume 1, part 3, edited by P.E. Easterling and B.M.W. Knox, 129–48. Cambridge: Cambridge University Press, 1989.

Loraux, Nicole. *The Divided City: Forgetting in the Memory of Athens*. Translated by Corinne Pache. New York: Zone Books, 2001.

– *The Experiences of Tiresias: The Feminine and the Greek Man*. Translated by Paula Wissing. Princeton, NJ: Princeton University Press, 1995.

Lord, George de Forest. *Heroic Mockery: Variations on Epic Themes from Homer to James Joyce*. Newark: University of Delaware Press, 1977.

– *Homeric Renaissance: The Odyssey of George Chapman*. New Haven, CT: Yale University Press, 1956.

– "Homer, *Paradise Lost*, and the Renaissance." In volume 4 of *A Milton Encyclopedia*, 9 vols. edited by William B. Hunter, 20–5. Lewisburg, PA: Bucknell University Press, 1978–83.

Louden, Bruce. *The Iliad: Structure, Myth, and Meaning*. Baltimore: Johns Hopkins University Press, 2006.

– "Milton and the Appropriation of an Epic Technique." *Classical and Modern Literature* 16, no. 4 (1996): 325–40.

– *The Odyssey: Structure, Narration, and Meaning*. Baltimore: Johns Hopkins University Press, 1999.

– "Pivotal Counterfactuals in Homeric Epic." *CA* 12, no. 2 (1993): 181–98.

Lovejoy, Arthur. *The Great Chain of Being: A Study of the History of an Idea*. Cambridge, MA: Harvard University Press, 1936.

Luxon, Thomas H. *Single Imperfection: Milton, Marriage, and Friendship*. Pittsburgh: Duquesne University Press, 2005.

MacCaffrey, Wallace. "Place and Patronage in Elizabethan Politics." In *Elizabethan Government and Society: Essays Presented to Sir John Neale*, edited by S.T. Bindoff, J. Hurstfield, and C.H. Williams, 95–126. London: Athlone Press, 1961.

MacDonald, Dennis. *Christianizing Homer: The Odyssey, Plato, and the Acts of Andrew*. Oxford: Oxford University Press, 1994.

Machacek, Gregory. "Royalist Homer." *Transactions of the Cambridge Bibliographical Society* 12 (2002): 331–3.

MacLure, Millar. *George Chapman: A Critical Study*. 2nd ed. Toronto: University of Toronto Press, 1969.

Mackie, Hilary. *Talking Trojan: Speech and Community in the "Iliad."* Lanham, Boulder, and New York: Rowman & Littlefield, 1996.

Maguire, Laurie E. "Performing Anger: The Anatomy of Abuse(s) in *Troilus and Cressida*." *Renaissance Drama* n.s. 31 (2002): 153–83.

Maier, Ida. "Une Page Inédite de Politien: La Note du Vat. Lat. 3617 sur Démétrius." *Bibliothèque d'Humanisme et Renaissance* 16 (1954): 7–17.

Marcus, Leah. *The Politics of Mirth: Jonson, Herrick, Milton, Marvell, and the Defence of Old Holiday Pastimes*. Chicago: University of Chicago Press, 1986.

Margolin, Jean-Claude. *Érasme: une abeille laborieuse, un témoin engagé*. Caen: Paradigme, 1993.

– ed. *Guerre et Paix dans la Pensée d'Érasme*. Paris: Aubier Montaigne, 1973.

Marsh, David. *Lucian and the Latins: Humour and Humanism in the Early Renaissance*. Ann Arbor: University of Michigan Press, 1998.

Martin, Richard. *Language of Heroes: Speech and Performance in the "Iliad,"* Ithaca, NY: Cornell University Press, 1989.

Martines, Lauro. *Strong Words: Writing and Social Strain in the Italian Renaissance*. Baltimore: Johns Hopkins University Press, 2003.

Martindale, Charles. *John Milton and the Transformation of Ancient Epic*. London and Sydney: Croom Helm, 1986.

– *Redeeming the Text: Latin Poetry and the Hermeneutics of Reception*. Cambridge: Cambridge University Press, 1993.

Martindale, Charles, and Richard F. Thomas, eds. *Classics and the Uses of Reception*. Oxford: Basil Blackwell, 2006.

Martinich, A.P. "Francis Andrewes's Account of Thomas Hobbes' Trip to the Peak." *NQ* 45, no. 4 (1998): 436–40.

– *Hobbes: A Biography*. Cambridge: Cambridge University Press, 1999.

– *A Hobbes Dictionary*. Oxford: Basil Blackwell, 1995.

– *The Two Gods of Leviathan: Thomas Hobbes on Religion and Politics*. Cambridge: Cambridge University Press, 1992.

Martz, Louis. *Milton: Poet of Exile*. 2nd ed. New Haven, CT: Yale University Press, 1986.

Masters, Mallary. *Rabelaisian Dialectic and the Platonic-Hermetic Tradition*. Albany: State University of New York Press, 1969.

McColley, Diane. "'All in All': The Individual of Creatures in *Paradise Lost*." In *'All in All': Unity, Diversity, and the Miltonic Perspective*, edited by Charles W. Durham and Kristin A. Pruitt, 21–38. Selinsgrove, PA: Susquehanna University Press, 1999.

– *Milton's Eve*. Urbana and Chicago: University of Illinois Press, 1983.

McCoy, Richard. *The Rites of Knighthood: The Literature and Politics of Elizabethan Chivalry*. Berkeley & Los Angeles: University of California Press, 1989.

McNeil, David. *Guillaume Budé and Humanism in the Reign of François I*. Geneva: Droz, 1975.

McPherson, David. "Ben Jonson's Library and Marginalia: An Annotated Catalogue." *SP* 71, no. 5 (1974): 1–106.

McQueen, William. "*Paradise Lost* V, VI: The War in Heaven." *SP* 71, no. 1 (1974): 89–104.

Ménager, Daniel. *La Renaissance et le Rire*. Paris: Presses Universitaires de France, 1995.

Mintz, Samuel J. *The Hunting of Leviathan: Seventeenth-Century Reactions to the Materialism and Moral Philosophy of Thomas Hobbes*. Cambridge: Cambridge University Press, 1962.

Moeck, William. "Bees in My Bonnet: Milton's Epic Simile and Intertextuality." *MQ* 32, no. 4 (1998): 122–35.

Monfasani, John. *Byzantine Scholars in Renaissance Italy: Cardinal Bessarion and Other Emigrés*. Aldershot, UK: Variorum, 1995.

Montiglio, Silvia. *Silence in the Land of Logos.* Princeton, NJ: Princeton University Press, 2000.

Morgan, Kathryn A. *Myth and Philosophy from the Presocratics to Plato.* Cambridge: Cambridge University Press, 2004.

Morgan, Llewelyn. *Patterns of Redemption in Virgil's Georgics*. Cambridge: Cambridge University Press, 1999.

Morrison, James V. "Alternatives to the Epic Tradition: Homer's Challenges in the *Iliad*." *TAPA* 122 (1992): 61–71.

– *Homeric Misdirection: False Predictions in the Iliad*. Ann Arbor: University of Michigan Press, 1992.

Moss, Ann. *Poetry and Fable: Studies in Mythological Narrative in Sixteenth-Century France*. Cambridge: Cambridge University Press, 1984.

Moul, Victoria. *Jonson, Horace, and the Classical Tradition*. Cambridge: Cambridge University Press, 2010.
Mueller, Martin. "Knowledge and Delusion in the *Iliad*." In *Essays on the Iliad: Selected Modern Criticism*, edited by John Wright, 105–23. Bloomington: Indiana University Press, 1978.
– "*Paradise Lost* and the *Iliad*." *CLS* 6 (1969): 292–316.
Murrin, Michael. *The Allegorical Epic: Essays in Its Rise and Decline*. Chicago: University of Chicago Press, 1990.
Nagler, Michael N. "Discourse and Conflict in Hesiod: Eris and the Erides." *Ramus* 21 (1992): 79–96.
– "Towards a Semantics of Ancient Conflict: Eris in the *Iliad*." *Classical World* 82 (1988): 81–90.
Nagy, Gregory. *The Best of the Achaeans: Concepts of the Hero in Archaic Greek Poetry*, 2nd ed. Baltimore: Johns Hopkins University, 1999.
– *Homeric Questions*. Austin: University of Texas Press, 1996.
– *Pindar's Homer: The Lyric Possession of an Epic Past*. Baltimore: Johns Hopkins University Press, 1990.
Nehamas, Alexander. "Eristic, Antilogic, Dialectic: Plato's Demarcation of Philosophy from Sophistry." *History of Philosophy Quarterly* 7, no. 1 (1990): 3–16.
Nelson, William. *The Poetry of Edmund Spenser*. New York: Columbia University Press, 1963.
Ng, Su Fang. *Literature and the Politics of Family in Seventeenth-Century England*. Cambridge: Cambridge University Press, 2007.
Nohrnberg, James. *The Analogy of The Faerie Queene*. Princeton, NJ: Princeton University Press, 1976.
Norbrook, David. "Rhetoric, Ideology, and the Elizabethan World Picture." In *Renaissance Rhetoric*, edited by Peter Mack, 140–64. New York: Warwick Studies, 1994.
Nünlist, René. *The Ancient Critic at Work: Terms and Concepts of Literary Criticism in the Greek Scholia*. Cambridge: Cambridge University Press, 2009.
Oates, J.C.T. *Cambridge University Library: A History from the Beginnings to the Copyright Act of Queen Anne*. 2 vols. Cambridge: Cambridge University Press, 1986.
Ong, Walter. *Fighting for Life: Contest, Sexuality, and Consciousness*. Ithaca, NY: Cornell University Press, 1981.
– *Interfaces of the Word*. Ithaca, NY: Cornell University Press, 1977.
– *Orality and Literacy: The Technologizing of the Word*. 2nd ed. London: Methuen, 1986.

Paganini, Gianni. "Hobbes among Ancient and Modern Skeptics: Phenomena and Bodies." In *The Return of Scepticism: From Hobbes and Descartes to Bayle*, edited by Paganini, 3–27. Kluwer Academic Publishing, 2003.

Parks, Ward. *Verbal Dueling in Heroic Narrative: The Homeric and Old English Traditions*. Princeton, NJ: Princeton University Press, 1990.

Pease, Arthur Stanley. "Things without Honor." *CP* 21, no. 1 (1926): 27–42.

Pépin, Jean. *Mythe et Allégorie: Les Origines Grecques et les contestations judéo-chrétiennes*. 2nd ed. Paris: Etudes Augustiniennes, 1976.

Peradotto, John. *Man in the Middle Voice: Name and Narration in the Odyssey*. Princeton, NJ: Princeton University Press, 1990.

Pérez, Brigitte. "Allégorie et Doxographie Sceptique." In *L'Allégorie de l'Antiquité à la Renaissance*, edited by Brigitte Pérez-Jean and Patricia Eichek-Lojkine, 243–53. Paris: Honoré Champion, 2004.

Pertusi, Agostino. *Leonzio Pilato fra Petrarca e Boccaccio: Le sue versioni omeriche negli autografi di Venezia e la cultura greca nel primo Umanesimo*. Venice: Istituto per la Collaborazione Culturale, 1964.

Pesic, Peter. "Shapes of Proteus in Renaissance Art." *HLQ* 73, no. 1 (2010): 57–82.

Pfitzner, Victor C. *Paul and the Agon Motif: Traditional Athletic Imagery in the Pauline Literature*. Leiden: Brill, 1967.

Pigman, George W. "Versions of Imitation in the Renaissance," *RQ* 33, no. 1 (1980): 1–32.

Plattard, Jean. *The Life of François Rabelais*. 2nd ed. New York: Humanities Press, 1968.

Pontani, Filippomaria. "From Budé to Zenodotus: Homeric Readings in the European Renaissance." *IJCT* 14, nos. 3–4 (2007): 375–430.

Porter, William. *Reading the Classics and "Paradise Lost."* Lincoln: University of Nebraska Press, 1983.

Pucci, Pietro. *Hesiod and the Language of Poetry*. Baltimore: Johns Hopkins University Press, 1976.

– *The Song of the Sirens: Essays on Homer*. Lanham, MD: Rowman & Littlefield, 1998.

Quint, David. *Epic and Empire: Politics and Generic Form from Virgil to Milton*. Princeton, NJ: Princeton University Press, 1993.

– "Expectation and Prematurity in Milton's Nativity Ode." *MP* 97, no. 2 (1999): 195–219.

– *Origin and Originality in Renaissance Literature: Versions of the Source*. New Haven, CT: Yale University Press, 1983.

– "Ulysses and the Devils: The Unity of Book Two of *Paradise Lost*." *MS* 49 (2009): 20–48.

Quitslund, Jon A. *Spenser's Supreme Fiction: Platonic Natural Philosophy and The Faerie Queene*. Toronto: University of Toronto Press, 2001.

Race, William. *Pindar*. Boston: Twayne, 1986.

Radzinowicz, Mary Ann. *Milton's Epics and the Book of Psalms*. Princeton, NJ: Princeton University Press, 1989.

Rankin, H.D. *Sophists, Socratics, and Cynics*. London: Croom Helm, 1983.

Reik, Miriam R. *The Golden Lands of Thomas Hobbes*. Detroit: Wayne State University Press, 1977.

Reinhardt, Karl. *Das Parisurteil*. Frankfurt, 1938.

Revard, Stella. "Milton, Homer, and the Anger of Adam." *MS* 41 (2002): 18–37.

– *Pindar and the Renaissance Hymn-Ode: 1450–1750*. Tempe, AZ: ACMRS, 2001.

– "Vergil's *Georgics* and *Paradise Lost*: Nature and Human Nature in a Landscape." In *Vergil at 2000: Commemorative Essays on the Poet and His Influence*, edited by John D. Bernard, 259–80. New York: AMS Press, 1986.

Reynolds, L.D., and N.G. Wilson, *D'Homère à Érasme. La transmission des classiques grecs et latins.* Paris: Centre National de la Recherche Scientifique, 1986.

Rhein, Stefan. "Melanchthon and Greek Literature." In *Philip Melanchthon (1497–1560) and the Commentary*, edited by Timothy J. Wengert and M. Patrick Graham, 149–70. Sheffield: Sheffield Academic Press, 1997.

Richardson, N.J. "The Contest of Homer and Hesiod and Alcidamas' *Mouseion*." *CQ* n.s. 31 (1981): 1–10.

– "Homer and His Ancient Critics." In volume 6 of *Homer's Iliad: A Commentary*, ed. Kirk, 25–49.

– "Literary Criticism in the Exegetical Scholia: A Sketch." In *Oxford Readings in Ancient Literary Criticism*, edited by Andrew Laird, 265–87. Oxford: Oxford University Press, 2006.

Richardson, Scott. *The Homeric Narrator*. Nashville, TN: Vanderbilt University Press, 1990.

Robinson, Christopher. *Lucian and His Influence in Europe*. Chapel Hill: University of North Carolina Press, 1979.

Roche, Thomas. *The Kindly Flame: A Study of the Third and Fourth Books of Spenser's Faerie Queene*. Princeton, NJ: Princeton University Press, 1964.

Romilly, Jacqueline de. *Magic and Rhetoric in Ancient Greece*. Cambridge, MA: Harvard University Press, 1975.

Rose, Margaret. *Parody: Ancient, Modern, and Post-Modern*. 2nd ed. Cambridge: Cambridge University Press, 1995.

Rothstein, Marian. "Homer for the Court of François I." *RQ* 49, no. 3 (2006): 732–67.

Rubenstein, Alice Levine. "The Notes to Poliziano's *Iliad*," *Italia medioevale e umanistica* 25 (1982): 205–39.

Rudhardt, Jean. *Themis et les Hôrai*. Geneva: Droz, 1989.

Rummel, Erika. "Argumentis, Non Contumeliis: The Humanistic Model for Religious Debate and Erasmus' Apologetic Letters." In *Self-Presentation and Social Identification: The Rhetoric and Pragmatics of Letter Writing in Early Modern Times*, edited by Toun Van Houdt and Jan Papy, 305–16. Leuven: Leuven University Press, 2002.

– "*Et cum Theologo bella poeta gerit*: The Conflict between Humanists and Scholastics Revisited." *SCJ* 23, no. 4 (1992): 713–26.

– *The Humanist-Scholastic Debate in the Renaissance and Reformation*. Cambridge, MA: Harvard University Press, 1995.

– "The Reception of Erasmus' *Adages* in Sixteenth-Century England." *Renaissance and Reformation* 18, no. 2 (1994): 19–30.

– ed. and trans. *Scheming Papists and Lutheran Fools: Five Reformation Satires*. New York: Fordham University Press, 1993.

– "The Use of Greek in Erasmus' Letters." *Humanistica Lovaniensia: Journal of Neo-Latin Studies* 30 (1981): 55–92.

Rumrich, John Peter. *Matter of Glory: A New Preface to Paradise Lost*. Pittsburgh: University of Pittsburgh Press, 1987.

Russell, Anthony Prusti. "Epic Agon and the Strategy of Reform in Folengo and Rabelais." *CLS* 34, no. 2 (1997): 119–48.

Rutherford, Richard. *Homer*. New Surveys in the Classics 26. Oxford: Oxford University Press for the Classical Association, 1996.

Ruzé, François. *Déliberation et Pouvoir dans la cité Grecque de Nestor à Socrate*. Paris: Publications de la Sorbonne, 1997.

Ryken, Leland. "*Paradise Lost* and Its Biblical Epic Models." In *Milton and Scriptural Tradition: The Bible into Poetry*, edited by James H. Sims and Leland Ryken, 43–81. Columbia: University of Missouri Press, 1984.

Saladin, Jean-Christophe. *La Bataille du Grec à la Renaissance*. Paris: Belles Lettres, 2000.

– ed. and trans. Guillaume Nesen, *Les Funérailles de la Muse*, and Ulrich von Hutten, *La Conférence Macaronique*. Paris: Belles Lettres, 2001.

Samuel, Irene. "The Dialogue in Heaven: a Reconsideration of *Paradise Lost*, III.1–41." *PMLA* 72 (1957), 601–11.

Sandys, J.E. *History of Classical Scholarship*. Volume 2. 3 vols. 2nd ed. New York: Hafner Publication Company, 1967.

Sansone, David. "How Milton Reads: Scripture, the Classics, and That Two-Handed Engine," *MP* 103, no. 3 (2006): 332–57.

Scalamandre, Raffaele. *Rabelais e Folengo e altri studi sulla letteratura francese del '500*. Rome: Edizioni di Storia e Letteratura, 1998.

Schlunk, Robin R. *The Homeric Scholia and the Aeneid: A Study of the Influence of Ancient Homeric Literary Criticism on Vergil*. Ann Arbor: University of Michigan Press, 1974.

Schmitt, Charles B. "Perennial Philosophy: From Agostino Steuco to Leibniz." *JHI* 27, no. 4 (1966): 505–32.

Schoell, Franck L. *Etudes sur l'Humanisme Continental en Angleterre à la Fin de la Renaissance*. Paris: Honoré Champion, 1926.

Schofield, John. *Philip Melanchthon and the English Reformation*. Aldershot: Ashgate, 2006.

Schofield, Malcolm. "Eubolia in the *Iliad*." *CQ* 36 (1986): 6–31.

Schwartz, Jerome. *Irony and Ideology in Rabelais: Structures of Subversion*. Cambridge: Cambridge University Press, 1990.

Scodel, Joshua. *Excess and the Mean in Early Modern English Literature*. Princeton, NJ: Princeton University Press, 2002.

Screech, M.A. *Laughter at the Foot of the Cross*. London and New York: Penguin, 1997.

– *Rabelais*. Ithaca, NY: Cornell University Press, 1979.

Seaford, Richard. *Reciprocity and Ritual: Homer and Tragedy in the Developing City-State*. Oxford: Oxford University Press, 1994.

Seeskin, Kenneth R. "The Comedy of Gods in the *Iliad*." *Philosophy and Literature* 1 (1977): 295–306.

Segal, Charles. "*Kleos* and Its Ironies in the *Odyssey*." *L'Antiquité Classique* 52 (1983): 22–47.

– *Singers, Heroes, and Gods in the Odyssey*. Ithaca, NY: Cornell University Press, 1994.

Seigel, Jerrold. *Rhetoric and Philosophy in Renaissance Humanism: The Union of Eloquence and Wisdom, Petrarch to Valla*. Princeton University Press, 1968.

Seiver, George O. "Cicero's *De Oratore* and Rabelais." *PMLA* 59, no. 3 (1944): 655–71.

Semenza, Gregory. *Sport, Politics, and Literature in the English Renaissance*. Newark: University of Delaware Press, 2003.

Seznec, Jean. *The Survival of the Pagan Gods: The Mythological Tradition and Its Place in Renaissance Humanism and Art*. Translated by Barbara F. Sessions. Princeton, NJ: Princeton University Press, 1953.

Shankman, Steven. *Pope's Iliad: Homer in the Age of Passion*. Princeton, NJ: Princeton University Press, 1983.

Shannon, Laurie. *Sovereign Amity: Figures of Friendship in Shakespearean Contexts*. Chicago: University of Chicago Press, 2002.

Shephard, S. "Scaliger on Homer and Virgil: A Study of Literary Prejudice." *Emerita* 29, no. 2 (1961): 313–40.
Shoulson, Jeffrey S. *Fictions of Conversion: Jews, Christians, and Cultures of Change in Early Modern England*. Philadelphia: University of Pennsylvania Press, 2013.
Simpson, Percy. "Ben Jonson on Chapman." *Times Literary Supplement*. 3 March 1932: 155.
Skinner, Quentin. *Reason and Rhetoric in the Philosophy of Hobbes*. Cambridge: Cambridge University Press, 1996.
– "Thomas Hobbes and His Disciples in France and England." *Comparative Studies in Society and History* 8 (1966): 153–67.
Slomp, Gabriella. "Hobbes, Thucydides, and the Three Greatest Things." *History of Political Thought* 11, no. 4 (1990): 565–86.
Smalley, Donald. "The Ethical Bias of Chapman's Homer." *SP* 36 (1939): 169–91.
Smith, Charles G. *Spenser's Theory of Friendship*. Baltimore: Johns Hopkins University Press, 1935.
Smith, Nigel. *Literature and Revolution in England, 1640–1660*. New Haven, CT: Yale University Press, 1994.
Snare, Gerald. *The Mystification of George Chapman*. Durham, NC: Duke University Press, 1989.
Snell, Bruno. *The Discovery of the Mind: The Greek Origins of European Thought*. Translated by T. G. Rosenmeyer. Oxford: Basil Blackwell, 1953.
Sowerby, Robin. "Chapman's Discovery of Homer." *Translation and Literature* 1 (1992): 26–51.
– "Early Humanist Failure with Homer (1)." *IJCT* 4, no. 1 (1997): 37–63.
– "Early Humanist Failure with Homer (II)." *IJCT* 4, no. 2 (1997): 165–94.
Spitz, Lewis W. *The Religious Renaissance of the German Humanists*. Cambridge, MA: Harvard University Press, 1963.
Sprague, Rosamond Kent. *The Older Sophists: A Complete Translation by Several Hands of the Fragments in Die Fragmente Der Vorsokratiker*. Edited by Diels-Krantz. Columbia: University of South Carolina Press, 1972.
Springborg, Patricia. "Hobbes and Historiography: Why the Future, He Says, Does Not Exist." In *Hobbes and History*, edited by G.A.J. Rogers and Tom Sorell, 44–72. London & NY: Routledge, 2000.
Stanford, W.B. *Ambiguity in Greek Literature.* 2nd ed. London and New York: Johnson Reprint Corp., 1972.
Steadman, John. "Achilles and Renaissance Epic: Moral Criticism and Literary Tradition." In *Lebende Antike: Symposium für Rudolf Sühnel*, edited by Horst Meller and Hans-Joachim Zimmermann, 139–54. Berlin: E. Schmidt, 1967.

– *Milton and the Paradoxes of Renaissance Heroism*. Baton Rouge: Louisiana State University Press, 1987.
Stephens, Walter. *Giants in Those Days. Folklore, Ancient History, and Nationalism*. Lincoln: University of Nebraska Press, 1989.
Stern, Virginia F. *Gabriel Harvey: His Life, Marginalia, and Library*. Oxford: Clarendon Press, 1979.
Stewart, Stanley. "Spenser and the Judgment of Paris." *Spenser Studies* 9 (1999): 161–209.
Strauss, Leo. *The Political Philosophy of Hobbes*. Chicago: University of Chicago Press, 1963.
Suter, Ann. "Paris and Dionysos: *Iambos* in the *Iliad*." *Arethusa* 26, no. 1 (1993): 1–18.
Swedenberg, H.T., Jr. *The Theory of the Epic in England 1650–1800*. 2nd ed. New York: Russell & Russell, 1972.
Szabari, Antonia. "Rabelais *Parrhesiastes*: The Rhetoric of Insult and Rabelais's Cynical Mask." *MLN* 120, no. 5 Supplement (2005): 84–123.
Terpening, Ronnie. *Lodovico Dolce, Renaissance Man of Letters*. Toronto: University of Toronto Press, 1997.
Terry, Richard. *Mock-Heroic from Butler to Cowper: An English Genre and Discourse*. Aldershot: Ashgate, 2005.
Tetel, Maurice. *Etude sur le Comique de Rabelais*. Florence: Leo Olschki, 1964.
– "The Function and Meaning of the Mock Epic Framework in Rabelais." *Neophilologus* 59, no. 2 (1975): 157–64.
Thalmann, William G. *The Odyssey: An Epic of Return*. New York: Twayne, 1992.
– *The Swineherd and the Bow: Representations of Class in the "Odyssey."* Ithaca, NY: Cornell University Press, 1998.
– "Thersites: Comedy, Scapegoats, and Heroic Ideology in the *Iliad*." *TAPA* 118 (1988): 1–28.
Thomson, Douglas F.S. "Erasmus and Paris." In *The Classical Heritage in France*, edited by Gerald Sandy, 109–36. Leiden: Brill, 2002.
Thomson, Patricia. "Rant and Cant in *Troilus and Cressida*." *Essays and Studies* 22 (1969): 33–56.
Thorpe, Clarence DeWitt. *The Aesthetic Theory of Thomas Hobbes*. Ann Arbor: University of Michigan Press, 1940.
Tilley, Arthur. "Greek Studies in England in the Early Sixteenth Century." *English Historical Review* 53 (1938): 221–39.
Tillyard, E.M.W. *The English Epic and Its Background*. New York: Oxford University Press, 1954.

Tonkin, Humphrey. *Spenser's Courteous Pastoral*. Oxford: Clarendon Press, 1972.

Tracy, James. *The Politics of Erasmus: A Pacifist Intellectual and His Political Milieu*. Toronto: University of Toronto Press, 1978.

Treip, Mindele Anne. "'Reason is Also Choice': The Emblematics of Free Will in '*Paradise Lost*'." *SEL* 31, no. 1 (1991): 147–77.

Turner, James Grantham. *One Flesh: Paradisal Marriage and Sexual Relations in the Age of Milton*. Oxford: Clarendon Press, 1987.

Vacca, Robert. "The Theology of Disorder in the *Iliad*." *Religion & Literature* 23, no. 2 (1991): 1–22.

Van Der Laan, Sarah. "Milton's Odyssean Ethics: Homeric Allusions and Arminian Thought in *Paradise Lost*." *MS* 49 (2009): 49–76.

– "'What virtue and wisdom can do': Homer's *Odyssey* in the Renaissance Imagination." PhD dissertation, Yale University, 2008.

Verdenius, W.J. "Gorgias' Doctrine of Deception." In *The Sophists and Their Legacy: Proceedings of the Fourth International Colloquium of Ancient Philosophy,* edited by G.B. Kerferd, 116–28. Wiesbaden: Franz Steiner Verlag, 1981.

Vernant, Jean-Pierre, ed. *Problèmes de la Guerre en Grèce Ancienne*. Paris: Editions de l'Ecole des hautes Etudes en Sciences Sociales, 1985.

– "Weaving Friendship." *Salmagundi* 130–1 (2001): 75–87.

Visa-Ondarçuhu, Valérie. *L'Image de l'Athlète d'Homère à la fin du Ve Siècle avant J.C.* Paris: Belles Lettres, 1999.

Vivante, Paolo. "On Homer's Winged Words." *CQ* 25, no. 1 (1975): 1–12.

Vredeveld, Harry. "Deaf as Ulysses to the Siren's Song: The Story of a Forgotten Topos." *RQ* 54, no. 3 (2004): 846–82.

Waddington, Raymond B. "Chapman and Persius: The Epigraph to *Ovids Banquet of Sence*." *Review of English Studies* n.s. 19 (1968): 158–62.

– *The Mind's Empire: Myth and Form in George Chapman's Narrative Poems*. Baltimore: Johns Hopkins University Press, 1974.

Walcot, Peter. *Envy and the Greeks: A Study of Human Behaviour*. Westminster, UK: Aris & Phillips, 1978.

Walsh, Thomas R. *Fighting Words and Feuding Words: Anger and the Homeric Poems*. Lanham, MD: Lexington Books, 2002.

Warner, J. Christopher. *The Augustinian Epic, Petrarch to Milton*. Ann Arbor: University of Michigan Press, 2005.

Waswo, Richard. *Language and Meaning in the Renaissance*. Princeton, NJ: Princeton University Press, 1987.

Watkins, John. *The Specter of Dido: Spenser and Virgilian Epic*. New Haven, CT: Yale University Press, 1995.

Watkins, J.W.N. *Hobbes's System of Ideas: A Study in the Political Significance of Philosophical Theories*. London: Hutchinson University Library, 1965.
Weidner, Henry M. "The Dramatic Uses of Homeric Idealism: The Significance of Theme and Design in George Chapman's *The Gentleman Usher*." *ELH* 28, no. 2 (1961): 121–36.
Weinberg, Bernard. *The History of Literary Criticism in the Italian Renaissance*. 2 vols. Chicago: University of Chicago Press, 1963.
– *Trattati di Poetica e Retorica del Cinquecento*. 4 vols. Bari: Laterza, 1970.
Weinberg, Florence. "Written on the Leaves: Rabelais and the Sibylline Tradition." *RQ* 43, no. 4 (1990): 709–30.
West, M.L. "The Contest of Homer and Hesiod." *CQ* n.s. 17, no. 2 (1967): 433–50.
– *Studies in the Text and Transmission of the Iliad*. Munich and Leipzig: K.G. Saur, 2001.
West, Michael. "Homer's *Iliad* and the Genesis of Mock-Heroic." *Cithara* 21, no. 1 (1981): 3–22.
– "Spenser's Art of War: Chivalric Allegory, Military Technology, and the Elizabethan Mock-Heroic Sensibility." *RQ* 41, no. 4 (1988): 654–704.
– "Spenser and the Renaissance Ideal of Christian Heroism." *PMLA* 88, no. 5 (1973): 1013–32.
Whelan, Frederick G. "Language and Its Abuses in Hobbes's Political Philosophy." *American Political Science Review* 75, no. 1 (1981): 59–75.
Whigham, Frank. *Ambition and Privilege: The Social Tropes of Elizabethan Courtesy Theory*. Berkeley: University of California Press, 1984.
Whitman, Jon. *Interpretation and Allegory: Antiquity to the Modern Period*. Leiden: Brill, 2000.
Wilson, Donna. *Ransom, Revenge, and Heroic Identity in the "Iliad."* Cambridge: Cambridge University Press, 2002.
Wilson-Okamura, David. *Virgil in the Renaissance*. Cambridge: Cambridge University Press, 2010.
Wind, Edgar. *Pagan Mysteries in the Renaissance*. New Haven, CT: Yale University Press, 1958.
Wolf, F.A. *Prolegomena to Homer* (1795). Edited and translated by Anthony Grafton, Glenn W. Most, and James E.G. Zetzel. Princeton, NJ: Princeton University Press, 1985.
Wolfe, Jessica. *Humanism, Machinery, and Renaissance Literature*. Cambridge: Cambridge University Press, 2004.
Wolff, Emil. *Die goldene Kette: die Aurea Catena Homeri in der englischen Literatur von Chaucer bis Wordsworth*. Hamburg: Hansischer Gildenverlag, 1947.

Wolin, Sheldon S. *Hobbes and the Epic Tradition of Political Theory*. Los Angeles: Clark Memorial Library, 1970.

Wood, Theodore E.B. *The Word "Sublime" and Its Context 1650–1750*. The Hague: Mouton, 1972.

Young, Philip H. *The Printed Homer*. London, McFarland, 2003.

Zappen, James P. "Aristotelian and Ramist Rhetoric in Thomas Hobbes's *Leviathan*: Pathos versus Ethos and Logos." *Rhetorica* 1, no. 1 (1983): 65–91.

Zatti, Sergio. *l'Ombra del Tasso: Epica e romanzo nel Cinquecento.* Milan: Bruno Mondadori, 1996.

Zegura, Elizabeth Chesney, ed. *The Rabelais Encyclopedia*. Westport, CT and London: Greenwood Press, 2004.

Zeitlin, Froma. "Visions and Revisions of Homer." In *Being Greek Under Rome: Cultural Identity, the Second Sophistic, and the Development of Empire*, edited by Simon Goldhill, 195–266. Cambridge: Cambridge University Press, 2001.

Zerba, Michelle. *Doubt and Scepticism in Antiquity and the Renaissance*. Cambridge: Cambridge University Press, 2012.

Zerbe, Gordon. "Paul's Ethic of Nonretaliation and Peace." In *The Love of Enemy and Nonretaliation in the New Testament*, edited by Willard Swartley, 177–222. Louisville, KY: Westminster-John Knox Press, 1992.

Index

www.ingramcontent.com/pod-product-compliance
Lightning Source LLC
LaVergne TN
LVHW010354080826
844660LV00015B/964/J

* 9 7 8 1 4 4 2 6 5 0 2 6 8 *